Accountability and Corporate Human Rights Violations in Tort and International Law

Accountability and Corporate Human Rights Violations in Tort and International Law

By

Emmanuel K. Nartey

Cambridge Scholars Publishing

Accountability and Corporate Human Rights Violations in Tort and International Law

By Emmanuel K. Nartey

This book first published 2021

Cambridge Scholars Publishing

Lady Stephenson Library, Newcastle upon Tyne, NE6 2PA, UK

British Library Cataloguing in Publication Data
A catalogue record for this book is available from the British Library

ISBN (10): 1-5275-7505-5
ISBN (13): 978-1-5275-7505-9

TABLE OF CONTENTS

ACKNOWLEDGEMENTS

I would like to extend thanks to the many people in Ghana and Abidjan, the Ghanaian and Ivorian Judo Federation, who so generously contributed to the work presented in this book. Special mention goes to my enthusiastic supervisor, Dr. Costantino Grasso and Prof. Kofi Kufuor. My PhD has been an amazing experience and I thank Juergen Klinger, Lt. Col. Campey, Mallika Singhal, Morgan Moone, The British Army, The Royal Tank Regiment and Team University of East London wholeheartedly, not only for their tremendous support but also for giving me so many wonderful opportunities. Similar, profound gratitude goes to Prof. Jeremie Gilbert, who has been a truly dedicated mentor. I am also hugely appreciative of Mr. Emmanuel Tetteh, especially for sharing his expertise so willingly, and for being so dedicated to his role as President of the Ghana Judo Federation.

Special mention goes to my Family, Fanni Simon, Urszula Piątek, Ekaterina Petrova, Matthew Tansley, Prisca Awiti-Alcaraz, Iveta Mogyorodiova, and TeamBath, The International Judo Federation and the African Judo Union. Finally, but by no means least, thanks go to mum, Enoyoma Nartey, late dad, Richard Kwame Nartey, and Séverine Nebie for almost unbelievable support. They are the most important people in my world, and I dedicate this book to them.

PREFACE

For over 60 years, issues around globalisation and multinational corporations (MNCs) have been at the fore of the most intense debates in international economics, international law, and international politics. Indisputably, they are the main catchphrases in terms of economics, environmental protection, and human rights law. The concept of globalisation has promoted an economic liberalisation that brought to light Adam Smith's theory of 'the invisible hand', which perceives that the market economy should regulate itself. Undoubtedly, this ideological concept has promoted economic development, trade liberalisation and the transfer of technology, knowledge, and finance across the globe.

However, it has also been observed that globalisation has brought economic inequality, social injustice, environmental damage, destruction of ecosystems and indigenous people's livelihoods, corruption, bad governance in developing countries, a lack of appropriate mechanisms to govern the global economy, and an imbalance of economic power between developed and developing countries. In the context of the international legal system and legal scholars' views, the self-regulatory perception of globalisation has led to violations of international law and human rights law by MNCs, either directly or indirectly, through their subsidiaries or host state governments. This concern indicates a need to develop an appropriate mechanism to regulate the conduct of MNCs at the international level. It should be noted that the idea of imposing private rights and duties under national and international law through collective jurisdiction and multinational trading systems, at both global and regional levels, signals the end of the Westphalian State System.

The primary aim of this book is to identify a coherent legal principle to establish a novel duty of care for corporate human rights violations and environmental damages. This book examines whether tort and civil law offer better accountability and remedy for victims of corporate human rights abuses. Over the course of the research, this book has attempted to carry out an in-depth and critical analysis of the concept of corporate accountability. Moreover, a fundamental part of this book is devoted to examining the extent to which international criminal law influences international human rights law in its use of tort law and civil law remedies. Finally, it attempts to set out a theoretical mechanism for duty of care as well as a proposal for the establishment of a Hybrid International Transnational Corporation Court that would have the potential to effectively interpret the concept of the corporate duty of care under tort law.

The central objective of the book is to strengthen the argument on MNC accountability and remedy, as well as to develop and present a new practical paradigm for international legal actions against human rights violations by MNCs in host or home states, in the context of the tort of negligence (the neighbourhood principles of duty of care). This book rests on the assumption that a corporation under a duty of care or its equivalent has the ability to control the business activities directly causing the harm. The ability to control, and not actual control, should be a good enough basis for legal liability. The control should be defined broadly to cover not only majority shareholding, but other situations that give entities either legal or factual control. In certain cases, including but not limited to when there is a majority ownership (over 50%), the ability to control should be assumed and the claimant should not have to prove it. Creating and structuring a relationship with a subsidiary, for example, through holding corporations or share companies so that there is no apparent control over its activities, should not be a defence. Suggestions in this book can also operate alongside direct regulatory actions by the state, and would help reinforce compliance. Lastly, the recommendation concerning applicable law is relevant and should be implemented in relation to all cases dealing with private claims under tort/non-contractual liability law.

Grateful acknowledgement is here made to those who helped this research and this book. This work would not have reached its present form without their invaluable help, especially to the Global Legal Review Editorial Team.

Emmanuel K Nartey PhD, BA, GDL, LLM, MSc and OLY.
30 October 2019
Email: maninartey@gmail.com

List of Abbreviations

ATCA – Alien Tort Claims Act
ATS – Alien Tort Statute
CCL – Control Council Law
ECHR – European Convention on Human Rights
FDI – Foreign Direct Investment
HITNCCC – Hybrid International Transnational Corporation Claim Court
ICC – International Criminal Court
ICESCR – International Covenant on Economic, Social and Cultural Rights
ICJ – International Court of Justice
ICT – International Criminal Tribunal
ICTR – International Criminal Tribunal for Rwanda
ICTY – International Criminal Tribunal for the former Yugoslavia
IFOR – Implementation Force
ILC – International Law Commission
ILO – International Labour Organisation
IMT– International Military Tribunal
JCE – Joint Criminal Enterprise
MNCs – Multi-National Corporations
NATO – North Atlantic Treaty Organisation
NGO – Non-Governmental Organisation
OECD – Organisation for Economic Co-operation and Development
PICC – Permanent International Criminal Court
RCO – Responsible Corporate Officer
RICO – Racketeer Influenced and Corrupt Organisations Act
SA – Standard on Auditing
SFOR – Stabilisation Force
TVPA – Torture Victims Prevention Act
UJ – Universal Jurisdiction
UK – United Kingdom
UN – United Nations
UNDHR 1948 – Universal Declaration of Human Rights
UNGA – UN General Assembly
UNGPs – United Nations Guiding Principles
UNSC – UN Security Council
UNSG – Secretary-General of the United Nations

US – United States
WCHR – World Court of Human Rights
WWII – World War II

INTRODUCTION

Remedies for human rights violations on matters such as the right to life, workers' rights, the right to food and shelter, the right to own property, the right to health and clean air, freedom from oppression, and freedom of expression, [1] together with freedom from environmental damages, are governed by international voluntary mechanisms under the auspices of a number of United Nations initiatives.[2] 'Human rights are the basic rights and freedoms that belong to every person in the world, from birth until death.'[3] They apply regardless of where you are from, what you believe or how you choose to live your life. They can never be taken away, although they can sometimes be restricted, such as when a person breaks the law or in the interests of national security. These basic rights are based on shared values like dignity, fairness, equality, respect and independence. These values are defined and protected by law. However, from the research carried out in this study, it appears that reparations[4] for victims who have suffered human rights abuses are ineffective and remedies are mostly unenforceable.[5] So far, states have been reluctant to offer an effective remedy, explicitly and in general, for victims of human rights violations and environmental damages. But, what is important to note is that the drafters

---

[1]UN General Assembly, *Universal Declaration of Human Rights*, 10 December 1948, 217 A (III), <http://www.refworld.org/docid/3ae6b3712c.html> Accessed 24 May 2018.

[2]Robert C Blitt, 'Beyond Ruggie's Guiding Principles on Business and Human Rights: Charting an Embracive Approach to Corporate Human Rights Compliance' (2012) 48 (1) Texas International Law Journal 33.

[3]The Equality and Human Rights Commission, 'What are human rights?' (2019). <https://www.equalityhumanrights.com/en/human-rights/what-are-human-rights#:~:text=Human%20rights%20are%20the%20basic,choose%20to%20live%20your%20life.&text=These%20basic%20rights%20are%20based,%2C%20equality%2C%20respect%20and%20independence> Accessed 19 April 2019.

4 Mijke De Waardt and Sanne Weber, 'Beyond Victims' Mere Presence: An Empirical Analysis of Victim Participation in Transitional Justice in Colombia' (2019) 11 (1) *Journal of Human Rights Practice* 209, 228.

[5]Liesbeth Zegveld, 'Remedies for Victims of Violations of International Humanitarian Law' (2003) 85 (851) Revue Internationale de la Croix-Rouge/International Review of The Red Cross 497, 527.

of the nineteenth-century human rights convention[6] already believed that humanity had inviolable rights that were protected under any jurisdiction.[7] However, human rights treaties do not expressly envisage causes of action for victims of human rights abuses under international or national law, and victims are hardly able to invoke their rights.

Critical observation of the development of human rights 'accountability can be noted at the conclusion of'[8] World War II, which created a crucial principle in the human rights accountability movement. 'The Nuremberg and Tokyo Tribunals tried military, civilian government and industrialist'[9] '(corporate) officials and found those in each category liable for their actions'[10] and inactions.[11] 'The inclusion of military, state and private officials in the trials held in the occupied zones continued into the 1950s, although Cold War politics led to the dismissal of charges against'[12] corporate officials in the early 1950s.[13] Other developments towards 'human rights accountability included the US Civil Rights Movement and increasing activism around human rights issues, including the formation of organisations such as Amnesty International in 1961, which saw the push for liability for human rights abuses.'[14] Human rights were also increasingly codified with the emergence of a growing number of human rights treaties in 1966[15] and the protocols on humanitarian law in

---

[6]AW Brian Simpson, *Human Rights and the End of Empire: Britain and the Genesis of the European Convention* (Oxford University Press on Demand 2004).
[7]Janet Holl Madigan, *Being Human, Being Good: The Source and Summit of Universal Human Rights* (Theses and Dissertations UMD 2004).
[8]Jennifer M Green, 'Corporate Torts: International Human Rights and Superior Officers' (2016) 17 Chicago Journal of International Law 447.
[9]*Ibid.*
[10]Jennifer M Green, 'Corporate Torts: International Human Rights and Superior Officers' (2016) 17 Chicago Journal of International Law 447.
[11]Michael R Marrus, *The Nuremberg War Crimes Trial, 1945-46: A Documentary History* (Macmillan 1997)
[12]Jennifer M Green, 'Corporate Torts: International Human Rights and Superior Officers' (2016) 17 Chicago Journal of International Law 447.
[13]Michael Bazyler and Jennifer Green, 'Nuremberg-Era Jurisprudence Redux: The Supreme Court in Kiobel v. Royal Dutch Petroleum Co. and The Legal Legacy of Nuremberg' (2012) 7 Charleston Law Review 23 and Jennifer M Green, 'Corporate Torts: International Human Rights and Superior Officers' (2016) 17 Chicago Journal of International Law 447.
[14]*Ibid.*
[15]Oona A Hathaway, 'Do Human Rights Treaties Make a Difference?' (2002) 111 Yale Law Journal 1935, and Beth Simmons, 'Treaty Compliance and Violation' (2010) 13 Annual Review of Political Science 273.

1977.[16] A complementary development was the increasing examination of the overlapping responsibilities for human rights violations of state and non-state actors, prominently in the context of gender rights, which examined and developed standards for due diligence in cases of domestic violence over the years.[17]

It is through the 'development of human rights law that the role of transnational corporations began to receive additional international attention. In 1972'[18], the United Nations 'Economic and Social Council ordered a study of the impact of transnational corporations on the development process and international relations.'[19] 'In 1979, the UN created an advisory body, the Commission on Transnational Corporations (UNCTC).'[20] 'From 1977 to 1990, the UNCTC developed a code of conduct for multinational corporations, but the final draft prepared in 1990 was never adopted.'[21] 'Country-specific standards included the 1977 Sullivan Principles to

[16]Protocol Additional to the Geneva Conventions of 12 August 1949 and Relating to the Protection of Victims of International Armed Conflicts (Protocol I), opened for signature June 8, 1977, 1125 UNT.S. 3 (entered into force Dec. 7, 1978) [hereinafter Protocol I]; Protocol Additional to the Geneva Conventions of 12 August 1949, and relating to the Protection of Victims of Non-International Armed Conflicts (Protocol II), opened for signature June 8, 1977, 1125 UNT.S. 609 (entered into force Dec. 7, 1978).

[17]Catherine Phuong, 'Hilary Charlesworth and Christine Chinkin, The Boundaries of International Law: a Feminist Analysis' (2002) 10 (2) Feminist Legal Studies 203.

[18]Jennifer M Green, 'Corporate Torts: International Human Rights and Superior Officers' (2016) 17 Chicago Journal of International Law 447.

[19]Jennifer M Green, 'Corporate Torts: International Human Rights and Superior Officers' (2016) 17 Chicago Journal of International Law 447. Also see: United Nation Economic and Social Council Res. 1721 (LIII) (July 28, 1972).

[20]*Ibid.* Also see: Karl P Sauvant, 'The Negotiations of The United Nations Code of Conduct on Transnational Corporations: Experience and Lessons Learned' (2015) 16 (1) Journal of World Investment & Trade 11, 87.

[21]Jennifer M Green, 'Corporate Torts: International Human Rights and Superior Officers' (2016) 17 Chicago Journal of International Law 447 and De La Vega Connie, Amol Mehra & Alexandra Wong, Holding Businesses Accountable for Human Rights Violations: Recent Developments and Next Steps (2011). <https://perma.cc/8WAA-SGCC> Accessed 13 June 2016.

address apartheid in South Africa'[22] and 'the 1984 MacBride Principles, the code of conduct for US companies doing business in Northern Ireland.'[23]

Furthermore, what has become clear in the past decades is that there is a substantial focus on actors with the highest levels of responsibility for human rights violations, which has translated into an important development for demanding greater accountability for human rights violations.[24] Together, these dynamics added to the momentum for a universal system of accountability for non-state actors,[25] a point which shall be argued throughout this book. This development was observed in the 1990s, when there was an increased focus on the rights of human rights victims to remedies for the violations perpetrated against them. Special international tribunals were created to address mass atrocities in the former Yugoslavia and in Rwanda,[26] followed by the 1998 establishment of the International Criminal Court (ICC).[27] The ICC statute, often referred to as the Rome Statute,[28] required the establishment of a trust fund so that victims of those convicted of human rights violations would benefit from the 'principles relating to reparations to, or in respect of, victims, including restitution, compensation and rehabilitation.'[29] Furthermore, in 2003 the ICC Prosecutor stated that these violations could include corporate

[22]Jennifer M Green, 'Corporate Torts: International Human Rights and Superior Officers' (2016) 17 Chicago Journal of International Law 447 and The Global Sullivan Principles, The University of Minnesota Human Rights Library (2016). <https://perma.cc/JU6X-WGCT> Accessed 24 May 2016.

[23]Father Sean McManus, 'The MacBride Principles, The University of Minnesota Human Rights Library' (2016). <https://perma.cc/JA8X-5HCM> Accessed 8 January 2016.

[24]Michael Bazyler and Jennifer Green (n 136).

[25]*Ibid.*

[26]John RWD Jones, *The Practice of The International Criminal Tribunals for The former Yugoslavia and Rwanda* (Transnational Pub Incorporated 2000).

[27]Cesare PR Romano, André Nollkaemper and Jann K Kleffner, eds. *Internationalized Criminal Courts and Tribunals: Sierra Leone, East Timor, Kosovo, and Cambodia* (Oxford University Press 2004).

[28]Mahnoush H Arsanjani, 'The Rome Statute of The International Criminal Court' (1999) 93 (1) American Journal of International Law 22, 43.

[29]Rome Statute of the International Criminal Court, art. 75, opened for signature July 17, 1998, 2187 UNT.S. 90 (entered into force July 1, 2002). <https://perma.cc/Z3ML-Q9FR> Accessed 7 March 2016.

officers,[30] and in September 2016, the ICC issued a policy paper discussing the liability of corporate officials for environmental crimes.[31]

In 1989, the UN Sub-Commission on the Prevention of Discrimination and Protection of Minorities began to research the right to restitution, compensation, and rehabilitation for victims of gross violations of human rights and fundamental freedoms.[32] The research by the Sub-Commission examined violations by those who were considered to have 'indirect' responsibility, or who might have violated rights by omission rather than by commission.[33] This ultimately led to a Resolution by the UN General Assembly which summarised the important steps towards an international system to advance the right of victims to remedies, including compensation and restitution.[34] The movement to impose transnational norms on corporations also intensified throughout this period. To date, several studies investigating corporate human rights violations illustrate that cases in the United States, Australia, England, and France against multinational corporations and corporate officers corroborate the push for corporate human rights accountability at the international level.[35] The UN continued to develop standards for businesses and their officers. In 2002, the UN Commission on Human Rights (Sub-Commission) drafted a set of principles that directly bound businesses and endorsed corporate officer responsibility.[36] The preamble reaffirmed that transnational corporations and other business enterprises, their officers including managers, members of corporate boards or directors and other executives, and persons working

---

[30]International Criminal Court, Policy Paper on Case Selection and Prioritisation (2003). <https://perma.cc/SDL9- A7B2 > Accessed 8 March 2017.

[31]International Criminal Court, Policy Paper on Case Selection and Prioritisation (2016). <https://perma.cc/SDL9- A7B2> Accessed 16 May 2017.

[32]Theo Van Boven, 'The United Nations Basic Principles and Guidelines on The Right to a Remedy and Reparation for Victims of Gross Violations of International Human Rights Law and Serious Violations of International Humanitarian Law' (2010) United Nations Audiovisual Library of International Law. New York, United Nations. <https://perma.cc/7U38- HQ8F> Accessed 2 September 2017.

[33] *Ibid.*

[34]G.A. Res. 60/147, Basic Principles and Guidelines on The Right to a Remedy and Reparation for Victims of Gross Violations of International Human Rights Law and Serious Violations of International Humanitarian Law (Dec. 16, 2005). <https://perma.cc/C49S-5MA3> Accessed 8 September 2017.

[35]Sarah Joseph, *Corporations and Transnational Human Rights Litigation* (Vol. 4. Hart Publishing 2004).

[36]Economic and Social Council, Commission on Human Rights, Sub-Commission on the Promotion and Protection of Human Rights, 55th Sess., UN Doc. E/CN.4/Sub.2/2003/12/Rev.2 (Aug. 26, 2003).

for them, have, inter alia, human rights obligations and responsibilities.[37] However, these standards were met with strong opposition and were obstructed at the UN Commission.[38]

Additionally, voluntary mechanisms such as the Guiding Principles (GPs),[39] the OECD Guidelines,[40] the ILO Tripartite Declaration of Principles Concerning Multinational Enterprises and Social Policy,[41] and the SA800 Standards[42] arguably have not helped victims gain access to justice and effective remedy. In fact, these initiatives have contributed to ongoing human rights violations in the international arena by allowing corporations to choose the methods and processes with which they respect human rights and the environment.[43] Some research has found that, while voluntary regulation has resulted in some substantive improvements in corporate behaviour, it cannot be regarded as a substitute for the more effective exercise of state authority at both national and international levels. The relevance of rights under international law and human rights law is questionable if victims have no legal capacity to enforce their rights before either a national or international court once they claim to have become a victim of human rights abuses.

International law has historically been between states, which are treated as subjects with legal personalities, allowing them to draft and consent to international agreements that regulate their affairs and relationships with each other. This relationship contrasts with domestic law, as international law goes beyond the internal affairs of a state to impinge

---

[37] David Weissbrodt and Muria Kruger, 'Norms on the Responsibilities of Transnational Corporations and other Business Enterprises with Regard to Human Rights' (2003) 97 (4) American Journal of International Law 901, 922.

[38] *Ibid.*

[39] United Nations, *Guiding Principles on Business and Human Rights: Implementing the United Nations "Protect, Respect and Remedy" Framework* (UN Press 2011).

[40] Kathryn Gordon, 'The OECD Guidelines and Other Corporate Responsibility Instruments: A Comparison' (OECD Working Papers on International Investment 2001).

[41] Jernej Letnar Cernic, 'Corporate Responsibility for Human Rights: Analyzing The ILO Tripartite Declaration of Principles Concerning Multinational Enterprises and Social Policy' (2009) 6 (1) Miskolc Journal of International Law 24.

[42] Grigoris Giannarakis, Nikolaos Litinas and Nikolaos Sariannidis, 'Evaluation of Corporate Social Responsibility Performance Standards' (2011) 5 (17) African Journal of Business Management 7367.

[43] David Vogel, 'The Private Regulation of Global Corporate Conduct: Achievements and Limitations' (2010) 49 (1) Business & Society 68, 87, also see: Steven R Ratner, 'Corporations and Human Rights: a Theory of Legal responsibility' (2001) 111 (3) Yale Law Journal 443.

upon the interests of other states and the international community as a whole. The right to a remedy and/or reparation is imperative for victims involved in human rights abuses, but the theory of international law and the exercise of state jurisdiction in domestic affairs has created a legal and jurisdictional impediment for victims' access to a remedy. The parameter of international law and state jurisdiction has contributed to the lack of effective remedies at both the national and international level. Also, voluntary regulation does not provide an effective remedy for state misconduct. As put by Lord Denning, a member of the British House of Lords, 'a right without a remedy is no right at all'.[44] Lord Denning's view stresses the importance of human rights and access to a remedy. Rights must be accompanied by a remedy.

Human rights abuses resulting from human activities, such as the disposal of toxic chemicals, the generation of power, and the exploitation of oil naturally produce violations without a remedy. Mismanagement of natural resources causes severe watershed erosion, desertification, and atmospheric pollution which severely impair human life.[45] Although human suffering associated with environmental destruction is growing, [46] international and regional human rights institutions have yet to clarify the obligations of governments to protect and provide remedies for the victims involved. A primary concern of this can be seen in the article 'ICC Widens Remit to Include Environmental Destruction Cases'.[47] The Hague International Criminal Court cited that it would prosecute governments and individuals for environmental crimes, including land grabs.[48] As put forward by Gallmetzer,[49] the ICC would establish jurisdiction based on the situations that produced human rights violations as opposed to whether or not the state that allowed the violation had agreed to ICC jurisdiction.

Recent evidence suggests that the ICC is extending its focus on corporate accountability to include Rome Statute crimes already in their

---

[44]*Gouriet v Union of Post Office Workers* [1978] AC 435, p. 435.

[45] Michelle Leighton Schwartz, 'International Legal Protection for Victims of Environmental Abuse' (1993) 18 Yale Journal of International Law 355.

[46] Michelle Leighton Schwartz, 'International Legal Protection for Victims of Environmental Abuse' (1993) 18 Yale Journal International Law 355.

[47]John Vidal and Owen Bowcott, *ICC Widens Remit to Include Environmental Destruction Cases* (2016) The Guardian. <https://www.theguardian.com/global/2016/sep/15/hague-court-widens-remit-to-include-environmental-destruction-cases> Accessed 15 June 2017.

[48]*Ibid.*

[49]Reinhold Gallmetzer, 'Prosecuting Persons Doing Business with Armed Groups in Conflict Areas: the Strategy of the Office of the Prosecutor of the International Criminal Court' (2010) 8 (3) Journal of International Criminal Justice 947, 956.

jurisdiction. The ICC, however, does not fully explain what it means by stating that the 'Office will also seek to cooperate and provide assistance to states, upon request',[50] with respect to conduct which constitutes a serious crime under national law, such as the illegal exploitation of natural resources, arms trafficking, human trafficking, terrorism, financial crimes, land grabbing or the destruction of the environment.[51] Thus, what does the ICC mean by 'assisting national governments' [52] in a form of legal prosecution or investigation? Nonetheless, the existence of false justice and equality before the law, in addition to the lack of cooperation by world powers and a lack of transparency in judicial systems, means enforcing this policy will be difficult.[53] Also, with the misrepresentation of the rule of law [54] that exists in developing country [55] judicial systems and the unwillingness of countries to cooperate with the ICC, it is hard to see how this policy will be effective in practice. Not to mention the various difficulties of holding corporations accountable for their misconduct under international criminal law.[56] Furthermore, without states and international institutions working together, it will be difficult for the ICC to promote direct interaction with victims, including coordinating preliminary examinations, investigations, pre-trials, trial and reparation arrangements.

The relationships between victims and the corporation, its subsidiaries and the environment require a renewed examination of the proper balance between corporate misconduct and solutions for victims.[57] It

---

[50]*Ibid.*

[51] ayal Patel, 'Expanding Past Genocide, Crimes Against Humanity, and War Crimes: Can an ICC Policy Paper Expand the Court's Mandate to Prosecuting Environmental Crimes?' (2016) 14 Loyola University Chicago International Law Review 175.

[52]Anna Stenning and Samantha Walton, *Introduction* (2017) iii-x. <http://www.tandfonline.com/doi/full/10.1080/14688417.2017.1310440> Accessed 15 June 2017.

[53]Tim Allen, Trial Justice: The International Criminal Court and the Lord's Resistance Army (Zed Books Ltd 2013).

[54]Antonin Scalia, 'The Rule of Law as A Law of Rules' (1989): 56 (4) University of Chicago Law Review 1175, 1188.

[55]United Nations, 'Economic Analysis & Policy Division' (2018) < <https://www.un.org/development/desa/dpad/least-developed-country-category.html> accessed 4 July 2016.

[56]Jonathan A Bush, 'The Prehistory of Corporations and Conspiracy in International Criminal Law: What Nuremberg Really Said' (2009) 109 Columbia Law Review 1094.

[57]Lucinda A Low, Sarah R. Lamoree and John London, 'The Demand Side of Transnational Bribery and Corruption: Why Levelling the Playing Field on the

is therefore likely that the connection between international criminal law and environmental crimes will not yield effective accountability for corporate human rights violations and environmental damages, but may provide some grounds for enforcing human rights obligations in the international community. Hence, it could be hypothesised that what is conceived as a violation or breach of a duty of care under civil and tort law will most likely not be conceived of as a violation of domestic criminal law, international criminal law, or criminal obligations under international law. Therefore, the need to create a legal principle for corporate accountability arises in the existing civil and tort law framework, which will give expression to new human rights treaties and existing obligations under the Universal Declaration of Human Rights.[58]

Nonetheless, the development of environmental crime has led many authors in the last two decades to see environmental law as the new legal framework for corporate human rights accountability and for the violations of human rights with respect to environmental law.[59] International environmental crime and environmental law have been identified as international mechanisms able to regulate corporate misconduct,[60] the protection of human rights, and the environment.[61] Commenters have

---

Supply Side Isn't Enough' (2015) 84 Fordham Law Review 563, DEP'T OF JUSTICE, CRIM. DIV., & SEC, ENF'T DIV., A RESOURCE GUIDE TO THE US FOREIGN CORRUPT PRACTICES ACT, at 71 (2012) [hereinafter DOJ & SEC RESOURCE GUIDE]. <https://www.sec.gov/litigation.shtml >Accessed 14 July 2017 and Joseph F Warin, Michael S Diamant, and Veronica Root, 'Somebody's Watching Me: FCPA Monitorships and How They Can Work Better' (2011).

[58]UN General Assembly, *Universal Declaration of Human Rights*, 10 December 1948, 217 A (III). <http://www.refworld.org/docid/3ae6b3712c.html> Accessed 15 June 2017.

[59]Alone Boyle, 'Human Rights and the Environment: Where Next?' (2012) 23 (3) European Journal of International Law 613: Lorand Bartels, 'Human Rights and Sustainable Development Obligations in EU Free Trade Agreements' (2013) 40 Legal Issues of Economics Integration 297 and Daniel Augenstein, 'Study of The Legal Framework on Human Rights and the Environmental Applicable to European Enterprise Operating Outside the European Union' (2014). <http://en.frankbold.org/sites/default/files/tema/101025_ec_study_final_report_en_0.pdf> Accessed on 28 May 2017.

[60]Joshua P Eaton, 'The Nigerian Tragedy, Environmental Regulation of Transnational Corporations, and The Human Right to a Healthy Environment' (1997) 15 Business and International Law Journal 261.

[61] Antonio Cardesa-Salzmann, 'Constitutionalising Secondary Rules in Global Environmental Regimes: Non-compliance Procedures and the Enforcement of Multilateral Environmental Agreements' (2011).

argued that the evolution of this field of international legal order, from substantive and institutional and legal procedural perspectives,[62] will provide victims of corporate human rights abuses with legal redress.[63] The recognition of corporate environmental abuses impacting human rights has led to the development of the principle of inter- and intra-generational equity. Inter- and intra-generational equity posits that previous generations have an obligation to maintain the earth in a reasonable condition for future generations, who inherit the earth from the preceding generation.[64] This has ultimately changed the traditional role of the state with its mutual relationship, towards a more practical role.

Inter- and intra-generational equity suggests that states should act in the interest of individuals and groups in society and in the common interest of humanity. Failure to meet this obligation may constitute a violation of the state's responsibility to protect its citizens under international law and human rights law.[65] With regards to cases for an enforceable international mechanism,[66] the studies of the accountability of transnational corporations in the developing world conducted so far have highlighted a potential inconsistency with this argument of corporate accountability because international environmental law cannot be used as a mechanism for corporate human rights obligations. A possible reason for this states that a country is limited in terms of solutions for corporate misconduct and criminal liability. Also, as will be explained, states have failed to establish effective mechanisms for regulating corporate misconduct linked to environmental crime. Typical examples include the Niger Delta,[67] the

---

<https://papers.ssrn.com/sol3/papers.cfm?abstract_id=2790886> Accessed 20 April 2017.

[62]*Ibid.*

[63]Beth Stephens, *The Amorality of Profit: Transnational Corporations and Human Rights*; *Human rights and Corporations* (Routledge 2017).

[64]Edith Brown Weiss, *Intergenerational Equity: a Legal Framework for Global Environmental Change* (United Nations University 1992).

[65]Ian Brownlie and Kathleen Baker, *Principles of Public International Law* (Vol. 1. Oxford Clarendon Press 1973).

[66]Kamil Omoteso and Hakeem Yusuf, 'Accountability of Transnational Corporations in the Developing World: The Case for an Enforceable International Mechanism' (2017) 13 (1) Critical Perspectives on International Business 54.

[67]Okechukwu Ibeanu, 'Oiling the Friction: Environmental Conflict Management in the Niger Delta, Nigeria' (2000) 6 Environmental Change and Security Project Report 19.

Bhopal disaster,[68] the Gulf Oil spill,[69] Lago Agrio,[70] Ok Tedi,[71] and the Sandoz spill.[72] Debates regarding environmental crimes argue that the application of human rights to international environmental law requires the creation of judicial balancing since environmental laws do not provide criminal standards themselves. Violations, therefore, become subject to judicial discretions which are difficult to implement in practice.

Taking the above into consideration, this book seeks to answer the following: what legal solutions should the national and international systems implement in order to remedy victims of corporate human rights abuses and environmental damage? Although voluntary mechanisms such as the Guiding Principles (GPs), the OECD Guidelines, the ILO Tripartite Declaration of Principles Concerning Multinational Enterprises and Social Policy, and the SA800 Standards have occasionally raised awareness of human rights violations and environmental damages, little has been done to prevent ongoing human rights abuses. Equally, it is only occasionally that a tort law such as The Alien Tort Statute (28 USC. § 1350) (ATS) provides an avenue for a tort claimant to obtain monetary compensation.[73] The fact remains that victims of human rights violations are often left without any remedy, specifically those victims located in developing countries that want to attract multinational corporations but lack the legal and judicial system necessary for regulating corporate business practices effectively.[74] Victims of corporate abuse face serious obstacles to obtaining legal remedy both in the jurisdiction where the harm occurred ('host state') as well as where multinational companies are headquartered ('home state'). When multinational companies commit human right abuses in host countries, host courts often remain the preferred forum for pursuing legal redress. However, for various reasons which include a lack of due process, political interference, mistrust

---

[68]Lee Wilkins, *Shared Vulnerability: The Media and American Perceptions of The Bhopal Disaster* (Vol. 8. Greenwood Press 1987).
[69]Bernard D Goldstein, Howard J Osofsky and Maureen Y Lichtveld, 'The Gulf Oil Spill' (2011) 364 (14) New England Journal of Medicine 1334.
[70]Cortelyou Kenney, 'Disaster in the Amazon: Dodging "Boomerang Suits" in Transnational Human Rights Litigation' (2009) 97 (3) California Law Review 857.
[71]Stuart Kirsch, 'Indigenous Movements and the Risks of Counter Globalization: Tracking the Campaign Against Papua New Guinea's Ok Tedi Mine' (2007) 34 (2) American Ethnologist 303.
[72] Aaron Schwabach, 'The Sandoz Spill: The Failure of International Law to Protect the Rhine from Pollution' (1989) 16 Ecology Law Quarterly 443.
[73]The Alien Tort Statute (28 USC. § 1350; ATS) 'The Alien Tort Statute (ATS; also known as the Alien Tort Claims Act) refers to 28 USC. § 1350.
[74]John Madeley, *Big Business, Poor Peoples: The Impact of Transnational Corporations on the World's Poor* (Palgrave Macmillan 1999).

of the courts or lack of affordable legal assistance, a claim in the host state may not be a viable option.[75] In these instances, legal options in the home state also need to be leveraged to ensure justice.

Victims of corporate human rights abuses and environmental damages come from a variety of backgrounds and experiences. These relationships may partly be explained by victims' perceptions of effective remedy and the process of remedy which may be varied and multidimensional in developing countries. Perhaps, cultural differences may also impact perceptions of remedies for victims of human rights abuses. In some cultures, active participation in criminal proceedings may be essential whereas, in others, the admission of guilt by the wrongdoer is most important. It can, therefore, be assumed that the fact that one can never undo what has been done or provide adequate remedies may mitigate against reparations, whereas in others, the symbolic effect is seen as extremely beneficial.[76] The context of the violation should give rise to specific perceptions of what kinds of remedies should be awarded. For example, a situation of massive population displacement and ethnic cleansing will necessitate a remedy for the return of people from the community and displaced persons, and/or provide alternative solutions for these victims. Many times, however, these remedies are not enacted. Great scrutiny and transparency is required in judicial procedures in order for effective remedies to be put in place for victims.

Another obstacle in seeking solutions with respect to corporate accountability includes the legal challenges victims of corporate misconducts face by both the host and home state jurisdiction in obtaining solutions from a company subsidiary. The 'corporate veil' or 'separate legal personality' doctrine is a major barrier to holding parent companies legally accountable for abuses committed by their subsidiaries. According to the corporate veil doctrine, each separately incorporated member of a corporate group is considered to be a distinct legal entity that holds and manages its own separate liabilities. This doctrine implies that the liabilities of one member of a corporate group will not automatically be imputed to another merely because one holds shares in the other, even if it holds the majority or all of those shares.[77]

---

[75]Amnesty International, 'Creating a Saradigm Shift: Segal Solutions to Improve Access to Remedy for Corporate Human Rights Abuse' (2017).

[76]Max F Perutz, *Redress: Torture Survivors Perceptions of Reparation: A Preliminary Survey* (2001) <http://www.redress.org/downloads/publications/TSPR.pdf> Accessed 4 July 2017.

[77]Henry W Ballantine, 'Separate Entity of Parent and Subsidiary Corporations' (1925) California Law Review 12.

International and national legal systems have failed to address the concept of parent corporations and subsidiary relations. Often, 'there will be cases in which a claim against a parent company may be the only way of securing an effective remedy for the human rights impacts of a subsidiary's activities.'[78] Conversely, whenever victims try to sue parent companies, parent companies invariably rely, amongst others, on two principles of corporate law: 'separate corporate personality'[79] and 'limited liability'. One of the consequences of the legal separation is that a company is generally not liable legally for the conduct (both acts and omissions) of its subsidiaries. On the other hand, the principle of limited liability limits the liability of a parent company for the wrongful conduct of its subsidiary company to the extent of its investment in the subsidiary.[80] It may be the case that victims who have suffered from corporate human rights abuses through corporate subsidiaries in developing countries,[81] which include environmental violations that have taken place in high-risk host states, may be denied access to remedies against the subsidiary in the host state.[82] This may be the case for varying reasons, which include: insufficient precautionary measures, lack of human rights regulatory mechanisms at the national level, judicial redress at the national level, lack of funds, underfunding, bankruptcy, or lack of enforcement.[83]

---

[78]Human Rights Council, 'Improving Accountability and Access to Remedy for Victims of Business-Related Human Rights Abuse: Report of The United Nations High Commissioner for Human Rights', A/HRC/32/19 (10 May 2016), para 22 ('OHCHR Guidance').

[79]David Millon, 'Theories of the Corporation' (1990) Duke Law Journal 201.

[80]Surya Deva, Fictitious Separation, Real Injustice: Why and How to Tame the Twin Principles of Corporate Law? (2017) and Amnesty International, 'Creating a Paradigm Shift: Legal Solutions to Improve Access to Remedy for Corporate Human Rights Abuse' (2017). <https://www.amnesty.org/download/Documents/POL3070372017ENGLISH.PDF> Accessed 09 March 2018.

[81]Michael Diamond, *Corporation 905* (3rd edn, Carolina Academic Press 2012); Special Representative on Business and Human Rights, United Nations Guiding Principles on Business and Human Rights: Implementing the United Nations "Protect, Respects, and Remedy" Framework, adopted by the Human Rights Council, 17th Sess., Mar. 21. 2011, U. N. Doc. A/HRC/17/. L.17/31 (2011).

[82]*Burnham v Superior Ct.*, 495 US 604, 628 (1990); *Kulko v Superior Ct.*, 436 U.S 84, 101 (1978. See also, *Daimler AG v Bauman*, 134 S. Ct., 746 (2014).

[83]Manby Bronwen, *The Price of Oil: Corporate Responsibility and Human Rights Violations in Nigeria's Oil Producing Communities* (Vol. 2156 Human Rights Watch 1999).

Further analysis demonstrates that multinational companies are normally structured in parent-subsidiary relationships for a variety of managerial, regulatory, and tax-related reasons,[84] which make it very difficult to hold them liable for business misconduct. Parent-subsidiary relationships have created a legal deficit that has contributed to a lack of solutions at the national level. This legal deficit remains within the sphere of a subsidiary not subject to the jurisdiction where the parent company is domiciled. The lack of effective remedy from the subsidiary could be due to the lack of identity of the parent corporation that is regulated by corporate law.[85] Further, human rights contained in multilateral agreements cannot be invoked by individuals against private companies because human rights can only be enforced against the state. Interestingly, the correlation between this legal theory of human rights law, international law and corporate law treats subsidiaries as separate from the parent corporation.[86] This distinct legal concept of corporate law treats business entities separately for the purposes of taxation, regulation, and liability. In other words, a subsidiary can sue and be sued separately from its parent, and its obligations will not normally be the obligations of its parent.[87]

Furthermore, complex corporate structures used to organise business subsidiaries within the transnational context often make access to justice for victims exceptionally difficult and even the establishment of a link between the violation and parent corporation very challenging.[88] One problem, and perhaps the key problem, is that no record of the violation is kept, and in most cases victims may not have the knowledge or legal expertise to examine complex legal issues, such as ones related to human rights violations and environmental damages.[89] It could also be that there is

---

[84]Alan O Sykes, 'Corporate Liability for Extraterritorial Torts under the Alien Tort Statute and Beyond: An Economic Analysis' (2011) 100 Georgetown Law Journal 2161.

[85]Murray A Pickering, 'The Company as a Separate Legal Entity' (1968) 31 (5) Modern Law Review 481.

[86]Henry W Ballantine, 'Separate Entity of Parent and Subsidiary Corporations' (1925) California Law Review 12.

[87] Jay Lawrence Westbrook, 'Theories of Parent Company Liability and The Prospects for an International Settlement' (1985) 20 University of Texas School of Law 321.

[88]Rolf H Weber and Rainer Baisch, 'Liability of Parent Companies for Human Rights Violations of Subsidiaries' (2015) <https://ssrn.com/abstract=2625536 or http://dx.doi.org/10.2139/ssrn.2625536> Accessed 25 September 2017.

[89]For more information see Chapter VI and VII of the book.

a lack of proximity to the victims and the corporation's business activities.[90] Difficulties arise when attempting to establish legal proximity[91] between the parent corporation and the subsidiary in order to bring a claim against the parent corporation. Moreover, the subsidiary may be underfunded or there may not be legal redress facilities in the host state legal system. Lastly, the presence of corruption and the ineffectiveness of domestic legal systems might represent another insurmountable obstacle for victims of corporate abuses.[92] This observation supports the hypothesis that, in considering legal options to establish the liability of a parent company, legislators and advocates must assess the following factors: 'duty of care'; the extent to which control or lack thereof was a proximate cause to the damage; how to establish liability and control; and whether damage must be proven or can be assumed in court.

The reasons acknowledged above indicate some of the main impediments for providing victims of corporate human rights abuses and environmental damages with effective remedies.[93] As has been mentioned in the above paragraph, in the parent corporation legal doctrine[94] and the organisational structure of corporate enterprises, both parties financially benefit from the subsidiary's business activities.[95] Therefore, it is legally and financially difficult for victims to gain access to an effective remedy against the parent corporation because of a deeply ingrained orthodox legal doctrine of corporate law[96] (i.e. parent corporation doctrine and the doctrine

---

[90]Ronen Shamir, 'Between Self-Regulation and The Alien Tort Claims Act: On the Contested Concept of Corporate Social Responsibility' (2004) 38 (4) Law & Society Review 635.

[91] Adrian Chan, *Who then–in Law–is my Neighbour? Lord Atkin's 'Neighbour Principle' as an Aid for the Principled Delineation of the Boundaries of Negligent Liability* (Diss 2011).

[92]Sarah Knuckey and Eleanor Jenkin, 'Company-Created Remedy Mechanisms for Serious Human Rights Abuses: A Promising New Frontier for the Right to Remedy?' (2015) 19 (6) International Journal of Human Rights 801.

[93]Joshua P Eaton, 'The Nigerian Tragedy, Environmental Regulation of Transnational Corporations, and The Human Right to a Healthy Environment' (1997) 15 Boston University International Law Journal 261.

[94]Christopher R Knight, 'International Human Rights Litigation after Bauman: The Viability of Veil Piercing to Hale Foreign Parent Corporations into US Courts' (2016) 41 University of Dayton Law Review 213.

[95] Julian Birkinshaw, Neil Hood and Stefan Jonsson, 'Building Firm-Specific Advantages in Multinational Corporations: The Role of Subsidiary Initiative' (1998) Strategic Management Journal 221.

[96]David. Millon, 'Theories of The Corporation' (1990) 2 Duke Law Journal 201.

of limited liability of shareholders),[97] which also applies to corporate shareholders.[98] Victims can only convince their home state court to pierce the corporate veil if the parent corporation is directly engaged in the abuse or if the subsidiary was acting as the parent's alter ego.[99] Without this, the parent corporation cannot be held liable or be required to provide a remedy to a victim of the subsidiary's action. Given these difficulties, the question that needs to be asked is, what is the legal principle for establishing the proximity between victims, parent corporations, and the subsidiary's misconduct?

It is difficult to explain how to address the issue of corporate law in this book, though it might be related to the idea of 'corporation as fiction' as seen in the *Case of Suttons*.[100] This theory arose by necessity from the idea that law regulates human beings and corporations do not constitute human beings. The representation of certain organisations as corporations, however, is justified by accepting that courts can treat them as living individuals. Consequentially, there is no limit to the jurisdiction of legal personality of courts and Parliament over laws as to what corporations are involved in.[101] Furthermore, the 'bracket theory' was taken to be an alternative vision, although it is not essentially so. It envisions 'corporation' as a shorthand for a whole set of rules with respect to its relationship to human beings. For instance, limited liability becomes a way of expressing an extraordinarily complicated set of terms in contracts.[102] Another source of uncertainty is the 'concession' theory,[103] which focuses on substance rather than form by acknowledging that corporations contain advantages,

---

[97]Bryan A Garner, *Black's Law Dictionary 1054* (10th ed. 2014), also see Robert B Thompson, 'Piercing The Corporate Veil: an Empirical Study' (1990) 76 Cornell Law Review 1036 and William O Douglas and Carrol M Shanks, 'Insulation from Liability Through Subsidiary Corporations' (1929) 39 Yale Law Journal 193.

[98]*United State v Bestfoods*, 524 US, 61-64 (1998). Also see; Phillip I Blumberg, 'Limited Liability and Corporate Groups' (1985) 11 Journal Corporation Law 573.

[99]*Bestfoods*, 524 US at 62. < https://caselaw.findlaw.com/us-2nd-circuit/1538603.html> Accessed 23 July 2016.

[100]*Case of Sutton's Hospital* (1612) 77 Eng Rep 960 and Grietje Baars, *Law (yers) Congealing Capitalism: On the (im) Possibility of Restraining Business in Conflict through International Criminal Law*. Diss. UCL (University College London 2012).

[101]*Ibid.*

[102]Petri Mäntysaari, 'Theories of Corporate Law and Corporations: Past Approaches' (Springer Berlin Heidelberg 2012).

[103]John Dewey, 'The Historic Background of Corporate Legal Personality' (1926) 35 (6) Yale Law Journal 655; see also: Stefan J Padfield, 'Corporate Social Responsibility & Concession Theory' (2015) 6 William & Mary Business Law Review 1.

whether or not in the form of default terms in implicit contracts. It directs attention to the bargain that the incorporating authority can offer in return for the advantages of incorporation regulation. It identifies that if the costs of regulation outweigh the benefits, firms will not be incorporated into bodies.[104] Finally, the 'realist theory', unlike the previous three legal theories, denies that society is comprised only of human beings.[105] The subjects of law include those institutions with the capacity to respect and apply the rules, as stated by the theory.

The first two theories of international law and corporate law place limitations on the capacity of the law to regulate by constructing an irreducible minimum of 'corporateness'.[106] This notion is derived 'from German sociology'[107] of the 1890s[108] and was implemented 'into common law jurisprudence only in'[109] translation 'form. It had the profound effect of facilitating an anthropomorphic approach to the acceptance of the corporate form in areas of law designed for human beings. Lord Denning, in particular, referred to companies'[110] 'and incorporations as having a 'head' and 'brain' when formulating reasons for why it might have intention for the purpose of intentional torts'[111] and crimes.[112] These theories assume that people, both collectively and individually, are a basic unit of society and are

---

104Stefan J Padfield, 'Corporate Social Responsibility & Concession Theory' (2015) 6 William & Mary Business Law Review 1.

105David Millon, 'Theories of the Corporation' (1990) 2 Duke Law Journal 201.

106*Chadwick v Pioneer Private Telephone Co. Ltd* [1941] 1 All E.R. 522, 523D, *Ready Mixed Concrete (South East) Ltd v Minister of Pension and National Insurance* [1968] 2 QB 497 and *Nethermere (St Neots) Ltd v Gardinier* [1984] ICR 612.

107 <https://www.oup.com.au/__data/assets/pdf_file/0006/163086/Wishart_ORC_theory_chapter.pdf> Accessed 8 May 2017.

108Harry Liebersohn, *Fate and Utopia in German Sociology 1870-1923* (Mit Press 1990).

109 <https://www.oup.com.au/__data/assets/pdf_file/0006/163086/Wishart_ORC_theory_chapter.pdf> Accessed 8 May 2017.

110*Ibid.*

111 Jake Dear and Steven E Zipperstein, 'Comparative Fault and Intentional Torts: Doctrinal Barriers and Policy Considerations' (1984) 24 Santa Clara Law Review 1 and <https://www.oup.com.au/__data/assets/pdf_file/0006/163086/Wishart_ORC_theory_chapter.pdf> Accessed 8 May 2017.

112*H.L Bolton (Engineering) Co Ltd v T.J Graham and Sons Ltd* [1957] 1QB 159 at 172 and *Lennard's Carrying Co. Ltd v Asiatic Petroleum Co. Ltd* [1915] AC 705 and <https://www.oup.com.au/__data/assets/pdf_file/0006/163086/Wishart_ORC_theory_chapter.pdf> Accessed 8 May 2017.

concerned with their legitimacy. Law regulates legitimate or 'legal' persons.[113] Given the assumptions of each theory, implications flow for that law. The law of legal persons is not otherwise explained in the definition, and its content is subject to debate.[114] However, the implications for each theory sometimes do not match existing or proposed legal doctrines for corporate accountability and remedy under international law.[115] They are, therefore, disproven. Nonetheless, the explanations are limited, for instance, and say little on how internal relations in corporations are to be regulated. This is because evidentiary difficulties may arise where the corporation concerned has a long-winded structure and because of the need to link the offence to a controlling officer/person. The smaller the corporation, the more likely it will be that guilty knowledge can be attributed to the controlling officer/person and, therefore, to the corporation itself. Thus, it will be difficult to establish corporate liability in this circumstance, and instead could be appropriate to find corporate liability through the duty of care.

The description of corporate legal personality in regards to human rights violations and environmental damages is inadequate, wrong, and incomplete.[116] Having said that, this book supports the reality approach to corporate legal personality and argues that corporations are capable of acquiring legal status under domestic and international law.[117] It can, therefore, be assumed that the substantial benefits that parent corporations receive through their subsidiaries' business activities[118] in the form of dividends, tax benefits, and preferential tax treatment, make them liable for subsidiary misconducts.[119] The growing acknowledgement that victims should be able to obtain a remedy against parent corporations for violations

113 Philip Allott, 'The Concept of International Law' (1999) 10 (1) European Journal of International Law 31, 50.
114 Steven R Ratner, 'Corporations and Human Rights: A Theory of Legal Responsibility' (2001) 111 (3) Yale Law Journal 443, 545.
115 Peter A French, 'The Corporation as a Moral Person' (1979) 16 (3) American Philosophical Quarterly 207.
116 Martin Wolff, 'On the Nature of Legal Persons' (1938) 54 Law Quarterly Review 494.
117 Max Radin, 'The Endless Problem of Corporate Personality' (1932) 32 (4) Columbia Law Review 643.
118 Phillip I Blumberg, 'Asserting Human Rights Against Multinational Corporations under United States Law: Conceptual and Procedural Problems' (2002) 50 American Journal of Comparative Law 493.
119 Nina A Mendelson, 'A Control-Based Approach to Shareholder Liability for Corporate Torts' (2002) 102 Columbia Law Review 1203.

of international human rights norms[120] and serious environmental damages,[121] specifically where they cannot obtain such a remedy against the corporate subsidiary in the host country,[122] should be seen as a valid legal argument. However, in the vast majority of corporate human rights violations cases, this has not been the case, as the legal theory of corporate law has restricted the development of corporate accountability under international law.[123] The majority of victims of human rights violations in developing countries have no appropriate remedy for corporate misconducts that have impacted on their life[124] because there is a lack of good governance, law and judicial mechanisms for corporate accountability.[125]

In addition, the doctrine of limited liability also restricts the accountability of corporate human rights violations no matter how great the harm, and no matter how much financial benefit the parent corporation receives from the business operations of the subsidiary.[126] The doctrine of limited liability advocates that a limited liability company is a company where the shareholder's liability towards the loss or deficit is limited by shares.[127]

---

[120]Gwynne Skinner, 'Beyond Kiobel: Providing Access to Judicial Remedies for Violations of International Human Rights Norms by Transnational Business in a New (Post-Kiobel) World' (2014).

[121]Hari M Osofsky, 'Environmental Human Rights Under the Alien Tort Claims Act: Redress for Indigenous Victims of Multinational Corporations' (1997) 20 Suffolk Transnational Law Review 335.

[122]Gwynne Skinner, 'Rethinking Limited Liability of Parent Corporations for Their Subsidiaries' Extraterritorial Violations of Human Rights Law' (2016) <http://clsbluesky.law.columbia.edu/2016/02/10/rethinking-limited-liability-of-parent-corporations-for-their-subsidiaries-extraterritorial-violations-of-human-rights-law/> Accessed 20 April 2017.

[123]Robert McCorquodale and Penelope Simons, 'Responsibility Beyond Borders: State Responsibility for Extraterritorial Violations by Corporations of International Human Rights Law' (2007) 70 (4) Modern Law Review 598, 625.

[124]Michael Blowfield and Jedrzej George Frynas, 'Setting New Agendas: Critical Perspectives on Corporate Social Responsibility in The Developing World' (2005) 81 (3) International affairs 499.

[125]Erik Berglöf and Stijn Claessens, 'Enforcement and Good Corporate Governance in Developing Countries and Transition Economies' (2006) 21 (1) World Bank Research Observer 123, 150.

[126] Robert B Thompson, 'Unpacking Limited Liability: Direct and Vicarious Liability of Corporate Participants for Torts of the Enterprise' (1994) 57 Vand Law Review 1.

[127]H. M. Curteis, 'The Doctrine of Limited Liability' (1938) 83 (532) Royal United Services Institution Journal 695.

Together, these theories and the principle of limited liability have created major obstacles for victims' access to effective remedies for corporate misconduct[128] and disclosure 'of human rights-relevant information, whether held by state authorities or private actors.'[129] Also, the lack of access to human rights-relevant information, including evidence of the detrimental impacts of companies' activities, has undermined the ability of affected individuals and communities to build robust lawsuits. This is particularly the case where the victims cannot identify the subsidiary causing the harm and cannot obtain a remedy in the host country.[130] As a consequence, many victims of business operations carried out in violation of international human rights norms who live in host countries with ineffectual and/or corrupt governments and judicial systems have faced serious obstacles in obtaining remedies against the subsidiary in the host country.[131] This is because there is either no mechanism for victims in host countries to obtain human rights-relevant information and remedies or there is no statutory or common law basis to bring a claim against the parent corporation.[132] As a result, many victims are unable to obtain judicial redress for the harm suffered. Also, even when victims are awarded a judicial judgment, there exists a lack of funds to provide remedies for the victims, the subsidiary of the parent corporation is underfunded, or there exists a lack of transparency and information.[133]

---

[128]John Ruggie, 'Report of the Special Representative of The Secretary-General on the Issue of Human Rights and Transnational Corporations and Other Business Enterprises: Guiding Principles on Business and Human Rights: Implementing the United Nations 'Protect, Respect and Remedy' Framework' (2011) 29 (2) Netherlands Quarterly of Human Rights 224.

[129]Amnesty International, 'Creating a Paradigm Shift: Legal Solutions to Improve Access to Remedy for Corporate Human Rights Abuse' (2017). <https://www.amnesty.org/download/Documents/POL3070372017ENGLISH.PDF> Accessed 9 April 2019.

[130]Ariadne K Sacharoff, 'Multinationals in Host Countries: Can They Be Held Liable under The Alien Tort Claims Act for Human Rights Violations' (1997) 23 Brooklyn Journal of International Law 927.

[131]Stephen J Kobrin, 'Private Political Authority and Public Responsibility: Transnational Politics, Transnational Firms, and Human Rights' (2009) 19 (3) Business Ethics Quarterly 349.

[132]Barbara A Frey, 'The Legal and Ethical Responsibilities of Transnational Corporations in The Protection of International Human Rights' (1997) 6 Minnesota Journal of Global Trade 153.

[133]Justice C Nwobike, 'The African Commission on Human and Peoples' Rights and The Demystification of Second and Third Generation Rights Under the African Charter: Social and Economic Rights Action Center (SERAC) and The Center for

To remedy this, the evaluation of the adequacy of a corporation's human rights duty of care should include an assessment of its disclosure practices. An adequate corporate human rights duty of care process should require the business disclosure of information about human rights policies, processes and their outcomes, as well as information about actual and potential adverse human rights impacts of specific business activities or operation. Furthermore, the corporate duty of care should include timely access to activity information that is reliable, useful and accessible to ensure genuine engagement and consultation with potentially affected individuals and communities. Corporate duty of care and disclosure are intrinsically connected and indispensable for each other. Disclosure failures are serious failures of the corporate duty of care.

Awareness by the international community of this issue is demonstrated by the fact that John Ruggie, the UN Special Representative on Business and Human Rights, was tasked with establishing an international framework as a common global standard for preventing and addressing the adverse human rights impact of business operations.[134] The main purpose behind Rep. Ruggie's work was to ensure businesses were accountable for human rights abuses related to corporate business operations. Rep. Ruggie sought to do this by developing the United Nations Guiding Principles on Business and Human Rights (GPs).[135] Interestingly, the framework of the GPs elaborated on the duty of states to protect against human rights violations by third parties in their jurisdictions, including the corporate responsibility to respect human rights through due diligence and effective judicial and non-judicial access to remedies for victims of business-related abuses.

Rep. Ruggie developed the Guiding Principles based on the UN concept of 'Responsibility to Protect'.[136] The concept adopts three pillars for examining the respective obligations and responsibilities of individuals with regard to human rights and business. Undoubtedly, Rep. Ruggie's GPs not only clarified the relationship between multinational corporations (MNCs) and human rights, but also highlighted several important issues regarding corporations and human rights in general. However, Ruggie's view on accountability and remedies for human rights abuses lacks substance

---

Economic and Social Rights (CESR) v Nigeria' (2005) 1 (2) African Journal of Legal Studies 129.

[134]John G Ruggie, 'Protect, Respect and Remedy: a Framework for Business and Human Rights' (2008) 3 (2) Innovations 189.

[135]Par Al Gedicks, *The New Resource Wars: Native and Environmental Struggles Against Multinational Corporations* (Vol. 210, Black Rose Books Ltd 1994).

[136]UNGA '2005 World Summit Outcomes' (24 October 2005) UN Doc A/RES/60/1.

as it does not provide clear mechanisms for cases when national states are reluctant or incapable of protecting citizens from human rights violations by MNCs. This is specifically in regard to Pillar 2 on 'corporate responsibility to respect, and Pillar 3, access to remedy. As such, this latest development has proven to be unsuccessful as well.'[137] It has failed, moreover, to fill the core gap that exists in the concept of corporate accountability for human rights abuses, which includes remedy and enforcement.

The last several decades have seen a rapid increase in the fears that voluntary implementation could allow too much discretion by corporate officers, and states have become quiet about establishing limits on corporate activity. The desire for quicker, more binding action led some governments and non-governmental organisations to renew calls for a binding treaty outlining corporate responsibility. In 2014, the Human Rights Council established an international working group to begin the drafting process for a treaty on business and human rights.[138] In July 2015, the working group held its first meeting to begin discussing the parameters of a treaty.[139] In February 2017, France adopted an unprecedented law that embodies some of the principles discussed above. Law 2017-399 (Duty of Vigilance law)[140] imposes a 'duty of vigilance' on French companies and subsidiaries whose head office is located in France or parent subsidiaries located abroad of a certain size to prevent serious human rights abuses and environmental damages resulting from their activities, the activities of companies they control, and those of established business relations.[141]

---

[137] Björn Fasterling and Geert Demuijnck, 'Human Rights in the Void? Due Diligence in The UN Guiding Principles on Business and Human Rights' (2013) 116 (4) Journal of Business Ethics 799.

[138] Open-Ended Intergovernmental Working on Transnational Corporations and Other Business Enterprises with Respect to Human Rights, UN Human Rights Council (2014). <https://perma.cc/GY7A-JB3R> Accessed 18 September 2015.

[139] *Ibid.*

[140] Loi n° 2017-399 Du 27 mars 2017 Relative au Devoir de Vigilance Des Sociétés Mères et Des Entreprises Donneuses d'Ordre. <https://www.legifrance.gouv.fr/affichTexte.do?cidTexte=JORFTEXT000034290626&dateTexte=&categorieLien=id. More information in English available at: https://business-humanrights.org/en/france-natl-assembly-adopts-law-imposing-due-diligence-on-multinationals-to-prevent-serious-human-rightsabuses-in-their-supply-chains> Accessed 5 June 2017.

[141] Amnesty International, 'Creating a paradigm shift: Legal Solutions to Improve Access to Remedy for Corporate Human Rights Abuse' (2017). <https://www.amnesty.org/download/Documents/POL3070372017ENGLISH.PDF> Accessed 09 March 2018.

To this end, companies must put measures in place to regularly identify and assess risks and take action to mitigate these risks and prevent serious abuses.[142] Importantly, any person whose human rights are allegedly affected as a result of a 'lack of vigilance' on the part of the French company can bring a civil claim against it before French courts. The law determines that a company has control over another when it (1) holds a majority of its voting rights, (2) has the right to elect the majority of the members of its administrative, executive or supervisory bodies, or (3) when it exercises a dominant influence over a subsidiary by virtue of a contract or statutory clauses.[143] Unfortunately, the range of companies captured by the law was defined too narrowly.[144] In effect, it applied to just 100 to 150 of France's largest companies. Nevertheless, this is the first law to establish an express duty for companies to prevent human rights abuses both domestically and abroad, and to account for the steps taken to achieve this objective. Significantly, this legislation recognises and takes steps to address the existing accountability gap of companies that operate across borders.[145]

Similarly, 'the Swiss government is considering a proposal from a large coalition of national civil society organisations to enact legislation to compel companies to undertake human rights and environmental due diligence in all their activities abroad.'[146] This follows a successful popular initiative (the 'Responsible Business Initiative') that was 'launched in 2015 and which gathered well over the required 100,000 signatures to prompt a national referendum on the proposal.'[147] 'The proposed legal text, if

---

142 *Ibid.* 5 Article 1 of the Duty of Vigilance law.

143 Amnesty International, 'Creating a paradigm shift: Legal solutions to Improve Access to Remedy for Corporate Human Rights Abuse' (2017). <https://www.amnesty.org/download/Documents/POL3070372017ENGLISH.PDF> Accessed 09 March 2018. Also see, *Ibid.*

144 Claire Bright, 'Creating a Legislative Level Playing Field in Business and Human Rights at the European Level: is the French duty of vigilance Law the Way Forward?' (2020).

145 Almut Schilling-Vacaflor, 'Putting the French Duty of Vigilance Law in Context: Towards Corporate Accountability for Human Rights Violations in the Global South?' (2020) Human Rights Review 1, 19.

146 <http://konzern-initiative.ch/?lang=en http://konzern-initiative.ch/swiss-quality-must-include-the-protection-of-human-rights-and-the-environment/?lang=en> Accessed 1 November 2017.

147 Amnesty International, 'Creating a paradigm shift: Legal Solutions to Improve Access to Remedy for Corporate Human Rights Abuse' (2017). <https://www.amnesty.org/download/Documents/POL3070372017ENGLISH.PDF> Accessed 09 March 2018 and <http://konzern-initiative.ch/over-140000-signatures-

enacted, would require Swiss-based companies to carry out human rights due diligence to identify actual and potential impacts on human rights and the environment, take appropriate measures to prevent and/or cease violations and account for the actions they took. These duties would apply to 'controlled companies' as well as all other business relationships.'[148] 'Unlike the French Duty of Vigilance law, the Swiss proposal does not define 'control'. 'Instead, it clarifies that control will be determined according to the factual circumstances of each case.'[149] 'Also, Swiss-based companies would be liable for damage caused by companies under their control unless they could prove that they carried out appropriate due diligence to avoid the'[150] the harm. This is another commendable effort to strengthen the prevention of corporate abuse across borders. [151]

Likewise, a useful precedent is the 'due diligence' defence established by the UK Bribery Act (2010). Section 7 of the Act determines that a commercial organisation will be liable if it fails to prevent bribery by an 'associated person' carried out on its behalf. However, the commercial organisation can invoke the defence that it 'had in place adequate procedures designed to prevent persons associated with [the commercial organisation] from undertaking such conduct'. [152] 'A 'due diligence' defence is also envisaged in the Swiss Responsible Business Initiative discussed above.' [153] Under the provision of Swiss law, it is the

---

for-the-swiss-responsible-business-initiative/?lang=en> Accessed 5 November 2017

[148]*Ibid.*

[149]*Ibid.*

[150]Amnesty International, 'Creating a paradigm shift: Legal Solutions to Improve Access to Remedy for Corporate Human Rights Abuse' (2017). <https://www.amnesty.org/download/Documents/POL3070372017ENGLISH.PDF> Accessed 09 March 2018 and <http://konzern-initiative.ch/initiativtext/?lang=en 21> Accessed 5 November 2017.

[151]Amnesty International, 'Creating a Paradigm Shift: Legal Solutions to Improve Access to Remedy for Corporate Human Rights Abuse' (2017)

[152]Amnesty International, 'Creating a Paradigm Shift: Legal Solutions to Improve Access to Remedy for Corporate Human Rights Abuse' (2017). <https://www.amnesty.org/download/Documents/POL3070372017ENGLISH.PDF> Accessed 06 April 2018 and Section 7 of the UK Bribery Act (2010) <http://www.legislation.gov.uk/ukpga/2010/23/contents 26> Accessed 30 October 2017.

[153] Amnesty International, 'Creating a paradigm shift: Legal solutions to improve access to remedy for corporate human rights abuse' (2017). https://justice-project.org/wp-content/uploads/2017/09/paradigm-shift-ai-2017.pdf > Accessed 12 April 2018.

responsibility of the company to prove that they are not liable for the harm caused. Hence the burden of proof is shifted to the parent corporation to prove it did all it could to prevent or stop the injury. Under this proposal, companies would not be liable for damages caused by entities under their control if they could prove that they took all due care to avoid the damage, or that the damage would have occurred even if all due care had been taken.[154]

Additionally, in May 2017, the EU passed Regulation (EU) 2017/821, requiring importers of certain raw minerals and metals (tin, tantalum, tungsten and gold) originating from conflict-affected and high-risk areas to 'carry out human rights' due diligence in accordance with the five steps required under the OECD Due Diligence Guidance for Responsible Supply Chains of Minerals from Conflict-Affected and High-Risk Areas.'[155] 'This was a welcome first step by the EU. However, enforcement of the law has been left entirely to member states, and it is unclear whether or how this will work in practice. EU member states must adopt rules dealing with infringements of the law by importers and issue a 'notice of remedial action''[156] 'to any importer that infringes the legislation. Authorities in each member state will also be responsible for undertaking 'ex-post checks' to ensure importers comply with the due diligence obligations. In practice, however, this means that the effectiveness of these mechanisms will depend on whether EU member states adopt adequate domestic laws and regulations to deter and address infringements (like effective penalties for non-compliance) and whether the relevant authorities take a proactive approach to ensuring compliance.'[157]

The German Green Party also tabled a proposal in the Bundestag in 2016 under which German companies of a certain size that operate directly, or through subsidiaries, in a high-risk sector or area, would be required to conduct human rights due diligence to identify and address risks

---

[154]<http://konzern-initiative.ch/initiativtext/?lang=en> accessed 30 November 2017.
[155]Amnesty International, 'Creating a paradigm shift: Legal Solutions to Improve Access to Remedy for Corporate Human Rights Abuse' (2017). <https://www.amnesty.org/download/Documents/POL3070372017ENGLISH.PDF> Accessed 09 March 2018 and Council of Europe Recommendation on Human Rights and Business, para. 22. <https://search.coe.int/cm/Pages/result_details.aspx?ObjectID=09000016805c1ad4> Accessed 22 November 2017.
[156]*Ibid.*
[157]<http://www.bhrinlaw.org/documents/amnestyinternational.creatingaparadigmshiftpol3070372017english.pdf> Accessed on 4 April 2018 and <http://eur-lex.europa.eu/legal-content/EN/TXT/?uri=OJ:L:2017:130:TOC> Accessed 22 November 2017.

of contributing to human rights abuses.[158] The Government's majority in the Bundestag rejected the motion, but civil society organisations continue to promote it.[159] The proposal broadly lays out the required due diligence steps, while also allowing for a number of factors, such as country and sector-specific risks, and the size of the company, to be taken into account in any assessment of the adequacy of the actual steps taken. Unlike the French Duty of Vigilance, which would be enforced through private claims, this would be enforceable by the state through a variety of instruments, including administrative orders and fines. However, public enforcement is supplemented by a provision that would allow or facilitate civil liability claims in cases of due diligence failures. According to the proposal, the due diligence duties established in the law would define the expected standard of conduct for tort/non-contractual liability claims.

Given all that has been mentioned thus far, one may suppose that the main problem arises when the host state is not able to apply its domestic law to MNCs operating on their soil[160] or when the home state is unwilling to impose accountability or restrict the operations of MNCs under its jurisdiction.[161] These findings suggest that legal rights and remedies are difficult to acquire in host states. Following the argument presented in this book, barriers to the implementation of human rights law may hinder the enforcement of judicial remedy and the stopping of MNCs from violating human rights in the countries in which they carry out their business operations. For the same reason, the focus of this book is centred on the legal rights and procedural rights to enforce remedies, while recognising

---

[158]The German Original of The Proposed Law can be Found in: Klinger/Krajewski/Krebs/Hartmann, Verankerung menschenrechtlicher Sorgfaltspflicht von Unternehmen im deutschen Recht (March 2016), pages 38 to 42. <https://germanwatch.org/de/download/14745.pdf> Accessed 20 November 2017.

[159]Business & Human Rights Resource Centre, '3 Entry Points to Implement the German National Action Plan'. <https://business-humanrights.org/en/3-entry-points-to-implement-the-germannational-action-plan> Accessed 20 November 2017.

[160]Dame Rosalyn Higgins, *Problems and Process: International Law and How We Use It* (Oxford University Press 1995).

[161]Laura A Dickinson, 'Government for Hire: Privatizing Foreign Affairs and The Problem of Accountability under International Law' (2005) 47 William & Mary Law Review 135, Markos Karavias, 'Shared Responsibility and Multinational Enterprises' (2015) 62 (1) Netherlands International Law Review 91, Cindy S Woods, 'It Isn't a State Problem: The Minas Conga Mine Controversy and The Need for Binding International Obligations on Corporate Actors' (2014) 46 Georgetown Journal of International Law 629, Danwood Mzikenge Chirwa, 'The Doctrine of State Responsibility as a Potential Means of Holding Private Actors Accountable for Human Rights' (2004) 5 Melbourne Journal of International Law 1.

that these are not the only rights victims seek. The victims of corporate human rights abuses and environmental damages may have a broad range of needs and may seek a variety of remedies under human rights law and environmental law. Likewise, a scenario that warrants the same solution is that of subsidiaries operating in countries that offer no realistic avenues to seek reparation against them if they cause harm. This may be the case of countries affected by or emerging from armed conflict, or where there is a total collapse of the rule of law.[162] In these circumstances, the level of inefficiency of the legal system, the degree of impunity for human rights abuse, or the level of arbitrariness in the promulgation, enforcement and adjudication of laws may be such that the prospects for achieving due process and justice in a given case may be very low.

In addition to the corporation's legal subjects, states have naturally sought to regulate them within their domestic legal systems. In these cases, home state laws should allow claims to be brought directly against the controlling corporation, or against both the controlling business and its subsidiary.[163] If allegations of wrongdoing against the subsidiary are proven,[164] the controlling corporation would be liable for the harm. Again, the element of fault of the controlling corporations in these cases would be irrelevant in court. However, due to the fact that corporations are steadily becoming more powerful, such efforts appear increasingly futile. Where a government's interests are concerned, corporations attempt to dominate the state, generating a paradoxical role reversal.[165] The pervasive influence of corporations and their ever-increasing effects on human rights globally 'is now the two hours' traffic of our stage.[166]

Evidence is accumulating that in the modern world, state power has been replaced by MNC economic power, where MNCs play an extensive role in the formation of regulations on business and human

---

[162]Richard A Cosgrove, *The Rule of Law: Albert Venn Dicey, Victorian Jurist* (UNC Press Books 2017).

[163]Ekaterina Aristova, 'Tort Litigation Against Transnational Corporations in the English courts: The Challenge of Jurisdiction' (2018) 14 Utrecht Law Review 6.

[164]Marieke van Hooijdonk and Peter V Eijsvoogel *Litigation in the Netherlands: Civil Procedure, Arbitration and Administrative Litigation* (Kluwer Law International BV 2009).

[165]Nicholas Connolly & Manette Kaisershot, 'Corporate Power and Human Rights' (2015) 19 (6) International Journal of Human Rights 663.

[166] *Ibid.*

rights.[167] Likewise, the expansion of international investment[168] and trade[169] has not promoted accountability, but has rather fuelled a system of corruption[170] and ineffective legal mechanisms for corporate governance.[171] The current level of corporate governance[172] has not resulted in effective corporate accountability or transparency in transnational business operations. Similarly, there is only a small amount of evidence to support the development and effectiveness of corporate governance in regulating corporate conduct. The continued development of trade agreements[173] and economic operations of MNCs[174] has produced many economic gains and benefits while simultaneously contributing to substantial human rights violations[175] and environmental damages.

---

[167]Ralph Nader, *The Case Against Free Trade: GATT, NAFTA, and The Globalization of Corporate Power (*Vol. 49. North Atlantic Books 1993).

[168] William Arthur Lewis, *The Evolution of The International Economic Order* (Princeton University Press 2015).

[169] John H Dunning, *The Globalization of Business (Routledge Revivals): The Challenge of the 1990* (Routledge 2014).

[170]Shang-Jin Wei, 'Corruption in Economic Development: Beneficial Grease, Minor Annoyance, or Major Obstacle?' (1999) World Bank Policy Research Working Paper No. 2048.

[171] Ian Bannon and Paul Collier, eds. *Natural Resources and Violent Conflict: Options and Actions* (World Bank publications 2003).

[172]<http://www.companydirectors.com.au/Help/Page-Not-Found?item=director-resource-centre%2fpublications%2fcompany-director-magazine%2fback-editions-2010%2fjuly-2010%2fjuly%2fopinion-good-governance-is-good-business&user=extranet%5cAnonymous&site=homesite&url=%252fDirector-Resource-Centre%252fPublications%252fCompany-Director-magazine%252fBack-editions-2010%252fJuly-2010%252fJuly%252fOpinion-Good-governance-is-good-business > Accessed 14 July 2016 and Van Lutgart den Berghe, *International Standardisation of Good Corporate Governance: Best Practices for the Board of Directors* (Springer Science & Business Media 2012).

[173]World Trade Report, 'Speeding Up Trade: Benefits and Challenges of Implementing the WTO Trade Facilitation' (2015). <https://www.wto.org/english/res_e/booksp_e/world_trade_report15_e.pdf> Accessed 12 August 2016.

[174]Tracey S Keys, Thomas W Malnight, and Christel K. Stoklund, 'Corporate Clout 2013: Time for Responsible Capitalism' (2013) Strategy Dynamics Global. <http://globaltrends.activatemedia.com/wp-content/uploads/2013/06/corporate%20clout%202013.pdf> Accessed 12 August 2016

[175]Jennifer A Zerk, *Multinationals and Corporate Social Responsibility: Limitations and Opportunities in International Law* (Vol. 48, Cambridge University Press 2006).

Although the past decades have seen a rapid development in MNCs' economic power, including financial institutions,[176] no effective mechanism has been developed for holding them accountable for human rights violations and environmental damages that are linked to their business operations.[177] Drawing on an extensive range of sources on MNCs' human rights violations,[178] most authors set out the different ways in which MNC operations and human rights abuses are linked, such as:

1. Forced eviction and displacement due to large infrastructure projects, specifically in energy and agriculture, which are mostly financed by international financial institutions (IFIs) and national development banks;
2. Loss of lands and livelihood as a result of extractive industry operations;
3. Adverse health impacts and environmental contamination caused by exploitation of natural resources, factory operations, or industrial accidents;
4. Loss of life, arbitrary detention and torture of community members and human rights campaigners by security forces who have been provided with equipment or employed by a company;
5. Poor and unsafe working conditions in factories which are part of the global supply chain for apparel and electronic retail brands; and
6. Violations of privacy, freedom of expression, and freedom of association resulting from technology companies complying with government surveillance or domestic law.[179]

The United Nations Guiding Principles on Business and Human Rights (UNGPs) advocate that all businesses across all sectors in the global economy be required to take the appropriate due diligence steps to 'identify, prevent, mitigate and account for how [they] address their impacts on human rights.'Pillar 2 of the UNGPs elaborates further on what is required

---

[176]Leslie Sklair, *Transnational Capitalist Class* (John Wiley & Sons Ltd 2012).
[177]Michael Anderson, 'Transnational Corporations and Environmental Damage: Is Tort Law the Answer?' (2001) 41 Washburn Law Journal 399.
[178]Layna Mosley and Saika Uno, 'Racing to the Bottom or Climbing to the Top? Economic Globalization and Collective Labour Rights' (2007) 40 (8) Comparative Political Studies 923.
[179]Andrew Clapham, *Human Rights Obligations of Non-State Actors* (OUP Oxford 2006).

under each of these steps. Intergovernmental organisations such as the Organisation for Economic Cooperation and Development (OECD) have begun elaborating sector- and issue-specific due diligence standards for companies, which lay out what is required to avoid harm in relation to particular situations. These standards provide guidance to assess liability to the extent that they elaborate on what 'reasonable steps' might look like in particular circumstances. These assessments of corporate due diligence should not be a 'box ticking' exercise, but should instead focus on the adequacy of the measures taken and the extent to which measures were genuinely geared towards preventing harm. However, in general, human rights violations and environmental damages caused by MNCs over the last few decades have exposed critical corporate accountability gaps,[180] with corporate accountability and the protection provided by international law and human rights mechanisms failing to keep pace with the rapid development of the economic power of MNCs. Corporate accountability literature abounds with descriptions of accountability; however, they avoid the reliable legal methodology and intellectual legal rigour that can provide a remedy for victims of human rights violations and environmental damages. The outcomes of these remedies, furthermore, are both predictable and consistent. In short, the current concept of corporate accountability has not identified the process or the legal methodology for identification and appraisal of the evidentiary rules of corporate liability under international law and human rights law.[181] What specifically needs to be questioned with respect to the MNC accountability gap is the effectiveness of the MNC liability under the current mechanism.

Also, 'corporate responsibility',[182] 'corporate social responsibility (CSR) and corporate accountability are sometimes confused or seen as synonymous.'[183] However, 'corporate social responsibility and corporate accountability are typically distinguished from one another along several lines. Corporate social responsibility, in its broadest sense, refers to varied practices that reflect the belief that corporations have responsibilities

---

[180] Wolfgang Kaleck and Miriam Saage-Maaß, 'Corporate Accountability for Human Rights Violations Amounting to International Crimes: the Status Quo and Its Challenges' (2010) 8 (3) Journal of International Criminal Justice 699, 724.

[181] Yvette Selim, 'Examining Victims and Perpetrators in Post-conflict Nepal' (2017) International Review of Victimology.

[182] Stephen Tully, ed. *Research Handbook on Corporate Legal Responsibility* (Edward Elgar Publishing 2005).

[183] Subhabrata Bobby Banerjee, 'Corporate Social Responsibility: The good, The Bad and The Ugly' (2008) 34 (1) Critical Sociology 51.

beyond generating profit for their shareholders.'[184] Such responsibilities include the negative duty to refrain from harm caused to the environment, individuals or communities, and sometimes also positive duties to protect society and the environment, such as protecting the human rights of workers and 'communities affected by business activities.'[185]

'Such responsibilities are generally considered to extend not only to direct social and environmental impacts of business activity, but also to more indirect effects resulting from relationships with [186]business partners, such as those involved in global production chains.'[187] In contrast, the term corporate accountability is commonly used to refer to more confrontational or enforceable strategies of influencing corporate behaviour. Often, the term corporate social responsibility is used to indicate voluntary approaches, albeit those supported by market-based incentives. [188] 'Corporate accountability typically implies that corporate behaviour is influenced by pressure exerted by social and governmental actors beyond the company itself.[189] Such actors can adopt a range of strategies, including but not limited to the mobilisation of legal mechanisms to enforce social standards.' [190] Together, these studies indicate that corporate social responsibility and corporate accountability illustrate different levels of liability in a legal context.

---

184 <https://corporateaccountabilityresearch.net/files/2011/09/What-is-corporate-accountability.pdf> Accessed 18 December 2020.

185<https://corporateaccountabilityresearch.net/files/2011/09/What-is-corporate-accountability.pdf > Accessed 9 June 2017 and Carmen Valor, 'Corporate Social Responsibility and Corporate Citizenship: Towards Corporate Accountability' (2005) 110 (2) Business and Society Review 191, 212.

186<https://corporateaccountabilityresearch.net/files/2011/09/What-is-corporate-accountability.pdf > Accessed 18 May 2018.

187Dirk Matten and Jeremy Moon, '"Implicit" and "explicit" CSR: A Conceptual Framework for a Comparative Understanding of Corporate Social Responsibility' (2008) 33 (2) Academy of Management Review 404, 424 and <https://corporateaccountabilityresearch.net/files/2011/09/What-is-corporate-accountability.pdf > Accessed 17 May 2018.

188 Doreen J McBarnet, Aurora Voiculescu and Tom Campbell, eds. *The New Corporate Accountability: Corporate Social Responsibility and the Law* (Cambridge University Press 2009).

189 Emeka Duruigbo, 'Corporate Accountability and Liability for International Human Rights Abuses: Recent Changes and Recurring Challenges' (2008) 6 (2) Northwestern University Journal of International Human Rights 222.

190 Julia Graff, 'Corporate War Criminals and The International Criminal Court: Blood and Profits in The Democratic Republic of Congo' (2004) 11 (2) Human Rights Brief 23.

'Perhaps, the most important innovation of the corporate accountability movement has been its'[191] demand 'for increased participation by affected groups.'[192] 'This has been shown to be extremely important in many contexts as a basis for effective compliance with specified norms.'[193] In the few and often short-lived cases in which a worker's organisation or representation has been established, positive outcomes for workers have often been achieved, both in factory settings and among homeworkers.[194] Participation in initiatives can feed into underlying changes to social power relations via their spill-over into campaigning activities, and their potential to create sustainable social alliances between workers, producers, and communities affected by transnational business activity.[195] However, such participatory, multi-stakeholder processes do tend to confront a range of practical challenges associated with both weak capacity among key stakeholder groups to engage effectively, and in some cases also difficulties in mediating conflicting priorities of affected stakeholders.[196] Clearly, significant challenges continue to confront all these different strategies of corporate accountability.[197] However, to view these initiatives as static institutional arrangements misunderstands their purpose and impact as both experimental, learning devices in specific governance contexts, and as broader vehicles for social transformation via their provision of ongoing

---

[191] <https://corporateaccountabilityresearch.net/files/2011/09/What-is-corporate-accountability.pdf> Accessed 19 June 2018.

[192] Craig N Smith, *Morality and The Market (Routledge Revivals): Consumer Pressure for Corporate Accountability* (Routledge 2014) and <https://corporateaccountabilityresearch.net/files/2011/09/What-is-corporate-accountability.pdf> Accessed 18 July 2019.

[193] David Weissbrodt and Muria Kruger, 'Norms on The Responsibilities of Transnational Corporations and Other Business Enterprises with Regard to Human Rights' (2003) 97 (4) American Journal of International Law 901.

[194] <https://corporateaccountabilityresearch.net/files/2011/09/What-is-corporate-accountability.pdf> Accessed 18 July 2019 and Lena Ayoub, 'Nike Just Does It and Why The United States Shouldn't: The United States' International Obligation to Hold MNCs Accountable for Their Labor Rights Violations Abroad' (1998) 11 DePaul Business Law Journal 395.

[195] Simon Chesterman, 'The Turn to Ethics: Disinvestment from Multinational Corporations for Human Rights Violations the Case of Norway's Sovereign Wealth Fund' (2007) 23 American University International Law Review 577.

[196] Esben Rahbek Pedersen, 'Making Corporate Social Responsibility (CSR) Operable: How Companies Translate Stakeholder Dialogue into Practice' (2006) 111 (2) Business and Society Review 137.

[197] John Gerard Ruggie, 'Business and Human Rights: The Evolving International Agenda' (2007) 101 (4) American Journal of International Law 819.

sources of knowledge and pressure that can leverage processes of progressive change within wider social and political institutions. Much uncertainty remains and a great deal more experimentation will be needed as corporate accountability initiatives continue to be formed and improved, either as stand-alone forms of corporate regulation or in conjunction with other strategies.[198]

Besides, the concepts of transparency in corporate responsibility and accountability are essential foundations for independent and responsible business conduct and auditing organisation operations. Business independence, accountability and transparency are essential prerequisites in corporate operations that are based on the rule of law and the credibility of international business practice.[199] Accountability and transparency are two important elements of good business governance.[200] 'Transparency is such a powerful force that when consistently applied'[201] it can help fight corruption, improve governance and human rights standards, and promote business accountability.[202] A possible explanation for this might be that accountability and transparency are not easily separated: they both encompass many of the same actions, including public reporting, respecting human rights and environmental law, observing financial law and avoiding business malpractices such as fraud and corruption.[203] The concept of accountability for corporate business operations refers to, among other things, legal and reporting frameworks, organisational structure, strategy, procedures and actions to help ensure that the business and organisation meet their legal obligations with regard to their audit mandate and required reporting within their budget.[204] It may also encompass evaluation and

---

[198]Rob Gray, Dave Owen and Carol Adams, *Accounting & Accountability: Changes and Challenges in Corporate Social and Environmental Reporting* (Prentice Hall 1996).

[199]Mark Casson, *A Theory of Cooperation in International Business* (Palgrave Macmillan UK 1989).

[200]Mark Bovens, 'Two Concepts of Accountability: Accountability as a Virtue and as a Mechanism' (2010) 33 (5) West European Politics 946.

[201]<http://www.issai.org/media(794,1033)/ISSAI_20_Endorsement_version_June.pdf> Accessed 9 June 2016.

[202] Yadong Luo, 'Corporate Governance and Accountability in Multinational Enterprises: Concepts and Agenda' (2005) 11 (1) Journal of International Management 1.

[203]Richard Welford, 'Corporate Social Responsibility in Europe and Asia: Critical Elements and Best Practice' (2004) 13 Journal of Corporate Citizenship 31.

[204] Andrew Crane and Dirk Matten, *Business Ethics: Managing Corporate Citizenship and Sustainability in The Age of Globalization* (Oxford University Press 2016).

follow-ups of the business's own performance as well as the impact of their audit, reports on the regularity and the efficiency of the use of funds, including their actions and activities, and the use of their resources to achieve business objectives.[205]

The notion of transparency refers to the timely, reliable, clear and relevant public reporting on a business's status, mandate, strategy, activities, financial management, operations and performance. It includes the obligation of public reporting on audit findings and conclusions and public access to information about the corporate business activities and dealings.[206] Thus, the notion of transparency itself is not the most important thing in business accountability; it is accountability that makes it possible. Transparency itself is, in fact, a metaphor based on the ability to make something clear without any hidden agendas. However, transparency reveals what is hiding in corporation business operations.[207] In practice, transparency allows the revelation of what otherwise might have been concealed, and it is applied in a social context to reveal human activity in which there is a valid public interest.[208] This theory can be applied to all of those who hold power and positions of authority in society, whether political or economic.[209] Therefore, the notion of business transparency is distinguished from open 'governance, procedural transparency, radical transparency, and systemic or total transparency.'[210] Transparency can be used to scrutinise the activity of businesses, including freedom of information laws, accounting and audit systems, and the protection of public interest disclosure (whistleblowing). However, whether transparency carries a legal duty, it is

---

[205]Stuart M Cooper and David L Owen, 'Corporate Social Reporting and Stakeholder Accountability: The Missing link' (2007) 32 (7) Accounting, Organizations and Society 649.

[206]David Hess, 'Social Reporting and New Governance Regulation: The Prospects of Achieving Corporate Accountability through Transparency' (2007) 17 (3) Business Ethics Quarterly 453.

[207]Paul Sturges, 'What is This Absence Called Transparency?' (2007) 7 (7) International Review of Information Ethics 1.

[208]Carolyn Ball, 'What is Transparency?' (2009) 11 (4) Public Integrity 293.

[209]Shantanu Dixit, Subodh Wagle and Girish Sant, 'The Real Challenge in Power Sector Restructuring: Instilling Public Control Through Transparency, Accountability and Public Participation (TAP)' (2001) 5 (3) Energy for Sustainable Development 95; Ronald J Krotoszynski Jr, 'Transparency, Accountability, and Competency: An Essay on The Obama Administration, Google Government, and The Difficulties of Securing Effective Governance' (2011) 65 (2) University of Miami Law Review 449.

[210]Paul Sturges (n 316).

a subject of legal[211] and literal interpretations,[212] which also need to be distinguished from each other when examining corporate accountability.

This book aims to examine corporate accountability and whether tort and civil law offer better accountability mechanisms and remedies for victims of corporate human rights abuses. In principle, the application of protected human rights in civil and tort law need not create any conceptual difficulty where corporate human rights violations and environmental damages are at stake. The doctrine of tort and the civil legal principle is capable of extending the obligation of corporations under international law and human rights law. The point of departure for the direct application of the duty of care[213] is that human rights law has always played a role in civil and tort law and vice versa. Therefore, at the foundation of the civil law and tort law systems are human rights obligations, self-relations, and human dignity.[214]

This can be seen with tort rules on protecting one image or protecting the rights of individuals (as is the case against state and non-state actors). [215] Likewise, the notion of taking care not to injure one's neighbour,[216] reasonableness, and negligence reflect, *inter alia*, an appropriate balance between corporate business conduct and human rights. Therefore, the notion of corporate duty of care under tort law is not a new concept, but is rather the evolution of an old legal principle. Thus, this book advocates for a content-dependent[217] conception of the principle of duty of care that is mindful of the demands of the legality of corporate liability as the best way forward for holding corporations accountable for human rights violations and environmental damages. The legal duty of care recommendation in this

---

[211]Percy Ellwood Corbett, *Law and Society in the Relations of States* (Harcourt Brace 1951).

[212]Gabriël Moens and John Trone, *Commercial Law of the European Union* (Vol. 4. Springer Science & Business Media 2010).

[213]Percy H Winfield, 'Duty in Tortious Negligence' (1934) 34 (1) Columbia Law Review 41, 66.

[214]Stephen D Sugarman, 'A New Approach to Tort Doctrine: Taking the Best from the Civil Law and Common Law of Canada' (2002) 17 Supreme Court Law Review 375, 388.

[215]Arthur R Miller, 'Simplified Pleading, Meaningful Days in Court, and Trials on The Merits: Reflections on The Deformation of Federal Procedure' (2013) 88 New York University Law Review 286. Also see: < https://www.blakemorgan.co.uk/a-brief-guide-to-the-tort-of-defamation/> Accessed 13 June 2016.

[216]*Donoghue (or McAlister) v Stevenson* [1932] All ER Rep 1; [1932] AC 562 and *Heaven v Pender* (11 Q. B. D. 503, 509

[217]Jain Neha, 'General Principles of Law As Gap-Fillers' (2014) 27 International Legal Theory Colloquium, New York Law School.

research is designed to operate in line with national law and international human rights law. The duty of care or 'duty to prevent' in this book is observed as an 'obligation of means'. This requires carefulness in fulfilling a duty, but not guaranteeing the attainment of a specific result. This allows a corporation to refute or limit the extent of its liability by demonstrating that it took all reasonable steps to avoid causing harm, including in relation to their subsidiaries' business activities. Nevertheless, these 'reasonable steps' must be 'outcome-oriented', that is, designed and implemented wit'h the express and overriding objective of preventing harm. They should be defined by reference to rigorous human rights standards that focus on the prevention of human rights abuses and environmental damages.

Overall, the obligations under tort and civil law indicate that the duty of care could ensure better prevention of adverse impacts by corporations and would also help victims of corporate human rights violations overcome some of the obstacles they face in achieving justice at the domestic court level. The duty of care requires corporations to identify key risks of impacts either linked to their business operations or those of the subsidiary, and the actions taken to prevent them.

This book goes further to argue *qui tacet consentire videtur si loqui debuisset ac potuisset* (he who is silent appears to consent if he should, and could, have spoken).[218] Thus, a reputable presumption of a duty of care exists where a corporation is engaged in business operations with a subsidiary that may directly or indirectly damage the environment or violate the human rights of the community. The legal argument under the neighbourhood principle of a duty of care will make it easier for victims of corporate human rights abuses to argue that the corporation could have influenced the business misconduct and that it should take the appropriate measures to mitigate adverse impacts.

Approaching corporate accountability under the notion of duty of care is an important step forward in a global context where achieving corporate accountability is hindered by the complexity, scale and reach of corporate structures, the absence of a level playing field, the legal and practical barriers faced by the victims to access remedies or the lack of enforcement of existing human rights standards, especially concerning MNCs with a myriad of subsidiaries and suppliers.[219] Admittedly, the reputable presumption of corporate duty of care must be preserved as a means of advancing human rights obligations at both the national and

---

[218]*Temple of Preah Vihear (Cambodia v Thailand)*, 1962 I.C.J. 6, 23 (June 15).

[219]Isabella D Bunn, 'Global Advocacy for Corporate Accountability: Transatlantic Perspectives from The NGO Community' (2004) 19 (6) American University International Law Review 1265.

international level. Thus, it appears inevitable that the flexibility needed for the growth of corporate accountability must be supplied by a greater degree of flexibility in identifying a novel duty of care in business operations. Therefore, for the purpose of this research on corporate accountability and remedy, the term accountability refers broadly to the international law that assigns accountability for certain specific serious corporate human rights violations under international law and human rights law.

So, the central objective of the book is to strengthen the argument on MNC accountability and remedy, as well as to develop and present a new practical paradigm for international legal action against human rights violations by MNCs in a host state or home state, in the context of the tort of negligence (the neighbourhood principle of duty of care). This book rests on the assumption that the corporation under a duty of care or equivalent has the ability to control the activities of the business directly causing the harm. The ability to control, and not actual control, should be enough of a basis for a legal liability. Control should be defined broadly to cover not only majority shareholding, but other situations that give entities either legal or factual control. In certain cases, including but not limited to when there is a majority ownership (over 50%), the ability to control should be assumed and the claimant should not have to prove it. Creating and structuring a relationship with a subsidiary, for example, through holding corporations or share companies so that there is no apparent control over its activities, should not be a defence. The suggestions in this research can also operate alongside the direct regulatory action by the state, and would help reinforce compliance. Lastly, the recommendation concerning applicable law is relevant and should be implemented in relation to all cases dealing with private claims under tort/non-contractual liability law.

CHAPTER I

The aim of this chapter is to introduce the concept of the Tort of Negligence and examine the arguments on the limitations, benefits and legal drawbacks on the applicability of the US Alien Tort Claims Act (ATCA) to corporate human rights violations and environmental damages. The ATCA, which allows for suits to be brought forward in the US by aliens for torts in violation of the law of nations or treaties of the United States, was enacted in 1789.[220] However, use of the ATCA remained dormant until 1980, when a federal court in *Filartiga v Pena-Irala*[221] allowed a Paraguayan woman to bring a suit against a Paraguayan government official who had tortured and killed her brother. Built on the *Filartiga v Pena-Irala* case, this chapter further assesses the federal court jurisprudence on corporate accountability under the Act, which has developed over the years, and reflects on the impact that the current uncertain state of the ATCA has on multinational corporate misconduct overseas. It concludes that *Kiobel*[222] does not mark the end of the ATCA. This is because the analysis of the ATCA in this book shows that it is not the end but rather the next step in the evolutionary process to develop a new concept of corporate liability through the Tort of Negligence. Thus, the chapter will first explain the notion of human rights law, the nature of human rights law and the rights protected under international human rights law before examining the application of the Tort of Negligence and the ATCA.

---

[220]Jeffrey M Blum, and Ralph G Steinhardt, Federal Jurisdiction over International Human Rights Claims: The Alien Tort Claims Act after Filartiga v. Pena-Irala' (1981) 22 Harvard International Law Journal 53.
'The Alien Tort Statute (ATS)'; also known as the Alien Tort Claims Act refers to 28 USC. § 1350. Also see: *Filártiga v Peña-Irala*, 630 F.2d 876 (2d Cir. 1980) and *Sosa v Alvarez-Machain,* 542 US 692 (2004).
[221]*Filártiga v Peña-Irala*, 630 F.2d 876 (2d Cir. 1980).
[222] *Kiobel v Royal Dutch Petroleum* Co., 133 S.Ct. 1659 (2013).

Definition of Human Rights Law

Even though the specific phrase 'human rights' is mostly traced back to the aftermath of World War II,[223] the idea is as old as humanity itself, and inevitably intertwined with the history of justice and law.[224] Human rights are rights that individuals have by virtue of being human.[225] The essence of human rights revolves around the question of what it is about being 'human' that gives rise to rights.[226] Human beings, thus, support the 'bottom-up' approach to human rights, starting from the essence of being human.[227] In this understanding, human rights are viewed as moral principles and as legal principles rooted in morality. Deriving from these moral and legal principles are the overarching and interrelated principles of 'human dignity' and 'equality'.[228]

As a consequence, human dignity as a concept is twofold. On the one hand, it serves as the foundational premise of human rights. On the other hand, it is a legal term, for instance serving as a tool for interpretation. This last strand is often criticised for its use in methods of interpretation and application of specific human rights because of its lack of clear content or meaning.[229] For the present purposes of human dignity, human rights law is referred to as the foundation of all human beings. These rules are fundamental rights that protect human beings and societies.[230] A possible implication of this is that 'human dignity is understood as an affirmation that every human being has an equal and inherent moral value or status',[231] a view shared by Kant, who stated that no human being could be used

---

[223]Henry J Steiner, Philip Alston and Ryan Goodman, *International Human Rights in Context: Law, Politics, Morals: Text and Materials* (Oxford University Press USA 2008).

[224]Reis A Monteiro, *Ethics of Human Rights* (Springer Science & Business Media 2014).

[225]James Griffin and James Thomas Griffin, *On Human Rights (*Oxford University Press 2008).

[226]Dinah L Shelton, ed. *Advanced Introduction to International Human Rights Law* (Edward Elgar Publishing 2014).

[227]*Ibid.*

[228]James Griffin and James Thomas Griffin (n 335).

[229]Justin Bates, 'Human Dignity an Empty Phrase in Search of Meaning?' (2005) 10 (2) Judicial Review 165, 168.

[230]Dinah L Shelton (n 336).

[231]Christopher McCrudden, 'Human Dignity and Judicial Interpretation of Human Rights' (2008) 19 (4) European Journal of international Law 655, 724.

merely as a means, but must always be used at the same time as an end in his classic work *The Metaphysics of Morals*.[232]

The concept of human dignity also has value as a true legal proposition.[233] Human dignity serves as one of the most fundamental concepts of international human rights law, exemplified by its widespread appearance in almost all human rights instruments and regular application by human rights bodies.[234] It is a principle recurring in binding human rights treaties as well as in jurisprudence.[235] The European Court of Human Rights (ECtHR)[236] for instance affirmed that 'the very essence' of the European Convention on Human Rights (ECHR) was 'respect for human dignity', as evidenced by the application of Article 3 of the ECHR.[237] Human dignity is also explicitly present in the other regional human rights documents.[238] The notion of human dignity not only provides for a measuring or interpretational tool in the application of civil rights but also has a role to play in respect of economic and social life in answering the question on the benefits needed for a dignified life.[239]

---

[232] Immanuel Kant, *Moral Law: Groundwork of the Metaphysics of Morals* (Routledge 2013).

[233] Jack Donnelly, 'Human Rights and Human Dignity: An Analytic Critique of Non-Western Conceptions of Human Rights' (1982) 76 (2) American Political Science Review 303, 316.

[234] Dinah Shelton, ed. *The Oxford Handbook of International Human Rights Law* (Oxford University Press 2013). Mentioning in international human rights treaties see for instance Art. 10 ICCPR, Art. 13 ICESCR and preambles of CERD, CEDAW, CRC and CRPD.

[235] Dinah L Shelton (n 336).

[236] Alastair Mowbray, *The Development of Positive Obligations under the European Convention on Human Rights by the European Court of Human Rights* (Bloomsbury Publishing 2004).

[237] 2 ECtHR (Merits), 29 April 2002, *Pretty v The United Kingdom*. App. No. 2346/02, para. 65; ECtHR (Judgment) 8 November 2011, VC v Slovakia, App 18968/07, para. 105.

[238] African charter on Human Rights and Peoples' Rights, OAU Doc CAB/LEG./67/3/Rev 5 reprinted in 21 ILM 59 (1982), preamble; Revised Arab Charter on Human Rights, May 22 2004, unofficial English translation 12 Int'L Hum Rts Reps 893, preamble, arts 3, 17, 20, 40;ASEAN Declaration on Human Rights, 18 Nov 2013 <www.asean.org/news/asean-statement-communiques/item/aseanhuman-rights-declaration> Accessed 3 June 2018.

[239] *The Social and Economic Rights Action Center and the Center for Economic and Social Rights v Nigeria*, No. 155/96. Furthermore: German Federal Constitutional Court, 9 February 2010, BverfGE 125, 175 at 222 with comment by Inga T Winkler and Claudia Mahler, 'Interpreting the Right to a Dignified Minimum Existence: A

Similarly, the concept of equality is inherently linked with human dignity, as exemplified by a reading of Article 1 of the Universal Declaration of Human Rights (UDHR) 1948: 'All human beings are born free and equal in dignity and rights.'[240] The moral principle underlying human rights is that we are all moral persons and therefore deserve equal respect, fittingly named 'the principle of equal respect.'[241] What is essentially being said here could be interpreted as the consequence of equality, which means a foundational principle that most human rights must be balanced against the rights of others. Equality holds in it a right of non-discrimination which is perceived as 'the most fundamental of the rights of man, the starting point of all other liberties.'[242] Such reasoning indeed lies at the foundation of the international concept of human rights, which is found for example in the abolition of slavery, minority rights and the right to self-determination.[243]

In this understanding, when considering human rights in legal terms we imagine that 'rights' exist as a counterpart of duties. Classically states are seen as the main duty holders in this regard since they exercise authority over persons and have the power to exercise a great degree of influence on them. However, when one keeps the moral foundations of human rights in mind we may imagine that states are not the only actors in the international sphere which have the power to exercise authority over individuals and the scope of duty bearers may thus be expanded,[244] an argument traced back to the moral foundation of human rights. In a more elaborate argument on human dignity, following up on Kant's views, Dworkin stipulates that human dignity has two faces: the intrinsic value of every human being and the moral responsibility to realise a successful life, which confirms the close interrelation of moral rights and moral duties. 'Based on this moral conception of human dignity, it leads to the argument that human rights constitute the legal face of human beings.[245] That is, human rights are not only the relational aspect of human dignity that

---

New Era in German Socio-Economic Rights Jurisprudence?' (2013) 13 (3) Human Rights Law Review 388, 401.

[240]Universal Declaration of Human Rights (UDHR), 1948, UNGA res 217 A, article 1.

[241]Dinah L Shelton (n 336).

[242]Hersch Lauterpacht, *An International Bill of the Rights of Man* (OUP Oxford 2013).

[243]Manouchehr Ganji, *International Protection of Human Rights* (No. 133. Geneve: Librairie E. Droz 1962).

[244]Andrew Clapham, *Human Rights Obligations of Non-State Actors* (OUP Oxford 2006).

[245]Robert Allen Rutland, *The Birth of the Bill of Rights, 1776-1791* (Northeastern University Press 1991).

justifies the interrelation of moral rights and moral duties; they are also the institutional aspect of implementing human moral rights and duties and the legitimate aspect to enforce a remedy for moral rights violation.'[246]

To conclude this passage, as Shelton states: 'human rights exist because human beings exist with goals and the potential for personal development based upon individual capacities which contribute to that personal development. This can only be accomplished if basic needs which allow for existence are met and if other persons refrain from interfering with the free and rational actions of the individual. Recognition of the fact that there are rational and legal limits to individual, corporate or state conduct that would interfere unreasonably with the free aims and life projects of others is a basic idea underlying contemporary understanding of human rights.'[247] Deriving from the moral foundation of human dignity, the main characteristics of human rights as they are known today stipulates that they are inherent, interdependent, and indivisible. This means first that they are of such a nature that they cannot be granted or taken away, a concept rooted in human dignity. Second, interdependence means that the enjoyment of one right influences the enjoyment of another right. This holds true not only when considering the rights of one person, but also when balancing the rights of one against the rights of another, a promulgation of the principle of equality. And third, human rights are indivisible which means that they must all be respected without exception. Though the notion of human rights throughout history has been founded in a social contract between individuals and the state,[248] it is only since World War II that human rights have become a part of the realm of international law, forming the 'international human rights law' branch of international law.

A possible implication might be that the 'term 'human rights' is used to denote a broad spectrum of rights ranging from the right to life to the right to a cultural identity. They involve all elementary preconditions for a dignified human existence.'[249] 'These rights can be ordered and specified in different ways.'[250] 'At the international level, a distinction has sometimes

---

[246]Manfred Nowak, 'On the Creation of World Court of Human Rights' (2012) 7 National Taiwan University Law Review 257.

[247]Dinah L Shelton (n 4).

[248]Alfons Söllner, 'Jean-Jacques Rousseau, Du Contrat Social ou Principes du Droit Politique, Amsterdam 1762' in *Key Works of Political Science* (VS Verlag for Social Sciences 2007).

[249]<https://www.abyssinialaw.com/about-us/item/943-theories-of-human-rights-and-justification> accessed 18 May 2016.

[250]<https://www.abyssinialaw.com/about-us/item/943-theories-of-human-rights-and-justification> accessed 18 May 2016 and Olivier De Schutter, 'Promotion and

been made between civil and political rights on the one hand, and economic, social and cultural rights on the other.'[251] 'One classification used is the division between 'classic' and 'social' rights.'[252] ''Classic' rights are often seen to require the non-intervention of the state'[253] (negative obligation), and 'social 'rights''[254] as requiring active intervention on the part of the state.'[255] 'Classifying human rights in terms of negative and positive obligations may have its own defects for a certain right may involve both negative and positive obligations for its effective realisation.'[256] 'In other words, classic rights entail an obligation for the state to refrain from certain actions, while social rights oblige it to provide certain guarantees.'[257]

Legal scholars and 'lawyers often describe classic rights in terms of a duty to achieve a given result ('obligation of result') and social rights in terms of a duty to provide the means ('obligations of conduct').'[258] 'The

---

Protection of all Human Rights, Civil, Political, Economic, Social and Cultural Rights, Including the Right to Development' (2010) Report Submitted by the Special Rapporteur on the Right to Food UN General Assembly.

[251] <https://www.abyssinialaw.com/about-us/item/943-theories-of-human-rights-and-justification> accessed 18 May 2016 and Kenneth Roth, 'Defending Economic Social and Cultural Rights: Practical Issues Faced by an International Human Rights Organization' (2004) 26 Human Rights Quarterly 63.

[252] <https://hrc.upeace.org/files/human%20rights%20reference%20handbook.pdf > Accessed 9 May 2016.

[253] <https://www.abyssinialaw.com/about-us/item/943-theories-of-human-rights-and-justification> accessed 18 May 2016.

[254] *Ibid.*

[255] Demelash Shiferaw and Yonas Tesfa, 'Human Rights Law Teaching Material' (2009) Prepared under the Sponsorship of the Justice and Legal System Research Institute and Jack Donnelly, *Universal Human Rights in Theory and Practice* (Cornell University Press 2013).

[256] <https://www.abyssinialaw.com/about-us/item/943-theories-of-human-rights-and-justification> accessed 18 May 2016 and Demelash Shiferaw and Yonas Tesfa, 'Human Rights Law Teaching Material' (2009) Prepared under the Sponsorship of the Justice and Legal System Research Institute and Jean-François Akandji-Kombe, 'Positive Obligations under the European Convention on Human Rights' (2007) 7 Human Rights Handbook

[257] Demelash Shiferaw and Yonas Tesfa, 'Human Rights Law Teaching Material (200) Prepared under the Sponsorship of the Justice and Legal System Research Institute. <https://chilot.files.wordpress.com/2011/06/human-rights-law.pdf> Accessed 28 May 2016.

[258] Demelash Shiferaw and Yonas Tesfa, 'Human Rights Law Teaching Material' (2009) Prepared under the Sponsorship of the Justice and Legal System Research Institute and David John Harris, *Cases and Materials on International Law* (Sweet & Maxwell 1998).

evolution of international law, however, has led to this distinction between 'classic' and 'social' rights becoming increasingly awkward.'[259] Classic rights, such as civil and political rights, often require considerable investment by the state.'[260] 'The state does not merely have the obligation to respect these rights, but must also guarantee that people can effectively enjoy them.'[261] 'Hence, the right to a fair trial, for instance, requires well-trained judges, prosecutors, lawyers and police officers, as well as administrative support. Another example is the organisation of elections, which also entails high costs.'[262]

'On the other hand, most 'social' rights contain elements that require the state to abstain from interfering with the individual's exercise of the right.'[263] 'As several commentators note, the right to food includes the right for everyone to procure their own food supply without interference; the right to housing implies the right not to be a victim of forced eviction; the right to work encompasses the individual's right to choose his/her own work and also requires the state not to hinder a person from working and to abstain from measures that would increase unemployment; the right to education implies the freedom to establish and direct educational establishments; and the right to the highest attainable standard of health implies the obligation not to interfere with the provision of health care.'[264]

---

[259]Paul Sieghart, *The International Law of Human Rights* (Oxford University Press 1983) and Demelash Shiferaw and Yonas Tesfa, 'Human Rights Law Teaching Material' (2009) Prepared under the Sponsorship of the Justice and Legal System Research Institute.

[260] Demelash Shiferaw and Yonas Tesfa, 'Human Rights Law Teaching Material (200) Prepared under the Sponsorship of the Justice and Legal System Research Institute. <https://chilot.files.wordpress.com/2011/06/human-rights-law.pdf> Accessed 28 May 2016.

[261] Gerard Quinn and Philip Alston, The Nature and Scope of States Parties' Obligations under the International Covenant on Economic, Social and Cultural Rights; *Economic, Social and Cultural Rights* (Routledge 2017) and Demelash Shiferaw and Yonas Tesfa, 'Human Rights Law Teaching Material' (2009) Prepared under the Sponsorship of the Justice and Legal System Research Institute.

[262]Demelash Shiferaw and Yonas Tesfa, 'Human Rights Law Teaching Material' (2009) Prepared under the Sponsorship of the Justice and Legal System Research Institute and David Weissbrodt, 'The Right to a Fair Trial under the Universal Declaration of Human Rights and the International Covenant on Civil and Political Rights' (2002) 21 Refugee Survey Quarterly.

[263]Demelash Shiferaw and Yonas Tesfa, 'Human Rights Law Teaching Material' (2009) Prepared under the Sponsorship of the Justice and Legal System Research Institute.

[264]Scott Leckie, 'Another Step Towards Indivisibility: Identifying the Key Features of Violations of Economic, Social and Cultural Rights' (1998) 20 (1) Human Rights

'In sum, the differentiation of 'classic' rights from 'social' rights does not reflect the nature of the obligations under each set of rights.'[265]

Also, the term 'civil rights' is often used by legal scholars and practitioners 'with reference to the rights set out in the first 18 articles'[266] of the Universal Declaration of Human Rights 1948 '(UDHR), almost all of which are also set out as binding treaty norms in the International Covenant on Civil and Political Rights 1966 (ICCPR).'[267] 'From this group, a further set of 'physical integrity rights' has been identified, which concern the right to life, liberty and security of the person, and which offer protection from physical violence against the person, torture and inhuman treatment, arbitrary arrest, detention, exile, slavery and servitude, interference with one's privacy and right of ownership, restriction of one's freedom of movement, and the freedom of thought, conscience and religion.' [268] Therefore, 'the difference between 'basic rights' and 'physical integrity rights' lies in the fact that the former include economic and social rights, but do not include rights such as protection of privacy and ownership.'[269] 'Although not strictly an integrity right, the right to equal treatment and protection in law certainly qualifies as a civil right.'[270] 'Moreover, this right

---

Quarterly 81, 124 and Demelash Shiferaw and Yonas Tesfa, 'Human Rights Law Teaching Material' (2009) Prepared under the Sponsorship of the Justice and Legal System Research Institute.

265Demelash Shiferaw and Yonas Tesfa, 'Human Rights Law Teaching Material' (2009) Prepared under the Sponsorship of the Justice and Legal System Research Institute.

266<https://hrc.upeace.org/files/human%20rights%20reference%20handbook.pdf> Accessed 9 April 2019.

267<https://hrc.upeace.org/files/human%20rights%20reference%20handbook.pdf> Accessed 9 April 2019 and Dominic McGoldrick, *The Human Rights Committee: Its Role in the Development of the International Covenant on Civil and Political Rights* (Oxford University Press USA 1991).

268<https://hrc.upeace.org/files/human%20rights%20reference%20handbook.pdf> Accessed 9 April 2019 and Linda Camp Keith, 'The United Nations International Covenant on Civil and Political Rights: Does It Make a Difference in Human Rights Behavior?' (1999) 36 (1) Journal of Peace Research 95, 118.

269<https://hrc.upeace.org/files/human%20rights%20reference%20handbook.pdf> Accessed 9 April 2019 and Rhoda Howard, 'The Full-Belly Thesis: Should Economic Rights Take Priority over Civil and Political Rights-Evidence from Sub-Saharan Africa' (1983) 5 Human Rights Quarterly 467.

270<https://hrc.upeace.org/files/human%20rights%20reference%20handbook.pdf> Accessed 9 April 2019 and Obinna B Okere, The Protection of Human Rights in Africa and the African Charter on Human and Peoples' Rights: A Comparative Analysis with the European and American Systems' (1984) 6 (2) Human Rights Quarterly 141.

plays an essential role in the realisation of economic, social and cultural rights. Another group of civil rights is referred to under the collective term of 'due process rights''.[271] '(Many modern due process cases deal with what is called procedural due process (fair process and procedures). Due process procedures do not guarantee that the result of government action will be to a citizen's liking. However, fair procedures do help prevent arbitrary and unreasonable decisions. Due process requirements vary depending on the situation.'[272] 'At a minimum, due process means that a citizen who will be affected by a government decision must be given notice of what the government plans to do and have a chance to comment on the action').[273]

'These pertain, among other things, to the right to a public hearing by an independent and impartial tribunal, the 'presumption of innocence', the *ne bis in idem* principle, and legal'[274] assistance[275] '(see Articles 9, 10, 14 and 15 of the ICCPR).'[276] 'Although the fundamental purpose of human rights is the protection and development of the individual (individual rights), some of these rights are exercised by people in groups (collective rights).'[277] For example, freedom of association and assembly, freedom of religion and, more especially, the 'freedom to form or join a trade union, fall into this category. Thus, the collective element is even more evident when human rights are linked specifically to membership of a certain group, such as the right of members of ethnic and cultural minorities to preserve

---

[271] *Ibid.*

[272] <http://webcache.googleusercontent.com/search?q=cache:yvDLcREIJPUJ:www.lincoln.edu/criminaljustic > Accessed 10 April 2016.

[273] Victor VRamraj, 'Four Models of Due Process' (2004) 2 (3) International Journal of Constitutional Law 492, 524. Also see, Henry Julian Abraham and Barbara Ann Perry, *Freedom and the Court: Civil Rights and Liberties in the United States* (Oxford University Press USA 1994). Also see: <http://webcache.googleusercontent.com/search?q=cache:yvDLcREIJPUJ:www.lincoln.edu/criminaljustic > Accessed 10 April 2016.

[274] <https://hrc.upeace.org/files/human%20rights%20reference%20handbook.pdf> Accessed 9 April 2019.

[275] <https://hrc.upeace.org/files/human%20rights%20reference%20handbook.pdf> Accessed 9 April 2019 and Bas Van Bockel, *The Ne Bis In Idem Principle in EU Law* (Vol. 72. Kluwer Law International 2010).

[276] Johann Bair, *The International Covenant on Civil and Political Rights and Its (first) Optional Protocol: A Short Commentary Based on Views, General Comments, and Concluding Observations by the Human Rights Committee.* (Peter Lang Publishing 2005).

[277] <https://hrc.upeace.org/files/human%20rights%20reference%20handbook.pdf > Accessed 30 April 2017.

their language and culture.'[278] Therefore, 'one must make a distinction between two types of rights, which are usually called collective rights: individual rights enjoyed in association with others, and the rights of a collective. The most notable example of a collective human right is the right to self-determination, which is regarded as being vested in peoples rather than in individuals (Articles 1 of the ICCPR and the ICESCR).'[279] 'The recognition of the right to self-determination as a human right is grounded in the fact that it is seen as a necessary precondition for the development of the individual. It is generally accepted that collective rights may not infringe on universally accepted individual rights, such as the right to life and freedom from torture.'[280]

Political rights

> 'In general, political rights are those set out in Articles 19 to 21 of the UDHR 1948[281] and also codified in the ICCPR. They include freedom of expression, freedom of association and assembly, the right to take part in the government of one's country, and the right to vote and stand for election at genuine periodic elections held by secret ballot (Articles 18, 19, 21, 22 and 25 of the ICCPR).'[282]

Economic and social rights

> 'The economic and social rights are listed in Articles 22 to 26 of the UDHR 1948,[283] and further developed and set out as binding treaty norms in the'[284] International Covenant on Economic, Social and Cultural Rights 1966 (ICESCR).[285] 'These rights provide the conditions necessary for prosperity and well-being. Economic rights refer, for example, to the right

---

[278]*Ibid.*
[279]*Ibid.*
[280]*Ibid.*
[281]Articles 19 to 21 of the UDHR 1948, Article 19.
[282]<https://hrc.upeace.org/files/human%20rights%20reference%20handbook.pdf> Accessed 9 April 2019 and Nahuel. Maisley, 'The International Right of Rights? Article 25 (a) of the ICCPR as a Human Right to Take Part in International Law-Making' (2017) 28 (1) European Journal of International Law 89, 113.
[283]Articles 22 to 26 of the UDHR 1948. Article 22.
[284]<https://hrc.upeace.org/files/human%20rights%20reference%20handbook.pdf> Accessed 9 April 2019.
[285]Kitty Arambulo, *Strengthening the Supervision of the International Covenant on Economic, Social and Cultural Rights: Theoretical and Procedural Aspects* (No. 3. Intersentia-Hart 1999).

to property, the right to work, the 'right to a fair wage,'[286] 'a reasonable limitation of working hours, and trade union rights. Social rights are those rights necessary for an adequate standard of living, including the right to health, shelter, food, social care, and education (Articles 6 to 14 of the ICESCR).'[287]

Cultural rights

The UDHR 1948 lists cultural rights in Article 27 – '(1) Everyone has the right freely to participate in the cultural life of the community, to enjoy the arts and to share in scientific advancement and its benefits. (2) Everyone has the right to the protection of the moral and material interests resulting from any scientific, literary or artistic production of which he is the author' – and Article 28 – 'everyone is entitled to a social and international order in which the rights and freedoms set forth in this Declaration can be fully realised'. 'These include the right to participate freely in the cultural life of the community, to share in scientific advancement, and the right to the protection of the moral and material interests resulting from any scientific, literary or artistic production of which one is the author (Article 15 of the ICESCR and Article 27 of the ICCPR).'[288]

The Assumption and Contradiction between Civil and Political Rights, and Economic, Social and Cultural Rights

Traditionally, it has been argued that there are fundamental differences between economic, social and cultural rights, and civil and political rights. These two categories of rights have been seen as two different concepts and their differences have been characterised as a

---

286<https://hrc.upeace.org/files/human%20rights%20reference%20handbook.pdf> Accessed 9 April 2019 and Demelash Shiferaw and Yonas Tesfa, 'Human Rights Law Teaching Material (200) Prepared under the Sponsorship of the Justice and Legal System Research Institute. <https://chilot.files.wordpress.com/2011/06/human-rights-law.pdf> Accessed 28 May 2016.

287<https://hrc.upeace.org/files/human%20rights%20reference%20handbook.pdf> Accessed 9 April 2019 and Egbert W Vierdag, 'The Legal Nature of the Rights Granted by the International Covenant on Economic, Social and Cultural Rights' (1978) 9 Netherlands Yearbook of International Law 69, 105.

288 Demelash Shiferaw and Yonas Tesfa, 'Human Rights Law Teaching Material (200) Prepared under the Sponsorship of the Justice and Legal System Research Institute. <https://chilot.files.wordpress.com/2011/06/human-rights-law.pdf> Accessed 28 May 2016.

dichotomy. According to this view, civil and political rights are considered to be expressed in a very precise language, imposing merely negative obligations which do not require resources for their implementation, and which, therefore, can be applied immediately. On the other hand, economic, social and cultural rights are considered to be expressed in vague terms, imposing only positive obligations conditional on the existence of resources and therefore involving a progressive realisation.

'As a consequence of these alleged differences, it has been argued that civil and political rights are justiciable whereas economic, social and cultural rights are not. In other words, this view holds that only violations of civil and political rights can be adjudicated by judicial or similar bodies, while economic, social and cultural rights are 'by their nature' non-justiciable. Over the years, economic, social and cultural rights have been re-examined and their juridical validity and applicability have been increasingly stressed.'[289] 'During the last decade, the world has witnessed the development of a large and growing body of case-law of domestic courts concerning economic, social and cultural rights.'[290] 'This case-law, at the national and international level, suggests a potential role for creative and sensitive decisions of judicial and quasi-judicial bodies with respect to these rights.'[291]

The Nature of Human Rights and the Law

Moving on, international human rights law is the structuration of human rights in the international legal order. The great leap of said structuration became apparent in the post-WWII period.[292] International human rights law has become an area of international law that encompasses a set of individual entitlements of persons against governments.[293] These entitlements – human rights – range from civil to political rights such as the

---

[289]<https://hrc.upeace.org/files/human%20rights%20reference%20handbook.pdf> Accessed 9 April 2019.

[290]Kenneth Roth, 'Defending Economic Social and Cultural Rights: Practical Issues Faced by an International Human Rights Organization' (2004) 26 Human Rights Quarterly 63 and <https://hrc.upeace.org/files/human%20rights%20reference%20handbook.pdf> Accessed 9 April 2019.

[291]*Ibid.*

[292]Paul Sieghart, *The International Law of Human Rights* (Oxford University Press 1983).

[293]Schachter Oscar, *International Law in Theory and Practice* (Vol. 13. Martinus Nijhoff Publishers 1991).

right to be free from arbitrary deprivation of life, torture and other ill-treatment, to the right to freedom of thought, conscience and religion, and to social and economic rights such as the right to health and education. Likewise, Globalisation has reconfigured the territoriality and sovereignty that has traditionally been associated with states.[294] Economic actors, such as transnational corporations, have become powerful actors within the world's economy and they are increasingly using their economic power to influence the actions of states.[295] Transnational corporations' business operations also directly affect the enjoyment of human rights by individuals, especially women.[296] One such case which is considered in the literature is that of the Bangladesh textile manufacturing factories,[297] which produces clothes for some of the world biggest retailers. As the case demonstrates, transnational corporations are increasingly escaping liability for abuses which happen within their corporate structures and supply chains.[298]

Substantively, international human rights law can be found in many different sources of moral and legal rules. These rules are either conventional or customary; some are binding, while others are non-binding, and these non-binding rules are the so-called 'soft' law.[299] Therefore, international human rights law has evolved both on the international and regional planes through several binding treaties, such as the International Covenant on Civil and Political Rights 1966 (ICCPR), the International Covenant on Economic, Social and Cultural Rights 1966 (ICESCR) and Convention on the Elimination of All Forms Racial Discrimination 1965 (CERD), centred around state obligations and rights for individuals.

---

[294] Wolfgang Kaleck and Miriam Saage-Maass, 'Corporate Accountability for Human Rights Violations Amounting to International Crimes. The Status Quo and Its Challenges' (2010)8 (3) Journal of International Criminal Justice 699.

[295] David L. Richards, Ronald D Gelleny and David H Sacko. 'Money with a Mean Streak? Foreign Economic Penetration and Government Respect for Human Rights in Developing Countries' (2001) 45 (2) International Studies Quarterly 219.

[296] Augustine Ikelegbe, 'Engendering Civil Society: Oil, Women Groups and Resource Conflicts in the Niger Delta Region of Nigeria' (2005) 43 (2) Journal of Modern African Studies 241.

[297] Mohammad Ali and Mamun Habib, 'Supply Chain Management of Textile Industry: A Case Study on Bangladesh' (2012) 1 (2) International Journal of Supply Chain Management.

[298] Zeenath Reza Khan and Gwendolyn Rodrigues, 'Human before the Garment: Bangladesh Tragedy Revisited. Ethical Manufacturing or Lack Thereof in Garment Manufacturing Industry' (2015) 5 (1) World.

[299] Andrew Clapham, *Human Rights Obligations of Non-State Actors* (OUP Oxford 2006).

Nowadays, a change in the international legal order can be perceived and the involvement of other actors is increasingly recognised.[300]

Now that the importance of human rights has been recognised in this book, the next question is: what is the law? Cassese identifies three steps toward legal positivism.[301] These steps are: identifying the substance of the rights, establishing binding duties for the protection of those rights and, finally, enforcing those duties.[302] The first step has been taken by the Universal Declaration of Human Rights 1948,[303] the second by the emergence of binding human rights treaties at the United Nations, the first of which was the Convention on the Elimination of All Forms Racial Discrimination (CERD) in 1965,[304] closely followed by the International Covenant on Civil and Political Rights (ICCPR) in 1966[305] and the International Covenant on Economic, Social and Cultural Rights (ICESCR) in 1966.[306] The last stage of enforcement is the most difficult one to take in the realm of international law; and it was made more difficult by the polarisation of the international community during the Cold War. Thus, international human rights law is a part of 'public international law, which is traditionally governed by and for sovereign states.[307] However, the role of other actors and the individual at the centre of international human rights law is undeniable.'[308] 'Indeed it is a field of law that is subject to constant

---

[300]Antonio Cassese, ed. *Realizing Utopia: The Future of International Law* (Oxford University Press 2012).

[301]*Ibid.*

[302]Christian Tomuschat, *Human Rights: between Idealism and Realism* (OUP Oxford 2014).

[303]UN General Assembly, *Universal Declaration of Human Rights*, 10 December 1948, 217 A (III) <http://www.refworld.org/docid/3ae6b3712c.html> Accessed 3 June 2018.

[304]UN General Assembly, *International Convention on the Elimination of All Forms of Racial Discrimination*, 21 December 1965, United Nations, Treaty Series, vol. 660, p. 195 <http://www.refworld.org/docid/3ae6b3940.html> Accessed 3 June 2018.

[305]UN General Assembly, *International Convention on the Elimination of All Forms of Racial Discrimination*, 21 December 1965, United Nations, Treaty Series, vol. 660, p. 195 <http://www.refworld.org/docid/3ae6b3940.html> Accessed 3 June 2018

[306]UN General Assembly, *International Covenant on Economic, Social and Cultural Rights*, 16 December 1966, United Nations, Treaty Series, vol. 993, p. 3 <http://www.refworld.org/docid/3ae6b36c0.html> Accessed 4 June 2018.

[307]Andrew Clapham (n 25).

[308]Dinah L Shelton (n 4).

evolution.'[309] 'However one conceives human rights law, it is surely not static. Human rights law is driven, not by the steady accretion of precedents and practice, but rather by outrage and solidarity.'[310] Nevertheless, the international legal system remains primarily governed by states.

In addition, human rights enforcement is a long-standing dilemma. Therefore, to address the irregularities in the in the current legal rules, human rights law should be enjoyed by everyone in the world. This enjoyment should also provide a mechanism for the enforcement of these rights. However, 'as the international community becomes increasingly integrated, the fundamental question that needs to be asked is how can the diversity and integrity of human rights be respected in all jurisdictions? Is global human rights enforcement inevitable?'[311] 'If so, is the world ready for it? How could'[312] an emerging global human rights mechanism 'based on and guided by human dignity and tolerance'[313] be accepted by all state parties? 'These are some of the issues, concerns and questions underlying the debate over universal human rights and the belief in effective enforcement.'[314] Relativism of enforcement 'is the assertion that human values, far from being universal, vary a great deal according to the different human rights perspectives. Some would apply this relativism to the promotion, protection, interpretation and application of human rights which could be interpreted differently within different jurisdictions and ethnic and

---

[309]Sophie Schiettekatte, Y Haeck, and A.Van Pachtenbeke, 'Do We Need a World Court of Human Rights? (2016) Universit Gent.

[310]*Ibid.*

[311]Sophie Schiettekatte, Y Haeck, and A.Van Pachtenbeke, 'Do We Need a World Court of Human Rights? (2016) Universit Gent.

[312]Demelash Shiferaw and Yonas Tesfa, 'Human Rights Law Teaching Material' (2009) Prepared under the Sponsorship of the Justice and Legal System Research Institute.

[313]*Ibid.*

[314]Demelash Shiferaw and Yonas Tesfa, 'Human Rights Law Teaching Material (200) Prepared under the Sponsorship of the Justice and Legal System Research Institute. <https://chilot.files.wordpress.com/2011/06/human-rights-law.pdf> Accessed 28 May 2016.

religious traditions.'[315] 'In other words, according to this view, human rights are'[316] related to the perception of a state party rather than universal.[317]

Taken to its extreme, the notion that human rights enforcement should be based on state discretion 'would pose a dangerous threat to the effectiveness of international law and the international system of human rights that has been painstakingly constructed over the last few decades.'[318] If state discretion and jurisdiction alone govern a nation's' 'compliance with international standards, then the widespread disregard, abuse and violation of human rights would be given legitimacy.'[319] 'Accordingly, the promotion and protection of human rights is perceived as'[320] a state obligation and should only be subject to national discretion on the grounds of security and public health. 'By rejecting or disregarding their legal obligation to promote and protect universal human rights, states advocating jurisdictional differences could raise their human rights norms and particularities above international law and standards.'[321] However, 'largely through the ongoing work of the United Nations, the universality of human rights has been clearly established and recognised in international law. Human rights are emphasised among the purposes of the United Nations as proclaimed in its Charter',[322] 'which states that human rights are 'for all without distinction'. Human rights are the natural-born rights of every human being, universally.

---

[315]Demelash Shiferaw and Yonas Tesfa, 'Human Rights Law Teaching Material (200) Prepared under the Sponsorship of the Justice and Legal Syste Sophie Schiettekatte, Y Haeck, and A.Van Pachtenbeke, 'Do We Need a World Court of Human Rights? (2016) Universit Gent.m Research Institute. <https://chilot.files.wordpress.com/2011/06/human-rights-law.pdf> Accessed 28 May 2016.

[316]*Ibid.*

[317]Sophie Schiettekatte, Y Haeck, and A.Van Pachtenbeke, 'Do We Need a World Court of Human Rights? (2016) Universit Gent.

[318] Demelash Shiferaw and Yonas Tesfa, 'Human Rights Law Teaching Material (200) Prepared under the Sponsorship of the Justice and Legal System Research Institute. <https://chilot.files.wordpress.com/2011/06/human-rights-law.pdf> Accessed 28 May 2016.

[319] *Ibid.*

[320]*Ibid.*

[321]Demelash Shiferaw and Yonas Tesfa, 'Human Rights Law Teaching Material (200) Prepared under the Sponsorship of the Justice and Legal System Research Institute. <https://chilot.files.wordpress.com/2011/06/human-rights-law.pdf> Accessed 28 May 2016.

[322]Demelash Shiferaw and Yonas Tesfa, 'Human Rights Law Teaching Material' (2009) Prepared under the Sponsorship of the Justice and Legal System Research Institute and Samuel Totten, *United Nations Charter; The Prevention and Intervention of Genocide* (Routledge 2008).

They are not privileges.'[323] Yet, 'an account of human rights enforcement by means of individual access to justice will be discussed later on in this book. After briefly explaining human rights law and its ramifications, the next section of this book will be devoted to the tort law doctrine and the ATCA.'[324]

Introduction into the Neighbourhood Principle under English Tort Law Doctrine

This section describes the neighbourhood principle under English tort law doctrine. The neighbourhood principle establishes conduct that falls below the standards of behaviour established by law for the protection of others against an unreasonable risk of harm.[325] A person has acted negligently if he or she has departed from the conduct expected of a reasonably prudent person acting under similar circumstances; if so, then a duty of care might exist, which is a doctrine established in the English legal system.[326]

The English legal system is a Common Law system. One of the most significant differences between Common Law, Religious Law[327] and Canon Law systems[328] and the Civil Law system (the principal legal system in continental Europe) is that former judicial decisions are binding on both the lower courts and on the court that made the decision. This is known as a system of precedent.[329]

The English legal system is divided into two: Public law and Private law.[330] Private Law is divided between Property Law and the Law

---

[323]Demelash Shiferaw and Yonas Tesfa, 'Human Rights Law Teaching Material' (2009) Prepared under the Sponsorship of the Justice and Legal System Research Institute and Sophie Schiettekatte, Y Haeck, and Van A Pachtenbeke, 'Do We Need a World Court of Human Rights? (2016) Universit Gent.

[324]Sophie Schiettekatte, Y Haeck, and Van A Pachtenbeke, 'Do We Need a World Court of Human Rights? (2016) Universit Gent.

[325]Cornelius J Peck, 'Negligence and Liability Without Fault in Tort Law' (1971) 46 Wash. L. Rev. 225.

[326]Robert FV Heuston, 'Donoghue v. Stevenson in Retrospect' (1957) 20 (1) Modern Law Review 1.

[327]Kent Greenawalt, 'Religious Law and Civil Law: Using Secular Law to Assure Observance of Practices with Religious Significance' (1998) 71 Southern California Law Review 781.

[328]James A Brundage, *Medieval Canon Law* (Routledge 2014).

[329]Catherine Elliott and Frances Quinn, *English Legal System* (Pearson Education 2008).

[330]Richard Ward, Amanda Akhtar and Amanda Wragg, *Walker & Walker's English Legal System* (Oxford University Press 2011).

of Obligation, with the law of obligation consisting of Contract, Tort, and Restitutions. The rationale behind this approach is that, introducing tort law in this section will help to understand the advantages of corporate accountability under the neighbourhood principle ('in the law of negligence, the neighbour principle enunciated by Lord Atkin in *Donoghue v Stevenson* (1932) AC 562, 580 provides an adequate basis on which to resolve duty of care questions'). It will offer an understanding into the concept of duty of care and how this can be applied to corporations in this book and in courts.

What Is Tort Law?

At its simplest, tort is the law of non-criminal wrongs.[331] The plural 'wrongs' here is deliberate. Tort law is the name given to the diverse collection of legal wrongs, such as negligence, trespass to land, assault, battery, libel, etc. (Rudden in 'Torticles' in the early 1990s counted 70 individual torts.[332]) Also, the boundaries between torts are fluid and the popularity of any individual tort can change. Old torts die out (the rule in *Rylands v Fletcher*[333] may be a case in point here) while new ones emerge (such as the tort of misuse of private information in *Vidal-Hall v Google Inc.*[334]). Tort law covers a lot of ground, so it could provide an appropriate mechanism for corporate accountability.

What is not clear is the extent to which the various individual torts (and the law of tort as a whole) share common features, principles, and justifications in relation to corporate accountability. The best view may be Weir's, who observed that 'tort is what is in the tort books, and the only thing holding it together is the binding.'[335] Weir's view is noted in tort cases, such as *Bourhill v Young*,[336] *Osman v United Kingdom*,[337] and *Hall v Simons*.[338] Therefore, in comparing tort law to international law and human rights law, tort law has the ability to address a variety of corporate human rights violations and cases of environmental damage.

---

[331]Dan B Dobbs, *The Law of Torts* (Vol. 2. West Group 2001).

[332]Bernard Rudden, 'Torticles' (1991) 6 /7 Tulane European and Civil Law Forum 105.

[333]*Rylands v Fletcher* [1868] UKHL 1.

[334]*Vidal -Hall & Ors v Google Inc* [2014] EWHC 13 (QB) (16 January 2014). <http://www.bailii.org/ew/cases/EWHC/QB/2014/13.html> Accessed 30 October 2016.

[335]Tony Weir, *An Introduction to Tort Law* (Oxford University Press 2006).

[336]*Bourhill v Young* [1943] AC 92.

[337]*Osman v United Kingdom* [1998] EHRR 101.

[338]*Arthur Hall v Simons* [2000] 3 WLR 543.

Also, in comparison to contract law (traditionally tort law's other half in the Law of Obligation),[339] which is grounded, *inter alia,* in the morality of promise-keeping, tort law appears to lack any such common theme or ambition, and resembles little more than a miscellaneous collection of relatively self-contained wrongs. Also, in recent years one particular tort, the tort of negligence,[340] has gained prominence and started to gain ground on other, older torts. This has extended the old tort of negligence to cover cause beyond the normal duty of care, in cases such as *Montgomery v Lanarkshire Health Board*[341] and *Caparo Industries v Dickman.*[342] If this development continues, it may be possible that national judicial systems will end up with a law of tort sharing a similar unity and coherence as is found in contract law. However, this move has not been universally welcomed.

The description of tort law as a collection of civil wrongs for which the law provides a remedy, as Cane suggests, is a way of protecting people's interests through 'a system of precepts about how people may, ought and ought not to behave in their dealing with others.'[343] This prompts another question: what wrongs or interests are protected under tort law? Does tort law protect rights under human rights law?

Tort law is concerned with civil wrongs, while criminal law is concerned with criminal conduct.[344] Unquestionably, the major (and most dynamic) field of law within tort is the law of negligence. In the context of personal injury claims, the injured person will be able to sue for negligence,[345] although there are other regimes that are relevant. Negligence in the English legal system expanded throughout the nineteenth and twentieth centuries, reflecting the pressures that arise out of an industrialised and urban society. It has been brought to bear upon the traditional groups of legal redress for interference with protected interests.[346] A possible implication of this might be that the orthodoxy approach to redress restricts

---

[339]Robert Stevens, *Torts and Rights* (OUP Oxford 2007).

[340]Frederick Pollock, *The Law of Torts: Treatise on The Principles of Obligations Arising from Civil Wrongs in The Common Law* (Banks & Brothers 1892).

[341]*Montgomery v Lanarkshire Health Board* (2015) UKSC 11.

[342]*Caparo Industries plc v Dickman* (1990) UKHL.

[343]Peter Cane, *The Anatomy of Tort Law* (Bloomsbury Publishing 1997).

[344]Henry M Hart, *The Aims of the Criminal Law* (1958) 23(3) Law and Contemporary Problems 401, 441.

[345]Richard A Posner, 'A Theory of Negligence' (1972) 1(1) Journal of Legal Studies 29.

[346]Simon F Deakin, Angus Johnston and Basil S Markesinis, *Markesinis and Deakin's Tort Law* (Oxford University Press 2012).

the protected rights that should be enjoyed by victims of human rights violations. These relationships may partly be explained by the flexibility it brought to the legal system. The flexibility allows the courts to find liability in a novel context to establish liability and effective remedy. However, for the court to make a finding of negligence, the claimant must prove a number of things, the primary one being that the defendant owed the claimant a duty of care. In this view, it is adequate to claim that tort law covers the rights derived from international law and human rights law.

Protected Rights Under Tort Law

Tort law might arise where someone has suffered an unwanted harm. Some cases involve physical injury, like the damage caused by an elderly resident getting her foot caught in a hole (*Sutherland Shire Council v Heyman*[347]). Another example is the case of the pedestrian killed by the speeding motorist (*Fitzgerald v Lane*[348]). In other examples, the harm can be psychological injury (*Page v Smith*[349] and *White v Chief Constable of South Yorkshire*[350]). Clearly not all cases involve physical or mental injury to the potential claimant; other types of harm include damage of property, for example the cause of explosion at the oil refinery (*Simaan General Contracting Co. v Pilkington Glass Ltd*[351]), financial loss, for example in the case of the buyer whose house is not worth as much they thought, or, more controversially, in the example of the student who has not been recognised as dyslexic (*Junior Books v Veitchi Co. Ltd*[352]).

In some of these examples, such *as Fitzgerald v Lane* and *White v Chief Constable of South Yorkshire* (this latter case arising 'from the disaster that occurred at Hillsborough football stadium in Sheffield during the FA Cup semi-final match between Liverpool and Nottingham Forest in'[353] 1989), there appears to be no damage or harm. However, even assuming, for the sake of argument, that ramblers walk over a farmer's land without causing damage (they do not, for example, tear at or pick flowers) or a drunk student's housemate unlocks the bathroom door before the drunk student wakes up the next morning and so is unaware of having been locked in all night, these can still be classified as interferences with the individual

[347]*Sutherland Shire Council v Heyman* (1985) HCA 4.
[348]*Fitzgerald v Lane* (1989) 1 AC 328.
[349]*Page v Smith* (1996) 1 AC 155.
[350]*White v Chief Constable of South Yorkshire* (1998) 3 WLR 1509.
[351]*Simaan General Contracting Co v Pilkington Glass Ltd* (1988) CA 17.
[352]*Junior Books Ltd v Veitchi Co Ltd* (1983) 1 AC 52.

rights. Other relevant cases include *Mitchell and Another v Glasgow City Council,*[354] *Stovin v Wise,*[355] *Norwich City Council v Harvey,*[356] and *Carmarthenshire County Council v Lewis.*[357] Thus, you have a right to determine who has access to or makes use of your land. The law says that you get to control the use of your land and the rights others have to your property. Similarly, each of us has a right to bodily freedom and autonomy; others are not entitled to touch us or confine our movement (subject to certain exceptions) without consent. Even though the farmer or the drunk student may not have been harmed, in the sense of being worse off, as a result of this action, it can be said that there had been wrong-doing.

As such, tort law is not only or primarily concerned with harm as much as it is with rights. Therefore, the question is: how are these rights protected and respected? The understanding of tort law as a system of rules protecting rights and interests will allow one to identify and apply tort law to fundamental human rights principles. Tort law presents the legal system with a neat, linear form of protecting rights and interests. It also involves a description of the way distinct torts are arranged and interrelated. Some torts exist and are defined to protect a single interest. For example, defamation protects the person and their reputation, and nuisance protects individual interests in enjoying their land. The tort of negligence offers protection to all legally recognised rights and interests.[358] Often, for any single harm or injury, there will be more than one tort upon which a claim may be founded. So, if someone hits another person, it may be possible to bring a claim in battery or negligence, as well as a criminal claim, depending on the circumstances of the case.[359]

The concept that established the duty of care was generalised in the famous case of *Donoghue v Stevenson.*[360] Tort law plays a role in deterring future tortious activity. The imposition of liability in relation to a particular

---

[354]*Mitchell v Glasgow City Council* (2009) UKHL 11.

[355]*Stovin v Wise* (1996) 3 WLR 389.

[356]*Norwich City Council v Harvey* (1988) 45 BLR 14.

[357] *Carmarthenshire County Council v Lewis* (1955) AC 549.

[358]Harold Luntz, David Hambly and Robert Alexander Hayes, *Torts: Cases and Commentary* (Butterworths 1992).

[359]Kenneth Mann, 'Punitive Civil Sanctions: The Middle ground between Criminal and Civil Law' (1992) Yale Law Journal 1795, 1873, William Geldart, *Introduction to English Law* (D.C.M. Yardley ed., 9th ed. 1984) 146 and Paul Skolnick and Jerry I Shaw, 'The OJ Simpson Criminal Trial Verdict: Racism or Status Shield?' (1997) 53(3) Journal of Social Issues 503, 516.

[360]Neil MacCormick, 'Donoghue v Stevenson and Legal Reasoning' in Burns P ed., *Donoghue v. Stevenson and The Modern Law of Negligence*, (Continuing Legal Education of British Columbia, Vancouver 1991).

activity enables others to regulate their behaviour accordingly. Thus, it is argued, the tort law case of *Woodroffe-Hedley v Cuthbertson* (also known as *Hedley v Cuthbertson*: Unreported, 20 June 1997), which was heard in the Queen's Bench Division of the High Court and where the claimant was a six-year-old child whose father had died in a mountaineering accident and the defendant was the victim's mountain guide who was found guilty of negligence,[361] has led to mountain guides being more likely to use two ice screws rather than risk liability by relying on one. Likewise, one might think that anything that encourages safe practice is, in itself, a good thing. Therefore, it seems that the effect of the imposition of tortious liability in such circumstances is not to deter potentially negligent conduct but to stop the activity altogether. Thus, could this be a mechanism to deter corporate human rights violations? The function of tort is often coupled with the idea of gaining publicity about what has happened to stop it from ever happening again. This is often the line claimants take if they have suffered as a result of someone's negligent actions; see the case of *Woodroffe-Hedley v Cuthbertson*[362] where Gerry Hedley's wife brought a negligence action against the defendant for the death of the claimant.[363]

Aims of Tort Negligence

Tort law seeks to protect an individual's interests both prospectively by deterring future harm, and retrospectively through the provision of compensation for past harm and the distribution of losses. Tort law has a number of disparate functions or purposes typically identified under the broad reading of compensation, deterrence, corrective justice and, less often, an inquiry and/or publicity.[364] The tort of negligence is the most frequently used of all torts and is therefore perhaps the most important. It has flourished in the latter part of the twentieth century, rising to a dominant position because of the flexible nature of its rules that allows judges to expand the tort to protect any claimants who would otherwise have been left

---

[361]Alistair Duff, '5 Legal Liability' (2003). <http://platform.rgs.org/NR/rdonlyres/A1732337-720E-4FCC-950D 0BC094B57FDA/0/06ch5.pdf> Accessed 30 October 2016.

[362]*Woodroffe-Hedley v Cuthbertson* [1997] QBD.

[363]Gary Younge 'Go Tell It on The Mountain' (1997) *The Guardian*; see also: Kirsty Horsey and Erika Rackley *Kidner's Casebook on Torts* (Oxford University Press USA 2015).

[364]Kirsty Horsey and Erika Rackley, *Kidner's Casebook on Torts* (Oxford University Press USA 2015).

unprotected by the law.[365] This combination of findings provides some support for the conceptual premise that applying this principle to corporate accountability could have the potential to restore the victims of corporate human rights abuses to the place they were prior to the wrongdoing or before the violations happened to them; however, this is not clear yet.

Torts are divided into three categories: Intentional,[366] Negligent[367] and Nuisance.[368] This book focuses on negligence, because it will provide victims of human rights violation with a mechanism to bring lawsuits against corporations. The tort of negligence forms one of the most dynamic and rapidly changing areas of liability in modern law.[369] It is defined as a careless behaviour with no intention of causing damage.[370] This careless behaviour makes others suffer, and as a result, the victim may be entitled to reparations and damages. That is the main concern of negligence,[371] hence why this book opts to focus exclusively on this aspect of tort law.

Definition of Negligence

The tort of negligence has been defined as 'a breach of a legal duty to take care which results in damage to the claimant.'[372] The tort is not usually concerned with harm inflicted intentionally on the claimant. Rather, it is a concern with injuries inflicted accidentally on the claimant or through a duty of care. However, establishing negligence involves much more than simply showing that the defendant behaved carelessly, as careless behaviour is only one ingredient of negligence.

To establish an intentional tort, the claimant must prove three things:

---

[365]Paula Giliker and Silas Beckwith, *Tort* (Sweet and Maxwell 2000).

[366]Peter Handford, 'Intentional Negligence: A Contradiction in Terms? (2010) 32 Sydney Law Review 29.

[367]Greg Walsh, *Tort of Negligence definitions* (2011).

[368] Nuisance in the form of smells , *Wheeler v JJ Saunders* (1996) Ch 19, Encroachment by tree branches or roots, *Lemmon v Webb* (1894) 3, Nuisance noise *Kennaway v Thompson* (1981) QB 88, Cricket balls – *Miller v Jackson* (1977) 3 WLR 20 and Disturbance from a brothel *Thompson-Schwab v Costaki* (1956) 1 WLR 335. *Sedleigh-Denfield* v O' Callaghan (1940) AC 880.

[369] Simon Whittaker, *Liability for Products: English Law, French Law, and European Harmonization* (Oxford University Press 2005).

[370] Joseph Carman Smith, *Liability in Negligence* (Carswell Legal Publications 1984).

[371]Robert A Leflar, 'Negligence in Name Only' (1952) 27 New York University Law Review 564.

[372] William Vaughan Horton Rogers and John Anthony Jolowicz, *Winfield and Jolowicz on Tort* (Sweet & Maxwell 2010).

a. The defendant owes the claimant a duty of care;
b. The defendant has acted in breach of that duty;
c. As a result, the claimant has suffered damage that is not too remote a consequence of the defendant's actions.

In order to impose a duty of care on the defendant, the claimant must make sure that the defendant has satisfied the above test. It is imperative to consider each element of the tort in turn. Rarely in practice, however, will disputes ever involve all three elements. Moreover, the court has a tendency to blur the distinction between each separate element of negligence, as shown in *Henderson v Merrett Syndicates Ltd.*[373] Quite often, a judgment may indicate each of the defendants liable but may not make it clear which of the three separate requirements of the tort has not been fulfilled,[374] which stems from the fact that the concept of reasonable foreseeability is used by the court in establishing all three elements of the tort.

The Application of Negligence

The tort of negligence covers such a wide range of factual situations that the search for a single set of rules applicable to all types of negligence cases is extremely difficult. The correct approach is to focus on the type of interest which the claimant is trying to use the tort to protect (physical, the safety of property, financial, livelihood, well-being, or psychological well-being), and then think about the policy reasons as to why the courts have felt either able or unable to extend the scope of negligence to protect that interest in a particular situation.[375] Therefore, the language of the judges and the pattern of their decision-making in corporate human rights violations will only begin to make sense when considered alongside the political and economic landscape, which in turn motivates decisions in negligence cases.

When one looks at what negligence is trying to achieve within society – the redistribution of certain risks within day-to-day activities – it becomes clear why the judges have difficulties in formulating workable rules for the tort. The point to grasp is that negligence is essentially concerned with conflicts of values/interests within society. In essence, therefore, in order to decide the question of negligence in corporate human rights abuses, the judge must make a political and moral value judgment as

[373] *Henderson v Merrett Syndicates Ltd* (1994) UKHL 5.
[374] *Sam (aka- Al-Sam) v Atkins* (2006) EWCA Civ 152, (2006) R.T. R14.
[375] Paula Giliker and Silas Beckwith (n 372).

to the relative merit of safety and protecting rights in society. So, the problem of corporate human rights violations is one of social, economic, and financial policy, not legal personality or treaty. Negligence exists to protect society from harm caused by any entity, including corporations.

Critical Overview of Negligence

In 1932, in the landmark *Donoghue v Stevenson*[376] case, Lord Atkin formulated a general principle known as the neighbour principle by which the existence of a legal duty to take care could be determined, thus effectively inventing the modern tort of negligence. The main strength of this argument is that Lord Atkin's general principle contained the logic that the limits of tort obligation could be confined.

As the tort of negligence developed, the courts sought to qualify Lord Atkin's general principles with a number of complexities, often inherently vague, and sometimes rather arbitrary rules. The courts have struggled to determine the proper scope of negligence, and have used the three elements of duty, breach, and causation as a control mechanism to try to set a limit to the tort.

The multifaceted approach can sometimes be rather confusing, but what is clear is that in recent times there has been a marked tendency to deal with the question of liability by reference to the scope of the duty of care. Logically, establishing the existence of a duty of care is the first hurdle a claimant must overcome.

In many situations, it will be obvious from case law that the defendant owes the claimant a duty of care. The real problem for the courts is how to decide whether a duty should be owed in a novel factual situation which is not covered by precedent. Because of the political and economic considerations involved, the courts have found it difficult both to decide this question and to express their decisions in the appropriate language.[377] In order to limit the scope of the duty of care, the courts have repeatedly asserted the importance of the relationship between the defendant and the claimant. This approach, however, has not resulted in a universally applicable test for determining the existence of a duty of care. The qualification on Lord Atkin's neighbourhood principle has become so frequently used that the House of Lords has been forced to abandon the

---

[376]*Donoghue v Stevenson* (1932) UKHL 100 (26 May 1932). <http://www.bailii.org/uk/cases/UKHL/1932/100.html> Accessed 31 October 2016, or (1932) UKHL 100, 1932 SC (HL) 31, (1932) AC 562, [1931] UKHL 3.

[377]Dominick R Vetri, *Tort Law and Practice* (LexisNexis/Matthew Bender 1998).

search for a single workable test. In *Caparo v Dickman*,[378] Lord Roskill concluded 'it has now to be accepted that there is no simple formula or touchstone to which recourse can be had in order to provide in every case a ready answer'.

However, critics of tort law argue that it created uncertainty and is unpredictable when one considers the requirements of the rule of law.[379] Although the legal principles that developed in relation to the imposition of a duty of care provide flexibility in the law, this book contests that the critics' views are invalid. The duty of care enables the incremental development of tort law in order to meet changing social needs. This development is not unconstrained, which provides for a level of consistency in negligence law. Furthermore, this book argues that critics' views of tort law are unjustified for two significant reasons. First, sceptical views of tort law lack robustness because, ultimately, judicial decisions in negligence cases are legitimate legal developments. Secondly, if one agrees with Fish, author of *There's No Such Thing as Free Speech: And It's a Good Thing, Too*, one may argue that judges are merely engaging with the incremental development of the law with relevance to existing doctrine.[380] Hence, such judicial activism merely develops the liability rules in conjunction with the purposes of tort law and social need. Finally, the imposition of a duty of care is an interpretive task due to the inherent ambiguities of language.

It is suggested here that the tort of negligence does not have a specific formula for each case, hence the concept of the tort of negligence is decided case-by-case, based on its merit. Bearing this in mind, it is perfectly acceptable to state that the tort of negligence offers a flexible approach to imposing a duty of care on an entity such as a corporation. Additionally, this book shall closely examine the historical development of duty of care, and the modern approach in *Caparo v Dickman*[381], to decide whether corporations can be held accountable under this principle.

Why Tort Law (Tort of Negligence)?

On the most basic level of corporate human rights accountability, the global human rights responsibility on all actors, including non-state actors in the international arena, overlaps with straightforward concepts of

[378] *Capara v Dickman* (1990) 2 AC 605, [1990] UKHL 2, (1990) 1 All ER 568.
[379] Christopher L Kutz, 'Just Disagreement: Indeterminacy and Rationality in The Rule of Law' (1994) 103(3) Yale Law Journal 997, 1030.
[380] Stanley Fish, *There's No Such Thing as Free Speech: And It's a Good Thing, Too* (Oxford University Press 1994).
[381] *Ibid.*

tort liability and civil responsibility for the wrongs one person causes another.[382] Tort law remedies provide crucial elements for the enforcement of international law both at international and domestic levels.[383] The analysis of the relationship between tort remedies and international law and human rights law is the multi-faceted nature of human rights legal process.[384] As noted by Coliver, Green and Hoffman, under the overlapping functions of The Alien Tort Statute 28 U.S.C. § 1350 (ATCA) and the Torture Victim Protection Act of 1991 (TVPA) in the US, a claimant can sue perpetrators, civilian and military superiors, and corporations and corporate officers for violations including genocide, war crimes, crimes against humanity, extrajudicial executions, disappearances, torture, slavery and forced labour, and human trafficking.[385]

The purpose of a lawsuit under ATCA/TVPA includes holding individuals and corporate perpetrators accountable for human rights violations.[386] Tort law provides the victims with official and legal acknowledgement and remedy for the harm caused to them.[387] This development has contributed to the development of international human rights law, building a legal pathway in the US to support tort litigation under the auspices of international law.[388] Similarly, tort litigation has added to a climate of deterrence, including supporting or catalysing efforts in other states for human rights accountability and remedy.[389] Minow in '*Between Vengeance and Forgiveness: Facing History after Genocide and Mass*

---

[382]Beth Stephens, Michael Ratner, Judith Chomsky, Jennifer Green and Paul Hoffman, *International Human Rights Litigation in US Courts* (Irvington-on-Hudson New York: Transnational publishers 1996).

[383]George P Fletcher, *Tort Lability for Human Rights Abuses* (Bloomsbury Publishing 2008).

[384]Craig Forcese, 'ATCA's Achilles Heel: Corporate Complicity, International Law and The Alien Tort Claims Act' (2001) 26 Yale Journal of International Law 487.

[385]Jennie M Green, Sandra Coliver, and Paul Hoffman, 'Holding Human Rights Violators Accountable by Using International Law in US Courts: Advocacy Efforts and Complementary Strategies' (2005) 19 Emory International Law Review 169.

[386]Mark W Bina, 'Private Military Contractor Liability and Accountability after Abu Ghraib' (2004) 38 John Marshall Law School Law Review 1237.

[387]Beth Stephens, Michael Ratner, Judith Chomsky, Jennifer Green, and Paul Hoffman, *International Human Rights Litigation in US Courts* (Irvington-on-Hudson, New York: Transnational publishers 1996).

[388]Brian C Free, 'Awaiting Doe v. Exxon Mobil Corp.: Advocating the Cautious Use of Executive Opinions in Alien Tort Claims Act Litigation' (2003) 12 (2) Pacific Rim Law & Policy Journal 467.

[389]Martha Minow, *Between Vengeance and Forgiveness: Facing History after Genocide and Mass Violence* (Beacon Press 1998.).

Violence'[390] explains how legal proceedings have promoted reconciliation and healing in a conflicted society.[391]

The concept of tort law allows victims of human rights violations and environmental damages or surviving family members to bring ligation against a perpetrator. This can provide an opportunity for financial remedy[392] that, while perhaps seeming routine and insufficient to victims, does provide an avenue for redress and an opportunity for remedy to help injured victims get back to where they were before the tort occurred.[393]

The enforcement of legal rights in tort law gives the victims the opportunity to have a court validate their claims by providing a formal legal judgment.[394] As stated by Haynes and Boone LLP 'in the case of punitive damages, a claimant will receive the added benefit of a public statement that reflects on the gravity of what the victims, survivors or their lost family member(s) have suffered.'[395] An implication for the defendants is that court proceedings will provide public accountability for what they have done, and for those who might be tempted to commit similar human rights violations and environmental damages in future. This will serve as a warning that any individual or corporation that violates human rights or damages the environment may face serious financial and reputational consequences for their actions.

Tort law also provides a duty of care for one person to avoid causing harm to another.[396] The notion of duty of care has developed jurisprudence on the doctrine of reasonable care, foreseeable harm, and duty of care.[397] It seems that the purpose of encouraging appropriate future corporate behaviour overlaps with the multiple functions of human rights law that contribute to the development of human rights norms and the

---

[390]Jennifer M Green, 'Corporate Torts: International Human Rights and Superior Officers' (2016) 17 Chicago Journal of International Law 447.

[391]*Ibid.*

[392]Avihay Dorfman, 'What is The Point of The Tort Remedy?' (2010) 55 (1) American Journal of Jurisprudence 105.

[393]Roger Paul Alford, *Apportioning Responsibility Among Joint Tortfeasors for International Law Violations* (2011).

[394]George P Fletcher, *Tort Liability for Human Rights Abuses* (Bloomsbury Publishing, 2008).

[395]William R Casto, 'The New Federal Common Law of Tort Remedies for Violations of International Law' (2006) 37 (3) Rutgers Law Journal 635. Also see, <Flaux-ting the Rules: Punitive Damages in English Law - Lexology> Accessed on 25 November 2017.

[396]*Ibid.*

[397]Joanne Conaghan and Wade Mansell, *The Wrongs of Tort* (Vol. 2. Pluto Press 1998).

deterrence of future human rights violations.[398] Another important aspect of tort law is that tort theory transcends legal systems and is commonly included in statutory or common law around the world.[399] In other legal systems, victims of human rights violations may be able to seek remedies both to punish the perpetrators of the abuse through criminal and civil remedies and receive compensation in a mechanism that is linked to their criminal claim.[400] For example, in the civil law system in France, the criminal system is the dominant system, with individuals able to be a *partie civile*, or civil party, to the criminal action.[401]

Also, Stephens, in her analysis of whether there were parallel options for human rights victims to the Alien Tort Statute in other countries, raised the notion of 'translation' among the different legal systems.[402] 'Translation of a legal concept from one system to 'another does not require identical implementation',[403] but rather requires 'adherence to the same underlying concept''.'[404] 'The mechanical transfer of legal procedure from one system to another is rarely effective.'[405] The common goals of a legal principle must be realised through procedures appropriate to each national judicial system and its universal applicability at international level.[406] It can thus be suggested that, at the core of judicial interpretation of legal rules, lies the commonalities.[407]

---

[398]Leon Gettler, 'Liability Forges a New Morality' *The Age* (3 August 2005).

[399]Paula Giliker, *Vicarious Liability in Tort–A Comparative Perspective* (Cambridge University Press 2010).

[400]Beth Stephens, *Translating Filartiga: A Comparative and International Law Analysis of Domestic Remedies for International Human Rights Violations* (2002). Explaining that the division between the civil and criminal actions should be eliminated by states, Robert C Thompson, Anita Ramasastry and Mark B Taylor, *Translating Unocal: The Expanding Web of Liability for Business Entities Implicated in International Crimes* (2009).

[401]Charles Howard, 'Compensation in French Criminal Procedure' (1958) 21 Modern Law Review 387.

[402]*Ibid.*

[403] Jennifer M Green, 'Corporate Torts: International Human Rights and Superior Officers' (2016) 447.

[404]*Ibid.*

[405] *Ibid.* Jennifer M Green, 'Corporate Torts: International Human Rights and Superior Officers' (2016) 447. < https://cjil.uchicago.edu/publication/corporate-torts-international-human-rights-and-superior-officers> Accessed 17 May 2017

[406]Craig M Scott, *Translating Torture into Transnational Tort: Conceptual Divides in The Debate on Corporate Accountability for Human Rights Harms* (2001).

[407]Beth Stephen (1123).

'Victims of human rights abuses around the world seek comparable results through varied procedural models, tailored to the requirements of their local legal systems, which is relevant to the principle in tort law.'[408] This can be seen in UN treaties and conventions which state 'the legal obligation is reaffirmed for all states to promote'[409] 'universal respect for, and observance and protection of, all human rights and fundamental freedoms for all.'[410] 'It is clearly stated 'that the obligation of states is to promote universal respect for and observance of human rights.'[411] 'Not selective, not relative, but universal respect, observance and protection.'[412] Thus, the enforcement of human rights law through the notion of tort law is a 'universal respect for, and observance and protection of, all human rights and fundamental freedoms for all', not a departure from the fundamental principles of the state's duties.[413]

The extensive critical analyses in this book have explored the common denominator of providing remedies to victims of corporate human rights violations in these multiple sources of law. However, it is acknowledged that to properly compare and translate the concept of corporate liability across jurisdictions, it is necessary to focus on the common core of parallel tests in international and domestic systems rather than the differences in implementation of tort law throughout the different systems. This book argues that tort law can facilitate corporate liability for

---

[408]Jennifer M Green, 'Corporate Torts: International Human Rights and Superior Officers' (2016) 447. <https://cjil.uchicago.edu/publication/corporate-torts-international-human-rights-and-superior-officers> Accessed 17 May 2017 and Robert C Thompson and Anita Ramasastry, and Mark B Taylor, *Translating Unocal: The Expanding Web of Liability for Business Entities Implicated in International Crimes* (2009).

[409] Demelash Shiferaw and Yonas Tesfa, 'Human Rights Law Teaching Material (200) Prepared under the Sponsorship of the Justice and Legal System Research Institute. <https://chilot.files.wordpress.com/2011/06/human-rights-law.pdf> Accessed 28 May 2016.

[410]Philip Alston, ed. *The United Nations and Human Rights: a Critical Appraisal* (Ardent Media 1996) and Demelash Shiferaw and Yonas Tesfa, 'Human Rights Law Teaching Material' (2009) Prepared under the Sponsorship of the Justice and Legal System Research Institute.

[411] Demelash Shiferaw and Yonas Tesfa, 'Human Rights Law Teaching Material (200) Prepared under the Sponsorship of the Justice and Legal System Research Institute. <https://chilot.files.wordpress.com/2011/06/human-rights-law.pdf> Accessed 28 May 2016.

[412]*Ibid.*

[413] James Frederick Green, *The United Nations and Human Rights* (Brookings institution 1956).

corporate human rights abuses and accountability for its supply chain and subsidiaries' misconduct, and that this concept is consistent with parallel standards in US law, such as ATCA and TVPA.[414] This notion also follows the obligation that are 'established for all states, in accordance with the Charter of the United Nations and other instruments of human rights and international law.'[415] 'No state is exempt from these obligations. All member states of the United Nations have a legal obligation to promote and protect human rights, regardless'[416] of the differences between the states' legal systems. 'Universal human rights protection and promotion are asserted in the Vienna Declaration as the 'first responsibility' of all governments.'[417] These findings suggest that common types of actions have resulted in common types of liability. Thus, there is an availability of remedies to victims of human rights violations, and of enforcement of human rights standard of tort principles through the concept of a duty of care.[418]

Link between Tort Duty of Care, International Human Rights Law, and International Criminal Law

'Human rights are the'[419] birth rights of 'every person. If a state dismisses universal human rights on the basis of'[420] the disparities that exist in its legal system, 'then rights would be denied to the persons living under

---

[414] Matthew H Murray, *Torture Victim Protection Act. Legislation to Promote Enforcement of The Human Rights of Aliens in US Courts* 25 Columbia Journal of Transnational Law 673 (1986).

[415] Demelash Shiferaw and Yonas Tesfa, 'Human Rights Law Teaching Material' (2009) Prepared under the Sponsorship of the Justice and Legal System Research Institute and Julie A Mertus and Dimitris Bourantonis, *The United Nations and Human Rights: a Guide for a New Era* (Routledge 2010).

[416] *Ibid.*

[417] Demelash Shiferaw and Yonas Tesfa, 'Human Rights Law Teaching Material' (2009) Prepared under the Sponsorship of the Justice and Legal System Research Institute and Arjun Sengupta, 'The Human Right to Development' (2004) 32 (2) Oxford Development Studies 179, 203.

[418] Philip Mariani, 'Assessing The Proper Relationship between The Alien Tort Statute and The Torture Victim Protection Act' (2008) 156 (5) University of Pennsylvania Law Review 1383.

[419] Demelash Shiferaw and Yonas Tesfa, 'Human Rights Law Teaching Material' (2009) Prepared under the Sponsorship of the Justice and Legal System Research Institute.

[420] *Ibid.*

that state's jurisdiction. The denial or abuse of human rights based'[421] on the existing difference in legal rules is wrong, regardless of the violator's link to the home or the host state. This is because the issue of the enforcement of human rights and remedies for victims have coexisted in many jurisdictions. For instance, in a common law jurisdiction, widespread acceptance of the relationship between tort and criminal law means that tort law provides remedy while punishment is primarily the role of the criminal system.[422] In jurisdictions such as the US and UK, punitive[423] remedies are for gross misconduct.[424] The awarding of a punitive remedy in this situation becomes more blurred because the goal of punitive damages is 'punishment; punitive damages also have the purpose of deterring future violations[425] and of naming and shaming the tortfeasor',[426] which enhance both the intentions of deterrence and the declarative function of the foundation of law.[427] Also, one of the most important questions being asked in recent decades surrounds the distinction between the criminal and tort law principles. This is due to the fact that crimes are considered to be committed against society as a whole.[428] Similarly, in civil legal systems, these functions are linked when

---

[421] *Ibid.*

[422] Duff RA, *Repairing Harms and Answering for Wrongs, in Philosophical Foundations of Tort Law,* 212, 16 (John Oberdiek, ed., Oxford University Press, 2014); and Duff RA, 'Torts, Crimes, And Vindication: Whose Wrong Is It?' *In Unravelling Tort and Crime 148-50* (Matthew Dyson ed., 2014).

[423] Clarence Morris, 'Punitive Damages in Tort Cases' (1931) 44 Harvard Law Review 1173 and *Rookes v. Barnard* [1964] AC 1129.
Kuddus v Chief Constable of Leicestershire Constabulary [2001] UKHL 29.
The House of Lords in *Kuddus v Chief Constable of Leicestershire Constabulary* [2001] 2 WLR 1789 over-ruled the decision of the Court of Appeal in *AB v South West Water Services Ltd* [1993] QB 507. Also see: *Rookes v. Barnard* [1964] AC 1129.

[424] Kenneth Mann, 'Punitive Civil Sanctions: The Middleground between Criminal and Civil Law' (1992) Yale Law Journal 1795.

[425] John C Coffee, 'Paradigms Lost: The Blurring of The Criminal and Civil Law Models. And What Can be Done About it' (1992) 101(8) Yale Law Journal 1875; Jerome Hall, 'Interrelations of Criminal Law and Torts: I' (1943) 43(3) Columbia Law Review 753; and John C. Coffee, 'Does "Unlawful Mean Criminal"?: Reflections on The Disappearing Tort/Crime Distinction in American Law' (1991) 71 Boston Law Journal 193.

[426] Jennifer M Green, 'Corporate Torts: International Human Rights and Superior Officers' (2016) 17 Chicago Journal of International Law 447.

[427] *Ibid.*

[428] Johannes Andenaes, *Punishment and Deterrence* (University of Michigan Press 1974).

a private party is able to join a criminal action.[429] It is possible, therefore, that the nature of human rights violations further blurs the common distinction between the criminal and civil legal systems.

What is clear in the development of tort and criminal liability law is that both have been set against each other in a way that can be seen as an attempt to avoid any accountability. Therefore, there is a valid argument for finding a legal basis for holding corporations liable in a tort lawsuit for international human rights law violations. As has been observed by Posner, 'those standing against criminal liability contend that there is no need for it because of civil liability'.[430] 'In a common law system such as the UK, tort and criminal law may complement each other and serve as different levers in building accountability within a particular jurisdiction, across national systems, and in the international legal system itself'.[431] For instance, states such as the US allow a claimant to bring tort claims alleging corporate responsibility for human rights violations and environmental damages in the last thirty years. However, there is still no provision for corporate liability for human rights violations in the US federal criminal code.[432]

Posner has mentioned several important treaties as examples that show the position of civil and administrative remedies where criminal remedies are unavailable.[433] The author cited the Organisation for Economic Cooperation and Development Convention on Combating Bribery of Foreign Public Officials in International Business Transactions,[434] the UN International

---

[429]Mann Kenneth (n 871).

[430]*Flomo v Firestone Nat. Rubber Co.*, LLC, 643 F.3d 1013 (7th Cir. 2011). Also see, Curtis A. Bradley and Mitu Gulati, 'Withdrawing from International Custom' (2010) Yale Law Journal 202, and William Blackstone, *Commentaries on The Laws of England* (Vol. 2. Collins & Hannay 1830).

[431] Jennifer M Green, 'Corporate Torts: International Human Rights and Superior Officers' (2016) 17 Chicago Journal of International Law 447 and Lillian Aponte Miranda, 'The Hybrid State-Corporate Enterprise and Violations of Indigenous Land Rights: Theorizing Corporate Responsibility and Accountability under International Law' (2007) 11 Lewis & Clark Law Review 135.

[432]Yadh Ben Achour to Pamela Hamoto, Permanent Representative of The United States to the United Nations (Oct. 6, 2015). <https://perma.cc/Z9HG-9C43> Accessed 3 September 2017.

[433] Jennifer M Green, 'The Rule of Law at a Crossroad: Enforcing Corporate Responsibility in International Investment Through the Alien Tort Statute' (2014) 35 (4) University of Pennsylvania Journal of International Law 1085.

[434] Organisation for Economic Cooperation and Development, *Convention on Combating Bribery of Foreign Public Officials in International Business Transactions*, Paris, November 20, 1997: 1–8 (1998) 3 Trends in Organized Crime 77, 82.

Convention for the Suppression of the Financing of Terrorism,[435] and the UN Convention Against Transnational Organized Crime.[436] These treaties permit civil and administrative remedies as substitutes to criminal liability.[437] Similarly, in some legal systems, tort standards may lead to criminal consequences or accountability for human rights violations.[438] Also, legal scholars such as Payne and Pereira have observed that there is a new development in how countries transitioning from dictatorships and/or civil conflicts have addressed corporate complicity.[439] Although 'transitional justice'[440] legal cases against state officials have been mainly criminal prosecutions, when it comes to corporate complicity, civil trials have outnumbered criminal trials.[441]

This observation supports the hypothesis that tort remedies do not contain the same restrictions as criminal prosecutions. Therefore, its application to corporations will breach the restrictions in the criminal law principle. The flexibility offered by tort law will allow courts to find legal

---

[435] UN General Assembly, *International Convention for The Suppression of The Financing of Terrorism*, 9 December 1999, No. 38349. <http://www.refworld.org/docid/3dda0b867.html > Accessed 3 September 2017.

[436] UN General Assembly, *Protocol to Prevent, Suppress and Punish Trafficking in Persons, Especially Women and Children, Supplementing the United Nations Convention against Transnational Organized Crime*, 15 November 2000. <http://www.refworld.org/docid/4720706c0.html> Accessed 3 September 2017. The United Nations Convention against Transnational Organized Crime, adopted by General Assembly resolution 55/25 of 15 November 2000, is the main international instrument in the fight against transnational organised crime. 'It opened for signature by Member States at a High-level Political Conference convened for that purpose in Palermo, Italy, on 12-15 December 2000 and entered into force on 29 September 2003'. <https://www.unodc.org/unodc/en/organized-crime/intro/UNTOC.html> Accessed 30 October 2017.

[437] *Flomo v Firestone Nat. Rubber Co., LLC*, 643 F.3d 1013, 1020 (7th Cir. 2011).

[438] Letter from Yadh Ben Achour to Pamela Hamoto, Permanent Representative of The United States to The United Nations (Oct. 6, 2015). <https://perma.cc/Z9HG-9C43> accessed 4 September 2017.

[439] Leigh A Payne and Gabriel Pereira, *Accountability for Corporate Complicity in Human Rights Violations: Argentina's Transitional Justice Innovation? In the Economic Accomplices to The Argentine Dictatorship: Outstanding Debts* (Horacio Verbitsky & Juan Pablo Bohoslavsky eds., 2016) 29, 44.

[440] Ruti G Teitel, *Transitional Justice* (Oxford University Press on Demand 2000). See also: 'The International Center for Transitional Justice assists countries pursuing accountability for past mass atrocity or human rights abuse to learn more. <https://www.ictj.org/sites/default/files/ICTJ-Global-Transitional-Justice-2009-English.pdf> Accessed 15 May 2017.

[441] Leigh A Payne and Gabriel Pereira (n 1148).

responsibility for corporations and their subsidiaries' misconduct. Where tort liability is established by the courts at both national and international level, effective remedies should be awarded to the victims. However, the significant difference in the balance of competing interests within a governmental office can serve as an impediment to the universal application of tort law.[442] Nonetheless, a note of caution is due here, as survivors of human rights violations may be able to secure private or public interest lawyers to file tort and civil claims on their behalf. Thus, these claims are more likely to overcome the political limitations than criminal prosecutions.[443]

There are several possible explanations for this legal reasoning. One of these is that the number of cases brought under the ATCA and TVPA far outstripped the number of criminal prosecutions for international human rights violations.[444] This is evident in the US government's prosecution and deportation of Nazi war criminals, as well as the prosecution of those accused of human rights violations for immigration fraud.[445] Nevertheless, only one person, Charles 'Chuckie' Taylor,[446] was criminally prosecuted for the underlying human rights violations he committed in Liberia.[447] In fact, no corporation or corporate official has been prosecuted in the US for international human rights violations except under the ATCA as a tort suit.[448] According to these findings, tort cases have the potential to provide remedies for human rights victims while moving the law forward and giving added impetus to criminal prosecutions.

---

[442] Anne-Marie Slaughter, 'Disaggregated Sovereignty: Towards the Public Accountability of Global Government Networks' (2004) 39 (2) Government and Opposition 159.

[443] Steven R Ratner, 'Belgium's War Crimes Statute: A Postmortem' (2003) 97 (4) American Journal of International Law 888.

[444] Douglas Donoho, 'Human Rights Enforcement in The Twenty-First Century' (2006) 35 Georgia Journal of International & Comparative Law 1.

[445] Kate Connolly, 'Trial of Man Deported from US to Germany for Nazi War Crimes to Begin' (London, 29 November 2009) The Guardian. See also: Jean Ancel, The History of The Holocaust in Romania (2016).

[446] Elise Keppler, Shirley Jean and Paxton J Marshall, 'First Prosecution in The United States for Torture Committed Abroad: The Trial of Charles 'Chuckie' Taylor, Jr' (2008) 15 (3) Human Rights Brief 4. See also: Alpha Sesay, United States Court of Appeals Judges Uphold Charles Taylor Jr.'s (Chuckie Taylor) Convictions And 97 Years Jail Sentence (2010). < https://www.ijmonitor.org/2010/07/united-states-court-of-appeals-judges-uphold-charles-taylor-jr-s-chuckie-taylor-convictions-and-97-years-jail-sentence/> Accessed 20th June 2017.

[447] The US federal extraterritorial torture statute, 18 USC. § 2340A (1994).

[448] Yolanda S Wu, *Genocidal Rape in Bosnia: Redress in United States Courts Under The Alien Tort Claims Act* (1993).

In addition to the flexibility offered by tort law, it is important to note that criminal prosecutions around the world vary according to the level of participation afforded to those harmed 'by the violations.'[449] 'Some countries, such as the US, Australia, Belgium, Canada, France, India, Indonesia, and South Africa give prosecutors complete enforcement discretion',[450] 'with little or no official participation by victims or their representatives.'[451]Contrarily, other countries, such as Argentina, Germany, Japan, the Netherlands, Spain, and Ukraine, allow higher levels of participation by victims, including participation in the criminal proceedings to the court decision and to the appeal of decisions not to prosecute.[452]

Lastly, one of the most vital assessments of the standards applied in human rights tort cases, the jurisprudence on human rights claims, looks to international criminal law to inform analysis in civil cases. For instance, in rulings on the definitions of human rights norms, US courts have frequently cited international criminal tribunal judgments to inform their rulings about the content of customary international law,[453] specifically in cases brought under the ATCA and TVPA.[454] International criminal law has been a primary source of developing standards, and US and other national courts have looked to international criminal tribunal jurisprudence for guidance when they are ruling on tort cases.[455] It can thus be suggested that in the international and national legal systems, accountability for human rights victims has integrated principles from the international criminal system as well as other sources of law. Therefore, including the concept of tort law into national legal system is not problematic, but rather an innovative approach to the development of a binding accountability concept for corporations.[456] Tort law remedies will reflect on the 'dynamic,

---

[449]Jennifer M Green, 'Corporate Torts: International Human Rights and Superior Officers' (2016) 17 Chicago Journal of International Law 447 and Leigh A Payne and Gabriel Pereira (n 1148).

[450]Jennifer M Green, 'Corporate Torts: International Human Rights and Superior Officers' (2016) 17 Chicago Journal of International Law 447.

[451]*Ibid.*

[452]*Ibid.*

[453]Andrea Bianchi, 'International Law and US Courts: The Myth of Lohengrin Revisited' (2004) 15 (4) European Journal of International Law 751.

[454]Eric Engle, 'The Torture Victim's Protection Act, The Alien Tort Claims Act, and Foucault's Archaeology of Knowledge' (2004) 67 Albany Law Review 501.

[455]Harold Hongju Koh, 'International Law as Part of Our Law' (2004) 09(1) American Journal of International Law 43.

[456]Doreen J. McBarnet, Aurora Voiculescu and Tom Campbell, *The New Corporate Accountability: Corporate Social Responsibility and the Law* (Cambridge University Press 2009).

coordinated efforts of the international community to achieve and advance a common standard and international system of law to protect human dignity.'[457]

The Application of Tort Law in Other Jurisdictions

In theory, 'the legal systems in most countries should offer victims of human rights violations the opportunity to seek tort and civil redress'[458] against the perpetrator(s).[459] Legal developments in the European Union, most notably the introduction of a unified private international law framework, suggest that European courts are better equipped and more likely to allow human rights victims access to justice in foreign-cubed scenarios.[460]

In *Lubbe*, the plaintiffs were employees of an English corporation with a South African subsidiary.[461] The plaintiffs alleged that the defendant had breached its duty of care by allowing the employees to be exposed to asbestos, despite *Lubbe* knowing that exposure 'was gravely injurious to health'.[462] The House of Lords granted the employees' claim for jurisdiction before the UK courts, even though all relevant conduct took place entirely in South Africa.

In *Akpan*, a Nigerian farmer, Friday Akpan, and a Dutch non-governmental organisation (NGO) *Milieudefensie,* jointly sued Royal Dutch

---

[457]Demelash Shiferaw and Yonas Tesfa, 'Human Rights Law Teaching Material (200) Prepared under the Sponsorship of the Justice and Legal System Research Institute. <https://chilot.files.wordpress.com/2011/06/human-rights-law.pdf> Accessed 28 May 2016.

[458]Amnesty International, 'Creating a Paradigm Shift: Legal Solutions to Improve Access to Remedy for Corporate Human Rights Abuse' (2017). <https://www.amnesty.org/download/Documents/POL3070372017ENGLISH.PDF> Accessed 06 April 2018.

[459]Beth Stephens, *Translating Filartiga: A Comparative and International Law Analysis of Domestic Remedies for International Human Rights Violations* (2002).

[460]Fiona Robertson, 'Access to Justice for Victims of Human Rights Abuse by Multinational; Does European Civil and Commercial Litigation Provide an Answer?' (2015) 9 (1) New Zealand Journal of Research on Europe.

[461]*Lubbe v Cape Plc* (2000) 1 WLR 1545 (HL) and Fiona Robertson, 'Access to Justice for Victims of Human Rights Abuse By Multinational Corporations: Does European Civil and Commercial litigation Provide and Answer? (2015) 9 (1) New Zealand Journal of Research on Europe. < Microsoft Word - ONLINE Access to justice for victims of human rights abuse by multinational corporations FINAL (auckland.ac.nz)> Accessed 13 May 2019.

[462]*Ibid.*

Shell Plc (RDS), which was headquartered in The Hague, and its Nigerian subsidiary, Shell Petroleum Development Company (SPDC), for tortious damage before The Hague District Court.[463] After applying Dutch procedural rules, the Hague District Court found that it had jurisdiction to hear the case against both RDS and the Nigerian subsidiary.

However, this has not happened in cases such as *Dakota Access Pipeline (DAPL),*[464] *Aguinda v Texaco, Inc.*, 850 F. Supp. 282 (SDNY 1994)[465] and *Coca-Cola*. 'Coca-Cola Company also leads in the abuse of workers' rights, assassinations, water privatisation, and worker discrimination.'[466]

'Between 1989 and 2002, eight union leaders from Coca-Cola bottling plants in Colombia were killed after protesting the company's labour practices.'[467] Hundreds of other Coca-Cola workers who joined or considered joining the Colombian union 'SINALTRAINAL have been kidnapped, tortured, and detained by paramilitaries who were hired to intimidate workers to prevent them from unionising.'[468]

In *Dow Chemical Co. v United States*, 476 US 227 (1986), 'the company, Dow Chemical, has been destroying lives and poisoning the planet for decades.'[469] 'The company is best known for the health disasters

---

[463]*Akpan v Royal Dutch Shell Plc Arrondissementsrechtbank* Den Haag (District Court of The Hague) C/09/337050/HA ZA 09-1580, 30 January 2013.

[464]Sam Levin, 'Dakota Access Pipeline: Native Americans Allege Cruel Treatment' *The Guardian* (31 October 2016) <https://www.theguardian.com/us-news/2016/oct/31/dakota-access-pipeline-protest-investigation-human-rights-abuses> Accessed 6 August 2017.

[465]*Aguinda v. Texaco, Inc.*, 850 F. Supp. 282 (SDNY 1994) and Judith Kimberling, 'Indigenous Peoples and The Oil Frontier in Amazonia: The Case of Ecuador, Chevron Texaco, and Aguinda v. Texaco' (2005) 38 New York University Journal of Law & Business 413.

[466] Terry Collingsworth, 'Separating Fact from Fiction in The Debate over Application of The Alien Tort Claims Act to Violations of Fundamental Human Rights by Corporations' (2002) 37 (3) USFL Review 563.

[467]Lesley Gill, 'Right There with You Coca-Cola, Labor Restructuring and Political Violence in Colombia' (2007) 27(3) Critique of Anthropology 235 and <https://www.malaysia-today.net/Blog-e/2005_12_16_MT_BI_archive.htm > Accessed 05 April 2016.

[468]Jonathan Hills and Richard Welford, 'Coca-Cola and Water in India' (2005) 12(3) Corporate Social Responsibility and Environmental Management 16 and <https://www.malaysia-today.net/Blog-e/2005_12_16_MT_BI_archive.htm> Accessed 05 April 2016.

[469]<https://www.malaysia-today.net/Blog-e/2005_12_16_MT_BI_archive.htm> Accessed 30 June 2018 and Rebecca S Katz, 'The Corporate Crimes of Dow Chemical and The Failure to Regulate Environmental Pollution' (2010) 18 (4)

inflicted on millions of Vietnamese people'[470] – as well as many US army veterans – by its lethal Vietnam War-era defoliant, Agent Orange. Dow also developed and perfected napalm, the brutal chemical weapon that burned many innocents to death during the Vietnam War and other wars.[471] In 1988, Dow provided pesticides to Saddam Hussein despite warnings that they could be used to produce chemical weapons.[472]

Nestle USA is involved in illegal and forced child labour, which is rampant in the chocolate industry. More than 40% of the world's cocoa supply comes from the Ivory Coast, a country that the US State Department estimates had approximately 109,000 child labourers working in hazardous conditions on cocoa farms.[473] In 2001, Save the Children Canada reported that 15,000 children between 9 and 12 years old, many from impoverished Mali, had been tricked or sold into slavery on West African cocoa farms, many for just $30 each.[474]

'Pfizer is the largest pharmaceutical company in the world; it is also one of the worst'[475] abusers of the human right of universal access to HIV/AIDS medicine.[476]

In September 2005, the International Labour Rights Fund filed a lawsuit on behalf of Wal-Mart supplier sweatshop workers in China,

---

Critical Criminology 295 and <https://www.malaysia-today.net/Blog-e/2005_12_16_MT_BI_archive.htm > Accessed 05 April 2016.

[470]<https://www.malaysia-today.net/Blog-e/2005_12_16_MT_BI_archive.htm> Accessed 30 June 2018

[471]Susan Schultz Huxman and Denice Beatty Bruce, 'Toward a Dynamic Generic Framework of Apologia: A Case Study of Dow Chemical, Vietnam, and the Napalm Controversy' (1995) 46 (1-2) Communication Studies 57.

[472]Takeshi Uesugi, 'Is Agent Orange a Poison? Vietnamese Agent Orange Litigation and the New Paradigm of Poison' (2013) 24 The Japanese Journal of American Studies.

[473] Adeline Zensius, *Inside The Cocoa Pod: An Analysis of The Harkin-Engel Protocol in Cote d'Ivoire* (Georgetown University 2012).

[474]Elliot J Schrage and Anthony P Ewing, 'The Cocoa Industry and Child Labour' (2005) 18 Journal of Corporate Citizenship, Ambika Zutshi, Andrew Creed and Amrik Sohal, 'Child Labour and Supply Chain: Profitability or (mis) Management' (2009) 21 (1) European Business Review 42, and Amanda A Humphreville, 'If The Question Is Chocolate-Related, The Answer Is Always Yes: Why Doe v. Nestle Reopens The Door for Corporate Liability of US Corporations Under The Alien Tort Statute' (2015) 65 American University Business Law Review 191.

[475]<https://www.malaysia-today.net/Blog-e/2005_12_16_MT_BI_archive.htm> Accessed 30 June 2018

[476]Michael A Santoro, 'Human Rights and Human Needs: Diverse Moral Principles Justifying Third World Access to Affordable HIV/AIDS drugs' (2006) 31 North Carolina Journal of International Law and Commercial 923.

Indonesia, Bangladesh, Nicaragua and Swaziland.[477] The workers were denied minimum wages, forced to work overtime without compensation, and were denied legally mandated health care.[478] Other worker rights violations that have been found in foreign factories that produce goods for Wal-Mart include locked bathrooms, starvation wages, pregnancy tests, denial of access to health care, and workers being fired and blacklisted if they try to defend their rights.[479]

The limitations of these cases observed above have shown that the vast majority of human rights abuse victims still have no or limited access to judicial remedy in the domestic court and at the international level.[480] Taken together, these findings do support strong recommendations to examine the law for bringing a claim and specifically focus on ATCA, which is the source for all human rights violation litigation. Other states have also instigated claims against perpetrators, but these have involved the filing of criminal complaints, which demand prosecution rather than a true tort and civil lawsuit.[481] Ensuring appropriate judicial systems, remedy, and support for victims of corporate human rights violations and environmental damages should be a priority for both domestic and international legal systems. Taken together, these findings of the ATCA suggest that the U.S. Federal Courts have relied on distinctive sources of authority to decide civil claiming arising from human rights violations committed abroad.[482]

The Alien Tort Statute is 'a unique, but ancient jurisdictional statute that authorises US federal courts to hear claims of violations against

---

[477]Molly Selvin, 'Wal-Mart Faces Suit by Labor Group' (2005) Los Angeles Times

[478]Naomi Jiyoung Bang, 'Unmasking the Charade of The Global Supply Contract: A Novel Theory of Corporate Liability in Human Trafficking and Forced Labor Cases' (2013) 35 Houston Journal of International Law 255.

[479]Kevin Kolben, Labour Rights as Human Rights? (2009) 50 (2) Virginia Journal of International Law 449 and *Wal-Mart v Dukes*, 564 US 338 (2011).

[480]Dinah Shelton, *Remedies in International Human Rights Law* (Oxford University Pres USA 2015).

[481]Luc Reydams, *Universal Jurisdiction over Atrocities in Rwanda: Theory and Practice* (1996) 4 European Journal of Crime, Criminal Law and Criminal Justice 18.

[482]The Alien Tort Claims Act (ATCA) of 1789, 28 USC. § 1350; ATS.

the'[483] "'law of nations' committed abroad against foreigners.'[484] Victims are able to bring civil lawsuits based on breaches of international law against private entities. For successful plaintiffs, US courts provide the gateway to potentially exorbitant remedy. Despite promises of the US as a legal forum for corporate accountability for human rights abuse victims, this book argues that the all too prevalent practice of resorting to US courts is not, in fact, the best way for human rights abuse victims to seek access to remedy and justice. This is because, in *Kiobel*, the Court was adamant to ensure that the fact pattern of the claim was suitable for the ATCA. In deciding whether the case could be brought under the ATCA, the Supreme Court's sole concern was to preserve the US foreign affairs interests.[485] Even the dissenting opinion's reference to victims deserving remedy for violations of the law of nations was subordinate to the preservation of the good international relations of the United States with other States.[486] The Court paid no regard to the availability (or lack thereof) of alternative forums for the victims of the human rights abuses in the case.

It is evident that the Court did not find the claimants' access to justice to be a matter of its responsibility. In the English legal system, 'on the other hand, Lord Bingham was anxious to ensure that the litigants did not face a denial of justice and refused a grant to stay in light of the risk that the litigants'[487] 'would not have adequate funding to represent their claim

---

[483] Fiona Robertson, 'Access to Justice for Victims of Human Rights Abuse By Multinational Corporations: Does European Civil and Commercial litigation Provide and Answer? (2015) 9 (1) New Zealand Journal of Research on Europe. < Microsoft Word - ONLINE Access to justice for victims of human rights abuse by multinational corporations FINAL (auckland.ac.nz)> Accessed 13 May 2019.

[484] Fiona Robertson, 'Access to Justice for Victims of Human Rights Abuse By Multinational Corporations: Does European Civil and Commercial litigation Provide and Answer? (2015) 9 (1) New Zealand Journal of Research on Europe and *Smith Kline & French Labs Ltd v Bloch* [1983] 1 WLR 730 at 733

[485] Eugene Kontorovich, 'Kiobel Surprise: Unexpected by Scholars but Consistent with International Trends' (2014) 89 Notre Dame Law Review 1671 and Fiona Robertson, 'Access to Justice for Victims of Human Rights Abuse By Multinational Corporations: Does European Civil and Commercial litigation Provide and Answer? (2015) 9 (1) New Zealand Journal of Research on Europe.

[486] *Kiobel v Royal Dutch Petroleum Co.* (n 810).

[487] Fiona Robertson, 'Access to Justice for Victims of Human Rights Abuse By Multinational Corporations: Does European Civil and Commercial litigation Provide and Answer? (2015) 9 (1) New Zealand Journal of Research on Europe. < Microsoft Word - ONLINE Access to justice for victims of human rights abuse by multinational corporations FINAL (auckland.ac.nz)> Accessed 13 May 2019.

properly in South Africa.'[488] Claims under tort law are common and while violations of the Alien Tort Claims Act (ATCA) may be framed as a violation of statutory law '(e.g. torture as battery) such redefining mutes the grave international law aspect of the tort, reducing it to no more (or less) than a garden variety municipal tort.'[489] 'Accordingly, the severity of the victim's harm may not be properly recognised by the'[490] ATCA and the 'stigma attached to the defendant as'[491] an alien is 'significantly less than if they were citizens'[492] of the home state, for instance. For the purposes of the study in this book, it is 'asserted that the most important factor for a human rights abuse'[493] victim is establishing jurisdiction. Therefore, framing atrocious abuse as a combination of garden variety torts, while unsatisfying, may be necessary in order to ensure that the victims have the right access to remedy and justice.[494]

It is argued in this book that tort litigation can create certainty in corporate accountability lawsuits, independence, and impartiality. It will also help to limit the restrictions on the presumption against extraterritorial jurisdiction, and help the enforcement of human rights law, health and safety legislation, and environmental protection. Thus, *Kiobel*, where the plaintiffs, citizens of Nigeria, claimed that Dutch, British, and Nigerian oil-exploration corporations aided and abetted the Nigerian government in the 1990s to commit violations of customary international law. '(The power to make a law having extraterritorial operation is conferred only on Parliament and not on the state legislatures. Hence an Act of the State Legislature, if it gives extra-territorial operation to its provisions, can be successfully

---

[488] *Lubbe v Cape Plc* [2000] 1 WLR 1545 (HL) and Fiona Robertson, 'Access to Justice for Victims of Human Rights Abuse By Multinational Corporations: Does European Civil and Commercial litigation Provide and Answer? (2015) 9 (1) New Zealand Journal of Research on Europe. < Microsoft Word - ONLINE Access to justice for victims of human rights abuse by multinational corporations FINAL (auckland.ac.nz)> Accessed 13 May 2019.

[489] William S Dodge, *Alien Tort Litigation: The Road Not Taken* (2014) and Fiona Robertson, 'Access to Justice for Victims of Human Rights Abuse By Multinational Corporations: Does European Civil and Commercial litigation Provide and Answer? (2015) 9 (1) New Zealand Journal of Research on Europe. < Microsoft Word - ONLINE Access to justice for victims of human rights abuse by multinational corporations FINAL (auckland.ac.nz)> Accessed 13 May 2019.

[490] *Ibid.*

[491] *Ibid.*

[492] *Ibid.*

[493] *Ibid.*

[494] Beth Stephens, *Translating Filartiga: A Comparative and International Law Analysis of Domestic Remedies for International Human Rights Violations* (2002).

challenged in the court, unless extra-territorial operation can be sustained on the ground of territorial nexus. It means that although the object to which the law applies may not physically be located within the territorial limits of a State, yet the State law will be valid if there exists a connection or nexus between the state and the object.)'[495] Corporate liability and territorial nexus are two unsettled areas in ATCA litigation. However corporate liability is unquestioningly accepted under the Brussels I Regulation, which considers the jurisdictional issues that arise when litigation has a foreign element. It sets out the rules which determine whether the English court will have jurisdiction, both under the common law and the European regime, including the Recast Brussels Regulation.[496]

In addition, following the minority judgment in *Kiobel*, it is unclear whether ATCA plaintiffs will also need to prove exhaustion of local remedies, or be precluded from attaining jurisdiction on the basis of *forum non conveniens* or international comity. The minority was not 'clear in identifying the other avenues that plaintiffs could pursue.'[497] The ATCA is a 'unique jurisdictional statute that assesses liability in accordance with international law'[498], and 'the lack of guidance is disconcerting. The requirement that a claimant exhaust local remedies, especially when the home state may have a corrupt judiciary, imposes additional costs on the claimant, who is already likely to be of limited means.'[499] 'There is also no guarantee that their claim will, in fact, be heard under the ATCA. On the

[495] <http://www.proud2bindian.in/indian-law-judiciary/4579-what-territorial-nexus.html> Accessed 8 January 2016 and Kenneth W Dam, *The Law-Growth Nexus: The Rule of Law and Economic Development* (Brookings Institution Press 2007).

[496]Brussels I Regulation. Recital 2; Case C-75/63 *Mrs MKH Hoekstra (Née Unger) v Bestur der Bedriifsvereniging voor Detaijhandel en Ambachten* [1964] ECR I-01519.

[497] Fiona Robertson, 'Access to Justice for Victims of Human Rights Abuse By Multinational Corporations: Does European Civil and Commercial litigation Provide and Answer? (2015) 9 (1) New Zealand Journal of Research on Europe. < Microsoft Word - ONLINE Access to justice for victims of human rights abuse by multinational corporations FINAL (auckland.ac.nz)> Accessed 13 May 2019.

[498]*Ibid.*

[499]Micaela L Neal, 'The Niger Delta and Human Rights Lawsuits: A Search for The Optimal Legal Regime' (2011) 24 Pacific McGeorge Global Business & Development Law Journal 343 and Fiona Robertson, 'Access to Justice for Victims of Human Rights Abuse By Multinational Corporations: Does European Civil and Commercial litigation Provide and Answer? (2015) 9 (1) New Zealand Journal of Research on Europe. < Microsoft Word - ONLINE Access to justice for victims of human rights abuse by multinational corporations FINAL (auckland.ac.nz)> Accessed 13 May 2019.

other hand, member state courts do not have such requirements and cannot stay proceedings in favour of any other court on the grounds of *forum non conveniens*.'[500] This common law doctrine allows a court to dismiss a civil action (even though the forum or venue is proper and the court has jurisdiction over the case and the parties) where an appropriate and more convenient alternative forum exists in which to try the action.[501] This is undoubtedly a critical and devastating obstacle for human rights plaintiffs.

'Foreign legislatures may try to thwart plaintiffs' access to justice by enacting laws prohibiting litigation of certain claims.'[502] Additionally, the ability to sue parties related to a foreign government's human rights abuses is far from certain under the ATCA given the United States Supreme Court's foreign policy concerns.[503] This discrepancy could be attributed to the fact that, when human rights abuse originates from a foreign government, national courts may be overly cautious when ruling on the question of jurisdiction, and dismiss a case entirely, even where corporate bodies played a role in the human rights abuse.[504] The possible interference of the national government in ATCA claims cannot be ruled out here. To the further disappointment of corporate human rights abuse plaintiffs, it is not clear whether they can sue corporations, especially where they have little or no connection to the United States. The inability to invoke the

---

[500]*Ibid.*

[501]Paxton Blair, 'The Doctrine of Forum Non Conveniens in Anglo-American law' (1929) 29 (1) Columbia Law Review 1, 34.

[502]Fiona Robertson, 'Access to Justice for Victims of Human Rights Abuse By Multinational Corporations: Does European Civil and Commercial litigation Provide and Answer? (2015) 9 (1) New Zealand Journal of Research on Europe. < Microsoft Word - ONLINE Access to justice for victims of human rights abuse by multinational corporations FINAL (auckland.ac.nz)> Accessed 13 May 2019 and Angela Walker, 'The Hidden Flaw in Kiobel, Under The Alien Tort Statute The Mens Rea Standard for Corporate Aiding and Abetting is Knowledg*e'* (2011) 10 Northwestern University Journal of International Human Rights 119; and Micaela L Neal, The Niger Delta and Human Rights Lawsuits: A Search for The Optimal Legal Regime' (2011) 24 Pacific McGeorge Global Business & Development Law Journal, 343.

[503]Beth Stephens, 'The Curious History of The Alien Tort Statute' (2014) 89 (4) Notre Dame Law Review 1467, and David Cole, Jules Lobel and Harold Hongju Koh, 'Interpreting the Alien Tort Statute: Amicus Curiae Memorandum of International Law Scholars and Practitioners in Trajano v. Marcos' (1988) 12 Hastings International & Comparative. Law Review 1; *Trajano v Marcos*, 978 F 2d 493; See *Filartiga v Pena-Irala,* 630 F.2d 876 (2d Cir.1980).

[504] Danielle Olson, 'Corporate Complicity in Human Rights Violations Under International Criminal Law' (2015) 1 International Human Rights Law Journal.

ATCA following state sanctioned human rights abuses severely compromises its utility for human rights abuse and environmental damage victims in the host country, seeking an impartial forum for their case. Furthermore, the US federal courts are constrained by foreign policy considerations when determining the question of jurisdiction.[505] Nonetheless, the problematic substantive law is not an issue in ATCA claims because ATCA jurisprudence has determined that applicable substantive law is customary international law and this is common to all countries. This combination of findings provides some support for the conceptual premise that the ATCA by far is the only mechanism that has the potential to provide remedies for corporate human rights abuses. Nevertheless, it still falls short.

The relationship between tort law, the ATCA and human rights principles forms the foundation of court decisions in corporate human rights abuse cases, particularly in understanding and approaching tort law rules and remedies for human rights violations. This is because, it could increase the propensity of claimants relying on human rights legislation, for example, in individual claims against the corporations. Legal practitioners should encourage the court to take into account tort law principles when deciding cases of corporate human rights violations. The court should consider attempts made by lawyers, as observed in *Daniels v Walker*, 'where the defendant appealed against the decision of the High Court judge refusing the defendant permission to obtain and rely upon the evidence of his care expert in response to a care report jointly obtained in a personal injury action brought by the claimant.'[506] Arguably, this case led to an expansion of tort law in common law, as it adapts a judicial interpretation that could be seen as meeting the dynamics of the modern world.

Moreover, if a plaintiff has relied on the breach of human rights where the negligence claim has failed earlier, then the judicial court may consider common law to balance the rights and interests of the associated parties. As shown in *X (Minors) v Bedfordshire County Council,*[507] the House of Lords held that children who had been subjected to prolonged physical and emotional abuse by their parents had no claim in the tort of negligence against a social services authority for alleged negligence in failing to take them into local authority care. The claimant, *X (Minor)*, forwarded the matter to the European Court of Human Rights (ECtHR). The

---

[505]Louis Henkin, 'The Foreign Affairs Power of the Federal Courts: Sabbatino' (1964). 64 (5) Columbia Law Review 805.

[506]*Daniels v Walker* (2000) 1 WLR 1382 CA. Also see: <https://www.brownejacobson.com/insurance/training-and-resources/legal-updates/2000/05/daniels-v-walker-c-a> Accessed 14 May 2016.

[507]*X (Minors) v Bedforshire County Council* (1995) 2 AC 633.

Court re-iterated that Article 3 of the European Convention enshrines one of the most fundamental values of democratic societies. It prohibits in absolute terms torture or inhuman or degrading treatment of punishment. 'The obligation on High Contracting Parties under Article 1 of the Convention to secure to everyone within their jurisdiction the rights and freedoms defined in the Convention, taken together with Article 3, requires States to take measures designed to ensure that individuals within their jurisdiction are not subjected to torture or inhuman or degrading treatment, including such ill-treatment administered by private individuals'[508] (See *A v the United Kingdom* judgement of 23 September 1998, Reports of Judgements and Decisions 1998-VI, para 22). 'These measures should provide effective protection, in particular, of children and other vulnerable persons and include reasonable steps to prevent ill-treatment of which the authorities had or ought to have had knowledge.'[509]

The Alien Tort Claims Act (ATCA) of 1789

The ATCA was enacted in 1789, 'and provides that district courts shall have original jurisdiction of any civil action by an alien for Tort only, committed in violation of the law of nations or a treaty of the United States.'[510] Therefore, the ATCA provides the US federal courts with subject matter jurisdiction over claims, provided that three basic requirements are met: (1) the claimant is an alien; (2) the defendant is liable for the tort; and (3) the tort violates the law of nations or a treaty to which the US is party.[511] Despite this, the ATCA remains ambiguous because the statute fails to provide clarity on the scope of the law, and courts have failed to provide consistent direction for parties to follow.[512]

In *Sosa v Alvarez-Machain*, the Supreme Court held that the detention of a foreign national, who was transferred to the custody of law

---

508< https://works.bepress.com/john_knox/1/download/> Accessed 8 April 2016.

509 <http://www.dcya.gov.ie/documents/Publications/SixthRapporrteurReport.pdf> Accessed 24 March 2018.

510<https://law.unimelb.edu.au/files/dmfile/download156e1.pdf> Accessed 27 October 2018 and 28 USC. § 1350; ATS.

511Jeffrey M Blum and Ralph G. Steinhardt, 'Federal Jurisdiction over International Human Rights Claims: The Alien Tort Claims Act after Filartiga v. Pena-Irala' (1981) 22(5) Harvard International Law Journal 3.

512Emily M Nellermoe, 'Balintulo v Daimler AG, 727 F. 3d 174 (2013): Second Circuit Closes the Door for Victims of International Rights Violations' (2014) 11 *South Carolina Journal of International Law and Business* and *Balintulo v Daimler AG*, US Dist. Lexis 17474 (2d Cir. Aug. 21, 2013).

enforcement officials in less than one day, did not clearly violate any norms of customary international law. Therefore, the plaintiff failed to establish a cause of action under the ATCA.[513] However, on appeal, a three-judge panel on the Ninth Circuit Court affirmed the ATCA judgment against *Sosa* but reinstated the claim against the US government. Preceding the *Sosa* case, some commentators read the ATCA as a jurisdictional grant and nothing more.[514] Hence, it is possible to suggest that, a federal claim under the ATCA must identify the source of a private right to sue to make out a cause of action, which is very difficult in practice because the act lacks clarity and consistency. This is partly because there is no uniform guideline of the text or case law that set out corporate accountability under the ATCA.[515]

An alternative approach located a new cause of action within the statute itself.[516] The Supreme Court in *Sosa* focused closely on the words of the statute as well as the intent behind the law.[517] The Court ultimately held that the ATCA does not create a statutory cause of action and merely grants subject matter jurisdiction.[518] Furthermore, the Court instructed district courts to exercise caution when deciding to hear claims allegedly based on the present day law of nations under the ATCA.[519] The Court required that any claim based on present day law of nations must also rest on a norm of international character accepted by the civilised world and defined with specificity comparable to the features of the eighteenth-century paradigms.[520] Moreover, comparing *Filártiga v Peña-Irala* in light of the *Kiobel* case, the Supreme Court concluded with the contrary.[521]

In *Filártiga v Peña-Irala* the Second District Court held that the ATCA merely provides federal jurisdiction over international law claims.[522] The court articulated that the ATCA does not grant new rights to aliens, but

---

[513]*Sosa v Alvarez-Machain*, 542 US 692, 738 (2004). 'The facts and procedural history are detailed in the first of the two *Alvarez-Machain* Supreme Court decisions, *United States v Alvarez-Machain*, 504 US 655, 657–59 (1992), and summarised in the recent opinion, *Sosa v Alvarez-Machain*, 542 US 692, 697–98 (2004)'.

[514]Beth Stephens, '*Sosa v Alvarez-Machain*-The Door Is Still Ajar for Human Rights Litigation in US Courts' (2004) 70 (5) Brooklyn Law Review, 33

[515]Hannah R Bornstein, 'The Alien Tort Claims Act in 2007: Resolving The Delicate Balance between Judicial and Legislative Authority' (2007) 82 Indiana Law Journal 1077.

[516]*Ibid.*

[517]*Ibid.*

[518]*Sosa v Alvarez-Machain*, 542 US 692, 712 (2004).

[519]*Ibid.*

[520]*Ibid.*

[521]*Ibid.*

[522]*Filártiga v Peña-Irala*, 630 F.2d 876 (2d Cir. 1980).

simply allows adjudication of the rights already recognised by international law.[523] This approach assumes international law can independently support a cause of action in federal court.[524]

Moreover, according to the *Sosa* holding, District Courts must determine issues of international law.[525] This, inevitably, will require District Courts to use their judgment regarding whether it is a good policy to make a cause of action available to victims of corporate human rights violations who bring their claim to the US federal court.[526] Therefore, it is vital when deciding whether a court, in absence of any treaty or any controlling executive or legislative act or judicial decision, should resort to the customs and usages of civilised nations to establish jurisdiction. This has not been the case in *Kiobel*.[527] The evidence from this study suggests that for the ATCA to meet the requirement of present international law and human rights law, the court must survey works of jurists and commentators for the actual application of substantive law.

The court, therefore, must consider whether the claimant identifies 'a specific, universal and obligatory norm of international law', and not a link with the US.[528] The following conclusions can be drawn from here: in order to trigger an effective ATCA jurisdiction, 'civilised nations'[529] must generally accept a clearly and unambiguously defined international norm.[530] Therefore, it is possible that global application of the ATCA requires a caution for several reasons.

First, the eighteenth-century understanding of both federal common law and the role of federal courts must change in order for the ATCA to meet the current dynamics of globalisation. Second, federal courts must avoid recognising new causes of action where Congress has not provided clear guidance on its global application. Thirdly, the Constitution assigns foreign affairs to the Executive and Legislative branches, and these cases often stray into this realm. This is because only the Executive and Legislative branches of government have authority over foreign affairs and

---

[523]*Ibid.*

[524]*Ibid.*

[525]*Sosa v Alvarez-Machain* (n 1210).

[526]*Ibid.*

[527]David P Stewart and Ingrid Wuerth, 'Kiobel v. Royal Dutch Petroleum Co.: The Supreme Court and the Alien Tort Statute' (2013) 107 (3) American Journal of International Law 601, 621.

[528]Emily M Nellermoe (n 938).

[529]Rudolf B Schlesinger, 'Research on The General Principles of Law Recognized by Civilized Nations' (1957) 51 (4) American Journal of International Law 734, 753.

[530]*Ibid.*

international politics. Lastly, 'Congress does not broadly support the idea that private rights of action provide the appropriate enforcement mechanism for international law norms.'[531] Consistent with this analysis, lower courts addressing the choice-of-law question have generally held that ATCA claims involve federal common law. This observation has also contributed to the uncertainty and the lack of clarity surrounding the ATCA.[532]

ATCA jurisdiction in US federal courts remained unchanged until the revolutionary case of *Filártiga v Peña-Irala* (1980).[533] In this case, the family of a Paraguayan man who had been tortured to death brought a civil action against the alleged perpetrators whilst his body was physically present in the US. The US Second Circuit Court of Appeals held that the ATCA provided the court with subject matter jurisdiction over the case. Ever since *Filártiga,* claimants have brought numerous civil lawsuit cases against perpetrators of human rights abuses committed on foreign soil through the ATCA. Likewise, many claims have been brought against high-ranking former and current foreign government officials, including presidents and ministers, as well as against MNCs.[534]

The federal courts have also entered judgments against Bosnian Serb President Radovan Karadzic; [535] Armando Fernandez-Larios, [536] a member of the Chilean army death squad known as the 'Cavaran of Death';[537] and Lui Qi, the former mayor of Beijing.[538] The US Supreme Court offered its first substantive opinion on the ATCA in *Sosa v Alvarez-Machain* in 2004.[539]

---

[531]<https://www.lexisnexis.co.uk/legal/search?query=enforcement%20mechanism%20for%20international%20law%20norms> Accessed 9 October 2017.

[532]*Sosa v Alvarez-Machain* (n 1177).

[533]Gabriel M Wilner, 'Filartiga v. Pena-Irala: Comments on Sources of Human Rights Law and Means of Redress for Violations of Human Rights' (1981) 11 Georgia Journal of International & Comparative Law 317.

[534]Natalie L Bridgeman, 'Human Rights Litigation under The ATCA as a Proxy for Environmental Claims' (2003) 6 Yale Human Rights & Development Law Journal 1.

[535]Sean D Murphy, 'Award of Damages Against Bosnian Serb Leader Radovan Karadzic' (2001) 95 (1) American Journal of International Law 143.

[536]Francisco Rivera, 'Inter-American Justice: Now Available in a US Federal Court Near You' (2005) 45 Santa Clara Law Review 889.

[537]Patricia Verdugo, Marcelo Montecino, and Paul E, Sigmund. *Chile, Pinochet, and The Caravan of Death* (North-South Center Press 2001).

[538] Beth Stephens, Michael Ratner, Judith Chomsky, Jennifer Green and Paul Hoffman, *International Human Rights Litigation in US Courts* (Irvington-on-Hudson New York: Transnational Publishers 1996).

[539]Beth Stephens, 'Sosa v. Alvarez-Machain-The Door Is Still Ajar for Human Rights Litigation in US Courts' (2004) 70 Brooklyn Law Review 533.

One source of weakness with the ATCA is the meaning of the term 'violations of the law of nations', and what constitutes an actionable violation of that law. This was never clarified or explained in any of the cases discussed above. In *Filártiga*, the court held that this phrase refers to 'international law not as it was in 1789, but as it has evolved and exists among the nations of the world today'[540]; thus, the court found that torture qualified because its prohibition was universally recognised, clear, and unambiguous.[541]

Furthermore, later courts adopted this standard and added extrajudicial killing, crimes against humanity, genocide, disappearance, unpaid forced labour, and prolonged arbitrary detention.[542] This is an indication that the ATCA does not confine itself to any universal principle of international law. Following a vigorous examination of congressional intent in 1789, the Supreme Court in *Sosa* categorised what had formerly been agreed in a court argument that the phrase 'violations of the law of nations' was indeed related to international law. It was found that federal common law gives a cause of action for violations of international law and human rights law, and that the ATCA gives the federal courts jurisdiction to hear such cases.[543] In addition, *Sosa* established a new condition for accountability for human rights violations. The violation must be accepted by the civilised world and must be comparable to three eighteenth-century cases of abuse Congress had in mind when it enacted the ATCA: '(1) abuse of safe behaviour; (2) breach of ambassador rights; and (3) piracy'.[544] However, the court did not explain a list of modern norms that met these conditions, leaving this assignment to the lower courts on a case-by-case basis but advising them to exercise control.[545] Nonetheless, the analysis here shows that US foreign affairs hold supremacy over the application of the ATCA.[546] The lower

---

[540]630 F 2d at 878,881, 884.

[541]Ralph G Steinhardt, 'Fulfilling the Promise of Filartiga: Litigating Human Rights Claims Against The Estate of Ferdinand Marcos' (1995) 20 Yale Journal of International Law 65 (1995).

[542]Armin Rosencranz and David Louk, 'Doe v. Unocal: Holding Corporations Liable for Human Rights Abuses on Their Watch' (2005) 8 Chapman Law Review 135; *Doe I v Unocal Corp.*, 395 F.3d 932, (9th Cir.2002); *Kadic v Karadzic*. 70 F.3.d 232 (2d Cir.1992); *Haliao v Marcos,* 25 F.3 1467 (9th Cir. 1994); *Trajano v Marcos,* 978 F.2d. (9th Cir. 1992).

[543]542 U.S at 724-25.

[544]*Ibid* at 725.

[545]*Ibid*; see also *South Africa Apartheid.*, 346 F. Supp. 2d 538, 547 (S.D.Y.2004).

[546]Harlan Grant Cohen, 'Supremacy and Diplomacy: The International Law of The US Supreme Court' (2006) 24 Berkeley Journal of International Law, 273 (2006).

courts were able to interpret the new standards to be consistent with the outcome of the case in *Filártiga* and applied it before *Sosa.*[547]

Likewise, the lower courts have reconfirmed a number of human rights abuses that are actionable under the ATCA, such as 'torture; cruel, inhuman, or degrading treatment; extrajudicial killing; a crime against humanity; genocide; and prolonged arbitrary detention.'[548] Therefore, a future lawsuit under the ATCA is likely to develop this list created by the lower courts, even though *Sosa* clearly indicates that the list should remain short.[549] The results of this study indicate that the ATCA allows victims of egregious human rights abuses committed abroad to sue those responsible in US federal courts.[550] Thus, the ATCA allows victims of human rights violations to bring forward lawsuits, which may be brought for serious violations of international law such as terrorism, state-sponsored torture and extrajudicial killings, war crimes, crimes against humanity, and genocide.[551] Taken together, this suggests that when the ATCA was drafted in the eighteenth century, international law dealt primarily with regulating diplomatic relations between states and outlawing crimes such as piracy. However, international law in the twenty-first century has expanded to include the protection of human rights.[552] In the 70-plus years since the signing of the Universal Declaration of Human Rights in 1948, universal human rights have moved from being an aspirational concept to a legal reality.[553]

This extraordinary evolution gave the ATCA renewed significance in the late twentieth century, allowing victims of human rights abuse to bring cases in US courts. Today, the ATCA gives survivors of egregious

---

[547]*Sare v Rio,* PLC, 487 F. 3d 1193, 1201-02 (9th Cir. 2007).

[548]*Calbello v Armando Fernandez-Larios*, 402 F. 3d 1148 (11th Cir.2005); *Almog v Arab Ban*, PLC 471 F. Supp. 2d 257 (E.D.N.Y. 2007); *Doe v Liu Qi*, 349 F. Supp. 2d 1258 (N.D. Cal 2004); *Doe v Rafael Saravia*, 348 F. Supp. 2d 1112 (E.D.N.Y. Cal. 2004); also see, *Aldana v Del Mont Fresh Produce*, N.A., Inc., 416 F. 3d 1242 (11th Cir. 2005) (Cruel, inhuman, or degrading treatment claims not actionable).

[549]*Sosa v Alvarez-Machain*, 542 US 692 (2004).

[550]William S Dodge, *The Historical Origins of the Alien Tort Statute: A Response to the 'Originalists'* (1996).

[551] Kenneth C Randall, 'Federal Jurisdiction over International Law Claims: Inquiries into the Alien Tort Statute' (1985) 18 New York University Journal of International Law and Politics 1.

[552]Thomas H Lee, 'The Safe-Conduct Theory of the Alien Tort Statute' (2006) Columbia Law Review 830.

[553]UN General Assembly, *Universal Declaration of Human Rights*, 10 December 1948, 217 A (III). <http://www.refworld.org/docid/3ae6b3712c.html> Accessed 6 August 2017.

human rights abuses, wherever committed, the right to sue the perpetrators in the United States, while other jurisdictions do not allow the victims to exercise their legal rights when their human rights are violated.[554] The ATCA can be seen as promoting the US goals of protecting human rights and denying safe haven to human rights abusers. Thus, it could be said that the modern goal of the ATCA is to protect human rights and this should not be negated by US foreign affairs interests.[555]

Even so, the ATCA does not provide universal jurisdiction over human rights abuses and the ATCA lawsuits typically apply ordinarily rules of civil liability. Therefore, ATCA lawsuits generally cannot be brought against foreign states.[556] However, without the ATCA, similar lawsuits would simply be brought in state courts and would result in confusing and conflicting rules that may not provide effective remedies for victims of human rights violations.[557] Likewise, ATCA cases that are legally unsound or factually unsupported could be dismissed by the courts.[558]

The ATCA allows MNCs from most industries to be sued, including Coca-Cola (accused of aiding murders by Colombian paramilitary groups);[559] ExxonMobil (accused of aiding human rights abuses by the Indonesian military);[560] General Motors (accused of aiding South Africa's apartheid government);[561] and Yahoo (accused of sharing subscriber data

---

[554]Curtis A Bradley, 'The Alien Tort Statute and Article III' (2001) 42 Virginia Journal of International Law 587.

[555]Marc Rosen, 'The Alien Tort Claims Act and The Foreign Sovereign Immunities Act: A Policy Solution' (1998) 6 Cardozo Journal of International and Comparative Law 461.

[556]Julian Ku and John Yoo, 'Beyond Formalism in Foreign Affairs: A Functional Approach to the Alien Tort Statute' (2004) Supreme Court Review, 153.

[557]Dinah Shelton, *Remedies in International Human Rights Law* (Oxford University Press USA 2015).

[558]Joanna E Arlow, 'The Utility of ATCA and The Law of Nations in Environmental Torts Litigation: Jota v. Texaco, Inc. and Large-Scale Environmental Destruction' (2000) 7 Wisconsin Environmental Law Journal 93.

[559] Terry Collingsworth, 'Separating Fact from Fiction in The Debate over Application of The Alien Tort Claims Act to Violations of Fundamental Human Rights by Corporations' (2002) 37 (3) US Florida Review 563.

[560]Brian C Free, 'Awaiting Doe v. Exxon Mobil Corp.: Advocating the Cautious Use of Executive Opinions in Alien Tort Claims Act Litigation' (2003) 12 (2) Pacific Rim Law & Policy Journal 467.

[561] Ariadne K Sacharoff, 'Multinationals in Host Countries: Can They Be Held Liable under The Alien Tort Claims Act for Human Rights Violations?' 23 (3) Brooklyn Journal of International Law 927 (1997).

with the Chinese government).[562] Almost all of these suits are based on 'aiding and abetting' abuses by foreign governments, rather than direct offences.

Comparing the effectiveness of the ATCA in corporate human rights violations to countries such as France,[563] Germany,[564] and the Netherlands,[565] it is argued here that the ATCA provides a better forum for corporate human rights abuses victims than the judicial systems in these states.

It can be inferred that international law does not allow courts of one country to exercise jurisdiction in civil cases over offences in other countries.[566] For this reason, foreign governments, including many close US allies, have filed more than 20 complaints with the State Department and Federal Courts in ATCA suits over the past decade.[567] The British, Dutch, and German governments are all strong advocates for human rights, and filed briefs in the *Kiobel* case, arguing that applying the ATCA to acts that take place in other countries and have no other connection to the United States is a violation of international law.[568] This has cast a cloud over the current dimension of the ATCA and its application in the international arena.

The current development in the courts suggests that the courts reject many proclaimed international law abuses, including temporary detention, parental abduction, sexual relations with a minor, wartime use of defoliants, and different types of environmental problems.[569] Could this be that the court thinks that national courts should have an applicable

[562]Chimène I Keitner, *Conceptualizing Complicity in Alien Tort Cases* (2008).

[563]William Laurence Craig, 'Application of The Trading with The Enemy Act to Foreign Corporations Owned by Americans: Reflections on Fruehauf v. Massardy' (1970) Harvard Law Review 579.

[564]Eric Engle, 'Extraterritorial Corporate Criminal Liability: A Remedy for Human Rights Violations' (2006) 20 (2) John's Journal of Legal Commentary 287.

[565]Arthur H Dean, 'The Role of International Law in a Metropolitan Practice' (1955) 103(7) University of Pennsylvania Law Review 886.

[566]David Wallach, 'The Irrationality of Universal Civil Jurisdiction' (2014) 46 Georgetown Journal of International Law 803.

[567]Daniel Prince, 'Corporate Liability for International Torts: Did the Second Circuit Misinterpret the Alien Tort Statute?' (2011) 8 Seton Hall Circuit Review 43.

[568]John B Bellinger III, 'Why the Supreme Court Should Curb the Alien Tort Statute' *The Washington Post* (Washington, 22 February 2012)

[569]*Sosa,* 542 US at 734-38, *Vietnam Asus'n for Victims of Agent Organ v Dow Chemical Co.,* 517 F. 3d 104 (2d Cir. 2008); *Taveras v Taveraz,* 477 F. 3d 767 (6th Cir. 2007); *Cisneros v Aragon,* 485 F.3d 1226 (10th Cir. 2007); *Flores v S. Peru Copper Corp.,* 343 F.3d 140 (2d Cir. 2003).

mechanism for these violations? What about a scenario where the national court is paralysed and has no power to enforce any human obligations in its jurisdiction?

One can argue that the court's view is too narrow and fails to adequately engage the issues facing most victims of human rights violations. Perhaps the appropriate question for the court should be, is there a particular relationship between the victims and the perpetrators to establish a duty of care? Is there any distinction between the acts of the perpetrators which give rise to the violations other than foreign affairs issues? Corporations should be liable for the violations of the former abuses but not those of the latter, which are related to foreign affairs. Likewise, the violations must be preferable to the relationship between the defendant, the tort, and the victims.

The Application of International Law and Human Rights Law in TVPA and ATCA Cases

In 1992, the US enacted the Torture Victim Protection Act (TVPA),[570] which provides authority for a civil action against an individual who, under the rule of law of any foreign state, tortured or summarily executed another person unlawfully.[571] The TVPA is a narrowly tailored law that authorises civil suits against foreign government officials for acts of torture or murder committed in their countries,[572] but the suits are subject to numerous procedural limitations.[573] The US Supreme Court limited the scope of the TVPA with regards to corporate liability and has effectively terminated claims made against corporations under the Act for allegations of aiding and abetting torture and extrajudicial killing committed abroad.[574]

This narrow statute is unprecedented in international law and risks reciprocal lawsuits against US officials and was specifically intended by Congress to apply to acts in other countries.[575] The advocates of the TVPA's

[570]The Torture Victims Protection Act (TVPA) 1991.

[571]*Cisneros v Araon*, 485, F. 3d 1226 (10th Cir. 2007); *Flore v S. Peru Copper Corp.*, 343 F. 3d 140 (2d Cir. 2003).

[572]Jennifer Correale, 'The Torture Victim Protection Act: A Vital Contribution to International Human Rights Enforcement or Just a Nice Gesture?' (1994) 6 Pace International Law Review School of Law 197.

[573]Robert F Drinan and Teresa T Kuo, 'Putting The World's Oppressors on Trial: The Torture Victim Protection Act' (1993) 15 (3) Human Rights Quarterly 605.

[574]*Mohamad v Palestinian Authority* 566 US (2012).

[575]Christopher W Haffke, 'The Torture Victim Protection Act: More Symbol Than Substance' (1994) 43 Emory Law Journal 1467.

application to organisations and corporations primarily argued that the TVPA was enacted to extend the Washington DC Circuit Court's *Tel-Oren v Libya Arab Republic* 'decision to US citizens. Here, plaintiffs who were foreign citizens and 'survivors or representatives of persons murdered in a foreign country filed suit against defendants seeking compensatory and punitive damages.'[576] The plaintiffs alleged that the 'defendants were responsible for multiple tortious acts resulting from violations of the law of nations, United States' treaties, United States' criminal law and the common law. The trial court dismissed the plaintiffs''[577] 'actions for lack of subject matter jurisdiction and for being time barred under the applicable statute of limitations.'[578]

Without a clear congressional mandate, 'the Supreme Court should not interpret the ATCA, which was enacted for a different purpose, to allow US courts to sit in judgment over acts that take place in foreign countries.'[579] Thus, the TVPA lays down four conditions: '(1) the defendant must have committed torture or extrajudicial killings; (2) the defendant must act under actual or apparent authority, or under the law of the foreign state; (3) the claimant is a victim, his or her legal representative, or a person who may be a claimant in a wrongful death action; and (4) the claimant must exhaust all

---

[576]Jennifer Hagerman, 'Navigating the Waters of International Employment Law: Dispute avoidance Tactics for United States-based Multinational Corporations' (2006) 41 Val. UL Rev 859.

[577]Jennifer Hagerman, 'Navigating the Waters of International Employment Law: Dispute avoidance Tactics for United States-based Multinational Corporations' (2006) 41 Val. UL Rev 859.

[578]*Tel-Oren v Libyan Arab Republic*, 726 F. 2d 774 – 1984, Jennifer Hagerman, 'Navigating the Waters of International Employment Law: Dispute avoidance Tactics for United States-based Multinational Corporations' (2006) 41 Val. UL Rev 859 and <http://www1.downloadmienphi.net/?tm=1&subid4=1614612095.0015547531&kw=Single+Click+Software+Download&KW1=Download%20from%20Cloud%20File%20Services&KW2=Download%20from%20High%20Security%20Cloud%20File%20Storage&KW3=Upload%20to%20Cloud%20File%20Sharing%20Services&searchbox=0&domainname=0&backfill=0> Accessed 9 October 2017.

[579]<https://www.washingtonpost.com/gdpr-consent/?next_url=https%3a%2f%2fwww.washingtonpost.com%2fopinions%2fwhy-the-supreme-court-should-curb-the-alien-tort-statute%2f2012%2f02%2f21%2fgIQA1leZWR_story.html> Accessed 19 November 2018.

available legal procedures and remedies at the national court where the violation giving rise to the lawsuit took place.'[580]

Congress did not intend the TVPA to be jurisdictional in nature, but rather to create a substantive cause of action. Similarly, the TVPA defines its cause of action with further details. Section 3 contains an in-depth definition of extrajudicial killing and torture.[581] The TVPA also contains an exhaustive list of remedies provision, requiring that the claimant exhausts all 'adequate and available remedies in the place in which the conduct giving rise to the claim occurred.'[582] A House of Representatives Report explains the need for this requirement, which 'ensures that U.S. courts will not intrude into cases more appropriately handled by courts where the alleged torture or killing occurred'.[583] This also 'avoids[s] exposing US courts to unnecessary burdens, and can be expected to encourage the development of meaningful remedies in other countries.'[584] Furthermore, the TVPA subjects claims to a ten year statute of limitations so that the courts 'will not have to hear stale claims.'[585] In this regard, in terms of form, the TVPA and the ATCA differ greatly.[586] Although the ATCA is short and unclear in nature, the TVPA provides more guidance on human rights accountability. While the ATCA does not provide definitions for what constitutes a 'law of nations' or a 'tort committed in violation' of that law, the TVPA contains a detailed definition of extrajudicial killing and torture as discussed above. In contrast, while the TVPA has a statute of limitation, the ATCA does not contain an express exhaustion of remedies requirement or a statute of limitations provision.[587]

---

[580]Jessica Grunberg, 'The Torture Victim Protection Act: A Means to Corporate Liability for Aiding and Abetting Torture' (2012) 61 Catholic University Law Review 235.

[581]Torture Victim Protection Act of 1991, Pub. L. No. 102-256, 106 Stat. 73 (1992) (codified at 28 USC. § 1350 (1994) (hereinafter referred to as TVPA).

[582]*Ibid.*

[583]John W Brooker, 'Ford v. Garcia: A Puzzling Fusion of the Command Responsibility Doctrine with the Torture Victim Protection Act' (2002) 28 North Carolina Journal of International Law and Commercial Regulation 701, and House Representative 2092, 102nd Congress (1991-1992).

[584]*Ibid.*

[585]TVPA § 2(c).

[586]Philip Mariani, 'Assessing the Proper Relationship between the Alien Tort Statute and the Torture Victim Protection Act' (2008) 156 (5) University of Pennsylvania Law Review 1383.

[587]Eric Engle, 'The Alien Tort Statute and the Torture Victims' Protection Act: Jurisdictional Foundations and Procedural Obstacles' (2006) 14 (1) Willamette Journal of International Law and Dispute Resolution 1.

Unlike the ATCA legislative history, which is largely unknown,[588] the TVPA has an extensive record of codification. Specifically, 'the House and Senate Reports list three main purposes for the TVPA'. [589] Unfortunately, the House and Senate Reports do not expressly clarify the relationship between the TVPA and the ATCA. Incidentally, 'however, the legislative history provides some guidance as to the interaction between the'[590] ATCA 'and the TVPA. Thus, the fact that the TVPA was codified'[591] as a note to the ATCA implies that they are intended to interact closely. The legislative history states that the ATCA 'has other important uses and should not be replaced'.[592] Both the Senate Report and the House Report state that the ATCA 'claims based on torture or summary executions do not exhaust the list of actions that may appropriately be covered by section 1350'. Accordingly, the statute should remain intact.[593]

These results provide further evidence that courts in different circuits diverge in their reading of the legislative history. Some courts have cited it in support of the suggestion that the TVPA and the ATCA provide two separate claims for torture and extrajudicial killing while other courts have interpreted it as weakening this proposition.[594] The minority view holds that claims for torture and extrajudicial killing must be brought exclusively under the TVPA. The United States Seventh Circuit Court endorsed this view in *Enahoro v Abubakar*. The Seventh Circuit held that all torture and extrajudicial killing claims should be brought under the TVPA[595] and plaintiffs must comply with all requirements of this statute. Thus, it found that the two statutes do not provide 'two bases for relief against torture and extrajudicial killing.'[596] 'In *Enahoro*, plaintiffs brought a suit against a general of the military junta in Nigeria for atrocities committed from 1993 to 1999.'[597] 'The plaintiffs only brought claims under

---

[588]*Sosa v Alvarez-Machain*, 542 US 692, 718-19 (2004).

[589] <https://scholarship.law.berkeley.educgi/viewcontent.cgi?article=1396&context=bjil > Accessed 29 June 2019 and House of Representatives Report No. 102-367, at 4. II and Senate Report No. 102-249, at 3(1991).

[590] <https://scholarship.law.berkeley.educgi/viewcontent.cgi?article=1396&context=bjil > Accessed 29 June 2019.

[591]*Ibid.*

[592]*Ibid.*

[593]Senate Report. No. 102-249, at 5.

[594]*Enahoro v Abubakar,* 408 F.3d 877, 884 (7th Cir. 2005).

[595]*Ibid.*

[596]*Ibid.*

[597] <https://www.lexisnexis.co.uk/legal/search?query=enforcement%20mechanism%20for%20international%20law%20norms> Accessed 9 October 2017 and Philip C Aka, 'Nigeria Since May 1999: Understanding the Paradox of Civil Rule and

the ATCA and did not make a simultaneous claim under the TVPA.'[598] 'The district court, following precedents from other circuits, held that the plaintiffs did not need to plead their case under the TVPA, suggesting that the two statutes offer two separate bases for remedy.'[599] Nonetheless, 'the Seventh Circuit disagreed with this proposition and overturned the decision of the district court. The US Seventh Circuit declared that unless the TVPA'[600] 'occup[ied] the field' for torture claims, it would be 'meaningless'.[601] The court further stated that '[n]o one would plead a cause of action under the Act and subject himself to its requirements if he could simply plead under international law.'[602] The court discussed the limitations the TVPA imposes in requiring exhausting the remedies in the jurisdiction where the conduct occurred and bringing the claim within ten years. The court also found support for its interpretation of the relationship between the ATCA and the TVPA in the legislative history of the TVPA and in *Sosa v Alvarez-Machain*.

The US Seventh Circuit interpreted the House and Senate Reports stating that the ATCA should 'remain intact' to mean that 'the enactment of the Torture Victim Protection Act did not signal that torture and killing are the only claims which can be brought under the Alien Tort Statute'.[603] Other claims can still be brought under the ATCA. The majority also interpreted *Sosa* as confirming the preclusive effect of the TVPA.[604] The court argued that since the US Supreme Court directed courts to exercise 'great caution' and 'vigilant door keeping' in finding what claims are allowed under the ATCA, and since the court also stated that 'a clear mandate' for suits for torture and extrajudicial killing exists under the TVPA,[605] in *Sosa* the court did not approve of utilising the ATCA for torture claims.[606]

Human Rights Violations under President Olusegun Obasanjo' (2003) 4 San Diego International Law Journal 209.

598 *Ibid.*

599 *Ibid.*

600 <https://www.lexisnexis.co.uk/legal/search?query=enforcement%20mechanism%20for%20international%20law%20norms> Accessed 9 October 2017.

601 *Ibid* at 884.

602 *Ibid.*

603 *Ibid* at 885.

604 Michael Garvey, 'Corporate Aiding and Abetting Liability under The Alien Tort Statute: A Legislative Prerogative' (2009) 29 BC Third World Law Journal 381.

605 (n 1252) at 885.

606 Eugene Kontorovich, 'Implementing Sosa v. Alvarez-Machain: What Piracy Reveals About the Limits of the Alien Tort Statute' (2004) 80 (1) Notre Dame Law Review 111.

The US Seventh Circuit then remanded the case to the district court because plaintiffs had to plead under the TVPA.[607] There are two main advantages to the US Seventh Circuit interpretation of the relationship between the ATCA and the TVPA. First, this interpretation clarifies the relationship between the two statutes in a very straightforward way.[608] By submitting that the TVPA 'occup[ies] the field' of claims for torture and extrajudicial killing, it becomes clear that all restrictions contained in the TVPA, such as the exhaustion of remedies and the statute of limitations, always apply. This simplifies the position taken in other circuits, which allows for claims to be brought under both of the statutes but which reads certain conditions from the TVPA into the ATCA in an ambiguous way.[609] Second, requiring all claims for torture and extrajudicial killing to be submitted under the TVPA ensures consistent treatment of aliens and US citizens.[610] 'The TVPA applies equally to aliens and US citizens while the ATCA applies only to aliens. Non-US citizens can circumvent the requirements under the TVPA by bringing claims under the ATCA. The US Second Circuit interpretation remedies this problem.'[611] 'In the dissenting opinion, Judge Cudahy disagreed with the majority holding'[612] in *Enahoro v Abubakar*. He argued that the legislative history of the TVPA shows Congress meant to expand the TVPA's reach to US citizens and not restrict the application of the ATCA to foreign citizens, on the grounds that the ATCA applies only to aliens.[613]

Consequently, the TVPA is not 'meaningless', as the majority asserted. Besides, the plain text of the TVPA did not contain any implicit amendment to the ATCA, and since repeals by implications are disfavoured, the relationship between the TVPA and the ATCA should not be interpreted as preclusive.[614] In addressing the Seventh Circuit argument that *Sosa* supports the majority holding, Judge Cudahy noted the majority 'stands

[607]*Ibid.*

[608]Matt A Vega, 'Balancing Judicial Cognizance and Caution: Whether Transnational Corporations are Liable for Foreign Bribery under The Alien Tort Statute' (2009) 31 Michigan Journal of International Law 385.

[609]Curtis A Bradley, *International Law in the US Legal System* (Oxford University Press USA 2015).

[610]*Ibid.*

[611]*Enahoro v Abubakar,* 408 F.3d 877, 886-88 (2005) (Cudahy, J., dissenting in part) and <https://scholarship.law.berkeley.educgi/viewcontent.cgi?article=1396&context =bjil > Accessed 29 June 2019.

[612]*Ibid.*

[613]*Ibid.*

[614]*Ibid* at 887.

Sosa on its head' by using it as a support.[615] Nothing in *Sosa* suggests the preclusive effect of the TVPA. Thus, Judge Cudahy argued that the two statutes 'are meant to be complementary and mutually reinforcing.'[616] The majority of circuit courts in the US have also rejected the view followed by the Seventh Circuit in *Enahoro*. They have ruled that the TVPA and the ATCA can be used simultaneously for claims of torture and extrajudicial killing.[617] More expressly with reference to the torture claims, the Eleventh Circuit has ruled that 'a plaintiff may bring distinct claims for torture under each statute'.[618] The Eleventh Circuit supported this interpretation of the relationship between the two statutes through an analysis of the plain meaning of the statutes, canons of statutory interpretation discouraging repeals by implication, *Sosa*, and the legislative history of the TVPA.[619]

The TVPA and the ATCA could be seen to share much in common. They serve similar purposes and the TVPA was enacted as a note to the ATCA.[620] In a critical examination, it could be argued that the TVPA was intended to codify the judgment from the *Filártiga* court's interpretation of the ATCA in a clear judicial basis, which gives the foundation for a civil claim against a wrongdoer. The TVPA, unlike the ATCA, covers only torture and summary execution, but it gives aliens and the US citizens the foundation to bring a civil action against individuals that violate it.[621]

The US courts have acknowledged that a defendant need not physically commit a given violation to be held liable under ATCA or TVPA.[622] Thus, both statutes can be applied to military and civilian leaders

---

[615]*Ibid* at 889.
[616]*Ibid* at 888.
[617]*Cabello v Femandez-Larios*, 402 F.3d 1148, 1154 (11th Cir. 2005).
[618]*Aldana v Del Monte Fresh Produce*, N.A., Inc, 416 F.3d 1242, 1249-50 (11th Cir. 2005).
[619] *Ibid.* see also: *Sosa v Alvarez-Machain*, 542 US 692, 734 (2004) (citing Paquete Habana, 20 S.Ct. 290, 299 (1900).
[620]Ekaterina Apostolova, 'The Relationship between the Alien Tort Statute and the Torture Victim Protection Act' (2010) 28 Berkeley Journal of International Law 640.
[621]28 USC. § 1350 (2006).
[622]Penny M Venetis, 'The Broad Jurisprudential Significance of Sosa v Alvarez-Machain: An Honest Assessment of The Role of Federal Judges and Why Customary International Law Can Be More Effective Than Constitutional Law for Redressing Serious Abuses' (2011*)* 21 Temple Political and Civil Rights Law Review 41; *Doe v Exxon Mobil Corp.*, 654 F.3d 11, 39-57 (D.C. Cir. 2011); *Romero v Drummond Co.*, 552 F.3d 1303, 1315 (11th Cir. 2008); *Flomo v Firestone Natural Rubber Co.,* 643 F.3d 1013, 1017-21 (7th Cir. 2011); *Sarei v Rio Tinto*, PLC, 2011 WL 5041927 (9th Cir. Oct. 25, 2011).

who fail to prevent, or punish, violations by subordinates under the doctrine of superior or command responsibility.[623] The courts have also looked at both international and national military law in deciding the definition of superior responsibility, which is close to that applied in the international criminal tribunals.[624]

The Nuremberg Court also confirmed that a defendant may aid and abet human rights abuses committed by others by giving assistance or moral support.[625] This has proven to be an important notion of accountability in cases against MNC defendants that might be connected with human rights violations by local governments or paramilitaries. The definition of aiding and abetting[626] human rights abuses is drawn from international law, in particular, International Criminal Tribunal for the former Yugoslavia (ICTY) jurisprudence and federal common law.[627] Likewise, the ICTY has also upheld claims that the defendant engaged in a conspiracy with others to commit actionable abuses.[628] In condoning the court's approach to ATCA and TVPA jurisdiction, the court is also confirming that the US is not obliged to entertain claims that would otherwise arise under universal civil jurisdiction or by virtue of forum of necessity laws. However, providing some 'silver lining', the court in the ATCA and TVPA cases itself appeared to address the potential ill-effects of its decision, which suggests that perhaps the United States should consider obliging courts to provide access to compensation in cases of this kind by endowing them with jurisdiction.

---

[623]Koji Kudo, *Command Responsibility, and the Defence of Superior Orders* (Diss. University of Leicester 2007).

[624]*Ford v Garcia*, 289 F.3d 1283, 1283, 1287-94 (11th Cir. 2002); *Doe* v *Liu Qi*, 349 F. Supp. 2d at 1328-34 (2004) (acknowledging that doctrine applies to military and civilian superior).

[625]Koji Kudo, *Command Responsibility and the Defence of Superior Orders* (DPhil thesis, University of Leicester 2007).

[626]George R Wright, 'Negotiating the Terms of Corporate Human Rights Liability Under Federal Law' (2016).

[627]*Khulumani v Barclay Nat. Bank Ltd* 504 F.3d 260, 270-82 ((2d Cir. 2007) (allegations that defendants aided South Africa's Apartheid-era government); *SAREI* v *Rio Tino* (9th Cir.2006) 487 F.3d at 1202-03 (9th Cir. Cal., 2007) (allegations that the defendant aided Papua New Guinea military); *Talisman Energy,* 453F. Supp. 2d at 665-68 (S.D.N.Y. 2006) (allegations that defendant aided Sudan).

[628]*Talisman Energy v Presbyterian Church of Sudan*, 453 F. Supp. 2d at 663-64 (S.D.N.Y. 2006) (citing *Hamdan v Rumsfeld*, 548 US 557, 609-10 (SC. 2006) *Cabello v Fernandez-Larios,* 402 F. 3d at 1159-60 (11th Cir. 2005).

Overview of ATCA in Human Rights cases

The US ATCA 1789 is a classic example of a domestic law with extraterritorial jurisdiction that is capable of holding MNCs liable for human rights violations in a foreign country.[629] Examples include the executives at the banana company Chiquita Brands International Inc. who pleaded guilty in 2007 to making payments to Colombian paramilitary groups and were ordered to face US lawsuits claiming they had played a role in the torture or killing of thousands of Colombians. Relatives of the victims could pursue their claims under the TVPA, a federal judge in West Palm Beach, Florida, ruled. The families claimed Chiquita paid $1.7 million to the United Self-Defense Forces of Colombia, or AUC, to quell labour unrest and prevent leftist sympathisers from infiltrating banana-plantation unions.[630] 'Another example saw residents of the island of Bougainville in Papua New Guinea (PNG) file suit against Rio Tinto under the ATCA in the' 'US federal court in 2000. The plaintiffs alleged that: Rio Tinto was complicit in war crimes and crimes against humanity committed by the PNG army during a secessionist conflict on Bougainville; environmental impacts from Rio Tinto's Panguna mine on Bougainville harmed their health in violation of international law; and that Rio Tinto'[631] 'engaged in racial discrimination against its black workers at Panguna.'[632] In *Doe v Unocal*, the complaint alleged that Myanmar's military subjected villagers to forced labour, rape, torture and murder with the knowledge and support of Unocal, the US oil and gas corporation, which created liability under the ACTA; 'whether to be liable under ATCA a non-state actor must engage in state action; whether Unocal was liable for aiding and abetting the Myanmar military in subjecting villagers to forced labour, rape, murder and torture;

---

[629]Alien Tort Claim Act 28 USC § 1350. <https://www.law.cornell.edu/uscode/pdf/uscode28/lii_usc_TI_28_PA_IV_CH_85_SE_1350.pdf> Accessed on 29 June 2015.

[630] Douglas M Branson, 'Holding Multinational Corporations Accountable? Achilles' Heels in Alien Tort Claims Act Litigation' (2011) 9 Santa Clara Journal of International Law 227.

[631] <https://www.businesshumanrights.org/en/Categories/Lawlawsuits/Lawsuits regulatoryaction/LawsuitsSelectedcases/RioTintolawsuitrePapuaNewGuinea/?sort_on=effective> Accessed 02 March 2016.

[632]Stuart Kirsch, 'Mining and Environmental Human Rights in Papua New Guinea' (Palgrave Macmillan UK 2003) and <https://www.business-humanrights.org/en/Categories/Lawlawsuits/Lawsuitsregulatoryaction/LawsuitsSelectedcases/RioTinto lawsuitrePapuaNewGuinea/?sort_on=effective> Accessed 02 March 2016.

Scope of the legal liability of transnational corporations for violations of human rights under ATCA.'[633]

Relating to those 'kidnapped or killed by terrorists in attacks against Israeli citizens overseas',[634] *Jesner v Arab Bank, PLC* saw the 'surviving aliens and the families of those who perished in the attacks accuse Arab Bank, PLC, a bank corporation headquartered in Jordan',[635] 'of financing and facilitating the various terrorist organisations involved in the attacks. The survivors sued Arab'[636] Bank in the New York federal court under the Alien Tort Statute (ATS), which provides for the federal district court jurisdiction over civil actions brought by aliens. 'Arab Bank moved to dismiss the ATS claims under the US Court of Appeals for the Second Circuit's decision in *Kiobel v Royal Dutch Petroleum Co.*'[637] In that case, the appellate court held that the ATS did not authorise claims against foreign corporations.[638] The ATCA permits US District Courts to hear civil proceedings of foreign citizens for damages caused by the business operations of MNCs 'in violations of the law of nations or a treaty of the [United States].'[639] Nonetheless, it is questionable whether victims of corporate human rights violations and environmental damages will be unable to bring a claim for harm under domestic law that they would otherwise be able to under the ATCA. This is because claims under the ATCA must amount to breaches of customary international law that are 'specific, universal and obligatory.'[640]

---

[633] *Doe v Unocal*, 395 F.3d 932, <https://www.business-humanrights.org/en/Categories/Lawlawsuits/Lawsuitsregulatoryaction/LawsuitsSelectedcases/RioTintolawsuitrePapuaNewGuinea/?sort_on=effective> Accessed 02 March 2016 and <https://www.escr-net.org/caselaw/caselaw_results.htm?focus=13675,13939,13961&order=dateDESC> Accessed 18 June 2017.

[634] <https://law.utexas.edu/humanrights/projects/bibliography-on-natural-resource-governance-inequality-and-human-rights/> Accessed 17 October 2018.

[635] *Ibid.*

[636] *Ibid.*

[637] The Bernard and Audre Rapoport Center for Human Rights and Justice, 'Bibliography on Natural Resource Governance, Inequality, and Human Rights' (2017). <https://law.utexas.edu/wp-content/uploads/sites/31/2017/06/Bibliography-NRG-Inequality-and-HR-Final-170825-1.pdf.> Accessed 18 April 2021.

[638] *Jesner v Arab Bank, PLC* 584 U.S. (2018) 138 S. Ct. 1386; 200 L. Ed. 2d 612. Several alien individuals were injured.

[639] Beth Stephens et al (eds), *International Human Rights Litigation in US Courts* (2nd ed., Martinus Nijhoff 2008).

[640] *Sosa*, 542 US at 734-38. <https://www.escr-net.org/caselaw/2009/john-doe-i-et-al-v-unocal-corp-et-al-395-f3d-932-9-cir-2002 > Accessed 29 June 2016.

Hence, it is likely that, with respect to member states of the UN, 'courts are likely to be critical of any nation that does not recognise equivalent liability in tort for such serious conduct.'[641] Therefore, 'state courts have the option of finding that this lack of recognition constitutes a violation of their mandatory public policy rules, and accordingly substitute their laws *(lex fori)*' [642] for the *lex loci damni*. '(*Lex loci damni* refers to the law of the place where the injury occurs.) 'In other words, if an injury appears in another country, the laws of that country govern.'[643] However, this rule is only applied if the tortfeasor had foreseen that the damage would have occurred there. This is a general rule applied under conflict of laws. *Nippon Fire & Marine Ins. Co. v M.V. Tourcoing,* 167 F.3d 99 (2d Cir. N.Y. 1999)' [644] is 'manifestly incompatible with the public policy of the forum'.[645]

Similarly, it is questionable whether it is fair to criticise the application of *lex loci damni* over international law considering the US Supreme Court's enthusiastic use of the presumption against extraterritoriality in *Kiobel.*[646] Since the US Supreme Court has acknowledged that the presumption against extraterritoriality applies to substantive statutes, it follows that the ATCA is recognised as the US substantive law when it applies international law.[647]

---

641 Simon Baughen, 'Holding Corporations to Account: Crafting ATS Suits in the UK' (2013) 2 British Journal of American Legal Studies 533 and Fiona Robertson, 'Access to Justice for Victims of Human Rights Abuse By Multinational Corporations: Does European Civil and Commercial litigation Provide and Answer? (2015) 9 (1) New Zealand Journal of Research on Europe. <Microsoft Word - ONLINE Access to justice for victims of human rights abuse by multinational corporations FINAL (auckland.ac.nz)> Accessed 13 May 2019.

642 Albert A Ehrenzweig, 'The Lex Fori - Basic Rule in the Conflict of Laws' (1960) 58 (5) Michigan Law Review 637 and also see, Fiona Robertson, 'Access to Justice for Victims of Human Rights Abuse By Multinational Corporations: Does European Civil and Commercial litigation Provide and Answer? (2015) 9 (1) New Zealand Journal of Research on Europe. < Microsoft Word - ONLINE Access to justice for victims of human rights abuse by multinational corporations FINAL (auckland. ac.nz)> Accessed 13 May 2019.

643 <https://definitions.uslegal.com/l/lex-loci-damni/ >accessed 20 June 2018.

644 <https://definitions.uslegal.com/l/lex-loci-damni/> Accessed 8 April 2020.

645 Ted M. De Boer, 'Party Autonomy and Its Limitations in The Rome II Regulation' (2007) 9 Yearbook of Private International Law 19, and *Nippon Fire & Marine Ins. Co. v M.V. Tourcoing*, 167 F.3d 99 (2d Cir. N.Y. 1999).

646 *Kiobel v Royal Dutch Petroleum* Co., 569 U.S. *108 (2013).*

647 Odette Murray, David Kinley, and Chip Pitts, 'Exaggerated Rumours of The Death of an Alien Tort: Corporations, Human Rights and The Peculiar Case of Kiobel' (2011).

Perhaps if the '*lex loci damni* applied instead, the US federal courts would be less concerned about imposing US law on other states. Courts, therefore, could not apply the presumption against extraterritoriality to the ATCA. According to the international legal scholar Dodge, choosing international law over *lex loci damni* as the substantive law under the ATCA provides'[648] the 'doctrinal hook'[649] for the US Supreme Court to enforce the presumption against extraterritoriality.[650] However, the presumption against extraterritoriality may not be very encouraging, as the disadvantage of *lex loci damni* is that domestic law, while applicable under the ATCA, may not be under international law. A 'claimant may be disadvantaged if they cannot frame a tortious claim under *lex loci damni* because domestic law does not recognise the relevant tort.'[651]

By contrast, there are a number of disadvantages that claimants in European member states and other states 'face compared to claims in the United States.'[652] 'First, for injuries occurring after January 2009, damages are assessed in accordance with the law of the state where damage arose.'[653] 'One can, therefore, envisage a situation where the damage occurred in a

---

[648]<https://definitions.uslegal.com/l/lex-loci-damni/> Accessed 13 April 2016.

[649]Tara M Stuckey, 'Jurisdictional Hooks in The Wake of Raich: On Properly Interpreting Federal Regulations of Interstate Commerce' (2006) 81 Notre Dame Law Review 2101.

[650]William S Dodge, *Alien Tort Litigation: The Road Not Taken* (2014).

[651]Fiona Robertson, 'Access to Justice for Victims of Human Rights Abuse By Multinational Corporations: Does European Civil and Commercial litigation Provide and Answer? (2015) 9 (1) New Zealand Journal of Research on Europe. < Microsoft Word - ONLINE Access to justice for victims of human rights abuse by multinational corporations FINAL (auckland.ac.nz)> Accessed 13 May 2019 and Jonathan Fitchen, 'Choice of Law in International Claims Based on Restrictions of Competition: Article 6 (3) of the Rome II Regulation' (2009) 5(2) Journal of Private International Law 337.

[652]Fiona Robertson, 'Access to Justice for Victims of Human Rights Abuse By Multinational Corporations: Does European Civil and Commercial litigation Provide and Answer? (2015) 9 (1) New Zealand Journal of Research on Europe. < Microsoft Word - ONLINE Access to justice for victims of human rights abuse by multinational corporations FINAL (auckland.ac.nz)> Accessed 13 May 2019 and Simon Baughen, 'Holding Corporations to Account: Crafting ATS Suits in the UK' (2013) 2 British Journal of American Legal Studies 533.

[653]Rome II Regulation, art 32 and Fiona Robertson, 'Access to Justice for Victims of Human Rights Abuse By Multinational Corporations: Does European Civil and Commercial litigation Provide and Answer? (2015) 9 (1) New Zealand Journal of Research on Europe. < Microsoft Word - ONLINE Access to justice for victims of human rights abuse by multinational corporations FINAL (auckland.ac.nz)> Accessed 13 May 2019.

developing state that rewards modest compensation, without the possibility of suing for punitive damages, such that it becomes uneconomical to sue before a foreign European forum.'[654] For 'some African nations, restorative redress, such as apologies,'[655] are valued more than monetary damages.[656]

Secondly, some member states in the European Union have introduced additional funding hurdles for plaintiffs by limiting the amount of legal aid they can claim.[657] However, the United States, in comparison, adopts a 'user pays' system such that it encourages victims of human rights violations to bring their case to court. Indeed, the financial advantages offered by the American legal system have been cited as a major reason why plaintiffs choose the United States as a forum.[658] On the other hand, litigation under the ATCA in the United States is likely to be higher than in the European Union because of the delays and inefficiencies in its legal system.[659] The additional uncertainties raised by the US Supreme Court Judgement in *Kiobel* will only add to the delays and expenses as lower courts struggle to apply the Supreme Court's cryptic decision.[660] Furthermore, ATCA lawsuits are a 'high risk-high return' investment based on the minuscule proportion of successful cases.[661]

Moreover, there may be less favourable disclosure requirements in accordance with the Member State forum's law as opposed to the United States. This is noted in *Akpan*, *Milieudefensie*,[662] a case where Nigerian farmers and Friends of the Earth filed suits against Royal Dutch Shell (Shell) and its Nigerian subsidiaries in a 'Dutch court seeking compensation for damage claimed to have been caused by leaking oil pipelines and an oil well in Nigeria. Initially, the Dutch Civil Procedural Code's restrictive

---

[654]*Ibid.*

[655]*Ibid.*

[656]Patrick J. Borchers, 'Conflict-of-Laws Considerations in State Court Human Rights Actions' (2013) 3 U.C. Irvine Law Review 45.

[657]Michael D. Goldhaber, 'Corporate Human Rights Litigation in Non-US Courts: A Comparative Score Card' (2013) 3 U.C. Irvine Law Review 127.

[658]David P Stewart and Ingrid Wuerth, 'Kiobel v. Royal Dutch Petroleum Co.: The Supreme Court and the Alien Tort Statute' (2013 107 (3) American Journal of International Law 601, 621.

[659]Samuel R Gross, 'The American Advantage: The Value of Inefficient Litigation' (1987) 85 Michigan Law Review 734.

[660]David P Stewart and Ingrid Wuerth, 'Kiobel v Royal Dutch Petroleum Co.: The Supreme Court and The Alien Tort Statute' (2013) 107 (3) American Journal of International Law 60.

[661]Michael D Goldhaber (n 1328).

[662]A.F. *Akpan v Royal Dutch Shell, plc,* Court of Appeal of The Hague (18 December 2015).

discovery rules meant that it could not access vital documents held by Shell.'[663] 'In *Akpan, 'Milieudefensie* it was alleged that disclosure of those documents would prove Shell's liability; hence disclosure requirements may play a significant role in the outcome of a case.'[664] Overturning a lower court decision, the Court of Appeal of the Hague ruled that Dutch courts have jurisdiction to consider the claims. It also directed Shell to provide the plaintiffs with access to documents pertaining to the oil spills.

Lastly, if a claim is regarding a truly foreign-cubed state of affairs, the Brussels and Rome Regulations – The Rome I Regulation can be distinguished from the Brussels Regime which determines which court can hear a given dispute, as opposed to which law it should apply. The regulation applies to all EU member states except Denmark, which has an opt-out from implementing regulations under the area of freedom, security and justice. The Danish government planned to join the regulation if a referendum on 3 December 2015 approved converting its opt-out into an opt-in, but the proposal was rejected – like the ATCA, are of no benefit. Nevertheless, claims can still be pursued under the Member State's national private international law rules. This is not a completely limiting disadvantage because of the willingness of Member State[665] courts to secure claimants' access to justice, as evidenced by *Lubbe*[666] and *Akpan.*[667]

In spite of the advantages offered by European civil and corporate human rights abuses jurisprudence, only a handful of claimants have

---

[663] Fiona Robertson, 'Access to Justice for Victims of Human Rights Abuse By Multinational Corporations: Does European Civil and Commercial litigation Provide and Answer? (2015) 9 (1) New Zealand Journal of Research on Europe. < Microsoft Word - ONLINE Access to justice for victims of human rights abuse by multinational corporations FINAL (auckland.ac.nz)> Accessed 13 May 2019 and Arthur S Hartkamp, 'Judicial Discretion under The New Civil Code of The Netherlands' (1992) 40 (5) American Journal of Comparative Law 554. See also: Dutch Civil Procedural Code's, Book 1 Litigation before the District Courts, the Courts of Appeal and the Supreme Court. Title 1 General provisions. Section 1 Jurisdiction of Dutch courts.

[664] Fiona Robertson, 'Access to Justice for Victims of Human Rights Abuse By Multinational Corporations: Does European Civil and Commercial litigation Provide and Answer? (2015) 9 (1) New Zealand Journal of Research on Europe. < Microsoft Word - ONLINE Access to justice for victims of human rights abuse by multinational corporations FINAL (auckland.ac.nz)> Accessed 13 May 2019.

[665] Regulation 44/2001 on Jurisdiction and the Recognition and Enforcement of Judgments in Civil and Commercial Matters [2001].

[666] *Lubbe v Cape Plc* [2000] UKHL 41.

[667] A.*F. Akpan v Royal Dutch Shell, plc,* Court of Appeal of The Hague (18 December 2015).

pursued the ATCA compared to lawsuits in European courts.[668] A possible explanation for this might be that the cultural dichotomy between Europe and the US is different. In the US, it is commonplace that harm done to a person is redressed 'privately through tort.'[669] Consequently, the 'US legal system recognises punitive damages and generally rewards higher overall compensation compared to other developed countries.'[670]

Contrarily, the prevailing belief in European cultures is that the State should be accountable for prosecuting wrongdoers through the criminal justice system, as opposed to private individuals through the civil system.[671] Even though tortious lawsuits have the ability to change social and legal practices in the US, historically they may have had little effect in European countries. Therefore, tort has not been acknowledged as the most effective way to remedy wrongs in European society.[672] With the increase in the number of MNCs since the advent of globalisation, however, this research argues that there is no reason victims should not utilise European civil and commercial litigation to secure effective redress.

Accordingly, the traditional differences between a civil lawsuit brought in the US compared to one brought in European legal systems are merely interesting reflections and should have little bearing on a claimant's choice of forum. Overall, the biggest problem facing activists of human rights claims against MNCs is uncertainty. The ATCA provides a possible avenue for bringing international human rights claims before the US Federal Courts. Nonetheless, the ATCA was enacted in 1789, a time very different

---

[668]Michael D Goldhaber (n 1294). See also Liesbeth Enneking, 'The Future of Foreign Direct Liability: Exploring the International Relevance of The Dutch Shell Nigeria Case' (2014) 10 Utrecht Law Review 44.

669Fiona Robertson, 'Access to Justice for Victims of Human Rights Abuse By Multinational Corporations: Does European Civil and Commercial litigation Provide and Answer? (2015) 9 (1) New Zealand Journal of Research on Europe. < Microsoft Word - ONLINE Access to justice for victims of human rights abuse by multinational corporations FINAL (auckland.ac.nz)> Accessed 13 May 2019.

[670]Vivian Grosswald Curran, 'Extraterritoriality, Universal Jurisdiction, and the Challenge of Kiobel v. Royal Dutch Petroleum Co.' (2013) 28 (1) Maryland Journal of International Law 76 and Fiona Robertson, 'Access to Justice for Victims of Human Rights Abuse By Multinational Corporations: Does European Civil and Commercial litigation Provide and Answer? (2015) 9 (1) New Zealand Journal of Research on Europe. < Microsoft Word - ONLINE Access to justice for victims of human rights abuse by multinational corporations FINAL (auckland.ac.nz)> Accessed 13 May 2019.

[671]*Ibid.*

[672]Pierre Legrand, 'European Legal Systems are Not Converging' (1996) 45(1) International & Comparative Law Quarterly 52.

from today, which means it requires innovation. Rather than expanding the decision on its applicability, the US Supreme Court has progressively restricted its scope. This has resulted in a frustrating journey for ATCA claimants who face numerous setbacks at the jurisdiction stage of the lawsuit. However, the US judicial system might have favourable legal fee rules and the ability to recover enormous damages, but examination should first and foremost be directed towards the plaintiff's ability to effectively pursue a claim for remedy.

Also, following *Filártiga*,[673] the ATCA's usefulness as a vehicle for securing human rights may have been 'somewhat inflated'.[674] A point of caution is due here, as only a small number of plaintiffs clear the jurisdictional hurdles. Even then, corporate defendants frequently encourage settlements (even though there exists uncertainty regarding corporate liability under the ATCA).[675] In regards to reparations, plaintiffs and their legal counsel should pursue a substitute avenue, such as tort lawsuit in another international court or the European Union Courts. This is because the U.S. judicial system is complex, especially regarding the division between federal and state courts. It is respectfully contested that there are no advantages to suing before U.S. federal courts over EU Member State courts or any other international forum. Furthermore, and significantly, other international fora and the Member State Courts can offer some extra certainty if the ATCA is not innovated to meet the current dynamics of international law.

Racketeer Influenced and Corrupt Organisations Act (RICO) and TVPA

In 1970, the U.S. passed the Racketeer Influenced and Corrupt Organisations Act (RICO), a federal law designed to combat organised crime in the US.[676] The Act permits prosecution and civil penalties for racketeering activity performed as part of an ongoing criminal enterprise.[677]

[673]Farooq Hassan, 'A Conflict of Philosophies: the Filartiga Jurisprudence' (1983) 32 (1) International & Comparative Law Quarterly 250.

[674]Nicola Jägers, Katinka Jesse, and Jonathan Verschuuren, 'The Future of Corporate Liability for Extraterritorial Human Rights Abuses: The Dutch Case Against Shell' (2014) 1 American Journal of International Law 36.

[675]Michael D Goldhaber (n 1328).

[676]Peter D Schellie, 'Racketeer Influenced and Corrupt Organizations Act (RICO)' (1986) Business Lawyer 1023.

[677] Robert G Blakey, and Brian Gettings, 'Racketeer Influenced and Corrupt Organizations (RICO): Basic Concepts-Criminal and Civil Remedies' (1980) 53 Temple Law Review 1009.

Such action may include illegal gambling, bribery, kidnapping, murder, money laundering, counterfeiting, embezzlement, drug trafficking, slavery, and a host of other illegal business practices.[678] Thus, US federal laws allow proceedings in US courts for violations of human rights in a foreign country, such as the Racketeer Influenced and Corrupt Organizations Act (RICO)[679] and the TVPA,[680] which offer some extraterritorial capability in regard to human rights violations, but only indirectly with regard to RICO.[681]

Consequently, the RICO Act provides both criminal and civil penalties for victims of human rights abuses.[682] Claims can potentially be brought by prosecutors on behalf of the government, or by private individuals.[683] Nonetheless, to succeed in RICO criminal prosecutions, the jury must be convinced of the defendant's guilt 'beyond a reasonable doubt'. This is the highest burden of proof that exists in the US legal standard.[684] Violations are punishable by up to 20 years in prison.[685] The sentence can be increased to life in prison if authorised by the underlying legislation or statute. Similarly, other offenders may also face a fine of either $250,000 or double the amount of the proceeds earned from the activity.[686]

'In general, liability for a RICO violation requires that a person be involved in an enterprise that operates through a pattern of racketeering activity.'[687] This raises a couple of questions that will prove important to

---

[678]Jeff Atkinson, 'Racketeer Influenced and Corrupt Organizations, 18 U.S.C. 1961-68: Broadest of The Federal Criminal Statutes' (1978) Journal of Criminal Law and Criminology 1.

[679]Racketeer Influenced and Corrupt Organizations Act, Title IX of Organised Crime Control Act (1970) PubLNo 91-452, 84 Stat. 922.

[680]Torture Victim Protection Act of 1991 Pub LNo 102-256, 106 Stat. 73 (1992) (codified at 28 USC. § 1350 (1994).

[681]Katie W Wood, 'Racketeer Influenced and Corrupt Organizations Act-Private Cause of Action-No Injury Required beyond Those Caused by Predicate Offenses for Section 1964 (c) Claim' (1985) 55 Mississippi Law Journal 167.

[682]Lan Cao, 'Illegal Traffic in Women: A Civil RICO Proposal' (1987) 96 Yale Law Journal 1297.

[683]Susan Rose-Ackerman and Bonnie J Palifka, *Corruption and Government: Causes, Consequences, and Reform* (Cambridge University Press 2016).

[684]Gerard E Lynch, 'RICO: The Crime of Being a Criminal, Parts I & II' (1987) 87(4) Columbia Law Review 661 and Susan W Brenner, 'RICO, CCE, and Other Complex Crimes: The Transformation of American Criminal Law' (1993) 2 (2) William & Mary Bill of Rights Law School Journals 239.

[685]Craig M Bradley, 'Racketeers, Congress, and the Courts: An Analysis of RICO' (1980) 65 Iowa Law Review 837.

[686]Paul H Rubin and Robert Zwirb, 'The Economics of Civil RICO' (1986) 20 UC Davis Law Review 883.

[687]RICO Law Racketeer Influenced and Corrupt Organizations Act.

anyone defending or pursuing a RICO case. The first is what qualifies as an 'enterprise'? Could the element requiring an enterprise be corporations, partnerships, and other businesses? Or can corporations, partnerships, and other businesses qualify as enterprises? What about informal organisations, like street gangs and rebels? The Supreme Court considered the issue of enterprises, and stated that an enterprise can be any group with members who are associated in a relationship in order to achieve a common purpose, provided the relationship lasts long enough to allow them to pursue that purpose. In this view, the meaning of enterprises in RICO law indicates that groups are known as 'association-in-fact' enterprises.[688]

Second, what constitutes 'a 'pattern' of racketeering activity? The RICO Act itself defines the term 'pattern' as 'two or more acts of'[689] 'racketeering activity within a 10-year period.'[690] 'The Supreme Court has considered this issue as well. According to the Court, to qualify as a pattern, criminal activities must be 'related and continuous.'[691] RICO law crimes have comparable features, with many including the same perpetrators, victims, and methods of commission. Therefore, continuity will be established if the crimes occurred over a substantial period of time. Some courts have interpreted this to mean at least one year.[692] This lack of consistency and contradiction questions the effectiveness of the RICO in combating human rights abuses, which does not even mention the high standards of proof required by the prosecution to establish liability.

Additionally, the US Supreme Court holds that private civil RICO suits must allege a 'domestic injury'.[693] In *Morrison v National Australia Bank Ltd*,[694] the US court sought to limit the circumstances in which US law

---

<https://www.hg.org/rico-law.html> Accessed 22 December 2017.
Gregory T Magarity, 'RICO Investigations: A Case Study' (1979) 17 American Criminal Law Review 367.

688 David B Smith and Terrance G Reed, *Civil RICO* (LexisNexis 1987).

689 < https://www.hg.org/rico-law.html> Accessed 09 March 2017.

690 Dorean Marguerite Koenig, 'The Criminal Justice System Facing the Challenge of Organized Crime' (1998) 44 Wayne Law Review 1351.

691 <https://www.hg.org/rico-law.html> Accessed 09 March 2017 and Barbara Black, 'Racketeer Influenced and Corrupt Organizations (RICO)-Securities and Commercial Fraud as Racketeering Crime after Sedima: What Is a Pattern of Racketeering Activity?' (1985) 6 Pace Law Review 365.

692 James L. Pray, 'Application of the Racketeer Influenced and Corrupt Organizations Act (RICO) to Securities Violations' (1982) 8 Journal of Corporation Law 411.

693 *RJR Nabisco Inc. v European Community*, 136 S. Ct. 2090 (2016).

694 *Morrison v National Australia Bank Ltd*, 561 US 247 (2010).

can be invoked to render foreign conduct actionable in the United States.[695] The US Supreme Court found that federal statutes do not apply in *Morrison*, beginning with the premise that federal statutes do not apply extraterritorially unless Congress has provided a clear indication of overcoming that presumption.

The Court applied that principle both to the provisions of the statute that define prohibited conduct and to the provisions that authorise a private cause of action.[696] The Court in its decision, through a majority of four Justices, decided that the RICO's 'civil remedy[697] is not consistent with §1962's substantive provisions', and therefore requires separate consideration.[698] The Court noted that 'a private right of action raises issues beyond the mere consideration whether underlying primary conduct should be allowed or not, entailing, for example, a decision to permit enforcement without the check imposed by prosecutorial discretion.'[699] Several lines of evidence also suggest that the Supreme Court perceived that permitting private claimants to bring claims for foreign injuries under civil RICO, including high damages, presents a 'danger of international friction'.[700] For these explanations, the US Supreme Court scrutinised §1964(c) and decided that it did not overcome the presumption against the extraterritorial application of US law. Considering this evidence, it seems that to sustain future civil RICO claims, claimants must have to assert and prove a domestic injury first before a claim under the Act can be established.

The Supreme Court's ruling may have numerous consequences for corporations that conduct their business operations outside the United States. However, it fails to address a number of essential questions; the first notable characteristic of the Court's verdict is its methodical framework.[701] Instead of examining the extraterritorial applicability of RICO in its entirety, or based solely on the 'substantive' terms of the statute that prohibit specified unlawful conduct, the Supreme Court distinctly measured the

---

[695] *Ibid.* William S Dodge, 'Presumptions Against Extraterritoriality in State Law' (2019) 53 UC Davis Law Review1389.

[696] Daniel R Peacock, 'RICO's Extraterritorial Application: From Morrison to RJR, Nabisco, Inc' (2017) 65 Drake Law Review 555.

[697] 18 USC. §1964(c).

[698] *Morrison v National Australia Bank Ltd* (n 1358).

[699] *Ibid.*

[700] *Ibid.*

[701] Genevieve Beyea, 'Morrison v. National Australia Bank and the Future of Extraterritorial Application of the U.S. Securities Laws' (2011) 72 Ohio State Law Journal 537 and *Morrison v National Australia Bank Ltd.*, US, No. 08-1191 (decided June 24, 2010).

scope of each statutory provision.[702] In examining each important section or subsection, the Supreme Court applied a two-step analysis outlined in *Morrison*.[703] First, the court determined whether Congress clearly provided for the statute's extraterritorial application. Second, the court did not assess whether a case was founded on a domestic application of the law.[704] The important themes that emerge from the studies, discussed so far, is that the method used by the US Supreme Court may generate supplementary prospects for perpetrators of human rights abuses to challenge the geographic reach of US statutes, especially in a civil lawsuit. An implication of this might be that such efforts will focus on whether a law prohibits foreign violations. They will also focus on other relevant components of any complex statutory scheme, which may include terms authorising causes of action, other enforcement mechanisms or remedies.

Likewise, the *RJR Nabisco* decision supports two related strategies for corporations looking for a way to resist RICO liability.[705] Undeniably, the Court's ruling is consistent with the position that the Justice Department advanced in its amicus brief.[706] It is likely that prosecutors will be considerably restricted, as compared to private claimants, in their use of RICO to target conduct occurring outside the United States, particularly in cases where much emphasis was placed on business undertakings of legitimate business operations.[707]

Moreover, given the extent to which criminal RICO cases are founded on established wrongdoings happening outside US borders, the courts will have to conclude whether the statutes barring such conduct apply extraterritorially, just as in the civil context.[708] Conceivably, even more prominently, courts will have to continue considering whether the offences

---

[702]*Ibid.*

[703]*Morrison v National Australia Bank Ltd* (n 1358).

[704]Katherine J Florey, 'State Law, US Power, Foreign Disputes: Understanding the Extraterritorial Effect of State Law in the Wake of Morrison v National Australia Bank' (2012).

[705]Franklin A Gevurtz, 'Building a Wall against Private Actions for Overseas Injuries: The Impact of RJR Nabisco v. European Community' (2017) 23 U.C. Davis Journal of International Law & Policy 1, *Morrison v National Australia Bank Ltd.*, 561 U. S. 247, 255 and *Morrison* and *Kiobel v Royal Dutch Petroleum Co.*, 569 U. S.

[706]*Ibid.*

[707]Richard G Strafer, Ronald R Massumi and Holly R Skolnick, 'Civil RICO in The Public Interest: Everybody's Darling' (1982) 19 American Criminal Law Review 655.

[708]Jed S. Rakoff and Howard W. Goldstein, *RICO: Civil and Criminal Law and Strategy* (Law Journal Press 2017).

alleged in civil or criminal cases call for the extraterritorial application of a specific statute, or whether claimants and prosecutors have to assume that the offences produce sufficient domestic injuries. Lawsuits surrounding these subjects will consequently continue and will not subside until the courts or Congress provide greater clarity on RICO.

RICO law closes any perceived loopholes that exempt individuals or organisations from prosecution who ordered or assisted others in a crime, but did not necessarily commit the crime outright. RICO also provides the US attorney prosecuting power to seek a pre-trial preventive order to temporarily seize a defendant's assets and other forfeitable property. The attorney may require the defendant to put up a performance bond, which ensures that there is something for the law enforcers to seize in case of a guilty verdict.[709] These procedures and sanctions satisfied the elements of an effective remedy.

However, the US judicial system remains unwilling to allow civil RICO claims. This is because of the fear that there would be deluge of plaintiffs bringing civil claims under RICO, where normal class civil actions would suffice.[710] Nonetheless, this research observes that even though RICO has achieved some crucial accountability for Racketeer Influenced and Corrupt Organisations Act offences,[711] it is restricted and cannot be the appropriate mechanism for corporate human violations and environmental damages.[712]

Other States with Extraterritorial Application and ATCA

A key strength of ATCA's accountability mechanism for corporate human rights violations and environmental damages is found in the enactment of implementing law dealing directly with corporate activities in

[709]Richard D Hartley, *Corporate Crime: A Reference Handbook* (ABC-CLIO 2008).
[710]U.S. Department of Justice. (2009). Criminal RICO: 18 USC. 1961-1968: *A Manual for Federal Prosecutors. Washington, D.C.: US Dept. of Justice, Criminal Division, Organized Crime and Racketeering Section*, 2 (23) 12.
[711]Arthur F Mathews, *Civil RICO Litigation* (Law & Business/Harcourt Brace Jovanovich 1985); Lee Coppola and Nicholas DeMarco, 'Civil RICO: How Ambiguity Allowed the Racketeer Influenced and Corrupt Organizations Act to Expand Beyond Its Intended Purpose' (2012) 38 New England Journal on Criminal and Civil Confinement 241.
[712]Michael N Glanz, *RICO and Securities Fraud:* 'A Workable Limitation' (1983) 83 Columbia Law Review 1513 (1983).

a foreign country. This is also enshrined in Australia's common law[713] and in UK law.[714] However, none of these laws have yet to make it into the statute books; the reason why is still unclear. It could be said that the refusal of developed countries to allow their national courts to become a platform for bringing litigation proceedings against corporations poses a significant obstacle to the application of the ATCA. This is because the US courts run the risk of being seen as an international forum for corporate liability,[715] thus overloading US courts and putting US corporations at a disadvantage.[716] These findings suggest that, in general, the international legal system may require a new international legal forum besides the ATCA and the US legal forum to hold corporations accountable for human rights abuses and environmental damages.[717]

Belgium distinguished between universal jurisdiction,[718] which is exercised by a State in the interests of the international community, and other types of extraterritorial jurisdiction, such as those deriving from the principle of protection or from the nationality of the perpetrator or of the

---

[713] Sarala Fitzgerald, 'Corporate Accountability for Human Rights Violations in Australian Domestic Law' (2005) 11(1) Australian Journal of Human Rights 2, Sarah Pritchard, 'The Jurisprudence of Human Rights: Some Critical Thought and Developments in Practice' (1995) 2(1) Australian Journal of Human Rights 3, *Workplace Relations Act 1996* (Cth) (WRA), the *Race Discrimination Act 1975* (Cth) (RDA), the *Sex Discrimination Act 1984* (Cth) (SDA), (Cth) (Affirmative Action Act) and the *Human Rights and Equal Opportunity Act 1986* (Cth) (HREOC Act) (Norris 2000: 132) and Sarala Fitzgerald, 'Corporate Accountability For Human Rights Violations in Australian Domestic Law' (2005) 11 (1) Australian Journal of Human Rights 2.

[714] Geoffrey Tweedale and Laurie Flynn, 'Piercing the Corporate Veil: Cape Industries and Multinational Corporate Liability for a Toxic Hazard, 1950–2004' (2007) 8 (2) Enterprise & Society 268, 296, *Lubbe v Cape Plc* [2000] UKHL 41 and *Guerrero v Monterrico Metals plc* [2009] EWHC 2475 (QB).

[715] Caroline Kaeb, 'The Shifting Sands of Corporate Liability under International Criminal Law' (2016) 49 George Washington International Law Review, 351; Elizabeth T. Lear, 'National Interests, Foreign Injuries, and Federal Forum Non Conveniens' (2007) 41 UC Davis School Law Review 559.

[716] Elliot J. Schrage, 'Judging Corporate Accountability in The Global Economy', (2003) 42 Columbia Journal of Transnational Law 153.

[717] Patrick Macklem, *Corporate Accountability under International Law: The Misguided Quest for Universal Jurisdiction; International Law Forum Du Droit International* (Vol. 7. No. 4. Brill Academic Publishers 2005).

[718] Kenneth C. Randall, 'Universal Jurisdiction under International Law' (1987) 66 Texas Law Review 78.

victim.[719] Belgium also considered that there are customary obligations which require States to incorporate rules of universal jurisdiction in their domestic law in order to try persons suspected of crimes of such seriousness that they threaten the international community as a whole,[720] such as grave crimes under international humanitarian law.[721]

Finally, in Belgian opinion, customary law enables States which are not parties to the 1984 Convention Against Torture to prosecute persons suspected of torture who are present in their territory, in view of the nature of the prohibition against torture as a peremptory norm of international law.[722] Similarly, customary law authorises States to exercise universal jurisdiction against persons suspected of acts of piracy, slavery, or trafficking of persons.[723] Thus, the argument that territorial connections also define the scope of extraterritorial jurisdiction is most obvious with respect to the Belgian court's 'effective control' cases, which turn on the premise that jurisdiction flows from the state's functional control over territory outside its borders.[724]

Belgium is one of the creators of universal jurisdiction with respect to grave crimes under international humanitarian law.[725] However, the application of this very far-reaching law gave rise to a number of problems

---

[719] Mark Summers, 'The International Court of Justice's Decision in Congo v Belgium: How Has It Affected the Development of a Principle of Universal Jurisdiction That Would Obligate All States to Prosecute War Criminals' (2003).

[720] Luc Reydams, 'Criminal Jurisdiction Universal Jurisdiction Crimes Against Humanity Immunity of Former Head of State Incorporation of Customary Law into Municipal Criminal Law Prescription (statutes of limitation)' (1999) 793(3) American Journal of International Law.

[721] Claus Kress, 'Universal Jurisdiction over International Crimes and The Institut de Droit International' (2006) 4(3) Journal of International Criminal Justice 561.

[722] Christine M. Chinkin, 'In Re Pinochet. United Kingdom House of Lords. Regina v. Bow Street Stipendiary Magistrate Ex Parte Pinochet Ugarte' (1999) American Journal of International Law 703.

[723] Stephen Macedo, ed. *Universal Jurisdiction: National Courts and the Prosecution of Serious Crimes under International Law* (University of Pennsylvania Press 2006).

[724] Sarah Miller, 'Revisiting Extraterritorial Jurisdiction: A Territorial Justification for Extraterritorial Jurisdiction Under The European Convention' (2009) 20(4) European Journal of International Law 1223.

[725] Malvina Halberstam, 'Belgium's Universal Jurisdiction Law: Vindication of International Justice or Pursuit of Politics?' (2003) 25 Cardozo Law Review 247. Also see: <https://www.un.org/en/ga/sixth/65/ScopeAppUniJuri_StatesComments/Belgium_E.pdf> Accessed 05 April 2016.

in practice, including that it interferes with foreign politics[726] and that it trumps the sovereign rights of a state.[727] Additionally, it has been observed that courts in Belgium have the capability to hear cases of human rights violations by or against any person, anywhere in the world.[728] Nevertheless, the Belgian legislature repealed provisions for extraterritorial corporate liability in 2003.[729] Earlier in 2003, Belgium offered jurisdiction over all humanitarian claims regardless of the crime's connection to the country, the nationality of the plaintiffs or defendants, or the absence of defendants from the proceedings.[730] However, this concept has come under constant attack about its scope and application. This has forced the Belgian court to accept a review of a case against *Total Fina Elf* that was based on the same facts underlying a claim brought in the French court.[731]

Similarly, following the outcomes 'of other controversial claims against high-ranking foreign officials,'[732] 'the US threatened to move the NATO headquarters out of Brussels unless Belgium revoked the rules.'[733] Without 'the extraterritorial jurisdiction that they had offered, the Belgian court could no longer adjudicate the case against *Total*.'[734] Similarly, it

---

[726] *F. Hoffman-La Roche Ltd. v Empagran S.A.*, 542 US 155, 164 (2004).

[727] Zachary D Clopton, 'Replacing the Presumption against Extraterritoriality' (2013) 1 Boston University Law Review 94.

[728] *Total lawsuit in Belgium.* In April 2002, four Myanmar refugees filed a lawsuit against TotalFinaElf (now Total).

[729] Steven R Ratner, 'Belgium's War Crimes Statute: A Post-mortem' (2003) 97(4) American Journal of International Law 888.

[730] Roemer Lemaitre, 'Belgium Rules the World: Universal Jurisdiction over Human Rights Atrocities' (2000) 37 (2) Jura Falconis 255.

[731] Jodie A. Kirshner, 'Why is The US Abdicating the Policing of Multinational Corporations to Europe? Extraterritorialism, Sovereignty, and The Alien Tort Statute' (2011).

[732] <https://www.lexisnexis.co.uk/legal/search?query=enforcement%20mechanism %20for%20international%20law%20norms> Accessed 9 October 2017 and Marlise Simons, 'Sharon Faces Belgian Trial after Term Ends' (2003) The New York Times and 'New War Crimes Suits Filed Against Bush, Blair in Belgium' *Deutsche Presse Agentur* 20 June 2003, <http://archives.dailytimes.com.pk/national/20-Jun-2003/war-crimes-suits-filed-in-belgiumagainst-bush-blair> Accessed 8 August 2017.

[733] Lorna McGregor, 'The Need to Resolve The Paradoxes of The Civil Dimension of Universal Jurisdiction' (2005) 99 American Society Of International Law Reviews 125.

[734] Antonio Cassese, 'The Belgian Court of Cassation v. The International Court of Justice: The Sharon and Others Case' (2003) 1 Journal of International Criminal Justice 437.

would not be able to pursue allegations brought by Burmese citizens against a French company for human rights violations in Burma.[735]

Also, when Spanish courts presented a forum for extraterritorial claims, the Spanish Parliament acted to restrict the jurisdiction over human rights cases in 2009.[736] Under the former provisions in Spain, which had been in force since 1985, allegations of the most serious crimes in violation of international law triggered jurisdiction, no matter where the actions had taken place.[737] Controversial cases against individuals followed, including against Augusto Pinochet, raising diplomatic concerns.[738] The new rules now require claims to allege either Spanish victims or perpetrators that are present in Spain before jurisdiction can arise.[739] The legal theoretical implications of these findings are unclear. However, what is clear is that the ATCA and the application of extraterritorial jurisdiction at present suffer from political interference and the unwillingness of states to prosecute.

Following this examination, the ATCA offers an anachronistic jurisdiction for human rights violations by MNCs because it has allowed cases such as *Turedi v The Coca-Cola Co.*,[740] *Roe v Bridgestone Corp.*,[741] *Abdullahi v Pfizer Inc.*,[742] *Sarei v Rio Tinto PLC*,[743] and *re South African Apartheid Litigation.*[744] However, the increasing caseload of the ATCA demonstrates that it is likely the US court will limit the application of the

---

[735] *Universal Jurisdiction in Europe, The State of The Art*, Human Rights Watch 37, 38. <http://www.hrw.org/sites/default/files/reports/ij0606web.pdf> Accessed 9 June 2006.

[736] Organic Law (L.O.P.J. 1985, art. 23.4), Ignacio de la Rasilla Del Moral, 'The Swan Song of Universal Jurisdiction in Spain' (2009) 9 (5) International Criminal Law Review 777.

[737] Joaquin Gonzalez Ibanez, 'Legal Pedagogy, The Rule of Law, and Human Rights: The Professor, The Magistrate's Robe, and Miguel de Unamuno' (2012) 7 (4) Interdisciplinary Journal of Human Rights Law 147.

[738] Naomi Roht-Arriaza, 'The Pinochet Precedent and Universal Jurisdiction' (2001) 35 New England Law Review 311.

[739] Máximo Langer, 'The Diplomacy of Universal Jurisdiction: The Political Branches and The Transitional Prosecution of International Crimes' (2011) 105 (1) American Journal of International Law 1.

[740] *Turedi v The Coca-Cola Co.*, 2009 US App. Lexis 14794 (2d Cir. July 7, 2009).

[741] *Roe v Bridgestone Corp.*, 257 F.R.D. 159, 172-73 (S.D. Ind. 2009).

[742] *Abdullahi v Pfizer Inc.,* 562 F.3d 163, 187 (2d Cir. 2009).

[743] *Sarei v Rio Tinto* PLC, 2009 WL 2762635 (C.D. Calif. July 31, 2009).

[744] *South African Apartheid Litigation,* 617 F. Supp. 2d 228, 296 (S.D.N.Y. 2009).

law to corporate human rights violations in the future.[745] It can also be noted that its jurisprudence is fragmented, lacks consistency, and is too ambiguous.[746] Nonetheless, no case has been decided on its merit and the US Supreme Court has not determined the scope of the ATCA and its practical content. The reason for this is yet to become clear and has created uncertainty around the ATCA application.

Previous studies of business and human rights accountability and remedy have also paid particular attention to the US ATCA,[747] which enables foreign nationals to bring claims in US Federal Courts for violations of customary international law or treaties to which the US is a party.[748] Following the ATCA, recent developments in European Union[749] human rights cases make such expositions unsatisfactory because it seems the US Supreme Court has ended most transnational claims under the ATCA, as seen in *Kioble v Royal Dutch Petroleum Co.*[750] The Supreme Court's application of the 'presumption against extraterritoriality' in the *Kiobel* case[751] will have a direct and immediate effect on future ATCA claims pending in the US courts, specifically in cases involving corporations accused of complicity in international human rights violations overseas. The Supreme Court issued a summary order in another large ATCA case, *Rio*

---

[745]David P Stewart and Ingrid Wuerth, 'Kiobel v. Royal Dutch Petroleum Co.: The Supreme Court and the Alien Tort Statute' (2013) 107(3) American Journal of International Law 601-621.

[746]Robert J. Delahunty and John Yoo, 'Against Foreign Law' (2005) 29 Harvard Journal of Law & Public Policy 291.

[747]Alien Tort Statute, 28 USC. § 1350.

[748]Sarah H. Cleveland, 'Alien Tort Statute, Civil Society, and Corporate Responsibility' (2004) 56 Rutgers Law Review 971.

[749]Markus Mayr, 'Extraterritorial Application of The European Convention on Human Rights and The Access to The Court for Victims of Human Rights Violations of ESDP Missions' (2010) BSIS Journal of International Studies 7 and Fiona Robertson, 'Access to Justice for Victims of Human Rights Abuse By Multinational Corporations: Does European Civil and Commercial litigation Provide and Answer? (2015) 9 (1) New Zealand Journal of Research on Europe. < Microsoft Word - ONLINE Access to justice for victims of human rights abuse by multinational corporations_FINAL (auckland.ac.nz)> Accessed 13 May 2019.

[750]*Kioble v Royal Dutch Petroleum Co.*, 133 S.Ct. 1659 (2013).

[751]*Kiobel v Royal Dutch Petroleum Co.*, 456 F. Supp. 2d 457, 465-67 (S.D.N.Y. 2006), *Kiobel v. Royal Dutch Petroleum Co.*, 642 F.3d 379 (2011), *Kiobel v Royal Dutch Petroleum Co.* No. 10–1491 (Breyer J., concurring), slip op. at 7-8 (US Apr. 17, 2013) (quoting *Tel-Oren v Libyan Arab Republic*, 726 F. 2d 774, 781 (D.C. Cir. 1984) (Edwards, J., concurring) and citing Pierre Leval, 'The Long Arm of International Law: Giving Victims of Human Rights Abuses Their Day in Court' (2013) 92 *Foreign Affairs*.

Tinto PLC v Sarei, No. 11-649,[752] a claim for alleged corporate responsibility for human rights abuses in Bouganville, Papua New Guinea. The US Court of Appeals for the Ninth Circuit held in 2011 that these violations are claims under the ATCA. In 2013, the Supreme Court granted Rio Tinto's *certiorari* petition and vacated the Ninth Circuit's 2011 decision, remanding the case to the Ninth Circuit 'for further consideration in light of *Kiobel*.'[753]

The most interesting thing about the *Kiobel* case[754] is that the US Supreme Court did not address other questions affecting corporations' conduct in international law. For instance, the US Second Circuit clearly acknowledged in *Kiobel* that international treaties may impose liability on corporations in certain subject matters, such as the prevention of bribery or organised crime. However, the Supreme Court's opinion did not address these specific policy areas. In *Kiobel*, the court was not asked to examine the potential international lawsuits that might be made in US courts in cases of expropriation by foreign governments.[755] Also, the court decision is likely not to deter current initiatives by international bodies and NGOs aimed at modifying corporate conduct in countries with substantial human rights records.

This may partly be the reason why the literature continues to address the concept of corporate accountability and the impact of the ATCA on MNCs.[756] Consequently, this is the beginning of a new accountability concept, rather than the end. In summary, the ATCA remains relevant to the understanding of the modern relationship between corporate and international law. It also explains the relationship between home and host states holding corporations accountable for human rights abuses. Even though it could be argued that the ATCA is outdated because it is an old legal doctrine, these two dimensions set a legal platform for holding corporations accountable for violations of international law.

However, the ATCA's aim to hold corporations accountable for human rights abuses abroad does suffer from a number of technical and

---

[752]*Sarei v Rio Tinto, PLC*, 671 F.3d 736 (2011).

[753]The Supreme Court granted certiorari in *Daimler Chrysler AG v Bauman, et al.* (docket 11-965).

[754]*Kiobel Case* (n 1151).

[755]See 28 USC. § 1605(a) (3). Also see, e.g., *Kalamazoo Spice Extraction Co. v. Provisional Military Gov't of Socialist Ethiopia*, 616 F. Supp. 660, 663 (W.D. Mich. 1985). <https://www.jdsupra.com/legalnews/us-supreme-court-greatly-restricts-scop-34703/> Accessed 08 February 2016.

[756]Bejamin Thompson, 'Was Kiobel Detrimental to Corporate Social Responsibility: Applying Lessons Learnt from American Exceptionalism' (2014) 30 Utrecht Journal of International and European Law 82 (2014).

practical limitations. Primarily, the act was enacted 200 years ago, and as such, was never designed to hold corporations accountable for human rights abuses.[757] Likewise, it is common that national courts, such those as in the UK[758] and in the Netherlands,[759] have extraterritorial application. Although it is less substantial for the operation of the ATCA, the cost is also a limiting factor.[760] The third restriction on the ATCA is that courts adopt a narrow interpretation of human rights violations that fall within their jurisdiction. For instance, Joseph and McBeth[761] stress that while some egregious human rights abuses fall within the realm of legislation, such as torture, summary executions, sexual assault, war crimes, crimes against humanity, forced labour, and slavery, others are included only if they are methodical, and some are not included at all, such as environmental damage, forced prison labour, expropriation of private property and restriction of freedom of speech.[762] This means that the application of *jus cogens* (customary international norms) does not have as significant an effect on the ATCA as it does for other national and international laws.

The ATCA is also restricted by State action requirements. Thus, non-state actors can only be accountable under the ATCA if they did not act in accordance with a state official or with significant state assistance.[763] This is a significant setback for the ATCA, because the establishment of state action requirement and state assistance is problematic in most ATCA cases. A possible explanation for this might be that state sovereignty and immunity from prosecution or liability[764] allow the corporation to escape liability

[757]Luisa Antoniolli, 'Taking Legal Pluralism Seriously: The Alien Tort Claims Act and the Role of International Law before U.S. Federal Courts' (2005) 12 (2) Indiana Journal of Global Legal Studies 651.

[758]Aleksandra Dorich, *Parent Company Responsibility of Corporations for the Acts of Their Overseas Group Subsidiaries* (The European Union/United Kingdom Perspective 2015).

[759]Larissa van den Herik, 'The Difficulties of Exercising Extraterritorial Criminal Jurisdiction: The Acquittal of a Dutch Businessman for Crimes Committed in Liberia' (2009) 9 (1) International Criminal Law Review 211, 226.

[760]Nadia Bernaz, 'Enhancing Corporate Accountability for Human Rights Violations: Is Extraterritoriality the Magic Potion?' (2013) 117 (3) Journal of Business Ethics 493.

[761]Sarah Joseph and Adam McBeth (eds), *Research Handbook on International Human Rights Law* (Edward Elgar 2010).

[762]*Ibid.*

[763]*Ibid.*

[764]Joanne Foakes, *Immunity for International Crimes?: Developments in The Law on Prosecuting Heads of State in Foreign Courts* (Chatham House 2011), *Ex-King*

where it acts under state authority.[765] The final limitation of the ATCA is that the court's ability to establish jurisdiction over foreign perpetrators (as with all courts) is limited under foreign relations and politics.[766] The US courts have the authority to decide whether or not there is a sufficient link between the foreign corporation(s) against which the case is brought. However, the majority of cases have been dismissed because of the lack of a close relationship between the parent company and its subsidiaries.[767] This approach by the courts is dismissed in this study because the supply chain and subsidiary's role in limiting liability is economically inefficient.[768]

In a more positive vein, the subsidiary is more than a device to limit liability; it is an extraordinarily powerful conflict device in the law of international business organisations. This aspect of the supply chain and subsidiary is independent of its risk-shifting function.[769] The subsidiary structure operates as a conflict device by minimising the number of forums in which a suit may be brought. A unitary firm that has 'minimum contacts'[770] with several forums is usually subject to jurisdiction in each of these forums. A firm may, however, conduct activities in one of these jurisdictions through a supply chain or subsidiary. If a suit against the firm 'arises from the subsidiary's activities, the firm is only subject to suit in this one jurisdiction, despite activities in other forums. The subsidiary thus serves a purpose similar to the one served'[771] by the *forum non conveniens* doctrine,[772] but yields far more predictable results.[773] It is possible therefore that limited liability is certainly justifiable at the shareholder level, but not

---

Farouk of Egypt v Christian Dior (1957) 24 I.L.R. 228; *Jimenez v Aristeguieta* (1962) 311 F.2d 547 and *Hatch v Baez* (1876) 7 Hun 596.

[765]Alan O Sykes, 'Corporate Liability for Extraterritorial Torts under The Alien Tort Statute and Beyond: An Economic Analysis' (2011) 100 Georgetown Law Journal 2161.

[766]Curtis A Bradley, 'The Costs of International Human Rights Litigation' (2001) 2 Chicago Journal of International Law 457.

[767]*Presbyterian Church of Sudan v Talisman Energy*, Inc., 244 F. Supp. 2d 289 (S.D.N.Y. 2003), *Sinaltrainal v Coca-Cola Company*, 578 F.3d 1252 (11th Cir. 2009) and *Bowoto v Chevron Corp.*, 621 F.3d 1116 (9th Cir. 2010). <https://www.abyssinialaw.com/about-us/item/943-theories-of-human-rights-and-justification> Accessed 23 May 2016.

[768]*Lemon v Kurtzman*, 403 602, 91 S. Ct. 2105, 29 L. Ed. 2d 745 (1971).

[769]*In International Shoe Co. v Washington*, 326 US 310 (1945).

[770]Ibid.

[771] Joseph H Sommer, 'The Subsidiary: Doctrine without a Clause' (1990) Fordham L aw Review59 227.

[772]*Islamic Republic of Iran v Pahlavi*, 62 N.Y.2d 474, 482-85 (1984).

[773]*Ibid.*

at the parent corporation liability level. For these reasons, the US Supreme Court wrongly ruled on these facts.

The ATCA is also subject to political and international relations between state governments.[774] In *Rendell-Baker v Kohn*,[775] Justice Marshall observed that '[t]he decisions of this Court clearly establish that where there is a symbiotic relationship between the State and a privately owned enterprise, so that the State and a privately owned enterprise are participants in a joint venture, the actions of the private enterprise may be attributable to the State'.[776] Consequently, uncertainty concerning the precise scope of state action has seen the doctrine of '*proximate cause*'[777] invoked by several circuit courts particularly in the Ninth Circuit as a key component of §1983 proceedings. As the Ninth Circuit put it in *Van Ort v. Estate of Stanewich*, 'although state action and causation are separate concepts, elements of the causation analysis have been used in determining state action.'[778]

The US political and international relations limitation was relevant in the Supreme Court decision in *United States v Curtiss-Wrights Export Corp.*[779] The court establishes by majority opinion that 'the President [is] the only organ of the US government in the field of international relations',[780] hence the ultimate decision maker. This means that it is only the President that has a *de facto* capacity to act in the name of a State. Thus, the ATCA is not applicable to State conduct because the State is immune from liability. The view on federal government power creates a conflict between the ATCA and the powers of the State to be use it as a full

[774]Matthew E Danforth, 'Corporate Civil Liability under the Alien Tort Statute: Exploring Its Possibility and Jurisdictional Limitations' (2011) 44 (3) Cornell International Law Journal 659, *Smith v Hooey* 513 US 374, 378 (1995) (*citing, Edmonson v Leesville Concrete Co.*, 500 US 614, 632 (1991)), *Gallagher v Neil Young Freedom Concert*, 49 F.3d 1442, 1448-51 (10th Cir. 1995), *Sandoval v Bluegrass Regional Mental Health-Mental Retardation Bd.*, 2000 US App. Lexis 17949 (6th Cir., 2011), *Lugar v Edmondson Oil Co.*, 457 US 922, 937 (1982), *Terry v Adams*, 345 US 461 (1953), *Marsh v Alabama*, 326 US 501, *Jackson v Metro. Edison* Co., 419 US 345, 352 (1974) and *Adickes v S.H. Kress & Co.*, 398 US 144, 170 (1970).

[775]*Rendell-Baker v. Kohn* 488 F.Supp. 764 (1980).

[776]*Rendell-Baker v Kohn* 457 US 830, 847 (1982).

[777]*Pawsey v Scottish Union & National Insurance Company* [1908] UKPC 60.

[778]*Van Ort v Estate of Stanewich* 92 F.3d 831, 836 (9th Cir. 1996) and *Arnold v IBM* 637 F.2d 1350, 1355 (9th Cir. 1981).

[779]*United State v Curtiss-Wrights Export Corp.*, 299 US 304 (1936). See also: Pierlings JT Menzel and J Hoffmann, *United States v Curtiss-Wright Export Corporation*, 299 US 304 (2005).

[780]*United State v Curtiss-Wrights Export Corp.*, 299 US 304 (1936).

accountability mechanism for human rights violations. However, this is not the case as most MNC cases can be linked to State immunity.

A possible way to overcome this obstacle is by allowing the ATCA an element of extraterritorial jurisdiction that permits the US District Court judges and the Supreme Court Justices to hear cases that may have an element of international relations. However, this would be very difficult to implement in practice because of the jurisdictional difference that exists at state level,[781] the fear that the state will become the new legal forum for corporate human rights violation cases,[782] and the foreign policy and political relations of the state.[783] As the recent *Kiobel* case has shown, the court has limited the jurisdiction of the ATCA in cases that may have the potential to upset foreign policy, international relations and the security of the federal government.[784] Furthermore, the ATCA does not offer a comprehensive solution for human rights violations by MNCs more broadly, especially when there is the likelihood of the defendant raising *forum non conveniens* as a defence mechanism.[785]

Černič and Ho argued that the US Supreme Court decision in *Kiobel v Royal Dutch Petroleum Co.*[786] signalled the end of future transitional human rights abuse claims under the ATCA.[787] However, this study has taken a contrary view; it is not the end of the ATCA, but rather the beginning of a new legal concept of tort liability under the duty of care. This is also seen in the literature, as it continues to address the concept of corporate accountability through the ATCA on the statute of corporate liability.[788] The ATCA remains relevant for developing corporate

---

[781]John Henry Merryman and Rogelio Pérez-Perdomo, *The Civil Law Tradition: An Introduction to The Legal Systems of Europe and Latin America* (Stanford University Press 2007).

[782]John B. Bellinger, 'Enforcing Human Rights in U.S. Courts and Abroad: The Alien Tort Statute and Other Approaches' (2009) 42 Vanderbilt Journal of Transnational Law 1.

[783]Donald Earl Childress, 'The Alien Tort Statute, Federalism, and the Next Wave of Transnational Litigation' (2012) 100 Georgetown Law Journal 709.

[784]Julian G Ku, 'Kiobel and The Surprising Death of Universal Jurisdiction under The Alien Tort Statute' (2013) 107(4) American Journal of International Law 835.

[785]John R. Wilson, 'Coming to America to File Suite: Foreign Plaintiffs and the Forum Non Conveniens Barrier in Transnational Litigation' (2004) 65 Ohio State Law Journal 659.

[786]*Kiobel v Royal Dutch Petroleum* Co., 133 S. Ct. 165.

[787]Jernej Letnar Černič and Tara Van Ho Draft (eds), 'Human Rights and Business: Direct Corporate Accountability for Human Right' (2015).

[788]Julian G. Ku, 'Kiobel and The Surprising Death of Universal Jurisdiction under The Alien Tort Statute' (2013) 107(4) American Journal of International Law 835,

accountability and corporate legal liability for human rights abuses. The development can be seen in two dimensions: the first is that the ATCA is the only mechanism that is capable of offering accountability for the victim of human rights violation; and the second is that the ATCA has the ability to offer an effective sanction on corporations irrespective of the state in which the violation happened. The indication for this is that the ATCA provides a basis for considering the relationship between the state, the corporation, society, international law, and legal norms, whereas the voluntary mechanism does not. This relationship can be summarised in two dimensions: the first is the state duty within international human rights law, which can be seen through tort and civil law liability as a duty of care; and the second is the relationship between the home and host states in holding corporation accountability for human rights abuses, which can be seen in the positive duty of states not to allow third parties to harm anyone in their jurisdictions.

A possible way of building on the success of the ATCA and its fundamental principles is to advocate a new paradigm for bringing an action against the corporation in the form of a tort and civil law principle (the Neighbourhood Principle), which has its route in the application of the tort of negligence. This principle is based purely on the Neighbourhood Principle under the English tort law system and other common law jurisdictions, such as Australia, Canada, Nigeria, South Africa, and New Zealand.[789] This approach has the potential to breach the accountability gap in corporate liability under international law. The neighbourhood principle[790] would provide victims with reparations; it would also put strong pressure on corporations to comply with international human rights laws and standards. It would also provide a standard to examine and develop accountability that will ensure adequate and effective protection for individuals and societies. By taking a tort and civil law approach to accountability, the principle could enhance the understanding of the human rights duties of corporations by assessing both underlying concepts as well as case studies that question and highlight the inadequacy of the current concept of corporate accountability.

---

841 and Muthucumaraswamy Sornarajah, *The International Law on Foreign Investment* (Cambridge University Press 2017).

[789]Jenny Steele, *Tort Law: Text, Cases, and Materials* (Oxford University Press 2010).

[790]*Donoghue v Stevenson* (1932) AC 562, 580.

Reasons for Accountability under Tort Law and Civil Law System

Following the discussion in this chapter so far, it is noted that the US ATCA has its limitations[791] and the current voluntary mechanism has failed to offer an appropriate solution for corporate human rights violations.[792] Additionally, international law has failed to both impose human rights obligations on corporations and provide a mechanism to regulate corporate conduct in the sphere of human rights.[793] A possible explanation for this might be that international law and international human rights law have solely addressed the affairs of states[794] while excluding private entities from human rights obligations.[795] There is no doubt that the current human rights accountability mechanism does not offer any remedy for the victims of corporate human rights abuses. There is no doubt corporate accountability should follow tort law and civil law systems. This is because corporate liability cannot be viewed through the current international law mechanisms, as it does not provide an adequate remedy for corporate human rights abuses.[796]

Tort and civil laws can offer two alternative approaches to corporate accountability and award remedy. The first is that remedy awarded by the court can be governed by different jurisdiction laws in tort and civil law principles. This is because tort and civil law can be enforced in most judicial systems and its legal principle is familiar to some states.[797] The second is that corporate accountability and remedy can be awarded

---

[791]Romesh J Weeramantry, 'Time Limitation under The United States Alien Tort Claims Act' (2003) 85 (851) International Review of the Red Cross 627, Forti *et al. v Suarez-Mason* (hereafter '*Forti*') and *Estate of Winston Cabello v Fernandez-Lorios*.

[792] Emeka Duruigbo, 'Corporate Accountability and Liability for International Human Rights Abuses: Recent Changes and Recurring Challenges' (2008) 6 (2) Northwestern Journal of Human Rights 222.

[793]*Ibid.*

[794]Tagle de Gonzalo Sánchez, 'The Objective International Responsibility of States in The Inter-American Human Rights System' (2015) 7 (2) Mexican Law Review 115.

[795]Sabina Anne Espinoza, *Should International Human Rights Law be Extended to Apply to Multinational Corporations and Other Business Entities?* (UCL University College London 2015).

[796] Barbara A Frey, 'The Legal and Ethical Responsibilities of Transnational Corporations in The Protection of International Human Rights' (1997) 6 Minnesota Journal of Global Trade 153.

[797]Oliver Wendell Holmes, *The Path of The Law* (The Floating Press 2009).

through the domestic and international judicial system. These are particularly important because international law structured in relation to civil liability has no specific stance on the appropriate mechanism for corporate accountability, but rather permits each state to take its stance and apply the law accordingly. This means that the state has the freedom to apply and enforce the principle in their jurisdiction without any significant constraint on the interpretation of the legal rule. The next chapter will address the concept of accountability and the role it can play in holding corporations liable for human rights violations.

CHAPTER II

The main aim of this chapter is to better understand the challenges that exist for corporate human rights accountability and environmental damages, as well as the initiatives likely to be most effective for the enforcement of human rights and environmental law, given the diversity of legal structures, traditions and approaches in different jurisdictions around the world. The research in this chapter attempts to analyse the concept of liability by critically examining the definitions of human rights law and tort law as well as examining the problems associated with the concept of corporate obligation, both in its legal and everyday use, with a view to developing a corporate liability mechanism under tort law. The research draws on empirical information from a wide range of general and legal literature on the concept of accountability. It examines the functioning of the general and legal concept of accountability, human rights law, tort of negligence, accountability systems, and relevant regimes. Adopting this approach to corporate liability allows the research to lay down the theoretical concept for the study by focusing on the substantive legal and practical issues that have an impact on the effectiveness of accountability and judicial mechanisms in achieving corporate accountability and effective remedy in cases of business-related human rights exploitations. There is a particular emphasis on the legal definition of accountability under public international law. This is because the definition is important in the recognition of an effective international legal framework on business and human rights as an essential step towards protecting victims' access to remedy for corporate wrongdoings. It will also serve as a legal instrument that could clarify the obligations of corporations to respect human rights.

The Notion of Accountability

The only area of international law that is capable of addressing the human rights violations of individuals' rights perpetrated by a state[798] is the

[798]Friends of the Earth, *'Briefing: Corporate Accountability'* (2005). <http://www.foe.co.uk/resource/briefings/corporate_accountability1.pdf> Accessed 16 November 2017.

action of the government or governmental actors against its citizens[799] and aliens. This doctrine falls into two parts. The first is the law of state accountability for injury to its citizens[800] and aliens,[801] which primarily deals with the disruption of property interests by aliens of foreign states, though this also includes attacks on individual persons in their jurisdiction (including its citizens). The second is the law and custom of war, which acknowledges certain limitations on the conduct of a state in war and is designed to promote some of the fundamental human rights of an individual during wartime.[802]

This concept is related to the principle of 'sovereignty'[803] that for many years has dominated international relations between states. Under current international law, sovereignty 'in the sense of contemporary public international law, denotes the basic international legal status of a state that is not subject, within its territorial jurisdiction, to the governmental, executive, legislative, or judicial jurisdiction of a foreign state or to foreign law other than public international law.'[804] This analysis indicates that it is only the state that is accountable for what happens in its jurisdiction and has a positive obligation to act. This positive obligation extends to the state's responsibility to protect not just its citizens,[805] but all aliens and actors in its jurisdiction. Hence, under the current concept of international law, it is adequate. However, it can be argued that the concept restricts the practical

---

[799]Karl Josef Partsch, 'Individuals in International Law' in Bernhardt R' (1995) Encyclopaedia of Public International Law 957.
Individuals in International Law, 2 Encyclopaedia of Public International Law 957, 962 (1995).

[800]Edith Brown Weiss, 'Invoking State Responsibility in the Twenty-First Century' (2002) 96 (4) American Journal of International Law 798 and Andrea Bianchi, 'Ad-Hocism and The Rule of Law' (2002) 13(1) European Journal of International Law 263.

[801]Cornelius F Murphy Jr, 'State Responsibility for Injuries to Aliens' (1966) 41 New York University Law Review 125.

[802]Myres Smith McDougal, Harold D Lasswell and Lung-chu Chen, *Human Rights and World Public Order: The Basic Policies of an International Law of Human Dignity* (New York Law School Press 1980).

[803]Virginie Guiraudon and Gallya Lahav, 'A Reappraisal of The State Sovereignty Debate: The Case of Migration Control' (2000) 33 (2) Comparative Political Studies 163.

[804]Helmut Steinberger, *Sovereignty* (2000) 4 Encyclopedia of Public International Law 500.

[805]Ramesh Thakur, *The Responsibility to Protect: Norms, Laws, and the Use of Force in International Politics* (London Routledge 2011).

and legal concept of accountability because it neglects the broader notion of accountability which includes non-state actors such as corporations.

It has departed from the 'concerted' approach for access to remedies and legal standards on businesses and human rights. Nevertheless, this does not undermine states' obligations to oversee the conduct of corporations, as they would operate under the international principle of subsidiarity, by which international institutions may exercise jurisdiction in cases where national legal systems are unwilling or unable to fulfil their primary obligation to protect human rights and redress human rights violations. This could enhance domestic efforts to protect human rights through international cooperation and legal coherence, as it would impose common international standards on the problem.[806] Thus, the current international legal framework has rejected the essential mechanism of accountability, which is an effective remedy and a fair and accessible justice system to hold a corporation or individual liable for misconduct.[807] Even though the reason for this deficiency was clear from the beginning of the creation of international law, could it be said that international law did not anticipate future dynamics with respect to the international legal obligations of non-state actors in relation to human rights accountability and environmental damage?

International law consists of the rules and principles of general application which apply to the conduct of states and international organisations, and their relations with one another and private individuals, minority groups, and transnational corporations.[808] Transnational corporations, however, do not have a legal personality under international law. The term 'international legal personalities' refers to the entities or legal persons that have rights and obligations under international law.[809]

A definition of state has the following characteristics: (1) a permanent population; (2) a defined territory; (3) a government; and (4) the capacity to enter relations with other states. The international legal system is a horizontal system dominated by states which are, in principle, considered sovereign and equal. International law is predominately made

[806]Luis Gallegos and Daniel Uribe, 'The Next Step Against Corporate Impunity: A World Court on Business and Human Rights?' (2016) 57 Harvard International Law Journal 7.

[807]Dinah Shelton, *Remedies in International Human Rights Law* (Oxford University Press 2015).

[808]Philip Allott, 'The Concept of International Law' (1999) 10 (1) European Journal of International Law 31.

[809]José E Alvarez, 'Are Corporations "Subjects" of International Law?' (2011) 9 Santa Clara Journal of International Law 1.

and implemented by states. Only states can have sovereignty over territory.[810] Only states can become members of the United Nations and other international organisations. Only states have access to the International Court of Justice.[811] Corporations do not meet the requirements under international law that allow them to acquire legal personality.[812]

This establishes a distinctive legal principle between the domestic legal system and the international legal framework for the liability of wrongful conduct.[813] Thus, international law and domestic law differ in terms of magnitude.[814] Domestic law governs the behaviour and actions of individuals within the state, whereas international law governs the behaviour and actions of bodies of government, including states.[815] National law, which can also be called municipal law, comes from legislature and customs, whereas international law consists of treaties and customs.[816] Legislature is a body of people who are able to make or enact laws. Treaties are formal agreements among and between countries.[817] Customs are practices which are deemed normal for individuals or states.[818] Corporations

---

[810] John Agnew, 'Sovereignty Regimes: Territoriality and State Authority in Contemporary World Politics' (2005) 95 (2) Annals of the Association of American Geographers 437.

[811] Kal Raustiala, 'States, NGOs, and International Environmental Institutions' (1997) 41(1) International Studies Quarterly 719.

[812] Karsten Nowrot, 'Legal Consequences of Globalization: The Status of Non-Governmental Organizations Under International Law' (1999) Indiana Journal of Global Legal Studies 579 and Ancietos Mwansa, 'Barotseland and the Advocacy for Statehood: A Case Entailing the Complexities of Statehood and State Recognition in Public International Law (2017) 11 (11) African Journal of Political Science and International Relations 317, 338. < African Journal of Political Science and International Relations - barotseland and the advocacy for statehood: a case entailing the complexities of statehood and state recognition in public international law (academicjournals.org)> Accessed 18 June 2017

[813] Roland Portmann, *Legal Personality in International Law* (Vol. 70. Cambridge University Press 2010).

[814] Friedrich V Kratochwil, *Rules, Norms, and Decisions: on The Conditions of Practical and Legal Reasoning in International Relations and Domestic Affairs* (Vol. 2. Cambridge University Press 1991).

[815] Ralph G Steinhardt, 'The Role of International Law as a Canon of Domestic Statutory Construction' (1990) 43 Vanderbilt Law Review 1103.

[816] Melvin A Eisenberg, *The Concept of National Law and The Rule of Recognition,* 29 Florida State University Law Review 1229 (2011).

[817] Visar Morina, Fisnik Korenica, and Dren Doli. 'The Relationship Between International Law and National Law in The Case of Kosovo: A Constitutional Perspective' (2011) 9(1) International Journal of Constitutional Law 274.

[818] Sally Engle Merry, 'Legal Pluralism' (1998) 22(5) Law & Society Review 869.

may nonetheless be a subject of national law in domestic courts and may have a legal obligation in domestic courts, though not in international legal settings.

Thus, the view of international law can be said to have resulted in the development of two distinct features of corporate accountability in domestic court and international legal settings: public and private accountability, and remedial mechanisms. The latter is divided into two parts, one related to the enforcement of public law offences and the other related to private law action by affected individuals and communities at the national level.[819] Although domestic legal regimes do not necessarily fall neatly into one or the other grouping, it can be argued that there is some element of accountability at the domestic legal system.

However, the concept of accountability in many domestic jurisdictions is limited[820] and falls short of the notion of accountability even though there are barriers common to both methods of enforcement of human rights accountability.[821] It is possible that there are sufficient differences between the two to warrant the development of a corporate accountability concept that has the ability to sanction and enforce a remedy. The problematic aspect of the concept of the corporate accountability lies in errors related to liability, sanction, enforcement, and the principle of duty of care. The duty of care in relation to corporate accountability is the notion that a parent corporation is liable for a subsidiary's violation of international law; the duty of care not to violate the human rights of the community and the environment.

Traditionally, a duty of care should protect victims of corporate human rights abuses. This is because where there is a particular relationship between the parties, such as parent corporation, supply chain, subsidiary and society, then there may be a duty to act positively[822] for the benefit of the

---

[819] OHCHR Accountability and Remedy Project: Improving Accountability and Access to Remedy in Cases of Business Involvement in Human Rights Abuses, 10 May 2016, A/HRC/32/19 <http://www.ohchr.org/Documents/Issues/Business/DomesticLawRemedies/A_HRC_32_19_AEV.pdf>.

[820] Henry J Steiner, Philip Alston and Ryan Goodman, *International Human Rights in Context: Law, Politics, Morals: Text and Materials* (Oxford University Press USA 2008).

[821] Steven R Ratner, 'Corporations and Human Rights: A Theory of Legal Responsibility' (2001). 111(3) Yale Law Journal 443.

[822] 'Liability for Omissions and Acts of Third Parties. <https://www.sixthformlaw.info/> Accessed 19 September 2016.

community the corporation operates in.[823] Closely connected with the parent corporation liability for the duty of care is the question of liability for the acts of the supply chain and the subsidiary.[824] This will typically arise when the corporation exercises control over the supply chain and subsidiary that committed the human rights violations.

This duty of care is most important in relation to the business activities of the corporation and its subsidiary. This is because corporate bodies, which may include state institutions as well as private corporations, are legal constructs which do not exist in the real physical world.[825] Therefore, if words and actions of a natural person cannot be attributed to a corporation, it is impossible to hold the corporation liable for anything.[826] Therefore, the duty of care is reflected in the maxim *qui facit per alium facit per se* (he who acts through another acts himself).[827] This was acknowledged by the House of Lords in Britain in *Launchbury v Morgan* in 1973,[828] where it was accepted as the true basis of the doctrine of liability for third party conduct.[829] Applying this to international human rights will allow parent corporations to be in physical proximity to the human rights violations and environmental damages caused by its business operation, which will thereby be abolished where there is a close relationship between the victims, the supply chain, the subsidiary, the parent corporation, and the human rights violations. This implied that the court should abandon attaching significance to whether the subsidiary's conduct is closely connected to the parent corporation. Thus, the question should be, does the conduct of the parent corporation and its subsidiary give rise to a duty of care?

If words or acts amount to a tort of negligence, the person to whom they are attributed by virtue of an economic or business relationship is responsible for the other party's conduct. With this view, the liability of the duty of care establishes a solid ground to hold any entity accountable for misconduct. The duty of care being advocated in this book can be seen in the theory of the *respondeat superior* (let the master answer) concept. The

---

[823]Henry W Ballantine, 'Separate Entity of Parent and Subsidiary Corporations' (1925) California Law Review 12.

[824]Maximilian Schiessl, 'The Liability of Corporations and Shareholders for The Capitalization and Obligations of Subsidiaries under German Law' (1986) 7 Northwestern Journal of International Law & Business 480.

[825]*Salomon v Salomon & Company Ltd* [1897] AC 2.

[826]*Marries v Martin* [1966] QB 716 (AC) 733.

[827]Robert Stevens, *Torts and Rights* (OUP Oxford 2007).

[828]See Chapter VIII, for the Application of the General Principle of Law.

[829]Glanville Williams, 'Vicarious Liability: Tort of the Master or of the Servant?' (1956) 72 (522) Law Quarterly Review.

duty of care and *respondeat superior* are legal notions, which can be used together with tort law to hold a corporation accountable for its misconduct. This is because it does not presume what the master must be accountable for, but rather, expresses the master's responsibilities. *Respondeat superior*[830] is used in the US to attribute liability to a legal person,[831] however, such criterion is rejected in the UK where it is used as identification doctrine.[832] The implication of this is that such a principle may not be widely accepted even within common law jurisdictions.

An effective remedy[833] is a fair and accessible judicial system, with a strong mechanism of accountability. The concept of accountability is a key guarantor of the human rights of people through the doctrine of a duty of care, which is the essential element of an effective sanction and remedy for victims whose rights have been violated by either a state or a non-state actor. Similarly, the relationships between accountability, effective sanctions[834] and remedies, which are missing in current international legal accountability of non-state actors, may partly be explained by the process of accountability, which has ignored the concept of a duty of care. Therefore, international law, human rights laws, norms and structures should require states and corporations to answer for their actions to other actors in the international community, which include the ordinary person whose rights have been violated, because it can be said that the corporation is under a duty of care to act in a reasonable and positive way and not to harm anyone who may be in its close proximity.

Consequently, if the duty of care is to be applied to accountability, it would be presumed that this approach would result in an effective accountability system. However, this has not been the case, as the current concept of accountability has resulted in a 'free for all' or excuse for

---

830Refer to Chapter V below for a Detail Explanation of Respondeat Superior.

831Anca Iulia Pop, 'Criminal Liability of Corporations - Comparative Jurisprudence' (2006) Michigan State University College of Law Review.

832Simon Parsons, 'The Doctrine of Identification, Causation and Corporate liability for Manslaughter' (2003) 67(1) Journal of Criminal Law 69, 81.

833General Comment No. 31 - Nature of the General Legal Obligation Imposed on States Parties to the Covenant. <project/humanrightscasesandmaterials/humanrightsconceptsideasandfora/theconceptsofhumanrightsanintroduction/definitionsandclassifications> Accessed 04 May 2016.

834Zachary D Clopton, 'Replacing the Presumption Against Extraterritoriality' (2014) 94 Boston University 1. Also see: <project/humanrightscasesandmaterials/humanrightsconceptsideasandfora/theconceptsofhumanrightsanintroduction/definitionsandclassifications> Accessed 25 May 2017.

vengeance against victims of human rights abuses.[835] In this understanding, the duty of care does indeed establish liability for corporations, and this liability extends to the misconduct of its subsidiaries through its business operations. But it comes with risks. The duty of care being advocated in this book will put the onus of proof in 'violations of human rights claims on corporations because the relevant information (and expertise to understand it) is in the hands of the corporate defendants. If claimants can *prima facie* demonstrate that they have suffered harm'[836] (injury) and that this is likely to have been the result of the corporation's activities (causation), the duty of care will shift the burden of proof to the corporate defendant.

The duty of care through accountability processes should lead to liability and sanctions. If the State or corporation does operate ethically and in accordance with human rights law, then sanctions should be put in place. However, the fundamental questions are: what is defined as duty of care or a reasonable state or corporation in the context of accountability? How does this fit with the concept of accountability?

'The reasonable state or corporation, in law, is compared to a reasonable person, reasonable man, or the man on the *Clapham omnibus,* '[837] which is a hypothetical person of legal fiction who is ultimately an anthropomorphic representation of the body of care standards crafted by the courts and communicated through case law and jury instructions.[838] The reasonable person is the longest established 'group of personalities who inhabit the legal system, which is available to be called upon when a problem arises that needs to be solved objectively,'[839] Thus, the reasonable

[835] Kyle Rex Jacobson, 'Doing Business with the Devil: The Challenges of Prosecuting Corporate Officials Whose Business Transactions Facilitate War Crimes and Crimes Against Humanity' (2005) 56 Air Force Law Review 167 and Joshua P. Eaton, 'Nigerian Tragedy, Environmental Regulation of Transnational Corporations, and The Human Right to a Healthy Environment' (1997) 15 Boston University International Law Journal 261. Amnesty International, 'Creating a paradigm shift: Legal solutions to Improve Access to Remedy for Corporate Cuman Rights Abuse' (2017). <https://justice-project.org/wp-content/uploads/2017/09/ paradigm-shift-ai-2017.pdf> Accessed 30 July 2016.

[836] Steven R Ratner, 'Corporations and Human Rights: a Theory of Legal Responsibility' (2001) 111 (3) *Yale Law Journal* 443, 545.

[837] Cynthia Lee, *Murder and the Reasonable Man: Passion and Fear in the Criminal Courtroom* (NYU Press 2007) and < https://lingualeo.com/pt/jungle/reasonable-person-523800> Accessed 08 April 2018

[838] *Blyth v Birmingham Waterworks Co* (1856) 11 Exch 781, also see *Hall* v *Brooklands Auto Racing Club* (1933) 1 KB 205.

[839] John Gardner, 'The Many Faces of The Reasonable Person' (2015) 131 Law Quarterly Review 563.

man could be the ordinarily prudent man of business,[840] the officious bystander,[841] the reasonable juror properly directed, and the fair-minded and informed observer.[842] All of these colourful characters and many others besides[843] provide important standard setting services to the law. The reasonable man standard is more than just a common law duty of care, but rather, a legal instrument to protect vulnerable citizens. As corporations are part of society, the law is created to protect society. As international law is the manifestation of domestic and customary law, the presumption here is that the reasonable corporation[844] test can also be applied to international law and standards. Both states and corporations should be held accountable if their conduct falls below the reasonable man standard, because the corporation is an entity and is required to act in accordance with the rule of law[845] and the moral principles of the society[846] where the corporation conducts its business operations.

Therefore, if the international legal system and domestic judicial systems are to hold corporations to a specific intent standard for human rights violations, as opposed to a knowledge standard or the reasonable man standard, the bar for corporate accountability for human rights violations in corporate human rights abuses would be substantially high.[847] It is difficult to impute specific intent on corporations for serious human rights abuses; arguably, the primary purpose of corporations is to maintain and increase corporate worth rather than commit human rights abuses. However, the pursuit of profits may lead to complicit behaviour. An example of this is where a government itself has the specific intent to perpetrate the criminal

---

[840]*Speight v Gaunt* (1883) LR 9 App Case 1 at 19, 20.

[841]*Shirlaw v Southern Foundries* [1939] 2 KB 206 at 227.

[842]*Webb v The Queen* (1994) 181 CLR 41.

[843]*Healthcare at Home Ltd v The Common Services Agency* (2014) UKSC 49.

[844]Cynthia Lee, *Murder and the Reasonable Man: Passion and Fear in the Criminal Courtroom* (NYU Press, 2007).

[845]Richard A Cosgrove, *The Rule of Law: Albert Venn Dicey, Victorian Jurist* (University of North Carolina Press 1980); Albert Venn, Dicey, John Humphrey Carlile Morris and Lawrence Antony Collins, *Dicey and Morris on The Conflict of Laws* (Vol. 1. Sweet & Maxwell 2000).

[846] John A Simmons, *Moral Principles and Political Obligations* (Princeton University Press 1981).

[847]David Scheffer and Caroline Kaeb, 'The Five Levels of CSR Compliance: The Resiliency of Corporate Liability under The Alien Tort Statute and The Case for a Counterattack Strategy in Compliance Theory', (2011) 29 Berkeley Journal of International Law 334.

act.[848] A note of caution is due here since criminal intent cannot be attributed to corporate accountability. Thus, if one accepts liability of legal persons before international tribunals and under international law, there remain many details that require further judicial rulings in terms of determining *actus reus* and imputing *mens rea* to the legal person. Questions include: what type of decision-making authority on the part of the individual person is required to attribute responsibility to the entity? Is corporate liability limited to the acts of 'organs' or 'representatives' of the corporation only, or does it extend also to acts of other agents?[849] Can a reasonable man be aggregated across the entire organisation, or do all elements of the human rights violations need to be present in one specific individual natural person in order to attribute responsibility to the entity? What are the appropriate and effective penalties for legal persons as perpetrators of international crimes?

The sanction and remedy in question is of vital significance when holding legal persons accountable for human rights abuses, as legal persons constitute a fiction. Therefore, the court must resort to tort and civil fines as a readily available sanction to levy against corporations because, as legal persons, they cannot be imprisoned or otherwise confined.[850] Sanctions and remedies can prove inadequate in changing corporate behaviour. Given that these analyses are used by corporations and for-profit business organisations, monetary fines could commoditise moral values, which can have perverse consequences.[851] A note of caution is due here in terms of sanctioning legal persons, and business organisations in particular. Corporate accountability is necessary to ensure that the objectives of international human rights law[852] are achieved, particularly in terms of retribution and deterrence. Also, it is questionable whether monetary fines are an appropriate means for punishing corporate involvement in human rights abuses.

If the State fails in its obligation to protect or the corporation fails in its responsibility to respect human rights, it has failed to uphold the

---

[848]Caroline Kaeb, 'The Shifting Sands of Corporate Liability under International Criminal Law' (2016) 49 George Washington International Law Review 351.

[849]In the *Case Against Al-Jadeed S.A.L. & Al Khayat,* STL-14-05/ T/CJ, Judgment, 61 (Special Trib. for Lebanon Sept. 18, 2015.

[850]John C Coffee, 'No Soul to Damn: No Body to Kick: An Unscandalized Inquiry into the Problem of Corporate Punishment' (1981) 79 (3) Michigan Law Review 386.

[851]Uri Gneezy and Aldo Rustichini, 'A Fine is a Price' (2000) 29 (1) Journal of Legal Studies 1.

[852]Rhona Smith, *International Human Rights Law* (Oxford University Press 2018).

actions of a reasonable person. However, in order to arrive at this conclusion, one needs to first establish: who is causing the violation and what are the causes; what accountability arises from failing to meet the reasonable person standard; and to whom must one account to? It should then be established who is responsible for the commission of the violation and who the duty-bearers are in order to assess the context of the violations and how they happened, in addition to determining what can be expected from a court/tribunal and its inherent limitations of the state and corporate duties. The final issue that needs to be established is the extent to which the victims or their representatives face reprisal. The extent to which the corporation complied with the duty of care test of liability and if the acts: (1) were within the scope of the business; (2) were committed or ordered by a superior agent (senior manager or solely owner); and (3) constituted human rights violations for which the punishments included fines and forfeitures of property.

Addressing these questions will result in an actor being identified, establishing who is to blame and what accountabilities arise from this blame. This will assist both international and national judicial bodies to have the authority and ability, in law and practice, to award a range of remedies in human rights law cases arising from business-related human rights abuses. These remedies may include monetary damages[853] and/or non-monetary remedial measures,[854] orders for restitution, aggravated damages,[855] exemplary damages, measures to assist with the rehabilitation of victims and/or resources, satisfaction and public apologies, and guarantees of non-repetition including mandated compliance programmes, education and training, and a criminal prosecution where appropriate.

It is recommended that the concept of accountability[856] should define, interpret, and enforce the formal legal norms and regulatory rules of international human rights.[857] According to this rationale, accountability should consist of a system of governance, meaning the standards, laws and

---

[853]John R Maley, 'Wrongful Adoption: Monetary Damages as a Superior Remedy to Annulment for Adoptive Parents Victimized by Adoption Fraud' (1987) 20 Indiana Law Review 709.

[854]Valerio Colandrea, 'On The Power of The European Court of Human Rights to Order Specific Non-Monetary Measures: Some Remarks in Light of The Assanidze, Broniowski and Sejdovic Cases' (2007) 7(2) Human Rights Law Review 396.

[855]For explanation of Aggravated Damages and Exemplary Damages.

[856]Richard Mulgan, 'Accountability': An Ever-Expanding Concept?' (2000) 78(3) Public Administration 555.

[857]Paul Sieghart, *The International Law of Human Rights* (Oxford University Press 1983).

norms that should be respected by all actors and all individuals and state officials operating in the international arena. Therefore, the notion of accountability should be seen as a legal framework that is capable of providing for the accountability of individuals, communities and other actors, including state and non-state actors, for its conduct. Consequently, accountability should have three essential components that are crucial for an effective enforcement of human rights law and remedy: international human rights law, norms and standards; accountability; and enforceability. This will aid in the establishment of a strong concept of accountability.

In terms of the first component, they should be used to assess the behaviour and performance of states, corporations, private individuals, and corporate officials. They should be based on universal values, such as the concept of human dignity.[858] The component of accountability sets the standard in laws and regulations for corporations. As for the second component – accountability or 'answerability' – different parties (State, corporation, claimant, NGO and witnesses) are called upon to answer and explain allegations of human rights violations. Finally, 'enforcement' means that adjudication should be followed by sanction or remedy where appropriate, i.e. a court or tribunal order that has a deterrent effect and is capable of stopping future human rights violations.

In each of these essential elements of accountability, international law and human rights have the ability to impose liability and award remedies for victims of human rights abuses through the duty of care by examining:

1. whether the corporate response was appropriate to the gravity of the abuse and the extent and nature of the loss and/or harm suffered by the victims;
2. whether it is to the extent permitted by the relevant legal system that reflects the degree of liability of the defendant corporation (for example, it can be demonstrated by whether the company exercised appropriate human rights duty of care, the strength and effectiveness of the company's legal compliance efforts, any history of similar conduct, whether the company responded adequately to warnings and other relevant factors);

---

[858]Jürgen Habermas, 'The Concept of Human Dignity and The Realistic Utopia of Human Rights' (2010) 41(4) Metaphilosophy 464. UN General Assembly, Universal Declaration of Human Rights, 10 December 1948, 217 A (III) <http://www.refworld.org/docid/3ae6b3712c.html > Accessed on 28 June 2016.

3. whether the concept of corporate accountability is designed in such a way as to minimise the risks of repetition or continuation of the harm; and
4. whether the corporation took account of issues of human rights duties and the needs of individuals or groups at risk of human rights abuses or vulnerable to environmental damage.

Evaluating accountability via the duty of care will allow effective control and punishment that give rise to assigning responsibility, sanctions, and remedies, which ensure control over a corporation's activities that have impacted on human rights. In turn, a duty of care will ensure that the corporation maintains openness and dialogue with victims of human rights abuses, while creating trust, affirming basic human rights standards and ethical standards, and improving corporate adherence to international standards. Therefore, the notion of accountability and criminal accountability under international law should be examined together with the doctrine of duty of care in order to propose a concept of corporate accountability that is based on tort and civil law principles of duty of care and duty bearer. This will ensure that national bodies and judicial bodies and/or relevant state agencies monitor corporate behaviour, implementation of international human rights law and duties, and effective remedies in an appropriate manner.

This will further ensure that there exists an effective mechanism by which interested persons can report and/or raise a complaint and/or seek remedial action with respect to any non-implementation of such remedies. This structured approach will act as guidance, based on a series of accountability and legal objectives, and the elements to demonstrate its flexibility in addition to the different ways in which corporate accountability for human rights can be achieved at both the domestic and international level. There are many differences among jurisdictions in terms of legal structures, cultures, traditions and resources, all of which have implications for corporate accountability.[859] However, approaching the question of what is accountability in this way will allow the development of a universal principle of corporate duty of care, which is based on the General Principle of Law.[860] This would allow global application of the concept of duty of care and the liability of the corporation, as well as developing a practical and legal approach to remedial action across a range of different legal

[859]Lauren Benton, *Law and Colonial Cultures: Legal Regimes in World History, 1400-1900* (Cambridge University Press 2002).

[860] Marcelo Kohen and Bérénice Schramm, *General Principles of Law* (Oxford University Press 2013).

systems and contexts, while at the same time adopting and reflecting international law, international human rights law and its concept of accountability.

Lastly, this approach resolves the deficiencies of accountability which, in many cases, are rooted in wider social, economic, and legal challenges in holding corporations accountable for human rights abuses. The suggested accountability in this book in relation to tort law can work together with international law and human rights law. 'However, some recommendations could be implemented on their own and still represent significant progress, such as a duty of care established by law and the automatic liability of a parent company. This can also operate alongside a direct' [861] regulatory action by the state and would help reinforce compliance. Similarly, international law and human rights law implemented in relation to recommendations dealing with private claims under tort/non-contractual liability law should be observed by both domestic and international courts. It links accountability to: sanctions and enforcement actions related to human rights abuses by corporations; legal developments; and improvements in the functioning of judicial mechanisms. The duty of care allows the legal system to establish a practical law enforcement mechanism for corporate liability at both the domestic and international level, which has the ability to connect corporate activities closely to international human rights obligations, and specifically to the concept of human dignity. Analysing this essential ingredient of accountability will also allow victims of human rights abuses access to justice and remedy for business-related human rights abuses.

Definition of the Concept of Accountability

Although the extensive definition of accountability has been highlighted and is partly explained in the sections above, this chapter will revisit this concept and adopt a twofold approach to accountability. The first definition of accountability is the common meaning found in the Oxford Advanced Learner's Dictionary: 'The fact or condition of being accountable; responsibility.' [862] This definition is limited; it means the duty of a corporation or corporate official to account for their undertakings and accept

---

[861] Amnesty International, 'Creating a paradigm shift: Legal Solutions to Improve Access to Remedy for Corporate Human Rights Abuse' (2017). <https://www.amnesty.org/download/Documents/POL3070372017ENGLISH.PDF> Accessed 09 March 2018.

[862] Albert Sydney Hornby and Sally Wehmeier, *Oxford Advanced Learner's Dictionary* (Vol. 1428 Oxford University Press 1995).

responsibility for their actions, as well as justifying their actions in an appropriate, fair, and honest manner in a business context without expecting other actors to be accountable. Accountability has also expanded beyond the basic definition which does not take into consideration other elements. Moreover, accountability cannot exist without vigorous mechanisms and procedures.[863] In other words, a lack of accountability means an absence of responsibility. Furthermore, the notion of accountability should be followed by responsibility, effective sanctions, and a remedy that leads to deterrence,[864] whereby the abuser could face a tribunal, court, or authorised judicial body. Also, the concept of accountability should result in effective reparations for the victims.[865]

The common definition of accountability cannot be because it does not: (1) communicate clearly the different modes and degrees of contribution to the harms perpetrated by the corporation and the subsidiary that will give rise to subordinate legal liability; and (2) take into account the extent to which the principles for assessing subsidiary liability are applicable to corporations. Moreover, it does not give clear principles to attribute knowledge, intentions, actions, and omissions to the corporation for the purposes of assessing corporate legal liability on the basis of theories of subordinate liability. It similarly does not treat causes of action based on subordinate liability as distinct causes of action both conceptually and procedurally separate from any wrongdoing committed by the primary corporation. Such third-party liability is not present in the definition of accountability or in any judicial finding of liability on the part of the primary offender.

Brooks provides the following definition of traditional accountability within Western organisations: 'Accountability is a mechanism to ensure that individuals can be called to account for their actions and that sanctions are incurred if the account is unsatisfactory.' [866] Brooks stresses that the traditional definition shows accountability as a procedural activity because

---

[863]Andreas Schedler, *The Self-Restraining Rate: Power and Accountability in New Democracies* (Lynne Rienner Publishers 1999).

[864]Sylvia Rich, 'Corporate Criminals and Punishment Theory' (2016) 29 Can JL & Jurisprudence 97.

[865]UN General Assembly, *Basic Principles and Guidelines on the Right to a Remedy and Reparation for Victims of Gross Violations of International Human Rights Law and Serious Violations of International Humanitarian Law: resolution / adopted by the General Assembly*, 21 March 2006, A/RES/60/147. <http://www.refworld.org/docid/4721cb942.html > Accessed 19 May 2016.

[866]Theo Brooks, *Accountability: It All Depends on What You Mean* (Akkad Press 1995).

the individual activity focuses on individuals, while also acknowledging that the collective characteristic of the term is that it is reasonable and essential, and that sanctions are the core element of accountability. Therefore, accountability should bring in the personal element of holding offenders to account. The author further argues that 'the purpose of sanctions is not to act as a threat to you but as a guarantee of protection to the individual.'[867] It is therefore imperative for accountability to have an element of deterrence and sanction; without this, accountability for misconduct is incomplete. Shotter contributes to the debate by stating that 'accountability is seen as a way of accounting for things that have a coercive quality to them'. Therefore, if one makes sense of things in certain permitted rules and regulations then it can be said that a person is to be accounted by others in the society as a capable, responsible member of the community.[868]

Following both authors' definitions, accountability should give rise to effective measures by the corporation to identify, prevent, and mitigate the adverse human rights impacts of their activities on individuals and society. Both authors also indicate that a corporation should take appropriate account of effective measures to supervise their officers and employees to prevent and mitigate adverse human rights impacts. Therefore, accountability should ensure the appropriate use of strict or absolute liability as a means of encouraging greater levels of vigilance in relation to business activities that carry particularly high risks of severe human rights impacts because the corporation has a duty of care to the society and the environment. In this respect, accountability should allow the international legal system, domestic courts, or international tribunals/courts to have access to and take proper account of robust, credible and, where appropriate, sector-specific liability as to the technical requirements of human rights accountability in different business operating contexts.

Consequently, accountability in this context will allow the distribution of evidential burdens of proof between the victims of human rights abuses and the defendants. Therefore, the concept of corporate accountability under this definition is contingent, in law and in practice, upon a prior finding of corporate legal liability under any legal regime (for example, finding corporate criminal liability or its functional equivalent). In contrast, the affected victims of human rights can be prevented, in law and in practice, from bringing an action against the corporation because of the existing deficiencies in both international law and domestic law. *Kiobel* is an example

---

[867] *Ibid.*

[868] John Shotter, 'Social Accountability and Selfhood' (1984) <http://philpapers.org/rec/SHOSAA> Accessed 04 April 2018.

of the deficiencies in accountability at the domestic and international level.[869] Additionally, these deficiencies in corporate accountability cannot be justified because a corporation can be involved in human rights abuses in many different ways. This includes the adverse impacts that business operations may cause or contribute through their activities or by virtue of their business relationships.[870] Therefore, the relationships mentioned above create an obligation to account to the government, judiciary, and society. This theoretical concept of accountability will ensure the legal accountability of business operations, and access to effective remedy for victims affected by such abuses is a vital part of a state's duty to protect against business-related human rights abuse.[871]

Scott and Lyman also took part in the debate by arguing that 'account is a linguistic device employed whenever an action is subjected to evaluative inquiry.'[872] The point they are making is that 'an account is not called for when people engage in routine, common-sense behaviour in a cultural environment that recognises that behaviour as such.'[873] The authors' understanding of accountability is that it is a concept that regulates the misconduct of individuals in society and organisations but is not mere guidelines. Therefore, 'evaluative inquiry' is not an essential element of accountability. This implies that accountability only happens after a breach of rule or misconduct behaviour indicates a punitive position.[874] Hence, the authors' views refer to a constructive disobedience or nonconformity to accountability as a separate conduct that is not acceptable in an organisation or society. Additionally, Scott and Lyman took into consideration the broader concept of accountability. The authors argued that the concept of accountability and evaluation was a process that happens after something has gone wrong. If one conducts a detailed analysis of accountability in this

[869]David P Stewart and Ingrid Wuerth, 'Kiobel v. Royal Dutch Petroleum Co.: The Supreme Court and the Alien Tort Statute' (2013) 107 (3) American Journal of International Law 601, 621 (2013).

[870]Jennifer Zerk, 'Corporate Liability for Gross Human Rights Abuses: Towards a Fairer and More Effective System of Domestic Law Remedies' (2013) 103.

[871]The Principle 25 and Commentary of The Guiding Principles on Business and Human Rights: Implementing the United Nations 'Protect, Respect and Remedy' Framework (A/HRC/17/31).

[872]Marvin B Scott and Stanford M. Lyman, 'Accounts' (1968) 33 (1) American Sociological Review 46.

[873]*Ibid.*

[874]Klaus J Beucher and John Byron Sandage, 'United States Punitive Damage Awards in German Courts: The Evolving German Position on Service and Enforcement' (1990-1991) 23 Vanderbilt Journal of Transnational Law 967. Also see, *Exxon Shipping Co. v Baker*, 554 US 471, (2008).

manner, the potential conclusion could be that accountability does create sanctions and enforcement, and so creates an implicit and/or explicit constraint on virtually everything that is done in society; a corporation should not be exempted from these rules.

As a critical observation, viewing accountability as an implicit and/or explicit constraint on either the individual or actor in society will address challenges that are exacerbated in cross-border corporate human rights violations cases, such as *Chiquita*,[875] *Lundin Petroleum*,[876] and *French Cement Company*.[877] It will also aid many domestic legal regimes to focus primarily on the enforcement of human rights obligations on business activities in the host state that may have a significant impact on society and the environment. The realities of global supply chains, cross-border trade, investment, communications, and movement of people are placing new demands on domestic legal regimes and those responsible for enforcing them. Therefore, examining corporate accountability for human rights abuses this way will help to clarify the process of accountability and the theoretical and practical mechanism to employ to achieve an effective remedy in an alternate forum, such as a court. These are positive legal measures that, if implemented and applied, will improve accountability and redress for corporate human rights violations.

Goffman's study on accountability pays particular attention to the frames of accounts. According to Goffman's frames, the concept can be understood as a specific form of accountability and liability in the context in which the act occurs; this conduct provides the basis for making an action sensible and meaningful.[878] Hence, an account (frame) can be a motivation/justification for action that makes it part of how people conduct themselves in society. Therefore, it is clear here that the purpose of the concept of accountability is to have a sanction, remedy, and enforcement element. However, the question is the extent to which the scope of legal accountability or determining corporate legal liability enforces human rights remedies on an actor? Another question is whether accountability responds adequately to the challenges of investigation and enforcement of

---

[875]Marco Were, 'Implementing Corporate Responsibility the Chiquita *Cas*e' (2003) 44 (2) Journal of Business Ethics 247, 260.

[876]Jennifer C Leary, 'Talisman's Sudanese Oil Investment: The Historical Context Surrounding Its Entry, Departure, and Controversial Tenure Diss' (2007).

[877] Nadia Bernaz, 'Criminal Complaint Against French Cement Company for Terrorism Financing, Complicity of Crimes against Humanity and War Crimes in Syria' (2016).

[878]Erving Goffman, *Frame Analysis: An Essay on the Organization of Experience* (Harvard University Press 1974).

human rights and environmental damages in international human rights cases.[879] It is also important to determine whether the judicial regimes provide the necessary coverage and the appropriate range of approaches with respect to business-related human rights impacts in the light of evolving circumstances and state obligations under international human rights treaties to which the country in question is a member. These questions allow one to examine the essential elements of accountability, which include state, judiciary, society, and corporate obligations.

The concept of accountability should be broad enough to incorporate liability, control, justification, sanction and legal remedy, whether criminal or civil. Likewise, accountability sanctions and remedies should arise directly from the relationship between the corporation and the society and environment where it operates. Hence, giving an appropriate definition to accountability will enable a tribunal or court to create a measure of remedy. Therefore, to establish accountability for corporations, there is a need to move this theoretical foundation of accountability to a broader legal framework that supports liability and remedy. The notion of accountability should aid in understanding corporate accountability but not the method of enforcement. The idea is that it will allow sanctions and other remedies to be ordered following a finding of corporate legal liability for human rights violations.

In this context, corporate accountability will acknowledge corporate duty and the possibility of corporate legal liability for human rights violations. This book does not dispute that there are differences from jurisdiction to jurisdiction in the kinds of violations for which a corporation can be liable and the types of legal liability that a corporation can attract, the legal concept of accountability, as well as administrative liability. In some jurisdictions such as the UK, [880] accountability may attach to individuals as natural persons. Therefore, the concept of accountability here is that it will make it possible for other kinds of public law regime liability and sanctions (such as regulatory, administrative or quasi-criminal) to play a vital role in holding corporations accountable for human rights abuses committed, either in a home or host state. For these reasons, the study is not confined to the common definition of accountability but encompasses a

[879]Stéphanie Lagoutte, 'New Challenges Facing States within the Field of Human Rights and Business' (2015) 33 (2) Nordic Journal of Human Rights 158.

[880]Stephen Griffin and Jon Moran, 'Accountability for Deaths Attributable to the Gross Negligent Act or Omission of a Police Force: The Impact of the Corporate Manslaughter and Corporate Homicide Act 2007' (2010) 74 (4) Journal of Criminal Law 358, 381.

variety of definitions of accountability applicable to the corporation, including regulatory, administrative and quasi-criminal liability.

Legal Definition of Accountability

Jowitt's Dictionary of English Law defines accountability as:

> (1) The condition of being answerable in law, or actually or potentially subject to a civil obligation, either generally, as including every kind of obligation, or, in a more special sense, to denote inchoate, future, unascertained or imperfect obligations, as opposed to debts, the essence of which is that they are ascertained and certain. Thus, when a person becomes surety for another, he makes himself liable, though it is unascertained in what obligation or debt the liability may ultimately result. The term can also mean the condition of being actually or potentially subject to a criminal sanction.
> (2) The obligation itself for judicial and statutory definitions and constructions in different contexts.[881]

Yarwood states that accountability means 'under international law: holding states accountable for a breach of *jus cogens* norms.'[882] *Black's Law Dictionary* gives the definition as: 'the state of being bound or obliged in law or justice to do, pay, or make good something; legal responsibility'.[883]

The *Black's Law* and Yarwood definitions of accountability relate directly to state accountability under public international law,[884] which is perfectly adequate because states and corporations have different levels and standards of accountability. Both can be adopted and applied to the accountability of corporations under private law.[885] However, accountability of states and corporations are different and corporations have no legal personality under international law.[886] Therefore, international human rights law cannot be enforced against corporations though it does have the ability to be enforced against states. Due to this, there is no international

[881] William Allen Jowitt, Clifford Walsh and John McDonald Burke, *Jowitt's Dictionary of English Law* (Vol. 1. Sweet & Maxwell 1977).
[882] Lisa Yarwood, *State Accountability under International Law: Holding States Accountable for a Breach of Jus Cogens Norms* (Routledge 2010).
[883] Henry Campbell, *Black's Law Dictionary* (St Paul Minn: West Publishing Co 1990).
[884] Alina Kaczorowska-Ireland, *Public International Law* (Routledge 2015).
[885] Martin Wolff, *Private International Law* (Clarendon Press 1950).
[886] John Dewey, 'The Historic Background of Corporate Legal Personality' (1926) 35 (6) Yale Law Journal 655, 673.

legal accountability mechanism for holding corporations either criminally or civilly liable for human rights abuses.

These definitions undoubtedly give an adequate explanation of the concept of accountability and how this can be applied in legal terms, but the question remains on how to apply this concept to non-state actors such as corporations. They are broad enough, include sanctions and remedies, and satisfy the constructive elements of state accountability. So, the indication is to apply this concept to corporate liability under international human rights law. This study, therefore, supports this definition of a strict and broad legal standard concept of finding a duty of care in a corporation's business activities.

Accountability exists when a relationship can be established between a corporation through its relationship with the government, society and the international community; this relationship establishes accountability links between society, the environment, and corporate conduct as well as with the subsidiary through business activities and economic transactions. This can be observed through the corporate control of the business operations. This control establishes the link to a prohibited conduct of the corporations and government of host nations. Making controlling businesses subject to a legal claim for alleged abuses by a subsidiary or automatically liable for 'proven' abuses by a subsidiary, regardless of their fault, is justified in these circumstances because it can be said that accountability exists. Lastly, the operation of the corporations is subject to corporate official oversight, and direction. In contrast, the problematic aspect of this approach is the relationship between the corporations and corporate misconduct, either through the subsidiary or the host government. This is because a parent company (in one country) and subsidiary (operating in another country) are treated as having separate legal personalities which has contributed to the obstacle of holding corporations accountable for human rights.[887]

Addressing these questions will allow the international legal systems and domestic judiciaries to ensure corporate human rights accountability and the fundamental human rights problem that is connected to their business operations to be dealt with. The basic element of human rights accountability is the existence of effective sanctions and remedies for victims of human rights abuses. It can also be argued that accountability covers the relationship between corporate responsibility and duty of care. This is a direct obligation of duty of care on the corporation and its

[887] Beth Stephens, 'Amorality of Profit: Transnational Corporations and Human Rights' (2002) 20 Berkeley Journal of International Law 45.

subsidiary. As a result of this duty of care, tort and civil liability should arise when a corporation violates human rights.

Establishing corporate legal liability in this theoretical concept of tort and civil law approach will ensure the requisite standard of proof that all elements of corporate human rights violations are satisfied. Human rights violations that include a criminal element, are likely to involve both mental and physical elements. The mental elements refer to the knowledge and intentions of the alleged offender. The physical elements refer to the offender's acts and whether they were the cause of the relevant harm. Taking this position is crucial because the corporation is a legal construction so the application of tests for establishing liability for human rights offences can be problematic in many jurisdictions. This is a particular problem in relation to human rights accountability in criminal law which requires proof that the corporation intended the harm or intended to commit the acts that caused the harm.

Consequently, the duty of care as a legal concept of accountability could aid in proving corporate intent and the identification of individuals working for or on behalf of the relevant corporation. This is referred to as the 'fault-finding' approach to corporate accountability. In addition, the principle of duty of care is widely applied as a standard for assessing tort liability,[888] whereby corporations may be liable for the acts of certain employees. On the basis that the corporation acts through those individuals or agents, this could play a vital role in establishing liability for a subsidiary act. While the tests for corporate liability vary from jurisdiction to jurisdiction, common limitations on this type of liability are that the corporate subsidiary must have been operating within the scope of its business responsibilities and/or for the benefit of the corporation.[889] However, this can be rebutted in the process of liability finding for corporate accountability in the concept of tort and civil law.

The notion of accountability has two distinct elements: liability and enforcement.[890] Liability refers to the duty of corporations and corporate officials to be held accountable for corporate misconduct that is closely linked to their business operations which may cause harm to society

---

[888] *Lister v Hesley Hall Ltd* [2001] UKHL 22. Also see; *Barker v Corus* (UK) plc [2006] UKHL 20, *Brazier v Dolphin Fairway Ltd* [2005] EWCA Civ 1469, Patrick Selim Atiyah, *Vicarious Liability in the Law of Torts* (Butterworths 1967).

[889] Ji Ma, 'Multinational Enterprises Liability for the Acts of Their Offshore Subsidiaries: The Aftermath of Kiobel and Daimler' (2015) 23 Michigan State International Law Review 397.

[890] Dennis Arroyo and Karen Sirker, 'Stocktaking of Social Accountability Initiatives in the Asia and Pacific Region' (2005) World Bank Institute Working Papers.

or the environment. The principle of the duty of care through tort and civil law can be seen as a legal doctrine that will aid in resolving the difficulties surrounding corporate accountability and the silence of international law on corporate liability for human rights abuses.[891] Enforcement refers to an official body, domestic court, tribunal/arbitration, international court or judiciary that can sanction a business entity that violates human rights or causes harm to society, livelihoods, and the environment. This sanction should give rise to an effective remedy, which under an accepted legal principle of accountability, should satisfy the 'eggshell skull rule'. The eggshell skull rule or eggshell plaintiff rule states that someone 'who harms another must pay for whatever damage the injured person suffered, even if it was much worse than anyone would have expected'.[892] Hence, evaluating the conduct of the corporation and imposing liability in such a manner will ensure accountability, enhance good business practice, protect the environment, and protect and prevent human rights violations in the short and long term. Furthermore, the indication behind this is that accountability is classified according to the type of accountability being exercised[893] by the corporations and corporate officials to give a justification to their actions.

The underlying question behind this approach is will the victims have suffered the harm caused if a corporation misconducts itself? By this principle, the defendant's conduct contributed to the result if and only if it was a necessary element in a set of conditions jointly sufficient to produce the harm caused,[894] also known in tort law by the acronym, the NESS[895] (Necessary Element of a Sufficient Set) test.[896] How does the test apply to corporations and the misconduct of their subsidiaries? If one replaces the careless conduct of one corporation with the conduct of the subsidiary then it is possible to say accountability might exist through the relationship. This means that certain business relationships might give rise to accountability/a duty of care.

---

[891]'Development in The Law Corporate Liability for Violations of International Human Rights Law' (2001) 114 Harvard Law Review 2025, 2030, 31.

[892]Stanley J McQuade, 'Eggshell Skull Rule and Related Problems in Recovery for Mental Harm in The Law of Torts' (2001) 24 Campbell Law Review 1.

[893]Ewan Ferlie, Laurence E. Lynn and Christopher Pollitt, *The Oxford Handbook of Public Management* (Oxford University Press USA 2005).

[894]Herbert Lionel Adolphus Hart and Tony Honoré, *Causation in the Law* (OUP Oxford 1985).

[895]Euan West, 'The Utility of the NESS Test of Factual Causation in Scots Law' (2013) 4 Aberdeen Student Law Review 39.

[896]Robert Stevens, *Torts and Rights* (OUP Oxford 2007) 140,144.

It is very difficult to think of anything in the physical world that alone is a sufficient cause of anything else, save perhaps God or the Big Bang Theory.[897] Once this includes things which are absent in the sufficient set, finding liability for corporate human rights abuses becomes obvious. An almost infinite number of things need to be absent for something else to occur. When describing something as sufficient to cause a consequence, it is sufficient with respect to the circumstances occurring at the time and/or in combination with a number of elements, to cause harm. A reputable presumption presumes: *but for* the corporation's business operations with the supply chain or subsidiary, the harm would not have occurred. The conceptual application of this theory of accountability follows the term 'behavioural approach'. (Behaviourism, also known as behavioural psychology, is a theory of learning based on the idea that all behaviours are acquired through conditioning. Conditioning occurs through interaction with the environment. Behaviourists believe that our responses to environmental stimuli shape our actions.) [898] The term 'behavioural approach' implies that people are motivated and shaped by forces external to themselves. As Gibson points out, 'in the presence of some external factors, individuals may not actively reason at all, but work according to habit, or obedience without a thought.'[899]

Applying behavioural approach to the concept of corporate accountability means that corporations and corporate officials that have a systematic knowledge of business operations have the potential to benefit or have a negative impact on the economic performance of the business because they work according to the business objectives of the corporations and are responsible for the corporation's misconduct through their decision-making. In the ordinary and legal interpretation, corporate officials, such as senior managers and directors, are the brain of the corporation and have control over what the corporation does; this makes them accountable for human rights violations through vicarious liability. In addition to the brain of the company, a corporation is accountable for the subsidiary conduct if that conduct is motivated at least in part by a desire to serve the corporation, but this need not be the sole motivation.[900] If the supply chain or subsidiary acted with intent to benefit the corporation in some way, the act is imputed

---

[897]John J Mackie, *The Cement of The Universe: A Study of Causation Clarendon* (Oxford Press 1974).

[898]Albert Bandura, 'Behavior Theory and the Models of Man' (1974) 29 (12) American Psychologist 859.

[899]Kevin Gibson, 'Excuses, Excuses: Moral Slippage in the Workplace' (2000) 43 (3) Business Horizons 65.

[900]*United States v Gold*, 743 F.2d 800, 813-14 (11th Cir. 1984).

to the principal of whether the corporation benefitted or not, or even if the result adversely affected the corporation`s interest.[901]

Accordingly, a corporation has the capacity and freedom to self-regulate decisions.[902] They are also capable of choosing their operational standards,[903] the business direction of the corporation, decision-making, and economic adjustments of the corporation's business with the supply chain and subsidiaries.[904] Looking at the notion of accountability as a behavioural approach will bridge the gap between the concept of international legal personality in the traditional view and the orthodox theory that stresses the position and capacity of the state as the sole bearer of international legal duties. Bridging the gap between corporate international legal personality and the duty of care will enable the judicial system to enforce human rights standards on all individuals, actors, and business organisations under international law through their domestic legal system or an alternate legal mechanism.

The corporation officials' ability to choose the process, the standards of business operations, the corporation's decision-making, the ability to control the business conduct and to demand operational information allow corporations and their officials to meet the legal definition of accountability and duty of care for liability for corporate misconduct. As Dobbs states, 'a duty of care refers to the circumstances and relationships which the law recognises as giving rise to a legal duty to take care. A failure to take such care can result in the defendant being liable to pay damages to a party who is injured or suffers loss as a result of their breach of the duty of care.'[905]

However, the key point of finding liability for corporate human rights violations depends on the corporation's ability to show that it complies with human rights law and standards. Merely having standards of conduct that prohibit human rights violations and environmental damages

---

[901] *Standard Oil Company of Texas v United States*, 307 F.2d 120 (5th Cir. 1962).

[902] Christine Parker, *The Open Corporation: Effective Self-Regulation and Democracy* (Cambridge University Press 2002).

[903] Pratima Bansal, 'The Corporate Challenges of Sustainable Development' (2002) 16 (2) Academy of Management Executive 122 <http://amp.aom.org/content/16/2/122.short> Accessed 6 July 2016.

[904] Richard Locke, Thomas Kochan, Monica Romis and Fei Qin, 'Beyond Corporate Codes of Conduct: Work Organization and Labour Standards at Nike's Suppliers' (2007) 146 (1) International Labour Review 21. <http://onlinelibrary.wiley.com/doi/10.1111/j.1564-913X.2007.00003.x/abstract> Accessed 15 July 2016.

[905] Dan B Dobbs, *The Law of Torts* (Vol. 2. West Group 2001).

is not good enough. A possible key for an effective adherence to human rights law and standards could include:

- A duty of care to detect and prevent human rights violations and environmental damages, or the promotion of an organisational culture that creates and enforces human rights standards in business operations that encourage ethical conduct and comply with the law.
- Oversight of the compliance standards by senior management.
- Responsible business practice and delegation.
- Adequate investigation of complaints and remediation of deficiencies, including self-disclosure and consistently applied discipline when appropriate.
- A robust monitoring and auditing process that sufficiently addresses the key areas for the corporation.

Examining accountability in this way helps to link the theoretical framework suggested in this book, to the Black Law, Yarwood and Anglo-Saxon concepts of liability, which involve an element of responsibility, effective sanctions and remedial actions.[906] Therefore, it is established here that the outline in this book will allow both the domestic and the international legal systems to hold corporations to account for business decisions that have rippling effects through affiliate business activities. Accountability for subsidiaries should arise in situations when such corporate decisions do not exist, but the parent companies are still connected to the subsidiary company that violated human rights. This is a fault-finding element of liability that establishes a corporate duty of care by differentiating the parent corporation's behaviour from the impact of its decision on the subsidiary's business operations and the influence it has on the supply chain or subsidiary by directly or indirectly controlling the business operation. The Court of Appeal in the UK addressed this issue with regard to the enforceability of a foreign judgment in England in *Adams v Cape Industries PLC.*[907] In this case, the subsidiary company Cape Industries PLC in South Africa employed the claimants. The complaint related to health hazards caused to the employees by asbestos. The complaint was filed against the parent company for personal injury.

---

906 Albert Jacob Meijer, *De Doorzichtige Overheid: Parlementaire en Juridische Controle in Het Informatietijdperk* (Eburon 2002).
907 *Adams v Cape Industries plc* [1990] Ch 43.

It is well established in tort law that companies are liable for torts committed by their employees during the scope of employment. While a company will not be liable for the acts of its subsidiary solely as a result of its ownership and shareholding, a company may be vicariously 'liable for its employees. In these circumstances, the court does not pierce the corporate veil ('Piercing the corporate veil' refers to a situation in which courts put aside limited liability and hold a corporation's shareholders or directors personally liable for the corporation's actions or debts.'[908] Veil piercing is most common in close corporations)[909] but instead identifies a free-standing duty of care owed by the parent company to the claimant arising out of the relationship between the parent and subsidiary.[910]

However, for a free-standing duty of care to be owed, the question that the court needs to ask is whether the corporate entity had proper systems and controls to prevent the human rights violation from occurring. Such systems and controls can operate to: (i) show there was no intent to commit the human rights violations on the part of a corporation; (ii) provide a defence; (iii) be a mitigating factor upon finding liability; or (iv) impact on decisions of the court and on penalties imposed if the corporation is found liable. There has been a recent raft of English case law which explores whether a wronged party can pursue a parent company for the actions of its subsidiary in tort; a tool used by some to their advantage where the parent company is located in a more favourable jurisdiction. [911]

The principle of accountability illustrates that even if the corporation's misconduct is that of the subsidiary's actions, the corporation should be responsible for its decision for conducting business with the subsidiary. When the corporation has the requisite knowledge of a potential human rights violation by the subsidiary through their business operation a duty of care can be established. This is also the case if the liability of the corporation or the words spoken to someone else is an impermissible fiction. It is no less of a fiction in the case of control and the exercise of influence over business operations in the host state.

---

[908] Daniel Uribe Terán, 'The Core Elements of a Legally Binding Instrument: Highlights of the Revised Draft of the Legally Binding Instrument on Business and Human Rights (2018). <https://www.southcentre.int/wp-content/uploads/2020/07/Designing-an-International-Legally-Binding-Instrument-on-Business-and-Human-Rights-REV.pdf> Accessed 17 March 2019.

[909] Robert BThompson, 'Piercing the Corporate Veil: An Empirical Study' (1990) 76 Cornell Law Review 1036.

[910] See Chapter VII.

[911] See Chapter VII. *Chandler v Cape* [2012] EWCA 525.

Finally, the concept of accountability can take the form of a single person's conduct outside of the rules imposing liability on the whole corporation.[912] Also, if the words or actions of another person are attributed to the defendant, and those actions infringe the claimant's rights, then the defendant will be liable. The principle of corporate accountability is like a game of football; it has rules which determine a player's accountability. The principle of corporate liability presupposes that what is being imputed is the responsibility for the wrongdoer and not the act itself. Therefore, the corporation must take responsibility for the action of its subsidiary against the rest of the world but not against the corporation itself. To put it another way, the position between the parties as to their relationship is not determined by the position of third parties to the relationship. The concept of accountability indicates that it does not matter whether it is the action of the corporation, supply chain, subsidiary or the liability which is attributed to the human rights violation and the environmental damage. The parent corporation should not be exempt from accountability just because its action does not touch and concern the home state.

Where there is a human rights violation or environmental damage as a result of the corporation or corporate misconduct, liability should be found according to the principle of accountability. If A's actions infringe B's right by carelessly injuring B, for example, and if A's actions are inputted to C, C and A are both tortfeasors. The attribution of A's acts to C means that C has control over or contributed to the infringement of B's rights. This means that the corporation could be held liable for the actions of the subsidiary or the corporate official that it has control over. Thus, the corporation is guilty of infringing the rights of the claimant. A and C become joint tortfeasors.

The duty of care enables accountability of corporate misconduct. It also helps to prevent individuals solely being held liable while the corporate entity escapes liability and continues its misconduct. The level of sanction and remedy contemplated under the duty of care could severely affect the continued operation and profitability of corporate entities. However, it is hard to determine whether the duty of care will prove to be an effective deterrent to human rights violations. Thus, the following chapter will analyse the definition of accountability, the mechanism of accountability, and its components.

---

[912]Dalia Palombo, 'Chandler v. Cape: An Alternative to Piercing the Corporate Veil Beyond Kiobel v. Royal Dutch Shell' (2015) 4 British Journal of American Legal Studies 453.

CHAPTER III

Following the analysis and definition of accountability, and the mechanism of accountability, it is now vital to extricate its components. This will allow for a better understanding of the practical concept of accountability (responsibility, answerability, blameworthiness, liability and sanctions). The aims and objectives of this chapter are to examine the key elements that are required for establishing accountability for non-state actors. A diagram will then be used to explain the components of the various forms of accountability and how accountability creates a legal duty of care for non-state actors, such as corporations.

Components of Accountability (The Link to Establish a Duty of Care)

Koppell perceives five different dimensions of accountability: transparency, liability, controllability, responsibility and responsiveness. Each of these factors forms the practical concepts of accountability in this book.[913] What is clear from the explanation by Koppell is that accountability is indeed an inclusive concept and includes different branches. In order to establish accountability and effective remedy, all the branches must be addressed. As explained above, the concept of accountability has provided some indication of this notion. However, such an explanation makes it difficult to establish empirically whether a corporation or corporate officials can be subject to accountability for a corporation's misconduct in relation to business operations under international law. This is because the different elements of accountability need widespread operationalisation to establish liability for the corporation's misconduct. After all, the different fundamentals of accountability cannot be measured along the same scale. For example, transparency may not carry the same effect as liability for human rights violations. Likewise, the difference between a corporation and its officials

[913]Jonathan GS Koppell, 'Pathologies of Accountability: ICANN and The Challenge of Multiple Accountabilities Disorder' (2005) 65 (1) Public Administration Review 94. <http://onlinelibrary.wiley.com/doi/10.1111/j.1540-6210.2005.00434.x/abstract> Accessed 3 July 2016.

makes it difficult to pinpoint the level of liability of either the corporation's or the official's misconduct in the course of the business operation.

Some dimensions, such as transparency,[914] are mechanisms for accountability but not indicative of it; others, such as responsiveness, are evaluative instead of representing the analytical dimension of accountability. Arguably, international criminal law accountability possesses elements of transparency, but this does not constitute accountability. One cannot incorporate transparency into the core aspect of accountability, such as liability and remedy, because liability and remedy arise as a result of one's misconduct, i.e. a corporation's or a corporation official's or a corporation's subsidiary and supply chain. Hence, accountability is an evaluation of corporate operations and their implications but not an analytical concept view of corporate accountability under international law. This also means that accountability should be based on the outcome of the evaluation of corporate business operations, which has a significant impact on human rights and the environment, and not on an analytical view of corporate activities. Viewing accountability in this conceptual premise will help to positively qualify the state of affairs[915] of the corporation, such as regulating the conduct of a corporation's activities based on its economic output, control, relationship with its subsidiaries, and impact it has on human rights and the environment. This could be the basis for establishing effective accountability and remedy for victims of human rights abuses.

These conceptual premises are closely connected to responsiveness, in the sense of the responsibility of the corporation and its officials in directing business operations, as well as the willingness of the corporation to act in a fair, honest, just, transparent and equitable way. Following this explanation of accountability, the notion of responsibility in this dimension will enable corporations to respect human rights and the environment because it will be assumed that the corporation owes a duty of care, which gives rise to liability and remedy. This is because the liability and remedy arise through corporate conduct, such as the exercise of its control over business operations and working procedures. However, there is no general agreement about the acceptable standard for corporately accountable behaviour and the difference from role to role, time to time, and place to place.[916]

---

[914]Transparency, in a business or liability context, is honesty and openness.

[915]*Duck v Peacock* [1949] 1 All ER 318.

[916]Elizabeth Fisher, 'The European Union in the Age of Accountability' (2004) 24 (3) Oxford Journal of Legal Studies 495. <http://www.jstor.org/stable/3600565?seq=1#page_scan_tab_contents> Accessed 3 July 2016.

It is vital to stress that in a legal definition of accountability, the main components are liability, remedy, and enforcement. These elements are crucial aspects of accountability and should not be exchanged for a less regulatory approach to accountability for human rights violations and environmental damages. The exemplification of corporate accountability in a legal and conceptual definition of accountability should be closely linked with corporate business operations but should be wider when it comes to imposing accountability on corporations, as this will enable courts to find liability and the control that the corporation exercises in its business operations. Corporate accountability should have a relationship with the impact of the corporation's business operations on society and the responsibility that is derived from this relationship gives rise to a duty of care not to cause harm. Hence, if the components of corporate accountability include liability, remedy, and enforcement, then the question is what is the scope of accountability? How does the definition of accountability aid corporate responsibility and sanctions in practice?

To answer these questions, it is vital to first look back at the definitions of accountability in duty of care, which help explain and justify conduct and sanctions. This implies a relationship between the state, corporate entities, and a forum, such as a tribunal or a court or society.[917] Also, the answer could be found in the roots of the etymological and historical definition of accountability that is related to specific social relations.[918] In this ideological concept, accountability will be seen as the relationship between actors, such as governments and corporations, and a forum, i.e. a judicial system, society, or the international community. Viewing accountability as a relationship gives rise to obligations to explain and justify one's conduct. Moreover, the forum will have the mandate to pose questions and pass judgment on corporate human rights abuse cases. Indeed, the corporation may face criminal or civil sanctions, specifically where it is found that a duty of care is owed.

This theoretical definition incorporates different actors, such as individuals, and situations in which corporate officials are involved in human rights violations. The forum in this rationale refers to the relationship between the domestic and international judicial systems. The actor is the corporation, and this can have the nature of a principal-agent relation, with the judicial system acting as the principal. Observing accountability in this ideology permits defining whether the implication of a sanction is a

[917] Christopher Pollitt, *The Essential Public Manage* (McGraw-Hill Education 2003).

[918] Patricia S Atkins, 'Regionalism' in JM Shafritz (ed.), *International Encyclopaedia of Public Policy and Administration* (Boulder Westview Press 1998).

constructive element of accountability.[919] It also allows identifying different levels of accountability for all the actors involved. This is crucial because effective accountability, sanctions, and remedies should in theory be based on the type and nature of accountability imposed on a particular actor through the actor's duty of care. This is purely due to the fact that accountability could fail on theoretical and practical interpretations if the essential elements are not taken into consideration when deciding whether an actor could be held accountable for its conduct or not.

Furthermore, transparency is about being understandable as well as being open and honest in all communications, transactions and operations. Accountability and transparency go hand-in-hand and involve being aware of who one is accountable to,[920] what the important pieces of information are, and how information can be communicated most effectively.[921] Transparency is about shedding light on rules, plans, processes and actions. It ensures that public officials, civil servants, managers, board members and businessmen act visibly and understandably and report on their activities. Additionally, it allows the general public to hold them accountable. It is the surest way of guarding against corruption and helps increase accountability in corporate business activities.[922] Transparency and accountability are considered critical not only to the workings of business and government, but also to the success of commercial enterprises, including in the agriculture sector. Through the practice of internationally established standards of corporate governance, private and state-owned enterprises can support robust foreign investment in agribusiness, along with economic growth.[923] The present study raises the possibility that transparency in the concept of accountability refers specifically to the substantive and administrative procedures through which institutions perform their functions, and whether they are documented and accessible,

---

[919]Mark Bovens, Robert E. Goodin and Thomas Schillemans (eds), *The Oxford Handbook of Public Accountability* (OUP Oxford 2014).

[920] Ella Armstrong, 'Integrity, Transparency and Accountability in Public Administration: Recent Trends, Regional and International Developments and Emerging Issues' (2005) United Nations, Department of Economic and Social Affairs 1,10.

[921]Antonino Vaccaro and Peter Madsen, 'Transparency in Business and Society: Introduction to the Special Issue' (2009) 11 (2) Ethics and Information Technology 101, 103.

[922] USAID, 'Transparency and Accountability' (2013) The US Government`s Hunger & Food Security Initiatives.

[923] Marcel Van Marrewijk, 'Concepts and Definitions of CSR and Corporate Sustainability: Between Agency and Communion' (2003) 44 (2) Journal of Business Ethics 95.

and where the government and publicly held companies are concerned, open to public scrutiny.

Accountability pertains to the relationship between citizens and government officials or, in the commercial context, shareholders and boards of directors along with a sense of obligation and a public service ethos among officials and the power of citizens or shareholders to sanction, impose costs, or remove officials for unsatisfactory performance or actions.[924] The concept of transparency in this view might involve two distinct stages: answerability and enforcement. Answerability refers to the obligation of the government, its agencies and public officials to provide information about their decisions and actions and to justify them to the public and those institutions of accountability tasked with providing oversight. Enforcement suggests that the public or the institution responsible for accountability can sanction the offending party or remedy the contravening behaviour. What this means is that, for one to achieve accountability, there should exist transparency as a facilitated procedure for corporate responsibility.

This finding, while preliminary, suggests that transparency is also used in ways that are closer to the scientific usage of transparency: transmission without distortion in its social terms.[925] Thus, the term transparency can be used to describe the way light passes through something (like glass or perspex) as if there were nothing there.[926] In other words, transparency 'can actually suggest concealment (of an intervening medium). This is the case in information technology where transparency usually refers to the operation of'[927] programmes[928] 'and applications that are not apparent to the user, as when the domain names system resolves authorised domain names into Internet Protocol addresses.'[929]

---

[924]Andrew Crane and Dirk Matten, *Business Ethics: Managing Corporate Citizenship and Sustainability in The Age of Globalization* (Oxford University Press 2016).
[925]Raymond T Hebert and Paul A Conrotto, 'Laser Scanner with Rotating Mirror and Housing Which is Transparent to the Scanning Radiation' (1989) 4 US Patent 870, 2694.
[926]Akira Fujishima, and Kenichi Honda, 'Electrochemical Photolysis of Water at a Semiconductor Electrode' (1972) 238 (5358) Nature 37.
[927]Paul Sturges, 'What is this absence called transparency?' (2007) 7 International Review of Information Ethics.
[928] Paul Sturges, 'What is This Absence called transparency?' (2007) 7 International Review of Information Ethics. <http://www.i-r-i-e.net/inhalt/007/24-sturges.pdf. > Accessed 23 May 2016.
[929]Floyd Backes, 'Transparent Bridges for Interconnection of IEEE 802 LANs' (1988) 2 (1) IEEE Network 5, 9 and Paul Sturges, 'What is this absence called transparency?' (2007) 7 International Review of Information Ethics.

'In this case, transparency shields the user from the complexity of the system, rather than reveals'[930] the human rights violations in the business operation. References to network transparency are common in the literature of computing and they too carry this sense that the user works in an environment where there seem to be no barriers or intervening changes of the system.[931] It is important to be aware that this usage contrasts directly with the common tendency to refer to open source applications in computing as transparent.[932] Open source is transparent because one is permitted to see through the surface and examine what is inside (the source code).[933] The definition of transparency here is referred to as clarity and unambiguous conclusion. Even though this definition has clarified the scientific meaning of transparency, it cannot be used in the legal context. This is because for transparency to serve as an element of accountability, it must have a legal meaning.[934]

Florini, for example, expresses that 'put simply, transparency is the opposite of secrecy. Secrecy means deliberately hiding your actions; transparency means deliberately revealing them.'[935] This is a pretty effective definition, except for the suggestion that transparency is always intentionally offered. Types of involuntary or imposed transparency undoubtedly exist. In addition, 'some definitions go further than merely contrasting transparency with secrecy and refer to it as the opposite of privacy. A crudely administered regime of transparency can damage privacy, but this is not usually the ostensible intent behind its introduction. The overwhelming weight of use of the word transparency is not to indicate that it throws light into legitimate privacy, but that it exposes the kind of secrecy that is 'detrimental to society''.[936] 'In fact, the particular value of transparency is its ability to reveal corrupt practices and show citizens how

---

[930]*Ibid.*

[931]LP Pitaevskii, 'Electric Forces in a Transparent Dispersive Dedium' (1961) 12 (5) Journal of Experimental and Theoretical Physics 1008, 1013.

[932]Giulio Giunta et al, 'A GPGPU Transparent Virtualization Component for High Performance Computing Clouds' (Springer Berlin Heidelberg 2010) European Conference on Parallel Processing.

[933]Andrian Marcus and Jonathan I Maletic, 'Recovering Documentation-to-Source-Code Traceability Links Using Latent Semantic Indexing' (2003) Software Engineering, 2003. Proceedings. 25th International Conference on IEEE.

[934]Carolyn Ball, 'What is Transparency?' (2009) 11 (4) Public Integrity 293.

[935]Ann Florini, *The End of Secrecy: Power and Conflict in The Age of Transparency* (Palgrave Macmillan US 2000). Also see: Paul Sturges, 'What is this absence called transparency?' (2007) 7 International Review of Information Ethics. <http://www.i-r-i-e.net/inhalt/007/24-sturges.pdf. > Accessed 23 May 2016.

[936]*Ibid.*

they can limit the damaging effects of corruption in their own lives.'[937] Florini sums up the relationship between transparency and privacy by saying, 'transparency is not about eliminating privacy. It is about giving us the power to hold accountable those who would violate it.'[938] Bosshard contributed to the debate by stating that the phrase 'sunshine is the best disinfectant' elegantly captures the cleansing potential of a regime of transparency, without yet explaining quite how that might work.[939]

Taken together, these definitions suggest that transparency is used in a context where conduct requires clear, honest, obvious, explicit, unambiguous, unequivocal and responsible action. However, what is not clear in this definition is where transparency could give rise to legal responsibility and liability. What is possible though, in this definition, is that transparency as an element of business accountability does give rise to a legal duty. The legal duty of transparency as an element of business accountability can be noted in the UK government passing the Modern Slavery Act of 2015, the first piece of UK legislation focusing on the prevention and prosecution of modern slavery and the protection of victims.

After much debate, the government included a provision on transparency in the supply chain.[940] The new transparency in supply chains provision in the Modern Slavery Act aims to stop slavery lurking in many supply chains. Increased transparency in the supply chains will push forced labour up the corporate agenda, but there are concerns it does not go far enough. Nonetheless, what is seen in this approach is that the UK recognised transparency as a legal tool to force corporations to respect human rights standards and adhere to international law. This suggests that the concept of transparency as an element of business accountability can be enforced in a court of law only where a statute explicitly demands transparency. The Bribery Act of 2010 is legislation of great significance for companies incorporated in or carrying on business in the UK. It presents heightened liability risks for companies, directors and individuals. To avoid corporate liability for bribery, companies must make sure that they have strong, up-

---

[937] Ivar Kolstad and Arne Wiig, 'Is Transparency the Key to Reducing Corruption in Resource-Rich Countries?' (2009) 37 (3) World Development 521. Also see: Paul Sturges, 'What is this absence called transparency?' (2007) 7 International Review of Information Ethics. <http://www.i-r-i-e.net/inhalt/007/24-sturges.pdf.> Accessed 23 May 2016.

[938] Paul Sturges, 'What is this Absence called Transparency' (2007) 7 (07) International Review of Information Ethics 1, 8.

[939] Peter Bosshard, 'The Environment at Risk from Monuments of Corruption' (2005) Global Corruption Report.

[940] Modern Slavery Act 2015.

to-date and effective anti-bribery policies and systems as transparency mechanisms.

The Bribery Act 2010, unlike previous legislation, places strict liability upon companies for failure to prevent active bribery. The only defence is that the company had adequate procedures designed to prevent persons associated with it from undertaking bribery.[941] The Foreign Corrupt Practices Act (FCPA) 1977[942] prohibits US citizens, permanent residents, public and private US companies and certain non-US individuals and entities from bribing foreign government officials in order to obtain a business advantage (*15 USC. §§ 78dd-1, et seq.*). Under some circumstances, the FCPA's jurisdiction extends to non-US individuals and companies, such as those who use the US capital markets, or those who use the US communications or banking networks in furtherance of improper payment schemes. Taken together, these acts suggest that greater emphasis is placed on the corporation to act in a transparent manner in its business operations. The theory that transparency as an element of business accountability therefore gives rise to a legal duty.

Also, certain aspects of the multi-faceted transparency principle are found in the 'rule of law principle', which can be defined as an 'umbrella principle' which contains numerous principles that aim at the rationale exercise of public power and protect qualified interests of the citizens.[943] In particular, the aspect of transparency which relates to the legal clarity in terms of setting clear, simple and understandable laws, is originated in 'rule of law' principles. This is due to its close relationship with the principle of legal certainty, which is recognised as an integral part of the rule of law principle and contributes to the creation of a 'foreseeable' legal environment.[944] Furthermore, the duty to give reasons in tort law and civil law, which is also recognised as a specific aspect of transparency, can be conceived both from the perspective of the 'rule of law' and the principle of democracy, because the knowledge of motives is fundamental both as a guarantee to the exercise of public power and as a prerequisite for effective democratic control by the citizens. In conclusion, it should be underlined that the different aspects of transparency can be recognised in the two most

---

[941]Bribery Act 2010.

[942]The Foreign Corrupt Practices Act of 1977.

[943]Armin von Bogdandy, 'Doctrine of Principles, Jean Monnet Working Paper 9/03' (2003) Max Planck Institute for Comparative Public Law and International Law. <http://centers.law.nyu.edu/jeanmonnet/archive/papers/03/030901-01.pdf> Accessed 20 August 2017.

[944]Takis Tridimas, *The General Principles of EC law* (Oxford University Press USA 1999).

fundamental principles of EU law.[945] What has to be examined, though, is whether the common core of these different aspects can constitute a new self-standing principle of democratic accountability and business accountability.

Transparency is a concept that is applied to 'international organisations, states, private corporations, civil society organisations,'[946] and individuals. Regulations for transparency abound at all these levels and the technology by which transparency can be enforced is hard to avoid. Businesses can no longer easily conceal their misconduct or offer misleading estimates of their business output when records and data can reveal corporation business activities. The 'main levels or types of transparency are as follows':[947]

1. 'adoption of openness in public and private sector governance. This encompasses a broad view of what transparency means, including both a mentality and a system or set of systems.'[948] A state's own disclosure structures are sometimes referred to as domestic transparency.[949] 'They are essentially directed towards permitting broad public knowledge of the actions of those who hold power, but also for purposes of crime detection and law enforcement.'[950]
2. 'A more limited procedural transparency can be identified in some usage of the word. In this sense, the simple existence of a set of provisions for making public, or allowing access to, details of the functioning of some or all of the activities of an organisation, is referred to as transparency.'[951]
3. 'Radical transparency, which is a management method by which almost all the decision making in an organisation is carried out publicly. The exceptions to transparency in such a

---

[945] *Ibid.*

[946] Paul Sturges, 'What is this absence called transparency?' (2007) 7 International Review of Information Ethics.

[947] *Ibid.*

[948] Robert M Bushman and Abbie J Smith, 'Transparency, Financial Accounting information, and Corporate Governance' (2003) and Paul Sturges, 'What is this absence called transparency?' (2007) 7 International Review of Information Ethics.

[949] Jeannine E Relly and Meghna Sabharwal, 'Perceptions of Transparency of Government Policymaking: A Cross-National Study' (2009) 26 (1) Government Information Quarterly 148.

[950] *Ibid.*

[951] *Ibid.*

system are matters such as personal privacy or the security of systems. It is regarded as more appropriate in working environments based on the Internet or intranets that do not suffer from the potential for the transmission of errors inherent in oral communication. It connects directly with the open source movement, which embodies the spirit of radical transparency.'[952]

4. The potential for a kind of systemic or total transparency in which the actions of absolutely everyone are exposed to the eye of interested parties. This idea is based on the existing capacity for deep surveillance that can provide detail about the life of anyone, in the interests of effective administration and policing, and to the private sector, for purposes of more accurately targeted business activity, to the state itself so that its policy can be monitored internationally. It is sometimes referred to as imposed transparency.[953] Although the meanings of transparency 'set out above undoubtedly have some negative connotations, it is chiefly used in a strongly positive[954] way'[955] to find liability for government and business misconduct.

Furthermore, there are a number of words that are regularly associated with transparency or are used in ways that share some of the meaning of the term. It is worth identifying the main ones here. They can be grouped according to what Oliver[956] identifies as the three elements in transparency: the observed, the observer and the means or method of observation. Broadly speaking, the 'observed' includes government, the corporate sector, and also those responsible for the dissemination of knowledge who might be referred to as the knowledge sector. A driving principle behind transparency in the public sphere is to allow the government

---

[952] Paul Sturges, 'What is this absence called transparency?' (2007) 7 International Review of Information Ethics. <http://www.i-r-i-e.net/inhalt/007/24-sturges.pdf. > Accessed 23 May 2016.

[953] John C Bertot, Paul T Jaeger and Justin M Grimes, 'Using ICTs to Create a Culture of Transparency: E-Government and Social Media as Openness and Anti-Corruption Tools for Societies' (2010) 27 (3) Government Information Quarterly 264.

[954] Paul Sturges, 'What is this absence called transparency?' (2007) 7 International Review of Information Ethics. <http://www.i-r-i-e.net/inhalt/007/24-sturges.pdf. > Accessed 23 May 2016.

[955] *Ibid.*

[956] Richard W Oliver, *What is Transparency?* (New York: McGraw-Hill 2004).

to set the context for transparency in the sphere of governance.[957] Systems of open government will usually include facilities for the observation of official meetings by members of the public and public consultation. In the processes of planning and decision making, it is possible for statutory rights to be granted for accessing public official information. Hence, these statutory rights expressed in freedom of information laws might restrict some of the rights enjoyed by the state.[958]

This forms a part of a national integrity system': a set of institutions and procedures that offers to check corporate accountability and its various forms.[959] A national integrity system includes at the most basic level the institutions of a democratically elected legislature, an executive answerable both to the legislative body and to an independent judiciary. 'It should also include a supreme audit institution, regulatory bodies, [960] ombudsmen'[961] (an official appointed to investigate individuals' complaints against a company or organization, especially a public authority),[962] and independent anti-corruption agencies.

'Corporations that embrace this concept monitor and offer their social performance, environmental impacts, employee relations and a range of other ethically sensitive aspects of'[963] business'[964] for regular auditing.[965] 'Formal reporting of non-financial matters complements the financial accounting already required by national laws and international agreements. This reporting is usually done on an annual basis, and is often verified by

---

[957] Jeannine E Relly and Meghna Sabharwal, 'Perceptions of Transparency of Government Policymaking: A Cross-National Study' (2009) 26 (1) Government Information Quarterly 148, 157.

[958] Barack Obama, 'Transparency and Open Government' (2009) Memorandum for The Heads of Executive Departments and Agencies.

[959] Jeremy Pope, *Confronting Corruption: The Elements of a National Integrity System* (Transparency International 2000).

[960] Paul Sturges, 'What is this absence called transparency?' (2007) 7 International Review of Information Ethics. <http://www.i-r-i-e.net/inhalt/007/24-sturges.pdf. > Accessed 23 May 2016.

[961] *Ibid.*

[962] Linda C Reif, *The Ombudsman, Good Governance, and the International Human Rights System* (Vol. 79. Martinus Nijhoff Publishers 2004).

[963] *Ibid.*

[964] Paul Sturges, 'What is this absence called transparency?' (2007) 7 International Review of Information Ethics. <http://www.i-r-i-e.net/inhalt/007/24-sturges.pdf. > accessed 23 May 2016.

[965] Pamela Bloomfield, 'The Challenging Business of Long-Term Public–Private Partnerships: Reflections on Local Experience' (2006) 66 (3) Public Administration Review 400.

independent and external third parties. It represents a considerable contribution to corporate transparency.'[966]

The analysis of the 'multi-faceted principle of transparency indicates that, although there is still a way for this principle'[967] to be recognised as a general principle of accountability, it has exerted significant regulative influence on the way that States, businesses, institutional bodies and agencies function.[968] 'Transparency goes further than ensuring openness of the decision-making processes and widest possible access to the relevant documents in a multi-level governance model.'[969] 'It also relates to some qualities that a legal duty of transparency should have, such as the cognoscibility of their context and the visibility of the motives of the legislator,'[970] qualities that can be seen as preconditions for both the acceptability and the effective application of the business standard itself.[971]

It should be underlined that although the multi-faceted principle of transparency builds upon well-established legal values, such as the rule of law and legal certainty, the elaboration of its elements in an integrated manner and in accordance with the particularities of business accountability gives it a new dynamic, although not yet fully crystallised, concerning the 'qualities' of the responsibility and business governance at national level. Such developments are also of importance for the accountability and liability for corporations at both domestic and international law level. Transparency is an accountability concept, but is only enforceable if it is included in business accountability or explicitly stated in the domestic law.

---

[966]Martin Lipton and Jay W Lorsch, 'A Modest Proposal for Improved Corporate Governance' (1992) Business Lawyer 59 and also see:

[967]Vasiliki Karageorgou, 'Transparency Principle as An Evolving Principle of EU law: Regulative Contours and Implications' (2006) Saatavissa. <https://www.right2info.org/resources/publications/eu-karageorgou-vasilikitransparency-principle-as-an-evolving-principle-of-eu-law> Accessed 16 June 2019.

[968]Adrienne Héritier, 'Composite Democracy in Europe: The Role of Transparency and Access to Information' (2003) 10 (5) Journal of European Public Policy 814.

[969]Vasiliki Karageorgou, 'Transparency Principle as an Evolving Principle of EU law: Regulative Contours and Implications' (2006) 18 Greece: Panteion University, Athens, Lecturer in European Administrative law and European Environmental Law, Panteion University and Liesbet Hooghe and Gary Marks, *Multi-Level Governance and European Integration* (Rowman & Littlefield 2001).

[970]*Ibid.*

[971]Vasiliki Karageorgou, 'Transparency Principle as an Evolving Principle of EU law: Regulative Contours and Implications' (2006) 18 Greece and Ans Kolk, 'Sustainability, Accountability and Corporate Governance: Exploring Multinationals' Reporting Practices' (2008) 17 (1) Business Strategy and the Environment 1.

Transparency can be a legal instrument to hold corporations accountable for business misconduct.

Accountability arises when the essential elements derived from the notion of accountability are met, such as liability, remedy and enforcement. A tribunal and court can hold an actor accountable for its conduct. Therefore, the consequences that flow from these elements are also determined by transparency, international standards and international norms. Hence, under wider moral and legal obligations, the tribunal or court must exercise extensive discretion to impose accountability on an actor, with an enforcement procedure either at the domestic or international level. This could include the freezing of company assets through consensus with the home state government or the state in which the headquarters of the corporation is located but only if it is established that a duty of care is owed, and was breached.

The sanction of fines or seizure of property should be imposed by an execution order issued by the court either at the domestic or international level. The fact that the sanction provided for the violation of international and human rights law is a fine or imprisonment of a corporate official in the discretion of the court, does not render it is inapplicable to a corporate human rights violation. Corporate officials may also be subject to liability for any violation of human rights law and standards under the theory that they failed to prevent the violation by neglecting to control the misconduct of those subject to their control. Under this concept of liability, a corporate official is liable based on his/her responsible relation to the human rights violation regardless of whether he/she has any knowledge of the misconduct.[972] Similarly, the duty of care should provide that the penalty for a violation of human rights may be read in conjunction with a general legal rule of remedy under tort law that allows the imposition of a fine, and the fine may be imposed on the corporation in civil and tort law.

Lastly, even an exercise of voluntary instruction such as stages of corporate report writing constitute a practical element of accountability. Also, this book concurs with Mulgan[973] and Strom[974] that sanctions form the main part of a practical element of accountability and on a broader spectrum are part of the conceptual component of accountability. Therefore, effective

---

[972]David G Owen, 'Deterrence and Desert in Tort: A Comment' (1985) 73 California Law Review 665.

[973]*Ibid.*

[974]Kaare Strøm, 'Delegation and Accountability in Parliamentary Democracies' (2000) 37 (3) European Journal of Political Research 261, 290. <http://link.springer.com/article/10.1023/A:1007064803327> Accessed 3 July 2016.

sanction and effective remedy should be the core element of accountability in a legal proceeding involving a state and a non-state actor. It is argued here that a tribunal or court has a moral and legal obligation to apply the conceptualisation of the practical element of accountability. The present study raises the possibility that the practical element of accountability should be a legal theory that is used to extend accountability to situations where a corporation has no hands-on supervision of the subsidiary's conduct, but, have direct or indirect control over the business operations.

It is now important to look at what is meant by the component of accountability and how this is linked with the corporate obligations that give rise to a duty of care. ***Diagram 1*** illustrates this concept by demonstrating how the various elements contained in the notion of practical corporate accountability ought to work in a broader concept to impose a legal duty of care on the corporation. The rationale behind this is that the components of accountability describe a relationship between a duty holder and a person or corporation to whom a duty is owed. It describes the capacity to demand that a person or corporation give reasons to justify their behaviour and the capacity to impose a sanction if they fail to give reasons, or if their performance falls below the reasonable man standard. The components of accountability involve three key elements. The first is 'delimitation of responsibility', defining over what, whom and how duty holders are responsible for their actions. The second is 'answerability', the obligation for duty holders to inform about and explain their actions. Accountability as answerability aims at creating transparency. It relies on information dissemination and the establishment of adequate monitoring and oversight mechanisms. The third is 'enforcement', or the capacity to subject power to the threat of sanctions or disciplinary actions. Legal and regulatory sanctions are at the core of enforcing accountability in the components described in this book. Following this explanation, ***Diagram 1*** lays out the obligations derived from the concept of accountability as:

1. Accountability by mandating;
2. Clear standards and legal duties that must be met by duty holders;
3. Requirements for effective accountability relationships;
4. Legal requirements for transparency and information disclosure;
5. Legal and formal institutions and mechanisms to hold duty holders to account; and
6. Legally established and effective sanctions for those who are not accountable

Diagram 1. Components of Accountability

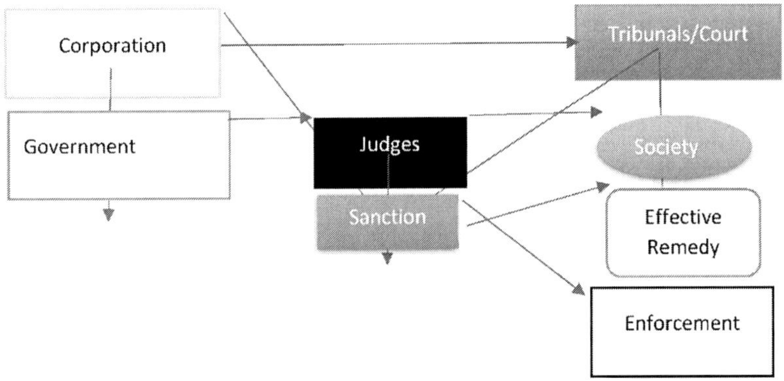

The Link between Government and Corporations

The link between government and corporations shows the law and regulation aspect of the corporation's duty of care; the company law, the government trade policy, as well as the business influence on the government by personal conduct and lobbying, forming trade unions, political action committees and large investments of the corporation. Breaking this down, the link between government and business is required for the welfare of the economy and the State. This link, which is established through government laws and regulations, establishes accountability. The corporation is required to be accountable to the government for its business operations through regulations and the corporate law of the state. Likewise, the link also means that the government has a responsibility to shape business practices through both the implementation of rules and regulations directly. This indicates that the link between government and corporations creates two dimensions of accountability: the first is the government regulatory mechanism for human rights conduct and the second is the corporation's duty not to violate human rights.

Therefore, the government must establish laws and rules that dictate what the business can and cannot do, such as implementing or enacting legislation that will either control or monitor some aspects of corporate business activities or enable courts to hold the corporation accountable for misconduct under some form of binding regulation. This could be either through environmental protection law, a labour commission, the implementation of conventions[975] and treaties[976] into domestic law or a governmental department for corporate human rights violations. However, it should be noted that this is just an illustrative view of binding regulations that are required to enforce human rights standards at the domestic level. This will allow governmental bodies to implement the law and monitor its application on businesses. The link between the government and businesses are legal regulations, enforcement, and the ability of the State to hold corporations accountable for human rights violations within its jurisdiction. The link establishes a corporate duty of care to the government, with the corporation's duty arising under this link to respect human rights standards both at the international and national levels. It, therefore, follows that the corporation's international business operation gives rise to a duty of the corporation to respect international human rights law.

The corporation should be liable, where it is at fault, for causing the claimant's injury or damaging the environment during the course of its business operations, unless there is a compelling human rights reason not to hold it liable. This doctrine is a core aspect of the duty of care principle, which was set out by Lord Wilberforce in *Anns v Merton London Borough Council*[977] as a two-stage test for the existence of a duty of care. The reasoning behind the recommendation of the common law approach of duty of care is that the test created the standard of duty of care, which undoubtedly can be applied in the international arena through the concepts

[975]UN General Assembly, *International Covenant on Civil and Political Rights*, 16 December 1966, United Nations, Treaty Series, vol. 999, p. 171. <http://www.refworld.org/docid/3ae6b3aa0.html> Accessed 6 July 2017, UN General Assembly, *International Convention on the Elimination of All Forms of Racial Discrimination*, 21 December 1965, United Nations, Treaty Series, vol. 660, p. 195. <http://www.refworld.org/docid/3ae6b3940.html> Accessed 6 July 2017, UN General Assembly, *International Covenant on Economic, Social and Cultural Rights*, 16 December 1966, United Nations, Treaty Series, vol. 993, p. 3. <http://www.refworld.org/docid/3ae6b36c0.html> Accessed 6 July 2017, UN General Assembly, International Covenant on Economic, Social and Cultural Rights, 16 December 1966, United Nations, Treaty Series, vol. 993, p. 3. <http://www.refworld.org/docid/3ae6b36c0.html> Accessed 6 July 2017.

[976]UN General Assembly, *Universal Declaration of Human Rights*, 10 December 1948, 217 A (III). <http://www.refworld.org/docid/3ae6b3712c.html> accessed 6 July 2017.

[977]*Anns v Merton London Borough Council* [1978] A.C. 728. <https://www.scribd.com/document/234563408/English-Tort-Law-Cases> Accessed 01 January 2017.

of the General Principle of Law and Positive Law.[978] Thus, the question should be, is there a sufficient relationship of proximity and foreseeability? If so, a *prima facie* duty of care should exist. Are there any considerations which could reduce or limit the scope of corporate liability?

The Link between Corporations and Society

This type of link establishes the responsibility of the corporation in the society in which it carries out its business activities. A corporation is part of a system that is affected by and affects other elements in society.[979] Corporate business operations are connected to or form part of society so that where the corporation violates human rights and the environment, a duty of care is owed in law to that society. Therefore, corporations need to work within the rules and regulations of society, as well as within international law and norms, in pursuit of economic goals in a way that will benefit both the corporation and society. This link demonstrates the practical accountability for corporate business activities on society, and so there exists a reputable presumption of a duty of care for the corporation not to cause harm to the society and the environment. This also means that corporations should be accountable to their stakeholders[980] in order to achieve improved economic, environmental, and human rights standards.[981] Thus, the corporation can be liable for a corporate act that may either harm society or destroy the environment, regardless of whether it is caused by a corporate official, supply chain or subsidiary if a duty of care is established.

---

[978]John Austin, *Lectures on Jurisprudence: Or, the Philosophy of Positive Law* (J. Murray 1875) and Andrei Marmor, *Positive Law and Objective Values* (Oxford University Press 2001).

[979]V Balachandran, *Corporate Governance, Ethics and Social Responsibility* (PHI Learning Pvt Ltd 2011).

[980]Mark Bandsuch, Larry Pate and Jeff Thies, 'Rebuilding Stakeholder Trust in Business: An Examination of Principle-Centered Leadership and Organizational Transparency in Corporate Governance' (2008) 113 (1) Business and Society Review 99.

[981] Doreen J McBarnet, Aurora Voiculescu and Tom Campbell, eds. *The New Corporate Accountability: Corporate Social Responsibility and the Law* (Cambridge University Press 2009).

The Link between the Judicial System, Government, and Corporations

Society influences law and so the law is a reflection of society. Therefore, the government is accountable to society through the judicial system and the law of the state, known as the doctrine of separation of power,[982] while a corporation is accountable to society either through the government or its judicial system. Of course, it is adequate that the doctrine of separation of powers is based on the acceptance of the constitutional doctrine of the separation of powers which is typically found in Western societies. Under the General Principle of Law (The appropriate answer depends on the nature or subject of the principle in question. However, whether a fundamental principle of justice rises to the level of a 'General Principle of International Law' can best, though not exclusively, be determined by its existence in the national laws of 'civilised nations').[983] and international law the separation of power is recognised by most judicial systems and can be applied in the concept of corporate liability here. This concept establishes an absolute duty of care for all the actors expressed in ***Diagram 1*** above. Hence, the link between corporations, the judicial system and society can simply be explained as a system of accountability for the corporation in the stakeholders' point of view, the government, and the judicial system in cases of corporate misconduct.

The Practical Extent of Accountability

Diagram 1 illustrates the practical link between the components in the concept of corporate accountability that give rise to a duty of care. This chapter has broadened the concept of accountability from a restrictive concept of liability to a wider one. Also, as shown in ***Diagram 1***, this study argues that the principle of corporate accountability extends to the various components in the chain of liability, such as the government, the judiciary and society, and not only to the corporation's business stakeholders. Therefore, the assumption is that where the court can establish a relationship and control, it can be inferred that corporate accountability exists through the duty of care it owes to the government, the judicial system, and society. The government and society in the chain can seek to hold the corporation

---

[982]Maurice John Crawley Vile, *Constitutionalism and the Separation of Powers* (Liberty Fund 2012).

[983]Anthony Clark Arend and Robert J Beck, *International Law and the Use of Force: Beyond the UN Charter Paradigm* (Routledge 2014).

accountable for its misconduct, specifically, where there is a substantial violation of human rights and environmental damage.

This further supports the fact that the corporation and corporate officials will have some relationship with and a degree of control over the corporation's business operations. Therefore, the degree of the relationship and control constitutes the guiding mind of the corporation.[984] As a result, there is a presumption that a corporation should be held accountable to the government and society that suffered from its business misconduct, including human rights violations[985] and environmental damages.[986] This is because it can be inferred that the corporation has an unwritten obligation to act in a manner that benefits society as a whole and not the contrary. Likewise, the corporation has an obligation to be accountable to its stakeholders. In other words, one's government and society arguably fall under the stakeholder definition. Thus, where it can be assumed that a corporation owes a duty of care to the government and society, there must be effective sanction and remedy.

As a practical observation, the link also shows how corporations have a duty of care. ***Diagram 1*** shows the interaction between the concept of accountability, the procedure of accountability and the mechanism which society could rely on to hold a corporation accountable for its actions. The theoretical concept deriving from this diagram is that corporate accountability is a step-by-step process, and at each stage, the corporation can be called to account for its misconduct. The concept of practical corporate accountability is an inclusive concept, which requires the corporation to be accountable to various actors, to whom they have legal and moral obligations.

The first theoretical question regarding ***Diagram 1*** is: what is the relationship between the actors and to whom is one made accountable to? This question is addressed by ***Diagram 1*** with the connection between each actor. This question regarding the diagram also yields a procedural query about the type of tribunal or court to which the actor is obliged to render account. The second theoretical question asks: who should the corporation be made accountable to? Is the corporation obliged to appear before the

---

[984] *Tesco Supermarkets Ltd v Nattrass* [1971] UKHL.

[985] Andrew Clapham and Scott Jerbi, 'Categories of Corporate Complicity in Human Rights Abuses' (2001) 24 (3) Hastings International and Comparative Law Review 339. <http://heinonline.org/HOL/LandingPage?handle=hein.journals/hasint24&div=20&id=&page=> Accessed 6 July 2016.

[986] William B Werther Jr and David Chandler, *Strategic Corporate Social Responsibility: Stakeholders in a Global Environment* (Sage Publications 2010).

tribunal or court of either the host state or the home state? In this rationale, the corporation's relationships to society make it clear who the corporation is to be made accountable to: the government, judiciary, judicial bodies, and any appropriate tribunal or court. In practice, however, this has proven to be a more complex question to answer. Therefore, the correct way to do this is to follow the argument in a systematic approach to accountability that ensures corporations and other actors know to whom they are accountable. This systematic approach will also allow victims of corporate misconduct to address their problems to a specific body on the link of corporate accountability, such as a tribunal or court. Therefore, to know whom to account to is part of the concept behind ***Diagram 1***. Likewise, ***Diagram 1*** gives a perfect suggestion about the systematic approach to accountability in terms of knowing your role as an actor. ***Diagram 1*** can be used to develop a cohesive accountability system which will ensure corporate conduct is checked and accounted for.

By applying this concept to corporate accountability, it can be argued that, in light of the above-mentioned, the primary aims pursued in corporate accountability should closely conform to the notion of legal accountability, which meets the changing sociological circumstances on the domestic and international scenes. Therefore, a rebuttable presumption arises already on the basis of the *de facto* influential position the corporation has in a domestic legal system and society. The actor, such as a corporation, is subject to the applicable legal obligations with regard to the promotion of community interests such as the protection of human rights, the environment, and the core labour and social standards. This, furthermore, is part of its business relationship with the government and society. The position this book shall adopt in conjunction with ***Diagram 1*** above is that there is a presumption that a corporation is legally accountable to the government and society in the way it carries out its business operations due to corporations owing a duty of care to society. This approach will ensure that the imposition of accountability by the state through the domestic civil legal system, which has the capacity to enforce treaty or customary international law, is a result of the interaction between the State, society, and corporations. Therefore, there is a *prima facie* case that the corporation is subject to domestic law, international law and human rights law, as well as other human rights treaties, and is obliged to be held accountable for its misconduct.

This will enable the state, through its judicial system, to fulfil its central purpose of comprehensively civilising relations between corporations, government and society in an effective way.[987] Attaching accountability to corporate conduct should impose upon corporations a positive obligation to take reasonable steps to ensure that such misconduct does not occur. In addition, any query about regulating corporate conduct in relation to human rights violations shall be first addressed through the judicial system established by the host government and, possibly, in the international system as a last resort. This is because under international law, a victim must first absorb all its rights in a domestic court before seeking judicial remedy at an international court.[988] An implication of this is that the victim 'must first have an opportunity to redress the situation complained of by its own means and within the framework of its own domestic legal system. The international court or tribunal may only deal with the matter after all domestic remedies have been exhausted'[989] or if the court suspected that the victims may not be provided with adequate remedy or justice at the domestic court.

Moving on, the final question related to ***Diagram 1*** concerns itself with the type and level of liability required, and the type of transparency and cooperation required to establish a corporate duty of care. This particular question relates to corporate business operations, corporate conduct in society, and corporate dealings with the government. This accountability should be in the form of providing information about corporate financial relations, the procedure of corporate operations, programmes, risk assessment, environmental risk assessment, economic impact on the livelihood of the people and trades, and steps taken to ensure the company adheres to human rights law: this is termed 'pragmatic accountability.'[990] This means that, in business operations, the corporation should have an obligation to provide information about its conduct when it is asked or required to do so either by the authorising domestic body or an international body. However, it should be noted that under domestic law,

---

[987]Stephen Tully, ed. *Corporations and International Law making* (Brill 2007).

[988]Silvia d'Ascoli and Kathrin Maria Scherr, 'The Rule of Prior Exhaustion of Local Remedies in the International Law Doctrine and Its Application in The Specific Context of Human Rights Protection' (2007).

[989]Martin Kuijer, 'Effective Remedies as a Fundamental Right' Seminar *on Human Rights and Access to Justice in the EU, Barcelona* (2014).

[990]Amanda Sinclair, 'The Chameleon of Accountability: Forms and Discourses' (1995) 20 (2) Accounting, Organizations and Society 19, 237.

international law, and human rights law, corporations may have a 'right to silence'.[991]

Nonetheless, the proposed duty of care advocated here should allow both domestic and international judicial systems to override the right to silence when it is established that the corporation has intentionally violated human rights for business benefits. The judicial institution at both domestic and international legal systems can impose a duty of care on the corporation to provide information about its business operations. Corporate duty of care is also about generating and disclosing information. The evaluation of the adequacy of a corporation's human rights duty of care should include an assessment of its disclosure practices. An adequate human rights duty of care process should require the disclosure of information about human rights policies, processes and their outcomes, as well as information about actual and potential adverse human rights impacts of specific activities or projects. Timely access to activity or project-specific information that is reliable, useful and accessible is critical to ensure genuine engagement and consultation with potentially affected individuals and communities. This, in turn, is essential for an accurate assessment of risk. Human rights duty of care and disclosure are intrinsically connected to accountability and indispensable for each other.

The last question regarding ***Diagram 1*** is why is the corporation obliged to render account to the appropriate authority (i.e. the domestic court, tribunal or international court)?[992] This particular question is linked to the nature of the relationship between the corporation, the government, society, and the tribunal or court. This obligation arises from the relationship between the corporation and the country it operates in.[993] This also means that where the corporation is engaged in business misconduct, it is obliged to be accountable to that host state court or any judicial body created for the purposes of regulating corporate conduct (through referral). If this is not possible, then there must be an international mechanism to hold the corporation accountable for its misconduct.

The connection between the corporation, the government, the judicial system, and society gives rise to accountability. There are several possible explanations for this. Corporations are part of society. This establishes a special relationship between the corporation and society

[991] Gregory W O'Reilly, 'England Limits the Right to Silence and Moves Towards an Inquisitorial System of Justice' (1994) 85 (2) Journal of Criminal Law and Criminology 402.

[992] Michael Blowfield and Alan Murray, *Corporate Responsibility: A Critical Introduction* (Oxford University Press 2008).

[993] Gabriel Moran, *A Grammar of Responsibility* (Crossroads 1996).

through the business operation. Therefore, the corporation can be held accountable where its actions have violated domestic or international law and human rights law in the country in which it operates. Similarly, the relationship between the corporation, the government, the judicial system and society gives rise to an effective, appropriate remedy, and sanction for the victims whose rights have been violated.

Therefore, the links establish that corporate accountability includes liability, which constitutes legal accountability, because legal accountability is a formalisation of social relations.[994] Corporate social relations is a blanket term for interactions between businesses, governments, people, groups, or organisations. Corporate social relationships are composed of an immense number of business operations and environmental interactions that create a climate for the exchange of goods and services in the global economy. ***Diagram 1*** has an element of social relations to prove this. Thus, the suggestion in this particular section of accountability is clear on the established relationship between the corporation and the other actors such as the government and society. This relationship has created the legal concept of accountability. However, the question is how ***Diagram 1*** can be used to plot accountability in such a way that the corporations can be held accountable for their actions in a host state's judicial system or an international tribunal or court.

Plotting Accountability

Understanding ***Diagram 1*** requires a mapping exercise. This is done by plotting accountability that closely matches ***Diagram 1***. This procedure is the relationship between the corporation, the government, the judicial system, and society. This is a dichotomous exercise that must follow a rationale of either/or.[995] Therefore, in following ***Diagram 1***, the main question that needs to be asked when plotting accountability is whether the corporation in question qualifies for legal corporate accountability (i.e. duty of care) or whether there is something else, such as the participation of other entities (supply chain/subsidiaries) or the responsibility of another entity. The next question concerns itself with the type of accountability. ***Diagram 2*** below illustrates this view in a hierarchical order.

---

[994]Lawrence M Friedman, *Total Justice* (Russell Sage Foundation 1985).

[995]Giovanni Sartori, 'Concept Misformation in Comparative Politics' (1970) 64 (4) American Political Science Review 1033, 1053. <http://journals.cambridge.org/action/displayAbstract?fromPage=online&aid=8935058&fileId=S0003055400133325> Accessed 4 July 2016.

Diagram 2. Plotting Corporate Accountability

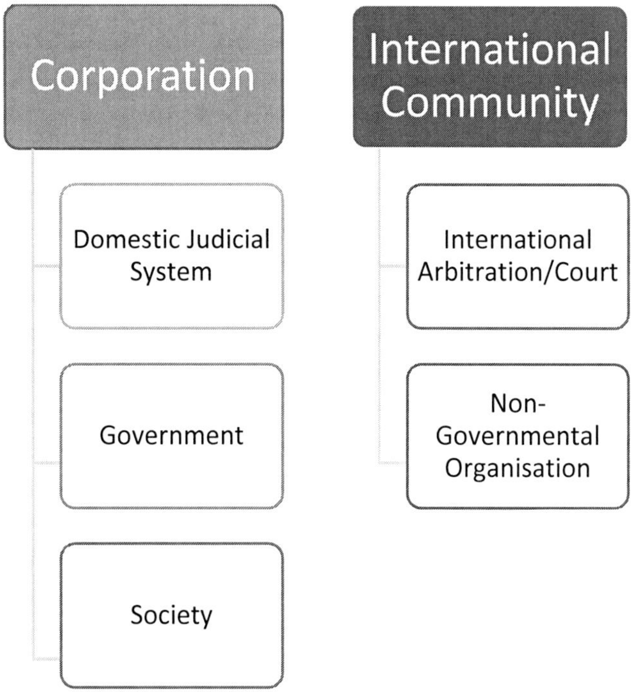

This is important in establishing liability for corporate human rights violations because having a strong accountability structure is paramount to the success of finding responsibility for any corporate human rights abuse. Accountability needs a structured hierarchy to establish internal and external control of the business operation. A hierarchical accountability allows lawyers and the court to identify the chain of the human rights abuses and serves as a reference point for decision making. Thus, corporate liability for human rights abuses without a hierarchy cannot effectively hold its business and subsidiary accountable. Lastly, in the most basic sense, a well-run business functions like the human body. The head instructs the various body parts on how to move and react in unison to perform the simplest of tasks. The notion of establishing corporate liability follows this idea, with the hierarchical decision-making flowing from the top (the head of the corporation) down to the employees who perform various tasks. Accountability is responsible for making the decisions that allow the corporation to function efficiently to achieve company objectives liable for the human rights abuses.

The theoretical conception behind ***Diagram 2*** is that accountability takes the form of social relations and business operations. ***Diagram 1*** and ***Diagram 2*** show that corporate accountability may have both horizontal and vertical interactions. Therefore, the concept of accountability is derived from the corporate relationship. This relationship forms the foundation of legal accountability and the basis for analysing the nexus between corporate conduct, government, and society. Hence, the concept as explained above confirms that accountability exists when corporations, government and society are operating within social relations. It is argued in this book that where social relations exist it does not matter whether there are other elements that aid or give rise to misconduct of the corporation or 'human rights violations'.[996] The corporation should be accountable to society through the government and judicial system.[997] This is based on the principle of separation of power.[998] However, corporations can also be held accountable through both the government and the judicial system. Therefore, the social relationship is an approach which allows society or the State to build accountability mechanisms which establish a duty of care to hold corporations liable for their misconduct.

Corporate accountability is the ability to ask the corporations and their officials, stakeholders, supply chains and subsidiaries to provide answers for their policies and actions as well as any human rights violations or environmental damages that might arise due to their misconduct. In summary, the duty of the state is to make sure that corporations are held accountable to the government and its citizens. This stems from the concepts: citizen rights, information rights, and human rights.[999] Accountability should offer mechanisms to monitor and 'protect human rights and the environment. The concept of accountability highlights citizens' rights to expect the government to act in the best interests of the people and to ensure that it does so in conjunction with other actors. Nonetheless, as interesting as this may sound, without domestic enforcement by the government, accountability will not be successful. Therefore, the question is: what is the

---

[996] *R v White* [1910] 2 KB 124.

[997] Anne Peters, *Beyond Human Rights: The Legal Status of the Individual in International Law* (Vol. 126 Cambridge University Press 2016).

[998] William B Gwyn, *The Meaning of The Separation of Powers: An Analysis of The Doctrine from Its Origin to The Adoption of The United States Constitution* (Vol. 9. Tulane University 1965).

[999] Jack Donnelly, *Universal Human Rights in Theory and Practice* (Cornell University Press 2013).

role of international law in enforcing human rights accountability in domestic jurisdictions? What legal principle can be applied to hold the corporation accountable for its misconduct?

Analysis of International Law Accountability for Multinational Corporations' Human Rights Violations across Different Jurisdictions

The International Criminal Court (ICC) demonstrates the international community's attempt to create an architecture of international criminal accountability through an international mechanism that presents an opportunity to enforce human rights by imposing a legal duty on those who violate human rights. However, many actors continue to violate human rights in spite of the fact that their actions will not be met with impunity. Examples of these actors are governments, governmental institutions, and non-state actors like MNCs.[1000] However, the ICC's jurisdiction must be submitted to; it is not automatic. So, a country can essentially 'opt out'. However, as a matter of history, the evidence does not easily support such a legal concept. What may be clear from this development is that the duties of states, the international community, and non-governmental organisations (NGOs) are indeterminate.[1001]

Corporate liability has been introduced in most jurisdictions enabling courts to 'sanction corporate entities for their criminal acts, but that there is also a general trend in most countries towards bringing corporate entities to justice for their human rights violations or the criminal acts of their business officers.'[1002] In those countries where there is no corporate liability per se, there is either quasi-criminal liability or the introduction of corporate criminal liability is being considered. A notable exception is Germany, where the strong feeling is that imposing corporate criminal liability would go against the basic principles of the German Criminal

---

[1000]Michael J Kelly, 'Ending Corporate Impunity for Genocide: The Case Against China's State-Owned Petroleum Company in Sudan' (2011) 90 Oregon Law Review 413.

[1001] David Weissbrodt and Muria Kruger, 'Norms on the Responsibilities of Transnational Corporations and Other Business Enterprises with Regard to Human Rights' (2003) 97 (4) American Journal of International Law 901, 922.

[1002]Clifford Chance, 'Corporate Liability in Europe' (2016) <https://www.cliffordchance.com/briefings/2016/04/corporate_criminalliability.html> Accessed 20 June 2017.

Code.[1003] Nevertheless, Germany's regulators have taken robust regulatory action against various German companies as a result of their criminal conduct, imposing large fines which have caused significant reputational damage. Arguably, this has been as effective as any criminal sanction.[1004]

In all jurisdictions where the concept of corporate or quasi-corporate criminal liability exists it is, with the exception of the UK and the Netherlands, a relatively new concept.[1005] 'France was the first European country to introduce the concept of corporate criminal liability in 1994',[1006] 'followed by Belgium in 1999, Italy in 2001, Poland in 2003, Romania in 2006 and Luxembourg and Spain in 2010. In the Czech Republic, an act creating corporate criminal liability became law as of 1 January 2012.'[1007] 'Even in the UK, 'where criminal liability for corporate entities has existed for decades, many offences focusing on corporate criminal liability have been created in recent years. In the Netherlands, only fiscal offences could be brought against corporate entities until 1976.'[1008]

In Belgium, except for offences of strict liability, a corporate entity can avoid criminal liability altogether by proving that it exercised proper due diligence in the hiring or supervising of the person that committed the offence and that the offence was not the consequence of defective internal systems and controls. In Germany, a corporate entity's owner or representative can be held liable within the regulatory context if they fail to take adequate supervisory measures to prevent a breach of duty by an employee. However, this is a defence for the owner and the representatives to show that they had taken adequate preventative measures.[1009] In Italy, the corporate entity has an affirmative defence if it can show that it had in place and effectively implemented adequate management systems and controls.

[1003] *The German Criminal Code: A Modern English Translation* (Bloomsbury Publishing 2008).

[1004] *Ibid.*

[1005] James Gobert and Ana-Maria Pascal, eds. *European Developments in Corporate Criminal Liability* (Taylor & Francis 2011).

[1006] <https://www.britishchamber.cz/data/1364207437484European_Technical_Bulletin.pdf> Accessed 30 Jun2 2016 and Guy Stessens, 'Corporate Criminal Liability: A Comparative Perspective' (1994) 43 (3) International and Comparative Law Quarterly 493, 520.

[1007] <https://www.britishchamber.cz/data/1364207437484European_Technical_Bulletin.pdf> Accessed 30 Jun2 2016 and Clifford Chance (n 608).

[1008] Sally S Simpson, *Corporate Crime, Law, and Social Control* (Cambridge University Press 2002) and see: <https://www.britishchamber.cz/data/1364207437484European_Technical_Bulletin.pdf> Accessed 30 Jun2 2016.

[1009] Clifford Chance (n 608).

Likewise, in Spain, corporate entities will not be criminally liable if they enforce appropriate supervision policies over their employees.[1010] In Poland the corporate entity is only liable if it failed to exercise due diligence in hiring or supervising the offender or if the corporate entity's representatives failed to exercise due diligence in preventing the commission of an offence. In Romania, the corporation is only liable if the commission of the offence is due to the corporation's lack of supervision or control.[1011]

In some jurisdictions, measures taken by a corporate entity to prevent the commission of offences may be mitigating factors upon sentence. For example, in Italy a fine imposed on a corporate entity will be reduced by 50% if, prior to trial, a corporation adopted necessary and preventative internal systems and controls.[1012] Even where it is not an express defence or it is not taken into account expressly as a mitigating factor, the adequacy of a corporate entity's processes and procedures is likely to be relevant both to regulators, prosecutors and courts in determining whether to prosecute and, if prosecuted, in deciding what penalty to apply. In France, the existence of adequate compliance procedures and control systems may be taken into account by the courts in considering the context of the offending, even though compliance procedures, of themselves, do not constitute an affirmative defence.[1013] The importance placed on adequate legal systems and controls by applicable legislation, and more broadly by prosecuting authorities and courts, demonstrates the importance of having an effective corporate accountability system in place at the corporate, domestic and international levels.

On the other hand, the work of other states, international institutions and NGOs since the 1980s has yielded an impressive body of treaties, conventions, self-regulatory mechanisms, judicial opinions and doctrines on corporate accountability.[1014] Even though there is a lack of coherent codification of international accountability for corporate human rights violations, domestics courts, international courts and hybrid tribunals for international crime have created significant case law that elaborates the substantive norms of human rights accountability.[1015] However, these

---

[1010] *Ibid.*

[1011] *Ibid.*

[1012] *Ibid.*

[1013] *Ibid.*

[1014] John Gerard Ruggie, *Just Business: Multinational Corporations and Human Rights* (Norton Global Ethics Series) (WW Norton & Company 2013).

[1015] Tawhida Ahmed and Israel de Jesús Butler. 'The European Union and Human Rights: An International Law Perspective' (2006) 17 (4) European Journal of International Law 771.

findings cannot be extrapolated to all corporate human rights violations due to the fact that the mechanism, while of great variety and now quite active, does not work with full vigour and regularity.

Examples of this include the Alien Tort Act,[1016] *Kiobel v Royal Dutch Petroleum*,[1017] and *Sosa v Alvarez-Machain*.[1018] This approach, while similar to the European states' criminal liability mechanism, has the potential to leave corporate accountability inconsistent and, in many ways, exceptional. In order to accelerate the prospects for corporate human rights accountability needs, national and international community decision-makers ought to take action based on developments that date back to Nuremberg[1019] and the European states' concept of corporate criminal liability. The burden of enforcing international law and human rights law, and of promoting corporate human rights accountability, should remain partly on governments and the international community,[1020] which include international courts and tribunals, but not necessarily treaties. The international community, international courts, and domestic courts should also seek to codify human rights violations and develop strategies, enforcement and remedies through the tort and civil law mechanism.

However, there are other possible explanations for the argument of corporate accountability dating back to Nuremberg in 1945 and 1946.[1021] Two possible reasons that can be observed in this study in addition to international corporate accountability doctrine are explained here. The first is that a domestic court, through a judicial panel implementing international norms, must include corporate obligations, the duty of care, and definitions of remedies from treaties as well as a universal jurisdiction[1022] that will allow international human rights violations to be heard in both the domestic judicial system and an international court. It must also be made clear that this will require states' willingness in addition to a meaningful sanctions process against the corporations involved. The second is that international

---

[1016]The Alien Tort Statute (28 USC. § 1350; ATS).

[1017]*Kiobel v Royal Dutch Petroleum*, No. 10–1491 (US Apr. 17, 2013) and *Morrison v National Australia Bank,* 561 US (2010).

[1018]*Sosa v Alvarez-Machain* 542 US 692.

[1019]Telford Taylor, *The Anatomy of The Nuremberg Trials: A Personal Memoir* (Knopf 2012).

[1020]Michel Rocard, 'What is The International Community?' (2013).

[1021] Gwynne. Skinner, 'Nuremberg's Legacy Continues: The Nuremberg Trials' Influence on Human Rights Litigation in US Courts under the Alien Tort Statute' (2008).

[1022]Schachter Oscar, *International Law in Theory and Practice* (Vol. 13. Martinus Nijhoff Publishers 1991).

law, through treaties on human rights and crimes against humanity, must permit the application of universal jurisdiction in tort law and should require states to extradite corporate officials or bring proceedings against corporations for human rights abuses committed abroad. Nonetheless, this book acknowledges that the application of universal jurisdiction[1023] can be problematic in domestic courts. This study reinforces the notion that international human rights law should have universal application.[1024] This will pave the way to a greater emphasis on activating the international mechanism in those situations where domestic courts cannot or will not function effectively.

In addition, in regard to MNCs' human rights accountability, this book advocates for corporate liability that is based purely on the current principle of tort and civil law accountability that has its liability and enforcement through negligence and the eggshell skull rule. The present study raises the possibility that tort and civil law will provide a better mechanism for corporation human rights violations than criminal law, because the tort and civil law may shift the burden of proof to the corporation. However, there is not much distinction between liability under tort law and criminal law, as their liability in legal principle coexists.[1025] Nevertheless, this book favours the tort and civil law system, because the requirement of intention and burden of proof is less substantial than criminal law. Therefore, in principle, the concept of MNCs' accountability for human rights abuses should be a discrete subject that must consist of the four interrelated bodies of law, such as: tort and civil law, international criminal law,[1026] humanitarian law,[1027] and human rights law.[1028] To pay too much attention to only one or two of these bodies of law, for the sake of clarifying a legal concept, will miss the full picture of accountability and

[1023]Cherif M Bassiouni, 'Universal Jurisdiction for International Crimes: Historical Perspectives and Contemporary Practice' (2001) 42 Virginia Journal of International Law 81.

[1024]Nihal Jayawickrama, *The Judicial Application of Human Rights Law: National, Regional and International Jurisprudence* (Cambridge University Press 2002).

[1025]Sanford H Kadish, Stephen J Schulhofer and Rachel E Barkow, *Criminal law and its processes: Cases and Materials* (Wolters Kluwer Law & Business 2016).

[1026]Jordan L Paust, Michael P Scharf, Leila Sadat, Cherif M Bassiouni, Jimmy Gurulé, Bruce Zagaris, and Sharon A Williams, *International Criminal Law* (Durham NC Carolina Academic Press 2000).

[1027]Jean-Marie Henckaerts and Louise Doswald-Beck, *Customary International Humanitarian Law* (Vol. 1. Cambridge University Press 2005).

[1028]Paul Sieghart, *The International Law of Human Rights* (Oxford University Press 1983).

remedy for MNCs under international law, and of human rights abuses committed in either the host or home state.

In relation to corporate liability, no uniform regulation exists at the international level. Some countries, such as Germany, do not provide for corporate liability at all, while other countries do have this provision, such as Switzerland. However, in the case of Switzerland, existing regulations have rarely been put into practice.[1029] Although some countries have successfully provided civil remedies for human rights violations caused by corporations, including the UK, the US and the Netherlands,[1030] this list remains limited. Consequently, in a broad analysis of corporate accountability, it is contested that corporate accountability does not exist and, even where it is present, is ineffective and lacks coherence.[1031] The current concept of corporate accountability is outdated, unrealistic and does not conform to the current expansion of the global economy. Therefore, there is a need for a concept of corporate accountability which implements a notion of social relations. This means moving the legal notion of corporate personality and impunity to a duty of care not to harm one's neighbour.

It is possible, therefore, that the examinations of liability for human rights violations by MNCs can be looked for in international human rights law, international humanitarian law, and international criminal law. This book will suggest future research in this area as this will help to measure the accountability of MNCs in the obligations that arise from these bodies of law. Having said that, this book will limit this part of the study to only international human rights law accountability as this notion is to develop corporate accountability and remedy through tort and civil law by applying the tort of negligence as the foundation to establish corporate liability for human rights abuses.

[1029] Art. 102 Schweizerisches Strafgesetzbuch, BBl. 2002 (Schweizerisches Gesetzesblatt).

[1030] P.M. Maduna, 'Declaration by Justice Minister Pennell Maduna on Apartheid Litigation in The United States', 11 July 2003. <www.info.gov.zajotherdocs/2003/apartheid.pdf > Accessed 15 November 2016; Minister Justice and Constitutional Development, 'Re South African Apartheid Litigation' (MDL 1499). <http://www. kosa. orgjdocuments/09~09~ OJ_MinJ usticeRSAto_J udgeBcheidlin. pdf > Accessed 15 November 2016. Also see, Magdalena Bexell, 'Distribution of Responsibility for Human Rights Protection: The Public-Private Distinction' (2004) Die Friedens-Warte 103.

[1031] Steven R Ratner, 'Corporations and Human Rights: A Theory of Legal Responsibility' (2001) 111 (3) Yale Law Journal 443.

Summary

Emerging findings from this chapter thus far state that corporations should be held accountable to the different players in the environments in which they operate, such as governments, judicial systems and society. It is also clear that the government, the corporation, society, and the court are key actors in what has been termed 'the concept of accountability'. However, it has also been found that for the corporation to be held accountable, it must meet the legal relationship laid down in ***Diagram 1*** and ***Diagram 2***; there must be a social relationship between the government, the corporation and society.[1032] Thus, if these relationships are established then there is accountability and there must be a legal implication as a result of this accountability. Lastly, it was also observed that where accountability exists, there must be sanctions and effective remedies for victims that have suffered through the principle of a duty of care. This is because of the particular act that arises from corporate business practice or corporate officials' conduct that is connected to the business purpose.

Furthermore, corporate accountability for human rights violations in international legal systems has proven to be a watershed. This is because there are inadequacies in the existing accountability mechanisms as well as several other legal problems and factual obstacles that hinder the enforcement of human rights law and international criminal law.[1033] This is also attributed to the problematic issues that persist, particularly with respect to the following: corporate criminal liability, the extraterritorial application of law, the attribution of criminal actions to specific agents, the requirements of accountability, the difficulties of extraterritorial investigations, and obtaining sufficient evidence for human rights violations.[1034] Hence, looking at corporate accountability in this concept of the duty of care will help to breach the gap that has existed in corporate liability for human rights abuses and environmental damages.

[1032]Zoltán Farkas, 'The Concept and Types of Social Relationship' (2014) 32 (1) Társadalomkutatás 10.

[1033] Wolfgang Kaleck and Miriam Saage-Maass, 'Corporate Accountability for Human Rights Violations Amounting to International Crimes The Status Quo and Its Challenges' (2010) 8 (3) Journal of International Criminal Justice 699.

[1034] Penelope Simons and Audrey Macklin, *The Governance Gap: Extractive Industries, Human Rights, and The Home State Advantage* (Routledge 2014).

Accountability in Relations to International Law and Human Rights Law

It appears that laws such as the UNDHR, the UN Covenant on Civil and Political Rights and the UN Covenant on Economic, Social, and Cultural Rights cohesively connect international criminal law with the social relations of humanity. The scope and extent of international criminal law and human rights law have generated much debate in the academic world.[1035] However, there has been less debate on the concept of corporate duty of care not to harm. Determining the extent to which international law acknowledges corporate accountability demands an inquiry that incorporates and elaborates the accountability of corporate human rights violations and prescribes the extensive and vigorous role for the state through the duty to act, but not merely a voluntary mechanism. It may be the case, therefore, that these could be explained through procedures which involve investigating the three subsidiary issues that in essence correspond to different strategies for providing corporate accountability and remedy in tort law:

1. To what extent does international human rights law directly provide corporate accountability for human rights violations?
2. To what extent does international human rights law obligate some or all states or the international community to try vigorously and sanction, or otherwise punish, perpetrators of human rights abuses?
3. To what extent does international human rights law authorise these same actors to try to extensively sanction and punish perpetrators of human rights violations within their control?

A typical example is noted in the Genocide Convention 1948,[1036] where international law explicitly allows a state to make a criminal act under the Convention a crime under domestic law. The Genocide Convention also obligates a state or an international court to carry out prosecutions or sanctions, as with the Genocide Convention, or to extradite or prosecute the

---

[1035]Robert Cryer, Håkan Friman, Darryl Robinson and Elizabeth Wilmshurst, *An Introduction to International Criminal Law and Procedure* (Cambridge University Press 2007).

[1036]UN General Assembly, *Convention on the Prevention and Punishment of the Crime of Genocide*, 9 December 1948, United Nations, Treaty Series, vol. 78, p. 277. <http://www.refworld.org/docid/3ae6b3ac0.html> Accessed 4 October 2016.

offender, as with the Torture Convention.[1037] Applying this to corporate accountability allows states or international courts to try and punish MNCs and their officials for a specific act, irrespective of normal jurisdictional limits.[1038] The approach by the international community is observed in the strategies adopted by the UN Security Council's statutes for the *ad hoc* tribunals in Yugoslavia and Rwanda and the Statute of the International Criminal Court[1039] to address the crimes under the Genocide Convention.[1040]

Although there is a substantial flaw in the principles of the Genocide Convention and the definition of these crimes, as well as its context and application,[1041] this study argues that this principle can form the basis of the universal application of a tort law norm. It can, therefore, be assumed that the methods by which the Convention provides for individual criminal responsibility can form the basis for a varied list of corporate accountability for human rights violations as well, though not the solution for liability and remedy. This is partly because tort law addresses individual rights to claim remedies, despite such rights for individual redress not existing under criminal law. Referring to the International Criminal Tribunal for Rwanda (ICTR) Statute, Article (6):

1. 'A person who planned, instigated, ordered, committed, or otherwise aided and abetted in the planning, preparation, or execution of a crime referred to in Articles 2 to 4 of the present Statute, shall be individually responsible for the crime.'[1042]

[1037]Thomas E Baker, 'A Primer on The Jurisdiction of The U.S. Courts of Appeals' (2009) 09 (01) *Florida International University Legal Studies Research Paper;* UN General Assembly, *Convention Against Torture and Other Cruel, Inhuman or Degrading Treatment or Punishment*, 10 December 1984, United Nations, Treaty Series, vol. 1465, 85. <http://www.refworld.org/docid/3ae6b3a94.html> Accessed 8 July 2017.

[1038]Yoram Dinstein, 'International Criminal Law' (1985) 20 Israel Law Review 206.

[1039]UN Security Council, *Resolution 827 (1993) Adopted by the Security Council at Its 3217th Meeting, On 25 May 1993*, 25 May 1993, S/RES/827 (1993) <http://www.refworld.org/docid/3b00f21b1c.html> Accessed 4 October 2016.

[1040]*Darfur, Prosecutor v Al Bashir (Omar Hassan)*; Case no ICC-02/05-01/09-139, ICL 912 (ICC 2011).

[1041] Oh Jongsok, 'The Prosecutor's Dilemma-Strengths and Flaws of The Genocide Convention' (2003) 10 (3) Murdoch University Electronic Journal of Law 4, David Chuter, *War Crimes* (Lynne Rienner Publishers 2003, Peter Quayle, 'Unimaginable Evil: The Legislative Limitations of the Genocide Convention' (2005) 5 (3) International Criminal Law Review 363 and David Chuter, *War Crimes: Confronting Atrocity in the Modern World* (Lynne Rienner Publishers 2003).

[1042] <https://www.nesl.edu/userfiles/file/wcmemos/2001/savastano.pdf> Accessed 20 April 2018.

2. 'The official position of any accused person, whether as Head of State or Government or as a responsible Government official, shall not relieve such person of criminal responsibility nor mitigate punishment.'[1043]

On the other hand, tort law implicitly concerns itself with individual responsibilities that people have with one another, as opposed to those responsibilities laid out in criminal law. Tort law provides legal remedies to those who have been damaged by someone else's failure to meet these implicit responsibilities, while criminal law exists to punish an individual for crimes against the state, not to provide remedies for individuals who have been inflicted with a criminal harm.[1044]

The international community's dependence on all three international law conventions[1045] indicates that a violation of international law becomes an international crime if the international community agreed through any of these laws,[1046] regardless of whether they are implemented through treaty, custom, or another prescriptive method, to hold individuals or any actors accountable[1047] for human rights violations. MNCs may be held accountable if these principles are to be adopted and enforced via tort or civil law. The presumption is that fundamental human rights are part of all domestic law.[1048] In a critical analysis, it can be assumed that accountability shares some of the goals and methods of international human rights, so holding MNCs liable under this principle of tort and civil law is an evolutionary process rather than a newly developing concept. This assumption is reached because human rights law and obligations and accountability for these

---

1043 <https://www.nesl.edu/userfiles/file/wcmemos/2001/savastano.pdf> Accessed 20 April 2018 and UN General Assembly, *Rome Statute of The International Criminal Court (Last Amended 2010)* (1998).
<http://www.refworld.org/docid/3ae6b3a84.html> Accessed 8 July 2017

1044 Arthur Ripstein, 'The Division of Responsibility and the Law of Tort' (2003) 72 Fordham Law Review 1811.

1045 International Law, International Humanitarian Law and International Criminal Law.

1046 International Criminal Tribunal for former Yugoslavia, *Prosecutor v Kunarac*, Judgment of 22 February 2001, para. 467: and *Coard et al. v United States*, Case No. 10.951, 29 September 1999, para. 39.

1047 Theodor Meron, 'International Criminalization of Internal Atrocities' (1995) 89 American Journal of International Law 554.

1048 Andrew Z Drzemczewski, *European Human Rights Convention in Domestic Law: A Comparative Study* (Oxford University Press 1985).

violations are incorporated into international law.[1049] Therefore, the fact that this study uses the term 'rights' to describe this civil wrong, rather than the language of a duty, indicates nothing important. Likewise, the duties of care acknowledged under the law of negligence can be said to be just as much about human rights as the rights derived from tort law. This means that the duty of care arising under the neighbourhood principles exists to protect the rights of people and the environment. Hence, a rebuttable presumption exists that where there is a duty of care to protect people and the environment, there is an effective remedy.

This means that corporate accountability gives rise to two duties of care. These duties fall into duties that are owed to other people and duties that are owed to no one in particular. The first is private duties[1050] and the second set is public duties.[1051] A given duty is owed to someone else if it was imposed for the benefit of that someone else, and a given duty is owed to no one in particular if it was imposed for the benefit of the community as a whole or for the benefit of some section of the community. Arguably, the corporate duty of care falls into both categories of duties of care imposed for the benefit of the individual or the community in order to not violate their rights through negligent conduct.[1052] The tort of negligence imposes a duty of care on the corporation for the benefit of the community in which the corporation is conducting its business operations. In contrast, if one takes two given individuals, A and B, A will have a duty under international law and human rights law not to pursue a course of conduct that will harm their (i) human rights and the environment which they live in and (ii) the harm which they know or ought to know may have amounted to a violation of international law and human rights law. A's duty is owed to B; it is imposed on A for the benefit of a particular individual, B.

Equally, international criminal law cannot be viewed as an alternative to substitute or enforce international human rights law on corporations, as demonstrated above in the concept of a duty of care and

---

[1049]Anthony D'Amato, 'Human Rights as Part of Customary International Law: A Plea for Change of Paradigms' (1995/96) 25 Georgia Journal of International & Comparative Law 47.

[1050]James D Barnett, 'The Foundations of The Distinction between Public and Private Functions in Respect to The Common-Law Tort Liability of Municipal Corporations' (1937) 16 Oregon Law Review 250.

[1051]Joseph W Glannon, 'Liability for "Public Duties" Under the Tort Claims Act: The Legislature Reconsiders The Public Duty Rule' (1994) 79 Massachusetts Law Review 17.

[1052]Brenda Mothersole and Ann Ridley, 'Tort of Negligence' *A-Level Law in Action* (Macmillan Education UK 1995) 211, 230.

further in the Khmer Rouge case study.[1053] (This concerned the 'genocide in Cambodia: By April 1975, a Communist group known as the Khmer Rouge, led by Pol Pot, seized control of Cambodia, renaming the country Democratic Kampuchea. Civil war had existed in Cambodia since 1970.'[1054]) Thus, findings here may help us to understand the relationship between the corporate duty of care, international law procedure, and human rights. The notion here is that tort and civil law can address a variety of acts[1055] beyond current human rights law, such as forced labour, other environmental-related acts, human rights offences, organised crime, corruption, mercenaries, and the initiation of an aggressive war through indirect corporate conduct.[1056] Tort law is based on reasonable conduct so that no one can be held liable in negligence for acting reasonably. It can also be argued that the tort of negligence may not apply to organised crime, corruption, or money laundering because these are offences under criminal law. This is also the case if one can prove that there exists an assumption that the corporation acted negligently, and that liability should be imposed on the corporation for breaching its duty of care. It is therefore not possible for the court to find that A owed B a duty to not cause harm if it was reasonable for A to act in such a way. In contrast, the fact that A acted reasonably will not always prevent them from being held liable for committing a tort.

This duty of care may be explained by the fact that a corporation is an artificial legal person,[1057] as noted by Lord Diplock in *Tesco Supermarket Ltd v Natrass*, and that 'it is incapable itself of doing any physical act or being in a state of mind'.[1058] If a corporation is to act, then it can only do so through a natural person, specifically, of course, through people who are capable of performing physical actions. Therefore, this creates a problem when one wishes to determine whether or not a corporation breached its duty of care owed to someone else.[1059] Hence, the

---

[1053]Ben Kiernan, *The Pol Pot Regime: Race, Power, and Genocide in Cambodia under The Khmer Rouge, 1975-79* (Yale University Press 2014).

[1054]<https://hmh.org/page.asp?id=41> Accessed 20 September 2019.

[1055]Peter Cane, 'Mens Rea in Tort Law' (2000) 20 (4) Oxford Journal of Legal Studies 533, 556.

[1056]Jordan L Paust, Michael P Scharf, Leila Sadat, Bassiouni M Cherif, Jimmy Gurulé, Bruce Zagaris and Sharon A Williams, *International Criminal Law* (Durham NC: Carolina Academic Press 2000).

[1057] Susan Mary Watson, 'The Corporate Legal Person' (2019) 19 (1) Journal of Corporate Law Studies 137, 166.

[1058]*Tesco Supermarkets Ltd v Nattrass* [1972] AC 153.

[1059]*Ibid.*

question arises as to whose actions should the court look towards in order to determine whether or not that duty of care was breached. The facts in *Tesco*[1060] illustrate the problem.

In the *Tesco* case, a customer at a Tesco store was charged Trade Descriptions Act 1968 3s 11d for a packet of washing powder when posters in the window of the store advertised that brand washing powder was on special offer at Trade Descriptions Act 1968 2s 11d per packet. The general manager of the store, Mr. Clement, was at fault for this; he had failed to take reasonable steps to ensure that the store was stocked with some packets with the mark of a lower price. Tesco was charged with committing an offence under Trade Descriptions Act 1968 s 11 (2) of the Trade Descriptions Act 1968 which provided that 'if any person offering to supply any good gives any indication likely to be taken in fact being offered he shall, subject to the provision of this Act, be guilty of an offence.' In their defence, Tesco sought to rely on s 24 (1) of the Act which provided that '[i]n any proceedings for an offence under this Act, it shall be a defence for the person charged to prove (a) that the commission of the offence was due to the act or default of another person and (b) that he took reasonable precautions and exercised all due diligence to avoid the commission of such an offence by himself or any person under his control.'

Tesco could establish that reference (a) was true; the crime was committed because of Clement's default. However, could it establish that reference (b) was true and that it took all reasonable care to ensure that its goods were not sold at a price higher than the advertised price? Clearly, Clement did not take such care, but did that mean that Tesco, Clement's employer, did not take such care? More generally, whose actions should be looked at to determine whether Tesco took reasonable care to ensure that its goods were not sold at a price higher than the advertised price? The House of Lords' answer was that one should look at the actions of those who represented Tesco's guiding mind or will. Only if they failed to take care to ensure that Tesco's goods were not sold at a price higher than the advertised price would it be proper to say that Tesco failed to take care in ensuring that its goods were sold at a price higher than the advertised price. Clement, the House of Lords held, did not 'function as the directing mind or will of the corporation' but he was being directed.[1061]

The principle endorsed in *Tesco* that the court could ascertain what a corporation did at a particular time by looking at the acts of those who represented the guiding mind or will of the corporation at that time is well

---

[1060]*Ibid.*
[1061]*Ibid.*

established.[1062] However, this principle was recently brought into question at the Supreme Court, as it has been suggested that how the court ascertains what a corporation did depends very much on the nature and purpose of the legal rule which requires one to find out what that corporation did. In *Re Supply of Ready Mixed Concrete (No.2)*,[1063] four corporations which were engaged in the supply of ready mixed concrete entered into agreements with each other which fixed the prices at which they would supply concrete to customers, and determined what share each corporation would enjoy on the market. These agreements were unlawful under s 35 (1) of the Restrictive Trade Practices Act 1976. The Director General of Fair Trade obtained an injunction against the four corporations which required them not to enter into or give effect to any such agreement in future.

In a subsequent Privy Council Case, *Meridian Global Funds Management Asia Ltd v. Securities Commission*,[1064] Lord Hoffmann, who gave the only judgment, endorsed the result in *Re Supply of Ready Mixed Concrete (No.2)* and reconciled it with the decision in the *Tesco* case by arguing that applying a particular legal rule to a company requires the courts to find out what that company did. This is always a matter of interpretation: given that the rule in question was intended to apply to a company, how was the application of the rule applied? One finds the answer to this question by applying the usual canons of interpretation and by taking into account the language of the rule and its content and policy.[1065] In every case where an artificial legal person owed someone else a duty of care, the courts are confronted with the problem of whose actions should be looked at to determine whether or not that person breached that duty.

In the case of corporate accountability, that problem is solved by adopting the guiding mind or will principle according to whether the court determines what a corporation did at a particular time by evaluating those in control of decisions. It can be suggested that elaborating on corporate accountability is derived directly from tort and civil law. The notion of a duty of care paves the way to holding a corporation accountable for its misconduct. However, the question remains, under what circumstance will international law hold corporations accountable for their human rights violations through the duty of care? The question of which violations of

[1062] It traces its origin to the judgement of Viscount Haldane LC in *Lennard's Carrying Co. Ltd v Asiatic Petroleum Co. Ltd* [1915] AC 705, 713 and Bolton *(Engineering) Co. Ltd v T J Graham & Sons Ltd* [1957] 1 QB 159, 172.

[1063] *Supply of Ready Mixed Concrete* [1992] QB 212.

[1064] *Meridian Global Funds Management Asia Ltd v Securities Commission* [1995] UKPC 5.

[1065] *Ibid.*

international law, including human rights law, require accountability mechanisms is somewhat unsettled in the current literature.[1066]

This present study raises the possibility that corporate accountability in tort and civil law overlaps with international human rights law, and so corporate accountability should follow the same concept when implementing international law and human rights obligations on non-state actors in the international arena, which include a corporation's duty of care to protect and respect human rights in the environment in which they operate. The explanation above supports the hypothesis that international human rights law is interrelated to other bodies of tort and civil law. Thus, international criminal law, international human rights, international humanitarian law and corporate accountability should not be considered separate but should be seen as part of one mechanism of enforcing human rights obligations in the international arena through tort and civil law mechanism. Likewise, it is argued that human rights obligations in the international arena have their foundation in the duty of care principle. Therefore, the corporate duty of care forms part of this correlation of international human rights. One of the emerging findings from this illustration is that when a MNC's accountability and remedy is viewed in the concept of tort and civil liability, it will provide international legal systems and domestic legal systems accountability and remedy procedures to follow.

Linking these accountability and remedy procedures to tort and civil law will ensure effective accountability and remedy for victims of human rights violations. Thus, tort and civil accountability should arise whenever a corporation violates human rights, damages the environment, or a state fails to comply with applicable international human rights law. Likewise, tort and civil law recognise exceptions of accountability for third-party behaviour; thus, drawing on this legal principle will put pressure on the corporation to make sure that its operation conforms to human rights duties. This approach is also further supported by international law that acknowledges group civil responsibility or tort liability for human rights abuses, in particular for organised non-state actors such as guerrilla or secessionist movements.[1067] Indeed, international law has also acknowledged

[1066]Nguyen Quoc, Dinh Daillier, Patrick Pellet, Alain Nguyen Quoc Dinh, Patrick Daillier and Alain Pellet, *Droit International Public* (No. 341.1/. 8. Librairie Générale de Droit et de Jurisprudence (1975).

[1067]Gerald G Fitzmaurice, 'Third Report on the Law of Treaties' (1958) 2 Yearbook of the International Law Commission 20, UN Doc. A/CN.4/115.

the determination of individual states to impose individual civil responsibility for human rights abuses through civil liability under national law.[1068]

With respect to the first research question set out in this book, it was found that the international criminal law, specifically that the Statute of Rome, provides some sort of accountability for an act against human dignity. The Nuremberg trials and other prosecutions of Axis defendants clearly established individual and corporate accountability for human rights abuses, but this is limited in regards to awarding liability and remedy. Also, the most important proven relevant finding in the Nuremberg principle was that it allows corporate officials to be held accountable for corporate misconduct. An implication of this is that Nuremberg established a semi perfect platform for MNCs' liability for human rights violations under international law. Therefore, enforcing human rights accountability through the tort and civil law concept forms the other part of international human rights accountable. The principle of international criminal law as a platform, in conjunction with tort and civil law principles, ensures fairness and justice for victims of human rights abuses. This is because of the failure of international criminal law to provide a direct remedy for the victim of human rights violations and environmental damages.

Part II will examine accountability in the context of a duty of care. It will critically analyse whether tort law, rather than international criminal law, could provide jurisdiction over corporate human rights violations, such as: 1. Summary executions; 2. Arbitrary detentions; 3. Draconian restrictions on the rights to freedom of expression, association and assembly; 4. Environmental damages; 5. Forced labour; 6. Torture; 7. Unfair trials; 8. Aiding and abetting domestic governments to violate rights; 9. Damage to livelihoods; 10. Complicity in the commission of torture; and 11. Extrajudicial killings. It will likewise focus on the fundamental rights enshrined in the International Covenant on Economic, Social and Cultural Rights,[1069] specifically:

- forcibly evicting people from their homes (the right to adequate housing);[1070]

[1068] Steven R Ratner and Jason S Abrams, *Accountability for Human Rights Atrocities in International Law: Beyond the Nuremberg Legacy* (Oxford University Press USA 2001).
[1069] UN General Assembly, *International Covenant on Economic, Social and Cultural Rights*, 16 December 1966, United Nations, Treaty Series, vol. 993, p. 3. <http://www.refworld.org/docid/3ae6b36c0.html> Accessed 24 September 2016.
[1070] *Ibid.*

- contaminating water, for example, with waste from state-owned facilities (the right to health);[1071]
- minimum wage (rights at work);[1072]
- failure to prevent employers from discriminating in recruitment (based on sex, disability, race, political opinion, class, social origin, HIV status, etc.) (the right to work);[1073]
- destroying or contaminating food and its source, such as arable land and water (the right to food);[1074]
- failure to provide for a reasonable limitation of working hours (rights at work);[1075]
- banning the use of minority or indigenous languages (the right to participate in cultural life); and
- arbitrary and illegal disconnection of water for personal and domestic use (the right to water).[1076]

[1071] *Ibid.*
[1072] *Ibid.*
[1073] *Ibid.*
[1074] *Ibid.*
[1075] *Ibid.*
[1076] *Ibid.*

CHAPTER IV

The aims and objectives of this chapter are to further argue that the tort of negligence, under the neighbourhood principle, could be an effective mechanism for holding corporations accountable for human rights violations. The relationship between the corporation, the supply chain, the government, society and the environment gives rise to a positive duty of care not to cause harm or damage.[1077] Adding to the minimal development in the field of tort law perspectives, this book expands on this concept by building on the idea of the duty of care in the framework set out in the neighbourhood principle, to analyse the options available for foreign nationals wishing to hold multinational corporations to account within home country jurisdictions, such as in the US, the UK, or the European Union. This chapter also builds on the legal principle of a duty of care and other legal cases to establish 'A Framework and Focus Approach' of assigning accountability for a supply chain corporation, its business partners and the parent corporation.

In a detailed reflection, it also observes that the relationship between corporate business operations, suppliers, subsidiaries and human rights violations give rise to a rebuttable duty of care. However, this can be limited in many different circumstances. Similarly, the nature, duration, and type of relationship in a supply chain may be different. Some corporations in the supply chain may have a higher level of influence over the corporation they do business with, while others may not. 'Some actors with special knowledge or skills might induce reliance by'[1078] victims from 'other'[1079] supply chain corporations, while other corporations will not. Thus, the supply chain relationship with a special characteristic that goes beyond an 'arm's length' transaction can trigger factors for legal liability of a

[1077]Ingrid De Poorter, 'Auditor's Liability towards Third Parties within the EU: A Comparative Study between the United Kingdom, The Netherlands, Germany and Belgium' (2008) 3 (1) Journal of International Commercial Law and Technology 68. Also see; <http://www.bhrinlaw.org/improving-paths-to-accountability-for-human-rights-abuses-in-the-global-supply-chains-a-legal-guide.pdf> Accessed 14 December 2017.
[1078]<http://www.bhrinlaw.org/documents/amnestyinternational.creatingaparadigmshiftpol3070372017english.pdf> Accessed 9 May 2016.
[1079]Ibid.

contractual partner for labour and human rights violations occurring in its supply business operations. Going beyond the 'arm's length' transaction between specific contractual parties in a special relationship does create a legal duty of care.

The purpose of the duty of care will help to establish the legal paths to accountability for human rights abuses in global supply chains. Therefore, the duty of care will provide an affirmative and interpretive instrument to support the push for tort liability for human rights violations in the global economy which is grounded in existing legal principles. The rationale behind this approach is an attempt to overcome the legal obstacle between the law and the economic and social realities prevailing in the global production network.

Additionally, through the use of the tort of negligence, this chapter highlights the positive grounds in which victims can bring a successful claim against corporations. It further argues that the tort of negligence should be expanded and modified to reflect the development of parent corporation and subsidiary accountability and the circumstances surrounding business operations. Finally, it establishes a *prima facie* case for corporate accountability and the role an international court/tribunal could play in a corporate duty of care case. In conclusion, this chapter offers a meaningful understanding of the duty of care and a practical solution for accountability and remedy of human rights violations through tort law if the corporation's (and its subsidiary's) undertakings are carried out negligently.

The Foundation of Tort Law

Generally, tort law can be observed well before the Roman times, when the law of ancient communities was based on the law of civil wrongs, rather than criminal law.[1080] Roman and Germanic tort laws have their origins in blood feuds and principles of vengeance.[1081] The French system was established through the basic principles of the Napoleonic Codes and the Anglo-American liability framework has its foundation in separate torts based on the Writ System.[1082] The law of tort varies from jurisdiction to jurisdiction, and it has evolved in very diverse ways, responding to different cultural, political, and social influences. As a result, the Industrial Revolution

---

[1080] Henry Sumner Maine, 'Ancient Law, It's Connection with The Early History of Society and Its Relation to Modern Ideas' (first published 1891, New York: Dorset 1986).

[1081] Wendell Holmes Oliver, *The Common Law* (Harvard University Press 2009).

[1082] Mark Lunney and Ken Oliphant, *Tort Taw: Text and Materials* (Oxford University Press 2008).

and the liberation of Western society brought the expansion of and significant changes to tort law.[1083] This resulted in the development of the tort of negligence,[1084] as acknowledged by Ennecking, and 'while industries and businesses grew with their technological and scientific know-how … [s]o did the groups of people, employees, and consumers, as well as other third parties that were exposed to the risk of the faulty product, hazardous materials, or potentially harmful production process.'[1085]

Tort law protects rights held by individuals. As noted by Blackstone, individual rights include the absolute rights of personal security, life, liberty and property,[1086] as well as the respective rights that individuals attain as members of the community and standing in innumerable relations to each other.[1087] These rights allow the victim of a private wrong to seek a remedy by bringing the appropriate form of action, such as a writ of trespass, for the breach of that right.[1088] However, a breach of the duty of care (*damnum*) alone is not enough to give rise to a judicial remedy. Rather it could warrant a cause of action only if the defendant suffered a legal injury, meaning a violation of a legal right (*injuria*).[1089]

A factual harm without a legal injury is known as *damnum absque injuria* and provides no basis for relief.[1090] While factual injury alone is not enough to give rise to redress, legal injury alone is enough to warrant action. A typical example of this is a trespass, where the appropriate action for redress is a direct, forcible invasion of a right; a claimant needs only to prove the violation of the legal right.[1091] An example of this rule is the 1348 case of *I de S et ux. v W de S*, where the defendant W de S went to the home of plaintiffs I de S and M de S at night to purchase wine, and upon finding the

[1083]*Ibid.*

[1084]*Ibid.*

[1085]Liesbeth FH Enneking, 'Foreign Direct Liability and Beyond-Exploring the Role of Tort Law in Promoting International Corporate Social Responsibility and Accountability' (2012).

[1086]William Blackstone, *Commentaries on the Laws of England* (Vol. 3. Garland Pub 1978. Also see, Caleb Nelson, 'Adjudication in the Political Branches' (2007) Columbia Law Review 559.

[1087]*Ibid.*

[1088]William Blackstone, *Tracts, Chiefly Relating to The Antiquities and Laws of England* (3d ed. Oxford Claredon Press 1771).

[1089]Andrew F Hessick, 'Standing, Injury in Fact, and Private Rights' (2008) 93 Cornell Law Review 275.

[1090]Theodore Sedgwick, Arthur G Sedgwick and Joseph Henry Beale, *A Treatise on The Measure of Damages* (Baker Voorhis 1891).

[1091]Ralph Sutton, *Personal Actions at Common Law* (Butterworth & Company Publishers 1929).

door closed, beat the door with a hatchet until M de S stuck her head outside and told him to stop. W de S swung the hatchet toward M de S but did not strike her, and the plaintiffs sued for assault.[1092] Additionally, in the English case *Ashby v. White,* Chief Justice Holt rejected the idea that a claimant could not bring an action in the case arising from the violation of a right if he suffered no harm.[1093] This implied that tort law and remedy for the violation of rights has been well-known in human existence, ever since the Romans.[1094] Chief Justice Holt clarified:

> '[i]f the plaintiff has a right, he must of necessity have a means to vindicate and maintain it, and a remedy if he is injured in the exercise or enjoyment of it; and indeed it is a vain thing to imagine a right without a remedy; for want of right and want of remedy are reciprocal.'[1095]

In response to the argument presented in this case, he contested that an action on the case was 'not maintainable because there is no hurt or damage to the plaintiff.' Chief Justice Holt further explained that 'surely every injury imports damage, though it does not cost the party one farthing, and it is impossible to prove the contrary; for damage is not merely pecuniary, but an injury imports damage, when a man is thereby hindered of his right.'[1096] Irrespective of the claim, the violation of the right is what must be taken into consideration. Therefore, Chief Justice Holt stated,

> 'in an action for slanderous words, though a man does not lose a penny by reason of the speaking them, yet he shall have an action. So, if a man gives another a cuff on the ear, though it cost him nothing, no not so much as a little diachylon, yet he shall have his action, for it is a personal injury. So, a man shall have an action against another for riding over his ground, though it does him no damage; for it is an invasion of his property, and the other has no right to come there.'[1097]

[1092]*I de S et ux. v W de S, Y.B.Lib.* Ass. folio 99, Placitum 60 (Assizes 1348), *reprinted* in William L Prosser, John W Wade and Victor E Schwartz, *Torts: Cases and Materials* (2010).

[1093]*Ashby v White* (1703) 92 ER 126.

[1094]David Ibbetson, 'How the Romans Did for Us: Ancient Roots of The Tort of Negligence' (2003) 26 (2) University of New South Wales Law Journal 475.

[1095]Ralph Sutton (n 1472).

[1096]*Ibid.*

[1097]*Ibid.*

A point to note: even though Chief Justice Holt's opinion was in dissent,[1098] his judgment succeeded on appeal in the House of Lords.[1099] Chief Justice Holt correctly stated the law books in relation to law in nineteenth-century England[1100] and the United States.[1101] Tort protects the rights of the individual from the unjustified interference of the enjoyment of the personal rights and personal property rights, which are derived from law.

In the twentieth and twenty-first centuries, tort litigation has been seen as a mechanism that evolved from private law and is now viewed as a mechanism for compensation in protecting modern rights. Therefore, in the brief foundation of tort law, it is argued that tort law is a mechanism and fundamental part of the socio-cultural framework in which it is rooted.[1102] The indication here is that tort law has a great ability to reflect on ever-changing societal and corporate behaviours and practices. This is evident in the realisation of women's rights by acknowledging them as individual persons before the law rather than as the property of their husbands. This allows women to sue in their own rights for personal injuries.[1103] Tort law could provide similar protection to victims of corporate human rights violations. This is because tort law places much emphasis on the judiciary to exercise a strong and effective remedy through reparation for victims whose rights have been violated.[1104]

The Different Theoretical Perceptions of Tort Law

As examined above, the foundation of tort law has been separated and scrutinised through a diverse viewpoint in order to establish the fundamental purpose of tort law. Following the foundation of tort law, it is observed that tort law is divided into two schools of thought: tort as an

1098See at 942–43, 92 Eng. Rep. at 129.

1099Louis L Jaffe, 'Suits Against Governments and Officers: Sovereign Immunity' (1963) Harvard Law Review 1, 39.

1100*Embrey v Owen* 6 Exch 353 at 370, 368, 155 Eng. Rep. 579, 585 [1851].

1101*Webb v Portland Mfg*. Co., 29 F. Cas. 506, 508 (Story, Circuit Justice, C.C.D. Me. 1838) (No. 17,322) and *Parker v Griswold*, 17 Conn. 288, 304 (1845).

1102Mauro Bussani and Marta Infantino, 'The Many Cultures of Tort Liability' in Mauro Bussani and Anthony J Sebok (eds) *Comparative Tort Law: Global Perspectives* (Publisher Edward Elgar 2015).

1103Leslie Bender, 'Tort Law's Role as a Tool for Social Justice Struggle' (1997) 37 Washburn Law Journal 249.

1104*Ibid*.

economic concept, and tort as justice concept,[1105] that offers remedy for victims whose rights have been breached by corporations. This principle creates two recognised duties under tort law that are as follows: the responsibility not to harm the people in your contemplations and strict liability, in which conduct is governed by a duty not to injure or cause harm to a person;[1106] and fault liability in which a person conducted to carry out a duty does not injure a person or cause harm to a person.[1107] Therefore, the fundamental claim is that tort law should be seen as an element to offer remedies for the victim and a deterrent element to stop the future breach of rights. In this understanding, strict liability and fault liability area are efficient mechanisms to protect personal rights. Likewise, it allows all actors to only take cost-justified precaution,[1108] not to harm their neighbour, as well as a deterrence mechanism,[1109] to prevent future harm.

Lastly, along similar lines, tort law should be seen as either a mechanism of social policy[1110] or as an expression of one's rights and duties, irrespective of the gravity of the rights and the duties.[1111] The non-instrumental theory of tort law should be seen as a mechanism derived to the interpretation of tort as a method of providing corrective justice,[1112] which should be at the core of every remedy for a wrongful act,[1113] such as corporate human rights violations. This is crucial because it challenges the core economic concept of tort by including tort of negligence in the ordinary moral conception of the corporate act and responsibility, carelessness, and wrongdoing, harm, and reparation.[1114]

Following this illustration, this book observed that tort law provides effective accountability, such as the right to truth, the right to

[1105]Gregory C Keating, 'Distributive and Corrective Justice in the Tort Law of Accidents' (2000) 74 Southern California Law Review 193.

[1106]Steven Shavell, 'Strict liability versus Negligence' (1980) 9(1) The Journal of Legal Studies 1. Also see: John J Kircher, Kenneth S Abraham, 'Strict Liability in Negligence' (2011).

[1107] Jules Coleman, Scott Hershovitz and Gabriel Mendlow, 'Theories of the Common Law of Torts' (2003).

[1108]I*bid.*

[1109]*Ibid.*

[1110]Gary T Schwartz, 'Reality in the Economic Analysis of Tort Law: Does Tort Law Really Deter' (1994) 42 UCLA Law Review 377.

[1111]*Ibid.*

[1112]Richard A Posner, 'Instrumental and Non instrumental Theories of Tort Law' (2013) 88 Indian Law Journal 469.

[1113]*Ibid.*

[1114]Jules L Coleman, 'Practice of Corrective Justice' (1995) 37 Arizona Law Review 5.

justice and the right to effective reparation. This can be extended to corporation and supply chain wrongful acts in home or host states. The principle of tort law in this book follows the conceptual parameter established under the rule of law, whereby 'effective remedies and effectiveness of justice, notably in providing effective recourse to anyone who alleges that her or his rights have been violated, are essential.'[1115]

The 'European Convention stipulates the right to access the court, which is an important element in remedying violations.'[1116] 'The European Convention on Human Rights Article 6, stipulates the right to an effective remedy in Article 13 and actual reparations in Article 41. Also, the ICCPR includes compensation in the article on fair trial (Article 14'),[1117] which also includes a condition with regard to access to court. In addition, Article 2 ICCPR stipulates the existence of effective remedies. Article 1 of the American Convention contains a general legal obligation to respect the Convention and Article 25 contains the right to judicial protection. Under the rule of law, effective remedies and effectiveness of justice, notably in providing effective recourse to anyone who alleges that her or his rights have been violated, are essential.[1118] Without such recourse, justice is of little use. While the American Convention stipulates in Article 25 that 'effective recourse to a competent court or tribunal', the ICCPR contains a broader general provision requiring states to respect and ensure to all individuals within their territory the rights recognised in the Covenant. States must ensure that individuals have accessible, effective and enforceable remedies and obtain reparations where violations have occurred. Hence, the nature of the duty of care will impose obligations on the states and non-state actors to protect and respect human rights.

Tort of Negligence

The lack of corporate accountability is further persevered by international voluntary mechanisms,[1119] such as corporate social responsibility

---

[1115]<https://www.humanrights.is/the-human-rightsrpoject/humanrightscasesand materials/comparativeanalysis/therighttodueprocess/effective/> accessed 30 June 2016.

[1116] *Ibid.*

[1117]<project/humanrightscasesandmaterials/humanrightsconceptsideasandfora/thec onceptsofhumanrightsanintroduction/definitionsandclassifications> Accessed 30 June 2017.

[1118]*Ibid.*

[1119]John Ruggie, 'Report of the Special Representative of The Secretary-General on The Issue of Human Rights and Transnational Corporations and Other Business

(CSR)[1120] initiatives,[1121] which are not legally binding. However, the concept of CSR is a subject that has links to many areas of law, including international law and European law, corporate law and corporate governance, tort law and contract law, procedural law, labour and environmental law, and criminal law.[1122] All of these areas contribute importantly to the development of CSR, and ultimately respond to the serious challenges victims face under corporate human rights abuses.[1123] Similarly, Detta 'offers a working definition for CSR which insists on going beyond the minimal in protecting and promoting human rights.'[1124] 'He proposes an approach to employing disclosures in regulating CSR to promote human rights.'[1125] 'His proposal is based on Section 116 of France's Nouvelles Régulations Économiques'[1126] and California's Transparency in Supply Chains Act of 2010.[1127] In reviewing Adeyeye's

---

Enterprises: Guiding Principles on Business and Human Rights: Implementing the United Nations 'Protect, Respect and Remedy' Framework' (2011) 29 (2) Netherlands Quarterly of Human Rights 224, 253.

[1120]Andreas Georg Scherer and Guido Palazzo, 'Globalization and Corporate Social Responsibility' (2008). Corporate Social Responsibility (CSR).

[1121]Justine Nolan, *The Corporate Responsibility to Respect Human Rights: Soft Law or Not Law Human Rights Obligations of Business: Beyond the Corporate Responsibility to Respect?* (Cambridge University Press 2013).

[1122]Tineke Elisabeth Lambooy, 'Legal Aspects of Corporate Social Responsibility' (2014).

[1123]Tineke Elisabeth Lambooy, '*Corporate Social Responsibility: Legal and Semi-Legal Frameworks Supporting CSR: Developments 2000-2010 and Case Studies* (Diss. Faculty of Law, Leiden University 2010), Earth Charter. <http://www.earthcharterinaction.org/content/pages/Read-the-Charter.html> Accessed 9 August 2017 and Tineke Lambooy, 'Legal Aspects of Corporate Social Responsibility (2014) 1 (30) Utrecht Journal of International and European Law.

[1124] Jeffrey A Van Detta, 'Sexual Orientation, Human Rights, and Corporate Sponsorship of the Sochi Olympic Games: Rethinking the Voluntary Approach to Corporate Social Responsibility' (2014) 30 (78) Utrecht Journal of International and European Law 99.

[1125]*Ibid.* also see: Tineke Lambooy, 'Legal Aspects of Corporate Social Responsibility (2014) 1 (30) Utrecht Journal of International and European Law.

[1126]Tineke Lambooy, 'Legal Aspects of Corporate Social Responsibility (2014) 1 (30) Utrecht Journal of International and European Law and Mary Lou Egan, et al. 'France's Nouvelles Regulations Economiques: Using Government Mandates for Corporate Reporting to Promote Environmentally Sustainable Economic Development' (2003) 25th Annual Research Conference for Public Policy and Management, Washington, DC.

[1127]Tineke Lambooy, 'Legal Aspects of Corporate Social Responsibility (2014) 1 (30) Utrecht Journal of International and European Law.

book *Corporate Social Responsibility of Multinational Corporations in Developing Countries: Perspectives on Anti-Corruption*,[1128] Ako describes how the author takes a stand that a CSR approach should be adopted to curb the involvement of multinational companies in corrupt practices, particularly in developing countries. Corruption is considered a CSR issue which should be regulated in an effective manner.[1129] The Earth Charter also promotes a corruption-free society: 'Eliminate Corruption in all Public and Private Institutions.'[1130]

It may be the case, therefore, that CSR and corporate due diligence[1131] traditionally focus on flagging the legal risks that might emerge from a company's contracts or financial obligations. A target company might express support for a set of voluntary third-party CSR protocols, but not give them much legal weight because they are not binding contracts or laws enforced by a government. Yet signing on to these statements brings legal risk. A typical example is where corporations can require their subsidiaries or suppliers to comply to minimum human rights stands, and publicly state that they monitor compliance and respond to recognised breaches by either requiring developments or ending the business relations. The importance of CSR for mining companies has changed rapidly. The government of Canada last year announced an 'enhanced' CSR strategy that threatens to cut off diplomatic support to Canadian companies with operations overseas who fail to comply with some recognised international standards.[1132]

[1128] Adefolake O Adeyeye, *Corporate Social Responsibility of Multinational Corporations in Developing Countries: Perspectives on Anti-Corruption* (Cambridge University Press 2012).

[1129] Rhuks Temitope Ako, 'Re-Defining Corporate Social Responsibility (CSR) in Nigeria's Post-Amnesty Oil Industry' (2012) 3 (1) African Journal of Economic and Management Studies 9.

[1130] Earth Charter, The Earth Charter also emphasises to: 'Ensure that decision making addresses the cumulative, long-term, indirect, long distance, and global consequences of human activities' (6.c) and to 'Act with restraint and efficiency when using energy and rely increasingly on renewable energy sources such as solar and wind' (7.b).

[1131] Ralph Hamann, Paresha Sinha, Farai Kapfudzaruwa and Christoph Schild, 'Business and Human Rights in South Africa: An Analysis of Antecedents of Human Rights Due Diligence' (2009) 87 (2) Journal of Business Ethics 453 and Peter Muchlinski, 'Implementing the New UN Corporate Human Rights Framework: Implications for Corporate Law, Governance, and Regulation' (2012) 22 (1) Business Ethics Quarterly 145.

[1132] David Scheffer and Caroline Kaeb, 'The Five Levels of CSR Compliance: The Resiliency of Corporate Liability under The Alien Tort Statute and The Case for a

Even then, however, it is hard to pin down the nature of those legal responsibilities. It is one thing for a public company to issue mandatory disclosure about events or risks that might be material to investors. Nonetheless, what about voluntary disclosures? What if a court determines that voluntary CSR compliance is akin to a form of advertising? The company making those statements would be held to the legal standard for false and misleading advertising. That is a different legal test from those that might arise in the tort claims. It is also be argued that the corporation that has undertaken to carry out subsidiary human rights duties could, nonetheless owe its victims a duty of care.[1133] As explained by Hasselback, 'CSR reporting has legal liability in a number of different manners, we are not there yet in terms of understanding what those mean.'[1134] The findings of this study suggest that CSR is going through an interesting transition from public relations to something that triggers concrete legal liabilities. While the precise nature of those legal responsibilities might be unclear, there is no doubt there is some legal liability when a corporation makes a CSR commitment. Thus, the obvious response for corporations is to abide by the statements made. Thus, the question is, do corporations owe a duty of care to the subsidiary and the community to act in a reasonable way so as not to harm society through its business operation, either directly or indirectly? When and where does this duty of care arise? This is perhaps a factual question.

A claim of a duty of care was rejected in the Ninth Circuit US Court of Appeal in *Doe I v Wal-Mart Store, Inc.* in 2009.[1135] Wal-Mart required its international suppliers to agree to follow Wal-Mart's work-conditions standards policy under the suppliers' contracts with Wal-Mart. The agreement with suppliers gave Wal-Mart the right to inspect the overseas facilities of suppliers and penalise suppliers for violating the policy. In general, it seems that Wal-Mart assumed responsibility and exercised control over the subsidiary's operational policy and working conditions. However, this judgment was not given a proper critical analysis by either the court or legal scholars. Likewise, the fundamental flaws in the Ninth Circuit decision have not been brought to light, as well as the flaw in

---

Counterattack Strategy in Compliance Theory' (2011) 29 Berkeley Journal of International Law 334.

[1133] Madeleine Conway, 'A New Duty of Care - Tort Liability from Voluntary Human Rights Due Diligence in Global Supply Chains' (2015) 40 (2) Queen's Law Journal 741.

[1134] Drew Hasselback, 'Investigating a Target Company's CSR Claims is now a Standard Part of Transaction Due Diligence, Lawyers say' (2015).

[1135] 572 (3d) 677 (9th Cir 2009) [Wal-Mart Stores 9th Cir].

applying the concept of a duty of care. The findings of this study suggest that the tort of negligence is not given proper consideration in the Wal-Mart case, especially where a corporation conducts its business activities in conjunction with its subsidiary, and where it has assumed responsibility to protect the victims from injury caused by the subsidiary (third party) and the victims can rely on the corporation undertaking for remedy. Another possible explanation for this is that the corporation may owe the victim a duty of care in the appropriate circumstances, where it is found that its conduct falls below the reasonable man standard and where it has indicated or shown to have taken responsibility of the subsidiary's business operations and policies.

Nonetheless, to understand where the duty of care arises, it is imperative to establish the concept of duty of care, how the duty of care is established, the situation that gives rise to a duty of care and the fundamental implications that underline a duty of care. This is because the liability element in the tort of negligence does not take the form of negation, but rather has a conditional form, which is manifested in the duty of care. Therefore, the tort of negligence encompasses a conduct-based approach. An intent-based duty of care is one that refers to an actor who possesses the ability to intentionally or knowingly comply with it, or to put it differently, has the ability but chooses not to exercise it. In this interpretation, where the duty of care is owed, negligence allows the imposition of liability for the foreseeable harmful outcomes of the negligent conduct.[1136]

In this notion the duty of care has two elements: harming and caring.[1137] These two elements impose a disjunctive norm, which demands that one does not cause or bring harm by one's negligent conduct.[1138] The disjunctive nature of negligence is reflected in 1) the evidence that avoiding breaching duty of care through negligent conduct can be achieved either by not causing harm (irrespective of whether one did or did not take care not cause harm); or 2) taking a reasonable care (to the appropriate extent) to alleviate the harm (irrespective of whether or not one action caused the harm). In a situation where an act that is subject to negligence fails to meet both disjunctives that compromise the negligence element – i.e. harm through careless conduct – it shall violate the duty of care and should be liable for its conduct. Therefore, a duty of care sets a standard for an actor's conduct. In a situation where an actor lacks the ability to perform as a

[1136]Herbert Lionel Adolphus Hart, *Punishment and Responsibility: Essays in the Philosophy of Law* (Oxford University Press 2008).

[1137]Dan B Dobbs, *The Law of Torts* (Vol. 2 West Group 2001).

[1138]Ori J Herstein, 'Responsibility in Negligence: Why the Duty of Care is Not a Duty "To Try"' (2010) 23 (02) Canadian Journal of Law and Jurisprudence 403.

rational agent or where the situation is such that the actor does not have the capacity to prevent harm (due to lack of ability), then the actor should not be responsible or should not be at fault for failing to comply with a duty of care and should not, therefore, be found liable for the negligent conduct.

The Neighbourhood Principle Duty of Care

The concept of duty of care has been established by legal precedent by courts over the years.[1139] Specifically, the law on duty of care has its origin in the famous case; *Donoghue v Stevenson* (1932).[1140] The facts of *Donoghue v Stevenson* began when Mrs. Donoghue and a friend went to a café for a drink. Mrs. Donoghue asked for a ginger beer, which her friend bought. It was supplied, as was customary at that time, in an opaque bottle. Mrs. Donoghue poured out and drunk some of the ginger beer, and then poured out the rest. At that point, the remains of a decomposing snail fell out of the bottle. Mrs. Donoghue became ill later and sued the manufacturer.[1141] In the case, the House of Lords agreed that manufacturers owed a duty of care to the consumer of their product.

Hence, the ginger beer manufacturers had breached the duty, causing harm to Mrs. Donoghue, and she was entitled to claim damages. In this view, the duty of care is about the relationship, and it must be shown that the particular wrongdoer stood in the required relationship to the victim such that he/she came under obligation to use care toward them. This relationship is referred to as proximity. Thus, to establish a duty of care, the victim must establish that the wrongdoer ought to have foreseen the breach of the duty of care to the victim. Therefore, duty means proximity, in the legal sense (this has nothing to do with geographical proximity) and proximity means the level of closeness of relationship required for that particular kind of violation.[1142] Accordingly, in order to establish a duty of care, it must be shown:

1. That some damage was foreseeable;
2. That there was a sufficiently close relationship between the parties to establish a duty in that class of case (proximity); and
3. That it was just and reasonable to impose a duty of care.[1143]

[1139]Harold Luntz, David Hambly and Robert Alexander Hayes (n 400).
[1140]*Donoghue v Stevenson* [1932] AC 562 (HL Sc).
[1141]Catherine Elliott and Frances Quinn, *English Legal System* (Pearson Education 2008).
[1142]John G Fleming, *An Introduction to The Law of Torts* (Clarendon P 1967).
[1143]Harold Luntz, David Hambly and Robert Alexander Hayes (n 400).

To be clear, the duty of care concept is a means of justifying or refusing to impose liability in law against a wrongdoer. Therefore, a duty of care protects against interference with the victim's rights, livelihood, environment, health, and the wellbeing of people close to them. In this understanding, it is argued that a duty of care protects against three types of harm: property and economic,[1144] human rights, and environmental.

Establishing the Neighbourhood Principle of Duty of Care

Donoghue v Stevenson *(1932)*

According to Lord Atkin, we are solely concerned with the question of whether, as a matter of law in the circumstance alleged, the tortfeasor-defendant owed any duty to the victim-plaintiff to take care. Lord Atkin went further to state that it is remarkable how difficult it is to find in the English authorities statements of general application defining the relations between parties that give rise to the duty. The Courts are concerned with the particular relations, which come before them in actual litigations, and it is sufficient to say whether the duty exists in that circumstance. The result is that the Courts have engaged in elaborate classifications of duties as they exist in respect of property, whether real or personal, with further divisions as to ownership, occupation or control, and distinctions based on the particular relations of the one side or the other. It can be ascertained at any time whether the law recognises a duty, but only where the case can be referred to some particular species which has been examined and classified.[1145]

Nonetheless, the duty which is common to all cases where liability is established must be based upon some element that is common to the cases where it is found to exist. To seek a complete logical definition of the general principle is probably to go beyond the function of the judge, for the more general the definition, the more likely it is to omit essential information or to introduce non-essential information. The attempt was made by Brett MR in *Heaven v Pender*, in a definition to which Lord Atkin referred to later in the judgment.[1146] As framed in *Heaven v Pender*, the duty of care was demonstrated as too wide, though it appears to Lord Atkin that if the concept of duty of care is properly limited, it will be capable of

[1144]John G Fleming, *The Law of Torts* (Vol. 1. Law Book Company for New South Wales Bar Association 1987).

[1145]Paula Giliker and Silas Beckwith, *Tort* (Sweet and Maxwell 2000).

[1146]*Heaven v Pender* [1883] 11 QBD 503.
<https://www.leeds.ac.uk/law/hamlyn/donoghue.htm> Accessed 18 December 2016.

affording a valuable practical guide. Lord Atkin further pointed out that in English law there must be some general conception of relations giving rise to a duty of care.[1147]

Therefore, the liability for negligence, whether it is styled as such or treated 'as a species of culpa, is no doubt based upon a general public sentiment of moral wrongdoing for which the offender must pay',[1148] 'but acts or omissions which any moral code would censure, cannot be treated so as to give a right to every person injured.'[1149] In this view, the rule of law arises which limits the range of complainants and the extent of their remedy.

Lord Atkin expounded on the neighbour principle. In laying down this principle, he said: The 'liability for negligence, whether you style it such or treat it as in other systems as a species of 'culpa', is no doubt based upon a general public sentiment of moral wrongdoing for which the offender must pay. But acts or omissions which any moral code would censure cannot in a practical world be treated so as to give a right to every person injured by them to demand relief. In this way rules of law arise which limit the range of complainants and the extent of their remedy. The rule that you are to love your neighbour becomes in law, you must not injure your neighbour; and the lawyer's question, who is my neighbour?'[1150] 'receives a restricted reply. You must take reasonable care to avoid acts or omissions which you can reasonably foresee would be likely to injure your neighbour. Who, then, in law is my neighbour? The answer seems to be – persons who are closely and directly affected by the act that the one ought reasonably to have them in contemplation as being so affected when one directing the mind to the acts or omissions which are called'[1151] into questions.[1152]

It appears to Lord Atkin that the doctrine of duty of care in *Heaven v Pender* is very broad, as laid down by Lord Esher (then Brett MR), when it is limited by the notion of proximity introduced by Lord Esher and Smith

[1147]Lord Atkin, 'Donoghue v Stevenson' [1932] 562 AC 580. <http://www.scienzegiuridiche.uniroma1.it/sites/default/files/docenti/alpa/Donoghue_Stevenson.pdf> Accessed 18 December 2016.

[1148]<https://fdslive.oup.com/www.oup.com/orc/resources/bin/9780199287888/kidner_chap02.pdf > Accessed 01 May 2016.

[1149]*Ibid.*

[1150]<https://fdslive.oup.com/www.oup.com/orc/resources/bin/9780199287888/kidner_chap02.pdf > Accessed 01 May 2016 and Robert FV Heuston, 'Donoghue v. Stevenson in Retrospect' (1957) 20 (1) Modern Law Review 1.

[1151]<https://fdslive.oup.com/www.oup.com/orc/resources/bin/9780199287888/kidner_chap02.pdf > Accessed 01 May 2016.

[1152]Neil MacCormick, 'Donoghue v Stevenson and Legal Reasoning' in Burns P (ed), *Donoghue v. Stevenson and The Modern Law of Negligence*, (Continuing Legal Education of British Columbia, Vancouver 1991).

LJ in *Le Lievre v Gould.*[1153] Lord Esher highlighted that, under certain circumstances, one may owe a duty to another man, even though there is no contract between them. Therefore, if one man is near another, or is near the property of another, a duty lies upon them not to do that which may cause a personal injury to that other or may injure his property.[1154] So for Smith LJ, the decision of *Heaven v Pender* was founded upon the principle that a duty to take care did arise when the person or property of one was in such proximity to the person or property of another that, if due care was not taken, damage might be done by the one to the other.[1155] In this view, the judgment sufficiently states the truth if proximity is not confined to merely physical proximity, but be used to extend to close and direct relations that the act complained of directly affects a person whom the person alleged to be bound to take care of would now be directly affected by his careless act.[1156]

Furthermore, Lord Macmillan humbly stated that the diversity of view exhibited in cases such as *George v Skivington* and *Blacker v Lack and Elliot*[1157] took two extreme instances in a duty of care. 'On the one hand, there is the well-established principle that no one other than a party to a contract can complain of a breach of that contract.'[1158] There is, contrarily, the equally well-established doctrine that negligence apart from contract gives a right of action to the party injured by that negligence, thus the use of negligence in the case implied a duty owed and neglected.[1159]

Therefore, the illustration from Lord Macmillian is that the fact that there is a contractual relationship between the parties which may give rise to an action for breach of contract does not exclude the co-existence of a right of action found on negligence. As between the same parties, independently of the contract, though arising out of the relationship in fact brought about the contract. Accordingly, in *George v Skivington* and *Blacker v Lack and Elliot*, the 'best illustration is the right of the injured

---

[1153]*Le Lievre v Gould* [1893] 1 QB 491. <http://www.iclr.co.uk/assets/media/vote/1915-1945/Donoghue_ac1932-1-562.pdf> Accessed 18 December 2016.

[1154]Dilan A Esper and Gregory C Keating, 'Putting "Duty" in Its Place: A Reply to Professors Goldberg & Zipursky' (2008) 41 Loyola of Los Angeles Law Review 1225.

[1155]Richard Kidner, *Casebook on Torts* (Oxford University Press 2012).

[1156]*Ibid.*

[1157]*Blacker v Lake &Elliot,* Ltd [1912] 106 L.T. 533. <http://www.scottishlawreports.org.uk/resources/dvs/page-text/pages/Respondents-Case-Page-10.html> Accessed 18 December 2016.

[1158]<https://fdslive.oup.com/www.oup.com/orc/resources/bin/9780199287888/kidner_chap02.pdf> Accessed 01 May 2016.

[1159]*Ibid.*

railway passenger to sue the railway company either for breach of the contract of safe carriage or for the negligence in carrying him.' [1160] Therefore, there is no reason why the same set of facts should not give a person a right of action in contract and another person a right of action in tort[1161] against corporations.

In cases like *Donoghue v Stevenson*, so much depends upon the approach to the question of the duty of care in tort of negligence case. If one begins 'with the sale by the manufacturer to the retail dealer, then the consumer who purchases from the retailer is at once seen to be a stranger to the contract between the retailer and the manufacturer and so disentitled to sue upon it.' [1162] 'There is no contractual relationship between the manufacturer and the consumer and thus, the plaintiff, if they are to succeed, is driven to try to bring himself or herself with one or other of the exceptional cases where the strictness of the rule that none but a party to the contract can be found on a breach of that contract has been mitigated in the public interest.'[1163] 'As it has been in the case of a person who issues a chattel which is dangerous or which he or she knows to be in a dangerous condition.'[1164] 'If then on the other hand, one disregards the fact that the circumstance of the case at one stage includes the existence of a contract of sales between the manufacturer and retailer and approaches the question by asking whether there is evidence of carelessness on the part of the manufacturer.'[1165] 'Or whether they are owed a duty to be careful in a question with which the party who has been injured in consequence of his want of care. The circumstance that the injured party who was not a party

---

[1160]Jenny Steele, *Tort Law: Text, Cases, and Materials* (Oxford University Press 2010).

[1161]Tony Weir, *A Casebook on Tort* (Sweet & Maxwell 2004).

[1162]<https://fdslive.oup.com/www.oup.com/orc/resources/bin/9780199287888/kidner_chap02.pdf> Accessed 01 May 2016 and Michael P Furmston and Greg Tolhurst, *Privity of Contract* (Oxford University Press 2015).

[1163]<https://fdslive.oup.com/www.oup.com/orc/resources/bin/9780199287888/kidner_chap02.pdf> Accessed 01 May 2016 and Simon Whittaker, 'Privity of Contract and the Tort of Negligence: Future directions' (1996) 16 (2) Oxford Journal of Legal Studies 191, 230.

[1164]<https://fdslive.oup.com/www.oup.com/orc/resources/bin/9780199287888/kidner_chap02.pdf > Accessed 01 May 2016 and William Lloyd Prosser, *Cases and Materials on Torts* (Foundation Press 1952).

[1165]*Ibid.*

to the incidental contract of sales becomes irrelevant, and his title to sue the manufacturer is unaffected by the circumstance of the injury.'[1166]

The law concerns itself with carelessness only where there is a duty to take care and where the failure in that duty has caused damage. Therefore, carelessness assumes the legal quality of negligence and entails the consequences in law of negligence.[1167] What, then, are the circumstances which give rise to this duty of care? In the daily contract of social and business life, human beings are thrown into, or place themselves in, an infinite variety of relations with their fellows, and the law can refer only to the standards of the reasonable man in order to determine whether any particular relations give rise to a duty of care as between those who stand in that relation to each other.[1168]

Hence, the ground of action may be as various and manifold as human errancy and legal responsibility may develop in altering social conditions and standards. The criterion of judgment must adjust and adapt itself to the changing circumstance of the human race. Therefore, the categories of negligence are never closed but constantly evolving. Consequently, the cardinal principle of liability is that the party complained of should owe to the party complaining a duty of care and that the party complaining should be able to prove that he has suffered damage in consequence of a breach of that duty. Likewise, where there is room for a variety of opinions, it is in determining what circumstance will establish such a relationship between the parties as to give rise to a duty of care. Hence, when the requirement of fault and duty of care is met, the tort will regulate the behaviour of actors in society when that behaviour falls within that sphere which it is the tort's purpose to regulate.

Anns v Merton London Borough Council *(1978)* *Test of a Duty of Care*

Following *Donoghue v Stevenson*, there was little development of duty of care concept until it was suggested in *Dorset Yacht v Home Office*[1169] that a duty should exist whenever damage was foreseeable.

1166<https://fdslive.oup.com/www.oup.com/orc/resources/bin/9780199287888/kidner_chap02.pdf> Accessed 01 May 2016 and Dominick R Vetri, *Tort Law and Practice* (LexisNexis/Matthew Bender 1998).

1167Kenneth S Abraham, *The Forms and Functions of Tort Law* (West Publishing Company 2002).

1168Brenda Mothersole and Ann Ridley, *Tort of Negligence A-Level Law in Action* (Macmillan Education UK 1995).

1169*Home Office v Dorset Yacht Co Ltd* [1970] AC 1004.

However, the concept of duty of care prompts the question: what is, or ought to be, reasonably foreseeable? This is something which may ultimately depend on the imagination of the individual judge. Thus, what one judge perceives to be reasonably foreseeable, another may consider unusual. Consequently, the modern reformulation of Lord Atkin's neighbourhood principle can be found in the dicta of Lord Wilberforce in *Anns v Merton London Borough Council*.

According to Lord Wilberforce, through the trilogy of cases *Donoghue v Stevenson*, *Hedley Byrne & Co. Ltd v Heller & Partners Ltd*, and *Dorset Yacht Co. Ltd v Home Office*, the position has now been reached that in order to establish that a duty of care arises in a particular situation, it is not necessary to bring the facts of that situation within those of previous situations in which a duty of care has been held to exist. Rather the question has to be about the approach in two stages. The first one has to ask whether, as between the alleged wrongdoer and the person who has suffered damage there is a sufficient relationship of proximity or neighbourhood such that, in the reasonable contemplation of the former, carelessness on his part may be likely to cause damage to the latter, in which a *prima facie* duty of care arises. Secondly, if the first question is answered affirmatively, it is necessary to consider whether there is any consideration which ought to negate or to reduce or limit the scope of the duty or the class of person to whom it is owed or the damages to which a breach of it may give rise.[1170]

The position was this: the wrongdoer owed the claimant a duty to take reasonable care unless there was a policy reason as to why not to impose a duty of care on the wrongdoer.[1171] This prompted Lord Goff in *Smith v Littlewood* to acknowledge that the broad general principle of liability for foreseeable damage is so widely applicable that the function of the duty of care is not so much to identify cases where liability is imposed as to identify those where it is not.[1172] The first stage test appeared to present almost no hurdle as almost everything is foreseeable if one is to think about it long enough. This meant that most of the work when it came to restricting claims was left to the second stage of the test. The fact that the first hurdle of Lord Wilberforce's test was so readily jumped was at the heart of the huge expansion of the tort of negligence in the late 1970s and early 1980s,

---

[1170]*Anns v Merton London Borough Council* [1978] AC 728.

[1171] Kirsty Horsey and Erika Rackley, *Kidner's Casebook on Torts* (Oxford University Press USA 2015).

[1172]*Smith v Littlewoods Organisation Ltd* [1987] UKHL 18. Also see; Harold Luntz, 'Torts Turnaround Downunder' (2001) 1 (1) Oxford University Commonwealth Law Journal 95.'< https://www.scribd.com/document/234563408/English-Tort-Law-Cases> Accessed 08 March 2016.

during which the court seemed reluctant to refuse claims of any vaguely sympathetic claimant who came before them.[1173] Lord Wilberforce's two-stage test soon fell into disfavour. This is because it was seen to be behind the unprecedented and increasingly unpopular expansion of the tort of negligence, as noted by Lord Roskill's leading opinion in *Junior Brooks v Veitchi.*[1174] Thus, the test was rejected in *Yuen Kun-yeu v Attorney General of Hong Kong*[1175] and *Anns* itself was subsequently overruled by *Murphy v Brentwood District Council.*[1176] Therefore, the broad general principle with its two-part test envisaged in *Anns* has been swept aside, leaving the courts to impose duties of care only when they could find precedent in comparable factual situations.

Modern Approach to the Law of Negligence

Tort law has developed over the years through case law in England; 'case law established that there are a number of factual situations in which a duty of care is owed. For example, drivers owe a duty of care not to injure pedestrians, and employers owe a duty of care to take a reasonable step to protect their employees from injury.' [1177] Nonetheless, 'there are still situations in which it is not clear whether there is a duty of care, and following'[1178] the move toward a tighter test after *Anns* was overruled, the Supreme Court set down a new test in *Caparo Industries plc v Dickman* (1990).

Caparo Industries plc v Dickman *(1990)*

In *Caparo*, the case raises an issue of law as opposed to an issue purely of fact. The defendant can make what is called a 'striking out application', which effectively argues that even if the facts of what the claimant says happened are true, this does not give them a legal claim against the defendant. Therefore, in cases where it is not clear whether there

---

[1173] *McLoughlin v O'Brian* [1983] 1 AC 410. <http://www.pierre-legrand.com/mcloughlin-v-obrian.pdf> Accessed 19 December 2016.

[1174] *Junior Books Ltd v Veitchi Co. Ltd* [1983] 1 AC 520.

[1175] *Anns and Others v Merton London Borough Council* [1978] AC 728

[1176] *Murphy v Brentwood District Council* [1991] 1 AC 398.

[1177] <https://www.scribd.com/doc/239277757/Catherine-Elliott-Frances-Quinn-Tort-Law-the-E-Bookos-org> Accessed 15 December 2019 and John Hamilton Baker, *An Introduction to English Legal History* (MICHIE 1979).

[1178] <https://www.scribd.com/doc/239277757/Catherine-Elliott-Frances-Quinn-Tort-Law-the-E-Bookos-org> Accessed 15 December 2019.

is a duty of care, the case may be struck out where essentially the defendant is saying that even if they had caused the harm alleged to the claimant, there was no duty of care to them and so there can be no successful claim in negligence.[1179]

'Where a striking out application is made, the court conducts a preliminary examination of the case, in which it assumes that the facts alleged by the claimant are true and decides whether they give rise to an arguable case in law.'[1180] In a case involving a duty of care, they would be deciding whether, on the facts before them, the defendant may owe a duty of care to the claimant. If not, the case can be dismissed without a full trial. If the court finds that there is an arguable case, the case can then proceed to full trial unless settled out of court.[1181]

The Notion of a Duty of Care in *Caparo Test*

The basic test for a duty of care is now the one set down in *Caparo v Dickman*. This applied the duty of care question in negligence cases and those which fall into any of the rules on the tort of negligence. In some cases, it is also applied alongside the special rules in a group of negligence cases, and some legal scholar suggests that those special rules are in fact simply a more detailed application of the principles in the *Caparo Test*.[1182] The test requires the court to ask three questions:

(1) Was the damage reasonably foreseeable?
(2) 'Was there proximity between the defendant and the claimant?'[1183]
(3) 'Is it just, fair, and reasonable to impose a duty in this situation?'[1184]

[1179] *Caparo Industries plc v Dickman* [1990] UKHL 2.
[1180] Catherine Elliott, *Tort Law/Catherine Elliott, Frances Quinn* (Pearson Education 2007).
[1181] Tom Allen, 'Liability for References: The House of Lords and Spring v. Guardian Assurance' (1995) 58 (4) Modern Law Review 553.
[1182] Catherine Elliott and Frances Quinn (n 1483).
[1183] <<https://www.scribd.com/doc/239277757/Catherine-Elliott-Frances-Quinn-Tort-Law-the-E-Bookos-org> Accessed 15 December 2019.
[1184] *Ibid.*

'All cases of negligence need the requisite level of proximity between the parties.'[1185] In cases of personal injury and damage to property, this requirement will be satisfied by foreseeability, but in other cases, such as psychiatric injury, and economic loss, a closer relationship between the parties will be necessary to establish liability. The dissatisfaction with the *Anns* test lay in the objection that there should, or indeed could, be any test for establishing a duty of care in negligence. Therefore, in *Caparo*, Lord Bridge stressed the inability of any single general principle to provide a practical test which could be applied to every situation to determine whether a duty of care was owed.[1186]

In his Lordship's opinion,[1187] in addition to the requirement of foreseeability of damage, necessary ingredients in any situation giving rise to a duty of care are that there should exist between the party owing the duty and the party to whom it is owed a relationship characterised by the law as one of 'proximity' or 'neighbourhood' and that the situation should be one in which the court considers it fair, just and reasonable that the law should impose a duty of a given scope upon the one party for the benefit of the other.[1188]

Furthermore, his Lordship stressed that 'novel categories of duty ought to be developed incrementally and by analogy with established categories of duty.'[1189] Lord Bridge immediately 'sought to halt any encouragement to view the foregoing as merely representing the substitution of one test of duty for another.'[1190] According to his Lordship:

> [T]he concepts of proximity and fairness are not susceptible of any such precise definition as would be necessary to give them utility as practical tests, but amount in effect to little more than convenient labels to attach to the features of different specific situations which, on a detailed examination of all the circumstances, the law recognises pragmatically as giving rise to a duty of care of a given scope.[1191]

This research shall argue that attempts to retard the expansion of liability through the abandonment of tests or principles will be viewed as

[1185]<https://fdslive.oup.com/www.oup.com/orc/resources/bin/9780199287888/kidner_chap02.pdf> Accessed 01 May 2016 and Kirsty Horsey and Erika Rackley, *Kidner's Casebook on Torts* (Oxford University Press USA 2019).

[1186]*Caparo Industries plc v Dickman* (n 1515).

[1187]*Ibid.* at 617, 618.

[1188]*Ibid.* at 617,618.

[1189]*Ibid.* at 618.

[1190]*Ibid.*

[1191]*Ibid.*

self-defeating. Regardless of Stapleton's view that there is no test for a duty of care and that there can be no 'duty test',[1192] over time, several Law Lords appear to have arrived at the inevitable conclusion that *Caparo* did indeed establish what may be described as a framework test for the creation of a duty.[1193] It may be seen therefore that the House of Lords has transmitted distinctly mixed signals to practitioners concerning whether the analysis of the duty question should take place according to tests and frameworks, or instead be decided with reference to the selection of factors.

This inconsistency has been unhelpful to legal representatives and lower court judges, to put it mildly. Steele has observed how 'in *Caparo* the elements of the test (especially the 'proximity' part of it) have been declared (whether boldly or despairingly) to have no content, yet at the same time, they continue to be talked about and apparently applied.'[1194] In the years following *Caparo*, however, the issues referred to in that case have not uniformly been adopted as the starting point for the analysis of whether a duty of care should be imposed in a novel situation. Putting to one side psychiatric harm cases where discrete guidelines have been developed,[1195] the case law reveals that other concepts such as assumption of responsibility and distributive justice have emerged to play an increasingly significant role in discussions about duty of care. However, as will be demonstrated in this book, diverging judicial viewpoints have rendered these concepts largely unintelligible to those whose task it is to apply them. That said, there is no doubt that the notion of duty of care is an appropriate doctrine for corporate accountability.

The Meaning of Reasonable Foreseeability

This element of the test has its foundation in the original neighbour principle developed in *Donoghue v Stevenson*.[1196] Essentially, the courts

---

[1192]Jane Stapleton, 'Duty of Care Factors: A Selection from The Judicial Menus' in Cane P and Stapleton J (eds), *The Law of Obligations: Essays in Celebration of John Fleming* (Oxford University Press 1998).

[1193]*Ibid*. *JD v East Berkshire Community Health NHS Trust* [2005] 2 AC 373 [2005] UKHL 23 and *Brooks v Commissioner of Police of the Metropolis* [2005] 1 WLR 1495; [2005] UKHL 24.

[1194]Jenny Steele, 'Scepticism and The Law of Negligence' (1993) Cambridge Law Journal 52, 437.

[1195]*Alcock v Chief Constable of South Yorkshire Police* [1992] 1 AC 310 and *Page v Smith* [1996] AC 155.

[1196]Percy H Winfield, 'Duty in Tortious Negligence' (1934) 34(1) Columbia Law Review 41.

must ask whether a reasonable person in the defendant's position would have foreseen the risk of harm. A modern case which shows how this part of the test works is *Langley v Draw*,[1197] where the claimant, a policeman, was injured in a car crash when he was chasing the defendant, who was driving a stolen car. The Court of Appeal held that the defendant knew, or should have known, that he was being pursued by the claimant, and therefore in increasing his speed he knew or should have known that the claimant would also drive faster and so risk injury. Therefore, the defendant had a duty not to create such risk and he was in breach of that duty.

Hence, for a duty to exist in negligent torts, it must be reasonably foreseeable that damage or injury would be caused to the particular defendant in the case, or to a class of people to which he or she belongs, rather than just to people in general.[1198] In other words, the duty is owed to a person or class of persons and not to the human race in general. A good, if old, example of this principle can be seen in *Palsgraf Long v Long Island Railroad*.[1199] The case arose from an incident where a man was boarding a train, and a member of the railway staff negligently pushed him, which caused him to drop a package he was carrying. The box contained fireworks, which exploded, and the blast knocked over some scales, several feet away. They fell on the claimant and she was injured. She sued, but the court held that it could not be reasonably foreseen that pushing the passenger would injure someone standing several feet away. It is reasonably foreseeable that the passenger himself might be injured, but that did not in itself create a duty to other people.

That does not, however, mean that the defendant has to be able to identify a particular individual who might foreseeably be affected by their actions; it is enough that the claimant is part of a class of people who might foreseeably be affected. This was the case in *Haley v London Electricity Board*.[1200] The defendant dug a trench in the street in order to do repairs. Their workmen laid a shovel across the hole to draw pedestrian's attention to it, but the claimant was blind, and fell into the hole, seriously injuring himself. It was agreed in court that the precautions taken would have been sufficient to protect a sighted person from injury, so the question is whether it was reasonably foreseeable that a blind person might walk by and be at risk of falling in. The Court of Appeal said that the number of blind people who lived in London and were used to walking about by themselves meant

---

[1197] *Langley v Dray* [1998] PIQR P 314.

[1198] Catherine Elliott and Frances Quinn, *As Law* (Pearson Education 2006).

[1199] *Palsgraf v Long Island Railroad Co.*, 248 N.Y. 339, 162 N.E. 99 (N.Y. 1928).

[1200] *Haley v London Electricity Board* [1965] AC 77. Also see: Mark Lunney and Ken Oliphant, *Tort Law: Text and Materials* (Oxford University Press 2008).

that the defendant owed a duty to that class of people. Thus, a duty is owed if the harm can be reasonably foreseeable by the defendant and it can be extended to all those who might reasonably be expected to be in his or her contemplation, including blind pedestrians.

The Meaning of Proximity

'In normal language, proximity means closeness, in terms of physical position. In law, however, it has a wider meaning, which essentially concerns the relationship, if any, between the defendant and the claimant.'[1201] Hence, in *Muirhead v Industrial Tank Specialities*, Goff LJ pointed out that this does not mean that the defendant and claimant must know each other. The situation they were both in meant that the defendant could reasonably be expected to foresee that his or her actions would cause damage to the claimant.[1202]

The notion of proximity can be seen as another simple way of showing the foreseeability test, as the case of *Caparo v Dickman* itself illustrated. The claimant, Caparo, was a company that had made a takeover bid for another firm, Fidelity, in which they already owned a large number of shares. When they were deciding whether to make the bid, they used figures prepared by Dickman for Fidelity's annual audit, which showed that Fidelity made a healthy profit. [1203] However, when the takeover was complete, Caparo discovered that Fidelity was in fact almost worthless. They sued Dickman, and the House of Lords had to decide whether Dickman owed them a duty of care. They pointed out that the preparation of an annual audit was required under the Companies Act 1985,[1204] for the purposes of helping existing shareholders to exercise control over a company. An audit was not intended to be a source of information or guidance for the prospective new investor, and therefore could not be intended to help existing shareholders, like Caparo, to decide whether to buy more shares. The audit was effectively a statement that was put into more or less general circulation and may foreseeably be relied on by strangers to the maker of the statement, for any one of a variety of purposes which the maker of the statement has no reason to contemplate.

[1201]Catherine Elliott and Frances Quinn (n 1563).

[1202]*Muirhead v Industrial Tank Specialties Ltd and Other* [1986] QB 507.

[1203]Margaret Brazier and Harry Street, *The Law of Torts* (Lexis Pub 1993).

[1204]Companies Act 1985.
<http://www.legislation.gov.uk/ukpga/1985/6/pdfs/ukpga_19850006_en.pdf> Accessed 19 December 2016.

Furthermore, proximity may also be expressed in terms of a relationship between the defendant and the activity which caused harm to the claimant, as defined by Lord Brennan in *Sutradhar v Natural Environmental Research Council*,[1205] or as proximity in the sense of a measure of control over and responsibility for the potentially dangerous situation.[1206] An example of this kind of proximity can be seen in *Watson v British Boxing Board of Control*, where the claimant was the famous professional boxer Michael Watson, who suffered severe brain damage after being injured during a match. He sued the Board, on the basis that they were in charge of safety arrangements at professional boxing matches, and evidence showed that if they had made immediate medical attention available at the ringside, his injuries would have been less severe. The Court of Appeal held that there was sufficient proximity between Mr Watson and the Board to give rise to a duty of care, because they were the only body in the UK which could license professional boxing matches and therefore had complete control of and responsibility over a situation which could clearly result to Mr Watson (the claimant) if the Board did not exercise reasonable care.[1207]

In *Sutradhar*, the claimant was a resident of Bangladesh, who had been made ill by drinking water contaminated with arsenic. The water came from wells near his home. 'Some years earlier, the plaintiff had carried out a survey of the local water system, and had neither tested for nor'[1208] revealed the presence of arsenic. The claimant argued that the defendant should have tested for arsenic, or made public the fact that they had not done so, so as not to lull the local people into a false sense of security. The Supreme Court in Bangladesh, however, held that the defendant had no duty of care to users of the water system because there was insufficient proximity.[1209] Mr Sutradhar himself had never seen the defendant's report, and so his claim had to be based on the idea that they owed a duty to the whole population of Bangladesh. The Supreme Court said this could not be the case, the defendant had no connection with the project that had provided the wells, and no one had asked them to test whether the water was safe to drink. They had no duty to the people or the government of Bangladesh to test the water for anything and were simply doing general research into the

[1205]*Sutradhar v Natural Environment Research Council* [2006] 4 All ER 490; [2006] UKHL 33 and *Customs and Excise Commissioners v Barclays Bank plc* [2006] 3 WLR 1; [2006] UKHL 28.

[1206]*Ibid.*

[1207]*Watson v British Boxing Board of Control* [2001] QB 1134.

[1208]<https://www.scribd.com/doc/239277757/Catherine-Elliott-Frances-Quinn-Tort-Law-the-E-Bookos-org> Accessed 15 December 2019.

[1209]*Sutradhar v Natural Environment Research Council* (n 1570).

performance of the type of wells that happened to be used in that area. Therefore, the fact that someone had expert knowledge of a subject did not impose on them a duty to use that knowledge to help anyone in the world who might require such help. Proximity required a degree of control of the source of Mr Sutradhar's injury, namely the drinking water supply of Bangladesh, and the defendants had no such control.

The Meaning of Fair, Just and Reasonableness

In practice, the requirement that it must be just and reasonable to impose a duty of care often overlaps with the previous two tests of reasonable foresight of harm and a relationship of proximity in *Watson* and *Sutradhar*. For example, the arguments made under the heading of proximity could equally well be seen as arguments relating to fair, just, and reasonableness.[1210] It was obviously more fair, just, and reasonable to expect the Boxing Board to supervise a match properly since that was their job, than it was to expect the researcher in *Sutradhar* to take responsibility for a task that was not their job and which they had never claimed to have done.

Where fair, just, and reasonableness are specifically referred to, it is usually because the case meets the requirements of foreseeability and proximity, but the court believes there is a sound public policy reason for denying the claim. An example is *McFarlane v Tayside Health Board*. The claimant had become pregnant after her partner's vasectomy failed and claimed for the cost of bringing up her child. The court denied her claim, on the basis that it was not fair, just, and reasonable to award compensation for the birth of the healthy child, something most people, they said, would consider a blessing.[1211]

Likewise, in *Commissioner of Customs and Excise v Barclays Bank Plc*, the government's Customs and Excise departments were owed large sums in unpaid VAT by two companies, who had accounts with the defendant bank. Customs and Excise went to the court and obtained what is called a freezing injunction, which restricted the two companies' access to the money they had in the bank. The bank was notified of the order, and should have prevented the companies from withdrawing money, but, apparently because of negligence, they failed to do so, which meant that the two companies were able to take out over two million pounds and Customs

[1210] Catherine Elliott and Frances Quinn (n 1563).

[1211] *MacFarlane and Another v Tayside Health Board* [2000] 2 AC 59.

and Excise were unable to recover all the money owed.[1212] They sued the bank, claiming that it owed them a duty of care. The Supreme Court held that it was foreseeable that Customs and Excise would lose the money if the bank was negligent in handling the freezing injunction, and that this suggested there was also a degree of proximity. However, the decisive issue was whether it was fair, just, and reasonable to impose a duty. The House of Lords stated that where a court order was breached, and the court had the power to deal with that breach, this would usually be enough to ensure that banks complied with such orders, and there was nothing to suggest that the order created any extra cause of action. In addition, it was unjust and unreasonable that the bank should become exposed to a liability which could amount to much more than the two million pounds that were at stake in this case when it had no way of resisting the court order and got no reward for complying with it.

In summary, the negligent act of a person that causes loss or damage to his or her human rights should give rise to a duty of care. The creation of danger,[1213] control over dangerous property,[1214] or a dangerous situation,[1215] may give rise to a duty of care. Therefore, as the law implied, you are to take care not to cause harm or injury your neighbour. Hence, in this context, the concept of duty of care imposes a legal obligation on humanity not to cause harm or bring harm to anyone in their contemplation, which extends to corporations, as well as another actor in society. In this notion, the currently established duty of care is also extended to a parent company to ensure that the operations of its foreign subsidiaries are conducted in an appropriate manner to protect the local citizens of the communities with whom the subsidiary interacts.[1216] Therefore the victim could argue that, under the principle of duty of care in tort law, if a duty of care can be established, then a parent corporation and its subsidiary can be found liable for negligence if the direct action of each result in human rights violations and environmental damages.[1217] Likewise, if these elements are

---

[1212]*Bellefield Computer Services Ltd v E Turner & Sons Ltd* refused to apply the theory, and that HHJ Humphrey Lloyd QC in *Payne v Setchell Ltd.*

[1213]Lord Hoffmann's Explanation of *Home Office v Dorset Yatch Co* [1970] AC 2004 in *Stovin v Wise* [1996] AC 923 at 948.

[1214]*Australia Safeway Stores Pty v Ltd v Zaluzna* (1987) 162 CLR 479.

[1215]*Ibid.*

[1216]José Engrácia Antunes, '*Liability of Corporate Groups: Autonomy and Control in Parent-Subsidiary Relationships in US, German and EU Law: An International and Comparative Perspective* (1994).

[1217]*X (Minors) v Bedfordshire County Council* [1995] 2 AC 633,13 and *Barrett v Enfield London Borough Council* [2001] 2 AC 550.

satisfied, the court should find that the victims had pleaded all the essentials required to support the establishment of a duty of care. Consequently, the court should allow the issue of whether a duty of care should be recognised in corporate and subsidiary human rights violations to proceed to trial.

The Modern Application of Tort Law to Corporate Human Rights Violations

Corporation Duty of Care in the Supply Chain/Agent

The complexities in the global supply chain and the structure of the supply chains may vary from one business operation to the other and can change over the duration of the business operation.[1218] The corporate supply structure may vary depending on the business model being used by a specific corporation, and the buying/selling agreements between the buyer and the seller, in relation to the business operation between the same supplier but with regard to different products. Thus, what might be clear in this scenario is that the volume of business between the purchasers and the suppliers can differ greatly. Furthermore, similar corporations in the supply chain may be a supplier and a purchaser at the same time with a varying level of market share and power in each product position. A possible effect of this might be that it will be impossible to offer a one size fits all approach to the question of corporate accountability for human rights violations in the supply chain. The duty of care has established legal paths that might enhance accountability, but it is also clear that it does not aim to provide definitive answers for every possible human rights violation that occurs in the supply chain.

Bearing these difficulties in mind and the different relationships in the supply chain, a duty of care provides a general legal tool and the flexibility, as far possible, to be used in connection with diverse supply chain relationships. However, what is important for the court to recognise is that the factual matrix of each case may differ, which can lead to different outcomes for corporate liability in the supply chain. Therefore, the aim of the duty of care is to establish a common ground for corporate accountability in the supply chain. This is because the key challenges facing victims of corporate human rights abuses in the supply chain arise from the contractual nature of the relationship and the indirect, weak connection

[1218]University of Essex, 'Improving the Paths to Business Accountability for Human Rights Abuses in The Global Supply Chains; A Legal Guide' (2017*)* Essex Business and Human Rights Project.

between the suppliers/buyers and their business partners that go beyond the first-tier relationships. In this situation, it is particularly difficult to establish when a supply chain corporation owes a duty of care to the victims in its supply chain; to find a causal link between the harm and the actions or omissions of the corporation, specifically for abuses happening beyond the first tier of their supply; or to strike the right balance in establishing accountability for victims of human rights abuses. This approach could be something that has the potential to prevent a corporation from working with a supplier who may engage in human rights violations. This is because the corporation will be able to use their power as leverage to improve the human rights standards of the supplier.

The risk of legal liability under the duty of care could push supply chain corporations to develop business ethics that incorporate human rights standards as the principle of its business operations in the supply chain. The important point to note here is that to prevent business from pushing their legal responsibility further down the supply chain tiers, the court must rely on the novel duty of care being advocated in this book to ensure that the supply chain corporations do not exempt themselves from human rights violations. Thus, the best approach for the court to establish legal liability is to consider the different levels of a duty of care for different supply chain relationships.

The supply chain duty of care is limited to four categories: (1) powerful influential purchasers and suppliers, or those that possess or should possess some types of expert knowledge or skills,[1219] including major brands falling under the group of what supply chain management literature calls 'lead firms' and SMEs[1220]; (2) social audit 'entities possessing special knowledge and instilling reliance on their expertise by businesses and third parties';[1221] (3) contractual partners of the firms recognised in (1); and (4) third parties whose human rights have been violated by the acts and omissions of corporations.

The criteria established here is aimed at recognising the concrete difference that can be made by taking a human rights-centred approach to holding corporations accountable for human rights abuses. The duty of care places an importance on the severity of the injuries suffered by victims. For example, the concept of duty of care will enable remedies for physical injuries in the notion of human rights violations and environmental

[1219]*Ibid.*

[1220]Offshoring Manufacturing SMEs, 'Manufacturing Small and Medium Size Enterprise's Offshore Outsourcing' (2013).

[1221]<http://www.bhrinlaw.org/improving-paths-to-accountability-for-human-rights-abuses-in-the-global-supply-chains-a-legal-guide.pdf> Accessed 17 May 2017.

damages. Bringing human rights duty of care into the interpretation of tort law principles will help the victims to show the severity of the human rights abuses and the injuries suffered. However, to establish a novel duty of care in the supply chain, the victims must prove a number of factors. These are:

- Number of tiers in the supply chain;
- Nature of the relationship between purchaser and suppliers/agent and third parties/social auditors and suppliers (contractual and non-contractual);
- Duration of the relationship;
- Size of the corporations involved, purchaser and supplier(s), of particular importance economic capacity;
- Nature of business activity and type of industry;
- The violation in question; labour rights and whether the claim can be formulated in civil liability terms.

The question for the court is to determine:

- Who are the claimants, and do they have legal standing: individual victims (for example employees in the supplier factory or consumer) or groups of individuals (for example indigenous communities)?;
- Who are the defendants, and do they have legal standing: purchasing corporation or supplier?;
- What are the standards for admissibility of evidence?;
- Who bears the burden of proof? Can the burden of proof be shifted towards the defendant?;
- What are the applicable laws to (a) the procedure and (b) the substance of the claim?;
- Are class actions or group claims admissible in the jurisdiction selected for the lawsuit?;
- Is legal aid available to cover the cost of litigation?

The Application of Duty of Care in the Supply Chain Context

What are the elements of a special relationship between the supply chain corporations that would enable holding one corporation responsible for human rights violations and environmental damages? While human rights and labour laws are distinctive in nature and scope, injuries or losses caused as a result of their breach can both give rise to a duty of care claim. For example, a violation of the right of life,[1222] prohibition of inhuman treatment, prohibition of slavery[1223] or respect for health can give rise to a duty of care claim for death, physical injury or psychiatric damages. A possible explanation for this might be that a violation of the right to a just and favourable condition of work could give rise to tort claims for property or personal damage. Therefore, what is important to prove in this case is whether:

- The defendant owes a duty of care to the claimant through an assumption (Focus Framework Approach) or imposition (Determinate Framework Approach) of responsibility; and
- When does the relationship between the parties give rise to an imposition or assumption of responsibility necessary for a duty of care?

Further to these questions, the court must apply the three-stage *Caparo Test* analysis to identify whether the defendant owes the claimant a duty of care. This three-stage analysis is:

1. Harm must be reasonably foreseeable;
2. Proximity of the relationship between the claimant and the defendant;
3. It must be fair, just, and reasonable that the law imposes a duty of a given scope on one party for the benefit of the other.

Further to this analysis, the court must also prove the defendant breached that duty and causation, which is the harm suffered by the claimant as the result of the defendant's breach of the duty. For the court to establish a supply chain accountability, three important conditions must be met:

1. The defendant owed a duty of care to the claimant;
2. Breach of that duty; and
3. Harm suffered by the defendant as a consequence of that breach.

[1222]Henry J Steiner, Philip Alston and Ryan Goodman, *International Human Rights in Context: Law, Politics, Morals: Text and Materials* (Oxford University Press USA 2008).

[1223]Marie-Bénédicte Dembour, *Who Believes in Human Rights: Reflections on the European Convention* (Cambridge University Press 2006).

However, the most challenging aspect of applying tort of negligence to supply chain relationship is to show that the supply chain corporation owed a duty of care to prevent/mitigate ham to the victims of the human rights violation in its supply chain business operations. Nonetheless, the court can address this complication by referring to the *Attorney General v Hartwell (British Virgin Islands)*,[1224] where it is observed by that 'a duty of care is a duty owed in law by one person or class of person to another particular person or class of person. This comprises an obligation to take reasonable care to ensure that the person or persons to whom the duty is owed do not suffer a particular type or types of damages.' [1225] The court held that to determine what the legitimate scope of the duty of care is, it is essential to ask whether a supply chain actor is within the cycle of people that owe a duty to take care to avoid damage to certain potential victims.

Of course, to date, there has not been a case or a judicial determination of this duty in the supply chain context. However, what is clear in a novel context in which a finding of negligence is possible, the courts have applied the three-stage test examined in *Caparo v Dickman*[1226] to determine whether a duty of care exists. When determining the existence of a novel duty of care, it is as vital for the court to bear in mind that 'categories of negligence are never closed'.[1227] Thus, Lord Bingham's view has been reaffirmed in English courts as an incremental approach to extended duties of care to a novel situation by analogy.[1228]

In this view, the tort of negligence draws a distinction between acts and omissions. 'Liability for positive acts of carelessness is well recognised, but liability for failure to act is treated differently with'[1229] "duties for affirmative action" 'being imposed only in exceptional circumstances.'[1230]

[1224]*Attorney General v Hartwell (British Virgin Islands)* [2004] 1 WLR 1273 Privy Council. <http://www.bhrinlaw.org/improving-paths-to-accountability-for-human-rights-abuses-in-the-global-supply-chains-a-legal-guide.pdf> accessed 17 May 2017.

[1225]*Ibid.*

[1226]*Caparo Industries plc v Dickman* [1990] 2 AC 605 HL.

[1227]Donoghue v Stevenson [1932] AC 562, per Lord Macmilan.

[1228]X and others (minors) v Bedfordshire County Council [1995] 3 All ER 353 and Chandler v Cape plc [2012] EWCA Civ 52.

[1229]<http://www.bhrinlaw.org/documents/amnestyinternational.creatingaparadigm shiftpol3070372017english.pdf> Accessed 19 June 2017.

[1230] <http://www.bhrinlaw.org/documents/amnestyinternational.creatingaparadigms hiftpol3070372017english.pdf> Accessed 19 June 2017 and Simon F Deakin, Angus Johnston and Basil Markesinis, Markesinis and Deakin's Tort Law (Oxford University Press 2012).

Most supply chain cases concerning human rights abuses are likely to fall under the 'omission' group of negligence. This is due to the fact that in the majority of cases, it is not the positive acts of the defendant that will cause the harm, but its failure to do its share to prevent the abuses taking place within the supply chain.

However, before the court moves to establish that a supply chain corporation failed to do its share to prevent the violation in question, the claimant must first determine whether the defendant had a legal duty to do something to prevent this harm in the first place. In order to examine the existence of such a duty to act, it is important for the court to assess whether a duty arises from the relationship between the parties, which gives rise to an imposition or assumption of responsibility. This position is vital because the facts of a case are of the utmost importance in deciding whether a new situation can be brought within the existing principle such that a duty of care will be held to exist. In determining whether such an imposition or assumption of responsibility exists, it is imperative for the court to resort to the principle that distinguishes between cases of physical injury, psychiatric injury[1231] and pure economic loss.[1232] If the court applies this principle, they will be able to find a duty of care where the injury in question is related to the supply chain operations.

To assess whether the relationship between a supply chain corporation and the victims of human rights violations in its business operations gives rise to an 'imposition or assumption of responsibility,'[1233] the court must examine the *Caparo* test. Thus, what is essential to determine is that there might be, in any given situation, two ways of fixing a duty of care on a supply chain corporation. The Focus Framework Approach means responsibility for damage done arises from an act that falls below a standard of reasonable care, with foreseeable damage, as could happen when a driver negligently causes an accident, injuring a pedestrian. The Determinate Framework Approach widens the enquiry for the imposition of a duty of care on the supply chain corporation. It determines the relationship between various actors that could share the responsibility for the harm caused to the victims. If a driver is an employee, then there must be a good reason for deciding that the employer shares responsibility, not because the latter helped cause the injury but because there is a good reason for policy for adding the employer as the responsible party. The latter might have a greater

---

[1231] *Alcock & Ors v Chief Constable of South Yorkshire* [1992] AC 310.

[1232] *Hedley Byrne & Co. Ltd v Heller & Partners Ltd* [1964] AC 465 HL.

[1233] *Smith v Littlewoods Organisation Ltd* [1987] AC 241 HL. See *Lamb v Camden London Borough Council* [1981] QB 625 and (*Dorset Yacht v Home Office* [1970] AC 1004).

resource available to remedy the victims, or might have a level of knowledge that will be desirable for the victims to rely on in order to prevent the accident. These two approaches are distinct, but are able to complement each other. The Focus Framework Approach can, for example, fix responsibility on a party who has taken a dangerous course of action, while the Determinate Framework Approach can ask which other parties should have taken action to prevent the danger from arising.

Assumption of Responsibility, the Determinate Framework and Efficient Approach

The Determinate Framework consists of a situation in which the supply chain corporation assumed responsibility through its actions vis-a-vis its business partner's employees, thus creating a special relationship between itself and its supply chain partners. Therefore, where the assumption of responsibility is not explicit, in order to assess whether the defendant is nevertheless deemed to have taken on or assumed such a responsibility towards the victims, the court must also resort to the *Caparo* test. The *Caparo* test is the ingredients of duty of care that set the standards for a reasonable foresight of the injury, the proximity of relationship between the supply chain corporation and the claimant, and the fairness/reasonableness of imposing a duty. However, it is important to also acknowledge that there is no specific definition of the legal text established in *Caparo*. Hence, they are viewed as 'convenient labels' to examine a duty of care in light of the circumstance of each case.[1234]

Foreseeability of Human Rights Abuses in Supply Chain Relationships

For a claimant to establish a duty of care, the harm must be reasonably foreseeable. The essential question to the court is whether the injury suffered is within the reasonable contemplation of the defendant. This question triggers two factors in a duty of care case; the subjective factor and the objective factor. The subjective factor in this book refers to the nature of the relationship; did the purchaser give specific instructions to suppliers, 'compliance monitoring, audits and human rights due diligence? The

---

[1234]*Caparo Industries plc v Dickman* [1990] 2 AC 605 HL, per Lord Bridge of Harwich. <http://www.bhrinlaw.org/improving-paths-to-accountability-for-human-rights-abuses-in-the-global-supply-chains-a-legal-guide.pdf> Accessed on 20 April 2018.

objective factor is about the level of risk for the human rights abuses'[1235], prevalence of labour and human rights abuses, industry-specific risks and the extent to which abuses are publicly known.

Applying the subjective and objective factors to a duty of care case will help to examine the foreseeability of the injury by the supply chain corporation. The defendant is required to investigate whether the injury suffered by the victim was within the reasonable contemplation of the supply chain corporation. In determining the reasonable foreseeability of human rights abuses, the focus should be on the knowledge that the person in the position of the defendant would be expected to possess in relation to the abuses suffered by the victims as a result of the supply chain corporation's act or failure to act. This approach was examined in *Attorney General v Hartwell.*[1236] The court stated:

> 'one of the necessary prerequisites for the existence of a duty of care is foresight that carelessness on the part of the defendant may cause damage of a particular kind to the plaintiff. Was it reasonably foreseeable that, failing the exercise of reasonable care, harm of the relevant description might be suffered by the plaintiff or member of a class including the plaintiff.'[1237]

However, the question here is what would make human rights violations and environmental damages foreseeable in the supply chain context? In this book, the answer to the question can be found in the examination of the knowledge that a person in the position of a particular supply chain corporation has or should have had in relation to the damaging consequences of its acts or omissions suffered in its supply chain. Addressing the duty of care by determining the knowledge of the defendant will potentially capture a wide group of victims, and thus the courts can also limit this requirement by the proximity and fairness element argued from the beginning of this chapter.

A possible way to achieve this is by the courts focusing on the relationship a purchaser has with the suppliers, including its suppliers beyond the first-tier. A purchaser's knowledge or presumed knowledge of human rights abuses as the result of it acts or omissions can be determined by first looking at the features of the relationship it has with its suppliers.

[1235]<http://www.bhrinlaw.org/documents/amnestyinternational.creatingaparadigmshiftpol3070372017english.pdf> Accessed 19 June 2017.

[1236]*Attorney General v Hartwell (British Virgin Islands)* [2004] 1 WLR 1273 and *Referring to Home Office v Dorset Yacht Co. Ltd* [1970] AC 1004.

[1237]*Ibid.*

This approach is adequate because not every purchaser will be in a position to reasonably foresee human rights abuses resulting from its act or omissions. The mere act of purchasing from a supplier is not likely to satisfy this prong of the *Caparo* test. When a purchaser gives specific instructions to its suppliers in relation to the standards concerning the way which the product is made (such as labour and human rights standards), and monitors suppliers compliance with its standards, then it can be inferred that this is an indication of the foreseeability of the harm, resulting from the suppliers' failure to comply with these standards.

The most important task is for the court to determine the type of standard-setting and monitoring that is relevant in the first-tier relationship. If this is clear, then there can be a strong 'presumption of foreseeability where the supply'[1238] chain corporation 'has carried out 'human rights due diligence' for its supply chain'[1239] relationship. A second contributory factor to the 'foreseeability examination in the supply chain context is the level of risk for labour and human rights violations prevalent in the country where the supplier is located or the level of risk inherent in the product or industry in question'[1240]; for example, conflict minerals and oppressive governments. This is an objective factor. Thus, 'if a purchaser is aware of or should be aware of such a risk, this is an indication of foreseeability of the harm. For example, sub-standard working conditions in garment factories in Bangladesh'[1241] 'are well-publicised. If a brand sub-contracted production of its branded goods to a garment factory'[1242] in Bangladesh, the foreseeability of the human rights violation is heightened. In these cases, foreseeability can be present for suppliers beyond the first-tier. This is so because brands often trace each stage of the production process in their supply chain to ensure a quality product. Even though the measurability of product quality and standards may be stronger than the measurability of labour and human rights standards, the ability to trace the former illustrates at least an ability to acquire knowledge concerning labour and human rights conditions in a supply chain. If the court is satisfied that all these elements

---

[1238]<http://www.bhrinlaw.org/documents/amnestyinternational.creatingaparadigmshiftpol3070372017english.pdf> Accessed 19 June 2017.
[1239]*Ibid.*
[1240]*Ibid.*
[1241] <http://www.bhrinlaw.org/documents/amnestyinternational.creatingaparadigmshiftpol3070372017english.pdf> Accessed 19 June 2017 and Muhammad Islam Azizul and Craig Deegan, 'Motivations for An Organisation Within a Developing Country to Report Social Responsibility Information: Evidence from Bangladesh' (2008) 21 (6) Accounting, Auditing & Accountability Journal 850, 874.
[1242]*Ibid.*

are present, then the court should be in a position to impose a duty of care on the defendant.

Proximity of Human Rights Abuses in Supply Chain Relationships

Proximity is shorthand for Lord Atkin's neighbour principle. It means that there must be legal proximity, i.e. a legal relationship between the parties from which the law will attribute a duty of care to protect a person from harm. What is essential in the examination of proximity is the question of whether the defendant has conducted itself in such a way that the claimant is entitled to rely upon the defendant relationship to give assumption of responsibility.

Also, the court must determine whether the person that suffers the harm has a close interest in a contract between the other parties and is affected by the non-compliance of one of those parties. In addition, it is recommended that the court must use the following parameters to establish proximity in the supply chain context. These parameters are:

- Monitoring and standard-setting through Code of Conduct;
- Monitoring compliance and imposition of a sanction for failure to comply;
- The volume of transactions and the duration of the relationship between the purchaser and supplier; and
- Outsourcing of the manufacture of self-branded product.

What is also important for the court to bear in mind before applying the principles indicated above is that proximity captures the closeness between the defendant and the claimant. It is not restricted to physical closeness, but also extends to certain close and direct relations where the human rights abuser knows or should have reasonably known that the careless act or omission complained of directly affects the victims.[1243] However, it is important to bear in mind that the element of foreseeability alone is not sufficient to find a duty of care. Therefore, there is a need for some indicators of proximity, which include physical, circumstantial or causal proximity.[1244]

The prerequisite for the proximity of relationship will also be fulfilled where it can be shown that the defendant has assumed responsibility to

---

[1243] J Steele, *Tort Law: Text, Cases and Materials* (3rd ed. OUP 2014).
[1244] *Sutherland Shire Council v Heyman* [1985] [1985] 50 ALR 1.

the claimant. This was explained by Deane J, in *Sutherland Shire Council v Heyman*:[1245] 'an assumption by one party of a responsibility to take care to avoid or prevent injury, loss or damage to the person or property of another or reliance by one party upon such care being taken where the other party ought to have known of such reliance'.[1246] In cases which conclude that a voluntary assumption of responsibility has been identified, the finding has been that the defendant has so conducted him/herself that the claimant is entitled to rely upon the defendant to act appropriately in relation to the subject matter of the duty of care. In Dam's view, 'in many of these situations, the "relier" is a person who has a close interest in a contract between other parties and is affected by the non-compliance of one of those parties.'[1247] An implication of this is that, where a purchaser sets labour and human rights standards in contract or purchase orders, the beneficiaries of these conditions would clearly have a close interest in the fulfilment of those contractual obligations.

However, a substantial challenge to establishing proximity between a purchaser and a victim of human rights abuse in the supply chain corporation is the difficulty of overcoming the argument that the defendant cannot be held liable for failing to prevent another party from abusing the human rights of a third party, which could be the supplier's employees or the indigenous people in the community. *Prima facie*, the purchaser is, at best, merely in a contractual relationship with the supplier, and as such has no duty to control the latter to prevent them inflicting harm on the third parties since in principle there can be no liability for an omission to act.[1248] However, if the relationship between the purchaser and the supplier goes beyond an 'arm's length' transaction, depending on the level of closeness of the relationship, there can be sufficient proximity between the human rights violation to the third party and the purchaser. Having said that, before the court determines proximity, the court must take into consideration a number of factors. It might be possible to take some or all these factors together in examining proximity. For example, a purchaser's monitoring of suppliers through standard-setting in supplier contracts and monitoring compliance, [1249] 'especially when non-compliance is attached to

---

[1245] *Ibid.*
[1246] *Ibid.*
[1247] Cees Van Dam, *European Tort Law* (OUP Oxford 2013).
[1248] *Sutradhar v Natural Environment Research Council* [2004] 4 All ER 490.
[1249] *Watson v British Boxing Board of Control* [2001] QB 1134.

sanctions,[1250]could illustrate closeness. The standard-setting might be via incorporating a Code of Conduct stipulating the labour and human rights standards expected from the supplier in the commercial contract, or by direct contractual reference to relevant international standards.'[1251]

Additionally, 'the volume of purchases and the long-term nature of a relationship with a supplier could also contribute to determining proximity.'[1252] Another indicator that the court can use for proximity could be the outsourcing of the manufactured goods by the supplier under its own brand. However, it is important for the court to bear in mind that in determining foreseeability and proximity, the correct approach is to focus on knowledge and closeness vis-à-vis the particular risks and injury in question. Thus, the purchaser might not be involved or have any influence over how the supplier runs its business in general but if it is involved in and has influence over, for example, working conditions or health and safety in the workplace of the supplier, then this might illustrate foreseeability and proximity to the victims for the injury suffered due to inadequate safety.

Fair, Just and Reasonable to Assign Human Rights Duty of Care in Supply Chain Relationships

The question here is whether it is fair, just and reasonable to assign human rights duty of care to a supply chain corporation? The answer to the question is subjective and objective, which requires the court to examine the elements of fairness in assigning a duty of care to an actor. The court needs to examine seven elements to determine whether it is fair, just and reasonable to assign a duty of care to supply chain corporation. These seven elements are:

- Allocation of responsibility between purchaser and supplier: who should bear the primary responsibility? Is it possible to hold both parties responsible jointly and severally?
- Damage recovery: can an adequate remedy be obtained from the primary wrongdoer?

1250Sarah A Altschuller and Amy K Lehr, 'The French Duty of Vigilance Law: What You Need to Know' (2017). <http://www.csrandthelaw.com/2017/08/03/the-french-duty-of-vigilance-law-what-you-need-to-know/> Accessed 28 February 2018.

1251 <52788_Legal_Guide_to_Human_Right_Accountability_Web.pdf (bhrinlaw.org)> Accessed 20 April 2020.

1252Simon F Deakin, Angus Johnston and Basil Markesinis, *Markesinis and Deakin's Tort Law* (Oxford University Press 2012).

- Leverage of certain supply chain corporations in the market can contribute to preventing future human rights abuses.
- Disparity between the public image promoted by the company and actual human rights performance (brand salience).
- Business relations: outsourcing the manufacture of branded goods.
- Severity of harm: violation giving rise to human rights abuse.
- Heightened risk due to the high volume of orders with an unreasonably short deadline at an unreasonably low price.

Fairness and reasonableness can be seen as another qualifier in identifying duty in a novel situation. Its role is to 'limit the duty of care in an exceptional situation where the criterion of proximity is satisfied, but where there is, nevertheless, an overriding public or general interest in denying a particular type of claim.'[1253] While in many cases fairness can be seen as a consequence of proximity of relationship,[1254] the role of this distinct element appears to act more as a guide against the expanding of the duty of care in novel situations. In a supply chain context, even if the claimant can establish foreseeability of the harm and proximity, the court might oppose fixing a duty on a supply chain corporation for human rights abuses taking place under the principle of fairness. The question to the court is whether it is fair to hold a purchaser of goods responsible for workplace human rights abuses suffered by the employee of its supplier. The responsibility of a supplier that arose from its own actions is not ruled out by also holding the purchaser liable. This is especially vital where damages cannot be recovered from the supplier itself, because the latter is bankrupt, ceased to exist, or remedies at the local level are unavailable or ineffective for other reasons.

There are several reasons that can contribute to the fairness assessment in the supply chain context. For example, if a purchaser is branding and marketing as its own the goods manufactured elsewhere under hazardous working conditions, it might be seen as fair to hold the purchaser responsible for the human rights violation that is committed in the name of producing that brand. It is also imperative for the court to bear in mind the fact that, while knowing intimately all aspects of the business from productions to sales, many brands might not be manufacturing any of their branded products themselves. They might have outsourced manufacturing entirely to a different state which has lower human rights standards than

---

[1253] *Stovin v Wise* [1996] UKHL 15.
[1254] *Ibid.*

there would be in the countries where the brands are sold.[1255] A duty on certain influential purchasers might promote better labour and human rights standards in the supply chain business operations. Another important consideration in examining fairness is the public image painted by the corporation to its investors, stakeholders and consumers. It is vital for corporate reputation and consumer confidence that the business in question does not profit from exploitation and human rights abuses. If a corporation acquires goodwill from its consumers after making public commitments that claim compliance with international minimum standard of labour and human rights throughout their supply chain[1256] but then fail to fulfil those commitments, arguably it would be fair to hold it accountable for its failings that caused the injury to employees and communities within their supply chain operations.

Similarly, courts should take into consideration the creation or heightening of the risk of injury when the purchaser sets strict and unreasonable deadlines, at an unreasonably low price. [1257] Another consideration often taken into account in the fairness examination is whether extending liability to novel situations would cause ‘floodgates’ of litigation and indeterminate liability. Courts have considered this argument especially when examining cases regarding pure economic loss[1258] and psychiatric injury, as they consider these types of cases to have a tendency to cause ‘ripple’ effects.[1259] Though, while many labour and human rights violations in the supply chain might come about in physical harm or property damage, some might merely result in a pure economic loss, like unpaid wages, forced overtime, debt-bondage, or psychiatric injury such as for family members of deceased victims. In these circumstances, it is adequate to say that the court should confine the duty to clearly restrict and set the parameter for a class of lawsuit, as set out in the *Caparo* case.

[1255]ITUC, ‘Frontlines Report: Why is The Global Business Model in Such Bad Shape?’ (2016). <https://www.ituc-csi.org/IMG/pdf/pdffrontlines_scandal_en-2.pdf> Accessed 28 February 2018.

[1256]Carolijn Terwindt, Sheldon Leader, Anil Yilmaz-Vastardis and Jane Wright, ‘Supply Chain Liability: Pushing The Boundaries of the Common Law?’ (2018) 8 (3) Journal of European Tort Law 261, 296.

[1257]Yann Queinnec and William Bourdon, ‘Regulating Transnational Companies: 46 Proposals’ (2010).

[1258]*Murphy v Brentwood District Council* [1991] 1 AC 398 and *Anns v Merton London Borough Council* [1978] AC 728.

[1259]*Woodland v Maxwell and Another* [2015] EWHC 273 (QB), [2015] All ER (D) 162 and *Spartan Steel & Alloys Ltd v Martin & Co (Contractors) Ltd* [1973] QB 27.

If the court follows the parameter set out in *Caparo*, at least the employees of first-tier suppliers with which the purchaser has a direct contractual relationship could be treated as a clearly limited and defined class of claimants.[1260] Therefore, an assumption of responsibility will more readily be recognised where the harm suffered is physical and where there is no threat that the burden of liability may be disproportionate to the conduct involved. What is clear is that, provided there is sufficient proximity and foreseeability of the injury, a duty to prevent or mitigate human rights abuses beyond the first-tier of the supplier might be seen as making it fair to impose on the purchaser a duty of care for the abuse resulting in the physical injury. Additionally, even the cases of pure economic losses and psychiatric injuries resulting from human rights violations can be treated by the court as serious injuries by examining the extent and scope of the defendant's involvement and by determining the fairness of attributing liability to the human rights abuse due to the gravity of the harm.

Applying the Principle of Duty of Care and *Chandler v Cape Industries* Case to The Supply Chain Context

The neighbourhood principle established in *Donoghue v Stevenson* and *Chandler v Cape Industries*[1261] grounds a duty of care within a supply chain business operation, if it can be determined that the following criteria are met in human rights abuse cases:

1) The business of the purchaser and supplier are in relevant aspects the same;
2) The purchaser had or ought to have had superior knowledge of some relevant aspect in a particular industry;
3) Supplier's system of work was unsafe as the purchaser knew or ought to have known; and
4) Purchaser/knew or ought to have foreseen that the supplier and/or supplier's employees would rely on the purchaser's using its superior knowledge for the employees' protection.

A vital precedent in examining proximity between the purchaser and employees of the supply chain corporation and fairness or reasonableness

[1260] *Wattleworth v Goodwood Road Racing Company Ltd and Others* [2004] EWHC 140 (QB).

[1261] *Chandler v Cape plc* [2012] EWCA Civ 525.

of finding a duty of care was observed in the decision in *Chandler v Cape Industries.*[1262] In *Chandler*, a parent corporation was held to have a duty of care to an employee of its subsidiary and a duty to intervene in order to fulfil that duty, where the employee had been made ill by asbestos dust on the subsidiary's workplace. The judge examined proximity, as well as fairness and reasonableness by reference to the role the parent corporation in directing policy on health and safety issues. Thus, assuming responsibility to prevent and mitigate injury from asbestos exposure to its subsidiaries' employees, should amount to a duty of care. Though the judge acknowledged that the subsidiaries themselves had a part to play in maintaining safety, especially through the implementation of the policies of the parent corporation, the parent corporation retained the overall responsibility for this part of health and safety policy, establishing a sufficient degree of proximity.[1263]

The Court applied the following parameters to find a duty of care in *Chandler*: 1. the business of the parent corporation and subsidiary were in relevant respects the same; 2. the parent corporation had, or ought to have had, superior knowledge of relevant aspect of health and safety in specific industry; 3. the subsidiary's system of work was unsafe as the parent corporation knew, or ought to have known; and 4. The parent corporation knew or should have known that the subsidiary or its employees would rely on its using that superior knowledge for employee protection. The Court of Appeal found that while the parent corporation had no *de jure* power to intervene in its subsidiary's business, simply because it was the parent corporation, it could still be held liable for failure to intervene to correct its subsidiary's unsafe practice. This was possible due to the *de facto* involvement of the parent in the health and safety policy of its subsidiary. In this respect, the court held that 'at any stage (the parent corporation) could have intervened and Cape Products (the subsidiary) would have bowed to its intervention. On this basis, the Claimant has established a sufficient degree of proximity between the Defendant and himself.'[1264] The question in this book is how can this legal rule, which the Court created in *Chandler*, be applied in supply chain corporate relationships? *Chandler* seems at first instance to be distinguishable from those in a purchaser/supplier relationship due to the fact that the purchaser does not have the power that a parent corporation has over its subsidiary. However, even though the supply chain relationship is simply one of seller and purchaser, the *Chandler* legal rule is still relevant here. Its operative

[1262]*Ibid.*
[1263]*Ibid.*
[1264]*Ibid.*

principles reach beyond the context of a parent corporation's relationship with its subsidiary.

The first step in the *Chandler* legal rule is determining whether the purchaser's business is in relevant parts the same as the supplier's. This point was both clear in *Chandler* and its precedent; English courts have avoided liability from parent corporations that are not operating in the same business sector, but 'merely hold shares in its subsidiaries as if [they] were an investment holding corporation'.[1265] Having said that, certain purchasers of goods in the supply chains will not play the passive role of an investment holding corporation. 'It is more likely that they will be actively carrying out business as retailers and manufacturers.'[1266] The important question for any legal counsellor is to ask whether the business of a purchaser can be viewed as being the same as the supplier's business. The *Chandler* court decision qualified 'sameness' of business with 'relevant aspect.' A possible implication of this is that the business of a purchaser and a supplier need not be the same in all aspects. For example, a purchaser and retailer of garments and a supplier of garments might be considered in the same line of business. It would be more difficult to establish sameness of business in 'relevant aspects' where a supplier is producing a component used in a final product; for example, a producer of a mineral used in an electronic product and a purchaser might have little in common.

Therefore, the vital point is to read the first legal rule in *Chandler's* judgement with the rest of the legal rules laid out in the court decision to find a duty of care in a tort of negligence case. What this means is that the purchaser having superior knowledge of the risk of certain types of injury in a specific industry or having an actual/presumed knowledge of the work conditions in the supplier's factory, where a risk assessment has been carried out, should amount to imposing a duty of care. The 'purchaser's actual or presumed awareness that the supplier or the injured'[1267] individual 'would partially rely on the purchaser acting on that knowledge in order to avoid'[1268] the injury. Hence, 'if the purchasing corporation has policies in place on workplace health and safety that it expects or requires its suppliers to follow, this could be evidence that the purchaser corporation has superior

[1265] *Thompson v The Renwick Group plc* [2014] EWCA Civ 635 and *Emere Godwin Bebe Okpabi and Others v Royal Dutch Shell PLC and Shell Petroleum Development Company of Nigeria Ltd* [2017] EWHC 89.

[1266] <http://www.bhrinlaw.org/improving-paths-to-accountability-for-human-rights-abuses-in-the-global-supply-chains-a-legal-guide.pdf> Accessed 18 April 2018.

[1267] *Ibid.*

[1268] *Ibid.*

knowledge of these issues as compared with that of its suppliers.'[1269] 'The drafters of the contract would then be seen as a quasi-regulator, which either defectively formulated the rules or failed to follow them through, and thus helped to create a risk.'[1270] In certain 'cases, superior knowledge could also be attributed to the purchaser if it audited the standards in the supplier's factory or workplace by itself or by hiring an auditing firm'.[1271] In each of these situations, 'the courts should examine whether the purchaser was in a line of business that overlapped with that of its supplier sufficiently to make it fair that its knowledge and experience should be brought to bear on improvements sought.'[1272]

When the courts are considering foreseeability the court can infer a duty of care by referring to the purchaser's level of engagement with its suppliers and by looking at the gravity and prevalence of the risk involved. A purchaser with vast experience in a particular sector could be in a position to evaluate the risk involved in producing a particular product. Where a purchaser requires its suppliers to adhere to its human rights standards and monitor compliance, this creates an environment where the supplier and third parties rely on the purchaser's efforts to avoid the injury caused. The latter could then be held liable for failing to bring that pressure to bear, thereby contributing to the injury caused to the victims. A conscious reliance by the injured third parties on the defendant is not considered necessary by the court to assign a duty of care on the actor.[1273] It is enough that 'where A advises B as to action to be taken which will directly and foreseeably affect the safety or well-being of C, a situation of sufficient proximity exists to found a duty of care on the part of A toward C. Whether in fact, such a duty arises will depend upon the facts of the individual case.'[1274]

[1269] *Ibid.*

[1270] <http://www.bhrinlaw.org/documents/amnestyinternational.creatingaparadigmshiftpol3070372017english.pdf> Accessed 19 June 2017 and Kenneth M Amaeshi, Onyeka K Osuji and Paul Nnodim, 'Corporate Social Responsibility in Supply Chains of Global Brands: A boundaryless Responsibility? Clarifications, Exceptions and Implications' (2008) 81(1) Journal of Business Ethics 223, 234.

[1271] *Ibid.*

[1272] Carolijn Terwindt, Sheldon Leader, Anil Yilmaz-Vastardis and Jane Wright (n 1612). Also see, <http://www.bhrinlaw.org/improving-paths-to-accountability-for-human-rights-abuses-in-the-global-supply-chains-a-legal-guide.pdf > Accessed 18 April 2020.

[1273] <http://www.bhrinlaw.org/documents/amnestyinternational.creatingaparadigmshiftpol3070372017english.pdf> Accessed 19 June 2017 and *Watson v British Boxing Board of Control* [2001] QB 1134.

[1274] *Ibid.*

Finding Liability in Supply Chain Business Operation Using the Focus Framework Approach

The theoretical focus here is connected to the previous findings in the above section, which discusses the approach of the Determinate Framework Approach in establishing proximity and foreseeability in supply chain business human rights abuses. In conjunction with the above evidence highlighted, finding liability through the concept of duty of care in supply chain businesses requires the corporation possessing certain business attributes to prevent, mitigate and remedy human rights violations in the supply chain. A liability for a supply chain breach of the duty of care can be triggered by:

- Outsourcing elements of the core business of the corporation;
- Special knowledge of the actor on labour and human rights standards in the supply chain, including industry-specific and country-specific knowledge; and
- Influence leverage.

The imposing of a duty of care on corporations using the Focus Framework Approach is an example of looking for the initial procedures the corporation took to regulate and mentor their supply chain business partner. This procedure could establish incentives for the corporation to take a hands-off approach to their supply chain partnership, which can result in no assumption of responsibility. Thus, the question to the court is whether in certain situations a duty to act could be imposed on the supply chain corporation if there is a certain type of relationship between the parties and if the defendant carries certain characteristics, irrespective of whether the corporation had actively taken certain steps to assume responsibility. This route could be considered when the purchaser or the supplier do not actively set standards and monitor compliance of its supply chain partnership but should do so.

The theoretical framework of the Focus Framework Approach is included in the UN Guiding Principles under the human rights due diligence requirement and applies to all business enterprises irrespective of the size.[1275] However, this book acknowledges that until such a due diligence

[1275] Björn Fasterling and Geert Demuijnck, 'Human Rights in the Void? Due Diligence in The UN Guiding Principles on Business and Human Rights' (2013) 116 (4) Journal of Business Ethics 799.

obligation is made mandatory by legislation[1276] it is hard to convince the courts that a business is under a duty to take those initial steps to identify, prevent, mitigate, and remedy abuses taking place within its supply chain business operations, as common laws only acknowledge a duty of affirmative action in tort in exceptional situations.[1277] Nevertheless, in the absence of statutory due diligence requirements, it might be possible to raise the parameter of existing legal doctrine so as to fix a duty of care on a certain corporation that carries superior knowledge and authority. However, in order to establish an affirmative duty of care aimed at preventing harm directly inflicted by the third parties, the tort of negligence often seeks to assess the 'pre-tort relationship between the parties.'[1278]

Relationships recognised as fixing affirmative duties have so far included occupiers' liability, employers' duty to ensure the safety of their employees, the relationship between parents and their children, between a school and the children in its care, and between prisons and similar authorities and those in their charge.[1279] These examples illustrate two types of duty: the first is a duty to ensure the safety of the other person in the relationship, and the second is to prevent the other party from causing harm to the third parties.[1280] In the first category of duty, the vulnerable party is in the care of the defendant; and in the second, the party causing harm is under the supervision of the parent or the custodial authority.[1281] In the second group, the English courts have also included certain situations where the defendant creates the risk of injury.[1282] In this case, it could appear far-fetched to argue that the victims of human rights abuses in the supply chain are in the purchaser's care or that the supplier is under the supervision of the purchaser where the latter has not actively assumed responsibility.

Nevertheless, as specified by the Privy Council in *AG of BVI v Hartwell*: the law of negligence is not an area where fixed absolutes of universal application are appropriate. In each case, the governing consideration is the underlying principle. The underlying principle is that reasonable foreseeability, as an ingredient of a duty of care, is a broad and flexible objective standard which is responsive to the infinitely variable circumstances of different cases. The nature and gravity of the damage foreseeable, the

---

[1276]Vanina Eckert, 'The French Attempt to Legalize Human Rights Due Diligence: Is France Leading The European Union in Business and Human Rights?' (2016).
[1277]*Smith v Littlewoods Organisation Ltd* [1987] UKHL 18.
[1278]Simon F Deakin, Angus Johnston and Basil Markesinis (n 1578).
[1279]*Ibid.*
[1280]*Ibid.*
[1281]*Ellis v The Home Office* [1953] 2 QB 135.
[1282]*Mitchell v Glasgow City Council* [2009] UKHL 11.

likelihood of its occurrence, and the ease or difficulty of eliminating the risk are all matters to be taken into account in court when deciding whether as a matter of legal policy a duty of care was owed by the defendant to the plaintiff in respect of the damage suffered by him.[1283]

In outsourcing the core elements of the business, a purchaser is delegating the task of complying with labour and human rights standards to others, while purchasing at the lowest cost possible, thus absolving itself from paying for the cost of compliance.[1284]

Also, special knowledge of labour and human rights issues in the supply chain need not just be the domain of a labour or human rights expert. If they have drawn up human rights and labour policies or recruited a human rights or a corporate social responsibility expert, these can give rise to a presumption of special knowledge. If a supply chain corporation is transacting with businesses in places where risks of abuse are higher,[1285] specifically if it carries on doing business with the corporation in environments where there are obvious failings, this should be taken into account in judging its affirmative duty. However, it has been held that the fact 'that one has expert knowledge does not in itself create a duty to the whole world to apply that knowledge in solving its problems'.[1286] If combined with other factors, knowledge can be an element for triggering liability. This is particularly so where the class of potential claimants is a clearly defined group like, for example, employees of suppliers. Furthermore, influence and leverage could be acknowledged as having a role in the purchaser's relationship with the supplier. It is not about being in control of the other entity but about the decisive influence exercised by a purchaser over aspects of supplier's business.[1287]

Evidence of this would be the volume of business between the parties, the duration of their business relationship, the special nature of the product manufactured by the supplier, or the 'level of revenue generated by the supplier from the purchaser's orders. These are elements that feed into the purchaser's ability to exert decisive pressure by ceasing the relationship with the supplier if the latter engages in labour and human

---

[1283] *Attorney General v Hartwell (British Virgin Islands)* [2004] 1 WLR 1273.

[1284] Yann Queinnec and William Bourdon (n 1613).

[1285] Jason Switzer, 'Armed Conflict and Natural Resources: The Case of The Minerals Sector' (2001) London: International Institute for Environment and Development.

[1286] *Sutradhar v Natural Environment Research Council* (n 1571).

[1287] Julia Hartmann and Sabine Moeller, 'Chain Liability in Multitier Supply Chains? Responsibility Attributions for Unsustainable Supplier Behaviour' (2014) 32 (5) Journal of Operations Management 281, 294.

rights abuses. Another important element of influence and leverage is whether an influential purchaser is contributing to the creation of a dangerous situation for the supplier's employees by, for example, placing excessive orders with tight deadlines.'[1288] In these cases, the purchaser would have constructive knowledge that this pressure would create an environment in which abuses are commonplace. The influence and leverage of some influential supply chain actors could trickle down, at various strengths, beyond the first-tier relationships, which will give rise to a duty of care.

The Breach of a Duty of Care in Supply Chain Business Operation

Once it is established that a supply chain corporation owes a duty of care to the victims of labour and human rights violations in its supply chain, then, it is necessary for the court to establish if the duty was breached. The most important aspect of determining whether the supply chain corporation has breached its duty of care is establishing the exact scope of the duty. However, this might differ from one case to another. In the most general terms, it would be a duty to prevent or mitigate human rights harm inflicted by its contractual partners to employees or other third parties in its supply chain. In cases of employees harmed in the factory, a specific duty would be to procure a healthy and safe working environment for the employees. In order to assess whether the duty was breached, English courts apply an objective standard of care based on what is required of the reasonable person.[1289] Under the principle of a reasonable man, if the person to whom the duty attaches is skilled or an expert, the standard of care will be determined by reference to a standard that would be expected from the ordinary skilled person 'exercising and professing to have that special skill.'[1290]

Whether the standard was followed or not is determined by looking at the facts of each case. It has been accepted by English courts that 'the degree of care required varies directly with the risk involved.'[1291] The risk of harm to human rights can arguably increase the standard of care required from the defendant. In the Focus Framework Approach, where a supply

---

[1288]ITUC Report (n 1577). Also see, <http://www.bhrinlaw.org/improving-paths-to-accountability-for-human-rights-abuses-in-the-global-supply-chains-a-legal-guide.pdf> Accessed 23 May 2020.

[1289]*Blyth v Birmingham Waterworks Company* [1856] 11 Ex Ch 78.

[1290]*Muir v Glasgow Corporation* [1943] SC (HL) 3.

[1291]*Barnett v Chelsea & Kensington Hospital Management Committee* [1968] 2 WLR 42.

chain actor assumes responsibility to prevent/mitigate labour and human rights abuses in its supply chain through codes of conduct, public statements, and 'monitoring processes such as audit and inspection, it shall carry out the requirements of such responsibility with reasonable care expected from the ordinary skilled person. If, during audits, it fails to identify the most obvious defects giving rise to human rights abuses, fails to follow up on corrective action plans and fails to impose the sanctions envisaged in the contract, it cannot be treated as acting with reasonable care.'[1292] For the Focus Framework Approach, the expected standard of care would also be that of the ordinary skilled person. In these cases, the breach of the duty might be due to failing to exercise a positive influence on the supply chain partner, contributing to precarious working conditions by placing excessive orders with short deadlines, or due to continuing business relationships with partners that severely abuse the rights of their workers.

Causation in Supply Chain Business Operation

The final step in establishing negligence liability is to show that the defendant's breach of duty caused the damage suffered. The first step is to establish causation in fact by applying the 'but-for' test. If the claimants would have suffered their injuries regardless of the defendant's negligence, the negligence has not caused the claimant's loss.[1293] The but-for causation is established on the balance of probabilities, so in assessing causation in the supply chain context, the courts would 'assess whether the harm could have been prevented or mitigated had the supply chain corporation not breached its duty. Where more than one corporation contributed to the damage, they could each be found liable (jointly and severally) for their contribution to the damage if each one's negligence had materially increased the risk of harm.'[1294] 'In these cases, the burden of proof is reversed, in that the defendant must show on a balance of probabilities that its negligence did not cause the harm.'[1295] 'Following this principle, a

---

[1292] <52788_Legal_Guide_to_Human_Right_Accountability_Web.pdf (bhrinlaw.org)> Accessed 13 June 2018.

[1293] *McGhee v National Coal Board* [1973] 1 WLR 1.

[1294] <http://www.bhrinlaw.org/documents/amnestyinternational.creatingaparadigmshiftpol3070372017english.pdf> Accessed 19 June 2017 and *Overseas Tankship (U.K.) Ltd v Morts Dock & Engineering Co., Ltd (Wagon Mound (No. 1)* [1961] A.C.388.

[1295] *Woodland v Essex County Council* [2013] UKSC 66 and <http://www.bhrinlaw.org/documents/amnestyinternational.creatingaparadigmshiftpol3070372017english.pdf> Accessed 19 June 2017.

purchaser, for instance, could be jointly liable with a supplier for injuries suffered by the latter's workers due to the negligent actions/omissions of each.'[1296]

'The second step in establishing causation is 'causation in law' which refers to the scope of liability. The damage suffered must be a foreseeable consequence of the breach of duty, sometimes described as requiring that any damage should not be too remote as a consequence of the harm.'[1297] This, again, will be decided by a factual inquiry by the court. The 'nature of loss, for example personal injury or pure economic loss, will play a role in deciding the foreseeability of the damage.'[1298] 'In supply chain human rights violation cases, one might look for a substantial effect on the outcome by assessing whether the ability to intervene would likely result in an improvement of behaviour on the part of its supply chain business partner. It will become more difficult to show causation in law if the human rights violation moves beyond the first tier in the supply chain.'[1299]

Non-Delegable Duty of Care in Supply Chain Business Operation

In certain supply-chain relationships, it is possible to argue that a supply chain business owed the employees of its contractual partners a non-delegable duty of care. This is because such a duty is personal to the defendant and not vicarious.[1300] A typical example of the non-delegable 'duty of care is the duty owed by an employer to its employees.'[1301] 'These duties particularly require providing a safe place and system of work.'[1302]

[1296] <http://www.bhrinlaw.org/documents/amnestyinternational.creatingaparadigmshiftpol3070372017english.pdf> Accessed 19 June 2017.

[1297] <http://www.bhrinlaw.org/documents/amnestyinternational.creatingaparadigmshiftpol3070372017english.pdf> Accessed 19 June 2017 and *Wilsons and Clyde Coal Ltd v English* [1937] UKHL 2.

[1298] *Ibid.*

[1299] *Ibid.*

[1300] Carolijn Terwindt, Sheldon Leader, Anil Yilmaz-Vastardis and Jane Wright (n 1578).

[1301] <http://www.bhrinlaw.org/documents/amnestyinternational.creatingaparadigmshiftpol3070372017english.pdf> Accessed 19 June 2017 and Patrick Selim Atiyah, *Vicarious Liability in the Law of Torts* (Butterworths 1967).

[1302] *Lochgelly Iron & Coal Co. v McMullan HL (Bailii* [1933] UKHL 4 and *Bartonshill Coal Co. v Reid* HL [1858] 3 Macqu 265.

'The underlying goal of non-delegable duties is'[1303] 'to protect those who are both inherently vulnerable and highly dependent on the observance of proper standards of care by those with a significant degree of control over their lives.'[1304] 'As they are recognised, non-delegable duties hinge on an antecedent relationship between the parties placing the defendant in a position of control over an aspect of the victim's life and it is owed to a limited class of claimants in a vulnerable position for a particular class of risks where the victim has no control over how the defendant chooses to perform its obligations.'[1305]

'Non-delegable duties are most relevant in the supply chain context where a purchaser appoints a social auditor to monitor compliance with the labour and human rights standards applied by its supplier.'[1306] However, 'the key question for the court is whether a purchaser can delegate all or parts of its duty to prevent or mitigate harm to the victims in its supply chain to an auditor. If, on the facts of a case, a purchaser exercises control over the conditions of safety in its supply chain partner's workplace',[1307] 'for example by assuming a quasi-regulator role, it arguably has a non-delegable duty to provide a safe place and system of work to its supplier's employee. Control can be manifested through the terms of the duty of care.'[1308] and threatened sanctions associated with codes of conduct, and the impacts on the workplace of the volume of orders generating the hours it was necessary to work in order to meet the orders. The employee of a supplier, for instance, will have no control over how a purchaser elects to discharge its duties, either itself or via its auditors. If an auditor carries out the monitoring negligently, liability for harm and losses arising from the auditor's negligence can be attributed to the purchaser/supplier. A supply chain corporation who has assumed responsibility for employee's safety and labour standards must not only appoint a suitable auditor but must take

---

1303<http://www.bhrinlaw.org/documents/amnestyinternational.creatingaparadigmshiftpol3070372017english.pdf> Accessed 19 June 2017.

1304Carolijn Terwindt, Sheldon Leader, Anil Yilmaz-Vastardis and Jane Wright (n 1648).

1305 <http://www.bhrinlaw.org/documents/amnestyinternational.creatingaparadigmshiftpol3070372017english.pdf> Accessed 19 June 2017 and *Woodland v The Swimming Teachers' Association and Others QBD (Bailii)* [2011] EWHC 2631 (QB), [2012] PIQR P3, [2012] ELR 76) and *Woodland v Essex County Council CA (Bailii)* [2012] EWCA Civ 239, [2013] 3 WLR 853, [2012] ELR 327, [2012] Med LR 419, [2012] PIQR P12, [2012] BLGR 879).

1306*Ibid.*

1307*Ibid.*

1308 <52788_Legal_Guide_to_Human_Right_Accountability_Web.pdf (bhrinlaw.org)> accessed 05 May 216.

adequate steps to assure that the auditor has carried out a suitable risk assessment.[1309] Careful selection of the auditor with the mission of assessing risk does not absolve the party which selected the auditor from the obligation itself to monitor the adequacy of the auditor's performance.[1310]

Vicarious Liability in Supply Chain Business Operation

In the supply chain business partnership context, vicarious liability might be an alternative ground for liability in cases involving the relationship between a purchaser and its suppliers or its auditors. In order to consider vicarious liability, there has to be a sufficiently close relationship between the tortfeasor and the party vicariously liable, and the tort committed must be sufficiently linked to that relationship. In its classic form, vicarious liability is a strict liability regime under which an employer is held liable for harm caused by the negligent conduct of its employees in the course of employment.[1311] Another relationship giving rise to vicarious liability is the relationship between a principal and an agent.[1312] English courts now accept that certain relationships that appear as one of 'independent contractor' might be classified as 'akin to employment' and give 'rise to vicarious liability.'[1313] However, 'there is a shift in focus from looking at the formal appearance of the relationship to the function exercised by the contractor.'[1314]

'A recent decision concerning the'[1315] relationship between *Uber BV* and its drivers from the employment tribunal shows how courts are willing to adapt the law to the modern economic conditions and relationships.[1316] If a supplier can be classified as having a relationship akin to employment with the purchaser, or if a social auditor can be classified as an agent of the purchaser, it might be possible to hold a purchaser

---

1309 *Uren v Corporate Leisure (UK) Ltd and Ministry of Defence (MOD)* [2011] EWCA Civ 66.

1310 *Ibid.*

1311 *Launchbury v Morgans CA* [1971] 2 QB 245.

1312 *JGE v The Trustees of the Portsmouth Roman Catholic Diocesan Trust* [2012] EWCA Civ 938.

1313 <http://www.bhrinlaw.org/documents/amnestyinternational.creatingaparadigmshiftpol3070372017english.pdf> Accessed 19 June 2017.

1314 *Ibid.*

1315 *Ibid.*

1316 *Aslam and Farrar and Others v Uber BV* (2202550/2015) [2016] Employment Tribunals.

vicariously liable for the torts committed by the supplier or the auditor.[1317] The rationale behind vicarious liability is to reach the deeper pockets of the party economically stronger than the tortfeasor, as well as to promote the improvement of behaviour on the part of the tortfeasor and the party held vicariously liable.[1318]

The relationship between a purchaser and its suppliers or auditors is not one of formal employment. Among other things, the relationship is one of 'independent contractor' and thus the parties would not be held accountable for human rights violations caused to third parties by each other's acts and omissions.[1319] However, it is important to observe that a formal employment relationship is not always necessary to establish vicarious liability.[1320] In extending vicarious liability to novel relationships, English courts give consideration to whether it would be fair, just and reasonable to extend liability. In *Various Claimants v Catholic Child Welfare Society,* Lord Phillips summarised these considerations as follows:

> (i) The employer is more likely to have the means to compensate the victim than the employee and can be expected to have insured against that liability; (ii) The tort will have been committed as a result of activity being taken by the employee on behalf of the employer; (iii) The employee's activity is likely to be part of the business activity of the employer; (iv) The employer, by employing the employee to carry on the activity will have created the risk of the tort committed by the employee; (v) The employee will, to a greater or lesser degree, have been under the control of the employer.[1321]

The court can overlook policy considerations in the supply chain context and find a novel duty of care in exceptional circumstances where it is fair, just and reasonable to impose a duty of care on the defendant.

[1317]Phillip Morgan, 'Vicarious Liability for Group Companies: The Final Frontier of Vicarious Liability?' (2015).

[1318]*Ibid.*

[1319]Ewan McKendrick, 'Vicarious Liability and Independent Contractors–A Re-Examination' (1990) Modern Law Review 53, 770.

[1320]*Ibid.*

[1321]*Catholic Child Welfare Society and Others v Various Claimants and The Institute of the Brothers of The Christian Schools* [2012] UKSC 56 on Appeal From [2010] EWCA Civ 1106.

Relationship between a Purchaser and its Suppliers Can Create a Duty of Care

Depending on the factual circumstances of each supply case, a relationship between a purchaser and a supplier might be similar to employment. In such cases, even if the relationship appears to be an independent contractor, one could argue that the purchaser is vicariously liable for the labour and human rights abuses inflicted by the supplier. The success of such an argument will also depend on the willingness of courts to take into consideration the changing social and economic realities that might justify new relationships akin to employment.[1322] One of the policy 'considerations identified by Lord Phillips in *Various Claimants* is having better means to compensate the victims'.[1323] It is contended in this book that in 'some cases the purchaser might be in a better position to compensate the victims.'[1324] However, 'this is not only because it has deeper pockets, but also because there might be no supplier to be held'[1325] liable for the human rights abuses. This is particularly so if, like the KiK and Rana Plaza cases, the supplier's business was run to the ground.[1326]

In determining the nature of the relationship between a purchaser and its supplier, the key question for the victims to answer is whether the supplier was under the supervision of and accountable to the purchaser.[1327] There are a number of elements in the relationship between a supplier and a purchaser that can indicate supervision and accountability. The first indicator is the level of control exercised over the policies and practices of the supplier. Control is understood as an 'entitlement' and as such, it is not necessary to show an actual exercise of control, but can be satisfied by showing an 'ability to control.'[1328] Control may not be exercised on all

---

1322Paula Giliker, *Vicarious Liability in Ttort: A Comparative Perspective* (Vol. 69. Cambridge University Press 2010).

1323<http://www.bhrinlaw.org/documents/amnestyinternational.creatingaparadigmshiftpol3070372017english.pdf> Accessed 19 June 2017.

1324<http://www.bhrinlaw.org/documents/amnestyinternational.creatingaparadigmshiftpol3070372017english.pdf> Accessed 19 June 2017.

1325*Ibid.*

1326Carolijn Terwindt and Miriam Saage-Maass, *Liability of Social Auditors in the Textile Industry* (Diss. Friedrich-Ebert-Stiftung Global Policy and Development 2016).

1327*JGE v The English Province of Our Lady of Charity and The Trustees of The Portsmouth Roman Catholic Diocesan Trust* [2011] EWHC 2871.

1328*Viasystems (Tyneside) Ltd v Thermal Transfer (Northern) Ltd* [2005] EWCA Civ 1151.

aspects of the supplier's business but it might be exercised with respect to the labour and human rights standards that must be followed in the supplier's workplace by assuming the role of a quasi-regulator. 'In other words, employment for one purpose is not necessarily employment for another purpose.'[1329] 'Other factors contributing to the control analysis would be the economic dependency of the supplier on the purchaser, its autonomy in taking decisions on labour and human rights standards, and the supplier's integration into the purchaser's overall organisational structure.'[1330]

'In *Aslam and Farrah v Uber BV*,'[1331] 'the employment tribunal found an employment relationship between Uber and its drivers, even though all the contractual arrangements between the relevant parties explicitly stated that the relationship was one of independent contractors. This finding was supported by the fact that the function provided by the drivers was at the heart of Uber's business.'[1332] 'The same could be said for some supply chain relationships where a business outsources a core function of its business to a contractor, in the hopes of offloading labour and human rights compliance requirements to the supplier.[1333]

An examination 'of this consideration can help determine whether the employer has created the risk by employing the supplier. The employment tribunal in the *Uber* case also took into consideration the public statements made by *Uber* about its drivers, which gave the impression that these drivers were employed by *Uber*. Similar public statements are sometimes made by supply chain corporations about the control they exercise over the labour and human rights policies of their partners. The employment tribunal also highlighted that *Uber* does not market transportation services provided via its software application for the benefit of any individual driver, but instead to promote its brand and sell its services. The same can be said where a supply chain corporation is outsourcing the production of branded products and markets goods produced in violation of labour and human rights standards as its own. The marketing is not done for the benefit of its suppliers, but for its brand name.

1329<http://www.bhrinlaw.org/documents/amnestyinternational.creatingaparadigmshiftpol3070372017english.pdf> Accessed 19 June 2017.

1330 <52788_Legal_Guide_to_Human_Right_Accountability_Web.pdf (bhrinlaw.org)> Accessed 20 April 2018.

1331*Aslam and Farrar and others v Uber BV* (n 1658).

1332<http://www.bhrinlaw.org/documents/amnestyinternational.creatingaparadigmshiftpol3070372017english.pdf> Accessed 19 June 2017.

1333*Ibid.*

This can arguably satisfy the condition that the activity was being[1334] carried out on behalf of the employer.'[1335]

'Another consideration for the *Uber* tribunal was the strict terms set by *Uber* which had to be followed by the drivers, otherwise, the drivers would face sanctions. Where a purchaser stipulates in contracts the conduct that must be followed by a supplier in discharging its obligations under the contract, and the party imposing the terms is in a superior bargaining position, this could result in a relationship akin to employment, as opposed to an arm's length contract between two independent businesses.'[1336] 'In these cases, while the supplier might be in a position to elect not to enter into a business relationship with the purchaser, if it does choose to enter into the relationship it will be required to follow the labour and human rights standards and instructions provided by the contract, especially if the failure to comply is accompanied by sanctions for breach of contract or otherwise.'[1337] 'This can show whether the employee' is under the control of the employer. All of these factors can indicate the integration of a supplier to its purchaser's organisational structure, not only in terms of what the supplier produces, but also how it produces the goods.[1338] The degree of economic integration of a business could assist in determining what is akin to employment. The required level of integration could be present even if the business relationship between the parties is not stable and long-term but are short-term and flexible, and the supplier is manufacturing goods for multiple purchasers, and not just one.[1339] In order to determine this, the courts should consider the existence of the above-mentioned conditions of supervision and accountability, as well as the mechanisms purchasers put in place for the regulation of their relationships with all their suppliers, particularly the organisational steps by which the purchaser investigates, evaluates, and approves or rejects a supplier. The consideration of these issues could help determine whether the employee's activity was a part of the business activity of the employer.

[1334] *Ibid.*
[1335] *Ibid.*
[1336] *Ibid.*
[1337] *Ibid.*
[1338] <http://www.bhrinlaw.org/documents/amnestyinternational.creatingaparadigmshiftpol3070372017english.pdf> Accessed 19 June 2017 and *JGE v The Portsmouth Roman Catholic Diocesan Trust* [2012] EWCA Civ 938.
[1339] *Ibid.*

Creating a Duty of Care through the Relationship between a Purchaser and its Auditors

It is a widespread practice for purchasers to engage social auditors to monitor supplier compliance with the labour and human rights standards they set in their supplier contracts.[1340] Negligently conducted audits might give rise to liability of the auditing company if it can be established that the auditors owed a duty of care to the employees of the supplier. Another route for accountability could be via the application of vicarious liability principles to the relationship between the purchaser and its auditor if the latter can be classified as the 'agent' of the former. An agent has the authority to represent the principal or act on the principal's behalf and can legally bind the principal vis-à-vis third parties.[1341]

An auditor might be classified as an agent if it is exercising the duty of monitoring supplier compliance on behalf of the purchaser. Acts carried out by the agent on behalf of the principal are attributed to the principal. If, in the course of exercising its authority, the agent signs a contract or commits a tort, the principal will directly be a party to these relationships with third parties. If an auditor's negligent conduct of audits acts as a cause of harm to the employees of the supplier, there might arguably be a case for the vicarious liability of the purchaser who appointed the auditor.[1342] The auditor is the 'conduit pipe' between a purchaser and the supplier and its injured employees, given that it was the purchaser's obligation to monitor compliance with labour and human rights standards, which it delegated to its auditor, 'either by finding faults that needed to be fixed or by giving clearance that the standards applied were systems fit for purpose.'[1343] 'Even where there are multiple purchasers from a supplier, and each engages their own auditor, each negligently conducted audit could give rise to a joint and'[1344] severe 'liability of the respective purchasers who have engaged the auditors if each audit has made a material contribution to increasing the risk of damage.'[1345]

[1340] Carol Murray and Barbara Cleave, *Schmitthoff's Export Trade* (Sweet & Maxwell 2005).

[1341] *Fairchild v Glenhaven Funeral Services Ltd* [2002] UKHL 22.

[1342] Rights of Third Parties Act 1999.

[1343] <http://www.bhrinlaw.org/documents/amnestyinternational.creatingaparadigmshiftpol3070372017english.pdf> Accessed 19 June 2017.

[1344] *Ibid.*

[1345] *Ibid.*

Human Rights Due Diligence and Reporting in Supply Chain Business Operation

Some national laws requiring companies to conduct human rights due diligence throughout their business operations, including their supply chains, have significant potential in improving the behaviour and accountability of corporation.[1346] 'Another contribution to improving accountability can come from reporting requirements on human rights. Non-financial reporting rules on human rights impacts have been introduced in the EU for certain large companies.'[1347] 'Under the EU Directive 2014/95/EU, covered companies are required to disclose information on the human rights impacts of their activities, including those arising from subsidiary and supply chain operations and how these impacts are managed, and the due diligence processes adopted to identify, prevent and mitigate any adverse impacts.'[1348] 'Reporting can be avoided where a company does not pursue policies relating to human rights, but it has to provide a clear and reasoned explanation of this choice.'[1349]

'In the UK, the Modern Slavery Act 2015 introduces a transparency obligation for'[1350] business organisations 'that fall within the scope of the Act.'[1351] Section 54 of the Act 'requires these entities to prepare an annual slavery and human trafficking statement. Pursuant to s 54 (4) of the Act, the statement could either state what steps were taken by the organisation 'to ensure that slavery and human trafficking is not taking place (i) in any of its supply chains, and (ii) in any part of its own business' or it could state that 'the organisation has taken no such steps.'[1352]

'While these are very positive steps, challenges remain. There is little clarity on the content of these reports and questions over sanctions for

---

[1346]Katherine Leanne Christ and Roger Leonard Burritt, 'Current Perceptions on The Problem of Modern Slavery In Business' (2018) Business Strategy & Development.
[1347]<http://www.bhrinlaw.org/documents/amnestyinternational.creatingaparadigmshiftpol3070372017english.pdf> Accessed 19 June 2017 and Directive 2014/95/EU. <http://www.bhrinlaw.org/improving-paths-to-accountability-for-human-rights-abuses-in-the-global-supply-chains-a-legal-guide.pdf> Accessed 13 December 2018.
[1348] <http://www.bhrinlaw.org/documents/amnestyinternational.creatingaparadigmshiftpol3070372017english.pdf> Accessed 19 June 2017.
[1349]*Ibid.*
[1350]*Ibid.*
[1351]<http://www.bhrinlaw.org/documents/amnestyinternational.creatingaparadigmshiftpol3070372017english.pdf> Accessed 19 June 2017 and Modern Slavery Act 2015.
[1352]*Ibid.*

failure to report accurately.’[1353] ‘The consequences for failing to report or misleading reporting are unclear. There is no clarity as to the substantive standards against which the reports shall be assessed and who shall conduct these assessments.’[1354] ‘Reporting has so far remained vague, with no actionable information coming out of company reports. On the other hand, there is still value in reporting and due diligence requirements. They urge companies to identify risks and take preventative measures. They can also aid in demonstrating knowledge and involvement of a company in its partners’ human rights performance.’[1355]

‘Lack of information is a serious challenge for victims seeking accountability against corporate groups’[1356] ‘and supply chain actors. In order to demonstrate ‘knowledge’ or even ‘assumption of responsibility’ in tort terms for human rights issues, claimants can make use of corporation reports that convey the relationship of a business with its supply chain partners.’[1357] ‘While potential liability can be a disincentive for corporations to disclose information, there is a growing pressure on businesses to become more transparent on human rights and labour issues, as well as a trend for introducing mandatory reporting requirements.’[1358] ‘These public and legislative pressures can have an impact on corporations’ attitude towards reporting. Beyond reporting, a mandatory due diligence obligation could result in a duty of care being attached to the corporation vis-à-vis the claimants.’[1359] ‘If states wish to establish a level playing field for business actors respecting human rights, mandatory due diligence and reporting obligations could make an important contribution to achieving such a level playing field.’[1360]

[1353] *Ibid.*
[1354] *Ibid.*
[1355] *Ibid.*
[1356] *Ibid.*
[1357] <http://www.bhrinlaw.org/documents/amnestyinternational.creatingaparadigmshiftpol3070372017english.pdf> Accessed 19 June 2017 and Yann Queinnec and William Bourdon (n 1579).
[1358] *Ibid.*
[1359] http://www.bhrinlaw.org/documents/amnestyinternational.creatingaparadigmshiftpol3070372017english.pdf> Accessed 19 June 2017 and Rachel Chambers and Anil Yilmaz Vastardis, ‘The New EU Rules on Non-Financial Reporting: Potential Impacts on Access to Remedy?’ (2015).
[1360] <http://www.bhrinlaw.org/improving-paths-to-accountability-for-human-rights-abuses-in-the-global-supply-chains-a-legal-guide.pdf> Accessed 10 June 2018.

The Application of Duty of Care to Multinational Corporations

'The UK courts' [1361] hear cases of overseas human rights violations.[1362] Most notably in 2016, Mr. Justice Coulson, sitting as a judge in the Technology and Construction Court, allowed a legal claim against the UK-based mining company Vedanta Resource Plc and its Zambian subsidiary Konkola Copper Mines to be tried in UK courts.[1363] This trend further supports the notion of tort law as an effective mechanism for corporate human rights violations and a tool for effective remedy.[1364] Also, US human rights violations litigation based on the ATCA has increased significantly.[1365] Other foreign direct liability cases have been heard in jurisdictions such as Canada, Australia, and the UK, as indicated in the previous chapters above, and other European Union jurisdictions.

In an examination of these cases, most of the legal suits have been based on a general doctrine of tort law and, more particularly, the tort of negligence. But these cases have lacked the core three principles of establishing a duty of care, as explained in the *Caparo v Dickman* case.[1366] Perhaps, this could be one of the reasons why the court has failed to establish liability of corporation subsidiary misconduct where there is a breach of the fundamental rights of humanity or environmental damages. Therefore, the question is: how can the court frame and address corporate misconduct in the context of the *Caparo v Dickman* test?

[1361] *Prest (Appellant) v Petrodel Resources Limited and others (Respondents)* [2013] UKSC 34 On appeal from: [2012] EWCA Civ 1395.

[1362] David P Forsythe *Encyclopedia of Human Rights* (Vol. 5. Oxford University Press 2009).

[1363] *Lungowe & others v Vedanta Resources PLC and Konkola Copper Mines PLC* [2016] EWHC 975 (TCC).

[1364] Liesbeth FH Enneking, *Foreign Direct Liability and Beyond-Exploring the Role of Tort Law in Promoting International Corporate Social Responsibility and Accountability* (Eleven International Publishing, The Netherlands 2012).

[1365] Halina Ward, 'Governing Multinationals: The Role of Foreign Direct Liability' (2001) 18 Briefing Paper.

[1366] Robyn Martin, 'Categories of Negligence and Duties of Care: Caparo in the House of Lords' (1990) 53 (6) Modern Law Review 824.

The Rationale behind the Corporate Neighbourhood Principle

The depth of international mechanisms for regulating corporate operations and providing remedies for the harm they may directly or indirectly cause society is ineffective and redundant in obtaining justice for the victims and environmental damages. The concept of foreign direct liability has been seen as an alternate method to the soft law initiative. However, it falls short due to jurisdiction limitations. The concept of tort is a collection of civil wrongs, for which the law provides a remedy for the victim, where the act of an actor falls below the reasonable man standard.[1367] Tort law allows the remedy to be enforced against a wrongdoer to the benefit of the victim who has suffered harm, which reflects on the harm committed by the wrongdoer.[1368] As explained by Ennecking in relation to human rights violation cases, tort law 'provides a legal framework or interference with the mutual relationship between private parties that is very flexible due to it open, standard-based structure and that may thus fairly easily accommodate shifting norms and values in a time of changes.'[1369]

As a result, in a legal application, tort is seen as a specific response to social change because of its flexibility and workable notion[1370] which has the potential to fill the gap between corporation liability and supply chain and subsidiary liability. Therefore, when applying this principle to human rights violations that are generally based on the norm of a duty of care, it will allow the court to take a range of factors into consideration, such as the whole business conduct of the corporations with the supply chain, the subsidiary and the government. That will effectively allow the court to pierce the corporate veil in a concept of the obligation to act reasonably in business activities and not to cause harm.[1371]

In the tort of negligence, it must be proven that the corporation owes a duty of care to the victims and the breach of this duty of care has resulted in the harm caused (see above section on the tort of negligence).[1372]

[1367]Jenny Steele, *Tort Law: Text, Cases, and Materials* (Oxford University Press 2010).

[1368]*Ibid.*

[1369]Liesbeth FH Enneking (n 1684).

[1370]*Ibid.*

[1371]Martin Petrin, 'Assumption of Responsibility in Corporate Groups: Chandler v Cape plc.' (2013) 76 (3) Modern Law Review 603, 619.

[1372] Richard Meeran, 'Tort Litigation against Multinational Corporations for Violation of Human Rights: An Overview of the Position Outside the United State' (2011) 3 City UHKL Review 1.

Applying this principle to corporate human rights abuse, what is clear is that accountability and remedy for the harm caused by a corporation, which can be anything from shock and inconvenience to illness or death,[1373] should give right to an effective sanction and remedy. However, this is currently not the case.[1374] The tort law in the notion of a duty of care can also accommodate different elements of harm caused by corporations, such as damage to the environment, damage to livelihood, toxic waste,[1375] oil spills,[1376] water pollutions,[1377] or even alleged corporate complicity in the kidnapping and torture of trade union leaders.[1378] Accordingly, the duty of care will provide victims with the different means so that the harm done to them does not have to fall into a standardised group, but can be acknowledged as an individual element of the tort of negligence, which requires effective sanction and remedy.

As well as the flexibility that the tort of negligence offers, the concept of a duty of care provides a legal instrument for greater accountability through the court system; it has the potential for universal applications. It provides the opportunity for the discovery and disclosure of the truth about corporate human rights abuses, which is a crucial factor in effective sanction and remedy for human rights violations.[1379] It is also a

---

[1373] *Bodo Community and Others v Shell Petroluem Development Company of Nigeria* [2014] EWHC 958 (TCC).

[1374] Gregory T Euteneier, 'Towards a Corporate "Law of Nations": Multinational Enterprises Contributions to Customary International Law' (2007) 82 (2) Tulane Law Review 757.

[1375] Frances Gibb, 'Trafigura's £30 Million Payout Approved After Slopes Dumped in Ivory Coast' (London, 24 September 2009) The Times. <http://www.thetimes.co.uk/tto/law/article22149990.ece> Accessed 21 December 2016.

[1376] *Bodo Community and Others v Shell Petroluem Development Company of Nigeria* (n 1659).

[1377] Norbert Fenzl, and Armin Mathis (eds), 'Pollution of Natural Water Resources in Amazonia: Sources, Risks and Consequences' In Aragon LE, and Clüsener-Godt M, *Issues of Local and Global Use of Water from the Amazon* (Montevideo 2004) 57.

[1378] Mary Carson, Adrian Gatton, Rodrigo Vázquez and Maggie O'Kane, 'Colombian Takes BP to Court in UK Over Alleged Complicity in Kidnap and Torture' (2015) *The Guadian.* <https://www.theguardian.com/environment/2015/may/22/colombian-takes-bp-to-court-in-uk-alleged-complicity-kidnap-and-torture> Accessed 21 December 2016.

[1379] Jaime E Malamud-Goti, Lucas Sebastian Grosman and P De Greiff, 'Reparations and Civil Litigation: Compensation for Human Rights Violations in Transitional Democracies' in Pablo de Greiff (ed) *The Handbook of Reparations* (OUP New York 2006).

method of providing a truth-seeking role for the victims in court, which places greater emphasis on transparency and the development of case law. Unlike many voluntary mechanisms, whose investigations rely on the willingness of the corporations, human rights violation cases brought before international courts provide a strong forum in which the truth can be revealed due to the independence of the court from the host and home state, the basis of the court and its rigorous fact-finding process.[1380]

Nonetheless, it can be acknowledged that procedural rules may vary between the judicial systems of states. However, following a close analysis of US civil law, religious law and other common law jurisdiction, the broad scope and extent of finding liability and revealing the truth about corporation misconducts will allow victims a comprehensive access to the corporate files,[1381] of which thorough investigation can lead to an 'airing of salient facts.'[1382]

This can be achieved in practice by applying the general principle of law.[1383] This evidence can, therefore, be presented and relied on in court to establish a novel duty of care for a particular misconduct that is in close relationship with the defendant and the plaintiff. The duty of care will ensure an appropriate balance between the need to discourage a 'claims culture' and 'fishing expeditions' on the one hand, and the need of victims of corporate abuse to access the corporate information and evidence they need to pursue legitimate claims on the other. The evidence rules must better consider the inherent inequality in access and control of information that exists between claimants and corporate defendants in human rights cases. Eventually, this will engage the state's own duty of care to guarantee access to justice, a fair trial, equality of arms and knowledge of the truth. Duty of care rules and the way in which they are interpreted by courts will address difficulties in accessing critical information by establishing broad and permissive discovery regimes. This view is partly supported with the development of the African Commission on Human and Peoples' Rights, which prepared model access to information that permits unqualified requests from private bodies where the information is necessary for the protection of human rights.[1384] South Africa is one of those countries that

---

[1380]*Ibid.*

[1381]Beth Stephens, 'Translating Filartiga: A Comparative and International Law Analysis of Domestic Remedies for International Human Rights Violations' (2002).

[1382]Sarah Joseph, *Corporations and Transnational Human Rights Litigation* (Hart-Publishing Oregon 2004).

[1383] For more information see Chapter VIII.

[1384]Section 12, Model Law for African States on Access to Information.

appear not to qualify access to information from private bodies on the basis of a relationship with the state.[1385]

Human rights litigation brought under the principle of duty of care in both national and international courts will facilitate the exposure of corporate misconduct and its perception in the public sphere. The difference is in what corporations advocate as its human rights duty to respect business operations.[1386] Of course, the media and NGOs play significant roles in publicising corporate human rights abuses, but this can only go as far as the social campaign element of corporate accountability. Therefore, tort elements enhance the gravity and consequences for corporations that engage in human rights abuses[1387] by imposing a duty of care on its business activities.

This can be supported by the current development of the publicities surrounding foreign direct liability in countries such as the UK[1388] and the US,[1389] comparing this to the voluntary mechanism such as United Nations Guiding Principles on Business and Human Rights. It can be observed that pressure from court judgments and media attention have damaging results for corporations because threats of civil litigation cause the corporation's share price to fall.[1390] This is further supported by Ward. The author noted that after the House of Lord's judgment in *Lubbe v Cape plc*,[1391] Cape's share dropped sharply.[1392] This suggestion follows similar patterns of

---

<http://www.achpr.org/instruments/access-information/> Accessed 10 December 2017. See also Toby Mendel 'Freedom of Information: A Comparative Legal Survey' UNESCO at 15 <http://unesdoc.unesco.org/images/0015/001584/158450e.pdf> Accessed 9 December 2017.

[1385]7 Section 32 of the Constitution of the Republic of South Africa 1996.

[1386]Halina Ward, 'Securing Transnational Corporate Accountability through National Courts: Implications and Policy Options' (2000) 24 Hastings International and Comparative Law Review 451.

[1387]*Ibid.*

[1388] Peter Muchlinski, 'Implementing the New UN Corporate Human Rights Framework: Implications for Corporate Law, Governance, and Regulation' (2012) 22 (01) Business Ethics Quarterly 145, 177.

[1389] Gregory GA Tzeutschler, 'Corporate Violator: The Alien Tort Liability of Transnational Corporations for Human Rights Abuses Abroad' (1998) 30 Columbia Human Rights Law Review 359.

[1390]Marisa McVey, 'A Powerful Retort: Foreign Direct Liability as an Essential Mechanism of Redress for Victims of Human Rights Violations by Multinational Extractive Corporations' (2015) Human Rights Commission 2015 Working Paper 1.

[1391]*Lubbe v Cape Plc* [2000] UKHL 41.

[1392]Halina Ward (n 1685).

Kappel, which found that UK and US corporations experience 'significant negative abnormal returns when human rights abuses become publicly known.'[1393] Nonetheless, this is only a detriment to the corporations and does not provide justice and remedy for the victim. Therefore, it is imperative to stress that the concept of corporate accountability is about justice and remedy for the victims, not the corporation or business activities. Thus, anything below this does not meet the minimum requirement of accountability.[1394]

The Opportunity for Victims under a Duty of Care

While the idea of corporate social responsibility and the growing body of voluntary mechanisms have focused on the soft law approach to regulating corporate conduct that is linked to their business operations, nothing has emerged from these spheres to provide a better solution for corporate human rights violations. There has been little done to directly address the environmental damages and abuses caused by corporations. However, it is also acknowledged here that the emphasis placed on tort law has portrayed tort law as a remedial instead of as an effective sanction and remedy mechanism for corporate human rights abuses. There is an element of truth in this view due to the current doctrine of tort law in Western society. Tort law is an ever-evolving concept and plays a significant role in the different social-legal challenges facing modern society. Therefore, tort law provides victims of human rights abuses a possible avenue for effective accountability and reparations, as well as being a source of deterrence for future corporate misconduct.

Adding to the minimal development in the field of tort law perspectives, this book expands on this concept by building on the idea of the duty of care in the framework set out in the neighbourhood principle, to analyse the options available for foreign nationals wishing to hold multinational corporations to account within home country jurisdictions, such as the US, the UK or the European Union. This will provide possible international standards that are directly related to victims' rights to truth, justice, and reparations, and which can be used as the metric for evaluating the effectiveness of accountability, whether at a host state or a home state

[1393]Vivien Kappel, Peter Schmidt and Andreas Ziegler, 'Human Rights Abuse and Corporate Stock Performance–an Event Study Analysis' (2009) 21 Whitepaper December.

[1394]Which is sanction and remedy, See Chapters II and III.

in the concept of foreign liability,[1395] or in an international forum, such as a court. Furthermore, the remedy for victims has been only addressed through the US ATCA after the *Kiobel* case, and no jurisdiction has yet to address and identify the extent and scope of the application of tort of negligence across the globe.[1396] There has already been a significant development in foreign liability in the UK and the Netherlands against Shell for the environmental damage and human rights abuses caused by the oil spill in Nigeria.[1397] Therefore, this is not to move away from this development but to argue that perhaps focusing on the duty of care element of human rights violations and environmental damages will establish the need for accountability and effective remedy for the victims. The duty of care creates a paradigm shift which paves the way for legal solutions to improve access to remedies for corporate human rights abuses and environmental damages, as demonstrated in the Focus and Determinate Framework Approach.

Summary of the Purpose of Tort Law

Following the discussion in this chapter so far, the study establishes that the tort law will fill the current gap created by the lack of an effective corporate accountability system. Furthermore, tort law covers all human rights abuses by a corporation in a socio-legal context. When used in a human rights context, the duty of care can be used to realise victims' rights to truth, justice, and reparations, specifically in bringing litigation against corporate extraction parent companies.

It has also been observed that the current human rights mechanisms cannot provide an effective remedy for victims of corporate human rights violations, because human rights obligations are primarily for states to abide by. Therefore, tort law can fill the needs of victims. Also, where a claimant has suffered harm and a mechanism already exists through which some form of redress may be sought, it can be argued that this makes it unnecessary for a civil law remedy in tort to be additionally created. This argument, of course, may only be deployed where a court feels that the existing means of redress offer an effective remedy. The next section of this chapter shall apply the concept of duty of care to corporate human rights violation cases

[1395] Gregory GA Tzeutschler, 'Corporate Violator: The Alien Tort Liability of Transnational Corporations for Human Rights Abuses Abroad' (1998) 30 Columbia Human Rights Law Review 359.

[1396] Beth Stephens, 'Corporate Liability: Enforcing Human Rights through Domestic Litigation' (2001) 24 (3) Hastings International and Comparative Law Review 401.

[1397] Liesbeth Enneking, 'Future of Foreign Direct Liability? Exploring the International Relevance of the Dutch Shell Nigeria Case' (2014) 10 (1) Utrecht Law Review 44.

in Canada and the UK, to illustrate how effective this mechanism will be in combating corporate human rights abuses.

The Application of Duty of Care to Multinational Corporations

The current development of corporate liability for human rights violations committed by subsidiaries is observed in Canadian courts, where Toronto-based Hudbay Minerals has assumed responsibility to protect the plaintiff from injury caused by a third party, and the plaintiff depended on the defendant's action.[1398] It was held that the defendant owed the plaintiff a duty of care.[1399] A Canadian corporation that has offered itself as a corporation that adheres to human rights duties in its global operation shall owe a duty to the victim of human rights abuses which are linked directly or indirectly to the business of the parent corporation. This is a novel duty and must be established using the two-step test in *Anns v London Borough Council*[1400]and *Caparo v Dickman.*[1401] Likewise, a case in the Canadian Supreme Court elaborates on the concept of duty of care in *Hill v Hamilton-Wentworth Regional Police Service Board*. ('Here Hill was investigated by the police, arrested, tried, wrongfully convicted, and ultimately acquitted after spending more than 20 months in jail for a crime he did not commit. Police officers suspected that Hill had committed ten robberies. The evidence'[1402] 'against Hill included a tip, a police officer's photo identification of Hill, eyewitness identifications, a potential sighting of Hill near the site of one of the robberies, and witness statements that the robber was aboriginal'.)[1403] These two cases show the principal example of where a corporation's duty of care arises from; they also indicate how the *Anns* and *Caparo* tests can be applied effectively in court to impose liability.

[1398]*Choc v Hudbay Minerals Inc.* [2013] ONSC 1414.

[1399]*Fullowka v Pinkerton's of Canada Ltd*, 2010 SCC 5, [2010] 1 SCR 132. <http://www.thecourt.ca/category/blogentry/torts/page/3/> Accessed 08 December 2017.

[1400]*Anns v Merton London Borough Council* [1978] AC. 728.

[1401]*Caparo* (n 1617).

[1402]<https://casebrief.fandom.com/wiki/Hill_v_Hamilton-Wentworth> Accessed 19 June 2019.

[1403]*Hill v Hamilton-Wentworth Regional Police Services Board*, 2007 SCC 41, [2007] 3 SCR 129. Supreme Court of Canada Torts Negligence Duty of care Police investigation. <http://www.lexisnexis.ca/documents/2007scc041.pdf> Accessed 15 August 2017.

Following this brief illustration, the study shall move on to address the steps that victims need to pass before bringing human rights violation cases against corporations under the concept of duty of care, as it has been shown in the duty of care in a supply chain business operation. It also examines whether the relationship between the plaintiff and the corporation discloses 'sufficient foreseeability and proximity to establish a *prima facie* case for corporate human rights violations'.[1404] Thus, given the inadequacy of case law [1405] addressing corporate human rights duty of care for operations in the foreign country,[1406] the book shall only focus on the case law from Canada, the United Kingdom, and the United States because these jurisdictions have applied the concept of duty of care in their domestic courts.[1407] It will then move on to address the second element of duty of care inquiry: observing whether there are 'any national policy considerations which are out to repudiate or restrict the duty of care.'[1408]

For the purposes of this book, the analysis follows the theoretical claim of the tort of negligence. Where a defendant corporation indicates that it requires its subsidiary to adhere to the basic minimum human right standards in its business operations, observing compliance with those standards and responding to acknowledged breaches of those standards by either asking the subsidiary to comply, improve, or terminate the business relationship if needs be, then the action establishes a novel duty of care. It is possible, therefore, that if corporation A failed to observe or respond to human rights impacts in its business operation, or if a corporate subsidiary did not monitor or respond to human rights impacts, if the plaintiff alleges that it did so negligently, then there exists a rebuttable duty of care for the negligent conduct of the subsidiary. The corporation's conduct should give rise to a duty of care and liability for human rights abuses. The question for the court is what the corporation knew or ought to have known at the time of the existence of a real and immediate risk of human rights violations from

---

[1404]*Ibid.*

[1405] Peter Muchlinski, 'Implementing the New UN Corporate Human Rights Framework: Implications for Corporate Law, Governance, and Regulation' 2012) 22 (1) Business Ethics Quarterly 145.

[1406]*Abu Ghraib lawsuits against CACI, Titan* (now L-3).

[1407]Shin Imai, Bernadette Maheandiran and Valerie Crystal, 'Access to Justice and Corporate Accountability: a Legal Case Study of HudBay in Guatemala' (2014) 35 (2) Canadian Journal of Development Studies/Revue canadienne d'études du développement 285; Robert McCorquodale, 'Waving Not Drowning: Kiobel Outside The United States' (2013) 107 (4) American Journal of International Law 846 and Julian Fulbrook, 'Chandler v Cape Plc: Personal Injury: Liability: Negligence' (2012) 3 Journal of Personal Injury Law C135.

[1408]*Ibid.*

the misconduct of a third party such as a subsidiary and if the corporation failed to take measures within its scope of power which, judged reasonably, it might have been expected to? Also, it is for the court to find whether a prior relationship between the victims and the corporation should be necessary at all in order to find negligence.

Third Party Liability: Corporation Foreseeability

The first leg of the *Anns* test is to ask whether there is a sufficient relationship between the plaintiff and the defendant to disclose sufficient foreseeability and proximity to establish a *prima facie* case of duty of care.[1409] Applying this to the Canadian case *Hill v Hamilton-Wentworth Regional Police Service Board*, if a Canadian corporation has undertaken to protect human rights in its business operations and has done so negligently, there is a rebuttable presumption that it is reasonably foreseeable that the corporate subsidiary's conduct could violate the human rights.

An illustration of this is *Shell*, which expressly recognises that while there was 'potential unethical social and environmental practice' in its business operations and its subsidiary's social responsibility programme in response to the concerns over human rights violations, the company did nothing to address it.[1410] In addition, it argued that a duty of care is created when a corporation has carried out a degree of human rights assessment as well as a degree of monitoring of human rights and environmental impacts of their business operation and the local community is aware of the specific risks attached to its business operation in such an environment. The corporation then has the requisite knowledge of the human rights abuse undertaken by its subsidiary. Thus, it can be said in court that this knowledge satisfies the first element of foreseeability in the *Anns* test. Therefore, the question for the court should be whether and if the event gained momentum to the extent that the harm that was reasonably foreseeable changed from harm of general human rights abuses and environmental damages to harm resulting from subsidiary human rights violations on that particular segment of society.

Consequently, if the court found that the reasonably foreseeable harm is present in the corporation's operations, the duty of care exists and any violations are only justifiable, if at all, within international human rights

---

[1409]Hazel McLean, 'Negligent Regulatory Authorities and the Duty of Care' (1988) 8 (3) Oxford Journal of Legal Studies 442.

[1410]Douglass Cassel, 'Corporate Initiatives: A Second Human Rights Revolution?' (1995) 19 Fordham International Law Journa*l* 1963. Also see: Ken Saro-Wiwa, *Genocide in Nigeria: The Ogoni Tragedy* (Vol. 18. Saros International Pub. 1992).

law obligations, as a duty not to harm your neighbour. This view followed the House of Lords' judgment in *Reeves v Commissioner of Police of the Metropolis*.[1411] A duty of care was established in respect of attempts of a prisoner known to be mentally ill but whom a doctor had found to be of sound mind. The police, who owed the defendant a duty of not physically harming him by their own actions, argued that they owed him no duty of care in respect of his suicide because he was not mentally ill and had deliberately taken his own life, even though the opportunity for him to do so had only arisen from their carelessness. The House of Lords disagreed, holding that police's duty to prisoners in its custody extends to a positive duty to take reasonable steps to assess the suicide risk of all prisoners. This was justified by the degree of control exercised over prisoners in custody and the known risk of suicide among prisoners, even those without a known mental illness. In a legal observation, the liability of corporate human rights and a subsidiary's acts do not need to touch and concern home states as advocated by the Supreme Court's judgment in *Kiobel*,[1412] because the duty of care is an action or conduct that violates the rights of people and the environment. The corporation's exercising of control and influence in the subsidiary's business operations gives rise to an effective remedy for the victims. It, therefore, seems that corporate foreseeability will negate a state's jurisdiction in imposing liability.

Comparing the concept of a duty of care to the decision in *Kiobel*, the US Supreme Court incorrectly applied tort law in the case of *Kiobel*.[1413] There is no general duty for the parent corporation to prevent other people from violating the human rights of others, but there are exceptions to this rule, many of which relate to and overlap with the concept foreseeability and stem from either special or pre-tort relations. For example, it is often because someone has not done something (an omission) that a third party is allowed the chance to lead to the harm suffered. Therefore, the question to the court in the parent corporation's scenario should be foreseeability: did the parent corporation foresee that its conduct will result in human rights abuses? In what circumstance should the general duty of care apply in the case or the general rule that people should not be liable for actions of the third party? If the US Supreme Court sought to address this issue at the initial stage of *Kiobel*, the presumption will be that a duty of care exists and

---

[1411] *Reeves v Commissioner of Police of the Metropolis* [2000] 1 AC 360. <https://www.scribd.com/document/234563408/English-Tort-Law-Cases> Accessed 08 June 2019.

[1412] David L Sloss, 'Kiobel and Extraterritoriality: A Rule without a Rationale' (2013) 28 (1) Maryland Journal of International Law, Forthcoming 241.

[1413] *Kiobel v Royal Dutch Petroleum Co.*, 133 S.Ct. 1659 (2013).

Shell Petroleum will be found liable for human rights violations by its subsidiary.

Hence, the concept of touch and concern is irrelevant to tort liability, and tort law does impose liability for the acts of the third party (the subsidiary) in exceptional circumstances. Having said that, the logical question for the court is if the liability for the third party[1414] act is broadly met by the conduct of the duty being a duty to control the third party or a duty to safeguard a dangerous thing. As noted by Lord Goff in *Smith v Littlewood* (1987), this is the case:[1415]

- where there is a special relationship between the defendant and the claimant;
- where there is a special relationship between the defendant and the third party such as control or supervision;
- where someone creates a source of danger that may be sparked by a third party; and
- where there is a failure to take a step to abate a known danger created by a third party.[1416]

Applying these rules to corporate human rights violations, the principle in *Smith v Littlewoods* established that corporate liability for misconduct should not be restricted because a parent corporation's accountability for its subsidiary may have political implications that are detrimental to international relations. This is because the finding of liability in this circumstance is based on the relationship, the control, the creation of the danger, and the steps taken to mitigate the danger. Thus, foreseeability and duty of care are about rule of law, remedy, deterrence, and protecting society from corporate conducts that are a detriment to the enjoyment of the fundamental human rights of humanity.

[1414]Sean W Martin, Reed Bates and Michael McMyne' 'Are You as Guilty as The Criminal? Liability for Criminal Acts of Third Parties and Employees' (2015) 64 (2) FDCC Quarterly 131 and *Posecai v. Wal-Mart Stores, Inc.*, 752 So. 2d 762, 766 (La. 1999). Also see: *Sturbridge Partners, Ltd. v Walker*, 482 S.E.2d 339 (Ga. 1997), *Lau's Corp, Inc. v Haskins*, 405 S.E.2d 474 (Ga. 199); *Ritz Carlton Hotel Co. v Revel*, 454 S.E.2d 183 (Ga. Ct. App. 1995) and *Grandma's Biscuits, Inc. v Baisden*, 386 S.E.2d 415 (Ga. Ct. App.).

[1415]*Smith v Littlewoods Organisation Ltd* [1987] UKHL 18.

[1416]*Ibid.*

Corporation Proximity

During the time of the writing this book, the UK and Canadian courts have not yet established whether the relationship between a UK or Canadian corporation and its subsidiary in conducting its business operations can be sufficiently proximate to give rise to a duty of care. However, it is acknowledged that there are existing authorities that have considered the imposition a duty of care to the corporation, for the misconduct of its subsidiary. Furthermore, this authority on the corporate duty of care has outlined the key tort of negligence principles for assuming a responsibility to protect human rights and the potential ground for holding corporations accountable for third-party misconduct.

Therefore, liability for the breach of the duty of care could arise where the corporations control the business operations (either directly or indirectly), where the corporation has assumed responsibility, and where the corporation's conduct has contributed to or created the violations of the basic human rights.[1417] An important point to note in the concept of liability and duty of care is that liability simply means having legal responsibility for one action and only attaches once all the elements of a tort are made out by the plaintiff. For example, while corporations who operate in an environment that has a very high record of human rights violations may owe a duty not to make the situation worse, their actions would be judged against the reasonable corporation in that circumstance. Hence, one way or another, these principles increase the degree of proximity between the corporation and the victims, creating a relationship between them in which the foreseeability of violation becomes greater, therefore justifying the corporation's potential liability to that specific victim for being involved either directly or indirectly in the human rights violations. Observing this development, this research will now move on to examine the accountability of a corporation and subsidiary before moving on to address the final leg of *Caparo* test, the fair, just, and reasonable principle.

Accountability for the Violation Inflicted by Third Party

The core question for the court in the proximity inquiry is whether the relationship was 'sufficiently close and direct to give rise to a legal duty of care, considering such a factor as expectation representation, trust, and the property or the interest involved.'[1418] *Saelzler v Advanced Group*

[1417] *Sutherland Shire Council v Heyman* [1985] 157 CLR 424.

[1418] *Fullowka v Pinkerton's of Canada Ltd.*, 2010 SCC 5, [2010] 1 S.C.R. 132.

'(Petition for review after the Court of Appeal reversed a summary judgment in a civil action. This case concerned (1) whether the Court of Appeal applied the proper standard in determining that evidence a property owner failed to provide security measures created a triable issue as to whether such failure was a contributing cause of an injury sustained as a result of a crime committed on the premises, and (2) whether a plaintiff may prove the required element of causation through expert testimony that the presence of proper security measures would have substantially reduced the probability that the crime would occur)'[1419]affirmed the summary judgment based on the plaintiff's failure to adequately demonstrate that the defendant's negligence was the proximate cause of her injuries in a case where the plaintiff was beaten and sexually assaulted while attempting to deliver a package to an apartment owned by the defendant. *Nola M. v University of S. Cal.*[1420] 'reversed the jury verdict in favour of the plaintiff because the plaintiff's security expert established the defendant's 'abstract negligence' but'[1421] did not establish a causal link between the negligence and plaintiff's injuries.

It can, therefore, be assumed that the act of a third person in committing an intentional tort or crime is a superseding cause of harm to another resulting therefrom.[1422] A vexing question in cases involving acts of third parties is the apportionment of fault among the co-defendants. A threshold question in analysing this issue, of course, is whether a particular jurisdiction applies the doctrine of vicarious liability or respondent superior and allows for apportionment of damages among joint tortfeasors/co-defendants.

Determining comparative fault and apportionment in cases of this type presents difficult issues, since it involves comparing the fault of an allegedly negligent actor with a party who acted intentionally. While courts in some states have held that fact finders may compare the fault of such parties,[1423] other states do not allow for the apportionment of fault between

---

[1419]*Saelzler v Advanced Group* 400, 107 Cal. Rptr. 2d 617, 623-24 (2001). <https://scocal.stanford.edu/opinion/saelzler-v-advanced-group-400-32181> Accessed 19 June 2018.

[1420]*Nola M. v Univ. of S. Cal.*, 20 Cal. Rptr. 2d 97 (Ct. App. 1993).

[1421]< https://www.starneslaw.com/pdf/Article-Salter-Bates-Feb2015.pdf> Accessed 18 October 2016

[1422]*Liberty Nat'l Life Ins. Co. v Weldon*, 100 So. 2d 696, 710 (Ala. 1957) (quoting Restatement (Second) of Torts § 448 (1977).

[1423]*Hutcherson v City of Phoenix*, 961 P.2d 449 (Ariz. 1998); *Field v Boyer Co.* L.C., 952 P.2d 1078 (Utah 1998).

negligent and intentional tortfeasors.[1424] In *Riley v Maison Orleans II*,[1425] relatives of a deceased nursing home resident alleged that the resident suffered injuries and ultimately died after being attacked with a steel pipe by another of the facility's residents. The trial court ruled that the deceased resident's injuries resulted from the conduct of another resident and from the absence of adequate supervision by the facility, and rendered a substantial damages award against the defendant's nursing facility.

The United States Court of Appeals for the Ninth Circuit addressed this issue in *Avitia v United States*.[1426] In that case, a patient was sexually assaulted by her doctor at a clinic receiving federal funds and sued the United States under the Federal Tort Claims Act. Applying California law, the trial court held the United States liable because the clinic and its employees failed to provide a chaperone for the patient during the gynaecological 'exam at which the alleged sexual assault occurred. The court found the clinic liable for its own negligence and, under respondent superior, for the negligence of the physician. The trial court awarded the plaintiff $210,000.00 in non-economic damages.'[1427]

The Supreme Court in *Childs Desormeaux*[1428] stated that it is uncommon for the court to find liability to protect others, without the essential element being present in the principle of proximity. 'Generally the mere fact that a person faces danger does not impose any kind of duty on those in a position to become involved.'[1429] Nonetheless, the Supreme Court concluded that liability for duty of care arises when these three factors are identified, which indicates a positive duty to protect, control, and provide self-sufficiency and trust. The factors developed by the court follow the principles of the *Anns* and *Caparo* tests.

The factors in *Childs* confirmed in the Supreme Court's later judgment in *Fullowka v Pinkerton's of Canada Ltd*. 'During a labour dispute at Yellowknife's Giant Mine in 1992, an employee named Roger Warren snuck into the mine and deliberately set a bomb that later killed nine miners who had crossed the picket line. Warren denied any knowledge of the bomb for many months, but eventually confessed and was convicted of nine

---

1424 <http://ww1.equalityrights.com/> Accessed 19 July 20220 and *Whitehead v Food Max*, 163 F.3d 265 (5th Cir. 1998); *Merrill Crossings Assocs. v McDonald*, 705 So. 2d 560 (Fla. 1997).

1425 *Riley v Maison Orleans II, Inc.* 2002 WL 31256411 (La. Ct. App. Sept. 25, 2002.

1426 *Avitia v United States*, No. 00-55240 (9th Cir. Dec. 14, 2001).

1427 <https://www.starneslaw.com/pdf/Article-Salter-Bates-Feb2015.pdf> Accessed 18 October 2016.

1428 *Childs v Desormeaux*, [2006] 1 S.C.R. 643.

1429 *Ibid.*

counts of murder.'[1430] The[1431] Supreme Court of Canada has dismissed a negligence claim brought against the CAW-Canada, holding that the national union should not be held liable for the acts of an affiliated local or its members.[1432] *Fullowka* arose from this bombing by a striking miner who was dismissed by the corporation.[1433] The family of one of the miners killed in the bombing brought a negligence claim against Pinkerton's, the security company hired to protect the mine during the strike, as well as against the trade union involved in the strike and the Government of the Northwest Territories.[1434] The Canadian Supreme Court rejected all the three tort claims, accepting that Pinkerton's owed a *prima facie* duty of care as a result of having assumed the responsibility of protecting the workers from the dangerous act of the miners during the strike.[1435]

To understand the concept of proximity, *Fullowka* is critical for a successful duty of care claim against the conduct of a third party because it addressed the same broad proposition of imposing a duty of care. Most importantly, however, it addresses the circumstance where a person could be found directly liable for failing to protect another person from harm caused by a third party. Thus, *Fullowka* is concerned with whether there existed, prior to the corporation misconduct or the misconduct of the subsidiary, failure to take care. The proximity in this context indicates the present pathways to harm and the existence of such pathways providing a reason for imposing a legal duty upon the corporation and the subsidiary.

Prior studies that have noted the importance of superior responsibility also have highlighted that one of the most important questions that arise before a defendant can be charged is whether the law or customary international law doctrine existed prior to an alleged violation of human rights.[1436] It is broadly acknowledged that it is unfair to hold someone accountable for something that was not a legal violation before they committed the act.[1437] Also, the notion of responsibility for the actions of a person under the command of another has a long and deep history in

---

[1430]<http://ww1.equalityrights.com/ >Accessed 18 September 2017.
[1431]*Ibid.*
[1432]*Ibid.*
[1433]*Fullowka v Pinkerton's of Canada Ltd* 2010 SCC 5, [2010] 1 SCR 132.
[1434]*Ibid.*
[1435]*Ibid.*
[1436]Allison Marston Danner and Jenny S Martinez, 'Guilty Associations: Joint Criminal Enterprise, Command Responsibility, and the Development of International Criminal Law' (2005) 93 California Law Review 75.
[1437]Ronald Slye and Beth Van Schaack, *International Criminal Law: Essentials* (Wolters Kluwer Law & Business 2009).

domestic and international law.[1438] Researchers have studied the roots of command responsibility back to the Roman Empire[1439] as well as Sun Tzu in the sixth century.[1440] 'Early responsibilities were connected to the state or military officials.' [1441] 'The responsibility of superiors (that were originally only military commanders) for failure to prevent or punish crimes committed by their subordinates, was conceived, in its first outline as a criminal law notion, as a form of complicity.'[1442] 'The doctrine was then spelt out by a US military commission in 1945, in the very controversial *Yamashita* case. General Yamashita, who was Commanding General of the Japanese Army in the Philippines between 1943 and 1945, was found culpable because he failed to provide effective control over his troops, permitting them to commit brutal atrocities and, as a consequence,'[1443] he was sentenced to death for the grave violations of the laws of war committed by his subordinates (and not considered 'only' as an accomplice).[1444]

In 1439, a proclamation from Charles VII of France, the Ordinance at Orleans, stated: 'each captain or lieutenant [is] held responsible for the abuses, ills and offences committed by members of his company' and must punish offences.[1445] This suggests that if there is a failure to punish or the

1438Hans Kelsen, 'Collective and Individual Responsibility in International Law with Particular Regard to The Punishment of War Criminals' (1942) 31 California Law Review 530.

1439Arthur Thomas O'Reilly, 'Command Responsibility: A Call to Realign Doctrine with Principles' (2004) 20 (1) American University International Law Review 71.

1440William H Parks, 'Command Responsibility for War Crimes' (1973) 63 Military Law Review 1. Also see: Victor H Mair, *The Art of War: Sun Zi's Military Methods* (Columbia University Press 2008).

1441Sidney G Buchanan, 'A Conceptual History of The State Action Doctrine: The Search for Governmental Responsibility (Part II of II)' (1997) 34 Houston Law Review 665.

1442Antonio Cassese, *The Human Dimension of International Law: Selected Papers of Antonio Cassese* (Oxford University Press 2008) and Micaela Frulli, 'Exploring the Applicability of Command Responsibility to Private Military Contractors' (2010) 15 (3) Journal of Conflict & Security Law 435, 466.

1443*Ibid.*

1444The judgment of the Military Commission in Law Reports of Trials of War Criminals. Selected and Prepared by the United Nations War Crimes Commission (HMSO, London 1948) (LRTWC) vol IV, 35.

1445Leslie C Green, 'Command Responsibility in International Humanitarian Law' (1995) 5 Transnational Law & Contemporary Problems 319. Also see: Zita Rohr, 'Playing the Catalan: The Rise of The Chess Queen; Queenship and Political Motherhood in Late Medieval Aragon and France' *Virtuous or Villainess? The Image of The Royal Mother from The Early Medieval to The Early Modern Era*

officer covers up the misdeed or delays taking action, or if, because of his negligence or otherwise, the offender escapes and thus evades punishment, the captain shall be deemed responsible for the offence as if he had committed it himself and shall be punished in the same way as the offender would have been.[1446]

Similarly, in 1621, the Articles of War delivered by Adolphus of Sweden stated that a commander could give no unlawful orders.[1447] Authors such as Grotius also contributed to the debate in 1625, observing that 'the state or the Superior Powers are accountable for the Crimes of their Subjects, if they know of them, and do not prevent them, when they can and ought to do so'.[1448] The notion of superior responsibility – *respondeat superior* – was not stated as a superlative but was a principle enforced in domestic law. In one early example in 1474, the Archduke of Austria ordered the trial of Peter von Hagenbach, who was charged with responsibility for atrocities committed by his subordinates while carrying out orders from his master.[1449]

Another central development in the evolution of the command responsibility doctrine was restitution for victims.[1450] Throughout the early twentieth century, many states ratified The Hague Convention of 1907 and the Geneva Convention of 1929.[1451] The most generally mentioned command responsibility inception of a positive duty of the state to prevent war crimes in a treaty is the Hague Convention.[1452] The Hague Convention also

(Palgrave Macmillan US 2016) 173-197 and Ralph Griffiths, 'Theodor Meron, Henry's Wars and Shakespeare's Laws' (1996) Nottingham Medieval Studies 198.

[1446] *Ibid.*

[1447] Norman G Cooper, 'Gustavus Adolphus and Military Justice' (1981) 92 Military Law Review 129.

[1448] Hugo Grotius, *Hugo Grotius on the Law of War and Peace* (Cambridge University Press 2012).

[1449] Leslie C Green (n 1758).

[1450] James C O'Brien, 'The international Tribunal for Violations of International Humanitarian Law in The Former Yugoslavia' (1993) 87 (4) American Journal of International Law 639.

[1451] International Conferences (The Hague), *Hague Convention (IV) Respecting the Laws and Customs of War on Land and Its Annex: Regulations Concerning the Laws and Customs of War on Land*, 18 October 1907. <http://www.refworld.org/docid/4374cae64.html > Accessed 5 September 2017 and International Committee of the Red Cross (ICRC), *Geneva Convention Relative to The Protection of Civilian Persons in Time of War (Fourth Geneva Convention)*, 12 August 1949, 75 UNTS 287. <http://www.refworld.org/docid/3ae6b36d2.html> Accessed 5 September 2017.

[1452] *Ibid.*

identified the duties for restitution to private parties: a belligerent party violating provisions 'shall if the case demands, be liable to pay compensation. What this means is that the defendant shall be responsible for all acts committed by persons forming part of its armed forces.'[1453] In addition, the Geneva Convention for the Amelioration of the Condition of the Wounded and Sick in Armies in the Field reinforced duties of military 'commanders in chief' to comply with the duties in the Convention.[1454] This observation may support the hypothesis that the concept of the responsibility of civilian superiors, and in particular private superiors, began to be more systematically implemented over the course of the twentieth century.

Furthermore, international treaties vary in the degree to which they mention corporate superior responsibility.[1455] Some research highlights them in groups such as defendants; this incorporates both state and non-state actors (corporations) but does not differentiate types of liability for all the different actors.[1456] Other treaties discuss both potential liability of non-state actors and superior responsibility.[1457] In addition to the Nuremberg[1458] trial that provided for the prosecution of superior officers, major international mechanisms offer further, longstanding support for the principle that private actors can be held accountable for their role in violations of international law.[1459] This observation is also valid when a private actor is in a position of superior responsibility.[1460]

This view is equivalent to the parent corporation and subsidiary relationship, where the parent corporation has significant control over the

---

[1453] *Ibid.*

[1454] Convention for The Amelioration of The Condition of The Wounded and Sick in Armies in The Field,118 L.N.T.S. 303, at art. 26 (June 19, 1931). Art 26.

[1455] Guénaël Mettraux, *The Law of Command Responsibility* (Oxford University Press USA 2009).

[1456] Jordan J Paust, 'Non-State Actor Participation in International Law and the Pretense of Exclusion' (2010).

[1457] William A Schabas, 'Punishment of Non-State Actors in Non-International Armed Conflict' (2002) 26 Fordham International Law Journal 907.

[1458] Gary Komarow, 'Individual Responsibility under International Law: The Nuremberg Principles in Domestic Legal Systems' (1980) International and Comparative Law Quarterly 21.

[1459] Jennifer M Green, 'Corporate Torts: International Human Rights and Superior Officers' (2016) 17 (2) Chicago Journal of International Law 447

[1460] Steven R Ratner, 'Corporations and Human Rights: A Theory of Legal Responsibility' (2001) 111 (3) Yale Law Journal 443.

subsidiary's business operation.[1461] The principle from Nuremberg and the body of law including international treaties and other sources focused on human rights and environmental law, as well as sources that deal with other substantive issues, such as maritime law, all come into play.[1462] This shows that it is possible for a corporation to be held accountable for human rights violations where it exercised control over a subordinate corporation.[1463] Even though the vast majority of case law, legislation and treaties do not make specific reference to *respondeat superior*, they contain comprehensive legal language that has been widely interpreted to include this form of liability.[1464] 'This body of law complements and strengthens the law codified by the founding documents of the international tribunals,'[1465] international courts and domestic courts decisions, which is further strengthened by the cases that have interpreted these laws in international and domestic tribunals.[1466]

Similarly, one of the treaties that addresses both superior responsibility and culpability for private actors is the Convention on Enforced Disappearances,[1467] which provides that State Parties:

> shall take the necessary measures to hold criminally responsible [superiors] who (i) Knew, or consciously disregarded information which clearly indicated, that subordinates under his or her effective authority and control were committing or about to commit a crime of enforced

---

1461Phillip I Blumberg, 'Accountability of Multinational Corporations: The Barriers Presented by Concepts of The Corporate Juridical Entity' (2001) 24 Hastings International and Comparative Law Review 297.

1462Michael A De Gennaro, 'Oil Pollution Liability and Control under International Maritime Law: Market Incentives as an Alternative to Government Regulation' (2004) 37 Vanderbilt Journal of Transnational Law 265.

1463Jennifer M Green, 'Corporate Torts: International Human Rights and Superior Officers' (2016) 17 Chicago Journal of International Law 447 and Brent Fisse and John Braithwaite, *Corporations, Crime and Accountability* (Cambridge University Press 1993).

1464 Brian Seth Parker, 'Applying the Doctrine of Superior Responsibility to Corporate Officers: A Theory of Individual Liability for International Human Rights Violations' (2012) 35 Hastings International and Comparative Law Review 1.

1465Jennifer M Green, 'Corporate Torts: International Human Rights and Superior Officers' (2016) 17 (2) Chicago Journal of International Law 447

1466Statute of the Special Court for Sierra Leone, S.C. Res. 1315, art. 6 3 (Aug. 16, 2000) and Jennifer M Green, 'Corporate Torts: International Human Rights and Superior Officers' (2016) 17 (2) Chicago Journal of International Law 447.

1467UN General Assembly, *International Convention for The Protection of All Persons from Enforced Disappearance*, 20 December 2006. <http://www.refworld.org/docid/47fdfaeb0.html> Accessed 6 September 2017

disappearance; '(ii) Exercised effective responsibility for and control over activities which were concerned with the crime of enforced disappearance; and (iii) Failed to take all necessary and reasonable measures within his or her power to prevent or repress the commission of an enforced disappearance or to submit the matter to the competent authorities for investigation and prosecution.'[1468] The Convention on Disappearances also noted that these provisions were 'without prejudice to the higher standards of responsibility applicable under international law to a military commander or to a person effectively acting as a military commander.'[1469]

Thus, there is no requirement of state action. What is essentially being said is that both governmental and non-state actors may be liable for false disappearances. For instance, the 1974 Athens Convention relating to the Carriage of Passengers and their Luggage by Sea[1470] provides that a carrier is liable for damage resulting from death or personal injury due to the fault or neglect of the carrier or his servants or agents acting within the scope of their employment.[1471]

Further, these sources of law are explicit about the application of superior responsibility to private actors. 'There is a body of law that includes the legal duties of private parties and the courts have observed the relationship of the superior commander.'[1472] 'These sources extend back almost two centuries; in particular, courts have established that rulings on the slave trade during the nineteenth century are an overlooked source of international law that addressed violations by private parties.'[1473] This development is also noted between 1817 and 1871 in the US, the UK, the Netherlands, and Portugal when these countries entered into treaties that established international courts to quash the slave trade.[1474] The courts were given authority to seize ships that engaged in the slave trade and divided the

---

[1468] *Ibid.*

[1469] Article 6.

[1470] International Maritime Organization (IMO), *International Convention for the Safety of Life At Sea*, 1. November 1974, 1184 UNTS 3. <http://www.refworld.org/docid/46920bf32.html> Accessed 6 September 2017 and Baris Soyer, 'Sundry Considerations on the Draft Protocol to The Athens Convention Relating to The Carriage of Passengers and Their Luggage by Sea 1974' (2002) 33 Journal of Air Law and Commerce 519.

[1471] *Ibid.*

[1472] Jenny S Martinez, 'Antislavery Courts and The Dawn of International Human Rights Law' (2008) Yale Law Journal 550, 641.

[1473] *Ibid.*

[1474] Jenny S Martinez, *The Slave Trade and The Origins of International Human Rights Law* (Oxford University Press 2011).

assets as a punishment for violating international law.[1475] In the twentieth century, most human rights treaties had provisions that specified that they were applied to private actors.[1476] Similarly, Article IV of the Convention on the Prevention and Punishment of the Crime of Genocide provides that: 'Persons committing genocide or any of the other acts enumerated in article III shall be punished, whether they are constitutionally responsible rulers, public officials or private individuals.' [1477] The Convention on the Prevention and Punishment of the Crime of Genocide in the US and international courts have held that genocide violates international law when it is committed by state or non-state actors[1478] and this also applies to those in positions of superior responsibility.[1479]

Also, the Convention against Torture (CAT) forbids torture 'inflicted by or at the instigation of or with the consent or acquiescence of a public official or other person acting in an official capacity'. [1480] The convention stipulates that public and private persons can be held accountable; the language is 'any person'.[1481] The Committee against Torture distinguished that the Convention recognised its enforcement against a private actor, arguing that 'acts of torture committed by non-state officials or private actors' is addressed by the Convention. [1482] Likewise, CAT General Comment 3, on the Convention's Article 14, explains the victim's right and

[1475] Eugene Kontorovich, 'The Constitutionality of International Courts: The Forgotten Precedent of Slave-Trade Tribunals' (2009) University of Pennsylvania Law Review 39.

[1476]Convention on the Prevention and Punishment of The Crime of Genocide, art. 4, *Opened for Signature* Dec. 9, 1948, 78 UNT.S. 277 (entered into force Jan. 12, 1951).

[1477]*Ibid.*

[1478]*Sosa v Alvarez-Machain,* 542 US 692, 732 & n. 20 (2004), *Kadic v Karadzic* 70 F.3d 232, 239 41 (2d Cir. 1995)); Case Concerning Application of Convention on Prevention and Punishment of Crime of Genocide (*Bosn. & Herz. v Serb. & Montenegro*), Judgment, 2007 I.C.J. 398 (Feb. 26).

[1479] Caroline Fournet, 'The Universality of The Prohibition of The Crime of Genocide, 1948-2008' (2009) 19 (2) *International Criminal Justice Review* 132,149 and Tahlia Petrosian, 'Secondary Forms of Genocide and Command Responsibility under the Statutes of the ICTY, ICTR and ICC' (2010) 17 Australian International Law Journal 29.

[1480]Convention against Torture and Other Cruel, Inhuman or Degrading Treatment or Punishment art. 1, *Opened for Signature* Dec. 10, 1984, 1465 UNT.S. 85 (entered into force June 26, 1985).

[1481]Article 6.

[1482]Committee against Torture, *General Comment No. 2: Implementation of Article 2 by States Parties* 18, UN Doc. CAT/C/GC/2/CRP.1/Rev.4 (Nov. 23, 2007).

the state's responsibility to provide redress, effective remedy, and reparations in situations in which 'state authorities knew or have reasonable grounds to believe that acts of torture or ill-treatment had been committed by non-state officials or private actors and failed to exercise due diligence to prevent, investigate and punish, the state bears responsibility to provide redress to the victims'.[1483]

Following these developments, a variety of treaties stipulate that all groups of 'persons' (natural and legal) are projected to be incorporated by their provisions. These treaties cover issues such as racial discrimination,[1484] apartheid,[1485] environmental hazards,[1486] and organised crime.[1487] Other treaties have generally incorporated the International Covenant on Civil and Political Rights (ICCPR),[1488] which advocates that each State party 'undertakes to respect and to ensure to all individuals within its territory and subject to its jurisdiction the rights recognised in the present Covenant;'[1489] the Convention for the Elimination of Racial Discrimination (CERD), which states that governments must 'prohibit and bring to an end, by all appropriate means 'including legislation racial discrimination by any

---

[1483]Committee against Torture, *General Comment No. 3: Implementation of Article 14 by States Parties*, 7, UN Doc. CAT/C/GC/3 (Dec. 13, 2012).

[1484] International Convention on The Elimination of All Forms of Racial Discrimination, *Opened for Signature* Dec. 21, 1965, 660 UNT.S. 195, 212; (entered into force Jan. 6, 1969) [hereinafter CERD]; Committee on The Elimination of Racial Discrimination, Consideration of Reports Submitted by States Parties under Article 9 of The Convention: Concluding Observations of The Committee on The Elimination of Racial Discrimination: United States of America, 30, UN Doc. CERD/C/USA/CO/6 (Mar. 5, 2008).

[1485]International Convention on The Suppression and Punishment of The Crime of Apartheid art. I (2), 2, *Opened for Signature* Nov. 30, 1973, 1015 UNT.S. 243 (entered into force July 18, 1976) (declaring apartheid criminal).

[1486]International Convention on Civil Liability for Oil Pollution Damage, *Opened for Signature* Nov.29, 1969, 973 UNT.S. 3 (entered into force June 19, 1975); Basel Convention on the Control of Transboundary Movements of Hazardous Wastes and Their Disposal, *Opened for Signature* Mar. 22, 1989, 1673 UNT.S. 57 (entered into force May 5, 1992); Convention on Third Party Liability in The Field of Nuclear Energy, *Opened for Signature* July 29, 1960, 956 UNT.S. 251. (Entered into force Apr. 1, 1968).

[1487]United Nations Convention against Transnational Organized Crime, art. 10 1, *Opened for Signature* Nov.15, 2000, 2225 UNT.S. 209 (entered into force Sept. 29, 2003).

[1488]Convention on The Elimination of All Forms of Discrimination Against Women art. 2(e), *Opened for Signature* Dec. 18, 1979, 1249 UNT.S. 13 (entered into force Sept. 3, 1981) [hereinafter CEDAW].

[1489]*Ibid.*

persons, group or'[1490] 'organisation;'[1491] and the Convention for the Elimination of Discrimination Against Women (CEDAW), which states its goal as to 'eliminate discrimination against women by any person, organisation or enterprise.'[1492] The present treaties raise the possibility that these sources of law, which provide for private liability, have been interpreted to cover superior officers (proximity). This interpretation strengthens the international legal basis for corporate superior officer liability in business operations. Lawyers and courts will be able to identify the legal and enforcement mechanisms required to hold a corporation liable for human rights abuses through the principles of superior officer.

Furthermore, the concept of due diligence in soft law[1493] in core human rights documents has also been an important characteristic of the recent development of business and human rights standards in the Organisation for Economic Co-operation and Development (OECD) Guidelines for Multinational Enterprises,[1494] the International Labour Organisation (ILO) Tripartite Declaration of Principles Concerning Multinational Enterprises and Social Policy,[1495] the UN Guiding Principles on Business and Human Rights, and the Voluntary Principles on Security and Human Rights.[1496] The due diligence principle in the UN Guiding Principles has supported the notion of the application of 'human rights' due diligence to identify, prevent, mitigate, and account for how to address business impacts on human rights.[1497] Also, the Guiding Principles include

---

[1490] Jennifer M Green, 'Corporate Torts: International Human Rights and Superior Officers' (2016) 17 (2) Chicago Journal of International Law 447.

[1491] *Ibid.*

[1492] UN Committee on The Elimination of Discrimination Against Women (CEDAW), *CEDAW General Recommendation No. 19: Violence against women*, 1992. <http://www.refworld.org/docid/52d920c54.html> Accessed 8 September 2017.

[1493] Ramona Elisabeta Cirlig, 'Business and Human Rights: from Soft Law to Hard Law?' (2016) 6 (2) Juridical Tribune 228 and *Lantz v Coleman* 2010 Conn. Super. Lexis 621 (Conn. Super. Ct. Mar. 9, 2010).

[1494] Richard Woodward, *The Organisation for Economic Co-Operation and Development (OECD)* (Routledge 2009).

[1495] Janelle M Diller, 'ILO Tripartite Declaration of Principles Concerning Multinational Enterprises And Social Policy' (2002) 41 (1) International Legal Materials 184.

[1496] Björn Fasterling and Geert Demuijnck, 'Human Rights in the Void? Due Diligence in The UN Guiding Principles on Business and Human Rights' (2013) 116 (4) Journal of Business Ethics 799.

[1497] Tanja Börzel and Jana Hoenke, 'From Compliance to Practice: Mining Companies and The Voluntary Principles on Security and Human rights in The Democratic Republic of Congo' (2010).

the identification of key risks related to the type of business and the geographical area of operation, and the existence of a plan of action to prevent or mitigate risks.[1498] The latter is based on both technical data and consultations with potentially affected people and other relevant stakeholders, specific actions triggered once abuses are reported, and disclosure of specific policies and processes undertaken to identify and address key risks.[1499] This suggests that the standards for business have also drawn increasing attention in regional bodies and within nation states.[1500]

The Working Group 'on Human Rights and Business has made important progress in seeking mutuality'[1501] 'among sectors and encouraging businesses to move towards respect for human rights.'[1502] Additionally, some 'sources of 'soft,' or non-binding, law such as UN declarations, have also supported the principles of private liability and superior responsibility for human rights violations.'[1503] For example, 'the Basic Principles and Guidelines on the Right to a Remedy and Reparation for Victims of Gross Violations of International Human Rights Law and Serious Violations of International Humanitarian Law'[1504] 'provide those who claim to be victims of a human rights or humanitarian law violation with equal and effective access to justice, irrespective of who may ultimately be the bearer of responsibility for the violation.'[1505] These various sources of soft

---

1498United Nations, *Guiding Principles on Business and Human Rights: Implementing the United Nations "Protect, Respect and Remedy" Framework* (UN 2011).

1499Radu Mares, ed. *The UN Guiding Principles on Business and Human Rights: Foundations and Implementation* (Martinus Nijhoff Publishers 2011.)

1500*Ibid.*

1501Jennifer M Green, 'Corporate Torts: International Human Rights and Superior Officers' (2016) 17 (2) Chicago Journal of International Law 447.

1502Jennifer M Green, 'Corporate Torts: International Human Rights and Superior Officers' (2016) 17 (2) Chicago Journal of International Law 447 and Human Rights Council Res. 17/4, UN Doc. A/HRC/RES/17/4, at 2 (July 6, 2011).

1503Jennifer M Green, 'Corporate Torts: International Human Rights and Superior Officers' (2016) 17 (2) Chicago Journal of International Law 447 and General Assembly Res. 60/147, 3(c) (Dec. 16, 2005).

1504Jennifer M Green, 'Corporate Torts: International Human Rights and Superior Officers' (2016) 17 (2) Chicago Journal of International Law 447.

1505Jennifer M Green, 'Corporate Torts: International Human Rights and Superior Officers' (2016) 17 (2) Chicago Journal of International Law 447 and Theo Van Boven, 'The United Nations Basic Principles and Guidelines on The Right to a Remedy and Reparation for Victims of Gross Violations of International Human Rights Law and Serious Violations of International Humanitarian Law' (2010) United Nations Audiovisual Library of International Law. New York, United Nations.

international law have detailed guidelines on business and human rights, which establish the obligations and procedures for due diligence standards to protect, respect and remedy human rights violations.[1506] Accountability for superior liability is established in both soft and hard law,[1507] as well as in case law in the past decades. This evidence establishes the possible ground for corporate superior responsibility for human rights abuses and environmental damages.

The Nuremberg trials, the continuation of the Allied Zone cases,[1508] and the Tokyo ('Far East')[1509] tribunals all included 'industrialists' as defendants, endorsing the early tribunals' application of international law irrespective of the status of the defendant (military, civilian governmental leader or private citizen).[1510] The judgement in the tribunals recognised in the case law is that conduct focused on whether superiors demonstrated a culpable failure to take reasonable steps to prevent or punish international crimes of those under their control.[1511] Also, the Nuremberg tribunals provided a new ground for holding individuals responsible for violating international law and human rights.[1512] Throughout World War II, the allies had delivered a number of statements signifying their intention to bring to trial the enemy personnel who were guilty of war crimes, including corporate defendants or 'industrialists'.[1513] The suggestion behind this principle is that a corporate structure did not provide a defence for

[1506] John Ruggic, 'Business and Human Rights: Towards Operationalizing the "Protect, Respect and Remedy" Framework' (2009) Report to The Human Rights Council, A/HRC/11/13.

[1507] Jon Birger Skjærseth, Olav Schram Stokke and Jørgen Wettestad, 'Soft law, Hard Law, and Effective Implementation of International Environmental Norms' (2006) 6 (3) Global Environmental Politics 104, 120.

[1508] Ann Tusa and John Tusa, *The Nuremberg Trial* (Skyhorse Publishing 2010).

[1509] John R Pritchard, 'The International Military Tribunal for The Far East and its Contemporary Resonances' (1995) 149 Military Law Review 25.

[1510] Bernard Victor Aloysius Röling and Christiaan F Rüter, eds. *The Tokyo Judgment: The International Military Tribunal for the Far East (IMTFE), 29 April 1946-12 November 1948* (Vol. 2. APA University Press Amsterdam 1977).

[1511] Allison Marston Danner and Jenny S Martinez, 'Guilty Associations: Joint Criminal Enterprise, Command Responsibility, and the Development of International Criminal Law' (2005) California Law Review 75, 169.

[1512] Michael R Marrus, *The Nuremberg War Crimes Trial, 1945-46: A Documentary History* (Macmillan 1997).

[1513] Quincy Wright, 'The Law of The Nuremberg Trial' (1947) 41 (1) American Journal of International Law 38.

prosecution.[1514] This was acknowledged by Justice Robert Jackson: 'While it is quite proper to employ the fiction of responsibility of a state or corporation for the purpose of imposing a collective liability, it is quite intolerable to let such a legalism become the basis of personal immunity.'[1515]

The superior responsibility principle was applied in military tribunals set up by the four Allied Powers under Allied Control Council Law No. 10.[1516] The cases that are most cited for the development of the doctrine are *US v List and Others* (The Hostages Cases)[1517] and *The High Command Case* (*officially, The United States of America v Wilhelm von Leeb et al.*).[1518] What is clear from both of these cases is that German military officers were held accountable because they were found to possess knowledge of their subordinates' abuses and had the power to stop the abuses but failed to exercise the power that they had.[1519] In the *US v List and Others,* it was observed that the duties of the supervisor included 'maintaining peace and order, and the prevention of crime' and that the 'should have known' standard was met: knowledge could be attributed to the commander because he ignored reports of terrorism and intimidation being carried out by units of the field.[1520]

The implication of the judgment is that it is the commander's duty to know 'any failure to acquaint themselves with the contents of such reports, or a failure to require additional reports where inadequacy appears on their face, constitutes a dereliction of duty which he cannot use in his

---

[1514]Francesca Gaiba, *The Origins of Simultaneous Interpretation: The Nuremberg Trial* (University of Ottawa Press 1998).

[1515]Michael Bazyler and Jennifer Green, 'Nuremberg-era Jurisprudence Redux: The Supreme Court in Kiobel v. Royal Dutch Petroleum Co. and the Legal Legacy of Nuremberg' (2012) 7 Charleston Law Review 23.

[1516]Deutschland Gebiet unter Alliierter Besatzung Kontrollrat, *Enactments and Approved Papers of The Control Council and Coordinating Committee* (1947).

[1517]*United States v List (Wilhelm) and others*, Trial Judgment, Case No 7, (1948) 11 TWC 757, (1950) 11 TWC 1230, (1948) 8 LRTWC 34, ICL 491 (US 1948), (1948) 15 ILR 632, 19th February 1948, International Military Tribunal [IMT]; Nuremberg Military Tribunal [NMT].

[1518]War Criminals, 'Law Report' (1949). <http://www.loc.gov/rr/frd/Military_Law/pdf/Law-Reports_Vol-12.pdf> Accessed 11 September 2017. *United States V Wilhelm von Leeb et al*, 12 LRTWC 1 at 59 (1948).

[1519]United Nations War Crimes Commission, *Law Reports of Trials of War Criminals* (Vol. 13. United Nations War Crimes Commission 1949).

[1520]*Ibid.*

own behalf'.[1521] Furthermore, the tribunal also observed that there was a duty to condemn and punish and provide a 'practical coercive deterrent'[1522] to high-ranking commanders ordering or complying with human rights violations.[1523] In respect of actions upon which the commander was on notice (in this case, the killings of innocent people): 'not once did he condemn such acts as unlawful. Not once did he call to account those responsible for these inhumane and barbarous acts. His failure to terminate these unlawful killings and to take adequate steps to prevent their recurrence constitutes a serious breach of duty and imposes criminal responsibility' on him.[1524]

The Nuremberg Military Tribunals (NMT) also held the defendants accountable where they did not have authoritative control over the state or military apparatus.[1525] The exemplary case, known as '*The Medical Trial*,' was when 16 medical doctors and officials were charged with responsibility for medical experiments, including subjecting people held in concentration camps to extreme temperatures and infecting them with diseases such as typhus.[1526] The defendants, including Siegfried Handloser, Chief of the Wehrmacht Medical Service were convicted of war crimes and crimes against humanity committed by subordinates. This is because they knew of the abuses, including those that resulted in the deaths of prisoners. Also, they knew that the abuses were likely to continue, and yet they failed to investigate, prevent, or punish the offences or 'exercise any proper degree of control over those conducting experiments within their *field of authority and competence*.'[1527] One interesting finding is that awareness was not sufficient for conviction; other defendants who were aware of the experiments were not convicted because they did not have supervisory authority.[1528] Thus, this awareness and the exercise of control and authority on the conduct of the subordinate is the legal proximity. Examining these

---

[1521]*Ibid.*

[1522]*Ibid.*

[1523]Allison Marston Danner and Jenny S Martinez, 'Guilty Associations: Joint Criminal Enterprise, Command Responsibility, and the Development of International Criminal Law' (2005) California Law Review 75, 169.

[1524]John A Appleman, *Military Tribunals and International Crimes* (Westport Conn: Greenwood Press 1971).

[1525]Kevin Jon Heller, *The Nuremberg Military Tribunals and The Origins of International Criminal Law* (Oxford University Press on Demand 2011).

[1526]Acquaviva G A Cassese, Fan M and A Whiting, *International Criminal Law: Cases and Commentary* (Oxford University Press 2011).

[1527]*Ibid.*

[1528]Matthew Lippman, 'Fifty Years after Auschwitz: Prosecutions of Nazi Death Camp Defendants' (1995) 11 Connecticut Journal of International Law 199.

convictions and acquittals together gives additional proof that the factors in culpability were knowledge and control (proximity) over subordinates (subsidiary) for a finding of corporate liability.[1529]

Analysing the tribunal, Nuremberg prosecutors were unequivocal about their ability to try civilian leaders.[1530] Drachsler pronounced Control Council Law No. 10 as expanding superior responsibility to 'industrialists in their representative capacity, as officers of the leading German economic institutions, as corporate officials of their own organisations, and as individuals'.[1531] This evidence suggested that 'industrialists could be held liable for acts undertaken as'[1532] supervisors.[1533] In one particular case, *Government Commissioner v Roechling*, the Tribunal found senior officials in the Roechling firm responsible for the abuse of labourers, who included prisoners of war, in spite of the fact that it was Gestapo soldiers who physically abused the labourers.[1534] The Tribunal held that 'Hermann Roechling and the other accused members of the Directorate of the Voelklingen works are not accused of having ordered this horrible treatment, but of having permitted it; and indeed supported it, and in addition, of not having done their utmost to put an end to these abuses.'[1535] Roechling's son-in-law was found to possess the authority 'to obtain an alleviation in the treatment of these workers, but, despite this authority, he did 'not address the violations.'[1536] Thus, the tribunal found the son-in-law

---

[1529]Chantal Meloni, *Command Responsibility in International Criminal Law* (TMC Asser press 2010).

[1530]Greg R Vetter, 'Command Responsibility of Non-Military Superiors in The International Criminal Court (ICC)' (2000) 25 Yale Journal of International Law 89 and Kai Ambos, 'General Principles of Criminal Law in the Rome Statute' (Vol. 10. No. 1. Springer Netherlands, 1999) Criminal Law Forum.

[1531]Jonathan A Bush, 'The Prehistory of Corporations and Conspiracy in International Criminal Law: What Nuremberg Really Said' (2009) Columbia Law Review 1094, 1262.

[1532]Jennifer M Green, 'Corporate Torts: International Human Rights and Superior Officers' (2016) 17 (2) Chicago Journal of International Law 447.

[1533]Kim Christian Priemel, '"A Story of Betrayal": Conceptualizing Variants of Capitalism in The Nuremberg War Crimes Trials' (2013) 85 (1) Journal of Modern History 69,

[1534]Rehan Abeyratne, 'Superior Responsibility and the Principle of Legality at the ECCC' (2012). Gov't Comm'r of the Gen. Trib. of The Military Gov't for the French Zone of Occupation in *Germany v Roechling*, Indictment, 14 Trials of War Criminals Before the Nuremberg Military Tribunals Under Control Council Law No. 10 1061 Appendix B (1950).

[1535]*Ibid.*

[1536]*Ibid.*

responsible because he had the authority to address the violations, but did not exercise his authority to halt the abuse. In examining the tribunal view, the standard applied to find these officials culpable had three elements defined in the statutes of the modern tribunals. The first is effective control, the second is knowledge of the abuse, and the third is the ability to stop the abuse but failing to do so.[1537] These three elements are referred to in tort law as reasonably foreseeable harm and proximity to impose a duty of care on the defendant.[1538]

Also, in the *Pohl* case, '18 defendants, all members of the WVHA (Wirtschaft und Verwaltungshauptamt, the Economic and Administrative Main Office), were indicted on 13 January 1947, and arraigned on 10 March.'[1539] ('In January 1947, Military Tribunal II, which had been created by the US Military Government for Germany on 14 December 1946, took on the trial of Oswald Pohl and the WVHA, the fourth Subsequent Nuremberg Proceeding.'[1540]) The defendants of the 'NMT included Karl Mummenthey, a Waffen SS officer[1541] who managed mining companies, factories, and quarries.'[1542] Mummenthey supervised labourers who were enslaved and presided over the administration of concentration camps.[1543] He attempted to escape liability by arguing that he was merely a 'private businessman in no way associated with the sternness and rigor of SS discipline and entirely detached from concentration camp routine'.[1544] The NMT did not accept this defence, and found that '[i]f excesses occurred in the industries under his control he was in a position not only to know about them, but to do something'.[1545] The Tribunal also rejected Mummenthey's claims of ignorance, stating that his 'assertions that he did not know what

[1537]Jennifer M Green (n 1475).

[1538]Martin Petrin, 'Assumption of Responsibility in Corporate Groups: Chandler v Cape plc' (2013) 76 (3) Modern Law Review 603, 619.

[1539]*POHL et al.* 'US Military Tribunal Nuremberg, Judgment of 3 November 1947. <http://holocaustresearchproject.org/holoprelude/pohl.html> Accessed 08 March 2017.

[1540]<https://encyclopedia.ushmm.org/content/en/article/subsequent-nuremberg-proceedings-case-4-the-pohl-case> Accessed 06 January 2016.

[1541]Bruce Campbell, *The SA Generals and The Rise of Nazism* (University Press of Kentucky 2015).

[1542]Jennifer M Green, 'Corporate Torts: International Human Rights and Superior Officers' (2016) 17 (2) Chicago Journal of International Law 447.

[1543]US Govt Printing Off., 5 Trial of War Criminals before The Nuremberg Military Tribunals Under Control Council Law No. 10 1052 (1950).

[1544]*Ibid.*

[1545]*Ibid.*

was happening in the labour camps and enterprises under his jurisdiction does not exonerate him. It was his duty to know.'[1546]

During the period from August 1947 to July 1948, the Tribunal in *United States v Krauch* put 24 directors of I.G. Farben on trial.[1547] In *Krauch*, 'Farben supplied Zyklon B poison gas to German concentration camps to murder millions.'[1548] Farben also 'conducted notorious medical experiments upon unwilling prisoners at Auschwitz, and operated a massive industrial complex next to Auschwitz that subjected prisoners to forced[1549] labour, 'most of whom died from hunger, disease, or exhaustion.'[1550] 'Ten corporate officers were acquitted, with the remainder found guilty and receiving prison terms ranging from eight years to time already served (one and a half years).'[1551] Thus, 'the court was clear about the accountability of these corporate officers'[1552]: in the case

> where private individuals, including juristic persons, proceed to exploit the military occupancy by acquiring private property against the will and consent of the former owner, such action, not being expressly justified, is in violation of international law. Similarly, where a private individual or a juristic person becomes a party to unlawful confiscation of public or private property by planning and executing a well-defined design to acquire such property permanently, acquisition under such circumstances subsequent to the confiscation constitutes conduct in violation of [international law].[1553]

[1546]*Ibid.*

[1547]*The United States of America v Carl Krauch et al.* (1950) Case No 6. 'US Gov't Printing Off., 5 Trial of War Criminals before the Nuremberg Military Tribunals Under Control Council Law No. 10 1052 (1950).

[1548]Jennifer M Green, 'Corporate Torts: International Human Rights and Superior Officers' (2016) 17 (2) Chicago Journal of International Law 447.

[1549]*Ibid.*

[1550]Jennifer M Green, 'Corporate Torts: International Human Rights and Superior Officers' (2016) 17 (2) Chicago Journal of International Law 447 and Records of the *United States Nuremberg War Crimes Trials, United States v Krauch* (Case IV) (Aug. 14, 1947–July 30, 1948). <https://perma.cc/PAZ2-VWSV> Accessed 12 September 2017.

[1551]*Ibid.*

[1552]Jennifer M Green, 'Corporate Torts: International Human Rights and Superior Officers' (2016) 17 (2) Chicago Journal of International Law 447.

[1553]*Ibid.*

In another notable trial, Alfried Krupp, the industrialist and sole owner of Krupp, was sentenced to 12 years imprisonment and ordered to forfeit all his property under Control Council Law No. 10.[1554]

In addition to the Nuremberg cases, another significant development of jurisprudence on superior responsibility was the legal system created to try war criminals in the Pacific region after World War II.[1555] The principle of superior accountability was termed in the founding documents for the tribunals, in one of the most cited cases against General Yamashita.[1556] The 'Pacific Region tribunals also put industrialists on trial for war crimes.'[1557] Similarly, 'the Chinese Law Governing the Trial of War'[1558] Criminals[1559] 'explicitly held superiors responsible for failing to prevent crimes of their subordinates and was stated in broad terms, applying to 'persons' and including omissions':[1560] 'Persons who occupy a supervisory or commanding position in relation to war criminals and in their capacity as such have not fulfilled their duty to prevent crimes from being committed by their subordinates shall be treated as the accomplices of such war criminals.'[1561]

[1554] *United States v Krupp* (The Krupp Case). 9 Trial of War Criminals before the Nuremberg Military Tribunals under Control Council Law NO. 10, 1449–50. (1950). <https://perma.cc/L9Q7-DHBU> Accessed 12 September 2017.

[1555] Jennifer M Green, 'Corporate Torts: International Human Rights and Superior Officers' (2016) 17 (2) Chicago Journal of International Law 447 and Ann Marie Prevost, 'Race and War Crimes: The 1945 War Crimes Trial of General Tomoyuki Yamashita' (1992) 14 Human Rights Quarterly 303.

[1556] Bruce D Landrum, 'The Yamashita War Crimes Trial: Command Responsibility Then and Now' (1995) 149 Military Law Review 293.

[1557] Jennifer M Green, 'Corporate Torts: International Human Rights and Superior Officers' (2016) 17 (2) Chicago Journal of International Law 447 and Arthur K Kuhn, 'International Law and National Legislation in The Trial of War Criminals the Yamashita Case' (1950) 44 (3) American Journal of International Law 559.

[1558] Jennifer M Green, 'Corporate Torts: International Human Rights and Superior Officers' (2016) 17 (2) Chicago Journal of International Law 447.

[1559] William H Parks, 'Command Responsibility for War Crimes' (1973) 1 Military Law Review 62.

[1560] Jennifer M Green, 'Corporate Torts: International Human Rights and Superior Officers' (2016) 17 (2) Chicago Journal of International Law 447.

[1561] Jennifer M Green, 'Corporate Torts: International Human Rights and Superior Officers' (2016) 17 (2) Chicago Journal of International Law 447 and *Prosecutor v Mucić et al.,* Case No. IT-96-21-T, Judgment, 337 (Int'l Crim. Trib. For the Former Yugoslavia Nov. 16, 1998). <https://perma.cc/BT86-GBWV> Accessed September 2017 (citing Art. IX of the Chinese Law of 24th October, 1946, Governing The Trial of War Criminals.

'Pursuant to the Tokyo Charter',[1562] which created the 'tribunals to try war crimes in the Pacific region, the Japanese General Tomoyuki Yamashita was tried for atrocities committed by troops under his command in the Philippines in the closing days of World War II.'[1563] 'The military commission found that 'there was a deliberate plan and purpose to massacre and exterminate a large part of the civilian population of Batangas Province and to devastate and destroy more than 25,000 men, women, children, all unarmed non-combatant'[1564] 'civilians were brutally mistreated'[1565] and killed.[1566] The Tribunal decided that 'the crimes were so extensive and widespread, both as to time and area, that they must either have been wilfully permitted by the accused, or secretly ordered by the accused.'[1567] Thus, it was held that Yamashita could be held responsible for the conduct of those under his command because a commander has a 'duty to take such appropriate measures as are within his power to control the troops under his command,' rather than those within his formal mandate or authority.[1568] The judgement was a contentious one, and some scholars have argued that 'in many ways, the evolution of command responsibility doctrine has consisted of reactions and counter-reactions to Yamashita.'[1569] The criticisms included the dissenting US Supreme Court justices in *Yamashita* case.[1570]

[1562]Jennifer M Green, 'Corporate Torts: International Human Rights and Superior Officers' (2016) 17 (2) Chicago Journal of International Law 447 and Robert Cryer and Neil Boister, eds. *Documents on The Tokyo International Military Tribunal: Charter, Indictment, and Judgments* (Vol. 1. Oxford University Press 2008).

[1563]Jennifer M Green, 'Corporate Torts: International Human Rights and Superior Officers' (2016) 17 (2) Chicago Journal of International Law 447 and United Nations War Crimes Commission, *Law Reports of Trials of War Criminals*. (Vol. 13. United Nations War Crimes Commission 1949).

[1564]Jennifer M Green, 'Corporate Torts: International Human Rights and Superior Officers' (2016) 17 (2) Chicago Journal of International Law 447.

[1565]*Ibid.*

[1566]In *re Yamashita*, 327 US 1, 14 (1946).

[1567]*re Yamashita*, 327 US at 15.

[1568]*Ibid.*

[1569]Allison Marston Danner and Jenny S Martinez, 'Guilty Associations: Joint Criminal Enterprise, Command Responsibility, and the Development of International Criminal Law' (2005) California Law Review 75, 169.

[1570]Jenny S Martinez, 'Understanding Mens Rea in Command Responsibility: From Yamashita to Blaškić and Beyond' (2007) 5 (3) Journal of International Criminal Justice 638, 664.

The Far East 'tribunals also included at least one case against officers of a corporation:[1571] the Kinkaseki Mine, which operated in Taiwan from 1942–1945.'[1572] 'Nine civilian Nippon employees were tried before the British War Crimes Court in Hong Kong in 1947'[1573] and 'charged with mistreating prisoners of war forced to work in the mines.'[1574] The perpetrators included the 'general manager, two production managers, a production supervisor and five foremen. Toda Mitsuga, the General Manager, was among those found guilty.'[1575] The tribunal rejected 'Toda's arguments that the military was responsible for the treatment of prisoners of war (POWs) at the mine'. 'The rejection was founded on Toda's testimony that POWs were paid by the company and that he received weekly or monthly reports from subordinate corporation officials about 'the amount of work done, the amount of ore extracted, purchases of stones and expenditures.'[1576] Toda was found guilty, but what is surprising is that the court provided no reasoning for its sentence.

The description of methods of responsibility in the Royal Warrant Regulation 8 (ii)[1577] took a procedural approach that 'where there was evidence that a war crime had been the result of concerted action on the part of a unit or a group of men,' it is '*prima facie* evidence of the responsibility of each member of that unit or group for that crime.'[1578] '[T]he Hong Kong indictments' have been interpreted 'to include a nascent version of the doctrine of command responsibility.'[1579] The tribunal decided that in the

---

[1571]Yuma Totani, *The Tokyo War Crimes Trial: The Pursuit of Justice in The Wake of World War II* (Vol. 299. Harvard Univ Council on East Asian 2009).

[1572]Jennifer M Green, 'Corporate Torts: International Human Rights and Superior Officers' (2016) 17 (2) Chicago Journal of International Law 447 and also see; Gary K Reynolds, *US Prisoners of War and Civilian American Citizens Captured and Interned by Japan in World War II: The Issue of Compensation by Japan* (Congressional Research Service Library of Congress 2002).

[1573]Sybilla Jane Flower, *British Prisoners of War of the Japanese*, 1941–45 *The History of Anglo-Japanese Relations, 1600–2000* (Palgrave Macmillan UK 2000).

[1574]Suzannah Linton, 'Rediscovering the War Crimes Trials in Hong Kong, 1946-48' (2012) 13 Melbourne Journal of International Law 284.

[1575]Yuma Totani, '*The Prisoner of War Camp Trials' Hong Kong's War Crimes Trials* (2013) 71, 94.

[1576]*Ibid.*

[1577]Anthony PV Rogers, 'War Crimes Trials under The Royal Warrant: British Practice 1945-1949' (1990) 39 (4) International and Comparative Law Quarterly 780.

[1578]Suzannah Linton, ed. *Hong Kong's War Crimes Trials* (Oxford University Press 2013).

[1579]*Ibid* at 207.

Hong Kong's War Crimes, the private mining company was liable for the conditions and mistreatment, including forced labour of prisoners of war who had been transferred to them by the Japanese Army.[1580] The tribunals established after the conclusion of World War II, including their prosecution of corporate officers in the ''industrialist trials' in both Europe and the Pacific'[1581], have become one of the most often cited bases in human rights law.[1582] The precedent of the courts provides a critical legal basis for applying superior responsibility to corporate officers committing war crimes and crimes against humanity.[1583] Furthermore, in the last two decades, a supplementary source of legal standards on superior responsibility has been the jurisprudence of international tribunals that were created to address genocide, war crimes, and crimes against humanity in particular countries or regions.[1584] The most common jurisprudence to be created so far has come out of the International Criminal Tribunal for the Former Yugoslavia (ICTY)[1585] and the International Criminal Tribunal for Rwanda.[1586]

In applying these legal standards, the tribunals have further developed the law on superior responsibility, which includes applicability to private corporate officials.[1587] In this development, the tribunals focus on the conduct itself rather than the status of the individual responsible for the violation, therefore, the elements of the test are whether a superior (1) has 'effective control' over subordinates, (2) knew or had reason to know about the alleged violation, and (3) failed to take measures to prevent the abuse or

---

[1580] Anita Ramasastry, 'Corporate Complicity: From Nuremberg to Rangoon-An Examination of Forced Labour Cases and Their Impact on the Liability of Multinational Corporations' (2002) 20 Berkeley Journal of International Law 91.

[1581] Jennifer M Green, 'Corporate Torts: International Human Rights and Superior Officers' (2016) 17 (2) Chicago Journal of International Law 447.

[1582] Paul Taucher, *Command Responsibility at The Sandakan-Ranau War Crimes Trial* (Diss. Murdoch University 2016).

[1583] Timothy Wu and Yong-Sung Kang, 'Criminal Liability for The Actions of Subordinates-The Doctrine of Command Responsibility and Its Analogues in United States Law' (1997) 38 Harvard International Law Journal 272.

[1584] Guénaël Mettraux, *International Crimes and The Ad hoc Tribunals* (Oxford University Press on Demand 2005).

[1585] George H Aldrich, 'Jurisdiction of The International Criminal Tribunal for the former Yugoslavia' (1996) 90 (1) American Journal of International Law 64.

[1586] Cecile Aptel, 'The International Criminal Tribunal for Rwanda' (1997) 37 (321) International Review of The Red Cross Archive 675.

[1587] William A Schabas, *The UN International Criminal Tribunals: The Former Yugoslavia, Rwanda and Sierra Leone* (Cambridge University Press 2006).

punish the perpetrator.[1588] Applying these elements in the context of tort law, the test set down in the ICTY, is equivalent to the House of Lord's test in *Caparo* (tort of negligence).

In 1998, the ICTY addressed the first contemporary judgement on the elements of superior responsibility.[1589] In the former Yugoslavia, a number of the defendants were non-state actors and in *Prosecutor v Delalic et al.* (*Celebici)* the ICTY ruled that 'the applicability of the principle of superior responsibility in Article 7(3) extends not only to military commanders but also to individuals in non-military positions of superior authority.'[1590] (In this case - which has become known as the *Celebici* case – the Trial Chamber pronounced its Judgement, which was 'the second Judgement upon trial to be rendered by the International Tribunal and the first to be completed involving more than one accused person. The trial of the four-accused commenced on 10 March 1997 and covered a period of some 19 months. The Trial Chamber was presented with a great quantity of evidence on the part of both the Prosecution and the Defence,'[1591] including the testimony of numerous witnesses and many hundreds of pages of documents, which it considered carefully, along with the arguments of the parties.)[1592] The applicability of superior responsibility to civilians as well as military officials was noted and the tribunal clarified that superior responsibility could apply whether or not there was a *de jure* hierarchical structure.[1593] The *Celebici* Appeals Chamber established that the essential relationship between superior and subordinate was one of 'effective control'.[1594] The ICTY observed the Nuremberg's *Pohl* case as a relevant precedent on superior responsibility and distinguished that the information

---

[1588]Ann B Ching, 'Evolution of The Command Responsibility Doctrine in Light of The Celebici Decision of The International Criminal Tribunal for the former Yugoslavia' (1999) 25 North Carolina Journal of International Law and Commercial Regulations 167.

[1589]Kelly D Askin, 'Reflections on Some of The Most Significant Achievements of the ICTY' (2003) 37 New England Law Review 903.

[1590]*Čelebici* Trial Judgment at 376 and <https://ihl-databases.icrc.org/customary-ihl/por/docs/v2_rul_rule153> Accessed 20 September 2016.

[1591]<https://legal.un.org/avl/studymaterials/rcil-thailand/2012/Book6.pdf> Accessed 08 January 2017.

[1592]*Prosecutor v Zdravko Mucic aka "Pavo", Hazim Delic, Esad Landzo aka "Zenga", Zejnil Delalic (Trial Judgement)*, IT-96-21-T, International Criminal Tribunal for the former Yugoslavia (ICTY), 16 November 1998. <http://www.refworld.org/cases,ICTY,41482bde4.html> Accessed 12 September 2017.

[1593]*Ibid* at 354.

[1594]*Ibid* at 376.

was available to put on notice for the need for further investigation.[1595] The tribunal's thinking shows that command responsibility is not a form of strict liability. Thus, although not strict liability, the standard for superior liability was greater than ordinary negligence and recklessness in this case.[1596]

In *Prosecutor v Blaskic*, the ICTY clarified that the 'indicators of effective control are more a matter of evidence than of substantive law.'[1597] Hence, what is clear in the court's judgment is that the elements of effective control recognised in this decision have the power to prevent international crimes, punish perpetrators, and to refer the offenders to appropriate authorities.[1598] The ICTY acknowledged the sources of customary international law with relation to superior responsibility and its application to cases involving both international and internal armed conflict, and to both military and civilian superiors.[1599] Its decisions repeated the elements of effective control between a superior and subordinate, whether the superior 'knew or had reason to know about a forthcoming or past violation, and the failure to prevent a predicted violation or punish violations within the superior's knowledge.'[1600]

Also, 'the International Criminal Tribunal for Rwanda (ICTR)'[1601], was formed to 'address genocide, war crimes, and crimes against humanity in Rwanda in 1994.'[1602] The tribunal 'clearly specified that superior

---

[1595]*Prosecutor v Blaškić,* Case No. IT-95-14-A, Appeal Judgment, 192–93, 262–63 (Int'l Crim. Trib. For the Former Yugoslavia, July 29, 2004). <https://perma.cc/Z8DM-MX56> Accessed 12 September 2017.

[1596]Allison Marston Danner and Jenny S Martinez (n 1545).

[1597]*Prosecutor v Blaškić,* Case No. IT-95-14-A, Appeals Chamber Judgement, 69 (Int'l Crim. Trib. For the Former Yugoslavia July 29, 2004). <https://perma.cc/L9VN-LWP6> Accessed 12 September 2017 hereinafter Blaskic Appeal Judgment.

[1598]*Ibid* at 69.

[1599]Greg R Vetter, 'Command Responsibility of Non-Military Superiors in The International Criminal Court (ICC)' (2000) 25 Yale Journal of International Law 89, James D Levine, 'The Doctrine of Command Responsibility and Its Application to Superior Civilian Leadership: Does the International Criminal Court Have The Correct Standard' (2007) 52 Military Law Review 193.

[1600]*Čelebici* Trial Judgment, at 379, 93.

[1601]Jennifer M Green, 'Corporate Torts: International Human Rights and Superior Officers' (2016) 17 (2) Chicago Journal of International Law 447.

[1602]Jennifer M Green, 'Corporate Torts: International Human Rights and Superior Officers' (2016) 17 (2) Chicago Journal of International Law 447 and Timothy Gallimore, 'The Legacy of The International Criminal Tribunal for Rwanda (ICTR) and Its Contributions to Reconciliation in Rwanda' (2008) 14 (2) New England Journal of International and Comparative Law 239.

responsibility applied to civilian as well as military officials.'[1603] In one 'crucial case, the *Prosecutor* v *Bagilishema'*[1604] panel indicated that, '[T]here can be no doubt, therefore, that the doctrine of command responsibility extends beyond the responsibility of military commanders to encompass civilian superiors in positions of authority'.[1605] The ICTR has found business leaders culpable under charges of superior responsibility where they had effective control over those committing the violations. Similarly, where superiors knew or had reason to know about the crimes and superior officers could have taken action to prevent or punish the violation, but failed to do so, have resulted in human rights abuses.[1606]

In the *Prosecutor v Musema* case against the director of the Gisovo Tea Factory, the ICTR Trial Chamber found the director Alfred Musema liable as a superior officer because he 'exercised *de jure* authority over [tea factory] employees' and because he 'was in a position, by virtue of these powers, to take reasonable measures, such as removing, or threatening to remove, an individual from his or her position at the Tea Factory if he or she was identified as a perpetrator of crimes punishable under the Statute.'[1607]

In another extensively discussed case, *The Media Case*,[1608] an ICTR Appeals Chamber examined the legal standards for superiors in a

---

[1603]Jennifer M Green, 'Corporate Torts: International Human Rights and Superior Officers' (2016) 17 (2) Chicago Journal of International Law 447 and also see; Gideon Boas, James L Bischoff and Natalie L. Reid, *Forms of Responsibility in International Criminal Law* (Cambridge University Press 2007).

[1604]Jennifer M Green, 'Corporate Torts: International Human Rights and Superior Officers' (2016) 17 (2) Chicago Journal of International Law 447 and *The Prosecutor v Ignace Bagilishema (Trial Judgement)*, ICTR-95-1A-T, International Criminal Tribunal for Rwanda (ICTR), 7 June 2001.
<http://www.refworld.org/cases,ICTR,48abd5170.html> Accessed 12 September 2017. Also see; Jennifer M Green, 'Corporate Torts: International Human Rights and Superior Officers' (2016) 17 (2) Chicago Journal of International Law 447

[1605]Jennifer M Green, 'Corporate Torts: International Human Rights and Superior Officers' (2016) 17 (2) Chicago Journal of International Law 447 and *Prosecutor v Bagilishema*, Case No. ICTR-95-1A-T, Judgment, 42 (Int'l Crim. Trib. for Rwanda June 7, 2001).

[1606]Catharine A MacKinnon, 'Prosecutor v Nahimana, Barayagwiza, & Ngeze. Case No. ICTR 99-52-T' (2004) 98 (2) American Journal of International Law 325.

[1607]*Prosecutor v Musema*, Case No. ICTR-96-13-T, Judgment and Sentence, 880, 894 (Int'l Crim. Trib. for Rwanda Jan. 27, 2000). <https://perma.cc/S2CL-BAUM> Accessed 13 September 2017.

[1608]Gabriele Della Morte, 'De-Mediatizing the Media Case: Elements of a Critical Approach' (2005) 3 (4) Journal of International Criminal Justice 1019.

private company running a Rwandan radio station and newspapers. The 'Chamber upheld the conviction of Ferdinand Nahimana, the radio station's founder and manager, for his subordinates' acts of inciting genocide.'[1609] The court held that superiors could be culpable for human rights violations committed by their subordinates.[1610] The Chamber held that corporate officials with effective control over their subordinates who 'knew or had reason to know' 'subordinates were about to commit crimes and failed to prevent or punish acts inciting genocide, could be held criminally responsible for these violations.'[1611] A vital characteristic of the Chamber judgement is its discrepancy between superior responsibility and direct instigation of genocide. Similarly, 'the Appeals Chamber dismissed charges of direct instigation due to lack of evidence against Nahimana, in spite of its finding of his responsibility as a superior.'[1612] The Appeals Chamber also highlighted 'that that this was not a case in which the defendant was a *de facto* military commander and that the army was not even in control.'[1613] '*The Media Case* permits 'double-derivative liability,'[1614] concluding that superior accountability applies even when the subordinate is merely an accomplice to a third-party perpetrator; that is, failing to prevent or punish a subordinate who aids and abets or incites another in the commission of a crime.'[1615]

In distinction, the Appeals Chamber found insufficient evidence against 'Jean-Bosco Barayagwiza, the radio station's co-founder, and Hassan Ngeze, who was alleged to be criminally liable for personally inciting genocide in the newspaper he controlled.'[1616] The Chamber established that

---

[1609]Jennifer M Green, 'Corporate Torts: International Human Rights and Superior Officers' (2016) 17 (2) Chicago Journal of International Law 447 and also see; *Ibid* at at 849–50, 853.

[1610]*Nahimana v Prosecutor*, Case No. ICTR 99-52-A, Appeals Judgment (Int'l Crim Trib for Rwanda Nov. 28, 2007). <https://perma.cc/VKG9-XKTB [hereinafter Media Case> Accessed September 2017.

[1611]*Ibid* at 589, 776, 822, 834, 840, 856, 942.

[1612]*Ibid.*

[1613]*Ibid.*

[1614]William H Painter, 'Double Derivative Suits and Other Remedies with Regard to Damaged Subsidiaries' (1961) 36 (3) Indian Law Journal 143 and *Hamilton Partners LP Englard* [2010] C.A. 4476 - VCL.

[1615]Diane F Orentlicher, 'Criminalizing Hate Speech in The Crucible of Trial: Prosecutor v. Nahimana' (2006) 21 (4) American University International Law Review 557.

[1616]Jennifer M Green, 'Corporate Torts: International Human Rights and Superior Officers' (2016) 17 (2) Chicago Journal of International Law 447 and also see:

'Barayagwiza had effective control over his subordinate merely at a time that was too distant from the genocide to hold him criminally responsible. Likewise, during the period of genocidal incitement at the radio station, he did not have effective control over his subordinates'.[1617] Even though Hassan Ngeze published 'criminal statements'[1618] in his newspaper and the Appeals Chamber endorsed his conviction for personally inciting genocide, the Chamber decided that it could not uphold the conviction for superior responsibility because he did not have effective control over his subordinates.[1619] The nuanced method adopted by the ICTR illustrates the careful application of the multi-pronged test of superior responsibility. Thus, if there is proof 'of effective control of subordinates, private actors, including corporate officers'[1620], will be 'held accountable for human rights violations that they were found to have known about and failed to attempt to prevent or punish.'[1621]

'In addition to the international tribunals created to address genocide and other violations in the former Yugoslavia and Rwanda, tribunals combining international and national laws and procedural aspects were created to address other patterns of atrocities across the world.'[1622] 'As these tribunals move forward, they are adopting theories of superior responsibility for corporate officials. One case that has been heard by the Special Tribunal for Lebanon has addressed corporate individuals'[1623] (Ayyash et al. STL-11-01 cases).[1624] In the first such Hybrid Tribunal case

---

Catharine A MacKinnon, 'Prosecutor V. Nahimana, Barayagwiza, and Ngeze. Case No. ICTR 99 52 A' (2004) 98 (2) American Journal of International Law 325.

[1617]Nahimana Prosecutor vBarayagwiza, & Ngeze (Media Case), Case No. ICTR-99-52-T (Dec. 3, 2003)' (2004) 117 Harvard Law Review 2769, 2773.

[1618]Stephen Porter and John C Yuille, 'Credibility Assessment of Criminal Suspects Through Statement Analysis' (1995) 1 (4) Psychology, Crime and Law 319.

[1619]Alexander Zahar, *The ICTR's "Media" Judgment and The Reinvention of Direct and Public Incitement to Commit Genocide (*Vol. 16. No. 1. Springer Netherlands 2005).

[1620]Jennifer M Green, 'Corporate Torts: International Human Rights and Superior Officers' (2016) 17 (2) Chicago Journal of International Law 447.

[1621]*Ibid.* Also see: Gregory S Gordon, 'A War of Media, Words, Newspapers, and Radio Stations: The ICTR Media Trial Verdict and a New Chapter in The International Law of Hate Speech' (2004) 45 Virginia Journal of International Law 139.

[1622]Jennifer M Green, 'Corporate Torts: International Human Rights and Superior Officers' (2016) 17 (2) Chicago Journal of International Law 447.

[1623]*Ibid.*

[1624]Jennifer M Green, 'Corporate Torts: International Human Rights and Superior Officers' (2016) 17 (2) Chicago Journal of International Law 447 and also see;

to address corporate officers, the Special Tribunal for Lebanon Tribunal proceeded against a private corporate official, Ms. Karma Mohamed Tahsin Al Khayat, for publishing the names of 'purported confidential witnesses.'[1625] In that case on contempt charges, the court convicted Ms. Khayat, who authorised the broadcasts on Al Jadeed TV and then authorised the transfer of the broadcasts onto Al Jadeed's website and YouTube page.[1626] She further had the authority to remove these broadcasts but failed to. In exercising her authority, she acted on behalf of Al Jadeed TV.

In addition to all the evidence presented above, the current tribunals, the ICTY, the ICTR and the Hybrid Tribunals have provided careful attention to legal standards of superior responsibility and its application to specific cases of private actors.[1627] The tribunals' conclusion was that business officials, as well as military and civilian government officials, can be found liable for human rights violations.[1628] What is clear is that these tribunals have applied multiple points of the test of superior responsibility to limit the application to those officials who had effective control over the subordinates who physically committed the violations.[1629] The indication presented in these cases so far is that corporate superiors can be held liable for human rights violations committed by their subordinates. What this means is that, in a legal context a reputable presumption may exist

Marko Milanović, 'An Odd Couple: Domestic Crimes and International Responsibility in the Special Tribunal for Lebanon' (2007) 5 (5) Journal of International Criminal Justice 1139.

1625 David Akerson and Nandish Wuetilleke, 'Contempt of Court a Digest of The Case Law of Contempt of Court at International Criminal Tribunals and The International Criminal Court' (2016) 44 Denver Journal of International Law and Policy 87.

1626 Matthew Gillett, 'Testing the Limits of The Law against Those Who Test The Tribunal's Limits: Contempt Proceedings at the Special Tribunal for Lebanon' (2017) Journal of International Criminal Justice 27.

1627 Ron H Davidson, 'The International Criminal Tribunal for Rwanda's Decision in The Prosecutor v. Ferdinand Nahimana et al.: The Past, Present, and Future of International Incitement Law' (2004) 17 (3) Leiden Journal of International Law 505.

1628 William A Schabas, 'International Criminal Tribunals: A Review of 2007' (2007) 6 Northwestern Journal of Human Rights 382.

1629 Yael Ronen, 'Superior Responsibility of Civilians for International Crimes Committed in civilian Settings' (2010) 43 Vanderbilt Journal of Transnational Law 313.

that parent corporations or corporate officials could be accountable for the actions of their subsidiaries.[1630]

Adding to these developments, the doctrine of superior responsibility in human rights cases in the US and other national courts runs an equivalent course to the developments in the international tribunals.[1631] This is evidenced in the first cases that focused on military superiority, and then expanded to civilian leaders and corporate officials.[1632] This is due to the fact that the principle of superior responsibility plays a central role in human rights cases in US courts.[1633] Thus, the US Courts' expression of General Yamashita's trial for war crimes in Asia during World War II is a common example for the test of the superior-subordinate relationship as one of 'effective control' and the 'knew or should have known' and 'failed to take action' standards.[1634]

The Yamashita military commission decision was appealed to the US Supreme Court.[1635] While controversial, the Supreme Court's ruling confirmed the important doctrine of superior responsibility that has been repeatedly cited other tribunals in human rights and humanitarian law cases.[1636] Importantly, 'one central point was the use of the 'effective control' test in *Yamashita.*'[1637] This test of superior responsibility still remains the core for the examination of superior and subordinate that international tribunals and national courts rely on to this day.[1638] However, the vast 'majority also focused much of its judgement on the deterrence purpose of holding commanders responsible by affirming that the goal of

---

[1630]Gideon Boas, James L Bischoff and Natalie L Reid, *Forms of Responsibility in International Criminal Law* (Cambridge University Press 2007).

[1631]Naomi Roht-Arriaza, ed. *Impunity and Human Rights in International Law and Practice* (Oxford University Press on Demand 1995).

[1632]John Haberstroh, 'In Re World War II Era Japanese Forced Labor Litigation and Obstacles to International Human Rights Claims in US Courts' (2003) 10 Asian Law Journal 253.

[1633]Michael L Smidt, 'Yamashita, Medina, and Beyond: Command Responsibility in Contemporary Military Operations' (2000) 164 Military Law Review 155.

[1634]Bruce D Landrum, 'The Yamashita War Crimes Trial: Command Responsibility Then and Now' (1995) 149 Military Law Review 293.

[1635]In *re Yamashita* 327 US 1 (1946).

[1636]*Ibid.*

[1637]Charles Fairman, 'The Supreme Court on Military Jurisdiction: Martial Rule in Hawaii and The Yamashita Case' (1946) 59 Harvard Law Review 833.

[1638]Michael L Smidt, 'Yamashita, Medina, and Beyond: Command Responsibility in Contemporary Military Operations' (2000) 164 Military Law Review 155.

protecting the civilian population'[1639] 'would largely be defeated if the commander of an invading army could with impunity neglect to take reasonable measures for their protection.'[1640] This is an illustration that the principle of superior responsibility is a legal doctrine that exists to protect the civil rights of society, as well as preventing impunity where the superior has effective control over the subordinate. What is important in regards to superior responsibility and tort law is that tort liability arises where there is a personal duty owed by the director or officer.[1641] Thus, the traditional doctrine provides that an officer is liable where he or she directs actions, participates or cooperates in an act, or has particular responsibilities.[1642] In the context of duties by officers to third parties, courts have acknowledged that such a duty might arise where there is direct or foreseeable contact with the third party, including where the corporation has delegated this duty to the officer.[1643] What this means is that the omissions and commissions may create tort liability. However, corporate officers are not generally liable merely because of their position in the corporation.[1644]

'Corporate officers can be personally liable to non-stakeholder third parties based on inadequate management or failure to supervise subordinates, including 'failure to stop misconduct they ought to know about.'[1645] 'Cases against directors and officers have been brought for decades for mass torts and products liability.'[1646] Hence, 'for supervision and management torts committed against third parties, the majority of courts

---

[1639] Jennifer M Green, 'Corporate Torts: International Human Rights and Superior Officers' (2016) 17 (2) Chicago Journal of International Law 447.
[1640]In *re Yamashita* 327 at 15.
[1641]Martin Petrin, 'Curious Case of Directors' and Officers' Liability for Supervision and Management: Exploring The Intersection of Corporate and Tort Law' (2009) 59 American University Law Review 1661.
[1642]3A Fletcher Cyc. Corp. § 1137 2016.
[1643]Restatement (Third) of Agency § 7.01 (2006) (individual personally liable for torts, including where acted as agent or under direction of another).
[1644]William E Knepper and Dan A. Bailey, *Liability of Corporate Officers and Directors* (LexisNexis 2004).
[1645]Jennifer M Green, 'Corporate Torts: International Human Rights and Superior Officers' (2016) 17 (2) Chicago Journal of International Law 447 and Martin Petrin, 'Curious Case of Directors' and Officers' Liability for Supervision and Management: Exploring The Intersection of Corporate and Tort Law' (2010) 59 (6) American University Law Review 1661.
[1646]Jennifer M Green, 'Corporate Torts: International Human Rights and Superior Officers' (2016) 17 (2) Chicago Journal of International Law 447 and Robert B Thompson, 'Unpacking Limited Liability: Direct and Vicarious Liability of Corporate Participants for Torts of the Enterprise' (1994) 47 Vanderbilt Law Review 1.

operate under a simple negligence standard.[1647] The Restatement (Second) on Torts (1965).'[1648] section 402(A) 'defines the manufacturer's duty to encompass when he has knowledge, or by the application of reasonable, developed human skill and foresight should have knowledge of possible harm through the use of the product.'[1649] Also, the 'duty to supervise is common in medical liability jurisprudence'.[1650] In 'comparison to the international law concept of 'effective control,' US supervisory responsibility is limited to when an individual is legally obliged to exercise control over a subordinate.'[1651]

'Theories of responsibility include a focus on a superior officer's participation in a tort where there was a breach of duty or on a court'[1652] exercising its discretion power to pierce the corporate veil.[1653] This research further contends that corporate superior liability is divided into groups, including cases in which a superior officer has 'constructive knowledge of a tort'[1654] or 'reasonably should have known that some hazardous condition or activity under their control could injure [a third party, but] they negligently failed to take or order appropriate action to avoid the harm.'[1655] A duty can be delegated by a corporation to a director or officer and then breached by officer conduct which causes injury to a third party; this liability can result from omissions such as failure to stop conduct that the officer ought to know about.[1656] Such duties to third parties, or 'external' duties, are derived from a principle I call 'moral hazard'. According to this

---

[1647]Richard A Posner, 'A Theory of Negligence' (1972) 1 (1) Journal of Legal Studies 29.

[1648]Jennifer M Green, 'Corporate Torts: International Human Rights and Superior Officers' (2016) 17 (2) Chicago Journal of International Law 447 and XXII. Restatement (Second) of Torts § 402A.

[1649]*Ibid.*

[1650]Jennifer M Green, 'Corporate Torts: International Human Rights and Superior Officers' (2016) 17 (2) Chicago Journal of International Law 447 and Dan B Dobbs, Robert E Keeton, Page W Keeton and David G Owen, *Prosser and Keeton on The Law of Torts* (West Publishing Company 1984).

[1651]Jennifer M Green, 'Corporate Torts: International Human Rights and Superior Officers' (2016) 17 (2) Chicago Journal of International Law 447.

[1652]*Ibid.*

[1653]Robert B Thompson, 'Piercing the Corporate Veil: An Empirical Study' (1990) 76 Cornell Law Review 1036.

[1654]John A Turcotte, 'When You Should Have Known: Rethinking Constructive Knowledge in Tort Liability for Sexual Transmission of HIV' (2000) 52 Maine Law Review 261.

[1655]*Frances T v Vill. Green Owners Ass'n,* 723 P.2d 573, 584 (Cal. 1986).

[1656]William E Knepper and Dan A. Bailey (n 1612).

principle, a consideration of the risk of personal liability may deter corporate misconduct in business practice.[1657]

Also, 'common law' application 'of negligent supervision' 'varies across state jurisdictions.[1658] Courts have differences in their focuses on input in the tortious conduct, breach of personal duty, or whether they treat supervision claims as separate from other tort liability.'[1659] In addition, the tort of negligent supervision is most used where there is a pattern and the officer 'had the opportunity to discover the wrongful acts'[1660] or where they are 'negligent in failing to learn of and prevent torts by employees.'[1661] Similarly, courts have held that officers were potentially liable for lack of reasonable diligence in the control and supervision of a business which resulted in a death caused by a warehouse explosion,[1662] or a death resulting from failure to properly train a machine operator, or company officers who decreased security measures to increase profits could be personally liable to a customer shot at a shopping mall.[1663]

Therefore, it can be assumed that corporate officers have a common law duty not to injure third parties.[1664] '[A] director could inflict injuries upon others and then escape liability behind the shield of his or her representative character, even though the corporation might be insolvent or irresponsible.'[1665] In *Bano v Union Carbide*, the United States Court of Appeals for the Second 'Circuit stated, under New York law a corporate officer who commits or participates in a tort, even if it is in the course of his

---

[1657]Kenneth J Arrow, 'Essays in the Theory of Risk-Bearing' (1970) No. 04; HB615, A7.

[1658]James D Barnett, 'The Foundations of The Distinction between Public and Private Functions in Respect to The Common-Law Tort Liability of Municipal Corporations' (1937) 16 Oregon Law Review 250.

[1659]Jennifer M Green, 'Corporate Torts: International Human Rights and Superior Officers' (2016) 17 Chicago Journal of International Law 447 and Martin Petrin (n 1613).

[1660]*Lowell Hoit & Co. v Detig*, 50 N.E.2d 602, 603 (Ill. App. Ct. 1943) and *Air Traffic Conference of Am. v Marina Travel, Inc.*, 316 S.E.2d 642, 645 (N.C. Ct. App. 1984).

[1661]*Avery v Solargizer Int'l, Inc.* 427 N.W.2d 675, 681 (Minn. Ct. App. 1988) and *Preston-Thomas Const., Inc. v Cent. Leasing Corp.* 518 P.2d 1125, 1127 (Okla. Ct. App. 1973).

[1662]*Cameron v Kenyon-Connel Commercial* Co., 56 P. 358, 361 (Mont. 1899)*; see Moak v Link- Belt* Co., 242 So. 2d 515 (La. 1970) (no negligence so no liability).

[1663]*Haire v Bonelli,* 870 N.Y.S.2d 591, 593 (N.Y. App. Div. 3d Dept. 2008).

[1664]*Frances T.,* 723 P.2d at 581–82.

[1665]*Ibid.*

duties on behalf of the corporation may be held individually liable.'[1666] What is clear from all these cases is that the general standards of tort liability for corporate superior officers under US law, which include negligence, would, in fact, allow a greater range of tort claims than the criminal international law standards.[1667]

The Responsible Corporate Officer (RCO) Principle

'The Responsible Corporate Officer (RCO)'[1668] 'principle provides accountability for an officer as well as a corporation if the officer participates in wrongful conduct or knowingly approves that conduct.'[1669] Hence, 'if there are joint participants then each can be held accountable. RCO liability involves the following elements[1670]: (1) the officer's position must allow influence on corporate policies or activities, (2) there must be a nexus between the officer and the violation, and (3) the defendant's actions or inactions facilitated the violations. [1671] The RCO was originally developed for 'public welfare' statutes, and now includes statutes such as the Clean Air Act, [1672] the Clean Water Act, [1673] the Comprehensive Environmental Response, Compensation and Liability Act (CERCLA),[1674] the Resource Conservation and Recovery Act, the Food, Drug and Cosmetic

1666Jennifer M Green, 'Corporate Torts: International Human Rights and Superior Officers' (2016) 17 (2) Chicago Journal of International Law 447 and *Lopresti v Terwilliger*, 126 F.3d 34, 42 (2d Cir. 1997).

1667Stuart M Speiser, Charles F Krause and Alfred W Gans, *The American Law of Torts* (Vol. 1. Lawyers Co-Operative Pub. Co 2003).

1668Jennifer M Green, 'Corporate Torts: International Human Rights and Superior Officers' (2016) 17 (2) Chicago Journal of International Law 447.

1669Jennifer M Green, 'Corporate Torts: International Human Rights and Superior Officers' (2016) 17 (2) Chicago Journal of International Law 447 and also see; 3A Fletcher Cyc. Corp. § 1135.

1670*Ibid.*

1671Tom McMahon and Katie Moertl, 'The Erosion of Traditional Corporate Law Doctrines in Environmental Cases' (1988) 3 (3) Natural Resources & Environment 29, Lynda J Oswald and Cindy A Schipani, 'CERCLA and The Erosion of Traditional Corporate Law Doctrine' (1991) 86 Northwestern University Law Review 259 and Marco Quazzo, 'Officers and Directors Face Personal Liability under The Responsible Corporate Officer Doctrine' (2013) 11 Corporation Accountability Report (BNA) 841.

1672Clean Air Act 1993.

1673Clean Water Act 33 USC. §1251 et seq. (1972). The Clean Water Act (CWA).

1674 Comprehensive Environmental Response, Compensation, and Liability Act (Superfund) 42 USC. §9601 et seq. (1980).

Act,[1675] and the Sherman Anti-Trust Act.[1676] Among all these acts, the common understanding is that these are public welfare statutes' enacted to prevent harm to the general public.[1677] In examining the concept of maximising deterrence, these statutes have turned to individual corporate officer liability.[1678] The evaluation of both the types of actions and the shared goal of deterrence points to these statutes as an important element of comparison with human rights cases.[1679]

RCO principle is not new. It was developed in the 1920s based on English cases from the nineteenth century.[1680] In *United States v Dotterweich*,[1681] the president of a pharmaceutical company was criminally convicted for shipping misbranded and adulterated drugs in interstate commerce.[1682] The court held that all those who had a 'responsible share' in the conduct could be held liable for corporate violations of the law.[1683] The essential elements required by the court to establish liability is 'foresight' and 'vigilance' that 'individuals who executed the corporate mission' would implement measures to prevent violations.[1684] Justice Frankfurter's opinion quantified that the Food, Drug and Cosmetic Act dispenses with the conventional requirement for criminal conduct awareness of some wrongdoing. Therefore, in the interest of the larger good, it puts the burden of the act creating the 'hazard upon a person otherwise innocent but standing in responsible relation to a public danger.'[1685]

In *United States v Park*,[1686] a chief executive officer was held liable for a national grocery chain's food storage conditions that violated federal

---

[1675]Resource Conservation and Recovery Act of 1976, Pub. L. 94-580, 90 Stat. 2795 (Codified as Amended in Scattered sections of 42 USC.).

[1676]Sherman Anti-Trust Act, 15 USC §§ 1–7 (2011).

[1677]Noel Wise, 'Personal Liability Promotes Responsible Conduct: Extending the Responsible Corporate Officer Doctrine to Federal Civil Environmental Enforcement Cases' (2002) 21 Stanford Environmental Law Journal 283.

[1678]*Ibid.*

[1679]*Celentano v Rocque*, 923 A.2d 709, 282 Conn. 645 (2007).

[1680]Noel Wise (n 1933).

[1681]*US v Dotterweich,* 320 US 277 283–84 (1943.
This Court so held in *United States v Morgan,* 222 US 274, 32 S. Ct. 81, 56 L. Ed. 198.

[1682]*Ibid.*

[1683]*Ibid.*

[1684]*US v Park*, 421 US 658, 672 (1975).

[1685]Jennifer M Green, 'Corporate Torts: International Human Rights and Superior Officers' (2016) 17 (2) Chicago Journal of International Law 447 and *Dotterweich,* 320 US at 281 (citing *United States v Balint,* 258 US 250, 252 (1922)).

[1686]*Park,* 421 US at 658.

law. The court held that 'individuals who execute the corporate mission' have a 'positive duty to seek out and remedy violations of [the Federal Food, Drug and Cosmetic Act] when they occur' and 'a duty to implement measures that will insure that violations will not occur.'[1687] The view of the court established that the public has a 'right to expect [foresight and vigilance] of those who voluntarily assume positions of authority in business enterprises whose services and products affect the health and well-being of the public that supports them.'[1688]

The court's approach can be connected to what has been labelled as a 'resurgence' of the RCO doctrine. In 2007, 'the Department of Justice brought charges against three officers for the misbranding and fraudulent marketing of OxyContin.'[1689] The executives pled guilty to misdemeanours and agreed to pay US$634,525,475 in fines.[1690] 'Additionally, the Office of the Inspector General (OIG) debarred the three executives from participation in federal healthcare programs for 12 years.'[1691] The exclusion was upheld by the US Court of Appeals for the District of Columbia.[1692] Furthermore, in 2009, a case against four executives of a medical devices manufacturer resulted in prison terms and $100,000 in fines.[1693]

The RCO principle was first applied in a civil case in 1985, in *United States v Hodges X-Ray*,[1694] where the defendants attempted to distinguish prior decisions on criminal liability, but the court rejected those

---

[1687]*Ibid* at 672.
[1688]*Ibid.*
[1689]Jennifer M Green, 'Corporate Torts: International Human Rights and Superior Officers' (2016) 17 Chi. *J. Int'l L.* 447. <https://cjil.uchicago.edu/publication/corporate-torts-international-human-rights-and-superior-officers> Accessed 30 May 2017. Also see, Thomas J Mortell and Michelle Gustavson, 'The Resurgence of The Corporate Officer Doctrine' (2012) 32 (55) Advocate (Citing *United States v Purdue Frederick Co*., Inc., 495 F. Supp. 2d 569, 573 (W.D. Va. 2007)). <http://www.hawleytroxell.com/2012/06/the-resurgence-of-the-responsible-corporate-officer-doctrine/> Accessed 14 September 2017.
[1690]Barry Meier, 'In Guilty Plea, OxyContin Maker to Pay $600 Million' (May 10, 2007) *New York Times*. <http://www.nytimes.com/2007/05/10/business/11drug-web.html> Accessed 14 September 2017.
[1691]Thomas J Mortell and Michelle Gustavson (n 1696) and <https://cjildev.uchicago.edu/publication/corporate-torts-international-human-rights-and-superior-officers > Accessed 15 May 2017.
[1692]*Friedman v Sebelius,* 686 F.3d 813 (D.C. Cir. 2012).
[1693]*United States v Norian Corp.,* No. 09-cr-403-LDD (E.D. Pa. 2009), Sentencing Nov. 21, 2011.
[1694]*United States v Hodges X-Ray*, Inc., 759 F.2d 557, 561 (6th Cir. 1985).

arguments, saying that 'the rationale for holding corporate officers criminally responsible for acts of the corporation, which could lead to incarceration, is even more persuasive where only civil liability is involved.'[1695] Also, in the 1990s, RCO was used for civil penalties in cases on a wide range of environmental statutes, including CERCLA, the Clean Air Act, and the Federal Hazardous Substances Act.[1696] The RCO doctrine has been labelled as a strict liability standard.[1697] This is because 'the primary unique feature of the responsible corporate officer doctrine is that it does not matter that such officer did not participate in or have knowledge of the alleged violation.'[1698]

Analysing 'RCO, one of the significant bases of the doctrine is that personal liability promotes responsible conduct.'[1699] Nonetheless, 'arguments against applying the RCO strict liability standards include that holding a superior responsible for genocide, war crimes, crimes against humanity, torture, or other serious human rights violations leads to more severe punishment'[1700] 'than RCO cases'.[1701] However, this study argues in favour of applying such a standard to human rights violations in a form of a strict liability standard, because it will demonstrate a zero-tolerance policy. Likewise, human rights violations should be treated as violations of the same level of severity as the conduct regulated by US public welfare

---

[1695] *Ibid.*

[1696] Noel Wise (n 1933).

[1697] Timothy Wu and Yong-Sung Kang, 'Criminal liability for The Actions of Subordinates-The Doctrine of Command Responsibility and Its Analogues in United States Law' (1997) 38 Harvard International Law Journal 272.

[1698] Kai Peters, *The Corporate Responsibility Doctrine: Handling Matters When Corporate Executives Are Involved in Criminal or Civil Matters*, in Protecting Corporation Against Management Liability Claims: Leading Lawyers on Analysing Development in Employment Regulation, Investigating and Responding to Allegation, and Creating Effective Compliance Strategies (2013). <https://www.gordonrees.com/Templates/media/files/pdf/The%20Corporate%20Responsibility%20Doctrine.pdf> Accessed 15 September 2017, *See Dotterweich,* 320 US at 284; Park, 421 US at 670–72.

[1699] Jennifer M Green, 'Corporate Torts: International Human Rights and Superior Officers' (2016) 17 (2) Chicago Journal of International Law 447 and Noel Wise (n 1933).

[1700] Jennifer M Green, 'Corporate Torts: International Human Rights and Superior Officers' (2016) 17 (2) Chicago Journal of International Law 447.

[1701] *Ibid.* And see: Timothy Wu and Yong-Sung Kang (n 1848).

statutes,[1702] which follow the principle of the duty not to harm thy neighbour.

There is also an argument that the criticism of unfair responsibilities is less applicable in the corporate context than it is for those in government service.[1703] Thus, where a corporate officer has power and responsibility and when the end objectives are the creation of profits, the situation is arguably different from the assumption of power in a military position or to serve a civilian government.[1704] Another central discrepancy is the difference between the consequences of a criminal conviction and a tort verdict against a corporate superior officer.[1705] In addition, liability is limited by what is feasible, notably by the 'objective impossibility defence'. A defendant may claim that he or she was 'powerless to prevent or correct a violation.'[1706] 'The defendant's duty does not require that which is objectively impossible'[1707], though it does need the highest standard of foresight and vigilance.[1708] 'The standards in US tort law for superior officer liability align with the standards under international law.'[1709] 'One of the essential comparable doctrines, RCO and the duty of care may, in fact, have a higher standard of liability than has been imposed by any of the international tribunals to date.'[1710] Therefore, it could serve as a model for corporate human rights accountability for subsidiary misconduct, in conjunction with the tort of negligence.

RCO from Other National Jurisdictions

The development of the doctrine of superior responsibility is not limited to US law. Legal systems around the world have recognised superior responsibility liability and a duty of care for corporate officers although,

---

[1702]Jennifer M Green, 'Corporate Torts: International Human Rights and Superior Officers' (2016) 17 (2) Chicago Journal of International Law 447.

[1703]*Ibid.*

[1704]*Ibid.* also see O'Brien Methven Claire and Sumithra Dhanarajan, 'The Corporate Responsibility to Respect Human Rights: A Status Review' (2016) 29 (4) Accounting, Auditing & Accountability Journal 542.

[1705]*Ibid.*

[1706]Jennifer M Green (n 1991).

[1707]Jennifer M Green, 'Corporate Torts: International Human Rights and Superior Officers' (2016) 17 (2) Chicago Journal of International Law 447.

[1708]*Ibid.*

[1709]Sean D Murphy, 'Contemporary Practice of the United States Relating to International law' (2001) 95 (2) American Journal of International Law 387.

[1710]Jennifer M Green, 'Corporate Torts: International Human Rights and Superior Officers' (2016) 17 (2) Chicago Journal of International Law 447.

similar to the US, these legal provisions have rarely been applied to human rights allegations against corporate officers. The developments in the international criminal tribunals are an important starting point in the assessment of national legal systems for RCO. This was highlighted in the International Committee of the Red Cross (ICRC) report, which is considered as one of the authoritative interpretive agencies of humanitarian law.[1711] The ICRC considered the legal systems around the world as they addressed violations in the context of armed conflicts.[1712] This report made it 'clear that superior responsibility is applicable to both civilian and military leaders who fail to take necessary and reasonable measures in their power' to prevent or punish subordinates.'[1713] Therefore, 'there is no requirement that the source of authority be military or governmental.'[1714]

However, 'tort law' systems differ, 'reflecting the different ideas, attitudes, trust, and beliefs that people in society hold with regard to litigation, institutions and social relationships in general'.[1715] 'Fletcher establishes that all western industrialised systems break down tort systems into intentional torts, negligence, and strict liability.'[1716] It is possible, therefore, that the 'traditional view' of duty-creating provisions for corporate officers 'inflicts liability on directors and senior officers if the corporation acted wrongfully and/or inflicted harm on their watch.'[1717] Thus, all jurisdictions include remedial mechanisms for violations of 'life,

---

[1711]Leah M Nicholls, 'The Humanitarian Monarchy Legislates: The International Committee of the Red Cross and Its 161 Rules of Customary International Humanitarian Law' (2006) 17 Duke Journal of Comparative & International Law 223.

[1712]Customary Law, 'The Red Cross 211' (2005) 87 International Law Review.

[1713]Jennifer M Green, 'Corporate Torts: International Human Rights and Superior Officers' (2016) 17 (2) Chicago Journal of International Law 447.

[1714]*Ibid.*

[1715]Jennifer M Green, 'Corporate Torts: International Human Rights and Superior Officers' (2016) 17 (2) Chicago Journal of International Law 447 and Mauro Bussani and Marta Infantino, 'Tort Law and Legal Cultures' (2015) 63 (4) American Journal of Comparative Law 77.

[1716]Jennifer M Green, 'Corporate Torts: International Human Rights and Superior Officers' (2016) 17 (2) Chicago Journal of International Law 447 and George P Fletcher, *Tort liability for Human Rights Abuses* (Bloomsbury Publishing 2008).

[1717]Harry Glasbeek, 'Looking for Responsibility in The Corporate World or The Corporation's Multiple Personality Disorder' in *Directors' Personal Liability for Corporate Fault–a Comparative Analysis. Austin/Boston/Chicago/New York/The Netherlands: Wolters Kluwer* (2008) 1, 43.

liberty, dignity, and physical and mental integrity.'[1718] All legal systems include some form of undisputable tort law (or delicts), therefore, none excuse corporate conduct as a category from superior liability.[1719] Similarly, in some countries around the world, corporate officers can be criminally prosecuted and victims are provided compensation for wrongs by corporate officers.[1720] These legal actions also permit the tendering of evidence of customary international law. Besides, in some jurisdictions, it is less common to impose liability on a corporate officer, instead of holding the entity itself liable.[1721]

The 'means of incorporation vary but there remains a core of commonality across jurisdictions.'[1722] Common types of 'implementation are direct provisions in law. For instance, Belgian law allows tort remedies for Belgian residents.'[1723] Also, 'some states incorporate international law through constitutional torts.'[1724] Additionally, in many 'European countries, bringing human rights principles into private law is described as the indirect third party effect.[1725] 'Public laws have indirect persuasive authority, create the general framework, and are intended to be enforceable by private

---

[1718] International Commission of Jurists, Report of the Expert Legal Panel on Corporate Complicity in International Crimes: Volume 3 (Civil Remedies) 4 (2008). <https://perma.cc/Q94M-FPZY> [hereinafter ICJ Report] Accessed 15 September 2017.

[1719] Jennifer Zerk, 'Corporate Liability for Gross Human Rights Abuses: Towards a Fairer and More Effective System of Domestic Law Remedies' (2013) Report Prepared for the Office of the UN High Commissioner for Human Rights 29.

[1720] Ronald C Slye, Corporations Veils and International Criminal Liability' (2008) 33 Brooklyn Journal of International Law 955.

[1721] William S Laufer, '*Corporate Bodies and Guilty Minds: The Failure of Corporate Criminal Liability* (University of Chicago Press 2008).

[1722] Jennifer M Green (n 1991).

[1723] Jennifer M Green, 'Corporate Torts: International Human Rights and Superior Officers' (2016) 17 (2) Chicago Journal of International Law 447 and International Commission of Red Cross, 'Customary International Humanitarian Law, *Belgium*: *Practice Relating to Rule 157: Jurisdiction over War Crimes*. <https://perma.cc/6UYY-5LMR> Accessed 15 September 2017.

[1724] Jennifer M Green, 'Corporate Torts: International Human Rights and Superior Officers' (2016) 17 (2) Chicago Journal of International Law 447 and Sathya Narayan, 'Christian von Bar, The Common European Law of Torts, Volume 1, Oxford University Press, Oxford/New York, 1983' (2000) 5 (2) Uniform Law Review-Revue de Droit Uniforme 396, 399.

[1725] Jennifer M Green, 'Corporate Torts: International Human Rights and Superior Officers' (2016) 17 (2) Chicago Journal of International Law 447 and Benedetto Conforti and Francesco Francioni, eds. *Enforcing International Human Rights in Domestic Courts*. (Vol. 49. Martinus Nijhoff Publishers 1970).

persons against other private persons.'[1726] 'Another common model of superior responsibility is for the law of tort and non-contractual responsibilities to be the primary bases for civil claims.'[1727] In addition, 'another model for liability'[1728] for superior responsibility is the compensation and other remedies for victims which are linked to criminal codes, such as in Spain,[1729] France,[1730] 'and the People's Republic of China.'[1731]

'A recent study of RCO found that [i]n the majority of jurisdictions, despite differences in terminology, for the purposes of civil liability an actor will often be considered to have acted intentionally if it voluntarily undertook a course of conduct knowing that it was more than likely to result in harm.'[1732] The 'common elements leading to liability are that a defendant knew or had reason to know about risk'[1733] 'and that the defendant failed to prevent the harm from occurring.[1734] This includes omissions, remaining silent, or failure to take precautionary measures.[1735] Similar to the US, 'other common law countries have RCO principles.'[1736]As indicated in the previous sections, the initial RCO cases in the US followed

---

[1726]Jennifer M Green, 'Corporate Torts: International Human Rights and Superior Officers' (2016) 17 (2) Chicago Journal of International Law 447 and Mauro Bussaniand and Anthony J. Sebok, eds. *Comparative Tort Law: Global Perspectives* (Edward Elgar Publishing 2015).

[1727]Jennifer M Green, 'Corporate Torts: International Human Rights and Superior Officers' (2016) 17 (2) Chicago Journal of International Law 447 and Andrew Dickinson, *The Rome II Regulation: The Law Applicable to Non-Contractual Obligations* (Vol. 1. Oxford University Press on Demand 2010).

[1728]*Ibid.*

[1729] Stephen Schafer, 'Victim Compensation and Responsibility' (1970) 43(1) Southern California Law Review 55.

[1730]Code de Procedure Penale [C. PR. PÉN.], art. 2 (French victim of an international tort can obtain remedy in France).

[1731]Zhonghua Renmin Gongheguo Xingfa [Criminal Law of the People's Republic of China] (promulgated by Order No. 83 of the President of the People's Republic of China, Mar. 14, 1997, effective Oct. 1, 1997), art. 36, P.R.C. LAWS. <https://perma.cc/ZT5U-2QLY> Accessed 15 September 2017.

[1732]Jennifer M Green, 'Corporate Torts: International Human Rights and Superior Officers' (2016) 17 Chicago Journal of International Law 447 and René David, ed. *International Encyclopaedia of Comparative Law* (Vol. 2 Brill Archive 1986).

[1733]*Ibid.*

[1734]*Ibid.*

[1735]Jennifer M Green, 'Corporate Torts: International Human Rights and Superior Officers' (2016) 17 Chicago Journal of International Law 447 and Jennifer A Zerk, *Multinationals and Corporate Social Responsibility: Limitations and Opportunities in International Law* (Vol. 48. Cambridge University Press 2006).

[1736]*Ibid.*

English law. Thus, under the laws of 'England, it is well-established that a person may be liable for authorising or inducing a tort committed by another.'[1737] 'In 1846, in *The Queen v Woodrow*, a tobacco dealer was charged with possession of adulterated tobacco.'[1738] 'The court determined that with regard to 'any matter that affected public health, persons could be required to act prudently in order to guard against injury to the public.'[1739] 'Australia applies RCO liability to environmental and health and safety legislation.'[1740]

The UK 'also has civil nationality jurisdiction for genocide, crimes against humanity, torture, war crimes, residence of offender and territorial jurisdiction.'[1741] In '*Chandler v Cape PLC*'[1742] 'and *Guerrero v Monterrico Metals PLC*',[1743] 'the English high court ruled that a parent company's Chief Executive Officer was in frequent contact with a local mine manager, so the parent company had the duty to take reasonable care to avoid foreseeable harm to the protestors.'[1744] 'In English law, for offences requiring criminal intent, corporate liability attributes through the identification principle, which requires that the natural person committing the offence is a director or otherwise entrusted with powers of company.'[1745]

[1737]*Ibid.*

[1738]Jennifer M Green, 'Corporate Torts: International Human Rights and Superior Officers' (2016) 17 (2) Chicago Journal of International Law 447.

[1739]*Ibid. Queen v Woodrow*, (1846) 153 Eng. Rep. 907, 912.

[1740]Jennifer M Green, 'Corporate Torts: International Human Rights and Superior Officers' (2016) 17 (2) Chicago Journal of International Law 447 and Karen Wheelwright, 'Corporate Liability for Workplace Deaths and Injuries-Reflecting on Victoria's Laws in The Light of The Esso Longford Explosion' (2002) 7 Deakin Law Review 323, also see Occupational Health and Safety Act 2004 (Vic) § 144. <https://perma.cc/7LCM-559R> Accessed 15 September 2017.

[1741]Jennifer M Green, 'Corporate Torts: International Human Rights and Superior Officers' (2016) 17 (2) Chicago Journal of International Law 447 and Michael P Scharf, 'Application of Treaty-Based Universal Jurisdiction on Nationals of Non-Party States.' (2001) 35 New England Law Review 363.

[1742]Jennifer M Green, 'Corporate Torts: International Human Rights and Superior Officers' (2016) 17 (2) Chicago Journal of International Law 447 and *Chandler v Cape plc* [2012] EWCA Civ 525.

[1743]*Ibid. Guerrero & Ors v Monterrico Metals Plc & Anor* (Rev 1) [2009] EWHC 2475 (QB) (16 October 2009).

[1744]*Ibid.*

[1745]Jennifer M Green, 'Corporate Torts: International Human Rights and Superior Officers' (2016) 17 (2) Chicago Journal of International Law 447 and Andrew Ashworth and Jeremy Horder, *Principles of Criminal Law* (Oxford University Press 2013).

'Some countries have stepped into the void of confronting violations committed during their own past.'[1746] For example, 'in Argentina, business executives were sued for their responsibility for abduction, detention, and murder during the country's 'Dirty War' against dissidents between 1976 and 1983.'[1747] 'In Argentina's Civil Code, Articles 43 and 1113 together provide for liability of persons for damage caused by their dependents.'[1748] 'Dependents have been interpreted to include a company's employees, agents, and other representatives who act under the instructions or direction of the company.'[1749] Therefore, 'the corporate veil is not a defence when corporate shares are used to breach the law, public order, good faith, or the rights of third parties. In a case in Colombia against the Urapalma palm oil company, Colombian corporate officers were ordered to pay compensation to each victim of dislocation caused by their actions.'[1750]

Other important examples of corporate superior responsibility can be noted in German law, which provides criminal and civil jurisdiction for individual officers and executives.[1751] This is evidenced in recent cases, such as when the manager of a Danzer Group subsidiary was alleged to have used security forces in the Congo when he should have foreseen violence due to his role as a member of the governing board of the subsidiary and head of the African Management Team for the Danzer Group.[1752] Under German law, senior managers may have criminal responsibility arising from a duty of care toward those affected by the actions of their employees.[1753]

[1746]*Ibid.*

[1747]Jennifer M Green, 'Corporate Torts: International Human Rights and Superior Officers' (2016) 17 (2) Chicago Journal of International Law 447 and Leigh A Payne and Gabriel Pereira, 'Corporate Complicity in International Human Rights Violations' (2016) 12 Annual Review of Law and Social Science 63.

[1748]Jennifer M Green, 'Corporate Torts: International Human Rights and Superior Officers' (2016) 17 (2) Chicago Journal of International Law 447.

[1749]*Ibid.* Cod. Rev. art. 43, 1113 (Arg.).

[1750]Jennifer M Green, 'Corporate Torts: International Human Rights and Superior Officers' (2016) 17 (2) Chicago Journal of International Law 447 and Leigh A Payne and Gabriel Pereira (n 2032).

[1751]Jennifer M Green, 'Corporate Torts: International Human Rights and Superior Officers' (2016) 17 (2) Chicago Journal of International Law 447 and Burgerliches Gesetzbuch [BGB] [Civil Code] Jan. 2, 2002, § 831, 1, *Translation.* <https://perma.cc/P24U-FSY8> Accessed 15 September 2017.

[1752]No Investigations Against Danzer Manager Over Human Rights Abuses Against Community in DRC, 'European Centre for Constitutional and human Rights'. <https://perma.cc/P33M-X97N> Accessed 20 September 2017.

[1753]German Jurisprudence Provides for The Liability of Leading Employees of a Company (*Geschaftsherrenhaftung*) and Gerhard Dannecker and Christoph Dannecker,

In the *Danzer* case, the European Centre for Constitutional and Human Rights eventually filed a criminal complaint with the public prosecutor's office that charged the Danzer Group senior manager with failure to issue clear directions. The complaint charged that the manager should have directed employees of the Siforco Company subsidiary that security forces must not be called in to deal with conflicts with the local population. The complaint specified that the call for security forces must be suspended until the results of any ongoing negotiations are clear; furthermore, the prerequisite to the use of security forces is that those forces must agree that no human rights violations will be committed. The complaint further charged that security forces must only receive payments if they commit no human rights violations.[1754]

Also, 'Japanese law can provide individual liability for gross human rights violations.'[1755] 'Article 709 of the Japanese Civil Code establishes tort liability and Article 715 provides for superior liability for a person who supervises the business or 'employs others'.'[1756] Zerk observed 'in 2014 that while no international law violations had been brought as torts, these violations could satisfy the Civil Code's requirement of 'illegality'[1757]

'The 'Distribution' of The Company's Criminal Liability in Business: The Criminal Responsibility of The Compliance Officer and (manager) Employee in The Take-Over of Company-Related Tasks, at The Same Time Review by BGH, Judgment of 17.7.2009-5 StR 394/08' (2010) Jurist Newspaper 981, 992.

[1754] Peter Muchlinski and Virginie Rouas, *Foreign Direct Liability Litigation: Toward the Transnationalisation of Corporate Legal Liability* (American Bar Association 2014), Newsletter: Criminal Complaint against Senior Manager of Danzer: Accountability for Human Rights Violations in the Democratic Republic of Congo, European Centre for Constitutional and Human Rights (Apr. 25, 2013). <https://perma.cc/26CW-57UV> Accessed 16 September 2017.

[1755] Jennifer M Green, 'Corporate Torts: International Human Rights and Superior Officers' (2016) 17 (2) Chicago Journal of International Law 447 and Mauro Bussani and Anthony J Sebok, eds. *Comparative Tort Law: Global Perspectives* (Edward Elgar Publishing 2015).

[1756] MINPÕ [MINPÕ] [CIV. C.] arts. 709 (tort liability), and 715 (superior liability). [Companies Act], Companies Act, Part II, Chapter 4, Section 11 (Liability for Damages of Officer to Third Parties) and Jennifer M Green, 'Corporate Torts: International Human Rights and Superior Officers' (2016) 17 (2) Chicago Journal of International Law 447.

[1757] Jennifer M Green, 'Corporate Torts: International Human Rights and Superior Officers' (2016) 17 (2) Chicago Journal of International Law 447 and Jennifer Zerk, 'Corporate Liability for Gross Human Rights Abuses: Towards a Fairer and More Effective System of Domestic Law Remedies' (2013) Report Prepared for The Office of the UN High Commissioner for Human Rights 29.

or 'infringement of rights.'[1758] 'The Japanese Companies Act, Part III, Section 11 on Liability for Damages of Officers to Third Parties, provides that officers with knowledge or grossly negligent in performing their duties may be liable to a third party for resulting damages.'[1759]

In a Korean case against Shinhan Bank directors, the court established that a chief executive officer has a duty to monitor[1760] the actions of subordinates.[1761] Hence, in order for corporate directors to be responsible to third parties as provided in Article 401(1) of the Commercial Code, they must have neglected to perform their duties wilfully or by gross negligence. 'If directors have neglected to perform their 'duty to monitor' wilfully or by gross negligence, they can be found liable for the damages incurred by a third party.'[1762] Additionally, the Indonesian Civil Code is similar, providing that a person is not only responsible for the damages caused by his own deed, but also for damages 'caused by the acts of the individuals for whom he is responsible, or caused by matters which are under his supervision.'[1763]

In the Netherlands, a corporate director is liable if he 'made a sufficiently serious mistake.'[1764] For instance, an attempt made to hold corporate officers accountable was in a case against the Trafigura company, which was domiciled in the Netherlands and sued for the dumping of toxic waste off the Ivory Coast that resulted in an estimated 12 deaths, with thousands of others made ill. Civil and criminal litigation was brought in the Ivory Coast,[1765] the Netherlands and the UK.[1766] In 2012, the Amsterdam Court of Appeal ruled that Claude Dauphin, founder and

---

[1758]*Ibid.*

[1759]Jennifer M Green, 'Corporate Torts: International Human Rights and Superior Officers' (2016) 17 (2) Chicago Journal of International Law 447 and Kaisha–Hō [Companies Act], Act No. 86 of 2005, Part III § 11.

[1760]Supreme Court [S. Ct.], 2006Da68636, Sept. 11, 2008. <https://perma.cc/RC9M-EF7X (S. Kor> Accessed 17 September 2017.

[1761]*Shinhan Bank Corporation v Kim Woo-Jjoong and Ten Others*, 2006 Da 6838, (S. Kor.).

[1762]*Ibid.*

[1763]Indonesian Civil Code, art. 1367.

[1764]Bastian F Assink, *Secondary Director Liability, the Defining Tension* (2009). <https://perma.cc/E9JU-8PFF> Accessed 17 September 2017.

[1765]Liesbeth Enneking, 'The Common Denominator of The Trafigura Case, Foreign Direct Liability Cases and The Rome II Regulation' (2008) 16 European Review of Private Law 283.

[1766]Nicola MCP Jagers and Marie-José van der Heijden, 'Corporate Human Rights Violations: The Feasibility of Civil Recourse in the Netherlands' (2008) 33 (3) Brooklyn Journal of International Law 833.

director of the Dutch company Trafigura, could be prosecuted.[1767] In November 2012, the company publicly denied culpability but paid £1.3 million in an out of court settlement in exchange for withdrawal of the charges against Dauphin.[1768]

In 'the past several decades, a broad range of defendants have faced civil claims in human rights cases. Those defendants have included those who were complicit in but did not physically commit acts such as torture, war crimes, and genocide.'[1769] Other types of 'indirect' involvement include those who knew or had reason to know about the abuse but failed to take action to prevent or punish the violations. The illustrations here from different national jurisdictions have underlying agreement in principle that there is a potential for greater use of superior corporate officer liability for human rights violations. Lastly, the purpose of corporate superior responsibility is to produce the elements recognised in the multiple sources of law detailed in this section so far and to determine that there is a consensus on the liability of superior corporate officers in international law and in US, UK, German and France domestic law as well as other national jurisdictions. Although there may be some differences in the *mens rea* element with regard to selected documents, the central question about enforcement of this standard is whether there is agreement on the duty of superior officers. Sources of law across international and national systems include duties for corporate superior officers to prevent and punish violations. Guidance from tort law further highlights the possibility of holding superior corporate officers liable. This standard is particularly relevant to human rights claims and serves an important function of providing remedies to human rights victims, punishing violators, and building a legal system that deters future violations.

International tribunals have commented on the efficacy of command responsibility on many occasions. For example, the International Military Tribunal at Nuremberg stated that 'command responsibility is the most effective method by which international criminal law can enforce responsible

---

[1767] *Trafigura Reaches Toxic Waste Settlement with Dutch,* REUTERS (Nov. 16, 2012). <https://perma.cc/QRE8-NG7J> Accessed 19 September 2017.

[1768] *Ibid.*

[1769] Jennifer M Green, 'Corporate Torts: International Human Rights and Superior Officers' (2016) 17 (2) Chicago Journal of International Law 447 and Michael P Healy, 'Direct Liability for Hazardous Substance Clean-ups Under CERCLA: A Comprehensive Approach' (1992) 42 (1) Case Western Reserve Law Review 65.

command.'[1770] In certain contexts, this applies to tort standards as well.[1771] The international tribunals have also focused on due process considerations, and defence attorneys and some commentators have also addressed whether superior responsibility is a standard which is fair to the defendant, and whether corporate officers are simply being made an example of for widespread corporate policy.[1772] The multipronged concentration on corporate accountability described in this study so far has incorporated references to corporate officers, though the different forms of accountability for officers and the corporations themselves have not been systematically examined together. The focus on corporate accountability has been on the actor itself. Hence, the liability of officers is sometimes assumed.[1773] The focus of accountability is frequently 'on the corporation because no individual officers are readily identifiable, or each officer did not act alone and did not individually perform sufficient acts to render them liable.'[1774]

A 'corporate officer liability and corporate institutional liability may serve the similar purposes of remedying the victim, punishing the responsible party, and deterring future abuses.'[1775] Similarly, it is suggested that both the officer and the corporation may be held liable for a tort; however, there are also differences between accountability from a corporation and an officer. This difference can be seen in the way the corporate officials conduct themselves. This could be collective,[1776] or it could be that the company itself must be the focus of liability. For this

---

[1770] *Prosecutor v Hadzihasanovic,* Case No. IT-01-47-AR72, Decision on Interlocutory Appeal Challenging Jurisdiction in Relation to Command Responsibility, 16, Int'l Crim. Trib. For the Former Yugoslavia (July 16 2003). <https://perma.cc/N62U-TYBZ> Accessed 15 September 2017.

[1771] Marcus L Plant, 'Comparative Negligence and Strict Tort Liability' (1979) 40 Louisiana Law Review 403.

[1772] Grahame Thompson, *The Constitutionalization of The Global Corporate Sphere?* (Oxford University Press on Demand 2012) and James Fanto, 'Organizational Liability' (2010) 19 Harvard Journal of Law & Public Policy 45.

[1773] Cynthia H Finn, 'The Responsible Corporate Officer, Criminal Liability, and Mens Rea: Limitations on The RCO Doctrine' (1996) 46 American University Law Review 543.

[1774] Jennifer M Green, 'Corporate Torts: International Human Rights and Superior Officers' (2016) 17 (2) Chicago Journal of International Law 447 and Aaron D Jones, 'Corporate Officer Wrongdoing and The Fiduciary Duties of Corporate Officers Under Delaware Law' (2007) 44 (3) American Business Law Journal 475.

[1775] Jennifer M Green, 'Corporate Torts: International Human Rights and Superior Officers' (2016) 17 (2) Chicago Journal of International Law 447.

[1776] Mark Osiel, 'The Banality of Good: Aligning Incentives Against Mass Atrocity' (2005) 105 Columbia Law Review 1751.

reason, punitive punishment might be a way to deter future human rights violations.[1777] It is clear that 'when an officer acts as the 'alter ego' of the corporation in carrying out corporate policy, it is the corporation that bears responsibility.'[1778] Additionally, it is also clear that individual officers bear singular responsibility for abuses under their watch, and the most appropriate form of accountability and deterrence is to focus on the corporate officers.[1779]

Thus, this study argues that holding the corporation accountable has been addressed as both an international and domestic obligation. Internationally, the role of the collective arises when particular human beings have not taken sufficient action for responsibility to be allocated to any particular individual,[1780] or where there is a responsibility on the corporation itself.[1781] There may be tactical reasons for actions against a corporation; some research has shown that corporations are more likely to be held liable for negligent actions than are individuals.[1782] Additionally, the conduct of a parent corporation and its subsidiary may be so closely connected so that it is difficult to pinpoint individual responsibilities and/or

---

[1777]George P Fletcher, 'The Storrs Lectures: Liberals and Romantics at War: The Problem of Collective Guilt' (2002) 111 Yale Law Journal 1499, Christian List and Philip Pettit, *Group Agency: The Possibility, Design, and Status of Corporate Agents* (Oxford University Press 2011). And William S Laufer, 'Corporate Bodies and Guilty Minds' (1994) 43 Emory Law Journal 647 and *MacPherson v Buick Motor Co.*, 111 N.E. 1050 (N.Y. 1916).

[1778]Jennifer M Green, 'Corporate Torts: International Human Rights and Superior Officers' (2016) 17 (2) Chicago Journal of International Law 447 and Yedidia Z Stern, 'Corporate Criminal Personal Liability-Who Is the Corporation' (1987) 13 Journal of Corporation Law 125.

[1779]Robert C Downs, 'Piercing the Corporate Veil - Do Corporations Provide Limited Personal Liability?' (1985) 53 UMKC Law Review 174.

[1780]Peter A French, *Collective and Corporate Responsibility* (1987) and Brent Fisse and John Braithwaite, 'The Allocation of Responsibility for Corporate Crime: Individualism, Collectivism and Accountability' (1986) 11 Sydney Law Review 468.

[1781] Harold Hongju Koh, 'Separating Myth from Reality About Corporate Responsibility Litigation' (2004) 7 (2) Journal of International Economic Law 263, Burt Neuborne, 'Of Singles Without Baseball: Corporations as Frozen Relational Moments' (2011) 64 (3) Rutgers Law Review 769 and Sara Sun Beale, 'Is Corporate Criminal Liability Unique?' (2007) 44 American Criminal Law Review 1503.

[1782]Pammella S Quinn, 'Rethinking Corporate Human Rights Accountability' (2014) 89 Tulane Law Review 603 and Valerie P Hans, *Business on Trial: The Civil Jury and Corporate Responsibility* (Yale University Press 2000).

formal separation between functions of a parent corporation and subsidiary, resulting in the parent company being held accountable.[1783]

Corporate officer liability has a specific deterrent effect. Thus, in pursuing and accepting positions as directors, corporate officers also assume positions of responsibility. Hence, superior officers have a central role and the authority to change business conduct throughout the organisation. This authority contains a positive duty to punish and prevent wrongs by subordinates.[1784] It is possible that these actions serve both the individual harmed and, more widely, deter future wrongs against the community.[1785] Also, when a specific officer has taken action that meets the standards for liability, that officer should be recognised and his or her actions, or failure to fulfil a duty, should be held up to public scrutiny and held accountable in the legal system.[1786] In this view, corporate officers should be more worried about individual liability rather than the liability of the corporation itself, due to the general belief that corporate liability is just passed along to shareholders.[1787] Where decisions may negatively impact individual corporate officers, the officers are more risk averse than when a decision affects third parties.[1788] So, litigation against individuals may also have heftier lawsuit costs in terms of time and potential reputational harm than suits against corporate entities.[1789]

Danner and Martinez observed that the law and economics group 'least-cost avoiders' as applied to the criminal prosecution of superior officer high-level officials are better placed to form policy and implement

[1783]Henry W Ballantine, 'Separate Entity of Parent and Subsidiary Corporations' (1925) California Law Review 12.

[1784]Roger S Clark, 'The Mental Element in International Criminal Law: The Rome Statute of The International Criminal Court and the Elements of Offences' (Vol. 12. No. 3. Springer Netherlands 2001).

[1785] Brent Fisse and John Braithwaite, 'The Allocation of Responsibility for Corporate Crime: Individualism, Collectivism and Accountability' (1986) 11 Sydney Law Review 468.

[1786]Cecil A Wright and Allen M Linden, *Canadian Tort law: Cases, Notes and Materials* (Butterworths 1975).

[1787] Henry Hansmann and Reinier Kraakman, 'Toward Unlimited Shareholder Liability for Corporate Torts' (1991) Yale Law Journal 1879.

[1788]Claire A Hill and Richard W Painter, *Better Bankers, Better Banks: Promoting Good Business Through Contractual Commitment* (University of Chicago Press 2015).

[1789]Robert J Rhee, 'Tort Arbitrage' (2008) 60 Florida Law Review 125.

it.[1790] Danner and Martinez also argued that there are moral duties when a government or military official assumes command. 'These leaders 'are not like everyone else' and have affirmative obligations related to the governance of society, such as monitoring persons under their control to ensure that they comply with certain standards of conduct.'[1791] 'The same is true for corporate officers' [1792] when one examines the psychological literature on group dynamics.[1793] Group dynamics generally reveal 'that individuals acting in groups are more likely to accept hazardous risks than are individuals acting for themselves.'[1794] 'Holding a superior responsible for the actions of a subordinate could enhance the ability of a group to avoid hazardous risks. This opinion here marries with the RCO doctrine developed in the UK and the US and other tort regimes applying the precautionary principle.'[1795]

Though 'a corporate officer has moral and legal duties to monitor subordinates and prevent and punish violations, a system should not be created or reinforced that allows certain individuals to be the sacrificial lambs for more widespread corporate behaviour when the corporation as a whole that must be held accountable.'[1796] Thus, 'the principle of vicarious liability holds that corporations are ultimately responsible for acts taken in the course of an officer's corporate duties. Law and economics'[1797] analysis

---

[1790] Allison Marston Danner and Jenny S Martinez, 'Guilty Associations: Joint Criminal Enterprise, Command Responsibility, and the Development of International Criminal Law' (2005) California Law Review 75.

[1791] Jennifer M Green, 'Corporate Torts: International Human Rights and Superior Officers' (2016) 17 (2) Chicago Journal of International Law 447.

[1792] Jennifer M Green, 'Corporate Torts: International Human Rights and Superior Officers' (2016) 17 (2) Chicago Journal of International Law 447.

[1793] Darwin Cartwritht and Alvin Zander, *Group Dynamics* (Harper and Row 1960).

[1794] Jennifer M Green, 'Corporate Torts: International Human Rights and Superior Officers' (2016) 17 (2) Chicago Journal of International Law 447 and Irving L Janis and Leon Mann, Decision Making: A Psychological Analysis of Conflict, Choice, and Commitment (Free Press 1977).

[1795] Herbert Hovenkamp, Enterprise and American Law, 1836-1937 (Harvard University Press 2009) and Jennifer M Green, 'Corporate Torts: International Human Rights and Superior Officers' (2016) 17 Chicago Journal of International Law 2. <https://chicagounbound.uchicago.edu/cgi/viewcontent.cgi?referer=&httpsredir=1&article=1714&context=cjil> Accessed 26 November 2017.

[1796] Jennifer M Green (n 1957). < https://cjil.uchicago.edu/publication/corporate-torts-international-human-rights-and-superior-officers> Accessed 27 November 2017.

[1797] Jennifer M Green, 'Corporate Torts: International Human Rights and Superior Officers' (2016) 17 (2) Chicago Journal of International Law 447.

finds 'that limited liability is a more efficient means of allocating responsibility and costs.'[1798] Therefore, 'singling out individuals to hold them liable is not a task to be undertaken lightly. A determination must be made about the control that the officer had over subordinates and whether the officer possessed the knowledge to allow prevention or punishment of the violation.'[1799] Hence, 'the question of superior officer liability must first address the duty the officer has.'[1800] 'In the context of a tort there is also the question of'[1801] foreseeability[1802] and 'the duty of reasonable care.'[1803] Also, the standard must be consistent and clear so as to give notice to any potential offenders.[1804] 'There is such a clear 'standard for superior responsibility for corporate officers.'[1805] The standard of superior responsibility does not undercut corporate institutional liability.'[1806] Together, these two forms of potential liability form important complementary pieces of a legal structure that can provide greater responsibility for corporate human rights violations and deter future corporations for violating human rights and the environment.

Corporation Control of Business Operations

This was the first factor established in the *Childs* case: 'the defendants' material implication in the creation of the risk or his or her

[1798] *Ibid.*
[1799] Jennifer M Green, 'Corporate Torts: International Human Rights and Superior Officers' (2016) 17 (2) Chicago Journal of International Law 447 and Christopher Leck, 'International Responsibility in United Nations Peacekeeping Operations: Command and Control Arrangements and the Attribution of Conduct' (2009) 10 Melbourne Journal of International Law 346.
[1800] Jennifer M Green, 'Corporate Torts: International Human Rights and Superior Officers' (2016) 17 (2) Chicago Journal of International Law 447 and Michael J Kelly, 'Grafting the Command Responsibility Doctrine onto Corporate Criminal Liability For Atrocities' (2010) 24 Emory International Law Review 671.
[1801] Jennifer M Green, 'Corporate Torts: International Human Rights and Superior Officers' (2016) 17 (2) Chicago Journal of International Law 447.
[1802] John CP Goldberg and Benjamin C Zipursky, 'Torts as Wrongs' (2010) 88 Texas Law Review 917.
[1803] Jennifer M Green, 'Corporate Torts: International Human Rights and Superior Officers' (2016) 17 (2) Chicago Journal of International Law 447.
[1804] Emily Sherwin, 'Interpreting Tort Law' (2011) 39 Florida State University Law Review 227.
[1805] Jennifer M Green, 'Corporate Torts: International Human Rights and Superior Officers' (2016) 17 (2) Chicago Journal of International Law 447.
[1806] *Ibid.*

control of a risk to which others have been invited.'[1807] Comparing this to the previous authorities established in cases such as *Fullowka*[1808] and the RCO principle, it was found that the defendant has control over the relevant risk, the defendant has both a physical presence at the site of the risk and was either liable for the operation of the mining site or contractually bound to protect the plaintiff from the risk created. Likewise, in *Fullowka*, Pinkerton's was particularly engaged to protect the mine and had employees stationed at the mine for that purpose.[1809]

In *Crocker Sundance Northwest Resorts Ltd*,[1810] the Canadian Supreme Court held that the operator of an inner tubing event owed a duty of care to a person who was harmed while engaging in a visibly drunk manner. It was further held that where the defendant operator's own employees were in charge of how the event was run, a duty of care was owed.[1811] Even though the corporation may not be morally responsible, it should be held accountable in the tort of negligence if it is found that the corporation fell below the objective standard of the reasonable man in relation to both the human rights violations and the control it exercises over the subsidiary.

Additionally, the plaintiff in a duty of care claim may be able to establish that the defendant (corporation subsidiary) was responsible for upholding the human rights standards and environmental assessment. For example, as noted above, Loblaw Companies Limited argued that if the parent corporation's own employee was responsible for monitoring workplace conditions in, for example, Bangladesh then the court should be able to impose liability on the defendant (corporation) for the conduct of the employees (subsidiary).[1812] Nonetheless, often the defendant would not have a physical presence in the relevant area where the corporation's subsidiary operates. Likewise, they may not have any contractual duty to protect the victims affected by the subsidiary's misconduct. Similarly, the Canadian corporation that determines the corporate employment policy through contractual obligations and has substantial control over its

[1807]*Childs v Desormeaux* (n 1746).

[1808]<https://goldblattpartners.com/experience/notable-cases/post/fullowka-v-pinkertons/ > Accessed 5 December 2016.

[1809]*Ibid.*

[1810]*Crocker v Sundance Northwest Resorts Ltd* [1988] 1 S.C.R. 1186.

[1811]*Crocker Case.*

[1812]Loblaw Companies Limited, 'Company Statement, Lonlaw Companies Limited Update Statement on Bangladesh' (2014). <www.loblaw.ac/English/Media-Centre/ announcement/default.aspx> Accessed 22 December 2016.

employee (subsidiary) will be liable for the conduct of the subsidiary.[1813] This could be seen to have sufficient control over the risk of human rights violations, regardless of the corporate not having a physical presence in the business environment.

Therefore, the question to the court should be whether in practice the defendant has control over the subsidiary's business conduct that has created harm, even if such control is not derived from physical presence, ownership, or a contractual obligation. This is particularly relevant when a parent corporation may owe a duty of care to victims of a human rights violation committed by its subsidiary. The parent corporation is liable for a duty of care that should give rise to a collective responsibility[1814] when it can be proven that the parent corporation exercises a high degree of contractual control and practical control over the operations of the subsidiary.[1815]

For example, a buyer has significant leverage over supplier operations, and it has the contractual capacity to ask the supplier to change its human rights standards and adopt a minimum human rights standard. In this context, a duty of care exists where the defendant has a position that allows it to exercise control over the subsidiary, exercise overall control, or control the business operations because the subsidiary's action exacerbates misconduct that is originally created by the defendant's influence. Therefore, there is a very high degree of foreseeability of harm, which, coupled with the corporation's proximate relationship to the subsidiary and the victims, could be seen as an assumption of responsibility through the corporation's control.

In this circumstance only in novel or contentious cases, will it be necessary to apply the first principle in order to determine whether a duty of care arises. In such cases, the test for duty of care comprises of three stages; reasonable foreseeability of the human rights violations and the environmental damages to the plaintiff, a sufficient relationship of proximity between the corporation and the plaintiff, and an inquiry into whether it would be fair, just, and reasonable to recognise a duty of care.

[1813]*Ibid.*

[1814]Joel Feinberg, 'Collective Responsibility' (1968) 65 (21) Journal of Philosophy 674.

[1815]Ian Sadler, *Logistics and Supply Chain Integration* (Sage 2007).

Corporation Self-sufficiency

The second essential element in the *Childs* case seeks to protect the independence of a person affected by imposing a positive duty of care on a defendant.[1816] In *Childs* this part of the judgment is concerned with protecting the right of a person 'engaged in risky activities' and the fundamental rights of a bystander to choose to intervene or not.[1817] This was also distinguished in the Canadian Supreme Court decision in *Fullowka*, where it rejected the concept that imposing a duty of care would interfere with the miner's autonomy, arguing that even though the miners had decided to continue working on the site while the risk was imminent, 'they made that choice in light of the assurance given to them'.[1818] Likewise, even though the plaintiff in a tort of negligence claim has knowledge about the presence of the risk and chosen to work there, they may have done so in light of the control being exercised by the defendant to monitor the compliance with specified minimum human rights standards and respond to breaches.

In this case, the assurance given by the defendant indicates that the defendant has assumed responsibility for the plaintiff and has knowledge about the ongoing human rights violations. Therefore, a duty of care is recognised. Additionally, a record of human rights abuses was shown to illustrate that the victims may not have had a choice about whether or not to work in an unsafe environment or for long labour hours and insufficient pay. Therefore, in such cases, it will be entirely inappropriate for the court to reject a duty of care out of concern for the victim's autonomy to engage in risky activities.[1819]

Accordingly, the concern for the victim's autonomy, if a duty were imposed in the tort of negligence claim, is a somewhat more cogent debate. Therefore, the Supreme Court in *Fullowka* held that imposing a duty on Pinkerton's would not conflict with Pinkerton's right to choose not to intervene, observing specifically that Pinkerton's had given up much of its freedom by entering into a contract to provide security for the miners.[1820] This position is valid because the victim of the tort of negligence may not be able to point to a contractual undertaking to inspect or monitor corporate

---

[1816] *Childs v Desormeaux* (n 1746).
[1817] *Ibid.*
[1818] *Fullowka v Pinkerton's of Canada Ltd.*, 2010 SCC 5, [2010] 1 S.C.R. 132.
[1819] *Ibid.*
[1820] *Ibid.*

adherence to human rights duties,[1821] but can rely on the principle of duty of care to exercise their human rights.

It is also observed that a Canadian corporation that has publicly stated it will monitor and respond to human right issues in its business operations and has benefited from this statement publicly (i.e., by improving public image) cannot be said to be innocent of the human rights abuse in its business conduct[1822] due to the fact that the public statement means it has assumed responsibility to the claimant. This position indicates a positive duty of care. Thus, it is adequate for one to infer that imposing a duty of care on the corporation in such circumstances will not be unreasonable, considering the corporation control exercised in the business operations with the subsidiary, the knowledge about the human rights abuse and the steps it claims to have taken to ensure human rights violation is negated in its business operations with the subsidiary.

Victims Reasonable Trust Test

Reliance, unlike an assumption of responsibility, is not a right-generating event. The common assumption is that it flows from the fact that in most cases where there has been an assumption of responsibility[1823] the claimant suffers loss as a result of relying on the undertakings. As an example, bailors rely on their employees to take care. (Bailment with respect to the contract act is essentially the delivery of goods (moveable property) by one person (bailor) to another person (bailee) for some specific purpose without any transfer of ownership. The bailor has certain duties when the goods bailed are defective.)[1824] Conscious patients rely on their doctor to be careful, as do the clients of a solicitor. Therefore, in claims for damages, it is necessary for the bailee, patient, or solicitor's client to establish reliance in the strong sense that they have acted upon the assumption of responsibility to them to their detriment. In particular, it is not necessary to show that an opportunity has forgone as a result of the assumption of responsibility. There is an entitlement to be placed in the better position which reasonable care would achieve, regardless of the

[1821]Paul Hoffman, and Beth Stephens, 'International Human Rights Cases Under State Law and in State Courts' (2012).

[1822]*Fullowka v Pinkerton's of Canada Ltd* (n 2097).

[1823]Russell Brown, 'Assumption of Responsibility and Loss of Bargain in Tort Law' (2006) Dalhousie Law Journal 29, 345.

[1824]Edwin Ames Jaggard, *Hand-book of the Law of Torts* (Vol. 2 West Publishing Company 1895).

availability of any alternative bailor, doctor, or lawyer who would have been careful.

Establishing loss through reliance on an assumption of responsibility is sufficient to find a duty of care. The concept of assumption of responsibility emerged from the landmark decision of the House of Lords in *Hedley Byrne & Co. Ltd v Heller & Partners Ltd*,[1825] which established that there could be a liability in negligence of carelessly produced statements resulting in a purely economic loss. Precisely what was entailed in this concept, along with the accompanying concepts of reasonable reliance and a special relationship, has never been entirely clear.[1826] However, up until 1994 this uncertainty was largely contained within the sphere of actions for negligent misstatements.

However, in *Spring v Guardian Assurance Plc*[1827] Lord Goff utilised the concept in a remarkable example of judicial creativity to find that the supplier of an employment reference owed a duty of care to its subject. In doing so, his Lordship commented:

[A]lthough *Hedley Byrne* itself was concerned with the provision of information and advice, it is clear that the principle in the case is not so limited and extends to include the performance of other 'services, as for example the professional services rendered by a solicitor to his client'.

Lord Goff 'later developed this approach in his leading judgment in *Henderson v Merrett Syndicates Ltd*,[1828] where underwriting members of Lloyd's Insurance were claiming against their underwriting agents'. His Lordship explained:

> [T]he concept provides its own explanation why there is no problem in cases of this kind of liability for pure economic loss; for if a person assumes responsibility to another in respect of certain services, there is no reason why he should not be liable in damages for that other in respect of economic loss which flows from the negligent performance of those services.

It follows that once the case is identified as falling within the *Hedley Byrne* principle, there should be no need to embark upon any further

[1825] *Hedley Byrne & Co. Ltd v Heller & Partners Ltd* [1964] AC 465.
[1826] Kit Barker, 'Unreliable Assumptions in the modern Law of Negligence' (1993) 109 (3) Law Quarterly Review 461, 484.
[1827] *Spring v Guardian Assurance plc* [1995] 2 A 296.
[1828] <https://lra.le.ac.uk/bitstream/2381/27596/4/J_Hartshorne_article_.pdf> Accessed 7 July 2018 and *Henderson v Merrett Syndicates Ltd* [1995] 2 AC 145.

enquiry into whether it is 'fair, just and reasonable' to impose liability for economic loss.[1829]

Additionally, Lord Goff clarified in *Henderson v Merrett Syndicates Ltd* 'that an objective test will be applied when asking the question whether, in a particular case, responsibility should be held to have been assumed by the defendant to the plaintiff.'[1830] In *Williams v Natural Life Health Foods Ltd*,[1831] 'this approach came to be referred to as the 'extended *Hedley Byrne* principle' and was described by Lord Steyn as the 'rationalisation or technique adopted by English law to provide a remedy for the recovery of damages in respect of economic loss caused by the negligent performance of services.'[1832]

'*Williams* appeared to secure the concept's position as a *bona fide* means of imposing a duty of care upon defendants in economic loss cases',[1833] 'and an attractive one at that, given the apparent absence of any requirement to consider whether it would be fair, just and reasonable to do so. In a further development, it is now clear that the assumption of responsibility concept is not necessarily restricted to economic loss cases.'[1834] 'What is less clear, however, is precisely when it would be more appropriate to utilise this approach towards a duty of care enquiry, and whether its application would necessarily lead to a different outcome.'[1835] For example, in *McFarlane v Tayside Health Board*,[1836] 'where the claimants were seeking compensation from hospital authorities for a combination of personal injuries and economic loss following a 'wrongful

---

[1829]Nicholas J McBride and Andrew Hughes, 'Hedley Byrne in The House of Lords: An Interpretation' (1995) 15 (3) Legal Studies 376 and <https://lra.le.ac.uk/bitstream/2381/27596/4/J_Hartshorne_article_.pdf > Accessed 7 July 2018.

[1830]*Ibid.*

[1831]*Williams v Natural Life Health Foods Ltd* [1998] 1 WLR 830 and <https://lra.le.ac.uk/bitstream/2381/27596/4/J_Hartshorne_article_.pdf > Accessed 7 July 2018.

[1832]*Ibid* at 834.

[1833]*White v Jones* [1995] 2 AC 207 and <https://lra.le.ac.uk/bitstream/2381/27596/4/J_Hartshorne_article_.pdf > Accessed 7 July 2018.

[1834]*Phelps v Hillingdon London Borough Council* [2001] 2 AC 619 and *Brooks v Commissioner of the Police for the Metropolis* [2005] 1 WLR 1495; [2005] UKHL 24.

[1835]In *McFarlane v Tayside* Health Board [2000] 2 AC 59 and <https://lra.le.ac.uk/bitstream/2381/27596/4/J_Hartshorne_article_.pdf > Accessed 7 July 2018.

[1836]*McFarlane v Tayside Health Board* [2000] 2 AC 59.

birth', their Lordships adopted a variety of differing approaches in resolving the dispute, notwithstanding that the claim had been brought under the extended *Hedley Byrne* principle'. Further 'uncertainty has been generated by judicial observations concerning the intelligibility of the concept. Even before Lord Goff's liberalisation of the concept in *Henderson*, several Law Lords had made such observations. For example, in *Caparo'*,[1837] Lord Roskill spoke of finding: 'considerable difficulty in phrases such as "voluntary assumption of responsibility" unless they are to be explained as meaning no more than the existence of circumstances in which the law will impose a liability upon a person making the allegedly negligent statement to the person to whom that statement is made'. In which case, 'the phrase does not help to determine in what circumstances the law will impose that liability or, indeed, its scope.'[1838]

In *Williams*, Lord Steyn noted that the concept had been subjected to such criticisms, and appeared to concede these arguments with the rejoinder that coherence 'must sometimes yield to practical justice.'[1839] Regardless of the development of the assumption of responsibility concept as a basis upon which to impose a duty of care, the nature and scope of the concept, and the circumstances in which it may be applied, are still a mystery. Barker has described the concept as a 'conceptual veil' which shrouds the true face of tort law.[1840] This may have been acknowledged by their Lordships in the *Customs and Excise Commissioners* case.[1841] The treatment of this concept by the House of Lords since 1994 represents merely one of several cautionary tales that warn that the desire to achieve practical justice may culminate in a legal landscape which is unintelligible to those lawyers who must work with it.

Nonetheless, the foreseeable possibility of detriment, whether by the reliance of the claimant or a third party, is relevant and will commonly be used in determining whether, as a matter of construction, the defendant has by his or her action implicitly assumed responsibility towards the claimant. Where the undertaking of a task means that it will not be undertaken by anyone else, this supports a finding that there is an implied assumption of responsibility in carrying it out. A finder who takes a lost car into his custody, or a surgeon who operates on the unconscious man,

---

[1837] *Ibid* at 628.

[1838] Lord Griffiths in *Smith v Eric S Bush* [1990] 1 AC 831 at 86. <https://inba.info/tort-cases-english-law_5745cbc0b6d87faab48b4588.html > Accessed 15 July 2016.

[1839] *Ibid* at 837.

[1840] Kit Barker (n 2104).

[1841] *Customs and Excise v Barclays Bank Plc* [2006] UKHL 28.

exclude the possibility of someone else undertaking this task. By contrast, in a case such as *Sutradhar v Natural Environment Research Council*,[1842] no one else was excluded from conferring the relevant benefit or was discouraged from doing so by the defendant's actions.[1843] Reliance is relevant to the true construction of what can legitimately be inferred from the defendant's conduct at the moment in time. The proof of actual reliance subsequent to the undertakings is unnecessary and is indeed irrelevant to the construction to be placed upon the defendant's prior actions.

Furthermore, it is unnecessary to show that expectation has been created by the assumption of responsibility. For example, where lost goods are found, goods are bailed, or a patient is admitted to the hospital, no expectations of reasonable care are generated in the mind of the owner of the good or the patient. Not only is reliance unnecessary, it is insufficient alone. The claimant must rely upon something. Someone who relies upon a promise made to someone else, for example, acquires no right by so doing. Further, reliance may cause another right to be infringed, but it does not generate a new right in itself. So, if someone calls an emergency hotline, and negligently assured that firefighters are on their way to the burning house, if the person has put out the fire themselves, if the person has not been given the assurance and the house burns down, as a result, this is actionable. It is the property right in the house that has been infringed. The reliance causes the person's right not to have their property carelessly destroyed to be infringed; but it did not generate a new right in itself, this was the third factor in the *Childs* case.

The factor recognised in the *Childs* case is reasonable trust,[1844] which falls under the principle of reasonable foreseeability. This factor entails that the plaintiffs establish that they have relied on the corporation's undertaking and that the corporation would reasonably expect such a trust.[1845] However, it is argued that the requirement for a plaintiff to establish dependence in a case will prove problematic, especially so, for example, in cases like the Canadian corporation in *Fullowka*, where employees are exposed to risks in their place of work and where the defendant has represented that it will protect them. Discerning from the Supreme Court decision in *Fullowka*, there is an assumption that perhaps

---

1842 *Natural Environment Research Council* [2006] UKHL 33.

1843 *Stovin v Wise* [1996] UKHL 15.

1844 *Childs v Desormeaux* (n 1746), also see, Peter Bowal and Preet Saini, 'Whatever Happened to Childs v. Desormeaux: Killer Hospitality' (2014), Kelsey Drozdowski, 'Liability for Impaired Driving: Expanding the Scope' (2004) 29 Law Now 62.

1845 *Fullowka v Pinkerton's of Canada Ltd* (n 2097.

the miners had a choice about whether or not to continue to participate in work-related activities.

However, the Supreme Court decision in *Fullowka* held that the miners continued to attend work with the assurance that the defendant's security contractors taking reasonable care would reduce the risk associated with working in such conditions.[1846] Thus, the employees in a negligence claim may not have a real choice about working for an employer that violates human rights in its business operations and may not have sufficient negotiating power to seek better working conditions. Hence, the Court approach to imposing a duty of care on the defendant is perfectly adequate. Likewise, the plaintiff would have reasonably required the corporation to act according to its publicised code of conduct on human rights,[1847] as it can be argued that the corporation assumed responsibility by publishing the code of conduct.

However, this could be difficult to apply in practice because the defendant needs to establish that he/she relied on the parent company's conduct. Therefore, some workers may be able to establish reasonable trust. In an empirical analysis, three specific challenges exist for a potential plaintiff in establishing reasonable foreseeability in a future claim: 1. lack of knowledge of human rights policies of the corporation; 2. lack of trust in the corporation's human rights policies in its business operations; and 3. unreasonable trust. These factors are all connected to the superior responsibility principle and to each other. Thus, the first hurdle for a future plaintiff would be to establish that he or she knew the corporation had a policy of protecting human rights in its business operations and control over the subsidiary business. This constitutes the reliance and assumption element of the tort. Even though a corporation often publishes its human rights policies in the media, it does not follow through to reflect on the human rights standards of its business with the subsidiary; this could be another mechanism to hold the corporation accountable for its public information.

Likewise, where an inspection was, in fact, carried out by or on behalf of a corporation, an employee's or the victim's litigation could be reinforced through the duty of care if he or she knew that the corporation was responsible for carrying out the human rights standards inspection. This would be easier for a plaintiff who was engaged in employment with the subsidiary of the parent company (for example, where the defendant – the corporation – is the main business partner), rather than for a plaintiff who

---

[1846]*Ibid.*

[1847]See above discussion on CSR.

works for a subsidiary that engages in business operations with multiple corporations, and where it is more difficult for the plaintiff to link the inspection to the parent corporation.

If the plaintiff could establish that they were aware of the defendant's business policy on human rights standards and control over that policy, then the next challenge is for them to establish that a duty of care existed – like the miners in *Fullowka* – and that they decided to work for the specific corporation or took some other action on the basis of the corporation's business policy at that particular time. Of course, this is very difficult to establish in practice. However, a plaintiff who has a choice about where to take up employment may be able to establish that they chose to work for a particular corporation because they believed the corporation would require its subsidiary to uphold the minimum human rights standards. Contrarily, victims of human rights abuses do not need to prove working relations if they can prove foreseeability, proximity, and the fair, just, and reasonable principle, because it can be presumed that a duty of care exists.

This can be supported by Philips and Lim's study of Vietnam's athletic footwear industry, where the authors found that 50% of surveyed workers indicated that comfortable working condition were the main reason why they choose to take up employment in a particular corporation. Comparing to the only 2.5% that stated the main reason why they choose to work for a particular corporation was a high salary.[1848] Additionally, Record, Kuttner and Phouxay observed that low wages and long working hours were the two main reasons as to why clothing employees in Laos decided to stop working for a particular corporation.[1849] Furthermore, where the workers are aware that the human rights inspection are in fact being carried out, they may argue that they have relied on that inspection as evidence that a particular human rights policy exists to protect their rights, therefore failure to adhere to this policy amounts to a failed duty of care to the employees. Hence, the court should be under obligation to pay attention to these failures, and whether this failure created or contributed to the harm suffered. A rebuttable presumption exists for a future plaintiff to argue that a duty of care exists when it is established that their dependence on the defendant's policy is reasonable.

Nonetheless, in *Fullowka*, the Canadian Supreme Court held that the miner's dependence was reasonable because of the defendant's presence

[1848]Joe Phillips and Suk-Jun Lim. 'Their "Brothers" Keeper: Global Buyers and the Legal Duty to Protect Suppliers' Employees' (2009) 61 Rutgers Law Review 333.

[1849]Richard Record, *Stephanie Kuttner and Kabmanivanh Phouxay, Voting with Their Feet? Explaining High Turnover and Low Productivity in the Lao Garment Sector* (Palgrave Macmillan UK 2014).

at the mine and the assurance given to the miners.[1850] A crucial point to note here though is that it would be very difficult for a plaintiff to establish that dependence was reasonable where he or she knew that the defendant was not responsible or engage in business activities with the subsidiary, monitoring, or enforcing minimum human rights standards. Likewise, it will also be very difficult for a plaintiff to establish that dependence is reasonable if it should be obvious to him or her that the corporation was turning a blind eye to human rights abuse that violated its business policy.

Even so, dependence on policy for duty of care is reasonable if the defendant appears to be engaging in business conduct with the subsidiary, monitoring and responding to human rights abuse in its business operations in accordance with its standard of business activities. However, if it can be established that there is foreseeability and proximity between the defendant and the victims then the presumption is that there is a duty of care.

Making the Situation Worse

If a claimant cannot establish that he or she reasonably trusted the corporate undertakings, a duty of care could still be possible to establish if there is evidence that the subsidiary relied on the undertaking and this dependence cause harm to the plaintiff or made the situation worse. Therefore, when one or more factors, including the defendant's negligence, are found to be a necessary condition of the plaintiff's harm, then the court should impose a duty of care on the corporation. This should involve two distinctive tests, the first is for the court to ask whether the harm was the result of the defendant's action through negligent conduct and the second is whether the subsidiary was acting in his own accord leading back to the defendant's (corporate) negligence. Each of these tests represents a value judgment on how far the court should think the defendant's liability should extend, that is, regarding the final question about whose responsibility it is, and whether the harm is appropriately allocated.

This was the case in *Goodwin v Godwin*, a decision of the British Columbia Court of Appeal.[1851] The defendant in *Godwin* was contracted by the local authority that it would keep roads clear from ice.[1852] The defendant advised the local authority that it would fulfil its contractual obligation of removing ice from a specific road, but, nonetheless, failed to do so once it recognised that work would fall outside its contract. The plaintiff was

---

[1850]*Fullowka v Pinkerton's of Canada Ltd* (n 2097).
[1851]Dean Wilson Edward and Shelly Tomic, *In the Supreme Court of Canada* (1990).
[1852]2007 BCCA 81at para 31, 279 DLR (4th) 227 [*Goodwin*].

injured in an accident as a result of the ice on the road.[1853] The Court held that there is a duty of care; if the defendant had not undertaken to remove the ice on the road, the local authority should have sought an alternative arrangement for the removal of the danger on the road.

Applying this to a corporation's duty of care, the relevant analysis is whether a harm is too far from the consequence of the defendant's negligence; or if there is an assumption of responsibility, whether the consequence of the negligent actions was so far from it as to have been unforeseeable by the defendant at the time the action occurred. The defendant can argue that the consequence of their action is not foreseeable. If this is the case, then cause in law is not established and the claimant's case cannot go further. The formulation of duty of care here means that whether something is too remote is judged in light of what was known at the time the breach occurred, with foresight, and not with the benefit of hindsight. This will be the case in a scenario where there was evidence that a trade union, NGO or the media have supervised or reported on human rights violations or advocated for workers in a particular corporate factory, but did not do so in dependence on the corporation's employees. Another example is where the subsidiary of a parent corporation would have carried out appropriate human rights standards but did not do so in dependence on the defendant corporation.[1854]

Similarly, if a negligent driver hits another person's vehicle, it is the evidence of the damage to the vehicle itself which would be foreseeable, as would be the damage to the contents of the vehicle. It would not matter what the contents of the vehicle are, so if a truck was transporting cheap beans or expensive designer clothing, the negligent driver would be liable for the full cost of whatever was damaged. Once the type of harm is judged to be foreseeable, the defendant should be held liable for all the harm caused, even where the extent itself was not. The duty of care to not harm a person, create a risk for a person, or cause injury or damage as a result of the misconduct of the corporation can be found where the parent corporation assumed responsibility. Also, a duty of care can arise where the subsidiary's parent corporation who is said to be under that duty has by its conduct assumed responsibility for the conduct of the subsidiary and the safety of its employees. Likewise, where the parent corporation has created or made the human rights abuses or environmental damages worse.

[1853]*Ibid.*

[1854]*Cooper v Hobart* [2001] 3 S.C.R. 537.

Fair, Just and Reasonable (Third Limb of *Caparo* Test)

The House of Lords established that for a duty of care to be imposed, the third limb of *Caparo v Dickman* should be satisfied, that it is fair, just, and reasonable that the law should recognise the duty of care on the defendant to take reasonable care not to cause that damage to the claimant.[1855] However, the question to the court is whether there is a mandatory factor, rather than the overriding question of whether it is fair, just, and reasonable to impose a duty of care on the corporation, having thoroughly considered the relationship (proximity) between the plaintiff and the defendant, to impose a duty of care on the defendant. The vital point here is that when a plaintiff is able to establish foreseeability and proximity, then the court should also apply a moral principle in conjunction to fair, just, and reasonable to impose a duty of care on the corporation.

In conjunction with the issues of control, corporate superior responsibility, the assumption of responsibility, and self-sufficiency as explained above, representations by the defendant that it will take action for the plaintiff's benefit can indicate proximity,[1856] as can be the case when the defendant has benefited economically from the circumstance giving rise to the violations.[1857] As also observed in the *Childs* case, 'the vulnerability of the plaintiff and the later subjection to the control of the defendant creates a situation where the latter has an enhanced responsibility to safeguard against risk', [1858] Even though this statement was made regarding a paternalistic relationship, it acknowledges that a duty can be established by the high level of control by the corporate, attached with the specific vulnerability and dependence of the victim.

Consequently, in a situation where it is not possible for the plaintiff to establish a duty of care due to the plaintiff own vulnerability, it may be fair, just, and reasonable to impose a duty of care. In the absence of evidence of the latter, the defendant receives an economic benefit from the subsidiary action. Through a reduced human rights standard, the corporation benefits from this, and establishes a reputation that has the ability to influence the human rights condition of the business operations. Furthermore, a claim would be strengthened if the defendant knew that its undertaking was the

[1855]John Murphy, 'Expectation Losses, Negligent Omissions and the Tortious Duty of Care' (1996) 55 (01) Cambridge Law Journal 43.

[1856]*Ibid.*

[1857]*Cooper v Hobart* (n 2132).

[1858]*Childs v Desormeaux* (n 1746).

main protective mechanism for employees and society in the subsidiary business operations.[1859]

The key factor for the court to consider when determining whether the defendant did act reasonably is the likelihood and the gravity of the harm that could reasonably have been foreseen. The greater the likelihood of human rights violations, the more the court should assume that care and discretion should be exercised to prevent and protect the rights of the victims. The best way for the court to make sense of this all is to understand that at each stage of foreseeability, proximity, and the fair, just, and reasonable principle, the court must ask slightly different questions in relation to the duty of care. The first question is whether the human rights violations were a reasonably foreseeable consequence of the defendant's careless action; the second question is whether the foreseeability was sufficiently grave and likely that the defendant should have done more than they did to avoid the human rights violation from happening.; and the third is asking not only if the violation was foreseeable but how likely was it that the violation might cause the serious harm that the defendant could reasonably have foreseen? If these questions are answered affirmatively then the court should conclude that it is fair, just, and reasonable to impose a duty of care on a corporation.

Parent Corporation Liability for Human Rights Violations Caused by Subsidiary Business Operations

Apart from the question of direct or collective corporate accountability for human rights abuses, international law and tort law acknowledge a special and substantial form of omission liability in the doctrine of superior or command responsibility. The doctrine seeks to enforce responsible command by extending criminal liability to a superior who fails in a duty to prevent, stop, or punish the crime of their subordinates.[1860] The doctrine of superior responsibility has ancient origins and has been included in the national military law as well.[1861] It is thus established that superior responsibility is not confined to military

[1859] *Ibid.*

[1860] Alphons MM Orie, 'Stare Decisis in the ICTY Appeal System? Successor Responsibility in the Hadžihasanović Case' (2012) 10 (3) Journal of International Criminal Justice 635.

[1861] Beatrice I Bonafé, 'Finding a Proper Role for Command Responsibility' (2007) 5 (3) Journal of International Criminal Justice 599.

commanders and wars but extended to civil superiors,[1862] such as corporate officials, and to crimes against humanity, genocide,[1863] and environmental damage.

The present study raises the possibility that the doctrine of command responsibility that has emerged in the international criminal law applies to corporate officials duties. It would impose a duty of care on the parent corporation, as the contractual obligation with the corporation would establish the command responsibility principle. This then makes a business liable for the corporate subsidiary's human rights violation.

This finding, while preliminary, suggests that three separate obligations will trigger the corporation's duty to protect and respect human rights. The first is the duty to prevent subordinate corporations and their officials from violating human rights; the second is the duty to intervene to stop ongoing human rights misconduct in its business operations; and the third is the duty to sanction a subordinate for having engaged in human rights abuses.[1864] A corporation may be liable for failing to prevent human rights violations in its business operations by failing to uphold even one of these elements. Specifically, where the corporation has assumed the overall responsibility for the operation of the business, there will be a rebuttable presumption that the corporation is liable for the misconduct, regardless of the knowledge of the abuses or the link between the home and host states.

The ICTY in the seminal 1998 *Celebic*[1865] judgment determined that this doctrine has three essentials.[1866] This study suggests that corporate accountability subsidiary conduct follows the three essential elements. First, the notion is that corporate officials and subordinates, including subsidiaries, must have a relationship where the former enjoyed effective control, that is, the material ability to prevent, stop or punish the subordinate for human rights violations.[1867] Effective control in this context means, for example,

---

[1862]Gideon Boas, James L Bischoff and Natalie L Reid, *Forms of Responsibility in International Criminal Law* (Cambridge University Press 2007).

[1863]Robert Cryer, *Prosecuting International Crimes: Selectivity and the International Criminal Law Regime* (Vol. 41. Cambridge University Press 2005).

[1864]ICC Statute Article 28 (a) (ii), (b) (iii); Volker Nerlich, 'Superior Responsibility Under Article 28 ICC Statute for What Exactly is The Superior Held Responsible?' (2007) 5(3) Journal of International Criminal Justice 665.

[1865]Marco Sassòli and Laura M. Olson, 'Prosecutor v. Tadić (Judgement) Case No. IT-94-aA. 38 ILM 1518 (1999) American Journal of International Law 571.

[1866]Jean-Marie Henckaerts, Louise Doswald-Beck and Carolin Alvermann, *Customary International Humanitarian Law* (Vol. 1. Cambridge University Press 2005).

[1867]Sonja Boelaert-Suominen, 'Prosecuting Superiors for Crimes Committed by Subordinates: A Discussion of The First Significant Case Law Since the Second World War'. (2000) 41 Virginia Journal of International Law 747.

the corporation official's power to issue an order to the alleged subordinates; that the subordinates have a tendency to follow these orders; the corporation official's influence among the subordinates; and the corporation official's ability to reprimand suspected subordinates for committing human rights abuses.[1868]

The second is: the corporate official must have either the knowledge or reason to know the subordinates' human rights misconduct.[1869] For the latter, two common standards that have been posited are: (1) negligence, where the corporation official bears liability if he should have known of the misconduct, implying a duty to stay informed of the subordinates;[1870] or (2) constructive knowledge, where the corporation official bears liability only if he had enough information at his disposal to suggest misconduct and still took no action to learn where the human rights abuse had been, were being, or were about to be committed,[1871] implying no duty to proactively seek out such knowledge.

The third and last element of the essential mechanism which seeks to hold corporations accountable for their subsidiaries' misconduct, is that the corporation must fail to take necessary and reasonable measures to prevent, stop, or punish subordinate human rights abuse.[1872] The assessment of this failure depends on the corporation's material ability to take action in the circumstance in question.[1873] Finally, this section strengthens the idea that parent corporate responsibility principles provide a strong avenue for corporate accountability for human rights violations under tort law. It also strengthens the idea that under the command responsibility doctrine, the assumption of responsibility, and the duty of care, the corporation can be held liable for human rights violations committed by its subordinates.

The development of English and Canadian law recognised that future plaintiffs could also be assisted in the emerging principle that a parent

---

[1868] Mohamed Elewa Badar, 'Drawing the Boundaries of Mens Rea in The Jurisprudence of The International Criminal Tribunal for The Former Yugoslavia' (2006) 6 (3) International Criminal Law Review 313, 348.

[1869] Jenny S Martinez, 'Understanding Mens Rea in Command Responsibility from Yamashita to Blaškić and Beyond' (2007) 5 (3) Journal of International Criminal Justice 638.

[1870] Brian Seth Parker, 'Applying the Doctrine of Superior Responsibility to Corporate Officers: A Theory of Individual Liability for International Human Rights Violations' (2012) 35 Hastings International and Comparative Law Review 1.

[1871] Protocol I, Article 43.

[1872] *Ibid.*

[1873] Volker Nerlich, 'Superior Responsibility Under Article 28 ICC Statute for What Exactly is The Superior Held Responsible?' (2007) 5 (3) Journal of International Criminal Justice 665.

company could be directly liable for human rights abuses caused by a subsidiary's business operation, especially where it has assumed responsibility either wholly or partly for the business operation as well as the protection of the plaintiff from the relevant human rights abuses. This is because the relationship between a parent corporation and subsidiary is very close, especially where the parent corporation has direct control over the actions of its subsidiary through finance, business policy, knowledge, or voting powers. Where a parent corporation, such as an oil or gas corporation, has significant control over its supplier's operations and, more specifically, its human rights standards, the relationship is parallel to the *Caparo* test's commander and servant relationship; thus a duty of care is owed in this instance.

However, neither the UK, the US, Canada nor the Netherlands courts have made a final determination on direct parent corporate responsibility. It is vital to note though, that the Ontario Superior Court has refused to strike out claims of this nature in the decisions in *United Canadian Malt Ltd v Outboard Marine Corporation of Canada Ltd*[1874] and *Choc v Hudbay Minerals*.[1875] Similarly, direct parent corporate liability is also noted in the recent decision in the English Court of Appeal in *Chandler v Cape PLC*.[1876] If, however, there is more specific knowledge about the relationship between the corporation and the subsidiary, then, the court should treat the relationship as possessing sufficient proximity to impose a duty of care on the parent corporations. After a careful examination of the supply chain, parent corporation and subsidiary liability throughout this part of the research, the study will now focus its attention on this principle and how it should alter corporate liability by piercing the corporate veil. The first part is to examine Canadian authority from the court, before assessing the English court authority on parent corporate liability.

Canadian Authority

Direct parent company liability for human rights violations caused by a subsidiary's operation was first heard in Canada by the Ontario

[1874] *United Canada Malt Ltd. v Outboard Marine Corp. of Canada* (2000), 48 O.R. (3d) 352 (S.C.). Can LII 22365 (ON SC) Environmental Protection Act struck out Environmental Protection Act, R.S.O. 1990, c. E.19, s. 99.
[1875] *Choc v Hudbay Minerals Inc.* 2013 ONSC 1414.
[1876] *Chandler v Cape plc* [2012] EWCA Civ 525.

Superior Court of Justice in *United Canadian Malt*.[1877] The defendant in *United Canadian Malt* was an American corporation with a Canadian subsidiary. The plaintiff alleged the parent corporation effectively controlled its subsidiary. The victim alleged that chemicals used on the Canadian subsidiary's property drifted into the plaintiff's property. Particularly, it was claimed that the American parent corporation management directed and controlled the clean-up of the subsidiary's property, had represented that it was responsible for the environmental problem that occurred as a result of improper environmental protection mechanisms by its subsidiary business, and had seized assets from the subsidiary after noticing the environmental contamination.[1878] Even though the Court was of the view that the plaintiff had an indisputable case for piercing the corporate veil and holding the parent corporation liable for the subsidiary's tort, the Court also suggested that the American parent corporation could be directly responsible for the fact that it had assumed responsibility for the environmental contamination issues.[1879]

The Ontario Superior Court of Justice considered this issue again in 2013 in *Hudbay Minerals*,[1880] which was another signal to strike the corporate veil. The claimants in *Hudbay Minerals* were indigenous Guatemalans who lived in a community where the Guatemalan subsidiary of Canadian Mining Corporation operated. The plaintiff claimed that a security company working for the Guatemalan subsidiary committed serious human rights violations, including rape and murder, when removing the indigenous residents from their own land for the purposes of the mining operation.[1881] The claimant brought an action against the Guatemalan subsidiary and the Canadian parent corporation.

The Superior Court refused to strike out the claim against the parent corporation. The Court specifically depended on the evidence that the parent corporation had made a public statement that it was committed to promoting human rights in its Guatemalan operations, including claiming to have conducted extensive training of security personnel, that led to a high

---

1877 Madeleine Conway, 'A New Duty of Care - Tort Liability from Voluntary Human Rights Due Diligence in Global Supply Chains' (2015) 40 (2) Queen's Law Journal 741.

1878 *United Canada Malt Ltd. v Outboard Marine Corp. of Canada* (n 1812).

1879 *Ibid.*

1880 Shin Imai, Valerie Crystal, and Bernadette Maheandiran, 'Access to Justice and Corporate Accountability: A Legal Case Study of HudBay in Guatemala' (2014) 35 (2) Canadian Journal of Development Studies/Revue canadienne d'études du development 285.

1881 *Ibid.*

expectation of adherence to human rights standards.[1882] The decision acknowledged that public statements by a corporation to protect a subsidiary can illustrate a relationship of proximity and assumption of responsibility.[1883] Consequently, liability for subsidiary misconduct is controlled by this similar concept. The relationship between the plaintiff and the defendant is important here also, as the court held that a high level of proximity is required before a duty of care is imposed. This works in two ways: either there is sufficient proximity between the defendant and the claimant that make it appropriate for the defendant to be liable when subsidiary causes harm to the claimant, or there is sufficient proximity between the defendant and the subsidiary. Likewise, the court should find a duty of care if there is a relationship of control and/or responsibility between the corporation and the subsidiary. Additionally, the corporation may be liable for the action of the subsidiary when either was involved in human rights violations that caused harm or have failed to abate a known human rights abuse by the subsidiary.

English Authority

Even though Canadian courts have yet to make a final determination on the direct liability of parent corporate responsibility, the English Court of Appeal recently affirmed in *Chandler* that under English law, a parent corporation may, in an appropriate situation, be directly liable for the subsidiary's workers.[1884] Even though the appropriate circumstance illustrated by the Court of Appeal are particularly related to the parent corporation and subsidiary relationship, the relevant parallels to the corporate duty of care in the tort of negligence are substantially the same.

The claimant in *Chandler* contracted asbestosis from exposure to dust while employed by Cape Products, a subsidiary of Cape Plc.[1885] The asbestos business was legally owned and operated by Cape Products, but Cape Plc maintained a significant level of control over Cape Products. Cape Plc was not responsible for executing the health and safety measures at Cape Products or for devising or implementing operational health and safety policies. Nonetheless, there was a fact to prove that Cape Plc was involved in specific problems relating to health and safety policy at Cape Products. Specifically, Cape Plc was engaged in a study of whether an employee

---

[1882]*Ibid.*
[1883]*Ibid.*
[1884]Martin Petrin, 'Assumption of Responsibility in Corporate Groups: Chandler v. Cape PLC' (2013) 76 (3) Modern Law Review 603.
[1885]*Ibid.*

diagnosed with asbestosis could continue to work in the corporation. The conclusion is that Cape Plc had a superior knowledge of the asbestos business because it operated its own asbestos factories and had greater knowledge and resources than Cape Products. Hence, Cape Plc was aware of the link between asbestos production and asbestosis because its group medical adviser was engaged in the study on this issue and was aware that Cape Products' asbestos business was carried out in a way that exposed the employee to the risk of health problems.[1886] The claimant brought a negligence claim against Cape Plc, contesting that it owed him the direct duty of care to advise on or ensure a safe work environment.[1887] The Court of Appeal upheld the plaintiff's claim.

What is relevant in *Chandler* is that there is a significant parallel between the amount of control the parent corporation has over its subsidiary's health and safety operations and the amount of control it has over some of its research regarding the employee, in comparison with the cases in the Ontario Superior Court. Reviewing these positions, the presumption is that a duty of care may exist in *Chandler*. Therefore, the court should use the appropriate human rights duty of care tests to determine the extent of the liability of the parent corporation.

Likewise, there could be a sufficient relationship to establish that the defendant has an ongoing involvement in the problem that is relevant to health and safety policy if the court applies the concept of proximity to the defendant's conduct. Thus, taking a more general approach, the corporate responsibility for on-the-ground implementation of health and safety policies and the management of human rights problem fulfil the three essential elements of imposing a duty of care, which include foreseeability, proximity, fairness, justness, and reasonability.

The Court of Appeal in *Chandler* also identified four factors relevant to a duty of care, two of which would be difficult to apply in a situation where the parent corporation does not engage with or have full control over the subsidiary's conduct.[1888] In summary to Cape Plc's involvement in Cape Products operations, the Court of Appeal concluded that 'in appropriate circumstance, the law may impose on a parent corporate responsibility for the health and safety of its subsidiary employee.'[1889] The

---

[1886]Charles Wild and Stuart Weinstein, *Smith and Keenan's Company Law* (Pearson Education 2013).

[1887]Robert McCorquodale, 'Waving Not Drowning: Kiobel Outside the United States' (2013) 107 (4) American Journal of International Law 846.

[1888]*Chandler v Cape plc* (n 2104).

[1889]*Ibid.*

Court then set out the four factors that, in the case before it, supported a duty of care:

1. the businesses of the parent and subsidiary are in a relevant respect the same;
2. the parent has, or ought to have, superior knowledge on the relevant aspect of health and safety in the particular industry;
3. the subsidiary's system of work is unsafe as the parent company knew, or ought to have known; and
4. the parent corporation knew or ought to have foreseen that the subsidiary or its employee would rely on its using that superior knowledge for the employee's protection[1890]

The Court of Appeal's first factor is the business operations of the parent and the subsidiary. The Court found that the business operations of the parent corporation were the same as the subsidiary, indicating that the parent corporation and the subsidiary operated as one, at least in regard to the relevant dangers posed by the nature of the business. However, in a critical analysis, it could be observed that the court did not intend such a high threshold. This is evidenced by the Court of Appeal's acceptance that health and safety was not, on the whole, centrally managed by Cape Plc.[1891]

The problem is whether Cape Plc was expected to take a step or give advice about the dangers of asbestos to the health of the employee working at the Cape Products factory, given that Cape Plc had involved itself in some of the health and safety policy. Another meaning of this is suggested by Sanger, who author stated that the parent corporation and subsidiary in *Chandler* produced the same product.[1892] However, this factor is not properly discussed in the judgment. Thus, it is difficult to see how the overlap in the business product is, of itself, vital to the establishment of a duty of care for the parent corporation. Having said that, if the Canadian court adopts this factor in a parent corporation and in a subsidiary context, it should satisfy a duty of care claim, where the parent corporation's business is the same as the subsidiary's.

The second challenging factor from *Chandler* concerns asymmetrical information that a parent corporation has or should have had, and superior knowledge of some aspect of health and safety in the specific

---

[1890] *Ibid.*

[1891] *Ibid.*

[1892] Andrew Sanger, 'Crossing the Corporate Veil: The Duty of Care Owed By a Parent Company to The Employees of Its Subsidiary' (2012) 71 (3) Cambridge Law Journal 478.

industry.[1893] A typical example of asymmetrical information would be where a defendant corporation knows more about the danger of a specific piece of equipment than its subsidiary. Nonetheless, the asymmetric information would not be present where the defendant corporation had allegedly failed to monitor or respond to a danger associated with the work or working environment. It is argued here that the purpose of the asymmetric information factor in the English Court of Appeal's reasoning was to limit its duty of care to a situation where it should have been obvious to the defendant that the relevant corporation would not address the risk unless the defendant intervened, which is relevant to a duty of care claim.

For that reason, it must be stressed that the Court of Appeal did not frame the four factors in *Chandler* as a requirement, but rather as an example of the situation, where it is appropriate to find a duty of care.[1894] Furthermore, when addressing a parent corporation and its subsidiary's relationship it may be appropriate for a court to find a duty of care even though not all of the factors observed in *Chandler* will be present. Specifically, if there is evidence of a high degree of control and involvement by the parent corporation in the subsidiary's business operation, it will be perfect for the court to seek the basic principle of duty of care, in order to arrive at a moral and legally justifiable conclusion. Recognition of a duty to avoid harm to a person or his property raises no unique problem of the neighbourhood principle in *Donoghue v Stevenson*,[1895]as it established the principle of finding a duty of care.

The Application of Duty of Care in Shell Nigeria Litigation

The Hague District Court recently rejected an attempt by Nigerian fisherman and farmers to apply the *Chandler* decision to three cases against Shell parent companies in situations similar to the Shell Nigeria litigation.[1896] The claimant in the Shell Nigeria lawsuit claims that they suffered harm due to oil pollution from installations operated by Shell in Nigeria and brought a lawsuit against two Shell parent companies, as well

---

[1893]*Chandler v Cape Plc* [2012] EWCA Civ 525.

[1894]*Ibid.*

[1895]*Donoghue v Stevenson* [1932] UKHL 100.

[1896]*A.F. Akpan v Royal Dutch Shell Plc*, NO C/09/337050/HA/ ZA 09-158 (Netherland), *Dooh v Royal Shell Plc*, No, NoC/09/337058 HA ZA 09-1581 (Netherland) and *Oguru v Royal Dutch Shell Plc*, No C/09?330891/ HA ZA 09 057.

as Shell Nigeria a subsidiary.[1897] What is interesting in the case is that The Hague Court applied Nigerian law, but depended on English jurisprudence, specifically *Chandler*. The claimant argued that the Shell parent corporations owed a duty of care because they were aware of the risk of the oil spillage in Nigeria[1898] and had publicly announced that they intended to prevent oil spillages in Nigeria, and in practice exercised influence on the subsidiary in Nigeria.[1899]

The Hague District Court found those factors were insufficient to give rise to a duty of care for five reasons:

1. The relationship between the parent corporation and the workers of its local subsidiary (as in *Chandler*) was not closer than the relationship between a parent corporation and a person living in the community where a local subsidiary carries out its business activities;[1900]
2. Shell's subsidiary was indirectly responsible for the oil spillage, as the court found the oil spillage was caused by sabotage,[1901] whereas in *Chandler* the subsidiary had directly harmed its workers by allowing them to work in a dangerous environment, that have caused harm to their health;[1902]
3. The business of the parent corporations and the subsidiary were not fundamentally the same because the parent corporations created general policy guidelines and were involved in a global strategy and risk management, whereas the subsidiary was involved solely in oil production in Nigeria;[1903]
4. It was not clear that the Shell parent corporations had more knowledge regarding the specific dangers of the oil spillage than the local subsidiary, which was directly engaged with the business operations in Nigeria;[1904] and

---

[1897]Liesbeth Enneking, 'Future of Foreign Direct Liability: Exploring the International Relevance of the Dutch Shell Nigeria Case' (2014) 10 Utrecht Law Review 44.
[1898] Judith Schrempf-Stirling and Florian Wettstein, 'Beyond Guilty Verdicts: Human Rights Litigation and Its Impact on Corporations' Human Rights Policies' (2015) Journal of Business Ethics 1, 18.
[1899]*Ibid.*
[1900]Lee J McConnell, 'Establishing Liability for Multinational Oil Companies in Parent/Subsidiary Relationships' (2014) 16 (1) Environmental Law Review 50.
[1901]*A.F. Akpan v Royal Dutch Shell Plc* (n 2140).
[1902]*Ibid.*
[1903]*Ibid.*
[1904]*Ibid.*

5. Because the Nigerian subsidiary was the party on the ground with the greatest awareness of local conditions, it was not clear why the community would rely on the parent corporation to protect them from oil spillage.[1905]

However, this study argues that the Hague District Court issued the judgment and interpretation of *Chandler* principles incorrectly. It did not correctly apply the principle of duty of care, or the concepts of foreseeability, proximity, and fair, just and reasonable to impose a duty of care on the parent corporation. The appropriate question for the court is to ask is: whether at any time, Shell exercised control over the subsidiary, both financial and in terms of the sharing of business knowledge; and did Shell assume responsibility at any time for the operation of the oil project in Nigeria?

Perhaps, if the court had asked the appropriate questions in this circumstance, they would have found that Shell did owe a duty of care to the subsidiary company and the plaintiff. This point is reached because another way someone can assume responsibility for the wellbeing of someone else is by actions or by doing nothing. What someone does in relation to someone else can indicate, by conduct, an assumption of responsibility. A clear example can be seen in the English case of *Barrett v Ministry of Defence* (MOD). Here the MOD was liable, but not through breach of a duty of care, for preventing the plaintiff becoming dangerously intoxicated. Until the deceased became unconscious, he alone carried the legal responsibility for his own actions. However, once the senior officer assumed a responsibility for him by ordering the petty officer to look after him a duty of care did arise. He was in breach of this duty by failing to ensure the deceased received the appropriate supervision.[1906]

Shell knew about the subsidiary's misconduct and knew about the danger posed by oil spillages. That is why it has developed a global strategy and policy to deal with the problem. Shell benefits from the subsidiary's business activities and has greater knowledge about the dangers and the protective guidelines for oil spillages; therefore, there is a presumption that Shell should owe a duty of care and that it is fair, just and reasonable to impose liability on Shell.

Also, in terms of turning a blind eye to the risk of an oil spillage, the established English case *Goldman v Hargrave* illustrates a similar idea. Here, a tree caught fire after being struck by lightning. The landowner

---

[1905] *Ibid.*

[1906] *Barrett v MOD* [1995] 1 WLR 1217.

ensured that the tree was cut down, but decided to let it burn itself out and took no further precaution to stop the fire from spreading. As a result, although he had not caused the fire, in deciding not to take any further steps to completely extinguish it he had adopted the risk that it might spread. Extensive damage was caused to a neighbouring property when the fire was revived by the wind and spread. The Privy Council found that a duty of care was owed in relation to adopted danger existing on one's land when that danger could spread to a neighbouring land.[1907]

The final question is: what did Shell do and not do. Answering this question could prove a vital point in the case. The court judgment lacks legal standing and moral merit in relation to the principle of a duty of care. Nonetheless, the Shell Nigeria lawsuit has limited persuasive value for a duty of care claim because it was decided by a Dutch Court applying English law via Nigerian law. Furthermore, the Dutch Court's reasoning is very confusing and lacks an understanding of the concept of the tort of negligence in three ways: 1. The Court appears to have treated the collection of factors identified in *Chandler* as mandatory and applied it incorrectly, rather than as guidelines to find a duty of care in an appropriate circumstance, as they were framed by the English Court of Appeal;[1908] 2. The difference between an offshore parent corporation and a local subsidiary is not supported by *Chandler*, therefore, the court should have resorted to the basic principle of finding a duty of care, as established in *Caparo*; and 3. The indirect cause of the oil spillage should not be relevant in assessing whether the parent corporation has a duty of care to take steps to prevent oil spillages as a result of its subsidiary's negligent operations.

The Dutch Court should have considered *Chandler* as part of Shell's breach of the duty of care. Considering the facts in the judgment, the Shell Nigeria lawsuit illustrates, at most, the factual difficulty in establishing a duty of care where a third party has caused harm to society and also has a degree of responsibility to protect the claimant. Consequently, for a corporation to be exempt or escape liability, its conduct must meet the standard of reasonable care. Accordingly, a corporation will breach the duty of care where their conduct falls below the standard the law set for all actors (the neighbourhood principle). The requirement that the corporation will be liable for the tort of negligence only where it has failed to exercise reasonable care suggests that negligence liability is premised and dependent on fault. For that reason, a claim should be successful if the plaintiff is able

[1907] *Goldman v Hargrave* [1967] Ch 645 Privy Council A 100.
[1908] *Chandler v Cape plc* [2012] EWCA Civ 525.

to establish the fault, and the essential elements of tort explained at the beginning of the chapter.

The Application of Duty of Care in The Ninth Circuit Court's Decision in *Doe I v Wal-Mart Stores*

The US Ninth Circuit Court's judgment in *Wal-Mart Stores* is the only decision to consider the duty of care to protect employees' rights in subsidiary business operations in America. However, this research argues that the Ninth Circuit Court's decision is in conflict with the undertakings to protect a contractual duty and inconsistent with the principle of duty of care. The claimants in *Wal-Mart Stores* were employed by Wal-Mart's subsidiaries in a number of countries such as China, Bangladesh, Indonesia, Swaziland, and Nicaragua.[1909] Wal-Mart's contract with the subsidiaries included a code of conduct requiring the subsidiaries to comply with the labour laws and industry standards set out in the Wal-Mart Standards.[1910]

The subsidiaries' contracts also provided that Wal-Mart would strictly monitor the labour law and industry standards, including on-site inspections of production facilities.[1911] The failure of the subsidiary to comply with these standards could result in Wal-Mart ending the contractual relationship. Also, the subsidiaries' contracts further required the subsidiaries to post local language copies of the Wal-Mart Standards in their workplaces.

Examining Wal-Mart's conduct, it is clear that the corporation had control over its subsidiaries and had assumed responsibility. Its failure to act to enforce these standards resulted in the creation of risks (i.e. human rights violations). In assessing the Ninth Circuit Court's judgment, the court depended on the California Supreme Court's summary of the principle of negligent undertaking in *Delgado v Trax Bar and Grill*, which concluded that 'a volunteer who, having no initial duty to do so, undertakes to provide protective services to another, will be found to have a duty to exercise due care in the performance of that undertakings if one of the two conditions is met: either 1.'[1912] 'the volunteer's failure to exercise such care increases the

[1909] *Wal-Mart Stores* (n 2011).
[1910] *Ibid.*
[1911] *Ibid.*
[1912] *Ibid.*

risk of harm to the person, or 2. the other person reasonably relies upon the volunteer's'[1913] 'undertakings and suffer injury as a result'.[1914]

As noted, the test overlaps significantly with the duty of care requirement for the third party under the English legal system or the reasonable man test rule. The Ninth Circuit Court focused on the initial problem of whether Wal-Mart had undertaken to provide a service to the claimant.[1915] Wal-Mart contested that this required a clear, express and active undertaking.[1916] Similarly, in the initial decision, the Ninth Circuit Court had rejected a different claim based on the third party beneficiary of the contract, arguing that Wal-Mart had simply reserved the right to inspect its subsidiary's workplace, but had not adopted a duty to inspect the factory. This was the court's initial finding, because the contract contained consequences for a subsidiary failing an inspection, but contained no consequence for Wal-Mart if it did not fulfil its contractual claims.[1917] This is very contradictory. It appears that the Ninth Circuit Court treated the claimant as negligent for undertaking the case essentially as a repeat of this third party beneficiary claim. It asserted that 'Wal-Mart merely reserved the right to cancel its supply contract if the inspection revealed contractual breaches by the supplier'.[1918] It seems that the court was of the view that any inspection carried out by Wal-Mart did not distort the conclusion as there was no duty to inspect, so any inspection carried out was gratuitous.[1919]

The fundamental flaw in the judgment is that the decision that there was no undertaking is surprising given that Wal-Mart publicly stated that the basic objective of its Factory Certificate Program, which it used to implement the Wal-Mart Standards, was to enhance the implementation of the necessary steps that would lead to the improvement of human rights standards for the employees who worked in its subsidiary's factory.

The *Wal-Mart Stores* case shows how difficult it is to establish a duty of care in corporate negligence conduct. It also shows the jurisprudential

---

1913 <https://www.queensu.ca/lawjournal/sites/webpublish.queensu.ca.qljwww/files/files/issues/10-Conway.pdf> Accessed 9 March 2017.

1914 *Delgado v Trax Bar & Grill* (2005) 36 C.4th 224 and *Ann M. v Pacific Plaza Shopping Centre* (1993) 6 C.4th 666, 25 C.R.2d 137, 863 P.2d 207, 6 *Summary* (10th), *Torts*, §1136, *Hassoon v Shamieth* (2001) 89 C.A.4th 1191, 107 C.R.2d 658 and *Isaacs v Huntington Memorial Hosp* (1985) 38 C.3d 112, 211 C.R. 356, 695 P.2d 653, 6 *Summary* (10th), *Torts*, §1134.

1915 *Wal-Mart Stores* (n 2201).

1916 *Ibid.*

1917 *Ibid.*

1918 *Ibid.*

1919 *Wal-Mart Stores* (n 2210). (Appellant's Reply Brief at para 48).

differences and the different interpretations of the concept of duty of care, but, the indication in this study suggests that the courts in America and the Netherlands have failed to establish *prima facie* legal justification for not finding a duty of care. In further analysis, it also found that the court applied the legal concept of a duty of care incorrectly. Duty of care should not be restricted or limited to particular contractual obligations but should be seen and examined through control, knowledge and conduct. Likewise, the Ninth Circuit Court did not consider whether the claimant relied on the undertakings in dismissing the lawsuit. This problem was briefly addressed in the hearing as well as from the bench during the oral argument. However, the duty of care should have required Wal-Mart to take reasonable steps to assess whether their conduct could lead to violations of rights or contribute to it, which it had failed to do. On the point of law, a duty of care could be said to exist. In certain situations, the relationship between the corporation and the subsidiary should meet the requirement for the three tests to impose a duty of care, especially where it is established that the defendant had sufficient control over the risk of human rights abuse of the claimant in the workplace.

Nonetheless, in England and Canada there is no threshold question of whether the corporation has assumed responsibility or undertaken to protect the claimant. However, such an argument can be negated, as the question is whether there is sufficient proximity between the plaintiff and the defendant. The UK House of Lords has addressed this point, 'holding that assumption of responsibility simply means that the law recognises that there is a duty of care. It is not so much that responsibility is assumed as that it is recognised or imposed by the law'.[1920] The Ninth Circuit Court considered that the employee duty of care claim was answered by the fact that there was no contractual duty to protect them,[1921] whereas the UK and Canada courts do not require a contractual duty or legal relationship to find a duty of care, even in a duty to act case or where the loss happened indirectly.[1922] An example is the case of *Godwin*, where the British Columbia Court of Appeal did not limit the defendant contractor's duty to protect simply because it had not contracted to remove the ice from the specific part of the road.[1923]

[1920] *Phelps v Hillingdon* [2001] 2 AC 619.

[1921] *Wal-Mart Stores* (n 1700).

[1922] Allen Linden and Bruce Feldthusen, *Canadian Tort Law* (8th ed. Markham: LexisNexis Butterworths 2006) 568.

[1923] *Goodwin v British Columbia (Superintendent of Motor Vehicles)* [2015] 3 SCR 250.

Finally, to some extent, the UK Court of Appeal's decision in *Chandler*, concerning direct parent liability to a subsidiary, set out a clear guideline for a future duty of care claim to follow. This research suggests that future corporate human rights violations decisions should follow the development in the UK Court of Appeal and the Neighbourhood Principle. Corporations must take reasonable care to avoid harming those to whom the harm can be reasonably foreseeable. Lord Atkin makes no reference to the specific type of damage in relation to whether a duty of care may arise or how the damage may be caused. The concept of duty of care suggests that if it was to be applied correctly to the above cases, then, the presumption would be that a reputable duty of care arises in these cases and the parent corporation should have been found liable for the misconduct of their subsidiaries and effective remedy should be awarded.

What is evident in all these cases is that the defendants could be said to owe a duty of care to the victim for the subsidiaries' misconduct. This also means the defendant's conduct falls below a certain standard: the standard of the reasonable care exercised by the corporation. Accordingly, a defendant breaches their duty of care where their conduct falls below the standards that have been set, and they should be liable for the harm caused. It is further suggested that the judgment of Equion Energia '(In July 2005 a group of Colombian farmers instituted proceedings in the English High Court against BP Exploration Company (Colombia) alleging that the construction of an oil pipeline by OCENSA (a consortium led by BP) caused severe environmental damage to their lands. In particular, the farmers claimed that the pipeline cut across key water sources which resulted in soil erosion, spoiled crops and fishponds being starved of water. Further, they alleged that BP, while not directly involved, benefited from the activities of paramilitaries employed to guard the pipeline.)'[1924] and Xstrata Ltd (A case brought by 22 indigenous Peruvians who allege human rights violations perpetrated by the Peruvian police for which they allege Xstrata Ltd (London) and its Peruvian subsidiary, Xstrata Tintaya S.A, should be held liable; two of the protestors were killed and a number of them were severely injured, assaulted and unlawfully detained by the Peruvian police during a

[1924] <ttps://www.businesshumanrights.org/en/Categories/Lawlawsuits/Lawsuitsregulatoryaction/LawsuitsSelectedcases/RioTintolawsuitrePapuaNewGuinea/?sort_on=effective> Accessed 02 March 2016 and also see: Philipp Wesche and Miriam Saage-Maass,'Holding Companies Liable for Human Rights Abuses Related to Foreign Subsidiaries and Suppliers before German Civil Courts: Lessons from Jabir and Others v KiK' (2016) 16 (2) Human Rights Law Review 370, 385.

protest at the Tintaya copper mine in May 2012.)[1925] and Vedanta (The UK's Supreme Court handed Vedanta Resources a lifeline in its bid to overturn previous court decisions which found that Zambian residents living near its operations were entitled to have their claims against the mining group's subsidiary heard in the UK. Some 1,826 Zambian residents say pollution from Konkola Copper Mines (KCM), which Vedanta owns, damaged their livelihoods. The High Court said the matter could be heard in the UK – a decision supported by the Court of Appeal. The latest judgement by the Supreme Court, however, finds that Vedanta can appeal the Court of Appeal's decision.)[1926] should follow the principle of duty of care laid down in this study.

This principle will allow the courts to be able to find a corporate duty of care without any jurisdiction or corporate impunity impediment. Also, courts in the past have proved a duty of care by using the '*but for test*', hence this not a new, developing concept. In cases from other jurisdictions raising the issue of the inability to prove which of two negligent defendants actually caused harm, the court long ago found another novel way to circumvent a duty of care impediment by using the '*but for test*'. In the US case of *Summers v Tice* [1927] and the similar Canadian case of *Cook v Levis*,[1928] the court shifted the burden of proof to the defendant. Shifting the burden of proof meant that the court asked the defendant to prove that he was not responsible and if neither could do this then, the court could hold both to be accountable. This means that if a parent corporation claims it was not liable or did not owe a duty of care, then the court can also resort to the '*but for test*' and impose a duty of care on both parties (meaning the parent corporation should be liable for the subsidiary's harm). In these circumstances, it is fair, just, and reasonable to impose liability on the parent corporation. This principle will also allow the court to examine the core context of corporate conduct and liability finding. It will also allow the court to pierce the corporate veil in certain circumstances when it is fair, just, and reasonable to impose a duty of care on the parent corporation.

[1925]Jonathan Kishen Gamu and Peter Dauvergne,'The Slow Violence of Corporate Social Responsibility: the Case of Mining in Peru' (2018) 39 (5) Third World Quarterly 959, 975.

[1926]Ekaterina Aristova, 'Tort Litigation against Transnational Corporations in the English Courts: The Challenge of Jurisdiction' (2018)14 (2) Utrecht Law Review.

[1927]*Summers v Tice*, 33 Cal.2d 80, 199 P.2d 1 (1948).

[1928]*Cook v Lewis* [1951] SCR 830.

Problematic Aspect of Duty of Care

Courts must decide, through the fundamental concept of duty of care, whether a defendant owes the claimant a duty not to cause harm. Therefore, if a *prima facie* duty of care is found, the next question for the court to ask is whether there is an outstanding policy issue to suggest that a duty of care should not be recognised or should be restricted. Possible policy issues include international politics, international relations, the opening the floodgate argument, deterring corporations from engaging in business operations with subsidiaries abroad, the existence of another avenue of judicial remedy, economic concerns and intrusion on the sovereignty of states in the country where the corporation conducts its business. These concerns will only negate the *prima facie* duty of care if they are compelling and a real potential for negative consequence is apparent, but it should not stop the court from finding a duty of care and awarding an appropriate remedy for the victims.

Floodgate

The most commonly relied on policy to deny a duty of care is that it would open the floodgates to an indeterminate number of similar claims at court.[1929] Even though this has served as an obstacle in many negligence claims, the proposed duty of care here, however, would not carry 'risk of liability for an indeterminate amount for an indeterminate time to an indeterminate class'.[1930] This is because a breach of the duty of care will lead to heavy sanctions and remedies for human rights violations. As a result, it will force the corporation to abandon business conduct or policy that will give rise to a breach of the duty of care. It will also promote good business practice and force the corporation to only conduct business with a subsidiary that respects and enforces human rights standards, as the corporation will know that it will be liable for the future misconduct of the subsidiary.

In the *prima facie* duty of care analysis above, a corporation will only owe a duty of care in its business operation with a subsidiary where it has indirectly or directly assumed responsibility or has controlled, created or contributed to the human rights violation. The floodgate argument would be more compelling if the duty of care was not required to establish proximity because a corporation would then owe a duty of care to everyone

---

[1929] *Hill v Hamilton-Wentworth Regional Police Services Boar* (1399).
[1930] *Ibid.*

in society, rather than only the victim that may have been affected by the misconduct. Nonetheless, even in this case, the proposed duty of care would be restricted to situations where there is a significant economic relationship between the corporation and its subsidiary. The corporation could constrain its exposure by making accurate and demonstrable facts about the extent to which it was involved in the subsidiary's operation, exercised control and protected human rights in the subsidiary's business activities.

Deterring Human Rights Violation in Corporation Business Operations

A more compelling policy concern is one that recognises that this duty of care would deter corporations from taking on the protective role in subsidiaries' business operations. However, this study argues the contrary and observes that a duty of care will promote good business practices and human rights standards. This argument was put forward in *Hudbay Minerals* '(On 28 March 2011 a group of 11 Guatemalan women filed a lawsuit in the Superior Court in Ontario, Canada, against Hudbay Minerals and its subsidiary HMI Nickel Inc. The women alleged that the companies were complicit in the gang rapes suffered by the women at the hands of security personnel hired by the defendant companies.'[1931] 'The women claim that the gang rapes occurred in January 2007 during forced evictions of members of the Mayan Q'eqchi' community living in El Estor. The companies' nickel mining project – the Fenix project – is located in El Estor. Members of this community have challenged the legitimacy of the mining concession granted for the Fenix project. Hudbay Minerals says it will vigorously defend itself against the allegations of rape).'[1932] Tort liability would be unlikely to put extreme responsibility on corporations. It will only impose a duty of care on corporations where their conduct is below what is seen as unreasonable in the eyes of the law and court, and where a corporation has foreseen that its conduct will violate human rights, yet still continues with its despicable business conduct.

Most importantly, a duty of care arises from a human rights violation in its subsidiary, where it has control, has assumed responsibility, or has created or contributed to the harm. Nonetheless, corporations are encouraged to carry out meaningful human rights policies and practices in all their business operations. A typical example is Nike, which has now

---

[1931]<https://www.business-humanrights.org/en/latest-news/hudbay-minerals-lawsuits-re-guatemala/#c74504> Accessed 13 August 2017.
[1932]*Choc v Hudbay Minerals Inc.* (n 2153).

arguably become an industry leader in addressing human rights problems in its subsidiary operations.[1933] The issue of effective human rights standards has the possibility to deter corporations from engaging with human rights standards and lacks effective remedy. More generally, there is not one single piece of empirical evidence to support the idea that a corporation will step back from a human rights responsibility initiative following the Nike litigation.[1934]

Other Avenue for Corporate Human Rights Liability

Another potential policy issue is whether an existing mechanism provides a sufficient path for a remedy for corporate human rights violations.[1935] As observed above, corporations that falsely claim to regulate human rights in their subsidiary business operations could potentially be liable to the investors and other stakeholders in society. Likewise, the workers and the communities that could allege that the corporation has failed to comply with the human rights standards are recognised universally by the international community. However, following the indication in ***Chapter III*** and the argument throughout this study, none of the existing instruments would provide an effective remedy to the victim that has suffered a loss due to a corporation's negligent conduct in its business operations with a subsidiary. Accordingly, it is unlikely that the existence of these instruments would be sufficient to displace a *prima facie* duty of care for victims of corporate human rights abuses.

Economic Concerns

The proposed corporate duty of care here could arguably have negative repercussions for international business. This argument was raised

---

[1933]Nicole Deitelhoff and Klaus Dieter Wolf, 'Business and Human Rights: How Corporate Norm Violators Become Norm Entrepreneurs' in Risse T, Ropp S.C. and Sikkink K (eds), *The Persistent Power of Human Rights: From Commitment to Compliance* (Cambridge University Press 2013).

[1934]David Hess and Thomas W Dunfee, 'The Kasky-Nike Threat to Corporate Social Reporting: Implementing a Standard of Optimal Truthful Disclosure as a Solution' (2007) 17 (1) Business Ethics Quarterly 5.

[1935]*Elliott v Insurance Crime Prevent Bureau*, 2005 NSCA 115 at para 84, 256 DLR (4th) 674.

by the US Chamber of Commerce, an amicus in the *Wal-Mart Stores* case.[1936] The Chamber argued that:

> If such as Plaintiffs' were actionable, companies operating in the United States will face a new burden in doing business overseas. Every time they entered into a commercial arrangement with a foreign company or in a foreign locale, they might be exposing themselves to potential liability, even when their action like the Defendant's, in this case, are far removed from alleged harm. A retailer like a defendant, which stocks myriad types of merchandise, has thousands of suppliers in countries all over the globe. Controlling labour practice of all of these companies is simply impossible. In addition to the immediate harms to global companies, secondary harms will likely fall on consumers in the form of higher prices, as companies attempt to pass on their extra cost.[1937]

Nonetheless, this contention will be ignored here because of the fact that the proposed duty of care would reflect only on the level of control the corporation has over its subsidiary and the particular relationship between the corporations and their subsidiaries' business operations. Likewise, the study contested that if the level of control is internationally erased, the court should exercise discretion in order to find a novel duty of care. Additionally, the proposed duty of care will not impose an absolute duty on the corporations to guarantee the human rights of the employees and the communities in which the subsidiary operates. Therefore, it is wholly appropriate to state that the proposed duty of care may increase the operational cost for a corporation who operates overseas, but the increased costs are only borne by the consumer and investors. Therefore, the corporation does not need to bear the cost for respecting human rights. As also observed by the former Supreme Court Justice Binnie, 'ordinary tort doctrine would call for the losses to allocate the ultimate cost of the products and borne by the consumers who benefit them, not disproportionately by the farmers and peasants of the Third World.'[1938]

Impediment of State Sovereignty on Duty of Care

The last policy argument is that it is not the jurisdiction of home state courts to regulate the human rights conduct of subsidiaries in the host

[1936] Anita Chan, 'Walmart Workers in China' (2008) Globalization & the Workplace 437.

[1937] *Wal-Mart Stores DC* (n 1700).

[1938] Ian Binnie, 'Judging and Judges; May the Boldly Go Where Ivan Rand Went Before' (2013) 26 (1) Canadian Journal of Law & Jurisprudence 5.

states. The general issue arising from human rights duty of care is the tension between the sovereignty of the states that the subsidiaries operate in and duties of the home states to uphold human rights in their jurisdictions. This tension can be seen in the recent stalemate over factory safety in Bangladesh between the Bangladeshi government and two subsidiary collectives that were created following the Rana Plaza building disaster.[1939]

Nevertheless, it is the corporations themselves that run the risk of intruding on state sovereignty by undertaking to carry out a voluntary human rights duty to respect human rights, as well as forcing states to reduce their human rights standards.[1940] Thus, the enforceability of such undertakings by victims of human rights violations in a home state court would not substantially aggravate this intrusion on sovereignty. In certain cases, it may be inappropriate for the home state court to refuse to hear human rights violations that are linked with parent corporations within its jurisdictions. Therefore, the duty of care has no significant bearing on the sovereignty of the state. This problem can be dealt with on a case-by-case basis.

The Evidence Supporting the Imposition of a Duty of Care

The problem discussed above must be balanced against policy matters that support the imposition of a duty of care.[1941] First, the imposition of a duty of care could deter corporations from turning a blind eye to human rights violations in its business operations and would additionally stop corporations from aiding and abetting human rights violations, as well as deterring corporations from falsely claiming to protect human rights in their business operations. Conversely, it will also encourage corporations to carry out more effective human rights and environmental impact assessments. This is consistent with the principle of tort law, which includes a disincentive to risk-creating behaviour.[1942] It is also consistent with the acknowledgement that corporations should carry out subsidiary human rights assessments and the general international commitment to promoting responsible business practices in the host states in which corporations carry out their operations.[1943]

[1939]Steven Greenhouse and Julfikar Ali Manik, 'Stalemate over Garment Factory Safety in Bangladesh' *New York Times* (New York, 25 June 2014).
[1940]Andrew Clapham, *Human Rights Obligations of Non-State Actors* (Oxford: OUP 2006).
[1941]*Choc v Hudbay Minerals Inc.* (n 2153).
[1942]*Resurfice Corp. v Hanke* [2007] 1 S.C.R. 333.
[1943]Radu Mares, ed. *The UN Guiding Principles on Business and Human Rights: Foundations and Implementation* (Martinus Nijhoff Publishers 2011).

Furthermore, imposing a duty of care would also provide a remedy in a situation where the plaintiff would otherwise be denied a remedy or justice for harm resulting from the negligent conduct of a parent corporation and its subsidiary, which is also the primary objective of tort law. Lastly, a defendant corporation would have benefited from the subsidiary's human rights abuses in its business operations, before a duty of care could be imposed. However, in the absence of control over, creation of, or contribution to the human rights violations, then the corporation should be given the benefit of the doubt without imposing a duty of care on them.

Summary

There are calls for binding obligations for corporations to respect human rights.[1944] This is formally highlighted in voluntary mechanisms such as the Guiding Principles,[1945] the OECD Guidelines,[1946] the ILO Tripartite Declaration of Principles Concerning Multinational Enterprises and Social Policy,[1947] the SA800 Standards,[1948] and now the proposed UN Binding Treaty on Transnational Corporations and Other Business Enterprises with Respect to Human Rights.[1949] The duty proposed in this book is much narrower. It would require corporations to ensure their conduct does not cause harm to those who could be affected by their business conduct; hence, it would only impose an obligation on a corporation whose conduct falls below the reasonable man standard. Additionally, the requirement of proximity would likely limit the number of

---

[1944]Cindy S Woods, 'It Isn't a State Problem: The Minas Conga Mine Controversy and The Need for Binding International Obligations on Corporate Actors' (2014) 46 Georgetown Journal of International Law 629.

[1945] United Nations, *Guiding Principles on Business and Human Rights: Implementing The United Nations 'Protect, Respect and Remedy' Framework* (UN 2008).

[1946]Elisa Morgera, 'OECD Guidelines for Multinational Enterprises' in Hale T and Held D, eds, *Handbook of Transnational Governance: Institutions and Innovations* (2011).

[1947]Hans Gunter, *Tripartite Declaration of Principles Concerning Multinational Enterprises and Social Policy (History, Contents, Follow-up and Relationship with Relevant Instruments of Other Organisations)* (No. 214282. International Labour Organization 1981).

[1948]Social Accountability International, 'SA8000 Standard Documents' (2014). <http://www.sa-intl.org/index.cfm?fuseaction=Page.ViewPage&PageID=937> Accessed 26 December 2016.

[1949]United Nations General Assembly, Doc A/HRC/RES/26/9 (2014). <https://www.ihrb.org/pdf/G1408252.pdf> Accessed 26 December 2016.

successful claims of victims of human rights abuses, as the victims would need to establish that the corporation foresaw the harm, establish the proximity between the victims and the corporation, and establish whether it was fair, just, and reasonable to impose a duty of care. However, it is argued here that this requirement should not be mandatory when it is absolutely clear that the corporation knows what it is doing or should have known what it ought to do and what it ought not to do. The court should in these cases find a novel duty of care.

In the right circumstances, tort law provides an effective remedy for victims who have suffered as a result of corporate negligence. The scope of the duty of care should expand through modification to incorporate the obligations which may arise in the proposed UN Binding Treaty on Transnational Corporations and Other Business Enterprises with Respect to Human Rights to reflect on the development of tort law and the reality of the global economy. Nonetheless, a duty of care could also promote effective subsidiary respect for human rights standards in business operations. Finally, tort law may, therefore, have a significant role to play in promoting the accountability of corporations for their human rights impact in the global economy more than the UN Binding Treaty on Transnational Corporations and Other Business Enterprises with Respect to Human Rights. Lastly, it is important for the courts to first consider the question of liability in light of the general principles of tort law and the theory of negligence, which is to impose liability for omissions parsimoniously. This demonstrates that the position of corporations can be considered without resorting to special immunities. This will allow the corporation to be held liable for most human rights violations caused by omissions. Therefore, the human rights law underlying the reluctance to impose liability for omissions in negligence more generally should be considered in the light of the human rights duty of care.

CONCLUSION

In conclusion, this book has attempted to analyse the concept of accountability by critically examining the literal and legal definitions of accountability. It draws on empirical information from a wide range of literal and legal literature on the concept of accountability. It examines the functioning of the literal and legal meaning of accountability, accountability systems, and relevant regimes. Adopting this approach to corporate accountability allows the book to lay down a theoretical concept for the study by focusing on the substantive legal and practical issues that have an impact on the effectiveness of accountability and judicial mechanisms in achieving corporate accountability and effective remedy in cases of business-related human rights exploitations, with a particular emphasis on corporate accountability under tort law.

Accountability in this theoretical framework for responsibility consists of liability, effective sanction, and remedy. An implication of this is that the flaws in the current liability for human rights violations, effective sanction, and remedy have presented an opportunity for the study in this book to include the enforcement of accountability, responsibility, and remedy – as well as enforcement mechanisms – into corporate human rights obligations under the concept of a duty of care. Adopting this explanation, it was possible to seek to improve the concept of corporate accountability with a notion of effective liability and enforcement.

The approach this study adopted emphasised a dynamic accountability mechanism that is accessible and can be updated and improved through the concept of the rule of law and through social changes. Likewise, it is intended to support the victims of human rights violations to enforce their rights and to encourage corporations to be involved in the sharing and exchange of responsibility with regards to the outcomes of human rights abuse cases. The book concluded that using this concept of accountability with the other overarching objective can ensure victims of human rights violations obtain the justice to which they are entitled, irrespective of who committed the abuse. However, this is very difficult to achieve in practice. Thus, it was suggested that a detailed analysis of the criminal and civil law accountability mechanism was required for further clarification of accountability under tort law. As a result, the book moved on to focus on the alternate forms of liability in tort law.

Following the analysis and definition of accountability, the research extracted the components of accountability through the definition of the notion of liability, which allows a better understanding of the practical concept of accountability (the practical concept of accountability in this context is referred to as responsibility, answerability, blameworthiness, liability, and sanctions).

Also, the idea that emerges from the book is one that can be subjected to an intense debate with regards to the concept of corporate human rights accountability and what it actually means in practice. The difficulties are the rocky connections between the appropriate procedural rights and the desire to provide an effective remedy for victims of international human rights violations.

In this rationale, international criminal law has failed to offer an appropriate system of accountability in both dimensions, namely accountability for the crime and remedy for the victims of human rights abuses. However, on the other hand, one could have thought there would be no reason to balance these two dimensions, as they coexist. Also, in the practical world, it can be argued that there is a trade-off between what constitutes accountability for international crimes and remedy for victims of human rights violations. Viewing international criminal law through these two dimensions of accountability for crime and remedy for human rights violations helps to clarify the process and the mechanism that needs to be implemented to ensure effective accountability; for example, the integration of both criminal and tort elements to ensure effective accountability.

This is because an attempt to restore the dignity of a victim of human rights violations and to provide them, or their relatives, with the appropriate forum, such as Tribunal or Court, to express their pain is, of course, a noble desire. Likewise, it is also significantly useful in reducing human rights violations as it has the potential to prevent future violations. It also gives victims the right to tell their stories in front of a judge, which also helps the judges in the chamber to gain a better understanding of the event on which they are required to pass judgment. Hence, there is no doubt that the international criminal legal system has fulfilled some of these elements. However, one needs to bear in mind that the problem of enforcing human rights has always been a challenge for the international community and legal system. Nonetheless, international criminal law provides some form of access to justice and enhances the effectiveness of bringing a legal proceeding against individuals who have violated human rights. Conversely, it should not be underestimated that international criminal law lacks on many grounds, such as enforcement, compliance, cooperation, effective prosecution procedures and the financial capacity to investigate and prosecute an individual that is found to have violated international law and international human rights law.

For that reason, it will be a flaw in this research to support the notion that international criminal law offers appropriate accountability systems for human rights violations and that this should be extended to corporate human rights accountability. Accordingly, it shall be suggested that the system is an indication of criminal justice, but its practical aspect is very difficult to implement due to the failures highlighted in this book. Also, international criminal accountability should consist of both criminal and tort law elements in its concept of accountability. Therefore, to address this gap in accountability, it is imperative to understand what constitutes accountability and human rights duty of care, and how to relate the practical meaning of accountability to human rights obligations. Moving on from the international criminal law accountability, the book addressed the tort element of accountability by examining the Alien Tort Statute.

It also examines the calls for binding obligations for corporations to respect human rights. It assessed the voluntary mechanisms such as the Guiding Principles, the OECD Guidelines, the ILO Tripartite Declaration of Principles Concerning Multinational Enterprises and Social Policy, the SA800 Standards, and now the proposed UN Binding Treaty on Transnational Corporations and Other Business Enterprises with Respect to Human Rights. Nonetheless, the duty proposed in this book is much narrower. It requires the corporation to only ensure their conduct does not cause harm to those who are in their close proximity; hence, it will only impose an obligation on a corporation whose conduct falls below the reasonable man standard.

Additionally, it is claimed that the requirement of proximity would likely limit the successful claims of victims of human rights abuse, as the victims would need to establish that the corporation foresaw the harm, establish the proximity between the victims and the corporation, and establish that it was fair, just and reasonable to impose a duty of care. However, it is observed in this book that this requirement should not be mandatory when it is absolutely clear that the corporation knew what it was doing or should have known what it ought to do and what it ought not to do; then the court should find corporate liability through a novel duty of care.

Even so, the book contests that, in the right circumstances, tort law provides an effective remedy for victims who have suffered as a result of corporate negligence and failure to respect human rights standards. It is further argued that the scope of the duty of care should expand through modification to incorporate the obligations which may arise in the UN Binding Treaty on Transnational Corporations and Other Business Enterprises with

Respect to Human Rights to reflect on the development of tort law and the reality of the global economy, if the treaty ever comes into force. A duty of care could also promote effective supply chain and subsidiary respect to human rights standards in business operations. Finally, tort law may, therefore, have a significate role to play in promoting the accountability of corporations with regards to their human rights impact in the global economy.

The indication of this book is that corporations normally violate human rights and damage the environment with some foresight. International corporations know or should know that if they engage or aid and abet governments to oppress their citizens' rights, or fail to conduct vigorous environmental damage assessments, the result will be substantial human rights violations and environmental damages. Therefore, the foresight of the corporation's conduct under legal principles does not exempt them from aggravated or exemplary liability.

Finally, it is suggested that the corporation that engages in human rights violations to maximise profits, at the expense of innocent victims and the environment, constitutes an unjust enrichment. Under the law of tort, it is prohibited that the defendant should benefit from a tort of negligence; therefore, tort does not pay or allow the corporation to enjoy unjust enrichment. Following this indication, it is imperative that the court, after assessing the circumstances surrounding the corporation's conduct, should be in a legal mandatory position to award either aggravated or exemplary damages for human rights violations. It is, therefore, recommended that aggravated or exemplary damages should be awarded if it is proven that the corporation has violated human rights or caused damage to the environment in the following circumstances:

1. Cases where corporations and their managers and staff have been accused of being directly responsible for acts amounting to gross human rights abuses;
2. Cases where governments and state authorities have engaged corporations to provide goods, technology, services or other resources which are then used in abusive or repressive ways;
3. Cases where companies have been accused of providing information, or logistical or financial assistance, to human rights abusers that have "caused" or "facilitated" or exacerbated the abuse; and
4. Cases arising out of situations where state security services have been called in to assist with the resolution of some dispute or conflict surrounding business activities where companies

> have been accused of being 'complicit' in human rights abuses by virtue of having made investments in projects or joint ventures with regimes with poor human rights records or with connections to known abusers.

After a careful consideration of the findings emerging in this book in relation to corporate accountability, it is concluded that the international community and global economic institutions will be best equipped to address corporate human rights violations through an international forum such as international corporation court and based on the principle of a duty of care under tort law. The present book was designed to determine whether tort and civil law could provide an appropriate tool for corporate human rights violations. In doing so, the book has dismissed the current mechanisms and views on corporate accountability and remedy as ineffective. They lack liability and enforcement. Therefore, to combat this deficiency of corporate accountability and remedy, the book concluded that there is a need to create an international court to implement a new notion of corporate accountability and remedy through tort and civil law. The book further observed that an international court for the purpose of corporate accountability is an appropriate mechanism to address corporate human rights violations through tort and the civil legal system. Finally, it is recommended that further research is carried out to examine the victim's perception of remedy, with a specific focus on victim-centric approach to judicial remedy. Similarly, further research is required to assess the effect of the proposed UN Binding Treaty on Transnational Corporations and Other Business Enterprises with Respect to Human Rights and the implications that this may have on national courts in developing countries.

APPENDIX

Tables

Table 1. The Extent of Accountability

If the following indications can be proven, then there exists an argument that accountability exists: When there is a relationship between the corporation and the host state; when the activity of the corporations' touch and concern the host state; when there is an economic transaction between the corporation and the government of the host nation; and when the corporate subsidiaries and corporate business operations have impacted on a particular sector of society (environment and factory operations). When the corporation has a duty of care to explain and justify its conduct to the national court of the host and home state, as well as an international tribunal or court if appropriate. The national courts of the host state, home state and international forum such as the arbitration or international court should have the authority under international law to investigate[1950] and sanction the corporation for its misconduct and contribution to human rights violations through tort and civil law. In this scenario, the national courts of the host state, home state, international tribunal or international court have the legitimate authority to pass judgment and sanction.[1951] The corporation must face sanctions if it is found that it has violated human rights, or assisted or aided the host government to violate the rights of its people. If found guilty, the corporation must compensate the victims through effective remedial action without undue delay.

[1950] Jorge Emilio Núñez, 'About the Impossibility of Absolute State Sovereignty' (2014) 27 (4) International Journal for the Semiotics of Law-Revue Internationale de Sémiotique Juridique 645.

[1951] Under the principle of a duty of care, the defendant can only be punished once. What this means is that only a single remedy shall be awarded against the corporation for a misconduct.

Table 2

ATCA	TVPA
Jurisdictional Definitions not detailed No exhaustion of remedies requirement No statute of limitations largely unknown legislative history	Substantive Detailed definitions Exhaustion of remedies requirement 10-year statute of limitations Detailed legislative history

Table 3. Civil Liability Treaties Adopted Since 1960[1952]

Treaty	Year of Adoption	Number of Signatures	Number of Ratification	Ratifications Necessary for Entry Into Force	Entry Into Force
IAEA Convention on Supplementary Compensation for Nuclear Damage	1997	13	3	5 states with a minimum of 400,000 units of installed nuclear capacity	Not in Force
Convention on Civil Liability for Oil Pollution Damage Resulting From the Exploitation of Seabed Mineral Resources	1977	6	0	4	Not in force
UNECE Convention on Civil Liability for Damage Caused During Carriage of Dangerous Goods by Road, Rail and Inland Navigated Vessels	1989	2	1	5	Not in Force

[1952]Convention on Biological Diversity, Montreal, Can., May 25-27 (2005), Status of Third-Party Liability Treaties and Analysis of Difficulties Facing Their Entry Into Force, UN Doc. UNEP/CBD/BS/WG-L&R/1? INF/ (2005) <https://www.biodiv.org/doc/meetings/bs/bswglr-01-inf-03-en-pdf> accessed 11 January 2017 [hereinafter Convention on Biological Diversity]. Ratifications for oil pollution damage treaties compile from 'The International Regime for Compensation for Oil Pollution Damage (2005).
<https://www.iopcfund.org/npdf/genE.pdf>. Information on the number of ratification necessary for entry into force was compile from the treaty texts.

IMO International Convention on Civil Liability for Oil Pollution Damage (Replaced 1969)	1992	10	122	10 states, including 4 states with more than 1million units of gross tonnage	1996
International Convention on the Establishment of an International Fund for Oil Pollution Damage (replaced 1972 Convention). Protocol	1992 2003	10 3	104 21	8 8	1996 2005
Council of Europe Lugano Convention on Civil Liability for Damage Resulting From Activities Dangerous to the Environment	1993	9	0	3 states, including at least 2 Council of Europe states	Not in Force
IMO Convention on Liability and Compensation in Connection with Carriage of Hazardous and Noxious Substances by Sea	1996	8	8	12 states, including 4 states that have at least two million unit of gross tonnage	
Basel Protocol on Liability and Compensation for Damage Resulting From Transboundary Movements of Hazardous Wastes	1999	13	8	20	Not in Force
IMO International Convention on Civil Liability for Bunker Oil Pollution Damage	2001	3	18	18 states, including 5 states with gross tonnage not less than 1 million units	Not in Force

UNCE Protocol on Civil Liability and Compensation for Damage Caused by the Transboundary Effect of Industrial Accident on Transboundary Waters	2003	24	1	16	Not in Force

Table 4. The State Stands in Connection to Civil Liability Treaty

National Economic Prevalence of the Targeted Business Operation Low High		
Low	I-Bystanders	II-Strong Opponent
High	III-Supporters	IV-Likely Operation

Table 5. Signatures and Parties that Choose to be Part of Civil Liability Treaties Since 1989

Treaty Name	Parties	Ratifying or Acceding States
UNECE Convention on Civil Liability for Damage Caused During Carriage of Dangerous Goods by Road, Rail and Inland Navigation Vessels (1989)[1953]	OECD: Germany Non-OECD: Morocco	OCED: None Non-OECD: Liberia
Convention on Liability and Compensation with Carriage Hazardous and Noxious Substance by Sea (1996)[1954]	OECD: Canada, Denmark, Finland, Germany, Netherlands, Norway, Sweden, United Kingdom Non-OECD: None	OECD: None Non-OECD: Angola, Cyprus, Morocco, Russian Federation, Saint Kitts and Nevis, Samoa, Slovenia and Tonga
Basel Protocol on Liability and Compensation for Damage Resulting from Transboundary Movement of Hazardous Waste (1999)[1955]	OECD: Denmark, Finland, France, Hungary, Luxembourg, Sweden, Switzerland and the United Kingdom Non-OECD: Chile, Columbia, Costa Rica, Macedonia, Monaco	OECD: None Non-OECD: Botswana, the Democratic Republic of the Congo, Ethiopia, Ghana, Liberia, Republic of Congo, Syria, Tonga

[1953]UNECE Convention on Civil Liability for Damage Caused During Carriage of Dangerous Goods by Road, Rail and Inland Navigation Vessels (1989) <https://www.unece.org/trans/danger/publi/crtd/crtd_e.html> accessed20 June 2017.
[1954]HNS Convention, <http://www.hnsconvention.org/en/status.html> accessed 16 January.
[1955]Basel Convention, Parties to the Basel Liability Protocol <http://www.basel.int/ratif/protocol.html> accessed 16 January 2017.

International Convention on Civil Liability for Bunker Oil Pollution Damage (2001)[1956]	OECD: Canada, Australia, Denmark, Finland, Germany, Italy, Norway, Sweden, Spain, United Kingdom Non-OECD: Brazil	OECD: Germany, Greece, Spain, Luxembourg, Poland, United Kingdom Non-OECD: Bulgaria, Croatia, Jamaica, Latvia, Lithuania, Samoa, Singapore, Slovenia, Tonga
Protocol on Civil Liability and Compensation for Damage Caused by the Transboundary Effects of Industrial Accidents on Transboundary Waters (2003)[1957]	OECD: Austria, Belgium, Denmark, Finland, Greece, Luxembourg, Norway, Poland, Portugal, Sweden, United Kingdom Non-OECD: Armenia, Bosnia, Bulgaria, Cyprus, Estonia, Georgia, Latvia, Moldova, Romania, Ukraine	OECD: Hungary Non-OECD: None

[1956] Transport Can., Maritime Law Reform Discussion Paper 15 n.12 (2005).<http:///www.tc.gc.ca/en/report/tp14370epdf> accessed 16 January 2017.

[1957] Protocol on Civil Liability and Compensation for Damage Caused by the Transboundary Effects of Industrial Accidents on Transboundary Waters to the 1992 Convention on the Protection and Use of Transboundary Watercourses and International Lakes and to the 1992 Convention on the Transboundary Effects of Industrial Accidents Kiev, 21 May (2003) <https://treaties.un.org/pages/ViewDetails.aspx?src=TREATY&mtdsg_no=XXVII-16&chapter=27&lang=en> accessed 16 October 2017.

BIBLIOGRAPHY

Addo MK, *Human Rights Standards and The Responsibility of Transnational Corporations* (The Hague: Kluwer 1999)

Andenaes J, *Punishment and Deterrence* (University of Michigan Press 1974)

Appleman JA, *Military Tribunals and International Crimes* (Westport Conn: Greenwood Press)

Arief, A, Margesson R, Browne MA, Weed MC *International Criminal Court Cases in Africa: Status and Policy Issues* (Diane Publishing 2010)

Askin KD, *War Crimes against Women: Prosecution in International War Crimes Tribunals* (Martinus Nijhoff Publishers 1997)

ASX Council, *Corporate Governance. Principles of Good Corporate Governance and Best Practice Recommendations* (Australian Stock Exchange Limited 2003)

Baker-Röben B, 'Civil Liability as a Control Mechanism for Environmental Protection at The International Level' in Morrison FL and Wolfrum K (eds), *International, Regional and National Environmental Law* (Kluwer Law International 2000)

Bass BSGJ, Everett CARO, Morris GRJ, Nash MWL, Sadat PSLN, Scharf MP and Scheffer DJ, *The United States and The International Criminal Court: National Security and International Law* (Rowman & Littlefield Publishers 2000)

Bassiouni CM, 'Historical Survey 1919-1998' in Bassiouni C (ed), *The Statute of The International Criminal Court: A Documentary History* (New York: Transnational Publishers 1998)

Bassiouni CM, *Introduction to International Criminal Law* (Brill 2012)

Becht AC and Miller FW, *The Test of Factual Causation in Negligence and Strict Liability Cases* (Committee on Publications Washington University 1961)

Beigbeder Y and Boven TV, *Judging War Criminals: The Politics of International Justice* (Macmillan Basingstoke and New Publishing 1999)

Berghe L, *International Standardisation of Good Corporate Governance: Best Practices for The Board of Directors* (Springer Science & Business Media 2012)

Bierzanek R, 'War Crimes: History and Definition' in Bassiouni C, *International Criminal Law: Enforcement* (New York: Transnational Publishers 1989)

Birnie P and Boyle A, *International Law and The Environment* (Oxford University Press 2002)

Bisschop, L. and Walle, G.V. (2013) 'Environmental victimisation and conflict resolution: A case study of e-waste'. In Westerhuis, D., Walters, R. and Wyatt, T. (eds) *Emerging Issues in Green Criminology: Exploring Power, Justice and Harm* (London: Palgrave Macmillan), pp. 34–57.

Blackstone W, *Commentaries on The Laws of England* (Vol. 2. Collins & Hannay 1830)

Blackstone W, Commentaries on the Laws of England: A Facsimile of the First Edition of 1765-1769, Vol. 1 [OF THE RIGHTS OF PERSONS - 1765] (University of Chicago Press, 1979)

Blowfield M and Murray A, *Corporate Responsibility: A Critical Introduction* (Oxford University Press 2008)

Boas G, Bischoff JL and Reid NL, *Forms of Responsibility in International Criminal Law* (Cambridge University Press 2007)

Boas G, *The Milošević Trial: Lessons for The Conduct of Complex International Criminal Proceedings* (Cambridge University Press 2007)

JH Franklin: Bodin J, *On Sovereignty,* ed. JH Franklin (Cambridge University Press 1992)

Bohlander M, ed. *International Criminal Justice: A Critical Analysis of Institutions and Procedures* (Cameron May 2007)

Bothe M, Karl Partsch KJ, and Solf WA, eds. *New Rules for Victims of Armed Conflicts: Commentary on The Two 1977 Protocols Additional to The Geneva Conventions of 1949* (Martinus Nijhoff Publishers 1982)

Boucher D, *Political Theories of International Relations* (Oxford University Press 1998)

Bovens M, Goodin RE and Schillemans T (eds), *The Oxford Handbook of Public Accountability* (Oxford: OUP 2014)

Bronwen M, *The Price of Oil: Corporate Responsibility and Human Rights Violations in Nigeria's Oil Producing Communities* (Vol. 2156. Human Rights Watch 1999)

Brooks T, *Accountability: It All Depends on What You Mean* (Akkad Press 1995)

Brownlie I and Baker K, *Principles of Public International Law* (Oxford: Clarendon 1980)

Burchill S, *Realism and Neo-Realism* (Palgrave 2001)

Bussani M. and Sebok AJ, eds. *Comparative Tort Law: Global Perspectives* (Edward Elgar Publishing 2015)

Campbell B, *The SA Generals and The Rise of Nazism* (University Press of Kentucky 2015)

Campbell HB, *Black's Law Dictionary* (St Paul Minn: West Publishing Co. 1990)

Cane P, *The Anatomy of Tort Law* (Bloomsbury Publishing1997)

Card R, *Card, Cross and Jones Criminal Law* (Oxford University Press 2016)

Cartwritht D and Zander A, *Group Dynamics* (Harper and Row 1960)

Cassese A, Acquaviva G, Fan M and Whiting A, *International Criminal Law: Cases and Commentary* (Oxford University Press 2011)

Cassese A and Gaeta P, *Cassese's International Criminal Law* (Oxford University Press 2013)

Cassese A, Gaeta P and Jones JRWD, eds. *The Rome Statute of The International Criminal Court: A Commentary* (Oxford University Press 2002)

Casson M, *A Theory of Cooperation in International Business* (Palgrave Macmillan UK 1989)

Cheng B, *General Principles of Law as Applied by International Courts and Tribunals* (Cambridge University Press 1994)

Chikulo BC and Hope KR, eds. *Corruption and Development in Africa: Lessons from Country Case-Studies* (Macmillan 1999)

Chuter D, *War Crimes: Confronting Atrocity in The Modern World* (Lynne Rienner Publishers 2003)

Ciorciari JD, eds. *The Khmer Rouge Tribunal* (No. 10. Phnom Penh: Documentation Center of Cambodia, 2006).

Clapham A, *Human Rights Obligations of Non-State Actors* (Oxford: OUP 2006)

Clarke KM and Goodale M, *Mirrors of Justice: Law and Power in The Post-Cold War Era* (Cambridge University Press 2010)

Cook K, 'Liability: No Liability, No Protocol' in Bail C., Falkner R. and Marquard H. (eds), *Cartagena Protocol on Biosafety: Reconciling Trade in Biotechnology with Environment and Development* (London, 2002) 371

Condorell L and Villalpando S, 'Relationship of The Court with The United Nations' in Cassese A, Gaeta P. and Jones J.R.W.D. (eds), *The Rome Statute of the International Criminal Court: A Commentary* (Oxford University Press, 2002) 221

Conforti B and Francioni F, eds. *Enforcing International Human Rights in Domestic Courts* (Martinus Nijhoff Publishers 1970)

Cosgrove RA, *The Rule of Law: Albert Venn Dicey, Victorian Jurist* (University of North Carolina Press 1980)

Cover RM, *Justice Accused: Antislavery and The Judicial Process* (Yale University Press 1975)

Cryer R and Boister N, eds. *Documents on The Tokyo International Military Tribunal: Charter, Indictment, and Judgments* (Oxford University Press 2008)

Cryer R, Friman H, Robinson D and Wilmshurst E*, An Introduction to International Criminal Law and Procedure* (Cambridge University Press 2007)

Cryer R, *Prosecuting International Crimes: Selectivity and The International Criminal Law Regime* (Cambridge University Press 2005)

David R, ed. *International Encyclopaedia of Comparative Law* (Vol. 2. Brill Archive 1986)

Deitelhoff N and Wolf KD, 'Business and Human Rights: How Corporate Norm Violators Become Norm Entrepreneurs' in Risse T, Ropp SC. and Sikkink K (eds), The Persistent Power of Human Rights: From Commitment to Compliance (Cambdrige University Press 2013)

Deva S and Bilchitz D (eds.)*, Building a Treaty on Business and Human Rights: Context and Contours* (Cambridge: Cambridge University Press 2017)

Deva S, *Regulating Corporate Human Rights Violations: Humanizing Business* (London Routledge 2012)

Diamond M, *Corporation 905* (3rd ed, Carolina Academic Press 2012)

Dicey AV, Humphrey J, Morris C and Collins LA*, Dicey and Morris on The Conflict of Laws* (Sweet & Maxwell 2000)

Dickinson A, *The Rome II Regulation: The Law Applicable to Non-Contractual Obligations* (Oxford University Press on Demand 2010)

Dobbs DB, Keeton RE, Keeton WP and Owen DG, *Prosser and Keeton on The Law of Torts* (West Publishing Company 1984)

Dobbs DB, *The Law of Torts* (Vol. 2. West Group 2001)

Donnelly J, *Universal Human Rights in Theory and Practice* (Cornell University Press 2013)

Drzemczewski AZ, *European Human Rights Convention in Domestic Law: A Comparative Study* (Oxford University Press 1985)

Dunbar-Brunton J, *The Tort of Nuisance: The Law and The Individual* (Macmillan Education UK 1979)

Dunning JH, *The Globalization of Business (Routledge Revivals): The Challenge of The 1990* (Routledge 2014)

Falk RA, *The Vietnam War and International Law, Volume 3: The Widening Context* (Vol. 3. Princeton University Press 2015)

Fawthrop T and Jarvis H, *Getting Away with Genocide? Elusive Justice and The Khmer Rouge Tribunal* (UNSW Press 2005)

Fenzl N and Mathis A, 'Pollution of Natural Water Resources in Amazonia: Sources, Risks and Consequences' in Aragon LE, and Clüsener-Godt M (eds), *Issues of Local and Global Use of Water from the Amazon* (Montevideo 2004) 57

Ferlie E, Lynn LE and Pollitt C, *The Oxford Handbook of Public Management* (Oxford University Press USA 2005)

Fisse B and Braithwaite J, *Corporations, Crime and Accountability* (Cambridge University Press 1993)

Fitzmaurice M, Elias OA and Merkouris P, *eds. Treaty Interpretation and The Vienna Convention on The Law of Treaties: 30 years on* (Vol. 1. Brill 2010)

Fleming JG, *The Law of Torts* (Vol. 1. Law Book Company for New South Wales Bar Association 1987)

Fletcher GP, *Tort Liability for Human Rights Abuses* (Bloomsbury Publishing 2008)

Friedman LM, *Total Justice* (Russell Sage Foundation 1985)

Gabriel Moran, *A Grammar of Responsibility* (Crossroads 1996)

Gaiba F, *The Origins of Simultaneous interpretation: The Nuremberg Trial* (University of Ottawa Press 1998)

Garner AB, *Black's Law Dictionary* (10th ed. Brand: Thomson West 2014)

Gedicks Pl, *The New Resource Wars: Native and Environmental Struggles Against Multinational Corporations* (Vol. 210. Black Rose Books Ltd 1994)

Giliker P and Beckwith S, *Tort* (Sweet and Maxwell 2000)

Giliker P, *Vicarious Liability in Tort, A Comparative Perspective* (Cambridge University Press 2010)

Glahn GV and Taulbee JL, *Law Among Nations: An Introduction to Public International Law* (Routledge 2015)

Global Environment (Sage Publications 2010)

Gloppen S, 'Courts, Corruption and Judicial Independence' in Soreide T and Williams A (eds), *Corruption, Grabbing and Development: Real World Challenges* (Edward Elgar Publishing 2014)

Goffman E, *Frame Analysis: An Essay on The Organization of Experience* (Harvard University Press 1974)

Gottesman E, *Cambodia after The Khmer Rouge: Inside the Politics of Nation Building* (Yale University Press 2004)

Gottesman E, *Cambodia after The Khmer Rouge: Inside the Politics of Nation Building* (Yale University Press 2004)

Gray R, Owen D and Adams C, *Accounting & Accountability: Changes and Challenges in Corporate Social and Environmental Reporting* (Prentice Hall 1996)

Grear A, *Redirecting Human Rights: Facing the Challenge of Corporate Legal Humanity* (Springer 2010)

Grotius H, *Hugo Grotius on The Law of War and Peace* (Cambridge University Press 2012)

Guzman AT, *How International Law Works: A Rational Choice Theory* (Oxford University Press 2008)

Gwyn WB, *The Meaning of The Separation of Powers: An Analysis of The Doctrine from Its Origin to The Adoption of The United States Constitution* (Tulane University 1965)

Hans VP, *Business on Trial: The Civil Jury and Corporate Responsibility* (Yale University Press 2000)

Harding C, *Hostis Humani Generis the Pirate as Outlaw in The Early Modern Law of The Sea Pirates? The Politics of Plunder 1550–1650* (Palgrave Macmillan UK 2007)

Harris KJ and Kushen R, *Surrender of Fugitives to The War Crimes Tribunals for Yugoslavia and Rwanda: Squaring International Legal Obligations with The US Constitution* (Kluwer Academic Publishers 1996)

Hart HLA and Honoré T, *Causation in The Law* (Oxford: OUP 1985)

Hawk D, 'The Cambodian Genocide' in Charny IW (ed), *Genocide: A Critical Bibliographic Review* (New York: Facts on File 1988) 137

Heller KJ, *The Nuremberg Military Tribunals and The Origins of International Criminal Law* (Oxford University Press on Demand 2011)

Henckaerts JM and Doswald-Beck L, *Customary International Humanitarian Law* (Cambridge University Press 2005)

Hill CA and Painter RW, *Better Bankers, Better Banks: Promoting Good Business through Contractual Commitment* (University of Chicago Press 2015)

Hill CA and Painter RW, *Better Bankers, Better Banks: Promoting Good Business Through Contractual Commitment* (University of Chicago Press 2015)

Hooghe L and Marks G, *Multi-Level Governance and European Integration* (Rowman & Littlefield 2001)

Hornby AS and Wehmeier S, *Oxford Advanced Learner's Dictionary* (Vol. 1428. Oxford University Press 1995)

Horne JN and Kramer A, *German Atrocities, 1914: A History of Denial* (Yale University Press 2001)

Hossain K, ed. *Human Rights Commissions and Ombudsman Offices: National Experiences Throughout the World* (Martinus Nijhoff Publishers 2000)

Hovenkamp H, *Enterprise and American Law 1836-1937* (Harvard University Press 2009)

Hunter D, Salzman J, Zaelke D, *Hunter, Salzman and Zaelke International Environmental Law and Policy* (Foundation Press 1998).

Jackson KD (ed.), *Cambodia, 1975-1978 Rendezvous with Death* (Princeton University Press 2014)

Jackson KD, 'The Ideology of Total Revolution' in Jackson KD (ed.), *Cambodia, 1975-1978: Rendezvous with Death* (Princeton University Press 1989)

Jackson RH, *Report of Robert H Jackson, United States Representative to The International Conference on Military Trials* (Washington DC US GPO 1949)

Janis IL and Mann L, *Decision Making: A Psychological Analysis of Conflict, Choice, and Commitment* (Free Press 1977)

Jayawickrama N, *The Judicial Application of Human Rights Law: National, Regional and International Jurisprudence* (Cambridge University Press 2002)

Jones JRWD and Powles S, *International Criminal Practice: The International Criminal Tribunal for The Former Yugoslavia, The International Criminal Tribunal for Rwanda, The International Criminal Court, The Special Court for Sierra Leone, The East Timor Special Panel for Serious Crimes, War Crimes Prosecutions in Kosovo* (Brill-Nijhoff 2003)

Jones M, *Textbook on Torts* (8th edn, Oxford University Press 2002)

Jönsson C, 'Cognitive Factors in Explaining Regime Dynamics' in Rittberger V, *Regime Theory and International Relations* (Oxford: Clarendon Press 1993)

Joseph S, *Corporations and Transnational Human Rights Litigation* (Hart Publishing 2004)

Jowitt WA, *Walsh C and Burke JM, Jowitt's Dictionary of English law* (Sweet & Maxwell 1977)

Keeton WP, et al. *Prosser and Keeton on The Law of Torts* (West Publishing Company 1984)

Kerr R, *The International Criminal Tribunal for The Former Yugoslavia: An Exercise in Law, Politics, and Diplomacy* (Oxford University Press on Demand 2004)

Kidner R, *Casebook on Torts* (Oxford University Press 2012)

Kiernan B, *The Pol Pot Regime: Race, Power, and Genocide in Cambodia under The Khmer Rouge, 1975-79* (Yale University Press 2014)

Kirsch S, *Mining and Environmental Human Rights in Papua New Guinea* (Palgrave Macmillan UK 2003)

Kohen M and Schramm B, *General Principles of Law* (Oxford University Press 2013)

Laufer WS, *Corporate Bodies and Guilty Minds: The Failure of Corporate Criminal Liability* (University of Chicago Press 2008)

Lee RSK, *ed. The International Criminal Court: The Making of The Rome Statute: Issues, Negotiations and Results* (Martinus Nijhoff Publishers 1999)

Lewis JR, *Uncertain Judgment: A Bibliography of War Crimes Trials* (Santa Barbara ABC Clio Inc 1979)

Lewis WA, *The Evolution of The International Economic Order* (Princeton University Press 2015)

Liebersohn H, *Fate and Utopia in German Sociology 1870-1923* (Mit Press 1990)

Linden AM and Feldthusen B, *Canadian Tort Law* (8th ed. Markham: LexisNexis Butterworths 2006) 568

Linderfalk U, *On the Interpretation of Treaties: The Modern International Law as Expressed in The 1969 Vienna Convention on The Law of Treaties* (Vol. 83. Springer Science & Business Media 2007)

Linton S, Cambodia, *East Timor and Sierra Leone: Experiments in International Justice* (Vol. 12. No. 2. Kluwer Academic Publishers 2001)

Linton S, ed. *Hong Kong's War Crimes Trials* (Oxford University Press 2013)

List C and Pettit P, *Group Agency: The Possibility, Design, and Status of Corporate Agents* (Oxford University Press 2011)

Macedo S, ed. *Universal Jurisdiction: National Courts and The Prosecution of Serious Crimes Under International Law* (University of Pennsylvania Press 2006)

MacCormick N, 'Donoghue v Stevenson and Legal Reasoning' in Burns P (ed.), *Donoghue v. Stevenson and The Modern Law of Negligence*, (Continuing Legal Education of British Columbia, Vancouver 1991)

Mackie JJ, *The Cement of The Universe: A Study of Causation Clarendon* (Oxford Press 1974)

Macklem P, *Corporate Accountability under International Law: The Misguided Quest for Universal Jurisdiction* (Brill Academic Publishers, 2005)

Madeley J, *Big Business, Poor Peoples: The Impact of Transnational Corporations on The World's Poo*r (Palgrave Macmillan 1999)

Maga TP, *Judgment at Tokyo: The Japanese War Crimes* Trials (University Press of Kentucky 2001)

Mair VH, *The Art of War: Sun Zi's Military Methods* (Columbia University Press 2008)

Maine HS, *Ancient Law, Its Connection with the Early History of Society and Its Relation to Modern Ideas* (first published 1891, New York: Dorset 1986)

Malekian F, *The Monopolization of International Criminal Law in The United Nations: A Jurisprudential Approach* (Coronet Books Inc 1995)

Mäntysaari P, *Theories of Corporate Law and Corporations: Past Approaches* (Springer Berlin Heidelberg 2012)

Mares R, ed. *The UN Guiding Principles on Business and Human Rights: Foundations and Implementation* (Martinus Nijhoff Publishers 2011)

Marks SP, 'The Human Rights Framework for Development: Seven Approaches' in Basu M, Negi A, and Sengupta A (eds), *Reflections on the Right to Development* (Sage Publications, New Delhi, 2005)

Marmor A, *Positive Law and Objective Values* (Oxford University Press 2001)

Marrus MR, *The Nuremberg War Crimes Trial, 1945-46: A Documentary History* (Macmillan 1997)

Martinez JS, *The Slave Trade and the Origins of International Human Rights Law* (Oxford University Press 2011)

Mathews AF, *Civil RICO Litigation* (Law & Business/Harcourt Brace Jovanovich 1985)

McBarnet DJ, Voiculescu A and Campbell T, eds. *The New Corporate Accountability: Corporate Social Responsibility and The Law* (Cambridge University Press 2009)

McCormack G, *Corporate Rescue Law: An Anglo-American Perspective* (Edward Elgar Publishing 2008)

McDougal MS, Lasswell HD and Chen L, *Human Rights and World Public Order: The Basic Policies of an International Law of Human Dignity* (1980)

McMahon WW, *Higher Learning, Greater Good: The Private and Social Benefits of Higher Education* (JHU Press 2009)

Meijer AJ, *De Doorzichtige Overheid: Parlementaire en Juridische Controle in Het Informatietijdperk* (Eburon 2002)

Meloni C, *Command Responsibility in International Criminal Law* (TMC Asser press 2010)

Mettraux G, *International Crimes and The Ad Hoc Tribunals* (Oxford University Press on Demand 2005)

Mettraux G, *The Law of Command Responsibility* (Oxford University Press USA 2009)

Miller R and Bratspies RM, *Transboundary Harm in International law: Lessons from The Trail Smelter Arbitration* (Cambridge University Press 2006)

Minear R, *Victors' Justice: The Tokyo War Crimes Trial* (Princeton: Princeton UniversityPress, 1971)

Minear RH, *Victors' Justice: Tokyo War Crimes Trial (Princeton University Press 2015)*

Minow M, *Between Vengeance and Forgiveness: Facing History After Genocide and Mass Violence* (Beacon Press 1998)

Moore SA, '*Global Garbage: Waste, Trash Trading, and Local Garbage Politics'* in Peet R, Robbins P. and Watts M, *Global Political Ecology* (2011)

Moran G, *A Grammar of Responsibility* (Crossroads 1996)

Mothersole B and Ridley A, *Tort of Negligence A Level Law in Action* (Macmillan Education UK 1995)

Muchlinski P and Rouas V, *Foreign Direct Liability Litigation: Toward the Transnationalisation of Corporate Legal Liability* (American Bar Association 2014)

Murphy SD, *Principles of International Law* (Thomson West 2006)

Nader R, *The Case Against Free Trade: GATT, NAFTA, and The Globalization of Corporate Power* (Vol. 49, North Atlantic Books 1993)

Nohria N and Ghoshal S, *The Differentiated Network: Organizing Multinational Corporations for Value Creation* (Jossey-Bass Publishers 1997)

Nohria N and Ghoshal S, *The Differentiated Network: Organizing Multinational Corporations for Value Creation* (Jossey-Bass Publishers 1997)

Obi CI, *Globalization and Local Resistance: The Case of Shell versus The Ogoni'* in Gills B.K. (eds) *Globalization and The Politics of Resistance* (Palgrave Macmillan UK 2000)

O'Flaherty M and Gisvold G, *eds. Post-War Protection of Human Rights in Bosnia and Herzegovina* (Vol. 53. Martinus Nijhoff Publishers 1998)

Olaniyan K, Corruption and Human Rights Law in Africa (Bloomsbury Publishing 2014)

Oliver RW, *What Is Transparency?* (New York: McGraw-Hill 2004)

Oxford Pro Bono Publico, *Obstacles to Justice and Redress for Victims of Corporate Human Rights Abuse* (University of Oxford 2008)

Papadatos PA, *The Eichmann Trial* (FA Praeger 1964)

Parker C, *The Open Corporation: Effective Self-Regulation and Democracy* (Cambridge University Press 2002)

Paust JJ, Scharf MP, Sadat L, Bassiouni CM, Gurulé J, Zagaris B and Williams SA, *International Criminal Law* (Durham NC: Carolina Academic Press 2000)

Peters A, *Beyond Human Rights: The Legal Status of The Individual in International Law* (Vol. 126 Cambridge University Press 2016)

Pitel SGA, Neyers JW and Chamberlain E, eds *Tort Law: Challenging Orthodoxy* (Bloomsbury Publishing 2013)

Phillips C, 'Nordic Co-Operation for The Protection of The Environment against Air Pollution and The Possibility of Transboundary Litigation' in Flinterman C, Kwiatkowska B and Lammers JG (eds), *Transboundary Air Pollution* (Nijhoff 1986)

Pollitt C, *The Essential Public Manager* (McGraw-Hill Education 2003)

Pope J, *Confronting Corruption: The Elements of A National Integrity System* (Transparency International 2000)

Quigley JB, *The Genocide Convention: An International Law Analysis* (Ashgate Publishing Ltd 2013)

Quoc N, Daillier D, Pellet P, Dinh ANQ, Daillier P and Pellet A, *Droit International Public. No. 341.1/. 8* (Librairie Générale de Droit et de Jurisprudence 1975)

Ramasastry A and Thompson RC, *Commerce, Crime and Conflict: Legal Remedies for Private Sector Liability for Grave Breaches of International Law: A Survey of Sixteen Countries: Executive Summary* (Fafo 2009)

Ratner SR, Abrams JS and Bischoff JL, *Accountability for Human Rights Atrocities in International Law: Beyond the Nuremberg Legacy* (Oxford University Press 2009)

Rehman J, *International Human Rights Law* (Pearson Education 2010)

Reichel PL, *Comparative Criminal Justice Systems: A Topical Approach. Upper Saddle River* (NJ Prentice Hall 2002)

Reiger C and Wierda M, *The Serious Crimes Process in Timor-Leste: In Retrospect* (New York International Center for Transitional Justice 2006)

Reynolds GK, *US Prisoners of War and Civilian American Citizens Captured and Interned by Japan in World War II: The Issue of Compensation by Japan* (Congressional Research Service Library of Congress 2002)

Riley D and Vennard J, *Triable Either-Way Cases: Crown Court or Magistrates' Court?* (No. 98. Bernan Press PA 1988)

Rochau AL, *Grundsätze der Realpolitik: Ausgewendet auf die Staatlichen Zustände Deutschlands* (K Göpel 1859)

Rogers WVH and Jolowicz JA, *Winfield and Jolowicz on Tort* (Sweet & Maxwell 2010)

Rohr Z, '*Playing the Catalan: The Rise of The Chess Queen; Queenship and Political Motherhood in Late Medieval Aragon and France'* in Fleiner C and Woodacre E (eds), *Virtuous or Villainess? The Image of The Royal Mother from The Early Medieval to The Early Modern Era* (Palgrave Macmillan US 2016)

Roht-Arriaza N, ed. *Impunity and Human Rights in International Law and Practice* (Oxford University Press on Demand 1995)

Röling BVA and Rüter CF, eds *The Tokyo Judgment: The International Military Tribunal for The Far East (IMTFE), 29 April 1946-12 November 1948* (Vol. 2. APA-UniversityPress Amsterdam 1977)

Roy SK Lee (ed.), *The International Criminal Court: The Making of the Rome Statute: Issues, Negotiations and Results* (Martinus Nijhoff Publishers1999)

Ruggie JG, *Just Business: Multinational Corporations and Human Rights* (Norton Global Ethics Series) (WW Norton & Company 2013)

Sands P and Peel J, *Principles of International Environmental Law* (Cambridge University Press 2012)

Santoro MA, *Profits and Principles: Global Capitalism and Human Rights in China* (Cornell University Press 2000)

Schabas WA, *An Introduction to The International Criminal Court* (Cambridge University Press 2011)

Schabas WA, *The UN International Criminal Tribunals: The Former Yugoslavia, Rwanda and Sierra Leone* (Cambridge University Press 2006)

Schachter O, *International Law in Theory and Practice* (Vol. 13. Martinus Nijhoff Publishers 1991)

Schedler A, *The Self-Restraining State: Power and Accountability in New Democracies* (Lynne Rienner Publishers 1999)

Shelton D, *Remedies in International Human Rights Law* (Oxford University Press USA 2015)

Sieghart P, *The International Law of Human Rights* (Oxford University Press 1983)

Simmons JA, *Moral Principles and Political Obligations* (Princeton University Press 1981)

Simons P and Macklin A, *The Governance Gap: Extractive Industries, Human Rights, and The Home State Advantage* (Routledge 2014)

Skinner G, McCorquodale R and De Schutter O, *The Third Pillar: Access to Judicial Remedies for Human Rights Violations by Transnational Business* (CORE 2013)

Skinner G, *Parent Company Accountability: Ensuring Justice for Human Rights Violations* (ICAR 2015)

Sklair L, *Transnational Capitalist Class* (John Wiley & Sons Ltd 2012)

Slye R and Schaack BV, *International Criminal Law: Essentials* (Wolters Kluwer Law & Business 2009)

Smith CN, *Morality and The Market (Routledge Revivals): Consumer Pressure for Corporate Accountability* (Routledge 2014)

Solaas IMG, *Transitional Justice in East Timor: A Case Study of Justice Versus Reconciliation and Its Consequences* (MS thesis 2009)

Spector BI, 'Deconstructing the Negotiations of Regime Dynamics' in Spector BI and Zartman IW (eds), *Getting It Done: Post-Agreement Negotiations and International Regimes* (Washington, DC, United States Institute of Peace Press 2003)

Speiser SM, Krause CF and Gans AW, *The American Law of Torts* (Vol. 1. Lawyers Cooperative Pub Co. 2003)

Stahn C, *The Law and Practice of The International Criminal Court* (Oxford University Press USA 2014)

Steinberger H, 'Sovereignty' in R Bernhardt (ed.) 4 Encyclopaedia of Public International Law (Amsterdam 2000) 500

Steiner HJ, Alston P and Goodman R, *International Human Rights in Context: Law, Politics, Morals: Text and Materials* (Oxford University Press USA 2008)

Stephens B, Ratner M, Chomsky J, Green J and Hoffman P, *International Human Rights Litigation in US Courts* (Irvington-on-Hudson New York Transnational publishers

Stevens R, *Torts and Rights* (Oxford: OUP 2007)

Tanaka Y, McCormack T and Simpson G, *eds., Beyond Victor's Justice? The Tokyo War Crimes Trial Revisited* (Leiden Martinus Nijhoff Publishers 2011)

Taucher P, *Command Responsibility at The Sandakan-Ranau War Crimes Trial* (Diss Murdoch University 2016)

Taylor T, *The Anatomy of The Nuremberg Trials: A Personal Memoir* (Knopf 2012)

Teitel RG, *Transitional Justice* (Oxford University Press on Demand 2000)

Thompson GF, *The Constitutionalization of The Global Corporate Sphere?* (Oxford University Press on Demand 2012)

Tonry MH, *Why Punish? How Much? A Reader on Punishment* (Oxford University Press on Demand 2011)

Totani Y, *The Tokyo War Crimes Trial: The Pursuit of Justice in The Wake of World War II* (Harvard University Asia Center 2009)

Tribunal (UNSW Press 2005)

Tully S (ed.), *Corporations and International Law-Making* (Brill 2007)

Tusa A and Tusa J, *The Nuremberg Trial* (Skyhorse Publishing Inc 2010)

UNCTAD, *World Investment Report, Non-Equity Modes of Production and Development* (New York/Geneva UN 2011)

United Nations, The Treaty Section of The Office of Legal Affairs, *Treaty Handbook* (United Nations Press 2006)

United Nations Office of the High Commission, *Guiding Principles on Business and Human Rights: Implementing the United Nations" Protect, Respect and Remedy"* Framework (UN 2011)

United Nations War Crimes Commission, *Law Reports of Trials of War Criminals* (Vol. 13 1949)

Veale FJP, *Advance to Barbarism: The Development of Total Warfare from Serajevo to Hiroshima* (Mitre P 1968)

Vile MJC, *Constitutionalism and The Separation of Powers* (Liberty Fund 2012)

Weiss EB, Intergenerational Equity: *A Legal Framework for Global Environmental Change* (United Nations University 1992)

Wells C, *Corporations and Criminal Responsibility* (Oxford University Press on Demand 2001)

Widyono B, *Dancing in Shadows: Sihanouk, The Khmer Rouge, and The United Nations in Cambodia* (Rowman & Littlefield Publishers 2007)

Wild C and Weinstein S, *Smith and Keenan's Company Law* (Pearson Education 2013)

Wilkins L, *Shared Vulnerability: The Media and American Perceptions of The Bhopal Disaster* (Vol. 8. Greenwood Press 1987)

Witting C, *Street on Torts* (Oxford University Press USA 2015)

Woods SL, Vietnam: *A Global Studies Handbook* (ABC-CLIO 2002)

Woodward R, *The Organisation for Economic Co-operation and Development* (OECD) (Routledge 2009)

Wright CA and Linden AM, *Canadian Tort law: Cases, Notes and Materials* (Butterworths 1975)

Yarwood L, *State Accountability under International Law: Holding States Accountable for a Breach of Jus Cogens Norms* (Routledge 2010)

Zahar A, The ICTR's *"Media" Judgment and the Reinvention of Direct and Public Incitement to Commit Genocide* (Vol. 16. No. 1. Springer Netherlands 2005)

Zensius A, Inside the Cocoa Pod: *An Analysis of The Harkin-Engel Protocol in Cote d'Ivoire* (Georgetown University 2012)

Zerk JA, *Multinationals and Corporate Social Responsibility: Limitations and Opportunities in International Law* (Vol. 48. Cambridge University Press 2006)

Articles

Abrams J, 'The Atrocities in Cambodia and Kosovo: Observations on The Codification of Genocide' (2001) 35 (2) New England Law Review 303

Agnew J, 'Sovereignty Regimes: Territoriality and State Authority in Contemporary World Politics' (2005) 95 (2) Annals of The Association of American Geographers 437

Ahmed T and Butler IJ, 'The European Union and Human Rights: An International Law Perspective' (2006) 17 (4) European Journal of International Law 771

Aka PC, 'Nigeria Since May 1999: Understanding the Paradox of Civil Rule and Human Rights Violations under President Olusegun Obasanjo' (2003) 4 San Diego International Law Journal 209

Akehurst M, 'Jurisdiction in International Law' (1972) 46 British Year Book of International Law 145

Akerson D and Wuetilleke N, 'Contempt of Court a Digest of The Case Law of Contempt of Court at International Criminal Tribunals and the International Criminal Court' (2016) 44 Denver Journal of International Law and Policy 87

Akhavan P, 'The Lord's Resistance Army Case: Uganda's Submission of The First State Referral to The International Criminal Court' (2005) 99 (2) American Journal of International Law 403

Ako RT, 'Re-Defining Corporate Social Responsibility (CSR) in Nigeria's Post-Amnesty Oil Industry' (2012) 3 (1) African Journal of Economic and Management Studies 9

Aldrich GH, 'Jurisdiction of the International Criminal Tribunal for the former Yugoslavia' (1996) 90 (1) American Journal of International Law 64

Alexander L, 'Reconsidering the Relationship Among Voluntary Acts, Strict Liability, and Negligence in Criminal Law' (1990) 7 (2) Social Philosophy and Policy 84

Allen T, 'Liability for References: The House of Lords and Spring v. Guardian Assurance' (1995) 58 (4) Modern Law Review 553

Allott P, 'The Concept of International Law' (1999) 10 (1) European Journal of International Law 31

Altholz R, 'Chronicle of a Death Foretold: The Future of US Human Rights Litigation Post Kiobel' (2014) 102 (6) California Law Review 1495

Alvarez JE, 'Are Corporations "Subjects" of International Law?' (2011) 9 Santa Clara Journal of International Law 1

Amann DM and Sellers MNS, 'The United States of America and The International Criminal Court' (2002) 50 American Journal of Comparative Law 381

Ambos K, 'International Criminal Procedure "Adversarial" "Inquisitorial" or Mixed?' (2003) 3 (1) International Criminal Law Review 1

Amer R, 'Border Conflicts between Cambodia and Vietnam' (1997) 5 (2) BRU Boundary and Security Bulletin 80

Anderson K., 'Kiobel v. Royal Dutch Petroleum: The Alien Tort Statute's Jurisdictional Universalism in Retreat' (2012) Cato Supreme Court Review Archives149

Anderson M, 'Transnational Corporations and Environmental Damage: Is Tort Law the Answer?' (2002) 41 Washburn Law Journal 399

Andrews OT, 'The Nigerian State, Oil Multinationals and The Environment: A Case Study of Shell Petroleum Development Company (SPDC)' (2015) 7 (2) Journal of Public Administration and Policy Research 24

Anoushirvani S, 'Future of The International Criminal Court: The Long Road to Legitimacy Begins with The Trial of Thomas Lubanga Dyilo' (2010) 22 Pace International Law Review 213

Antoniolli L, 'Taking Legal Pluralism Seriously: The Alien Tort Claims Act and The Role of International Law before U.S. Federal Courts' (2005) 12 (2) Indiana Journal of Global Legal Studies 651

Apostolova E, 'The Relationship between The Alien Tort Statute and The Torture Victim Protection Act' (2010) 28 Berkeley Journal of International Law 640

Aptel C, 'The International Criminal Tribunal for Rwanda' (1997) 37 (321) International Review of the Red Cross Archive 675

Arbour L, 'The Crucial Years' (2004) 2 Journal of International Criminal Justice 396

Arlow JE, 'The Utility of ATCA and The Law of Nations in Environmental Torts Litigation: Jota v. Texaco, Inc. and Large Scale Environmental Destruction' (2000) 7 Wisconsin Environmental Law Journal 93

Armstrong E, 'Integrity, Transparency and Accountability in Public Administration: Recent Trends, Regional and International Developments and Emerging Issues' (2005) United Nations, Department of Economic and Social Affairs 1

Arroyo D and Sirker K, 'Stocktaking of Social Accountability Initiatives in The Asia and Pacific Region' (2005) World Bank Institute Working Papers

Arsanjani MH and Michael RW, 'Interpreting Treaties for The Benefit of Third Parties: The "Salvors Doctrine" and The Use of Legislative History in Investment Treaties' (2010) 104 (4) American Journal of International Law 597

Ascencio–Herrera A, 'The Transboundary Movement of Living Modified Organisms: Issues Relating to Liability and Compensation' (1997) 6 (3) Review of European Community & International Environmental Law 293

Ashford HA and Risinger MD, 'Presumptions, Assumptions, and Due Process in Criminal Cases: A Theoretical Overview' (1969) 79 (2) Yale Law Journal 165

Ashworth A and Blake M, 'The Presumption of Innocence in English Criminal Law' (1996) Criminal Law Review 306

Askin KD, 'Reflections on Some of The Most Significant Achievements of the ICTY' (2003) 37 New England Law Review 903

Atkinson J, 'Racketeer Influenced and Corrupt Organizations, 18 U.S.C. 1961-68: Broadest of The Federal Criminal Statutes' (1978) Journal of Criminal Law and Criminology 1

Ayoub L, 'Nike Just Does It and Why the United States Shouldn't: The United States' International Obligation to Hold MNCs Accountable for Their Labour RightsViolations Abroad' (1998) 11 DePaul Business Law Journal 395

Azzam F, 'The Duty of Third States to Implement and Enforce International Humanitarian Law' (1997) 66 (1) Nordic Journal of International Law 55

Baer HU and Hostettler P, 'International Humanitarian Law: An Introduction' (2002) 167 (8) Military Medicine 7

Baghi VG and Mruthi TR.,'Nullum Crimen sine Lege in The International Criminal Court' (2010) 6 (3) Acta Universitatis Danubius. Juridica 65

Baker TE, 'A Primer on The Jurisdiction of The U.S. Courts of Appeals' (2009) 09 (01) Florida International University Legal Studies Research Paper

Ball C, 'What is Transparency?' (2009) 11 (4) Public Integrity 293

Ballantine HW, 'Separate Entity of Parent and Subsidiary Corporations' (1925) California Law Review 12

Bandsuch M, Pate L and Thies J, 'Rebuilding Stakeholder Trust in Business: An Examination of Principle-Centered Leadership and Organizational Transparency in Corporate Governance' (2008) 113 (1) Business and Society Review 99

Banerjee SB, 'Corporate Social Responsibility: The Good, The Bad and The Ugly' (2008) 34 (1) Critical Sociology 51

Bang G, Hovi J and Sprinz DF, 'US Presidents and The Failure to Ratify Multilateral Environmental Agreements' (2012) 12 (6) Climate Policy 755

Bang NJ, 'Unmasking the Charade of The Global Supply Contract: A Novel Theory of Corporate Liability in Human Trafficking and Forced Labour Cases' (2013) 35 Houston Journal of International Law 255

Bansal P, 'The Corporate Challenges of Sustainable Development' (2002) 16 (2) Academy of Management Executive 122 <http://amp.aom.org/content/16/2/122.short> accessed 6 July 2016

Banteka N, 'Mind the Gap: A Systematic Approach to The International Criminal Court's Arrest Warrants Enforcement Problem' (2016) 49 Cornell International Law Journal 521

Barnett JD, 'The Foundations of The Distinction between Public and Private Functions in Respect to The Common-Law Tort Liability of Municipal Corporations' (1937) 16 Oregon Law Review 250

Bartels L, 'Human Rights and Sustainable Development Obligations in EU Free Trade Agreements' (2013) 40 (4) Legal Issues of Economic Integration 297

Bartelson J, 'The Concept of Sovereignty Revisited' (2006) 17 (2) European Journal of International Law 463

Bassiouni CM, 'Legal Control of International Terrorism: A Policy-Oriented Assessment' (2002) 43 Harvard International Law Journal 83

Bassiouni CM, 'Universal Jurisdiction for International Crimes: Historical Perspectives and Contemporary Practice' (2001) 42 Virginia Journal of International Law 81

Baughen S, 'Holding Corporations to Account: Crafting ATS Suits in the UK' (2013) 2 British Journal of American Legal Studies 533

Bazyler M and Green J, 'Nuremberg-era Jurisprudence Redux: The Supreme Court in Kiobel v. Royal Dutch Petroleum Co. and the Legal Legacy of Nuremberg' (2012) 7 Charleston Law Review 23

Beale SS, 'A Response to The Critics of Corporate Criminal Liability' (2009) 46 American Criminal Law Review 1484

Beale SS, 'Is Corporate Criminal Liability Unique' (2007) 44 American Criminal Law Review 1503

Beever A, 'The Structure of Aggravated and Exemplary Damages' (2003) 23 (1) Oxford Journal of Legal Studies 87

Bellinger JB III, 'Why the Supreme Court Should Curb The Alien Tort Statute' *The Washington Post* (Washington, 22 February 2012)

Bellinger JB, Enforcing Human Rights in U.S. Courts and Abroad: The Alien Tort Statute and Other Approaches' (2009) 42 Vanderbilt Journal of Transnational Law 1

Bender L, 'Tort Law's Role as a Tool for Social Justice Struggle' (1997) 37 Washburn Law Journal 249

Bernaz N, 'Corporate Criminal Liability under International Law: The New TV SAL and Akhbar Beirut SAL Cases at The Special Tribunal for Lebanon' (2015) 13 (2) Journal of International Criminal Justice 313

Bernaz N, 'Enhancing Corporate Accountability for Human Rights Violations: is Extraterritoriality the Magic Potion?' (2013) 117 (3) Journal of Business Ethics 493

Berryman J, 'The Case for Restitutionary Damages over Punitive damages: Teaching The Wrongdoer That Tort Does Not Pay' (1994) 73 Canadian Bar Review 320

Bertot JC, Jaeger PT and Grimes JM, 'Using ICTs to Create a Culture of Transparency: E Government and Social Media as Openness and Anti-Corruption Tools for Societies' (2010) 27 (3) Government Information Quarterly 264

Bethell L, 'The Mixed Commissions for The Suppression of The Transatlantic Slave Trade in the Nineteenth century' (1966) 7 (1) Journal of African History 79

Beucher KJ and Sandage JB, 'United States Punitive Damage Awards in German Courts: The Evolving German Position on Service and Enforcement' (1990-1991) 23 Vanderbilt Journal of Transnational Law 967

Bexell M, 'Distribution of Responsibility for Human Rights Protection: The Public-Private Distinction' (2004) Die Friedens-Warte 103

Beyea G, 'Morrison v. National Australia Bank and The Future of Extraterritorial Application of The U.S. Securities Laws' (2011) 72 Ohio State Law Journal 537

Bianchi A, 'Ad-Hocism and The Rule of Law' (2002) 13 (1) European Journal of International Law 263

Bianchi A, 'International Law and US Courts: The Myth of Lohengrin Revisited' (2004) 15 (4) European Journal of International Law 751

Bina MW 'Private Military Contractor Liability and Accountability after Abu Ghraib' (2004) 38 John Marshall Law School Law Review 1237

Binnie I, 'Judging and Judges; May the Boldly Go Where Ivan Rand Went Before' (2013) 26 (1) Canadian Journal of Law & Jurisprudence 5

Birkinshaw J, Hood N and Jonsson S, 'Building Firm-Specific Advantages in Multinational Corporations: The Role of Subsidiary Initiative' (1998) Strategic Management Journal 221

Black B, 'Racketeer Influenced and Corrupt Organizations (RICO)-Securities and Commercial Fraud as Racketeering Crime after Sedima:

What Is a Pattern of Racketeering Activity' (1986) 6 Pace Law Review 365

Blakey RG, and Gettings B, 'Racketeer Influenced and Corrupt Organizations (RICO): Basic Concepts-Criminal and Civil Remedies' (1980) 53 Temple Law Review 1009

Blattmann R and Bowman K, 'Achievements and Problems of The International Criminal Court: A View from Within' (2008) 6 (4) Journal of International Criminal Justice 711

Blay S and Green J, 'Development of a Liability Annex to The Madrid Protocol' (1995) 25 Environmental Policy and Law 24

Blitt RC, 'Beyond Reggie's Guiding Principles on Business and Human Rights: Charting an Embracive Approach to Corporate Human Rights Compliance' (2012) 48 (1) Texas International Law Journal 33

Bloomfield P, 'The Challenging Business of Long-Term Public–Private Partnerships: Reflections on Local Experience' (2006) 66 (3) Public Administration Review 400

Blowfield M and Frynas JG, 'Setting New Agendas: Critical Perspectives on Corporate Social Responsibility in The Developing World' (2005) 81 (3) International Affairs 499

Blum JM, and Steinhardt RG, 'Federal Jurisdiction over International Human Rights Claims: The Alien Tort Claims Act after Filartiga v. Pena-Irala' (1981) 22 Harvard International Law Journal 53

Blumberg PI, 'Accountability of Multinational Corporations: The Barriers Presented by Concepts of The Corporate Juridical Entity' (2001) 24 Hastings International and Comparative Law Review 297

Blumberg PI, 'Asserting Human Rights against Multinational Corporations under United States Law: Conceptual and Procedural Problems' (2002) 50 American Journal of Comparative Law 493

Blumberg PI, 'Limited Liability and Corporate Groups' (1985) 11 The Journal of Corporation Law 573

Blumer M. and Sass J, 'Oil Pollution: Persistence and Degradation of Spilled Fuel Oil' (1972) 176 Science 1120

Bockers E, Stammel N, and Knaevelsrud C, 'Reconciliation in Cambodia: Thirty Years after The Terror of The Khmer Rouge Regime' (2011) 21 (1) Torture Journal 71

Bodansky D, 'The Legitimacy of International Governance: A Coming Challenge for International Environmental Law?' (1999) 93 (3) American Journal of International Law 596

Boelaert-Suominen S, 'Commentary: The Yugoslavia Tribunal and The Common Core of Humanitarian Law Applicable to All Armed Conflicts' (2000) 13 (3) Leiden Journal of International Law 619

Boer MD, 'Party Autonomy and Its Limitations in The Rome II Regulation' (2007) 9 Yearbook of Private International Law 19

Bogdandy AV, 'Pluralism, Direct Effect, and The Ultimate Say: On the Relationship between International and Domestic Constitutional Law' (2008 6 (3-4) International Journal of Constitutional Law 397

Bohnet I, Frey BS and Huck SH, 'More Order with Less Law: On Contract Enforcement, Trust, and Crowding' (2001) 95 (1) American Political Science Review 131

Boister N, 'The Application of Collective and Comprehensive Criminal Responsibility for Aggression at The Tokyo International Military Tribunal: The Measure of The Crime of Aggression?' (2010) 8 (2) Journal of International Criminal Justice 425

Bonafé BI, 'Finding a Proper Role for Command Responsibility' (2007) 5 (3) Journal of International Criminal Justice 599

Bondzie-Simpson E, 'A Critique of The African Charter on Human and Peoples' Rights' (1988) 31 Howard Law Journal 643

Borchers PJ, 'Conflict-of-Laws Considerations in State Court Human Rights Actions' (2013) 3 UC Irvine Law Review 45

Bornstein HR, 'The Alien Tort Claims Act in 2007: Resolving the Delicate Balance between Judicial and Legislative Authority' (2007) 82 Indiana Law Journal 1077

Bosshard P, 'The Environment at Risk from Monuments of Corruption' (2005) Global Corruption Report

Bothe M, 'The Protection of the Civilian Population and NATO Bombing on Yugoslavia: Comments on a Report to the Prosecutor of the ICTY' (2001) 12 (3) European Journal of International Law 531

Boven TV, 'Basic Principles and Guidelines on The Right to a Remedy and Reparation for Victims of Gross Violations of International Human Rights Law and Serious Violations of International Humanitarian Law' (2005) United Nations Audiovisual Library of International Law New York, United Nations

Bovens M, 'Two Concepts of Accountability: Accountability as a Virtue and as a Mechanism' (2010) 33 (5) West European Politics 946

Boyd KL, 'The Inconvenience of Victims: Abolishing Forum Non Conveniens in US Human Rights Litigation' (1998) 39 Virginia Journal of International Law 41

Boyle A, 'Human Rights and The Environment: Where Next?' (2012) 23 (3) European Journal of International Law 613

Boyle AE, 'Globalising Environmental Liability: The Interplay of National and International Law' (2005) 17 (1) Journal of Environmental Law 3

Boyle AE, 'Saving the World? Implementation and Enforcement of International Environmental Law Through International Institutions' (1991) 3 Journal of Environmental Law and Litigation 229

Boyle AE, 'State Responsibility and International Liability for Injurious Consequences of Acts Not Prohibited by International Law: A Necessary Distinction?' (1990) 39 (1) International and Comparative Law Quarterly 21

Bradley CA and Gulati M, 'Withdrawing from International Custom' (2010) Yale Law Journal 202

Bradley CA, 'The Alien Tort Statute and Article III' (2001) 42 Virginia Journal of International Law 587

Bradley CA, 'The Costs of International Human Rights Litigation' (2001) 2 Chicago Journal of International Law 457

Bradley CM, 'Racketeers, Congress, and The Courts: An Analysis of RICO' (1980) 65 Iowa Law Review 837

Branson DM, 'Holding Multinational Corporations Accountable? Achilles' Heels in Alien Tort Claims Act Litigation' (2011) 9 Santa Clara Journal of International Law 227

Bratspies RM, 'Organs of Society: A Plea for Human Rights Accountability for Transnational Enterprises and Other Business Entities' (2005) 13 (1) Michigan State Journal of International Law 9

Brenner SW, 'RICO, CCE, and Other Complex Crimes: The transformation of American Criminal Law' (1993) 2 (2) William & Mary Bill of Rights Law School Journals 239

Bridgeman NL, 'Human Rights Litigation under The ATCA as a Proxy for Environmental Claims' (2003) 6 Yale Human Rights & Development Law Journal 1

Brooker JW, 'Ford v. Garcia: A Puzzling Fusion of the Command Responsibility Doctrine with the Torture Victim Protection Act' (2002) 28 North Carolina Journal of International Law and Commercial Regulation 701

Brown BS, 'Primacy or Complementarity: Reconciling the Jurisdiction of National Courts and International Criminal Tribunals' (1998) 23 (2) Yale Journal of International Law 383

BrunnEee J, 'Of Sense and Sensibility: Reflections on International Liability Regimes as Tools for Environmental Protection' (2004) 53 (02) International & Comparative Law Quarterly 351

Buchanan SG, 'A Conceptual History of The State Action Doctrine: The Search for Governmental Responsibility (Part II of II)' (1997) 34 Houston Law Review 665

Bujra J, 'Leo Igwe: Interview with a Nigerian Humanist' (2006) 33 (110) Review of African Political Economy 740

Bunn ID, 'Global Advocacy for Corporate Accountability: Transatlantic Perspectives from The NGO community' (2004) 19 (6) American University International Law Review 1265

Bush JA, 'The Prehistory of Corporations and Conspiracy in International Criminal Law: What Nuremberg Really Said' (2009) 109 (5) Columbia Law Review 1094

Bussani M and Infantino M, 'Tort Law and Legal Cultures' (2015) 63 (4) American Journal of Comparative Law 77

Caesius A, 'The Statute of The International Criminal Court: Some Preliminary Reflections' (1999) 10 (1) European Journal of International Law 144

Campbell M, 'Witnessing Death: Ken Saro-Wiwa and The Ogoni Crisis' (2002) 5 (1) Postcolonial Studies: Culture, Politics, Economy 39

Cancik H, '"Dignity of Man" and "Persona" in Stoic Anthropology: Some Remarks on Cicero, De Officiis I 105-107' (2002) The Concept of Human Dignity in Human Rights Discourse 19

Cao L, 'Illegal Traffic in Women: A Civil RICO Proposal' (1987) 96 Yale Law Journal 1297

Cassel D, 'Corporate Initiatives: A Second Human Rights Revolution?' (1995) 19 Fordham International Law Journal 1963

Cassese A, 'The Belgian Court of Cassation v. The International Court of Justice: The Sharon and Others Case' (2003) 1 (2) Journal of International Criminal Justice 437

Castiglione M, 'Corporate Liability, Extraterritorial Jurisdiction and The Future of The Alien Tort Claims Act: Some Remarks after "Kiobel"' (2013) 2 Diritti Umani e DirittoInternationale 401

Casto WR, 'The New Federal Common Law of Tort Remedies for Violations of International Law' (2006) 37 (3) Rutgers Law Journal 635

Caswell M, 'Khmer Rouge Archives: Accountability, Truth, and Memory in Cambodia' (2010) 10 (1) Archival Science 25

Cernic JL, 'Corporate Responsibility for Human Rights: Analyzing The ILO Tripartite Declaration of Principles Concerning Multinational Enterprises and Social Policy' (2009) 6 (1) Miskolc Journal of International Law 24

Cerone J, 'The Jurisprudential Contributions of The ICTR to The Legal Definition of Crimes against Humanity: The Evolution of The Nexus Requirement' (2007) 14 New England Journal of International and Comparative Law 191

Chan A, 'Walmart Workers in China' (2008) Globalization & The Workplace 437

Chehab M, 'Finding Uniformity Amidst Chaos: A Common Approach to Kiobel's Touch and Concern Standard' (2016) 93 University of Detroit Mercy Law Review 119

Chesterman S, 'The Turn to Ethics: Disinvestment from Multinational Corporations for Human Rights Violations - The Case of Norway's Sovereign Wealth Fund' (2008) 23 American University International Law Review 577

Chigara BA and Nwankwo CM, '"To Be or Not to Be?" The African Union and Its Member States Parties' Participation as High Contracting States Parties to The Rome Statute of The International Criminal Court (1998)' (2015) 33 (3) Nordic Journal of Human Rights 243

Childress DE, 'The Alien Tort Statute, Federalism, and The Next Wave of Transnational Litigation' (2012) 100 Georgetown Law Journal 709

Ching AB, 'Evolution of The Command Responsibility Doctrine in Light of The Celebici Decision of The International Criminal Tribunal for the former Yugoslavia' (1999) 25 North Carolina Journal of International Law and Commercial Regulations 167

Chinkin CM, 'In Re Pinochet. United Kingdom House of Lords. Regina v. Bow Street Stipendiary Magistrate ex parte Pinochet Ugarte (No. 3) [1999] 2 WLR 827' (1999) American Journal of International Law 703

Chirwa DM, 'The Doctrine of State Responsibility as a Potential Means of Holding Private Actors Accountable for Human Rights' (2004) 5 Melbourne Journal of International Law 1

Chu BSP, 'The BHP and Ok Tedi Case 1984-2000: Issues, Outcomes and Implications for Corporate Social Reporting' (2001) 7 (1) News Journal of The Asia Pacific Centre for Environmental Accountability 11

Cirlig RE, 'Business and Human Rights: From Soft Law to Hard Law?' (2016) 6 (2) Juridical Tribune 228

Clapham A. and Jerbi S, 'Categories of Corporate Complicity in Human Rights Abuses' (2001) 24 (3) Hastings International and Comparative Law Review 339 <http://heinonline.org/HOL/LandingPage?handle=hein.journals/hasint24&div=20&id=&page=> accessed 6 July 2016

Cleveland SH, 'Alien Tort Statute, Civil Society, and Corporate Responsibility' (2004) 56 Rutgers Law Review 971 <http://heinonline.org/HOL/LandingPage?handle=hein.journals/rutlr56&div=35&id=&page=> accessed 14 August 2016

Clough J, 'Punishing the Parent: Corporate Criminal Complicity in Human Rights Abuses' (2008) 33 Brooklyn Journal of International Law 899

Coffee JC, 'Does "Unlawful Mean Criminal"?: Reflections on The Disappearing Tort/Crime Distinction in American law' (1991) 71 Boston Law Journal 193

Coffee JC, '"No Soul to Damn: No Body to Kick": An Unscandalized Inquiry into The Problem of Corporate Punishment' (1981) 79 (3) Michigan Law Review 386

Coffee JC, 'Paradigms Lost: The Blurring of The Criminal and Civil Law Models. And What Can be Done About it' (1992) 101 (8) Yale Law Journal 1875

Cohen LA, 'Application of The Realist and Liberal Perspectives to The Implementation of War Crimes Trials: Case Studies of Nuremberg and Bosnia' (1997) 2 UCLA Journal of International Law & Foreign Affairs 113

Colandrea V, 'On the Power of The European Court of Human Rights to Order Specific Non-Monetary Measures: Some Remarks in Light of The Assanidze, Broniowski and Sejdovic Cases' (2007) 7 (2) Human Rights Law Review 396

Cole D, Lobel J and Koh HH, 'Interpreting the Alien Tort Statute: Amicus Curiae Memorandum of International Law Scholars and Practitioners in Trajano v. Marcos' (1988) 12 Hastings International & Comparative Law Review

Cole WM, 'Mind the Gap: State Capacity and The Implementation of Human Rights Treaties' (2015) 69 (2) International Organization 405

Coleman JL, 'Practice of Corrective Justice' (1995) 37 Arizona Law Review 5

Collingsworth T, 'Separating Fact from Fiction in The Debate over Application of The Alien Tort Claims Act to Violations of Fundamental Human Rights by Corporations' (2002) 37 (3) USFL Review 563

Connolly K, 'Trial of Man Deported from US to Germany for Nazi War Crimes to Begin' The Guardian (London, 29 November 2009) <https://perma.cc/4T4E-NDT6> accessed 4 September 2017

Connolly N & Kaisershot M, 'Corporate Power and Human Rights' (2015) 19 (6) International Journal of Human Rights 663

Conway M, 'A New Duty of Care - Tort Liability from Voluntary Human Rights Due Diligence in Global Supply Chains' (2015) 40 (2) Queen's Law Journal 741

Cook WW, 'Act, Intention, and Motive in The Criminal Law' (1916) 26 (8) Yale Law Journal 645

Cooper NG, 'Gustavus Adolphus and Military Justice' (1981) 92 Military Law Review 129

Cooper SM and Owen DL, ‘Corporate Social Reporting and Stakeholder Accountability: The Missing link’ (2007) 32 (7) Accounting, Organizations and Society 649

Coppola L and DeMarco N, ‘Civil RICO: How Ambiguity Allowed the Racketeer Influenced and Corrupt Organizations Act to Expand Beyond Its Intended Purpose’ (2012) 38 New England Journal on Criminal and Civil Confinement 241

Correale J, ‘The Torture Victim Protection Act: A Vital Contribution to International Human Rights Enforcement or Just a Nice Gesture?’ (1994) 6 Pace International Law Review School of Law 197

Craig WL, ‘Application of The Trading with The Enemy Act to Foreign Corporations Owned by Americans: Reflections on Fruehauf v. Massardy’ (1970) 83 Harvard Law Review 579

Crisan J, ‘The Principles of Legality “Nullum Crimen, Nulla Poena Sine Lege” and Their Role’ (2010) 5 Effectius Newsletter 1

Crossette B, ‘UN Report Says New Democracies Falter’ New York Times (New York, 24 July 2002) A8

Curran VG and Sloss D, ‘Reviving Human Rights Litigation after Kiobel’ (2013) 107 (4) American Journal of International Law 858

Curran VG, ‘Extraterritoriality, Universal Jurisdiction, and The Challenge of Kiobel v. Royal Dutch Petroleum Co.’ (2013) 28 (1) Maryland Journal of International Law 76

Currie DP, ‘Positive and Negative Constitutional Rights’ (1986) 53 The University of Chicago Law Review 864

Curteis HM, ‘The Doctrine of Limited Liability’ (1938) 83 (532) Rusi Journal 695

Damaska M, ‘What is The Point of International Criminal Justice?’ (2008) 83 Chicago-Kent Law Review 329

D'Amato A, ‘Human Rights as Part of Customary International Law: A Plea for Change of Paradigms’ (1995/96) 25 Georgia Journal of International & Comparative Law 47

Danforth ME, ‘Corporate Civil Liability under The Alien Tort Statute: Exploring Its Possibility and Jurisdictional Limitations’ (2011) 44 (3) Cornell International Law Journal 659

Daniel A, ‘Civil Liability Regimes as a Complement to Multilateral Environmental Agreements: Sound International Policy or False Comfort?’ (2003) 12 (3) Review of European Community & International Environmental Law 225

Danner AM and Martinez JS, ‘Guilty Associations: Joint Criminal Enterprise, Command Responsibility, and the Development of International Criminal Law’ (2005) 93 California Law Review 75

Davidson RH, 'The International Criminal Tribunal for Rwanda's Decision in The Prosecutor v. Ferdinand Nahimana et al.: The Past, Present, and Future of International Incitement Law' (2004) 17 (3) Leiden Journal of International Law 505

De Gennaro MA, 'Oil Pollution Liability and Control under International Maritime Law: Market Incentives as An Alternative to Government Regulation' (2004) 37 Vanderbilt Journal of Transnational Law 265

De Maglie C, 'Models of Corporate Criminal Liability in Comparative Law' (2005) 4 Washington University Global Studies Law Review 547

De Poorter I, 'Auditor's Liability towards Third Parties within the EU: A Comparative Study between the United Kingdom, The Netherlands, Germany and Belgium' (2008) 3 (1) Journal of International Commercial Law and Technology 68

Dean AH, 'The Role of International Law in a Metropolitan Practice' (1955) 103 (7) University of Pennsylvania Law Review 886

Dear J and Zipperstein SE, 'Comparative Fault and Intentional Torts: Doctrinal Barriers and Policy Considerations' (1984) 24 Santa Clara Law Review 1

Delahunty RJ and Yoo J, 'Against Foreign Law' (2005) 29 Harvard Journal of Law & Public Policy 291

Deva S, 'Socially Responsible Business in India: Has the Elephant Finally Woken Up to The Tunes of International Trends?' (2012) 41 (4) Common Law World Review 299

Dewey J, 'The Historic Background of Corporate Legal Personality' (1926) 35 (6) Yale Law Journal 655

Dickinson LA, 'Government for Hire: Privatizing Foreign Affairs and The Problem of Accountability under International Law' (2005) 47 William & Mary Law Review 135

Diller JM, 'ILO Tripartite Declaration of Principles Concerning Multinational Enterprises and Social Policy' (2002) 41 (1) International Legal Materials 184

Dimitrov RS, 'Knowledge, Power, and Interests in Environmental Regime Formation' (2003) 47 (1) International Studies Quarterly 123

Dine J, 'Jurisdictional Arbitrage by Multinational Companies: A National Law Solution?' (2012) 3 (1) Journal of Human Rights and The Environment 44

Dinstein Y, 'International Criminal Law' (1985) 20 Israel Law Review 206

Diskant EB, 'Comparative Corporate Criminal Liability: Exploring the Uniquely American Doctrine Through Comparative Criminal Procedure' (2008) Yale Law Journal 126

Dixit S, Wagle S and Sant G, 'The Real Challenge in Power Sector Restructuring: Instilling Public Control Through Transparency, Accountability and Public Participation (TAP)' (2001) 5 (3) Energy for Sustainable Development 95

Doane D and Abasta-Vilaplana N, 'The Myth of CSR' (2005) 3 (3) Stanford Social Innovation Review 22

Dodge WS, 'Understanding the Presumption against Extraterritoriality' (1998) 16 Berkeley Journal of International Law 85

Doeker G and Gehring T, 'Private or International Liability for Transnational Environmental Damage - The Precedent of Conventional Liability Regimes (1990) 2 Journal of Environmental Law and Litigation 1

Donoho D, 'Human Rights Enforcement in The Twenty-first Century' (2006) 35 Georgia Journal of International & Comparative Law 1

Dorfman A, 'What is The Point of The Tort Remedy?' (2010) 55 (1) American Journal of Jurisprudence 105

Douglas WO and Shanks CM, 'Insulation from Liability Through Subsidiary Corporations' (1929) 39 Yale Law Journal 193

Downs RC, 'Piercing the Corporate Veil - Do Corporations Provide Limited Personal Liability?' (1985) 53 UMKC Law Review 174

Drinan RF and Kuo TT, Putting the World's Oppressors on Trial: The Torture Victim Protection Act' (1993) 15 (3) Human Rights Quarterly 605

Drozdowski K, 'Liability for Impaired Driving: Expanding the Scope' (2004) 29 Law Now 62

Duncan RN, 'The 1972 Convention on The Prevention of Marine Pollution by Dumping of Wastes at Sea' (1973) 5 Journal of Maritime Law and Commerce 299

Dunn FS, 'International Law and Private Property Rights'. (1928) 28 Columbia Law Review 166

Duruigbo E, 'Corporate Accountability and Liability for International Human Rights Abuses: Recent Changes and Recurring Challenges' (2008) 6 (2) Northwestern University Journal of International Human Rights 222

Eaton JP, 'The Nigerian Tragedy, Environmental Regulation of Transnational Corporations, and The Human Right to a Healthy Environment' (1997) 15 Boston University International Law Journal 261

Edelman JJ, 'Unjust Enrichment, Restitution, and Wrongs' (2001) 79 Texas Law Review 1869

Ehrenzweig AA, 'The Lex Fori - Basic Rule in The Conflict of Laws' (1960) 58 (5) Michigan Law Review 637

Eisenberg MA, 'The Concept of National Law and The Rule of Recognition' (2002) 29 (4) Florida State University Law Review 1229

Emeseh E, 'Globalisation and Resource Development in Africa: Assessing the Facilitator - Protector Roles of International Law and International Institutions' (2008) 25 (5) Development Southern Africa 561

Engle E, 'Corporate Social Responsibility (CSR): Market-Based Remedies for International Human Rights Violations' (2004) 40 Willamette Law Review 103

Engle E, 'Extraterritorial Corporate Criminal Liability: A Remedy for Human Rights Violations' (2006) 20 (2) John's Journal of Legal Commentary 287

Engle E, 'The Alien Tort Statute and The Torture Victims' Protection Act: Jurisdictional Foundations and Procedural Obstacles' (2006) 14 (1) Willamette Journal of International Law and Dispute Resolution 1

Engle E, 'The Torture Victim's Protection Act, The Alien Tort Claims Act, and Foucault's Archaeology of Knowledge' (2004) 67 Albany Law Review 501

Enneking L, 'The Common Denominator of The Trafigura Case, Foreign Direct Liability Cases and The Rome II Regulation' (2008) 16 European Review of Private Law 283

Enneking L, 'Future of Foreign Direct Liability? Exploring the International Relevance of The Dutch Shell Nigeria Case' (2014) 10 (1) Utrecht Law Review 44

Ensign RL, 'How Daimler Got "A Very Good Report Card' *The Wall Street Journal* (New York, 29 May 2013) <https://blogs.wsj.com/riskandcompliance/2013/05/29/how-daimler-got-avery-good-report-card/> accessed 15 July 2017

Epstein RA, 'A Theory of Strict Liability' (1973) 2 (1) Journal of Legal Studies 151

Epstein RA, 'The Tort/Crime Distinction: A Generation Later' (1996) 76 BUL Review 1

Esper DA and Keating GC, 'Putting "Duty" in Its Place: A Reply to Professors Goldberg & Zipursky' (2008) 41 Loyola of Los Angeles Law Review 1225

Euteneier GT, 'Towards a Corporate "Law of Nations": Multinational Enterprises Contributions to Customary International Law' (2007) 82 (2) Tulane Law Review 757

Fagan DN, 'Achieving Restitution: The Potential Unjust Enrichment Claims of Indigenous Peoples against Multinational Corporations' (2001) 76 New York University Law Review 626

Fagbohun OA, 'The Regulation of Transboundary Shipments of Hazardous Waste: A Case Study of The Dumping of Toxic Waste in Abidjan, Cote d'Ivoire' (2007) 37 Hong Kong Law Journal 831

Fairman C, 'The Supreme Court on Military Jurisdiction: Martial Rule in Hawaii and The Yamashita Case' (1946) 59 Harvard Law Review 833

Fanto J 'Organizational Liability' (2010) 19 Harvard Journal of Law & Public Policy 45

Faqir RSA, 'The Criminal Liability of Parent Corporations for Acts of Its Subsidiaries under Criminal Law in Jordan: A Comparative Study' (2016) 7 Beijing Law Review 212

Farkas Z, 'The Concept and Types of Social Relationship' (2014) 32 (1) Társadalomkutatás 10

Fasterling B and Demuijnck G, 'Human Rights in the Void? Due Diligence in The UN Guiding Principles on Business and Human Rights' (2013) 116 (4) Journal of Business Ethics 799

Feeney P, 'Business and Human Rights: The Struggle for Accountability in The Future and The Future Direction of The Advocacy Agenda' (2009) 6 (11) South International Journal of Human Rights 174

Feinberg J, 'Collective Responsibility' (1968) 65 (21) Journal of Philosophy 674

Finch GA, 'Nuremberg Trial and International Law, The' (1947) 41 American Journal of International Law 20 <http://heinonline.org/HOL/LandingPage?handle=hein.journals/ajil41&div=6&id=&page=> accessed 21 September 2016

Finkelman P, 'Prigg v. Pennsylvania and Northern State Courts: Anti-Slavery Use of a Pro-Slavery Decision' (1979) 25 Civil War History 5

Finn CH, 'The Responsible Corporate Officer, Criminal Liability, and Mens Rea: Limitations on The RCO Doctrine' (1996) 46 American University Law Review 543

Fisher E, 'The European Union in The Age of Accountability' (2004) 24 (1) Oxford Journal of Legal Studies 495 <http://www.jstor.org/stable/3600565?seq=1#page_scan_tab_contents> accessed 3 July 2016

Fisse B and Braithwaite J, 'The Allocation of Responsibility for Corporate Crime: Individualism, Collectivism and Accountability' (1986) 11 Sydney Law Review 468

Fitchen J, 'Choice of Law in International Claims based on Restrictions of Competition: Article 6 (3) of The Rome II Regulation' (2009) 5 (2) Journal of Private International Law 337

Fitzgerald S, 'Corporate Accountability for Human Rights Violations in Australian Domestic Law' (2005) 11 (1) Australian Journal of Human Rights 2

Fitzmaurice GG, 'Third Report on The Law of Treaties' (1958) 2 Yearbook of the International Law Commission 20, U.N. Doc. A/CN.4/115

Fletcher GP, 'The Storrs Lectures: Liberals and Romantics at War: The Problem of Collective Guilt' (2002) 111 Yale Law Journal 1499

Forcese C, 'ATCA's Achilles Heel: Corporate Complicity, International Law and The Alien Tort Claims Act' (2001) 26 Yale Journal of International Law 487

Ford C and Hess D, 'Can Corporate Monitorships Improve Corporate Compliance?' (2008) 34 Journal of Corporation Law 679

Free BC, 'Awaiting Doe v. Exxon Mobil Corp.: Advocating the Cautious Use of Executive Opinions in Alien Tort Claims Act Litigation' (2003) 12 (2) Pacific Rim Law & Policy Journal 467

Freeman B, Pica MB and Camponovo CN. 'A New Approach to Corporate Responsibility: The Voluntary Principles on Security and Human Rights' (2001) 24 Hastings International and Comparative Law Review 423

French PA, 'The Corporation as A Moral Person' (1979) 16 (3) American Philosophical Quarterly 207

Frey B, 'Motivation Crowding Theory-a New Approach to Behaviour' (2008) Behavioural Economics and Public Policy: Roundtable Proceedings. Australian Government Productivity Commission

Frey BA, 'The Legal and Ethical Responsibilities of Transnational Corporations in The Protection of International Human Rights' (1997) 6 Minnesota Journal of Global Trade 153

Frynas JG, 'Political Instability and Business: Focus on Shell in Nigeria' (1998) 19 (3) Third World Quarterly 457

Fuentes X, 'International Law-Making in The Field of Sustainable Development: The Unequal Competition Between Development and The Environment' (2002) 2 (2) International Environmental Agreements: Politics, Law and Economics 109

Fujishima A and Honda K, 'Electrochemical Photolysis of Water at A Semiconductor Electrode' (1972) 238 (5358) Nature 37

Fulbrook J, 'Chandler v Cape Plc: Personal Injury: Liability: Negligence' (2012) 3 Journal of Personal Injury Law C135

Gaeta P, 'Is NATO Authorized or Obliged to Arrest Persons Indicted by The International Criminal Tribunal for the former Yugoslavia?' (1998) 9 (1) European Journal of International Law 174

Gaines SE, International Principles for Transnational Environmental Liability: Can Developments in Municipal Law Help Break the Impasse?' (1989) 30 Harvard International Law Journal 311

Gallegos L and Uribe D, 'The Next Step Against Corporate Impunity: A World Court on Business and Human Rights?' (2016) 57 Harvard International Law Journal 7

Gallimore T, 'The Legacy of The International Criminal Tribunal for Rwanda (ICTR) and Its Contributions to Reconciliation in Rwanda' (2008) 14 (2) New England Journal of International and Comparative Law 239

Gardner J, 'The Many Faces of The Reasonable Person' (2015) 131 Law Quarterly Review 563

Garvey M, 'Corporate Aiding and Abetting Liability Under the Alien Tort Statute: A Legislative Prerogative' (2009) 29 (2) BC Third World Law Journal 381

Gehring T and Jachtenfuchs M, 'Liability for Transboundary Environmental Damage Towards a General Liability Regime?' (1993) 4 (1) European Journal of International Law 92

Gettler L, 'Liability Forges a New Morality' *The Age* (3August 2005)

Gevurtz FA, 'Building a Wall against Private Actions for Overseas Injuries: The Impact of RJR Nabisco v European Community' (2017) 23 U.C. Davis Journal of International Law & Policy 1

Giannarakis G, Litinas N and Sariannidis N, 'Evaluation of Corporate Social Responsibility Performance Standards' (2011) 5 (17) African Journal of Business Management 7367

Gibb F, 'Trafigura's £30 Million Payout Approved after Slopes Dumped in Ivory Coast' *The Times* (London, 24 September 2009) <http://www.thetimes.co.uk/tto/law/article22149990.ece> accessed 21 December 2016

Gibson K, 'Excuses, Excuses: Moral Slippage in The Workplace' (2000) 43 (3) Business Horizons 65

Giesel GM, 'The Legal Advice Requirement of The Attorney-Client Privilege: A Special Problem for In-House Counsel and Outside Attorneys Representing Corporations' (1997) 48 Mercer Law Review 1169

Gillett M, 'Testing the Limits of The Law against Those Who Test the Tribunal's Limits: Contempt Proceedings at The Special Tribunal for Lebanon' (2017) 15 (4) Journal of International Criminal Justice 27

Glannon JW, 'Liability for" Public Duties" Under the Tort Claims Act: The Legislature Reconsiders The Public Duty Rule' (1994) 79 Massachusetts Law Review 17

Glanz MN, 'RICO and Securities Fraud: A Workable Limitation' (1983) 83 Columbia Law Review 1513

Gneezy U and Rustichini A, 'A Fine is a Price' (2000) 29 (1) Journal of Legal Studies 1

Goldberg JCP and Zipursky BC, 'Torts as Wrongs' (2010) 88 Texas Law Review 917

Goldenberg SL, 'Crimes against Humanity 1945-1970: A Study in the Making and Unmaking of International Criminal Law' (1971) 10 Western Ontario Law Review 1

Goldhaber MD, 'Corporate Human Rights Litigation in Non-US Courts: A Comparative Scorecard' (2013) 3 U.C. Irvine Law Review 127

Goldstein BD, Osofsky HJ and Lichtveld MY, 'The Gulf Oil Spill' (2011) 364 (14) New England Journal of Medicine 1334

Gordon GS, 'A War of Media, Words, Newspapers, and Radio Stations: The ICTR Media Trial Verdict and a New Chapter in The International Law of Hate Speech' (2004) 45 Virginia Journal of International Law 139

Gordon GS, 'Hong Kong's War Crimes Trials' (2014) 15(2) Melbourne Journal of International Law 560

Graff J, 'Corporate War Criminals and The International Criminal Court: Blood and Profits in The Democratic Republic of Congo' (2004) 11 (2) Human Rights Brief 23

Granatino KG, 'Corporate Responsibility Now: Profit at The Expense of Human Rights with Exemption from Liability?' (1999) 23 Suffolk Transnational Law Review 191

Grear A and Weston BH, 'The Betrayal of Human Rights and The Urgency of Universal Corporate Accountability: Reflections on a Post-Kiobel Lawscape' (2015) 15 (1) Human Rights Law Review 21

Grear A, 'Challenging Corporate "Humanity": Legal Disembodiment, Embodiment and Human Rights' (2007) 7 (3) Human Rights Law Review 511

Green JM, 'Corporate Torts: International Human Rights and Superior Officers' (2016) 17 (2) Chicago Journal of International Law 447

Green JM, 'The Rule of Law at a Crossroad: Enforcing Corporate Responsibility in International Investment Through the Alien Tort Statute' (2014) 35 (4) University of Pennsylvania Journal of International Law 1085

Green JM, Coliver S., and Hoffman P, Holding Human Rights Violators Accountable by Using International Law in US Courts: Advocacy Efforts and Complementary Strategies' (2005) 19 Emory International Law Review 169

Green LC, 'Case Analysis: Dražen Erdemovic: The International Criminal Tribunal for The Former Yugoslavia in Action' (1997) 10 (2) Leiden Journal of International Law 363

Green LC, 'Command Responsibility in International Humanitarian Law' (1995) 5 Transnational Law & Contemporary Problems 319

Greenawalt K, 'Religious Law and Civil Law: Using Secular Law to Assure Observance of Practices with Religious Significance' (1998) 71 Southern California Law Review 781

Greene J, 'Hostis Humani Generis' (2008) 34 (4) Critical Inquiry 683

Greenhouse S and Manik JA, 'Stalemate over Garment Factory Safety in Bangladesh' *New York Times* (New York, 25 June 2014)

Gross SR, 'The American Advantage: The Value of Inefficient Litigation' (1987) 85 Michigan Law Review 734

Grossman DI, 'Would a Corporate Death Penalty Be Cruel and Unusual Punishment' (2016) 25 (3) Cornell Journal of Law and Public Policy 697

Grunberg J, 'The Torture Victim Protection Act: A Means to Corporate Liability for Aiding and Abetting Torture' (2012) 61 Catholic University Law Review 235

Guiraudon V and Lahav G, 'A Reappraisal of The State Sovereignty Debate: The Case of Migration Control' (2000) 33 (2) Comparative Political Studies 163

Habermas J, 'The Concept of Human Dignity and The Realistic Utopia of Human Rights' (2010) 41 (4) Metaphilosophy 464, 480

Haberstroh J, 'In Re World War II Era Japanese Forced Labour Litigation and Obstacles to International Human Rights Claims in US Courts' (2003) 10 Asian Law Journal 253

Haffke CW, 'The Torture Victim Protection Act: More Symbol than Substance' (1994) 43 Emory Law Journal 1467

Hagemann TA and Grinstein J, 'The Mythology of Aggregate Corporate Knowledge: A Deconstruction' (1997) 65 (2) George Washington Law Review 210

Haggard S and Simmons BA, 'Theories of International Regimes' (1987) 41 (03) International Organization 491

Halberstam M, 'Belgium's Universal Jurisdiction Law: Vindication of International Justice or Pursuit of Politics?' (2003) 25 Cardozo Law Review 247

Hall J, 'Interrelations of Criminal Law and Torts: I' (1943) 43 (3) Columbia Law Review 753

Hamann R, Sinha P, Kapfudzaruwa F, and Schild C, 'Business and Human Rights in South Africa: An Analysis of Antecedents of Human Rights Due Diligence' (2009) 87 (2) Journal of Business Ethics 453

Handford P, 'Intentional Negligence: A Contradiction in Terms? (2010) 32 Sydney Law Review 29

Handl G, 'Transboundary Nuclear Accidents: The Post-Chernobyl Multilateral Legislative Agenda' (1988) 15 Ecology Law Quarterly 203

Hannum H and Hawk H, 'The Case against The Standing Committee of The Communist Party of Kampuchea' (1986) New York: Cambodia Documentation Commission

Hansmann H and Kraakman R, 'Toward Unlimited Shareholder Liability for Corporate Torts' (1991) Yale Law Journal 1879, 1934

Koh HH, 'President Versus The Senate in Treaty Interpretation: What's All the Fuss About?' (1990) 15 Yale Journal of International Law 331

Hartkamp AS, 'Judicial Discretion Under The New Civil Code of The Netherlands' (1992) 40 American Journal of Comparative Law 554

Hathaway OA, 'Do Human Rights Treaties Make a Difference? (2002) 111 Yale Law Journal 1935

Hawk D, 'International Human Rights Law and Democratic Kampuchea' (1986) 16 (3) International Journal of Politics 3

Haynes J, 'Power, Politics and Environmental Movements in The Third World' (1999) 8 (1) Environmental Politics 222

Healy MP, 'Direct Liability for Hazardous Substance Clean-ups under CERCLA: A Comprehensive Approach Case' (1992) 42 (1) Western Reserve Law Review 65

Hebert RT and Conrotto PA, 'Laser Scanner with Rotating Mirror and Housing Which is Transparent to The Scanning Radiation' (1989) 4 US Patent 870 2674

Henkin L, 'The Foreign Affairs Power of The Federal Courts: Sabbatino' (1964) 64 (5) Columbia Law Review 805

Héritier A, 'Composite Democracy in Europe: The Role of Transparency and Access to Information' (2003) 10 (5) Journal of European Public Policy 814

Herstein OJ, 'Responsibility in Negligence: Why the Duty of Care is Not a Duty "To Try"' (2010) 23 (02) Canadian Journal of Law and Jurisprudence 403

Herz RL, 'Litigating Environmental Abuses Under The Alien Tort Claims Act: A Practical Assessment' (2000) 40 Virginia Journal of International Law 545

Hess D and Dunfe TW, 'The Kasky-Nike Threat to Corporate Social Reporting: Implementing a Standard of Optimal Truthful Disclosure as A Solution' (2007) 17 (1) Business Ethics Quarterly 5

Hess D, 'Social Reporting and New Governance Regulation: The Prospects of Achieving Corporate Accountability Through Transparency' (2007) 17 (3) Business Ethics Quarterly 453

Hessick AF, 'Standing, Injury in Fact, and Private Rights' (2008) 93 Cornell Law Review 275

Heuston RFV, 'Donoghue v. Stevenson in Retrospect' (1957) 20 (1) Modern Law Review 1

Higgins G, 'Fair and Expeditious Pre-trial Proceedings the Future of International Criminal Trials' (2007) 5 (2) Journal of International Criminal Justice 394

Higgins DR, 'Human Rights in The International Court of Justice' (2007) 20 (2) Leiden Journal of International Law 745

Higgins DR, 'International Law in A Changing International System' (1999) 58 (1) Cambridge Law Journal 78

Hills J and Welford R, 'Coca-Cola and Water in India' (2005) 12 (3) Corporate Social Responsibility and Environmental Management 168

Hinton AL, 'A Head for An Eye: Revenge in The Cambodian Genocide' (1998) 25 (3) American Ethnologist 352

Hirschl R, '"Negative" Rights vs. "Positive" Entitlements: A Comparative Study of Judicial Interpretations of Rights in An Emerging Neo-Liberal Economic Order' (2000) 22 (4) Human Rights Quarterly 1060

Hodas DR, 'Enforcement of Environmental Law in A Triangular Federal System: Can Three Not Be a Crowd When Enforcement Authority Is Shared by The United States, and Their Citizens?' (1995) 54 (4) Maryland Law Review 1552

Holzer B, 'Framing the Corporation: Royal Dutch/Shell and Human Rights Woes in Nigeria' (2007) 30 (3) Journal of Consumer Policy 281

Hovi J and Areklett I, 'Enforcing the Climate Regime: Game Theory and the Marrakesh Accords' (2004) 4 (1) International Environmental Agreements: Politics, Law and Economics 1

Howard C, 'Compensation in French Criminal Procedure' (1958) 21 Modern Law Review 387

Hughes AG, 'Drawing Sensible Borders for The Definition of "Foreign Official" Under the FCPA' (2013) 40 (3) American Journal of Criminal Law 253

Humphreville AA, 'If the Question Is Chocolate-Related, The Answer Is Always Yes: Why Doe v Nestle Reopens the Door for Corporate Liability of US Corporations Under The Alien Tort Statute' (2015) 65 American University Business Law Review 191

Huxman SS and Bruce DB, 'Toward a Dynamic Generic Framework of Apologia: A Case Study of Dow Chemical, Vietnam, and The Napalm Controversy' (1995) 46 (1-2) Communication Studies 57

Ibanez JG, 'Legal Pedagogy, The Rule of Law, and Human Rights: The Professor, The Magistrate's Robe, and Miguel de Unamuno' (2012) 7 (4) Interdisciplinary Journal of Human Rights Law 147

Ibbetson D, 'How the Romans Did for Us: Ancient Roots of The Tort of Negligence' (2003) 26 (2) University of New South Wales Law Journal 475

Ibeanu O, 'Oiling the Friction: Environmental Conflict Management in The Niger Delta, Nigeria' (2000) 6 Environmental Change and Security Project Report 19

ILC, 'Report of The International Law Commission on The Second Part of Its Seventeenth Session and on Its Eighteenth Session' (1966) Yearbook of the International Law Commission II 219 <http://untreaty.un.org/ilc/texts/instruments/english/commentaries/1_1_1966.pdf> accessed 21 September 2017

Imai S, Maheandiran B and Crystal V, 'Access to Justice and Corporate Accountability: A Legal Case Study of HudBay in Guatemala' (2014) 35 (2) Canadian Journal of Development Studies/Revue canadienne d'études du développement 285

Imoedemhe O, 'Unpacking the Tension between The African Union and The International Criminal Court: The Way Forward' (2015) 23 (1) African Journal of International and Comparative Law 74

Islam MA and McPhail K, 'Regulating for Corporate Human Rights Abuses: The Emergence of Corporate Reporting on The ILO's Human Rights Standards within The Global Garment Manufacturing and Retail Industry' (2011) 22 (8) Critical Perspectives on Accounting 790

Issacharoff S and Rave DT, 'The BP Oil Spill Settlement and The Paradox of Public Litigation' (2014) 74 (2) Louisiana Law Review 397

Jackson KT, 'A Cosmopolitan Court for Transnational Corporate Wrongdoing: Why Its Time Has Come' (1998) 17 (7) Journal of Business Ethics 757

Jackson KT, 'Global Corporate Governance: Soft Law and Reputational Accountability' (2010) 35 Brooklyn Journal of International Law 41

Jackson RH, 'Nuremberg in Retrospect: Legal Answer to International Lawlessness' (1949) 35 American Bar Association Journal 813

Jacobson KR, 'Doing Business with The Devil: The Challenges of Prosecuting Corporate Officials Whose Business Transactions Facilitate War Crimes and Crimes against Humanity' (2005) 56 Air Force Law Review 167

Jaffey P, 'The Law Commission Report on Aggravated, Exemplary and Restitutionary Damages' (1998) 61 (6) Modern Law Review 860

Jägers NMCP, Jesse KD and Verschuuren JM, 'The Future of Corporate Liability for Extraterritorial Human Rights Abuses: The Dutch Case against Shell' (2014) 1 American Journal of International Law E36

Jagers NMCP and Heijden MJ, 'Corporate Human Rights Violations: The Feasibility of Civil Recourse in The Netherlands' (2008) 33 (3) Brooklyn Journal of International Law 833

Johnston BR, 'Reparations and The Right to Remedy' (2000) World Commission on Dams Contributing Report, Thematic Review

Jones AD, 'Corporate Officer Wrongdoing and The Fiduciary Duties of Corporate Officers under Delaware Law' (2007) 44 (3) American Business Law Journal 475

Jongsok O, 'The Prosecutor's Dilemma-Strengths and Flaws of The Genocide Convention' (2003) 10 (3) Murdoch University Electronic Journal of Law 4

Jordon J, 'Recent Developments in The Foreign Corrupt Practices Act and The New UK Bribery Act: A Global Trend Towards Greater Accountability in The Prevention of Foreign Bribery' (2010) 7 New York University Journal of Law & Business 845

Jorgensen NHB, 'Right of The Accused to Self-Representation before International Criminal Tribunals' (2004) 98 American Journal of International Law 711

Juergensmeyer JC, 'Control of Air Pollution Through the Assertion of Private Rights' (1967) Duke Law Journal 1126

Kaeb C, 'The Shifting Sands of Corporate Liability under International Criminal Law' (2016) 49 George Washington International Law Review 351

Kalleberg AL, 'Precarious Work, Insecure Workers: Employment Relations in Transition' (2009) 74 (1) American Sociological Review 1

Kappel V, Schmidt P and Ziegler A, 'Human Rights Abuse and Corporate Stock Performance An Event Study Analysis' (2009) Whitepaper, December 21

Karaba FA, 'Negligent Homicide or Manslaughter: A Dilemma' (1950) 41(2) Journal of Criminal Law and Criminology 183

Karavias M, 'Shared Responsibility and Multinational Enterprises' (2015) 62 (1) Netherlands International Law Review 91

Katz RS, 'The Corporate Crimes of Dow Chemical and The Failure to Regulate Environmental Pollution' (2010) 18 (4) Critical Criminology 295

Kaleck W and Saage-Maass M, 'Corporate Accountability for Human Rights Violations Amounting to International Crimes. The Status Quo and Its Challenges' (2010) 8 (3) Journal of International Criminal Justice 699

Keating GC, 'Distributive and Corrective Justice in The Tort Law of Accidents' (2000) 74 Southern California Law Review 193

Keegan MJ, 'Preparation of Cases for the ICTY' (1997) 7 Transnational Law & Contemporary Problems 119

Kelly MJ, 'Ending Corporate Impunity for Genocide: The Case Against China's State-Owned Petroleum Company in Sudan' (2011) 90 Oregon Law Review 413

Kelly MJ, 'Grafting the Command Responsibility Doctrine onto Corporate Criminal Liability For Atrocities' (2010) 24 Emory International Law Review 671

Kelsen H 'Collective and Individual Responsibility in International Law with Particular Regard to The Punishment of War Criminals' (1942) 31 California Law Review 530

Kende MS, 'The South African Constitutional Court's Embrace of Socio-Economic Rights: A Comparative Perspective' (2003) 6 Chapman Law Review 137

Kennedy D, 'International Human Rights Movement: Part of the Problem? (2002) 15 Harvard Law School Human Rights Journal 101

Kenney C, 'Disaster in The Amazon: Dodging "Boomerang Suits" in Transnational Human Rights Litigation' (2009) 97 (3) California Law Review 857

Keohane RO, 'The Demand for International Regimes' (1982) 36 (02) International Organization 325

Keys TS, Malnight TW and Stoklund CK, 'Corporate Clout 2013: Time for Responsible Capitalism' (2013) Strategy Dynamics Global <http://globaltrends.activatemedia.com/wpcontent/uploads/2013/06/corporate%20clout%202013.pdf> accessed 12 August 2016

Khanna V and Dickinson TL, 'The Corporate Monitor: The New Corporate (2006) 105 University of Michigan Law School 1713

Kiernan B, 'Bringing the Khmer Rouge to Justice' (2000) 1 (3) Human Rights Review 92.

Kimberling J, 'Indigenous Peoples and The Oil Frontier in Amazonia: The Case of Ecuador, ChevronTexaco, and Aguinda v. Texaco (2005) 38 New York University Journal of Law & Business 413

Kircher JJ, 'The Four Faces of Tort Law: Liability for Emotional Harm' (2006) 90 Marquette Law Review 789

Kirsch A, 'Criminal Liability for Corporate Bodies in French Law' (1998) 9 European Business Law Review 38

Kirsch S, 'Indigenous Movements and The Risks of Counter Globalization: Tracking the Campaign against Papua New Guinea's Ok Tedi Mine' (2007) 34 (2) American Ethnologist 303

Klabbers J, 'International Legal Histories: The Declining Importance of Travaux Préparatoires in Treaty Interpretation?' (2003) 50 (3) Netherlands International Law Review 267

Klein KM, 'Bringing the Khmer Rouge to Justice: The Challenges and Risks Facing the Joint Tribunal in Cambodia' (2006) 4 Northwestern Journal of Human Rights 549

Klimchuk D, 'Unjust Enrichment and Reparations for Slavery' (2004) 84 Boston University Law Review 1257

Knight CR, 'International Human Rights Litigation after Bauman: The Viability of Veil Piercing to Hale Foreign Parent Corporations into US Courts' (2016) 41 (2) University of Dayton Law Review 213 <http://heinonline.org/HOL/LandingPage?handle=hein.journals/udlr41&div=13&id=&page=> accessed 25 September 2017

Knop K, 'Here and There: International Law in Domestic Courts' (1999) 32 New York University Journal International Law & Politics 501

Knuckey S and Jenkin E, 'Company-Created Remedy Mechanisms for Serious Human Rights Abuses: A Promising New Frontier for The Right to Remedy?' (2015) 19 (6) International Journal of Human Rights 801

Kobrin SJ, 'Private Political Authority and Public Responsibility: Transnational Politics, Transnational Firms, and Human Rights' (2009) 19 (3) Business Ethics Quarterly 349

Koenig DM, 'The Criminal Justice System Facing the Challenge of Organized Crime' (1998) 44 Wayne Law Review 1351

Koh HH, 'How is international Human Rights Law Enforced' (1999) 74 Indian Law Journal 1397

Koh HH, 'International Law as Part of Our Law' (2004) 98 American Journal of International Law 43

Koh HH, Chayes A, Chayes AH and Franck TM, 'Why Do Nations Obey International Law?' (1997) 106 (8) Yale Law Journal 2599

Koh HH, 'Separating Myth from Reality about Corporate Responsibility Litigation' (2004) 7 (2) Journal of International Economic Law 263

Kolben K, 'Labour Rights as Human Rights?' (2009) 50 (2) Virginia Journal of International Law 449

Kolk A, 'Sustainability, Accountability and Corporate Governance: Exploring Multinationals Reporting Practices' (2008) 17 (1) Business Strategy and the Environment 1

Kolstad I and Wiig A, 'Is Transparency the Key to Reducing Corruption in Resource-Rich Countries?' (2009) 37 (3) World Development 521

Komarow G' 'Individual Responsibility under International Law: The Nuremberg Principles in Domestic Legal Systems' (1980) International and Comparative Law Quarterly 21

Kontorovich E, 'Implementing Sosa v. Alvarez-Machain: What Piracy Reveals About the Limits of The Alien Tort Statute' (2004) 80 Notre Dame Law Review 111

Kontorovich E, 'Kiobel Surprise: Unexpected by Scholars but Consistent with International Trends' (2014) 89 Notre Dame Law Review 1671

Kontorovich E, 'The Constitutionality of International Courts: The Forgotten Precedent of Slave-Trade Tribunals' (2009) 158 (1) University of Pennsylvania Law Review 39

Koppell JGS, 'Pathologies of Accountability: ICANN and The Challenge of "Multiple Accountabilities Disorder"' (2005) 65 (1) Public Administration Review 94 <http://onlinelibrary.wiley.com/doi/10.1111/j.1540-6210.2005.00434.x/abstract> accessed 3 July 2016

Kress C, 'Universal Jurisdiction over International Crimes and the Institut de Droit International' (2006) 4 (3) Journal of International Criminal Justice 561

Kritz NJ, 'Coming to Terms with Atrocities: A Review of Accountability Mechanisms for Mass Violations of Human Rights' (1996) 59 (4) Law and Contemporary Problems 127

Krotoszynski Jr RJ, 'Transparency, Accountability, and Competency: An Essay on The Obama Administration, Google Government, and The Difficulties of Securing Effective Governance' (2011) 65 (2) University of Miami Law Review 449

Ku J and Yoo J, 'Beyond Formalism in Foreign Affairs: A Functional Approach to The Alien Tort Statute' (2004) Supreme Court Review 153

Ku JG, 'Kiobel and The Surprising Death of Universal Jurisdiction under The Alien Tort Statute' (2013) 107 (4) American Journal of International Law 835

Kuckes N, 'Civil Due Process, Criminal Due Process' (2006) 25 (1) Yale Law & Policy Review 1

Kuhn AK, 'International Law and National Legislation in the Trial of War Criminals the Yamashita Case' (1950) 44 (3) American Journal of International Law 559

Kuziemko I and Werker E, 'How Much is a Seat on The Security Council Worth? Foreign Aid and Bribery at The United Nations' (2006) 114 (5) Journal of Political Economy 905

Kyriakakis J, 'Corporate Criminal Liability and The ICC Statute: The Comparative Law Challenge' (2009) 56 (3) Netherlands International Law Review 333

Lagoutte S, 'New Challenges Facing States within The Field of Human Rights and Business' (2015) 33 (2) Nordic Journal of Human Rights 158

Landrum BD, 'The Yamashita War Crimes Trial: Command Responsibility Then and Now' (1995) 149 Military Law Review 293

Langer M, 'The Diplomacy of Universal Jurisdiction: The Political Branches and the Transitional Prosecution of International Crimes' (2011) 105 (1) American Journal of International Law 1

Langevoort DC, 'On Leaving Corporate Executives "Naked, Homeless and Without Wheels": Corporate Fraud, Equitable Remedies, and The Debate over Entity versus Individual Liability' (2007) 42 Wake Forest Law Review 627

Larguier J, 'Civil Action for Damages in French Criminal Procedure' (1964) 39 Tulane Law Review 687

Laufer WS, 'Corporate Liability, Risk Shifting, and The Paradox of Compliance' (1999) 52 Vanderbilt Law Review 1341

Laufer WS, 'Social Accountability and Corporate Greenwashing' (2003) 43 (3) Journal of Business Ethics 253

Lear ET, 'National Interests, Foreign Injuries, and Federal Forum Non Conveniens' (2007) 41 UC Davis School Law Review 559

Leck C, 'International Responsibility in United Nations Peacekeeping Operations: Command and Control Arrangements and The Attribution of Conduct' (2009) 10 Melbourne Journal of International Law 346

Lee TH, 'The Safe-Conduct Theory of The Alien Tort Statute' (2006) Columbia Law Review 830

Lee TH, 'The Three Lives of The Alien Tort Statute: The Evolving Role of The Judiciary in US Foreign Relations' (2014) 89 Notre Dame Law Review 1645

Leflar RA, 'Negligence in Name Only' (1952) 27 NYUL Rev. 564

Legrand P, 'European Legal Systems are Not Converging' (1996) 45 (1) International & Comparative Law Quarterly 52

Lemaitre R, 'Belgium Rules the World: Universal Jurisdiction over Human Rights Atrocities' (2000) 37(2) Jura Falconis 255

Levine JD, 'The Doctrine of Command Responsibility and Its Application to Superior Civilian

Leadership: Does the International Criminal Court Have The Correct Standard' (2007) 52 Military Law Review 193

Levin S 'Dakota Access Pipeline:Native Americans Allege Cruel Treatment' *The Guardian* (31 October 2016) <https://www.theguardian.com/us-

news/2016/oct/31/dakota-accesspipeline-protest-investigation-human-rights-abuses> accessed 6 August 2017

Linton S, 'Rediscovering the War Crimes Trials in Hong Kong, 1946-48' (2012) 13 Melbourne Journal of International Law 284

Lippman M, 'Fifty Years after Auschwitz: Prosecutions of Nazi Death Camp Defendants' (1995) 11 Connecticut Journal of International Law 199

Lippman M, 'The Other Nuremberg: American Prosecutions of Nazi War Criminals in ccupied Germany' (1992) 3 Indiana International & Comparative Law Review 1

Lipton M and Lorsch JW, 'A Modest Proposal for Improved Corporate Governance' (1992) Business Lawyer 59

Locke R, Kochan T, Romis M and Qin F, 'Beyond Corporate Codes of Conduct: Work Organization and Labour Standards at Nike's Suppliers' (2007) 146 (1-2) International Labour Review 21 <http://onlinelibrary.wiley.com/doi/10.1111/j.1564-913X.2007.00003.x/abstract> accessed 15 July 2016

Locke RM, Qin F and Brause A, 'Does Monitoring Improve Labour Standards? Lessons from Nike' (2007) 61(1) Industrial & Labour Relations Review 3, 31

London L, 'Human Rights, Environmental Justice, and The Health of Farm Workers in South Africa' (2003) 9 (1) International Journal of Occupational and Environmental Health 59

Lopez C and Shea B, 'Negotiating a Treaty on Business and Human Rights: A Review of The First Intergovernmental Session' (2016) 1 (01) Business and Human Rights Journal 111

Low LA, Lamoree SR and London J 'The Demand Side of Transnational Bribery and Corruption: Why Levelling the Playing Field on The Supply Side Isn't Enough' (2015) 84 Fordham Law Review 563

Luftglass S, 'Crossroads in Cambodia: The United Nation's Responsibility to Withdraw Involvement from The Establishment of a Cambodian Tribunal to Prosecute the Khmer Rouge' (2004) Virginia Law Review 893

Luntz H, 'Torts Turnaround Downunder' (2001) 1 (1) Oxford University Commonwealth Law Journal 95

Luo Y, 'Corporate Governance and Accountability in Multinational Enterprises: Concepts and Agenda' (2005) 11 (1) Journal of International Management 1

Lustig D, 'The Nature of The Nazi State and The Question of International Criminal Responsibility of Corporate Officials at Nuremberg: Revisiting Franz Neumann's Concept of Behemoth at The Industrialist

Trials' (2010) 43 New York University Journal of International Law and Politics 965

Lynch C, 'UN Warns Cambodia on War Crimes Tribunal' *Washington Post* (Washington DC, 3 February 2001)

Lynch GE, 'RICO: The Crime of Being a Criminal, Parts I & II' (1987) 87(4) Columbia Law Review 661

Ma J, 'Multinational Enterprises' Liability for The Acts of Their Offshore Subsidiaries: The Aftermath of Kiobel and Daimler' (2015) 23 Michigan State International Law Review 397

Macek EE, 'Scratching the Corporate Back: Why Corporations Have No Incentive to Define Human Rights' (2002) 11 Minnesota Journal of Global Trade 101

MacKinnon CA, 'Prosecutor v Nahimana, Barayagwiza, & Ngeze. Case No. ICTR 99-52-T' (2004) 98 (2) American Journal of International Law 325

Magarity GT, 'RICO Investigations: A Case Study' (1979) 17 American Criminal Law Review 367

Magliveras KD, 'The Interplay between The Transfer of Slobodan Milosevic to The ICTY and Yugoslav Constitutional Law' (2002) 13 (3) European Journal of International Law 661

Mahmoudi S, 'Some Private International Law Aspects of Transboundary Environmental Disputes' (1990) 59 Nordic Journal of International Law 128

Maier HG, 'Extraterritorial Jurisdiction at a Crossroads: An Intersection between Public and Private International Law' (1982) 76 (2) American Journal of International Law 280

Maizels A and Nissanke MK, 'Motivations for Aid to Developing Countries' (1984) 12 (9) World Development 879

Maley JR, 'Wrongful Adoption: Monetary Damages as A Superior Remedy to Annulment for Adoptive Parents Victimized by Adoption Fraud' (1987) 20 Indiana Law Review 709

Mann K, 'Punitive Civil Sanctions: The Middle Ground between Criminal and Civil Law' (1992) 101 (8) Yale Law Journal 1795

Mares R, 'Gap in The Corporate Responsibility to Respect Human Rights' (2010) 36 Monash University Law Review 33

Mariani P, 'Assessing the Proper Relationship between The Alien Tort Statute and The Torture Victim Protection Act.' (2008) 156 (5) University of Pennsylvania Law Review 1383

Mark SP, 'Forgetting the Policies and Practices of The Past: Impunity in Cambodia' (1994) 18 Fletcher Forum of World Affairs 17

Marrewijk MV, 'Concepts and Definitions of CSR and Corporate Sustainability: Between Agency and Communion' (2003) 44 (2) Journal of Business Ethics 95

Martin R, 'Categories of Negligence and Duties of Care: Caparo in the House of Lords' (1990) 3 (6) Modern Law Review 824

Martin SW, Bates R and McMyne M, 'Are You as Guilty as The Criminal? Liability for Criminal Acts of Third Parties and Employees' (2015) 64 (2) FDCC Quarterly 131

Martinez JS, 'Antislavery Courts and The Dawn of International Human Rights Law' (2008) 117 (4) Yale Law Journal 550

Martinez JS, 'Understanding Mens Rea in Command Responsibility from Yamashita to Blaškić and Beyond' (2007) 5 (3) Journal of International Criminal Justice 638

Mason M, 'Civil Liability for Oil Pollution Damage: Examining the Evolving Scope for Environmental Compensation in The International Regime' (2003) 27 (1) Marine Policy 1

Matten D and Moon J, 'Implicit" and "Explicit" CSR: A Conceptual Framework for a Comparative Understanding of Corporate Social Responsibility' (2008) 33 (2) Academy of Management Review 404

Mayr M, 'Extraterritorial Application of The European Convention on Human Rights and The Access to The Court for Victims of Human Rights Violations of ESDP Missions' (2010) BSIS Journal of International Studies 7

McConnell LJ, 'Establishing Liability for Multinational Oil Companies in Parent/Subsidiary Relationships' (2014) 16 (1) Environmental Law Review 50

McCorquodale R and Simons P, 'Responsibility Beyond Borders: State Responsibility for Extraterritorial Violations by Corporations of International Human Rights Law' (2007) 70 (4) Modern Law Review 598

McCorquodale R, 'Waving Not Drowning: Kiobel Outside the United States' (2013) 107 (4) American Journal of International Law 846

McDougal MS, Lasswell HD and Chen L, 'Human Rights and World Public Order: The Basic Policies of An International Law of Human Dignity' (1980) Northwestern University Law Review <http://digitalcommons.law.yale.edu/cgi/viewcontent.cgi?article=3674&context=fss_papers> accessed March 2016

McGregor L, 'The Need to Resolve the Paradoxes of The Civil Dimension of Universal Jurisdiction' (2005) 99 American Society of International Law Reviews 125

McIntyre G, 'Equality of Arms - Defining Human Rights in The Jurisprudence of The International Criminal Tribunal for The Former Yugoslavia' (2003) 16 (2) Leiden Journal of International Law 269

McLachlan C, 'The Principle of Systemic Integration and Article 31 (3) (c) of The Vienna Convention' (2005) 54 (2) International & Comparative Law Quarterly 279

McLean H, 'Negligent Regulatory Authorities and The Duty of Care' (1988) 8 (3) Oxford Journal of Legal Studies 442

McMahon T and Moertl K, 'The Erosion of Traditional Corporate Law Doctrines in Environmental Cases' (1988) 3 (3) Natural Resources & Environment 29

McQuade SJ, 'The Eggshell Skull Rule and Related Problems in Recovery for Mental Harm in The Law of Torts' (2001) 24 Campbell Law Review 1

McVey M, 'A Powerful Retort: Foreign Direct Liability as An Essential Mechanism of Redress for Victims of Human Rights Violations by Multinational Extractive Corporations' (2015) Human Rights Commission 2015 Working Paper 1

Meeran R, 'Tort Litigation against Multinational Corporations for Violation of Human Rights: An Overview of The Position Outside the United State' (2011) 3 City UHKL Review 1

Meernik J and King K, 'The Sentencing Determinants of The International Criminal Tribunal for The Former Yugoslavia: An Empirical and Doctrinal Analysis' (2003) 16 (04) Leiden Journal of International Law 717 <https://www.cambridge.org/core/journals/leiden-journal-of-internationallaw/article/the-sentencing-determinants-of-the-international-criminal-tribunal-for-theformer-yugoslavia-an-empirical-and-doctrinalanalysis/6F736144D4226AE6056594718177C8AA> accessed 25 September 2016

Mendelson NA, 'Control-Based Approach to Shareholder Liability for Corporate Torts' (2002) 102 Columbia Law Review 1203

Menzel PJT and Hoffmann J, 'United States v Curtiss-Wright Export Corporation, 299 US 304' (2005) Völkerrechtssprechung Mohr Siebeck 265

Meron T, 'International Criminalization of Internal Atrocities' (1995) 89 American Journal of International Law 554

Meron T, 'Procedural Evolution in the ICTY' (2004) 2 Journal of International Criminal Justice 520 <http://heinonline.org/HOL/LandingPage?handle=hein.journals/jicj2&div=63&id=&page=> accessed 25 September 2016

Meron T, 'Reflections on The Prosecution of War Crimes by International Tribunals' (2006) 100 (3) American Journal of International Law 551

Meron T, 'The Time Has Come for The United States to Ratify Geneva Protocol I' (1994) 88 (4) American Journal of International Law 678

Meron T, 'War Crimes in Yugoslavia and The Development of International Law' (1994) 88 (1) American Journal of International Law 78

Merrill TW, 'Golden Rules for Transboundary Pollution' (1997) 46 (5) Duke Law Journal 931

Merry SE, 'Legal Pluralism' (1988) 22 (5) Law & Society Review 869

Mickelson K, 'Rereading Trail Smelter' (1993) 31 Canadian Yearbook of International Law 219

Miller AR, 'Simplified Pleading, Meaningful Days in Court, and Trials on The Merits: Reflections on The Deformation of Federal Procedure' (2013) 88 New York University Law Review 286

Miller S, 'Revisiting Extraterritorial Jurisdiction: A Territorial Justification for Extraterritorial Jurisdiction Under The European Convention' (2009) 20 (4) European Journal of International Law 1223

Millon D, 'Theories of The Corporation' (1990) 2 Duke Law Journal 201

Mills J, 'Starting at Secondary School' (1996) 13 (1) British Journal of Music Education 5

Mills K, 'Bashir is Dividing Us: Africa and The International Criminal Court' (2012) 34 (2) Human Rights Quarterly 404

Miranda LA, 'The Hybrid State-Corporate Enterprise and Violations of Indigenous Land Rights: Theorizing Corporate Responsibility and Accountability Under International Law' (2007) 11 Lewis & Clark Law Review 135

Morina V, Korenica F, and Doli D. 'The Relationship Between International Law and National Law in The Case of Kosovo: A Constitutional Perspective' (2011) 9 (1) International Journal of Constitutional Law 274

Morris C, 'Punitive Damages in Tort Cases' (1931) 44 Harvard Law Review 1173

Mortell TJ and Gustavson M, The Resurgence of The Corporate Officer Doctrine, (2012) 32(55) Advocate (Citing *United States v Purdue Frederick Co*., Inc., 495 F. Supp. 2d 569, 573 (W.D. Va. 2007)) <http://www.hawleytroxell.com/2012/06/the-resurgence-of-theresponsible-corporate-officer-doctrine/> accessed 14 September 2017

Mosley L and Uno S, 'Racing to The Bottom or Climbing to The Top? Economic Globalization and Collective Labour Rights' (2007) 40 (8) Comparative Political Studies 923

Muchlinski P, 'Implementing the New UN Corporate Human Rights Framework: Implications for Corporate Law, Governance, and Regulation' (2012) 22 (1) Business Ethics Quarterly 145

Mueller GOW, 'Tort, Crime and The Primitive' (1955) 46 Journal of Criminal Law, Criminology, and Police Science 303

Mulgan R, 'Accountability': An Ever-Expanding Concept?' (2000) 78 (3) Public Administration 555

Müller FL, 'The Spectre of a People in Arms: The Prussian Government and The Militarisation of German Nationalism, 1859–1864' (2007) 122 (495) English Historical Review 82

Murphy J, 'Expectation Losses, Negligent Omissions and The Tortious Duty of Care' (1996) 55 (1) Cambridge Law Journal 43

Murphy J, 'The Nature and Domain of Aggravated Damages' (2010) 69 (2) Cambridge Law Journal 353

Murphy Jr CF, 'State Responsibility for Injuries to Aliens' (1966) 41 New York University Law Review 125

Murphy MC and Dweck CS, 'Mindsets Shape Consumer Behaviour' (2016) 26 (1) Journal of Consumer Psychology 127

Murphy SD, 'Award of Damages against Bosnian Serb Leader Radovan Karadzic' (2001) 95 (1) American Journal of International Law 143

Murphy SD, 'Contemporary Practice of The United States Relating to International law' (2001) 95 (2) American Journal of International Law 387

Murray MH, 'Torture Victim Protection Act: Legislation to Promote Enforcement of The Human Rights of Aliens in US Courts' (1987) 25 Columbia Journal of Transnational Law 673

Musila GM, 'The Right to An Effective Remedy under The African Charter on Human and Peoples' Rights' (2006) 6 (2) African Human Rights Law Journal 442

Naldi GJ, 'The Regulation of The Transnational Trade in Hazardous Wastes: The African Response' (2000) 7 South African Journal of Environmental Law and Policy 213

Neal ML, 'The Niger Delta and Human Rights Lawsuits: A Search for the Optimal Legal Regime' (2011) 24 Pacific McGeorge Global Business & Development Law Journal 343

Neha J, 'General Principles of Law As Gap-Fillers' (2014) 27 International Legal Theory Colloquium, New York Law School

Nellermoe EM, 'Balintulo v Daimler AG, 727 F.3d 174 (2013). Second Circuit Closes the Door for Victims of International Rights Violations' (2014) 11 South Carolina Journal of International Law and Business

Nelson C, 'Adjudication in The Political Branches' (2007) 107 (3) Columbia Law Review 559

Nelson WE, 'The Impact of The Antislavery Movement Upon Styles of Judicial Reasoning in Nineteenth Century America' (1974) 87 Harvard Law Review 513

Nerlich V, 'Superior Responsibility under Article 28 ICC Statute for What Exactly is The Superior Held Responsible?' (2007) 5(3) Journal of International Criminal Justice 665

Neuborne B, 'Of Singles Without Baseball: Corporations as Frozen Relational Moments' (2011) 64 (3) Rutgers Law Review 769

'New War Crimes Suits Filed Against Bush, Blair in Belgium' *Deutsche Presse Agentur* (20 June 2003) <http://archives.dailytimes.com.pk/national/20-Jun-2003/war-crimes-suits-filed-inbelgiumagainst-bush-blair> accessed 8 August 2017

Nicholls LM, 'The Humanitarian Monarchy Legislates: The International Committee of The Red Cross and Its 161 Rules of Customary International Humanitarian Law' (2006) 17 Duke Journal of Comparative & International Law 223

Nill DA, 'National Sovereignty: Must It be Sacrificed to The International Criminal Court?' (1999) 14 Brigham Young University Journal of Public Law 119

Nowrot K, 'Legal Consequences of Globalization: The Status of Non-Governmental Organizations under International Law' (1999) Indiana Journal of Global Legal Studies 579

Núñez JE, 'About the Impossibility of Absolute State Sovereignty' (2014) 27 (4) International Journal for The Semiotics of Law-Revue Internationale de Sémiotique Juridique 645

Nwobike JC, 'The African Commission on Human and Peoples' Rights and The Demystification of Second and Third Generation Rights under The African Charter: Social and Economic Rights Action Center (SERAC) and The Center for Economic and Social Rights (CESR) v Nigeria' (2005) 1 (2) African Journal of Legal Studies 129

Nye JS, 'Corruption and Political Development: A Cost-Benefit Analysis' (1967) 61 (2) American Political Science Review 417

Obama B, 'Transparency and Open Government' (2009) Memorandum for The Heads of Executive Departments and Agencies

O'Brien CM and Dhanarajan S, 'The Corporate Responsibility to Respect Human Rights: A Status Review' (2016) 29 (4) Accounting, Auditing & Accountability Journal 542

O'Brien JC, 'The international Tribunal for Violations of International Humanitarian Law in The Former Yugoslavia' (1993) 87 (4) American Journal of International Law 639, 659

O'Connell J, 'Gambling with The Psyche: Does Prosecuting Human Rights Violators Console Their Victims?' (2005) 46 Harvard International Law Journal 295

O'Connell ME, 'Enforcement and The Success of International Environmental Law' (1995) 3 (1) Indiana Journal of Global Legal Studies 47

Oh J, 'The Prosecutor's Dilemma-Strengths and Flaws of The Genocide Convention' (2003) 10 Murdoch University Electronic Journal Law 4

Okere OB, 'The Protection of Human Rights in Africa and The African Charter on Human and Peoples' Rights: A Comparative Analysis with The European and American Systems' (1984) 6 (2) Human Rights Quarterly 141

Okoye A, 'Corporate Enterprise Principles and UK Regulation of Modern Slavery in Supply Chains' (2017) 28 (5) International Company and Commercial Law Review 196

Olson D, 'Corporate Complicity in Human Rights Violations under International Criminal Law' (2015) 1 International Human Rights Law Journal

Olugbuo BC. 'Implementation of The Rome Statute of The International Criminal Court in Africa: An Analysis of The South African Legislation' (2004) 1 Eyes on The ICC 220

Ong DM, 'The Impact of Environmental Law on Corporate Governance: International and Comparative Perspectives' (2001) 12 (4) European Journal of International Law 685

O'Reilly AT, 'Command Responsibility: A Call to Realign Doctrine with Principles' (2004) 20 (1) American University International Law Review 71

O'Reilly GW, 'England Limits the Right to Silence and Moves Towards an Inquisitorial System of Justice' (1994) 85 (2) Journal of Criminal Law and Criminology (1973) 402

Orentlicher DF, 'Criminalizing Hate Speech in The Crucible of Trial: Prosecutor v Nahimana' (2006) 21 (4) American University International Law Review 557

Orentlicher DF, 'Swapping Amnesty for Peace and The Duty to Prosecute Human Rights Crimes' (1996) 3 ILSA Journal of International and Comparative Law 713

Orie AMM, 'Stare Decisis in The ICTY Appeal System? Successor Responsibility in The Hadžihasanović Case' (2012) 10 (3) Journal of International Criminal Justice 635

Osiel M, 'The Banality of Good: Aligning Incentives Against Mass Atrocity' (2005) 105 Columbia Law Review 1751

Osofsky HM, 'Environmental Human Rights Under The Alien Tort Claims Act: Redress for Indigenous Victims of Multinational Corporations' (1997) 20 Suffolk Transnational Law Review 335

Osofsky HM, Baxter-Kauf K, Hammer B and Mailander A, 'Environmental Justice and The BP Deepwater Horizon Oil Spill' (2012) 20 New York University Environmental Law Journal 99

Oswald LJ and Schipani CA, 'CERCLA and The "Erosion" of Traditional Corporate Law Doctrine' (1992) 86 Northwestern University Law Review 259

Owen DG, 'Response, Aggravating Punitive Damages' (2010) 158 (1) University of Pennsylvania Law Review 181

Oye KA, 'Explaining Cooperation under Anarchy: Hypotheses and Strategies' (1985) 38 (01) World politics 1

Padfield SJ, 'Corporate Social Responsibility & Concession Theory' (2015) 6 William & Mary Business Law Review 1

Paine LS, 'Managing for Organizational Integrity' (1994) 72 (2) Harvard Business Review 106

Painter WH, 'Double Derivative Suits and Other Remedies with Regard to Damaged Subsidiaries' (1961) 36 (2) Indian Law Journal 143

Parker BS, 'Applying the Doctrine of Superior Responsibility to Corporate Officers: A Theory of Individual Liability for International Human Rights Violations' (2012) 35 Hastings International and Comparative Law Review 1

Parks WH, 'Command Responsibility for War Crimes' (1973) 1 Military Law Review 62

Parrish AL, and Hsu SL, 'Litigating Canada-U.S. Transboundary Harm: International Environmental Lawmaking and The Threat of Extraterritorial Reciprocity' (2007) Virginia Journal of International Law 1

Parsons S, 'The Doctrine of Identification, Causation and Corporate Liability for Manslaughter' (2003) 67 (1) Journal of Criminal Law 69

Patel P, 'Expanding Past Genocide, Crimes against Humanity, and War Crimes: Can an ICC Policy Paper Expand the Court's Mandate to Prosecuting Environmental Crimes?' (2016) 14 Loyola University Chicago International Law Review 175

Payne LA and Pereira G, 'Corporate Complicity in International Human Rights Violations' (2016) 12 Annual Review of Law and Social Science 63

Peck CJ, 'Negligence and Liability without Fault in Tort Law' (1971) 46 (2) Washington Law Review 225

Pedersen ER, 'Making Corporate Social Responsibility (CSR) Operable: How Companies Translate Stakeholder Dialogue into Practice' (2006) 111 (2) Business and Society Review 137

Pejic J, 'Accountability for International Crimes: from Conjecture to Reality' (2002) 84 (845) Revue Internationale de la Croix-Rouge/International Review of the Red Cross 13, 33

Pejic J, 'Tribunal and the ICC: Do Precedents Matter?' (1996) 60 Albany Law Review 841

Perry SR, 'Protected Interests and Undertakings in the Law of Negligence, (1992) 42 (3) University of Toronto Law Journal 247

Petrin M, 'Assumption of Responsibility in Corporate Groups: Chandler v. Cape Plc' (2013) 76 (3) Modern Law Review 603

Petrin M, 'Curious Case of Directors' and Officers' Liability for Supervision and Management: Exploring the Intersection of Corporate and Tort Law' (2010) 59 (6) American University Law Review 1661

Phillips J and Lim SJ, 'Their Brothers' Keeper: Global Buyers and The Legal Duty to Protect Suppliers' Employees' (2009) 61 Rutgers Law Review 333

Phuong C, 'Hilary Charlesworth and Christine Chinkin, The Boundaries of International Law: A Feminist Analysis' (2002) 10 (2) Feminist Legal Studies 203

Pickering MA, 'The Company as A Separate Legal Entity' (1968) 31 (5) Modern Law Review 481

Plant ML, 'Comparative Negligence and Strict Tort Liability' (1979) 40 Louisiana Law Review 403

Polgreen L and Simons M, 'Global Sludge Ends in Tragedy for Ivory Coast' (2006) 2 New York Times

Porter S and Yuille JC, 'Credibility Assessment of Criminal Suspects Through Statement Analysis' (1995) 1 (4) Psychology, Crime and Law 319

Posner RA, 'A Theory of Negligence' (1972) 1 (1) Journal of Legal Studies 29

Posner RA, 'Cost-Benefit Analysis: Definition, Justification, and Comment on Conference Papers' (2000) 29 (S2) Journal of Legal Studies 1153

Posner RA, 'Instrumental and Noninstrumental Theories of Tort Law' (2013) 88 Indian Law Journal 469

Pray JL, 'Application of The Racketeer Influenced and Corrupt Organizations Act (RICO) to Securities Violations' (1982) 8 Journal of Corporation Law 411

Prevost AM, 'Race and War Crimes: The 1945 War Crimes Trial of General Tomoyuki Yamashita' (1992) 14 Human Rights Quarterly 303

Priemel KC, '"A Story of Betrayal": Conceptualizing Variants of Capitalism in The Nuremberg War Crimes Trials' (2013) 85 (1) Journal of Modern History 69.

Prince D, 'Corporate Liability for International Torts: Did the Second Circuit Misinterpret the Alien Tort Statute?' (2011) 8 Seton Hall Circuit Review 43

Pritchard JR, 'International Military Tribunal for The Far East and Its Contemporary Resonances' (1995) 149 Military Law Review 25

Pritchard S, 'The Jurisprudence of Human Rights: Some Critical Thought and Developments in Practice' (1995) 2 (1) Australian Journal of Human Rights 3

Putnam RD, 'Diplomacy and Domestic Politics: The Logic of Two-Level Games' (1988) 42 (03) International Organization 427

Quayle P, 'Unimaginable Evil: The Legislative Limitations of The Genocide Convention' (2005) 5 (3) International Criminal Law Review 363

Quazzo M, 'Officers and Directors Face Personal Liability under The Responsible Corporate Officer Doctrine' (2013) 11 Corporate Accountability Rep (BNA) 841

Wright Q, 'The Law of The Nuremberg Trial' (1947) 41 (1) American Journal of International Law 38, 72

Quintal AL, 'Rule 61: The Voice of The Victims Screams Out for Justice' (1998) 36 Columbia Journal of Transnational Law 723

Quinn PS, 'Rethinking Corporate Human Rights Accountability' (2014) 89 (3) Tulane Law Review 603

Radin M, 'The Endless Problem of Corporate Personality' (1932) 32 (4) Columbia Law Review 643, 667

Railsback K, 'Genocide Convention Action against The Khmer Rouge: Preventing a Resurgence of The Killing Fields' (1989) 5 Connecticut Journal of International Law 457

Ramasastry A, 'Corporate Complicity: From Nuremberg to Rangoon-An Examination of Forced Labour Cases and Their Impact on The Liability of Multinational Corporations' (2002) 20 Berkeley Journal of International Law 91

Ramasastry A, 'Corporate Social Responsibility versus Business and Human rights: Bridging The Gap between Responsibility and Accountability' (2015) 14 (2) Journal of Human Rights 237

Randall KC, 'Universal Jurisdiction under International Law' (1987) 66 Texas Law Review 785

Rasilla Del Moral, 'The Swan Song of Universal Jurisdiction in Spain' (2009) 9 (5) International Criminal Law Review 777

Ratner S, 'Corporations and Human Rights: A Theory of Legal Responsibility' (2001) 111 (3) Yale Law Journal 443

Ratner SR, 'Belgium's War Crimes Statute: A Post-Mortem' (2003) 97 (4) American Journal of International Law 888

Ratner SR, 'The Schizophrenias of International Criminal Law' (1998) 33 Texas International Law Journal 237

Raustiala K, 'States, NGOs, and International Environmental Institutions' (1997) 41 (1) International Studies Quarterly 719

Rees C, 'Mediation in Business-Related Human Rights Disputes: Objections, Opportunities and Challenges' (2010) 56 Corporate Social Responsibility Initiative Working Paper

Regan DH, 'Siamese Essays:(I) CTS Corp. v Dynamics Corp. of America and Dormant Commerce Clause Doctrine: (II) Extraterritorial State Legislation' (1987) 85 (8) Michigan Law Review 1865

Reiger C and Wierda M, 'The Serious Crimes Process in Timor-Leste: In Retrospect. NewYork: International Center for Transitional Justice' (2006) International Center for Transitional Justice

Relly JE, and Sabharwal M, 'Perceptions of Transparency of Government Policymaking: A Cross-National Study' (2009) 26 (1) Government Information Quarterly 148

Reydams L, 'Criminal Jurisdiction Universal Jurisdiction Crimes against Humanity Immunity of Former Head of State Incorporation of Customary Law into Municipal Criminal Law Prescription (Statutes of limitation)' (1999) 93 (3) American Journal of International Law 700.

Reydams L, 'Universal Jurisdiction over Atrocities in Rwanda: Theory and Practice' (1996) 4 European Journal of Crime, Criminal Law and Criminal Justice 18

Rhee RJ, 'Tort Arbitrage' (2008) 60 Florida Law Review 125

Ripstein A, 'The Division of Responsibility and The Law of Tort' (2003) 72 Fordham Law Review 1811

Rivera F, 'Inter-American Justice: Now Available in a US Federal Court Near You' (2005) 45 Santa Clara Law Review 889

Roach GP, 'How Restitution and Unjust Enrichment Can Improve Your Corporate Claim' (2007) 26 Review of Litigation 265

Roberts A, 'Comparative International law? The Role of National Courts in Creating and Enforcing International Law' (2011) 60 (1) International & Comparative Law Quarterly 57

Robertson F, 'Access to Justice for Victims of Human Rights Abuse by Multinational; Does European Civil and Commercial Litigation Provide an Answer?' (2015) 9 (1) New Zealand Journal of Research on Europe

Robinson PH, 'Imputed Criminal Liability' (1984) 93 (4) Yale Law Journal 609

Rogers APV, 'War Crimes Trials under The Royal Warrant: British practice 1945-1949' (1990) 39 (4) International and Comparative Law Quarterly 780

Roht-Arriaza N, 'Institutions of International Justice' (1999) Journal of International Affairs 473

Roht-Arriaza N, 'The Pinochet Precedent and Universal Jurisdiction' (2001) 35 New England Law Review 311

Ronen Y, 'Superior Responsibility of Civilians for International Crimes Committed in Civilian Settings'. (2010) 43 Vanderbilt Journal of Transnational Law 313

Rosen M, 'The Alien Tort Claims Act and The Foreign Sovereign Immunities Act: A Policy Solution' (1998) 6 Cardozo Journal of International and Comparative Law 461

Rosenblum P, 'Save The Tribunals; Salvage the Movement, a Response to Makau Mutua' (1997) 11 Temple International & Comparative Law Journal 189

Rosencranz A and Louk D, 'Doe v. Unocal: Holding Corporations Liable for Human Rights Abuses on Their Watch' (2005) 8 Chapman Law Review 135

Rott P and Ulfbeck V, 'Supply Chain Liability of Multinational Corporations?' (2015) 23 (3) European Review of Private Law 415

Rubin PH and Zwirb R, 'The Economics of Civil RICO' (1986) 20 UC Davis Law Review 883

Rubin SJ, 'Developments in The Law and Institutions of International Economic Relations' (1974) 68 (3) American Journal of International Law 475

Rudden B, 'Torticles' (1991) 6 /7 Tulane European and Civil Law Forum 105

Ruffin S, 'Royal Dutch Shell Environmentally Degrades Nigeria's Niger Delta Region: A Land of Blacks' (2012) 5 (3) Environmental Justice 140

Ruggie J, 'Business and Human Rights: Towards Operationalizing The "Protect, Respect and Remedy" Framework' (2009) Report to The Human Rights Council A/HRC/11/13

Ruggie J, 'Report of The Special Representative of The Secretary-General on The Issue of Human Rights and Transnational Corporations and Other Business Enterprises: Guiding Principles on Business and Human Rights: Implementing the United Nations 'Protect, Respect and Remedy' Framework' (2011) 29 (2) Netherlands Quarterly of Human Rights 224

Ruggie JG, 'Business and Human Rights: The Evolving International Agenda' (2007) 101 (4) American Journal of International Law 819

Ruggie JG, 'Protect, Respect and Remedy: A Framework for Business and Human Rights' (2008) 3 (2) Innovations 189

Ryu PK, 'Causation in Criminal Law' (1958) 106 (6) University of Pennsylvania Law Review 773

Sacharoff AK, 'Multinationals in Host Countries: Can They Be Held Liable under The Alien Tort Claims Act for Human Rights Violations?' (1997) 23 (3) Brooklyn Journal of International Law 927

Sachs N, 'Beyond the Liability Wall: Strengthening Tort Remedies in International Environmental Law' (2008) 55 UCLA Law Review 837

Salas-Fouksmann O, 'Corporate Liability of Energy/Natural Resources Companies at National Law for Breach of International Human Rights Norms' (2013) 2 (1) UCL Journal of Law and Jurisprudence 201

Sánchez de Tagle G, 'The Objective International Responsibility of States in The Inter-American Human Rights System' (2015) 7(2) Mexican Law Review 115

Sanger A, 'Crossing the Corporate Veil: The Duty of Care Owed by a Parent Company to the Employees of Its Subsidiary' (2012) 71 (3) Cambridge Law Journal 478

Santner AL, 'A Soft Law Mechanism for Corporate Responsibility: How the Updated OECD Guidelines for Multinational Enterprises Promote Business for The Future' (2011) 43 George Washington International Law Review 375

Santoro MA, 'Human Rights and Human Needs: Diverse Moral Principles Justifying Third World Access to Affordable HIV/AIDS Drugs' (2006) 31 North Carolina Journal of International Law and Commercial 923

Sartori G, 'Concept Misformation in Comparative Politics' (1970) 64 (4) American Political Science Review 1033 <http://journals.cambridge.org/action/displayAbstract?fromPage=online&aid=8935058&fileId=S0003055400133325> accessed 4 July 2016

Sassòli M and Olson LM, 'Prosecutor v. Tadić (Judgement) Case No. IT-94-aA. 38 ILM 1518' (1999) American Journal of International Law 571

Sayre FB, 'Mens Rea' (1932) 45 (6) Harvard Law Review 974

Scalia A, 'The Rule of Law as a Law of Rules' (1989) 56 (4) University of Chicago Law Review 1175

Schaack, BV 'The Principle of Legality in International Criminal Law' (2010) 10(8) Santa Clara University Legal Studies Research Paper

Schabas WA, 'International Criminal Tribunals: A Review of 2007' (2007) 6 North-western Journal of Human Rights 382

Schabas WA, 'National Courts Finally Begin to Prosecute Genocide, The 'Crime of Crimes' (2003) 1 (1) Journal of International Criminal Justice 39

Schabas WA, 'Problems of International Codification-Were the Atrocities in Cambodia and Kosovo Genocide?' (2000) 35 New England Law Review 287

Schabas WA, 'Punishment of Non-State Actors in Non-International Armed Conflict' (2002) 26 Fordham International Law Journal 907

Schafer S, 'Victim Compensation and Responsibility' (1970) 43 (1) Southern California Law Review 55

Scharf MP, 'Application of Treaty-Based Universal Jurisdiction on Nationals of Non-Party States' (2001) 35 New England Law Review 363

Scheffer D and Kaeb C, 'The Five Levels of CSR Compliance: The Resiliency of Corporate Liability under The Alien Tort Statute and The Case for a Counterattack Strategy in Compliance theory' (2011) 29 (1) Berkeley Journal of International Law 334

Scheffer D, 'Corporate Liability under The Rome Statute' (2016) 57 Harvard International Law Journal 35

Schellie PD, 'Racketeer Influenced and Corrupt Organizations Act (RICO)' (1986) Business Lawyer 1023

Schick FB, 'Crimes against Peace' (1948) 38 Journal of Criminal Law and Criminology 445

Schiessl M, 'The Liability of Corporations and Shareholders for The Capitalization and Obligations of Subsidiaries under German Law' (1986) 7 Northwestern Journal of International Law & Business 480

Schlesinger RB, 'Research on The General Principles of Law Recognized by Civilized Nations' (1957) 51 (4) American Journal of International Law 734

Schrage EJ and Ewing AP, 'The Cocoa Industry and Child Labour' (2005) 18 Corporate Citizenship Journal 99

Schrage EJ, 'Judging Corporate Accountability in The Global Economy' (2003) 42 Columbia Journal of Transnational Law 153

Schrempf-Stirling J and Wettstein F, 'Beyond Guilty Verdicts: Human Rights Litigation and Its Impact on Corporations' Human Rights Policies' (2015) Journal of Business Ethics 1

Schwabach A, 'The Sandoz Spill: The Failure of International Law to Protect the Rhine from Pollution' (1989) 16 (2) Ecology Law Quarterly 443

Schwartz GT, 'Reality in The Economic Analysis of Tort Law: Does Tort Law Really Deter' (1994) 42 UCLA Law Review 377

Schwartz ML, 'International Legal Protection for Victims of Environmental Abuse' (1993) 18 Yale Journal of International Law 355

Scott MB and Lyman SM, 'Accounts' (1968) 33 (1) American Sociological Review 46

Seipp DJ, 'The Distinction between Crime and Tort in The Early Common Law' (1996) 76 BUL Review 59

Selim Y, 'Examining Victims and Perpetrators in Post-conflict Nepal' (2017) 23 (3) International Review of Victimology

Selvin M, 'Wal-Mart Faces Suit by Labour Group' (2005) Los Angeles Times

Shear MD, 'Trump Will Withdraw US from Paris Climate Agreement' (2017) New York Times <https://www.nytimes.com/2017/06/01/climate/trump-paris-climate-agreement.html> accessed 13 October 2017

Setear JK, 'Responses to Breach of a Treaty and Rationalist International Relations Theory: The Rules of Release and Remediation in The Law of Treaties and The Law of State Responsibility' (1997) 83 Virginia Law Review 1

Shamir R, 'Between Self-Regulation and The Alien Tort Claims Act: On the Contested Concept of Corporate Social Responsibility' (2004) 38 (4) Law & Society Review 635

Shavell S, 'Strict Liability Versus Negligence' (1980) 9(1) Journal of Legal Studies 1

Shaw C, 'Uncertain Justice: Liability of Multinationals under The Alien Tort Claims Act' (2002) Stanford Law Review 1359

Sherwin E, 'Interpreting Tort Law' (2011) 39 Florida State University Law Review 227

Sherwin E, 'Reparations and Unjust Enrichment' (2004) 84 (5) Boston University Law Review 1443

Silberman LJ and Lowenfeld AF, 'A Different Challenge for the ALI: Herein of Foreign Country Judgments, An International Treaty, and An American Statute' (2000) 75 India Law Journal 635

Simmons B, 'Treaty Compliance and Violation' (2010) 13 (1) Annual Review of Political Science 273

Simons KW, 'Does Punishments for "Culpable Indifference" Simply Punish for "Bad Character"? Examining the Requisite Connection Between Mens Rea and Actus Reus' (2002) 6 (1) Buffalo Criminal Law Review 219

Simons KW, 'The Crime/Tort Distinction: Legal Doctrine and Normative Perspectives' (2007) 17 Widener Law Journal 719

Simons M, 'Sharon Faces Belgian Trial After Term Ends' (2003) The New York Times

Sinclair A, 'The Chameleon of Accountability: Forms and Discourses' (1995) 20 (2-3) Accounting, Organizations and Society 219

Singer PW, 'War, Profits, and The Vacuum of Law: Privatized Military Firms and International Law' (2004 42 Columbia Journal of Transnational Law 521

Skelding A, 'The Elusive Standard of Reasonableness' (2015) 3 Legal Issues Journal 72

Skinner G, 'Beyond Kiobel: Providing Access to Judicial Remedies for Violations of International Human Rights Norms by Transnational Business in a New (Post-Kiobel) World' (2014) 46 Columbia Human Rights Law Review 158.

Skjærseth JB, Stokke OS and Wettestad J, 'Soft law, Hard Law, and Effective Implementation of International Environmental Norms' (2006) 6 (3) Global Environmental Politics 104

Skolnick P and Shaw JI, 'The OJ Simpson Criminal Trial Verdict: Racism or Status Shield?' (1997) 53 (3) Journal of Social Issues 503

Skupski GR, 'The Senior Management Mens Rea: Another Stab at A Workable Integration of Organisational Culpability into Corporate Criminal Liability' (2011) 62 Case Western Reserve Law Review 267

Slaughter AM, 'Disaggregated Sovereignty: Towards the Public Accountability of Global Government Networks' (2004) 39 (2) Government and Opposition 159

Sloss DL, 'Kiobel and Extraterritoriality: A Rule without a Rationale' (2013) 28 (1) Maryland Journal of International Law, Forthcoming 241

Sluiter G, 'ICTY and Offences against The Administration of Justice' (2004) 2 Journal of International Criminal Justice 631

Slye RC, 'Corporations Veils, and International Criminal Liability' (2008) 33 Brooklyn Journal of International Law 955

Smidt ML, 'Yamashita, Medina, and Beyond: Command Responsibility in Contemporary Military Operations' (2000) 164 Military Law Review 155

Smith J, 'Tort and Absolute Liability: Suggested Changes in Classification' (1916 30 (3) Harvard Law Review 241

Soyer B, 'Sundry Considerations on The Draft Protocol to The Athens Convention Relating to The Carriage of Passengers and Their Luggage by Sea 1974' (2002) 33 Journal of Maritime Law and Commerce 519

Spector BI and Korula AR, 'Problems of Ratifying International Environmental Agreements: Overcoming Initial Obstacles in The Post-

Agreement Negotiation Process' (1993) 3 (4) Global Environmental Change 369
Sprinz D and Vaahtoranta T, 'The Interest-Based Explanation of International Environmental Policy' (1994) 48 (01) International Organization 77
Squillante AM and Congalton FM 'Force Majeure' (1975) 80 Commercial Law Journal 4
Starke JG, 'Monism and Dualism in the Theory of International Law' (1936) 17 British Year Book of International Law 66
Steinhardt RG, 'Determining Which Human Rights Claims Touch and Concern the United States: Justice Kennedy's Filartiga' (2014 89 Notre Dame Law Review 1695
Steinhardt RG, 'Fulfilling The Promise of Filartiga: Litigating Human Rights Claims Against The Estate of Ferdinand Marcos' (1995) 20 Yale Journal of International Law 65
Steinhardt RG, 'Kiobel and The Weakening of Precedent: A Long Walk for a Short Drink' (2013) 107 (4) American Journal of International Law 841
Stephens B, 'Amorality of Profit: Transnational Corporations and Human Rights' (2002) 20 (1) Berkeley Journal of International Law 45
Stephens B, 'Corporate Liability: Enforcing Human Rights Through Domestic Litigation' (2001) 24 (3) Hastings International and Comparative Law Review 401
Stephens B, 'Sosa v Alvarez-Machain: "The Door Is Still Ajar" for Human Rights Litigation in US Courts' (2005) 70 (2) Brooklyn Law Review 533
Stephens B, 'The Curious History of The Alien Tort Statute' (2014) 89 (4) Notre Dame Law Review 1467
Stern YZ, 'Corporate Criminal Personal Liability-Who Is the Corporation' (1987) 13 Journal of Corporation Law 125
Stewart DP and Wuerth I, 'Kiobel v Royal Dutch Petroleum Co.: The Supreme Court and TheAlien Tort Statute' (2013) 107(3) American Journal of International Law 601
Stewart JG, 'The End of 'Modes of Liability' for International Crimes' (2012) 25 (1) Leiden Journal of International Law 165
Stone CD, 'The Place of Enterprise Liability in The Control of Corporate Conduct' (1980) 90 (1) Yale Law Journal 77
Strafer RG, Massumi RR and Skolnick HR, 'Civil RICO in The Public Interest: Everybody's Darling' (1982) 19 American Criminal Law Review 655
Strøm K, 'Delegation and Accountability in Parliamentary Democracies' (2000) 37 (3) European Journal of Political Research 261

<http://link.springer.com/article/10.1023/A:1007064803327> accessed 3 July 2016

Stuckey TM, 'Jurisdictional Hooks in The Wake of Raich: On Properly Interpreting Federal Regulations of Interstate Commerce' (2006) 81 Notre Dame Law Review 2101

Sturges P, 'What is This Absence Called Transparency' (2007) 7 (07) International Review of Information Ethics 1, 8

Sugarman SD, 'A New Approach to Tort Doctrine: Taking the Best from The Civil Law and Common Law of Canada' (2002) 17 Supreme Court Law Review 375

Sykes AO, 'Corporate Liability for Extraterritorial Torts Under The Alien Tort Statute and Beyond: An Economic Analysis' (2012) 100 Georgetown Law Journal 2161

Symposium ECS, '1945-1995: Critical Perspective on The Nuremberg Trial and State Accountability' (1995) 12 New York Law School Journal of Human Rights 631

Szasz PC, 'Proposed War Crimes Tribunal for Ex-Yugoslavia' (1993) 25 New York University Journal of International Law and Politics 405

Terblanche P, 'Lex Fori or Lex Loci Delicti? The Problem of Choice of Law in International Delicts' (1997) 30 (3) Comparative and International Law Journal of Southern Africa 243

Thompson B, 'Was Kiobel Detrimental to Corporate Social Responsibility: Applying Lessons Learnt from American Exceptionalism' (2014) 30 Utrecht Journal of International and European Law 82

Thompson RB, 'Piercing the Corporate Veil: An Empirical Study' (1991) 76 Cornell Law Review 1036

Thompson RB, 'Unpacking Limited Liability: Direct and Vicarious Liability of Corporate Participants for Torts of The Enterprise' (1994) 47 Vanderbilt Law Review 1

Thürer D, 'The "Failed State" and International Law' (1999) 81 (836) International Review of the Red Cross 731

Tierney S, 'Reframing Sovereignty? Sub-state National Societies and Contemporary Challenges to The Nation-State' (2005) 54 (1) International & Comparative Law Quarterly 161

Tigar ME, 'It Does the Crime but Not the Time: Corporate Criminal Liability in Federal Law' (1990) 17 American Journal of Criminal Law 211

Tolbert D, 'Reflections on The ICTY Registry' (2004) 2 Journal of International Criminal Justice 480

Townsend PK and Townsend WH, 'Assessing an Assessment: The Ok Tedi Mine' (2004) Bridging Scales and Epistemologies: Linking Local

Knowledge and Global Science in Multi-Scale Assessments, Alexandria, Egypt 17

Tsimplis M, 'Liability and Compensation in The International Transport of Hazardous Wastes by Sea: The 1999 Protocol to The Basel Convention' (2001) 16 (2) International Journal of Marine and Coastal Law 295

Turcotte JA, 'When You Should Have Known: Rethinking Constructive Knowledge in Tort Liability for Sexual Transmission of HIV' (2000) 52 Maine Law Review 261

Tweedale G and Flynn L, 'Piercing the Corporate Veil: Cape Industries and Multinational Corporate Liability for a Toxic Hazard, 1950–2004' (2007) 8 (2) Enterprise & Society 268

Tzeutschler GGA, 'Corporate Violator: The Alien Tort Liability of Transnational Corporations for Human Rights Abuses Abroad' (1998) 30 Columbia Human Rights Law Review 359

Ulmer SS, 'The Supreme Court's Certiorari Decisions: Conflict as a Predictive Variable' (1984) 78 (4) American Political Science Review 901

Uesugi T, 'Is Agent Orange a Poison? Vietnamese Agent Orange Litigation and The New

Paradigm of Poison' (2013) 24 The Japanese Journal of American Studies

USAID, 'Transparency and Accountability' (2013) The US Government`s Hunger & Food Security Initiatives

Vaccaro A and Madsen P, 'Transparency in Business and Society: Introduction to The Special Issue' (2009) 11 (2) Ethics and Information Technology 101

Valor C, 'Corporate Social Responsibility and Corporate Citizenship: Towards Corporate Accountability' (2005) 110 (2) Business and Society Review 191

Van Detta JA, "Sexual Orientation, Human Rights, and Corporate Sponsorship of The Sochi Olympic Games: Rethinking the Voluntary Approach to Corporate Social Responsibility' (2014) 30 (78) Utrecht Journal of International and European Law 99

Van den Herik L and Černič JL, 'Regulating Corporations under International Law: from Human Rights to International Criminal Law and Back Again' (2010) 8 (3) Journal of International Criminal Justice 725

Van den Herik L, 'The Difficulties of Exercising Extraterritorial Criminal Jurisdiction: The Acquittal of a Dutch Businessman for Crimes Committed in Liberia' (2009) 9 (1) International Criminal Law Review 211

Vega MA, 'Balancing Judicial Cognizance and Caution: Whether Transnational Corporations Are Liable for Foreign Bribery Under the Alien Tort Statute' (2009) 31 Michigan Journal of International Law 385

Venetis PM, 'The Broad Jurisprudential Significance of Sosa v Alvarez-Machain: An Honest Assessment of The Role of Federal Judges and Why Customary International Law Can Be More Effective Than Constitutional Law for Redressing Serious Abuses' (2011) 21Temple Political and Civil Rights Law Review 41

Vetter GR, 'Command Responsibility of Non-Military Superiors in the International Criminal Court (ICC)' (2000) 25 Yale Journal of International Law 89

Vidal J and Owen Bowcott, 'ICC Widens Remit to Include Environmental Destruction Cases' (2016) The Guardian <https://www.theguardian.com/global/2016/sep/15/hague-courtwidens-remit-to-include-environmental-destruction-cases> accessed 15 June 2017

Vogel D, 'The Private Regulation of Global Corporate Conduct: Achievements and Limitations' (2010) 49 (1) Business & Society 68

Walker A, 'The Hidden Flaw in Kiobel, Under the Alien Tort Statute the Mens Rea Standard for Corporate Aiding and Abetting is Knowledge' (2011) 10 (2) Northwestern Journal of International Human Rights 119

Walker H, 'Treaties for The Encouragement and Protection of Foreign Investment: Present United States Practice' (1956) 5 (2) American Journal of Comparative Law 229

Wallach D, 'The Irrationality of Universal Civil Jurisdiction' (2014) 46 Georgetown Journal of International Law 803

Warbrick C and Rowe P, 'The International Criminal Tribunal for Yugoslavia: The decision of The Appeals Chamber on The Interlocutory Appeal on Jurisdiction in The Tadic Case' (1996) 45 (03) International and Comparative Law Quarterly 691

Ward H, 'Governing Multinationals: The Role of Foreign Direct Liability' (2001) The Royal Institute of International Affairs,18 Briefing Paper 1

Ward H, 'Securing Transnational Corporate Accountability Through National Courts: Implications and Policy Options' (2001) 24 Hastings International and Comparative Law Review 451

Warin FJ, Diamant MS and Root VS, 'Somebody's Watching Me: FCPA Monitorships and How They Can Work Better' (2011) 13 University of Pennsylvania Journal of Business Law 321

Waters MA, 'Creeping Monism: The Judicial Trend Toward Interpretive Incorporation of Human Rights Treaties' (2007) Columbia Law Review 628

Weeramantry RJ, 'Time Limitation Under The United States Alien Tort Claims Act' (2003) 85 (851) International Review of The Red Cross 627

Wei SJ, 'Corruption in Economic Development: Beneficial Grease, Minor Annoyance, or Major Obstacle?' (1999) World Bank Policy Research Working Paper No. 2048

Weinrib EJ, 'The Disintegration of Duty' (2006) 31 Advocates' Quarterly 212

Weiss EB, 'Invoking State Responsibility in The Twenty-First Century' (2002) 96 (4) American Journal of International Law 798

Weissbrodt D and Kruger M, 'Norms on The Responsibilities of Transnational Corporations and Other Business Enterprises with Regard to Human Rights' (2003) 97 (4) American Journal of International Law 901

Welford R, 'Corporate Social Responsibility in Europe and Asia: Critical Elements and Best Practice' (2004) 13 Journal of Corporate Citizenship 31

Were M, 'Implementing Corporate Responsibility the Chiquita Case' (2003) 44 (2) Journal of Business Ethics 247-260

West E, 'The Utility of The NESS Test of Factual Causation in Scots Law' (2013) 4 Aberdeen Student Law Review 39-62

Westbrook JL, 'Theories of Parent Company Liability and The Prospects for An International Settlement' (1985) 20 University of Texas School of Law 321

Wheelwright K, 'Corporate Liability for Workplace Deaths and Injuries-Reflecting on Victoria's Laws in The Light of The Esso Longford Explosion' (2002) 7 (2) Deakin Law Review 323

Wiener JB, 'Global Environmental Regulation: Instrument Choice in Legal Context' (1999) 108 (4) Yale Law Journal 677-800

Williams G, 'Finis for Novus Actus?' (1989) 48 (3) Cambridge Law Journal 391-416

Williams G, 'Vicarious Liability: Tort of The Master or of The Servant?' (1956) 72 Law Quarterly Review 522

Williams S, 'Genocide: The Cambodian Experience' (2005) 5 (3) International Criminal Law Review 447-461

Wilner GM, 'Filartiga v. Pena-Irala: Comments on Sources of Human Rights Law and Means of Redress for Violations of Human Rights' (1981) 11 (2) Georgia Journal of International & Comparative Law 317

Wilson JR, 'Coming to America to File Suite: Foreign Plaintiffs and The Forum Non Conveniens Barrier in Transnational Litigation' (2004) 65 Ohio State Law Journal 659

Winfield PH, 'Duty in Tortious Negligence' (1934) 34 (1) Columbia Law Review 41

Wise N, 'Personal Liability Promotes Responsible Conduct: Extending The Responsible Corporate Officer Doctrine to Federal Civil Environmental Enforcement Cases' (2002) 21 Stanford Environmental Law Journal 283

Wolff M, 'On the Nature of Legal Persons' (1938) 54 Law Quarterly Review 494 <http://heinonline.org/HOL/LandingPage?handle=hein.journals/lqr54&div=37&id=&page=> accessed 4 July 2017

Wood KW, 'Racketeer Influenced and Corrupt Organizations Act-Private Cause of Action-No Injury Required Beyond Those Caused by Predicate Offenses for Section 1964 (c) Claim' (1985) 55 Mississippi Law Journal 167 <http://heinonline.org/HOL/LandingPage?handle=hein.journals/mislj55&div=16&id=&page=> accessed 29 June 2015

Wood SG and Scharffs BG, 'Applicability of Human Rights Standards to Private Corporations: An American Perspective' (2002) 50 The American Journal of Comparative Law 531-566

Woods CS, 'It Isn't a State Problem: The Minas Conga Mine Controversy and The Need for Binding International Obligations on Corporate Actors' (2014) 46 Georgetown Journal of International Law 629

Wouters J and Chanet L, 'Corporate Human Rights Responsibility: A European Perspective' (2008) 6 Northwestern Journal of International Human Rights 262

Wouters J and Ryngaert C, 'Litigation for Overseas Corporate Human Rights Abuse in The European Union: The Challenge of Jurisdiction' (2008) 40 George Washington International Law Review 939

Wu T and Kang YS, 'Criminal Liability for The Actions of Subordinates-The Doctrine of Command Responsibility and Its Analogues in United States Law' (1997) 38 Harvard International Law Journal 272

Wu YS, 'Genocidal Rape in Bosnia: Redress in United States Courts under The Alien Tort Claims Act' (1993) 4 (1) UCLA Women's Law Journal 101

Young OR, 'The Politics of International Regime Formation: Managing Natural Resources and The Environment' (1989) 43 (03) International Organization 349

Zappalà S, 'Prosecutor's Duty to Disclose Exculpatory Materials and The Recent Amendment to Rule 68 ICTY RPE' (2004) 2 Journal of International Criminal Justice 620

Zartman WI, 'Negotiating the Rapids: The Dynamics of Regime Formation' (2001) 11 (1) Japan Negotiation Journal 3

Zegveld L, 'Remedies for Victims of Violations of International Humanitarian Law' (2003) 85
(851) Revue Internationale de la Croix-Rouge/International Review of The Red Cross 497
Zerk J, 'Corporate Liability for Gross Human Rights Abuses: Towards a Fairer and More Effective System of Domestic Law Remedies' (2013) Report Prepared for Office of The High Commissioner for Human Rights (United Nations) 103
Zietsman JC, 'Vicious Dogs A Case Study from 2000 BC to AD 2000' (2000) 45 (1) Akroterion 75
Zutshi A, Creed A and Sohal AS, 'Child Labour and Supply Chain: Profitability or (mis)Management' (2009) 21 (1) European Business Review 42

Legislation

European Union

Art. 102 Schweizerisches Strafgesetzbuch, BBl. 2002 (Schweizerisches Gesetzesblatt), at 5390
Brussels I Regulation
Burgerliches Gesetzbuch [BGB] [Civil Code] Jan. 2, 2002, § 831, 1, translation at <https://perma.cc/P24U-FSY8> accessed 15 September 2017 (Ger.)
Code de Procedure Penale [C. PR. PÉN.], art. 2
Council Directive 2014/95/EU O.J. (L 330)
Organic Law (L.O.P.J. 1985, art. 23.4)
Regulation (EC) No 864/2007 of the European Parliament and of the Council of 11 July 2007 on the law applicable to non-contractual obligations (Rome II)
Regulation 44/2001 on Jurisdiction and the Recognition and Enforcement of Judgments in Civil and Commercial Matters [2001] OJ L12/1
Regulation 593/2008 on the Law Applicable to Contractual Obligations [2008] OJ L177/6;
Regulation 864/2007 on the Law Applicable to Non-Contractual Obligations [2007] OJ
L199/40. E
Rome II Regulation, art
Rome II Regulation, art 32
International law
Article 121(5) of the Rome Statute

Article 2 of The ICTY's Statute, Grave Breaches of the Geneva Convention of 1949
Article 25(1) of the Rome Statute
Article 25(2) of the Rome Statute
Article 3 of the Geneva Convention
Article 38(1)(c) of the Statute of the ICJ (UN 1945)
Australia Criminal Code Act 1994, s. 12.3(2) (c)
Basel Protocol on Liability and Compensation for Damage Transboundary Movements of Hazardous Wastes 1999
Convention on Civil Liability for Oil Pollution Damage Not Resulting From the Exploration Force for and Exploitation of Seabed Mineral Resources 1977
Convention on the Prevention of Marine Pollution by Dumping of Wastes and Other Matter 1972
Convention on the Protection and Use of Transboundary Watercourses and International Lakes (ECE Water Convention) 1992
Council of Europe Lugano Convention on Civil Liability including Damage Resulting from Activities Dangerous to the Environment 1993
Geneva Convention I and Article 13
Geneva Convention III and Article 85
Geneva Convention IV and Article 4
Geneva Convention IV and Article 4
Genocide Convention, Art. II
IAEA Convention Supplementary Compensation installed Force for Nuclear Damage, IAEA Vienna Convention on Civil Liability 1963
ICC Statute, Preamble, Arts. 1, 11(1), 126(1)
IMO Convention on Liability & Compensation in Connection with Carriage Hazardous and Noxious Substances by Sea 1996
IMO International Convention on Civil Liability for Bunker Oil Pollution Damage 2001
IMO International Convention on Civil Liability for Oil Pollution Damage one million (replaced 1969 units of gross Convention) 1992
IMT Charter, Article 2, 4 (C), 14 16, 26-29
Indonesian Civil Code, art. 1367
International Convention on Civil Liability for Oil Pollution Damage (CLC) Adoption: 29
November 1969; Entry into force: 19 June 1975; Being replaced by 1992 Protocol: Adoption: 27 November 1992; Entry into force: 30 May 1996
International Convention on the Establishment of an International Fund for Oil Pollution Damage (replaced 1971 Convention) 1992
International Criminal Courts Act 2001 s 51-52

International Maritime Organization (IMO), International Convention on Maritime Search and Rescue, 27 April 1979, 1403 UNTS, http://www.refworld.org/docid/469224c82.html accessed 6 September 2017

Kaisha–hō [Companies Act], Act No. 86 of 2005, Part III § 11

Ley Organica 5/2010 art. VII (B.O.E. 2010, 152) (Spain)

MINPÕ [MINPÕ] [CIV. C.] arts. 709 (tort liability), and 715 (superior liability). [Companies Act], Companies Act, Part II, Chapter 4, Section 11 (Liability for Damages of Officer to Third Parties)

Paris Convention on Third Party Liability in the 1960

Statute of the Special Court for Sierra Leone, S.C. Res. 1315, art. 6 3 (Aug. 16)

Supplementary Convention, Amending Protocol 1964 Amending Protocol 1982

The Affirmative Action (Equal Employment Opportunity for Women) Act 1986 (Cth) (Affirmative Action Act)

The Australian legislation relevant to employment rights is the Workplace Relations Act 1996 (Cth) (WRA)

The Human Rights and Equal Opportunity Act 1986 (Cth) (HREOC Act) (Norris 2000: 132)

The Race Discrimination Act 1975 (Cth) (RDA)

Tokyo Charter, Article 2

UNECE Convention on Civil Liability for Damage Caused During Carriage of Goods by Road, Rail and Inland Navigation Vessels 1989

UNECE Protocol on Civil Liability and Compensation for Damage Caused by Transboundary Effects of Industrial Accidents on Transboundary Waters 2003

United Nations Convention on the Law of the Sea LOS Convention, 1982

Zhonghua Renmin Gongheguo Xingfa [Criminal Law of the People's Republic of China] (promulgated by Order No. 83 of the President of the People's Republic of China, Mar. 14, 1997, effective Oct. 1, 1997), art. 36, P.R.C. LAWS, https://perma.cc/ZT5U-2QLY accessed 15 September 2017

United Kingdom

Companies Act 1985 <http://www.legislation.gov.uk/ukpga/1985/6/pdfs/ukpga_19850006_en.pdf> accessed 19

December 2016

Criminal Justice Act 1988

Criminal Law Act 1977
Dangerous Drugs Act 1965
Firearms Act 1968
Halsbury's Corporations' Laws of England (2006).
Modern Slavery Act 2015
Office of Secretes Act 1989
Protection from Harassment Act 1997, s4 (1)
Public Order Act 1986
Sentencing and Punishment of Offenders Act 2012 (UK)
The Sexual Offences Act 2003 (SOA 2003)

United States

3A Fletcher Cyc. Corp. § 1137 2016
Alien Tort Statute (28 USC. § 1350; ATS)
Articles of War (10 USC. §§ 1471-1593
Bribery Act 2010
Clean Air Act 1993
Comprehensive Environmental Response, Compensation, and Liability Act (Superfund) 42
USC. §9601 et seq. (1980)
Espionage Act of 1917, 50 USC. § 38. Article 2
Fed. R. Civ. P. 12(b) (6)
Federal Rule of Civil Procedure 12(b) (6)
Federal Tort Claims Act
Food and Drugs Act of 1906, 34 Stat. 768, 21 USC.A. § 1 et seq
Foreign Corrupt Practices Act of 1977
IX of Organised Crime Control Act (1970) Pub L No 91-452, 84 Stat. 922
Occupational Health and Safety Act 2004 (Vic) § 144, https://perma.cc/7LCM-559R accessed 15 September 2017
Racketeer Influenced and Corrupt Organizations Act
Resource Conservation and Recovery Act of 1976, Pub. L. 94-580, 90 Stat. 2795 (codified as amended in scattered sections of 42 USC.)
Restatement (Third) of Agency § 7.01 (2006)
Restatement (Third) of Foreign Relations Law § 102(2) (1987
Rules and Regulation under Securities Exchange Act of 1934, 17 C.F.R. § 240.16a-1
Sherman Anti-Trust Act, 15 USC §§ 1–7 (2011).
The Torture Victims Protection Act (TVPA) 1991
US Federal Extraterritorial Torture Statute, 18 USC. § 2340A (1994)
XXII. Restatement (Second) of Torts § 402A

United Nations

Basel Convention on the Control of Transboundary Movements of Hazardous Wastes and their Disposal, Opened for Signature Mar. 22, 1989, 1673 UNT.S. 57 (entered into force May 5, 1992)

Committee against Torture, General Comment No. 2: Implementation of Article 2 by States Parties 18, UN Doc. CAT/C/GC/2/CRP.1/Rev.4 (Nov. 23, 2007)

Committee against Torture, General Comment No. 3: Implementation of Article 14 by States Parties, 7, UN Doc. CAT/C/GC/3 (Dec. 13, 2012).

Committee on Economic, Social and Cultural Rights, General Comment 15, The right to water (Twenty-ninth session, 2003), UN Doc. E/C.12/2002/11 (2002)

Committee on the Elimination of Racial Discrimination, Consideration of Reports Submitted by States Parties under Article 9 of the Convention: Concluding Observations of the Committee on the Elimination of Racial Discrimination: United States of America, 30, UN Doc. CERD/C/USA/CO/6 (Mar. 5, 2008

Convention against Torture and Other Cruel, Inhuman or Degrading Treatment or Punishment art. 1, Opened for Signature Dec. 10, 1984, 1465 UNT.S. 85 (entered into force June 26, 1985)

Convention for Co-operation in the Protection and Development of the Marine and Coastal Environment of the West and Central African Region, Abidjan, (1981).

Convention for the Amelioration of the Condition of the Wounded and Sick in Armies in the Field, 118 L.N.T.S. 303, at art. 26 (June 19, 1931). Art 26

Convention for the Protection and Development of the Marine Environment of the Wider Caribbean Region, Cartagena de India's, (1983)

Convention on Biological Diversity, Montreal, Can., May 25-27 (2005), Status of Third-Party Liability Treaties and Analysis of Difficulties Facing Their Entry Into Force, UN Doc. UNEP/CBD/BS/WG-L&R/1?INF/ (2005) <https://www.biodiv.org/doc/meetings/bs/bswglr01-inf-03-en-pdf> accessed 11 January 2017

Convention on the Elimination of All Forms of Discrimination Against Women art. 2(e), Opened for Signature Dec. 18, 1979, 1249 UNT.S. 13 (entered into force Sept. 3, 1981) [hereinafter CEDAW]

Convention on the Prevention and Punishment of the Crime of Genocide, art. 4, Opened for Signature Dec. 9, 1948, 78 UNT.S. 277 (entered into force Jan. 12, 1951)

Convention on the Protection and Use of Transboundary Watercourses and International Lakes and to the 1992 Convention on the Transboundary Effects of Industrial Accidents Kiev, 21 May (2003) https://treaties.un.org/pages/ViewDetails.aspx?src=TREATY&mtdsg_no=XXVII16&chapter=27&lang=en accessed 16 October 2017

Convention on Third Party Liability in the Field of Nuclear Energy, opened for signature July 29, 1960, 956 UNT.S. 251 (entered into force Apr. 1, 1968)

Declaration, Joint Four Nations, 'The Moscow Conference; October 1943' (1943).

Draft Convention on the Crime of Genocide, June 26, 1947, UN Doc. E/447, at 66

European Agreement Concerning the International Carriage of Dangerous Goods by Inland Waterways AND), Geneva, (2000)

General Assembly Res. 60/147, 3(c) (Dec. 16, 2005)

General Assembly Resolution, 260B (II), UN Doc.A/760, at 12-13 (1948)

General Assembly Resolution, 44/39, para. (1990), General Assemble Resolution, 44/41, (1991

General Assembly, Rome Statute of the International Criminal Court (last amended 2010), 17 July 1998, ISBN No. 92-9227-227-6, http://www.refworld.org/docid/3ae6b3a84.html accessed 8 July 2017

General Assembly, United Nations Convention Against Corruption, 31 October 2003, A/58/422 http://www.refworld.org/docid/4374b9524.html accessed 23 September 2016].

Genocide Convention, Art. VI; Apartheid Convention, Art. V

Hague Conference on Private International Law, Civil Liability Resulting From Transfontier

Environmental Damage: A Case for the Hague Conference? 5-16 Preliminary Doc 8 (2000) <http://www.hcch.net/upload/wop/gen_pd8e.pdf.> Accessed 07 January 2017

HNS Convention, <http://www.hnsconvention.org/en/status.html> accessed 16 January

Human Rights Council Res. 17/4, UN Doc. A/HRC/RES/17/4, at 2 (July 6, 2011)

International Atomic Energy Agency [IAEA], Vienna Convention on Civil Liability for Nuclear Damage (2007) <www.iaea.org/Publications/Documents/Conventions/liability_status.pdf> access on 12 January 2017

International Committee of the Red Cross (ICRC), Geneva Convention Relative to the Protection of Civilian Persons in Time of War (Fourth Geneva Convention), 12 August 1949, 75 UNTS 287 http://www.refworld.org/docid/3ae6b36d2.html accessed 5 September 2017

International Conferences (The Hague), Hague Convention (IV) Respecting the Laws and Customs of War on Land and Its Annex: Regulations Concerning the Laws and Customs of War on Land, 18 October 1907 http://www.refworld.org/docid/4374cae64.html accessed 5 September 2017

International Convention on Civil Liability for Oil Pollution Damage, opened for signature Nov.29, 1969, 973 UNT.S. 3 (entered into force June 19, 1975)

International Convention on the Elimination of All Forms of Racial Discrimination, opened for signature Dec. 21, 1965, 660 UNT.S. 195, 212; (entered into force Jan. 6, 1969) [hereinafter CERD]

International Convention on the Suppression and Punishment of the Crime of Apartheid art. I (2), 2, opened for signature Nov. 30, 1973, 1015 UNT.S. 243 (entered into force July 18, 1976) (declaring apartheid criminal)

International Covenant on Economic, Social and Cultural Rights Adopted and opened for signature, ratification and accession by General Assembly resolution 2200A (XXI) of 16 December 1966

International Covenant on Economic, Social and Cultural Rights Adopted and opened for signature, ratification and accession by General Assembly resolution 2200A (XXI) of 16 December 1966 entry into force 3 January 1976

Kyoto Protocol to the United Nations Framework Convention on Climate Change Kyoto, 11 December (1997) <https://treaties.un.org/pages/ViewDetails.aspx?src=TREATY&mtdsg_no=XXVII-7-a&chapter=27&lang=en> accessed 12 October 2017.

OHCHR Accountability and Remedy Project: Improving Accountability and Access to Remedy in Cases of Business Involvement in Human Rights Abuses, 10 May 2016, A/HRC/32/19 <http://www.ohchr.org/Documents/Issues/Business/DomesticLawRemedies/A_HRC_32_19_AEV.pdf> accessed 5 November 2016

Protocol on Civil Liability and Compensation for Damage Caused by the Transboundary Effects of Industrial Accidents on Transboundary Waters to the 1992

Report of the Committee on International Criminal Jurisdiction, 1-31 August 1951, UN Doc. A/2645 (1954)

Report of the International Law Commission on the Work of Its Forty-Fourth Session, UN Doc. A/47/10(1992)/

Rome Statute of the International Criminal Court art. 20, July 17, 1998, 2187 UNT.S. 90 SPSC Regulation SS 3-9, 22

The Principle 25 and Commentary of the Guiding Principles on Business and Human Rights: Implementing the United Nations 'Protect, Respect and Remedy' Framework (A/HRC/17/31)

Transport Can., Maritime Law Reform Discussion Paper 15 n.12 (2005) <http:///www.tc.gc.ca/en/report/tp14370epdf > accessed 16 January 2017

U.N Conference on the Human Environment, Stockholm, Swed., June 5-16, 1972, Declarationof the United Nations Conference on the Human Environment, princ. 22, U.N Doc. A/CONF.48/14/REV. 1 (1972.)

UN Committee on the Elimination of Discrimination Against Women (CEDAW), CEDAW General Recommendation No. 19: Violence against women, 1992, http://www.refworld.org/docid/52d920c54.html accessed 8 September 2017

UN Doc. S/2000/915, ((2000), para 1 and 6, 14 August 2000

UN General Assembly Resolution, 49/53 (1995); UN General Assembly Resolution, 50/46 (1996)

UN General Assembly Resolution, 52/160 (1997); Report of the Preparatory Committee on the Establishment of an International Criminal Court, Apr. 14, 1998, UN Doc. A/CONF.183/2/Add.1

UN General Assembly, 51/207 (1996)

UN General Assembly, Convention on the Prevention and Punishment of the Crime of Genocide, 9 December 1948, United Nations, Treaty Series, vol. 78, p.277 http://www.refworld.org/docid/3ae6b3ac0.html accessed 4 October 2016

UN General Assembly, International Covenant on Economic, Social and Cultural Rights, 16 December 1966, United Nations, Treaty Series, vol. 993, p. 3 <http://www.refworld.org/docid/3ae6b36c0.html> accessed 6 July 2017

UN General Assembly, Protocol to Prevent, Suppress and Punish Trafficking in Persons, Especially Women and Children, Supplementing the United Nations Convention against Transnational Organized Crime, 15 November 2000 <http://www.refworld.org/docid/4720706c0.html> accessed 3 September 2017

UN General Assembly, Convention Against Torture and Other Cruel, Inhuman or Degrading Treatment or Punishment, 10 December 1984, United Nations, Treaty Series, vol. 1465, p.85, http://www.refworld.org/docid/3ae6b3a94.html >accessed

UN General Assembly, International Convention for the Suppression of the Financing of Terrorism, 9 December 1999, No. 38349 http://www.refworld.org/docid/3dda0b867.html accessed 3 September 2017

UN General Assembly, International Convention on the Elimination of All Forms of Racial Discrimination, 21 December 1965, United Nations, Treaty Series, vol. 660, p. 195 <http://www.refworld.org/docid/3ae6b3940.html> accessed 6 July 2017

UN General Assembly, International Covenant on Civil and Political Rights, 16 December 1966, United Nations, Treaty Series, vol. 999, p. 171 <http://www.refworld.org/docid/3ae6b3aa0.html> accessed 6 July 2017]

UN General Assembly, International Covenant on Economic, Social and Cultural Rights, 16 December 1966, United Nations, Treaty Series, vol. 993, p. 3, <http://www.refworld.org/docid/3ae6b36c0.html> accessed 6 July 2017

UN General Assembly, Prevention and Punishment of the Crime of Genocide, 9 December 1948, A/RES/260 <http://www.refworld.org/docid/3b00f0873.html> accessed 7 November 2016.

UN General Assembly, Protocol to Prevent, Suppress and Punish Trafficking in Persons, Especially Women

UN General Assembly, Rome Statute of the International Criminal Court (last amended 2010), 17 July 1998 http://www.refworld.org/docid/3ae6b3a84.html accessed 3 November 2016]

UN General Assembly, United Nations Conference on the Human Environment, 15 December

UN General Assembly, United Nations Convention against Transnational Organized Crime: resolution / adopted by the General Assembly, 8 January 2001, A/RES/55/25 http://www.refworld.org/docid/3b00f55b0.html accessed 23 September 2016

UN General Assembly, Universal Declaration of Human Rights, 10 December 1948, 217 A (III) <http://www.refworld.org/docid/3ae6b3712c.html > accessed 15 June 2017

UN General Assembly, Universal Declaration of Human Rights, 10 December 1948, 217 A (III) <http://www.refworld.org/docid/3ae6b3712c.html> accessed 6 July 2017

UN Security Council, Resolution 827 (1993) Adopted by the Security Council at Its 3217th Meeting, On 25 May 1993, 25 May 1993, S/RES/827 (1993) <http://www.refworld.org/docid/3b00f21b1c.html >accessed 4 October 2016

UNECE Convention on Civil Liability for Damage Caused During Carriage of Dangerous Goods by Road, Rail and Inland Navigation Vessels (1989) <https://www.unece.org/trans/danger/publi/crtd/crtd_e.html> accessed20 June 2017

UNGA '2005 World Summit Outcomes' (24 October 2005) UN Doc A/RES/60/1

United Nations Conference on Environment and Development, Rio De Janerio, Braz., June 3-14, 1992, Rio Declaration on Environment and Development, princ 13, UN Doc. A/CONF.151/26 (Vol. 1) (1992)

United Nations Conference on the Human Environment, UN Conference on Environment and Development (1992) <https://sustainabledevelopment.un.org/content/documents/Agenda21.pdf> accessed 14 January 2017

United Nations Convention against Transnational Organized Crime, art. 10 1, opened for signature Nov. 15, 2000, 2225 UNT.S. 209 (entered into force Sept. 29, 2003)

United Nations Declaration on the Rights of Indigenous Peoples (A/RES/61/295) was adopted by the General Assembly on Thursday, 13 September 2007

United Nations Environmental Programme [UNEP], Liability and Compensation Regimes Related to Environment Damage 63 (2002) [hereinafter] <www.unep.or/DEPI/programmes/Liability-compen-papers.pdf.> accessed 07 January 2017

United Nations General Assembly, Doc A/HRC/RES/26/9 (2014) https://www.ihrb.org/pdf/G1408252.pdf> accessed 26 December 2016

United Nations Human Rights Council, Elaboration of an International Legally Binding Instrument on Transnational Corporations and Other Business Enterprises with Respect to Human Rights, 26th Session, 14/07/2014. A/HRC/RES/26/9.

United Nations, Treaty Series, Vol. 993, p. 3 <http://www.refworld.org/docid/3ae6b36c0.html>

accessed 24 September 2016

United Nations, Charter of the International Military Tribunal – Annex to the Agreement for the prosecution and punishment of the major war criminals of the European Axis ("London Agreement") 8 August 1945 http://www.refworld.org/docid/3ae6b39614.html accessed 5 November 2016

United Nations, Charter of the United Nations, 24 October 1945, 1 UNTS XVI <http://www.refworld.org/docid/3ae6b3930.html>accessed 30 August 2016

United Nations, Vienna Convention on the Law of Treaties, 23 May 1969, United Nations, Treaty Series, vol. 1155, p. 331, http://www.refworld.org/docid/3ae6b3a10.html accessed 10 January 2017

Vienna Convention on the Law of Treaties, signed on 23 May 1969, entered into force on 27 January 1980, UN Doc A/CONF. 39/27; 1155 UNTS 331, <http://untreaty.un.org/cod/avl/ha/vclt/vclt.html> accessed 21 September 2017

Cases

International Cases

2007 BCCA 81 at para 31, 279 DLR (4th) 227 [Goodwin]

Abu Ghraib lawsuits against CACI, Titan (Now L-3)

Akpan v Royal Dutch Shell Plc Arrondissementsrechtbank Den Haag [District Court of The Hague] C/09/337050/HA ZA 09-1580, 30 January 2013

Australia Safeway Stores Pty v Ltd v Zaluzna (1987) 162 CLR 479

Avery v Solargizer Int'l, Inc. 427 N.W.2d 675, 681 (Minn. Ct. App. 1988)

Baldeón García v Peru Case. Judgment of April 6, 2006. Series C No. 147, paragraph 81

Ballantyne, Davidson, McIntyre v Canada Communications Nos. 359/1989 and 385/1989

Bemba Case, The Prosecutor v Jean-Pierre Bemba Gombo. ICC-01/05-01/08<https://www.icc-cpi.int/car/bemba?ln=en> accessed 6 November 2016

Cameron v Kenyon-Connel Commercial Co., 56 P. 358, 361 (Mont. 1899)

Case against Al-Jadeed S.A.L. & Al Khayat (The Al-Jadeed Case), STL-14-05/ T/CJ

Case C-75/63 Mrs MKH Hoekstra (Née Unger) v Bestur der Bedriifsvereniging voor

Detaijhandel en Ambachten [1964] ECR I-01519

Case Concerning Military and Paramilitary Activities In and Against Nicaragua (Nicaragua v United States of America); Merits, International Court of Justice (ICJ), 27 June 1986 <http://www.refworld.org/cases,ICJ,4023a44d2.html >accessed 25 October 2017

Case of González et al. ("Cotton Field") v Mexico. Preliminary Objection, Merits, Reparations and Costs. Judgment of November 16, 2009. Series C No. 205, paragraph 252. I/A Court H.R

Central African Republic II Situation in Central African Republic II, ICC-01/14<https://www.icc-cpi.int/carII> accessed 6 November 2016.

Choc v Hudbay Minerals Inc. 2013 ONSC 1414

Coard et al. v United States, Case No. 10.951, 29 September 1999

Corfu Channel Case (United Kingdom v Albania); Assessment of Compensation, 15 XII 49, International Court of Justice (ICJ), 15 December 1949 <http://www.refworld.org/cases,ICJ,402398c84.html > accessed 25 October 2017

Dooh v Royal Shell Plc, No, NoC/09/337058 HA ZA 09-1581 (Netherland)

Ejolt, 'The Trafigura Case' (2015) <http://www.ejolt.org/wordpress/wpcontent/uploads/2015/08/FS-45.pdf>accessed 8 July 2017

Ex-King Farouk of Egypt v Christian Dior (1957) 24 I.L.R. 228

Fullowka v. Pinkerton's of Canada Ltd., 2010 SCC 5, [2010] 1 SCR 132 686

Georgia Situation in Georgia, ICC-01/15 <https://www.icc-cpi.int/georgia> accessed 6 November 2016

González et al ("cotton field") v Mexico Case. Series C No. 205, Judgment November 16, 2009, paragraph 280

I/A Court H.R, Velásquez Rodríguez v Honduras Case. Judgment of July 29, 1988, Series C No. 4, paragraph 166; Perozo et al. v Venezuela Case

Indigenous Community Sawhoyamaxa v Paraguay Case. Judgment of March 29, 2006. Series C No. 146, paragraph 155

Kalamazoo Spice Extraction Co. v Provisional Military Gov't of Socialist Ethiopia, 616 F. Supp. 660, 663 (W.D. Mich. 1985)

Keays v Honda Canada Inc., [2006] O.J. No. 3891 (C.A.), leave to appeal to S.C.C. Granted, [2006] S.C.C.A. No. 470 [Keays]

Mali Situation in the Republic of Mali, ICC-01/12 <https://www.icc-cpi.int/mali> accessed 6 November 2016

Massacre of Pueblo Bello v Colombia Case. Judgment of January 31, 2006. Series C No. 140

Nahimana Prosecutor V Barayagwiza, & Ngeze (Media Case), Case No. ICTR-99-52-T (Dec. 3, 2003)

Nahimana v Prosecutor, Case No. ICTR 99-52-A, Appeals Judgment (Int'l Crim Trib. for Rwanda Nov. 28, (2007) <https://perma.cc/VKG9-XKTB [hereinafter Media Case > accessed September 2017

Oguru v Royal Dutch Shell Plc, No C/09/ 330891 / HA ZA 09 057

Prosecutor v Šešelj (Vojislav), Decision on the Financing the Defence of The Accused, Case No IT-03-67-PT, ICL 116 (ICTY 2007), 30th July 2007

Prosecutor v Bagilishema, Case No. ICTR-95-1A-T, Judgment, 42 (Int'l Crim. Trib. for Rwanda June 7, 2001)

Prosecutor v Blaškić, Case No. IT-95-14-A, Appeal Judgment, 192–93, 262–63 (Int'l Crim. *Trib. For the Former Yugoslavia*, July 29, 2004) <https://perma.cc/Z8DM-MX56> accessed 12 September 2017

Prosecutor v Dusko Tadic (Appeal Judgement), IT-94-1-A, International Criminal Tribunal for the former Yugoslavia (ICTY), 15 July 1999 <>accessed 25 September 2016

Prosecutor v Hadzihasanovic, Case No. IT-01-47-AR72, Decision on Interlocutory Appeal *Challenging Jurisdiction in Relation to Command Responsibility, 16, Int'l Crim. Trib. For the Former Yugoslavia* (July 16 2003) <https://perma.cc/N62U-TYBZ> accessed 15 September 2017

Prosecutor v Miroslav Kvocka et al. (Appeal Judgement), IT-98-30/1-A, International *Criminal Tribunal for The Former Yugoslavia* (ICTY), 28 February 2005,
http://www.refworld.org/docid/48ad2b772.html accessed 25 September 2016

Prosecutor v Mucić et al., Case No. IT-96-21-T, Judgment, 337 (Int'l Crim. Trib. For the *Former Yugoslavia* Nov. 16, 1998)
<https://perma.cc/BT86-GBWV> accessed September 2017, (citing Art. IX of the Chinese Law of 24th October, 1946, Governing the Trial of War Criminals

Prosecutor v Musema, Case No. ICTR-96-13-T, Judgment and Sentence, 880, 894 (Int'l Crim. Trib. for Rwanda Jan. 27, 2000)
<https://perma.cc/S2CL-BAUM > accessed 13 September 2017

Prosecutor v Sam Hinga Norman, Case No. SCSL-2004-14-AR72 (E)

Prosecutor v Tihomir Blaskic (Appeal Judgement), IT-95-14-A, International Criminal *Tribunal for the former Yugoslavia* (ICTY), 29 July 2004
http://www.refworld.org/docid/4146f0eb4.html

accessed 25 September 2016

Prosecutor v Zdravko Mucic aka "Pavo", Hazim Delic, Esad Landzo aka "Zenga", Zejnil Delalic (Trial Judgement), IT-96-21-T, International Criminal Tribunal for The former *Yugoslavia* (ICTY), 16 November 1998 http://www.refworld.org/cases,ICTY,41482bde4.html accessed 12 September 2017

Prosecutor v Zlatko Aleksovski (Appeal Judgement), IT-95-14/1-A, International Criminal Tribunal For The Former Yugoslavia (ICTY), 24 March 2000

Re Yamashita, 327 US 1, 14 (1946)

Shinhan Bank Corporation v Kim Woo-Jjoong and Ten Others, 2006 Da 6838, (S. Kor.)

Slobodan Milošević (IT-02-54) <http://www.icty.org/case/slobodan_milosevic/4> accessed 2 November 2016

Temple of Preah Vihear (Cambodia v Thailand), 1962 I.C.J. 6, 23 (June 15)

The Prosecutor v Germain Katanga. ICC-01/04-01/07 https://www.icccpi.int/iccdocs/PIDS/publications/KatangaEng.pdf accessed 6 November 2016

The Prosecutor v Ignace Bagilishema (Trial Judgement), ICTR-95-1A-T, International Criminal Tribunal for Rwanda (ICTR), 7 June 2001 <http://www.refworld.org/cases,ICTR,48abd5170.html >accessed 12 September 2017.

The Prosecutor v Mathieu Ngudjolo Chui. ICC-01/04-02/12 <https://www.icccpi.int/drc/ngudjolo?ln=en>accessed 6 November 2016

The Prosecutor v Omar Hassan Ahmad Al Bashir ICC-02/05-01/09, ICC-PIDS-CIS-SUD-02-005/17

Trafigura Reaches Toxic Waste Settlement with Dutch, REUTERS (Nov. 16, 2012), https://perma.cc/QRE8-NG7J > accessed 19 September 2017

United States Nuremberg War Crimes Trials, United States v Krauch (Case IV) (Aug. 14, 1947–July 30, 1948) <https://perma.cc/PAZ2-VWSV> accessed 12 September 2017

United States of America v Carl Krauch et al (1950) Case No 6

United States v Canada 1941, UN Rep. Int'L Arb. Awards 1905 (1949)

United States v List (Wilhelm) and ors, Trial Judgment, Case No 7, (1948) 11 TWC 757, (1950) 11 TWC 1230, (1948) 8 LRTWC 34, ICL 491 (US 1948), (1948) 15 ILR 632, 19th February 1948

United States V Wilhelm von Leeb et al, 12 LRTWC 1 at 59 (1948)

Valle-Jaramillo and et al. v Colombia Case. Merits, Reparations and Costs. Judgment of
November 27, 2008. Series C No. 192, paragraph 78
Williams v State Farm Mut. Auto. Ins. Co., 229 Conn. 359 (Conn. 1994)

European Union Cases

Complaint, SEC v Siemens Aktiengesellschaft, No. 1:08-cv-02167 (D.D.C. 2008)
ECHR, Case of Kiliç v. Turkey, Judgment of 28 March 2000, paragraphs 62 and 63 ECHR
Case of Osman v. the United Kingdom, Judgment of 28 October 1998, paragraphs 115 and 116. I/A Court H.R.
Factory At Chorzów, Germany v Poland, Judgment, Claim for Indemnity, Merits, Judgment No 13, (1928) PCIJ Series A No 17, ICGJ 255 (PCIJ 1928), 13th September 1928, League of *McIntyre v Grigg* [2006] O.J. No. 4420

United States Cases

572 (3d) 677 (9th Cir 2009) [Wal-Mart Stores 9th Cir].
A. v New York, 252 N.Y.S.2d 800, 810 (Ct. Cl. 1964)
Abdullahi v Pfizer Inc., 562 F.3d 163, 187 (2d Cir. 2009)
Adickes v S.H. Kress & Co., 398 US 144, 170 (1970)
Aguinda v Texaco, Inc., 850 F. Supp. 282 (SDNY 1994)
Air Traffic Conference of Am. v Marina Travel, Inc., 316 S.E.2d 642, 645 (N.C. Ct. App. 1984)
Aldana v Del Mont Fresh Produce, N.A., Inc., 416 F. 3d 1242 (11th Cir. 2005)
Almog v Arab Ban, PLC 471 F. Supp. 2d 257 (E.D.N.Y. 2007)
Ann M. and Sharon P v Arman Ltd. (1999) 21 C.4th 1181, 91 C.R.2d 35, 989 P.2d 121,6 Summary (10th)
Arnold v IBM 637 F.2d 1350, 1355 (9th Cir. 1981)
Avitia v United States, No. 00-55240 (9th Cir. Dec. 14, 2001)
Balintulo v Daimler AG, US Dist. Lexis 17474 (2d Cir. Aug. 21, 2013)
Bank of New England, 821 F.2d at 856
Bano v Union Carbide, 273 F.3d 120, 133 (2d Cir. 2001)
Bowoto v Chevron Corp., 621 F.3d 1116 (9th Cir. 2010). 690
Burnham v Superior Ct., 495 US 604, 628 (1990)
Cabello v Femandez-Larios 402 F.3d 1148, 1154 (11 th Cir. 2005)
Calcagno v Kuebel, Fuchs P'Ship, 01-691 (La. App. 5 Cir. 11/14/01)

Casey v Manson Constr. & Engineering Co., 247 Ore. 274 (Or. 1967)
Celentano v Rocque 923 A.2d 709, 282 Conn. 645 (2007)
Cisneros v Aragon 485 F.3d 1226 (10th Cir. 2007)
Delgado v Trax Bar & Grill (2005) 36 C.4th 224
Della Ratta v Della Ratta, 927 So.2d 1055 (Fla. 4th DCA 2006)
Doe I v Unocal Corp 395 F.3d 932, (9th Cir.2002)
Doe v Liu Qi 349 F. Supp. 2d 1258 (N.D. Cal 2004)
Doe v Rafael Saravia 348 F. Supp. 2d 1112 (E.D.N.Y. Cal. 2004)
Doe v Unocal Corp 963 F. Supp. 880, 883–84, 892 (C.D. Cal. 1997)
Doe v Unocal Corp Nos. BC 237980, BC 237679, 2002 WL 33944506 at 13–14 (Cal. Super.
Ct. June 11 2002)
Dotterweich 320 US at 281 (citing United States v Balint, 258 US 250, 252 (1922)
Dreyfus v Von Finck 534 F.2d 24 (2d Cir.), cert. denied, 429 US 835, 97 S. Ct. 102, 50 L. Ed. 2d 101 (1976)
Dunn v United States, 284 US 390, 52 S.Ct. 189, 76 L.Ed. 356, 80 A.L.R. 161
E.E.O.C. v Arabian American Oil Co., 499 US 244 (1991)
Edmonson v Leesville Concrete Co., 500 US 614, 632 (1991)
Egan v United States, 137 F.2d 369, 379 (8th Cir. 1943), cert denied, 320 US 788 (1943)
Elliott v Insurance Crime Prevent Bureau, 2005 NSCA 115
Exchange v M'Faddon, 11 US (7 Cranch) 116, 3 L. Ed. 287 (1812)
Exxon Shipping Co. v Baker, 554 US 471, 128 S. Ct. 2605, 171 L. Ed. 2d 570 (2008) 691
F. Hoffman-La Roche Ltd. v Empagran S.A., 542 US 155, 164 (2004)
Field v Boyer Co. L.C 952 P.2d 1078 (Utah 1998)
Filártiga v Peña-Irala, 630 F.2d 876 (2d Cir. 1980)
Flomo v Firestone Nat. Rubber Co., LLC, 643 F.3d 1013 (7th Cir. 2011)
Flores v S. Peru Copper Corp., 343 F.3d 140 (2d Cir. 2003)
Foley Bros., Inc. v Filardo 336 US 281, 285 (1949)
Ford v Garcia, 289 F.3d 1283, 1283, 1287-94 (11th Cir. 2002)
Frances T v Vill. Green Owners Ass'n 723 P.2d 573, 584 (Cal. 1986).
Friedman v Sebelius 686 F.3d 813 (D.C. Cir. 2012)
Fullowka v Pinkerton's of Canada Ltd 2010 SCC 5, [2010] 1 S.C.R. 132
Gallagher v Neil Young Freedom Concert, 49 F.3d 1442, 1448-51 (10th Cir. 1995)
Georgia Malone & Co. v Rieder, 132, 2012 NY Slip Op 05200 (N.Y. June 28, 2012)
Grandma's Biscuits, Inc. v Baisden, 386 S.E.2d 415 (Ga. Ct. App

Haire v Bonelli, 870 N.Y.S.2d 591, 593 (N.Y. App. Div. 3d Dept. 2008)
Haliao v Marcos, 25 F.3 1467 (9th Cir. 1994)
Hassoon v Shamieth (2001) 89 C.A.4th 1191, 107 C.R.2d 658
Hutcherson v City of Phoenix, 961 P.2d 449 (Ariz. 1998)
*IIT v Vencap Lt*d 519 F.2d 1001 (2d Cir. 1975)
In International Shoe Co. v Washington, 326 US 310 (1945)
Isaacs v Huntington Memorial Hosp. (1985) 38 C.3d 112, 211 C.R. 356, 695 P.2d 653, 6 Summary (10th)
Islamic Republic of Iran v Pahlavi, 62 N.Y.2d 474, 482-85, 478 N.Y.S.2d 597, 602-03, 467
N.E.2d 245, 250-51 (1984)
Jackson v Metro. Edison Co., 419 US 345, 352 (1974)
Jesner v Arab Bank, PLC 16-499 (2d Cir. Oct 11, 2017) TBD 692
Jimenez v Aristeguieta (1962) 311 F.2d 547
Kadic v Karadzic 70 F.3.d 232 (2d Cir.1992)
Kiobel v Royal Dutch Petroleum Co 133 S.Ct. 1659 (2013)
Kollias v D & G Marine Maintenance 29 F.3d 67, 71 (2d Cir. 1994), cert. denied, 513 US 1146 (1995)
Kulko v Superior Ct 436 U.S 84, 101 (1978)
Labour Union of Pico Korea, Ltd. v Pico Prods., Inc., 968 F.2d 191, 194 (2d Cir.), cert. denied, 506 US 985 (1992)
Lantz v Coleman 2010 Conn. Super. Lexis 621 (Conn. Super. Ct. Mar. 9, 2010)
Lau's Corp, Inc. v Haskins 405 S.E.2d 474 (Ga. 199)
Lawton v Steele 152 US 133, 14 S. Ct. 499 (1894)
Lemon v Kurtz Man 403 US 602, 91 S. Ct. 2105, 29 L. Ed. 2d 745 (1971).
Liberty Nat'l Life Ins. Co. v Weldon, 100 So. 2d 696, 710 (Ala. 1957)
Linder v Calero Portocarrero, 963 F.2d 332, 333–34 (11th Cir. 1992)
Liu Qi 349 F. Supp. 2d at 1328-34
Lopresti v Terwilliger, 126 F.3d 34, 42 (2d Cir. 1997)
Lowell Hoit & Co. v Detig 50 N.E.2d 602, 603 (Ill. App. Ct. 1943)
Lugar v Edmondson Oil Co 457 US 922, 937 (1982)
MacPherson v Buick Motor Co 111 N.E. 1050 (N.Y. 1916)
Mandarin Trading Ltd. v Wildenstein 16 NY3d 173, 182 (2011)
Marsh v Alabama 326 US 501)
Maryland v Baltimore Radio Show 338 US 912 (1950)
Merrill Crossings Assocs. v McDonald 705 So. 2d 560 (Fla. 1997)
Moak v Link- Belt Co., 242 So. 2d 515 (La. 1970) (no negligence so no liability).
Mohamad v Palestinian Authority 566 US (2012) 693
Morrison v National Australia Bank 561 US (2010)

Morrison v National Australia Bank Ltd 130 S. Ct. 2869, 561 US 247, 177 L. Ed. 2d 535 (2010)
Morrison v National Australia Bank Ltd 561 US 247 (2010)
Namba v McCourt 204 P.2d 569, 583 (Or. 1949)
Nippon Fire & Marine Ins. Co. v M.V. Tourcoing 167 F.3d 99 (2d Cir. N.Y. 1999)]
Nola M. v Univ. of S. Cal 20 Cal. Rptr. 2d 97 (Ct. App. 1993)
Palsgraf v Long Island Railroad Co 248 N.Y. 339, 162 N.E. 99 (N.Y. 1928)
Park 421 US at 658.
Parker v Griswold 17 Conn. 288, 304 (1845)
Posecai v Wal-Mart Stores, Inc 752 So. 2d 762, 766 (La. 1999)
Presbyterian Church of Sudan v Talisman Energy, Inc 244 F. Supp. 2d 289 (S.D.N.Y. 2003
Preston-Thomas Const., Inc. v Cent. Leasing Corp 518 P.2d 1125, 1127 (Okla. Ct. App. 1973)
Reed v Littleton 289 N. Y. Supp. 798, 159 Misc. 853 (1932)
Rendell-Baker v Kohn 457 US 830, 847 (1982).
Richards v United States 369 US 1 (US 1962)
*Riley v Maison Orleans II Inc.*2002 WL 31256411 (La. Ct. App. Sept. 25, 2002)
Ritz Carlton Hotel Co. v Revel 454 S.E.2d 183 (Ga. Ct. App. 1995)
RJR Nabisco, Inc. v European Community 136 S. Ct. 2090 (Supreme Court 2016)
Roe v Bridgestone Corp 257 F.R.D. 159, 172-73 (S.D. Ind. 2009)
Saelzler v Advanced Group 400 107 Cal. Rptr. 2d 617, 623-24 (2001)
Salas v United States 974 F. Supp. 202, 209 (W.D.N.Y. 1997)
Sampson v Federal Republic of Germany 250 F.3d 1145, 1149-50 (7th Cir. 2001)
Sandoval v Bluegrass Regional Mental Health-Mental Retardation No. 99-5018, 2000 US
App. Lexis 17949 (6th Cir. July 11)
Sarei v Rio PLC 487 F. 3d 1193, 1201-02 (9th Cir. 2007) 694
Sarei v Rio Tinto PLC 2011 WL 5041927 (9th Cir. Oct. 25, 2011)
Sarei v Rio Tinto PLC, 2009 WL 2762635 (C.D. Calif. July 31, 2009)
Sinaltrainal v Coca-Cola Company 578 F.3d 1252 (11th Cir. 2009)
Sosa v Alvarez-Machain 542 US 692
South Africa Apartheid 346 F. Supp. 2d 538, 547 (S.D.Y.2004)
Staples v United States 511 US 600 (1994).
Sturbridge Partners, Ltd. v Walker 482 S.E.2d 339 (Ga. 1997)
Summers v Tice 33 Cal.2d 80, 199 P.2d 1 (1948)
Tachiona v Mugabe 234 F. Supp. 2d 401 (S.D.N.Y. 2002)

Taveras v Taveraz 477 F. 3d 767 (6th Cir. 2007)
Tel-Oren v Libyan Arab Republic 726 F. 2d 774 (1984)
Terry v Adams 345 US 461 (1953)
The Paquete Habana 175 US 677, 700, 20 S. Ct. 290, 44 L. Ed. 320 (1900)
Touchard v Slemco Electric Found, 99- 3577, 1 (La. 10/17/00); 769 So. 2d 1200, 1202
Trajano v Marcos 978 F.2d. (9th Cir. 1992)
Turedi v The Coca-Cola Co US App. Lexis 14794 (2d Cir. July 7, 2009)
United Canada Malt Ltd. v Outboard Marine Corp. of Canada (2000), 48 O.R. (3d) 352 (S.C.)
United State v Bestfoods 524 US, 61-64 (1998)
United State v Curtiss-Wrights Export Corp 299US 304 (1936)
United States v Daimler AG No. 1:10-cr- 00063-RJL (D.D.C. 2010)
United States v Hodges X-Ray Inc 759 F.2d 557, 561 (6th Cir. 1985)
United States v Morgan 222 US 274, 32 S.Ct. 81, 56 L.Ed. 198
United States v Norian Corp No. 09-cr-403-LDD (E.D. Pa. 2009), Sentencing Nov. 21, 2011.
United States v Purdue Frederick Co Inc 495 F. Supp. 2d 569, 573 (W.D. Va. 2007)
United States government v Bowman 260 US 94 (1922)
United States v Dotterweich 320 US 277 283–84 (1943)
United States v Gatlin 216 F.3d 207, 211-12 (2d Cir. 2000)
United States v Park 421 US 658, 672 (1975)
Van Ort v Estate of Stanewich 92 F.3d 831, 836 (9th Cir. 1996), cert. denied 519 US 1111 (1997)
Vietnam Asus'n for Victims of Agent Organ v Dow Chemical Co 517 F. 3d 104 (2d Cir. 2008)
Wal-Mart v Dukes 564 US 338 (2011)
Webb v Portland Mfg. Co 29 F. Cas. 506, 508 (Story, Circuit Justice, C.C.D. Me. 1838) (No. 17,322)
Whitehead v Food Max 163 F.3d 265 (5th Cir. 1998)

United Kingdom Cases

2 Travel Group plc (in liquidation) v Cardiff City Transport Services Ltd [2012] CAT 19
38, TAkitota v A-G [2009 26 BHRC578
A v Bottrill [2002] UKPC 44, [1978] 2 All ER 437, 438
AB v South West Water Services Ltd [1993] 1 All ER 609
Acher v Brown [1985] QB 401
Adams v Cape Industries Plc [1990] Ch 433

A-G Trindade and Tobago v Ramanoop [2006] 1 AC 328
Anns v Merton London Borough Council [1978] AC 728
Archer v Brown [1984] QB 401(deceit)
Arthur Hall v Simons [2000] 3 WLR 543
Ashby v White [1703] 92 ER 126
AT v Gavril Dulhieru [2009] EWHC 225 696
B V DPP [2000] 2 AC 428
Bailey v MOD [2009] 1 WLR 1052
Barker v Corus (UK) Plc [2006] UKHL 20
Barnett v Chelsea & Kensington Hospital [1969] 1 QB 428
Barrett v MOD [1995] 1 WLR 1217
Blacker v Lake & Elliot, Ltd [1912] 106 L.T. 533 <http://www.scottishlawreports.org.uk/resources/dvs/page-text/pages/Respondents-CasePage-10.html>
Blyth v Birmingham Waterworks Co [1856] 11 Exch 781
Bodo Community and Others v Shell Petroleum Development Company of Nigeria [2014]
EWHC 958 (TCC)
Bolton (Engineering) Co. Ltd v T J Graham & Sons Ltd [1957] 1 QB 159
Borders (UK) Ltd v MPC [2005] EWCA Civ 197
Bourhill v Young [1943] AC 92
Brazier v Dolphin Fairway Ltd [2005] EWCA Civ 1469
Caparo Industries plc v Dickman [1990] 2 AC 605
Carmarthenshire County Council v Lewis [1955] AC
Case of Sutton's Hospital [1612] 77 Eng Rep 960
Cassell & Co Ltd v Broome and Another [1971] 2 All ER 187, 198
Cf Merest v Harvey [1814] 5 Taunt 442, 128 ER 761
Chadwick v Pioneer Private Telephone Co. Ltd [1941] 1 All E.R. 522, 523D
Chandler v Cape plc [2012] EWCA Civ 525
Childs v Desormeaux, [2006] 1 S.C.R. 643
Choc v Hudbay Minerals Inc [2013] ONSC 1414
Cook v Lewis [1951] SCR 830 697
Cooper v Hobart [2001] 3 S.C.R. 537
Crocker v Sundance Northwest Resorts Ltd [1988] 1 S.C.R. 1186
Customs and Excise v Barclays Bank Plc [2006] UKHL 28
Devenish Nutrition Ltd v Sanofi-Aventis SA [2007] EWHC 239
DHN Food Distributors Ltd v Tower Hamlets London Borough Council [1976] 1 WLR 852
Donoghue (or McAlister) v Stevenson [1932] All ER Rep 1; [1932] AC 562
Donoghue v Stevenson [1932] AC 562 (HL Sc)
DPP v Smith [1961] AC 290

Drane v Evangelou and Others [1978] 2 All ER 437
Duck v Peacock [1949] 1 All ER
Duck v Peacock [1949] 1 All ER 318
Edwards v Ddin [1976] 63 Cr App R 218
Embrey v Owen 6 Exch 353 at 370, 368, 155 Eng. Rep. 579, 585 [1851]
Fidler v Sun Life Assurance Company of Canada [2006] SCC 30
Fitzgerald v Lane [1989] 1 AC 328
George and Wife v Skivington [1869] LR 5 Ex 1
Gibbons v Proctor [1891] 64 LT 594
Goldman v Hargrave [1967] Ch 645
Goodwin v British Columbia (Superintendent of Motor Vehicles) [2015] 3 SCR 250
Gouriet v Union of Post Office Workers [1978] AC 435
Guerrero & Ors v Monterrico Metals Plc & Anor (Rev 1) [2009] EWHC 2475 (QB) (16 October 2009)
H L Bolton (Engineering) Co Ltd v T.J Graham and Sons Ltd [1957] 1QB 159
Haley v London Electricity Board [1965] AC 77
Hall v Brooklands Auto Racing Club [1933] 1 KB 205 698
Hamilton Partners LP v. Englard [2010] C.A. 4476-VCL
Harold Holdsworth & Co (Wakefield) Ltd v Caddies [1955] 1 WLR 352
Healthcare at Home Ltd v The Common Services Agency [2014] UKSC 49
Heaven v Pender (1883) 11 QBD 503 <https://www.leeds.ac.uk/law/hamlyn/donoghue.htm> accessed 18 December 2016
Henderson v Merrett Syndicates Ltd [1994] UKHL 5
Hill v Hamilton-Wentworth Regional Police Services Board, 2007 SCC 41 [2007] 3 SCR 129
Holden v Chief Constable of Lancashire [1987] QB 380
Home Office v Dorset Yacht Co Ltd [1970] AC 1004
Horsford v Bird & Ors (Antigua and Barbuda) [2006] UKPC 3
Hudson 1 QB 448 CCA
Hyam v DPP [1975] AC 55
Innis v A-G St Christopher and Nevis [2008] UKPC 38
John v MGN Ltd [1996] 1 All 35, at 57
Junior Books Ltd v Veitchi Co Ltd [1983] 1 AC 520
KD v Chief Constable of Hampshire [2005] EWHC 2550
Kennaway v Thompson [1981] QB 88
Khodaparast v Shad [2000] 1 All ER 545 (malicious falsehood)
Kuddus v Chief Constable of Leicestershire Constabulary [2001] 2 WLR 1789

Kudus v Chief Constable of Leicestershire [2002] 2 AC 122
Langley v Dray [1998] PIQR P 314
Le Lievre v Gould [1893] 1 QB 491 <http://www.iclr.co.uk/assets/media/vote/1915-1945/Donoghue_ac1932-1-562.pdf> accessed 18 December 2016
Lennard's Carrying Co. Ltd v Asiatic Petroleum Co. Ltd [1915] AC 705
Lister v Hesley Hall Ltd [2001] UKHL 22 699
Lubbe v Cape Plc [2000] UKHL 41
Lungowe & Others v Vedanta Resources PLC and Konkola Copper Mines Plc [2016] EWHC 975 (TCC)
MacFarlane and Another v Tayside Health Board [2000] 2 AC 59
Marries v Martin [1966] QB 716 (AC) 733
McLoughlin v O'Brian [1983] 1 AC 410 <http://www.pierre-legrand.com/mcloughlin-vobrian.pdf> accessed 19 December 2016
Meridian Global Funds Management Asia Ltd v Securities Commission [1995] UKPC 5
Miller v Jackson [1977] 3 WLR 20
Mitchell v Glasgow City Council [2009] UKHL 11
Montgomery v Lanarkshire Health Board [2015] UKSC 11
Motto v Trafigura Ltd [2011] EWCA Civ 1150
MPC v Caldwell [1982] AC 341
Muirhead v Industrial Tank Specialties Ltd and Other [1986] QB 507
Murphy v Brentwood District Council [1991] 1 AC 398
Muuse v Secretary of State for The Home Department [2010] EWCA Civ 453
Norton v Corus UK Ltd [2006] EWCA Civ 1630
Norwich City Council v Harvey [1988] 45 BLR 14.
O'Hara v Chief Constable of Royal Ulster Constabulary [1997] AC 286
Ord v Belhaven Pubs Ltd [1998] 2 BCLC 447
Osman v United Kingdom [1998] EHRR 101
Owens v Liverpool Corp [1939] 1KB 394
Page v Smith [1996] 1 AC 155
Phelps v Hillingdon [2001] 2 AC 619
Queen v Woodrow [1846) 153 Eng. Rep. 907, 912 700
Queen v Stephens [1884] 14 QBD 273
R (on the application FWL Congo) v Secretory of State for Home Dept [2011] 2 WLR 671 [1972] AC 102
R v Dytham 1979] QB 722
R v Fenton [1830] 1 Lew CC 179
R v Franklin [1883] 15 Cox CC 163
R v G & R [2003] 3 WLR

R v Goodfellow [1986] 83 Cr App R 23
R v Hancock and Shankland [1986] 2 WLR 257
R v Inglis [2011] 1 WLR 1110, DPP v Smith [1961] AC 290
R v Lamb [1967] 2 QB 981
R v Larsonneur [1933] 24 Cr App R 74
R v Lowe [1973] QB 702
R v Miller [1983] 2 AC 161
R v Mitchell [1983] QB 741
R v Moloney [1985] AC 905
R v Nedrick (1986) 83 Cr App 267
R v Pittwood [1902] TLR 37
R v Saik [2006] UKHL 18
R v Scalley [1995] Crim LR 504
R v Tolson [1889] 23 QBD 168
R v Walker and Hayles (1990) 90 Cr App R 226
R v White [1910] 2 KB 124
R v Larsonneur [1933] 24 Cr App R 74
Racz v Home Office [1993] 2 WLR 23 701
Ramzan v Brookwide [2012] 2 All ER 903
Ready Mixed Concrete (South East) Ltd v Minister of Pension and National Insurance [1968] 2 QB 497
Reaney v University Hospital of North Staffordshire NHS Trust [2014] EWHC 3016
Reeves v Commissioner of Police of the Metropolis [2000] 1 AC 360
Regina v Woodrow 15 M. & W [1846]40*4* Exch.
Resurfice Corp. v Hanke [2007] 1 S.C.R. 333
Rookes v Barnard [1964] AC 1129
Roper v Taylor's Central. Garages (Exeter) Ltd [1951] 2 T.L.R. 284
Rowlands v Chief Constable of Merseyside Police [2007] 1 WLR 1065
Rylands v Fletcher [1868] UKHL 1
Salomon v Salomon and Co. Ltd [1897] A.C 22
Sam (aka- Al-Sam) v Atkins [2006] EWCA Civ 152, [2006] R.T.R14
Sedleigh-Denfield v O' Callaghan [1940] AC 880
Shirlaw v Southern Foundries [1939] 2 KB 206
Simaan General Contracting Co v Pilkington Glass Ltd [1988] CA 17
Smith Kline & French Labs Ltd v Bloch [1983] 1 WLR 730
Smith v Littlewoods Organisation Ltd [1987] UKHL 18
Speight v Gaunt (1883) LR 9
Stovin v Wise [1996] 3 WLR 389
Stovin v Wise [1996] AC 923 at 948.
Supply of Ready Mixed Concrete ([1992] QB 212

Sutcliffe v Pressdram Ltd [1991] 1 QB 153
Sutherland Shire Council v Heyman (1985) 157 CLR 424
Sutherland Shire Council v Heyman [1985] HCA 4 702
Sutradhar v Natural Environment Research Council [2006] UKHL 33
Sweet v Parsley [1970] AC 132
Takitota v A-G [2009 26 BHRC578
Tesco Supermarkets Ltd v Nattrass [1971] UKHL 1
Thompson v Commissioner of Police of Metropolis [1998] QB 498
Thompson v Hill [1870] LR 5 CP564
Thompson-Schwab v Costaki [1956] 1 WLR 335
Turner v Shearer [1973] 1 All ER 397
Vaughan v Menlove [1837] 3 Bing NC 468, 132 ER 490 (CP)
Vidal -Hall & Ors v Google Inc [2014] EWHC 13 (QB) (16 January 2014) <http://www.bailii.org/ew/cases/EWHC/QB/2014/13.html > accessed 30 October 2016
Watkins v Home Office and others [2006] UKHL 17.
Watkins v Secretary of State for the Home Dept [2006] 2 WLR 807
Watson v British Boxing Board of Control [2001] QB 1134
*Webb v The Queen (*1994) 181 CLR 41
Wheeler v JJ Saunders [1996] Ch 19
White v Chief Constable of South Yorkshire [1998] 3 WLR 1509
*Whitehous*e (1999) Times, 10 December, CA
Williams v Natural Life Health Foods Ltd [1998] UKHL 17
Winzar v Chief Constable of Kent [1983]
Woodroffe-Hedley v Cuthbertson [1997] QBD
Young [1984] 2 All ER 164.
Yuen Kun Yeu v Attorney-General of Hong Kong [1988] AC 175

Miscellaneous

Abeyratne R, 'Superior Responsibility and The Principle of Legality at The ECCC' (2012)
Abraham KS, 'Strict Liability in Negligence' (2011)
Alford RP, 'Apportioning Responsibility among Joint Tortfeasors for International Law Violations' (2011)
Amegatcher N, 'Ghana Gets Tough on Judicial Corruption' (2016) <http://www.ibanet.org/Article/NewDetail.aspx?ArticleUid=2c8eb0c5-3ba2-4619-a7ac-b5c2d117633d> accessed 18 January 2017
Amnesty International, 'Creating a Paradigm Shift: Legal Solutions to Improve Access to Remedy for Corporate Human Rights Abuse' (2017)

<https://www.amnesty.org/en/documents/pol30/7037/2017/en/> accessed 15 October 2-17.

Antunes JE, 'Liability of Corporate Groups: Autonomy and Control in Parent-Subsidiary Relationships in US, German and EU law: An International and Comparative Perspective' (1994)

Arrow KJ, 'Essays in The Theory of Risk-Bearing' (1970) No. 04; HB615, A7

Assink BF, 'Secondary Director Liability, The Defining Tension' (2009) <https://perma.cc/E9JU-8PFF > accessed 17 September 2017

Associated Press in Addis Ababa, 'African Leaders Plan Mass Withdrawal from International Criminal Court' (2017) https://www.theguardian.com/law/2017/jan/31/africanleaders-plan-mass-withdrawal-from-international-criminal-court accessed 8 July 2017

Augestein D, 'Study of The Legal Framework on Human Rights and The Environmental Applicable to European Enterprise Operating Outisde The European Union' (2014) <http://en.frankbold.org/sites/default/files/tema/101025_ec_study_final_report_en_0.pdf> accessed on 28 May 2017

BDO Consulting, 'Independent Evaluation of The Gulf Coast Claims Facility: Executive Summary' (2012) <http://media.nola.com/2010_gulf_oil_spill/oth> accessed 20 September 2017

Bella BN and Dabelko GD, 'UN Special Rapporteur Calls for Business & Human Rights Treaty to Protect Human Rights Defenders' (2016) https://business-humanrights.org/en/unspecial-rapporteur-calls-for-business-human-rights-treaty-to-protect-human-rightsdefenders accessed 10 January 2017

Bernaz N, 'Criminal Complaint against French Cement Company for Terrorism Financing, Complicity of Crimes against Humanity and War Crimes in Syria' (2016)

Bettelli P, 'Summary of The Fifth Conference of The Parties to The Basel Convention on The Control of Transboundary Movements of Hazardous Wastes and Their Disposal' (1999)

Bogdandy A, 'Doctrine of Principles, Jean Monnet Working Paper 9/03' (2003) <http://centers.law.nyu.edu/jeanmonnet/archive/papers/03/030901-01.pdf > accessed 20 August 2017

Boolieris E, 'To Punish or Not Punish: A Comparative Analysis of The Legislative Treatment of Exemplary Damages in Commonwealth Jurisdictions' (2013)

Börzel T and Hoenke J, 'From Compliance to Practice: Mining Companies and The Voluntary Principles on Security and Human rights in The Democratic Republic of Congo' (2010)

BP Statement on Deepwater Horizon Settlement with US, WALL ST. J. (Nov. 15, 2012)

Bradley CA, 'US Announces Intent Not to Ratify International Criminal Court Treaty' (2002)

Bushman RM and Smith AJ, 'Transparency, Financial Accounting Information, and Corporate Governance' (2003)

Cardesa-Salzmann A, 'Constitutionalising Secondary Rules in Global Environmental Regimes: Non-compliance Procedures and The Enforcement of Multilateral Environmental Agreements' (2011) <https://papers.ssrn.com/sol3/papers.cfm?abstract_id=2790886> accessed 20 April 2017

Carson M, Gatton A, Vázquez R and O'Kane M, 'Colombian Takes BP to Court in UK over Alleged Complicity in Kidnap and Torture' (2015). The Guardian <https://www.theguardian.com/environment/2015/may/22/colombian-takes-bp-tocourt-in-uk-alleged-complicity-kidnap-and-torture> accessed 21 December 2016

Cassin SR, 'ENI in $365 Million Settlement' THE FCPA BLOG (July 27,

Clapham A, 'The Question of Jurisdiction under International Criminal Caw over Legal Persons: Lessons From The Rome Conference on An International Criminal Court' (2000) <https://www.academia.edu/24513911/_The_Question_of_Jurisdiction_Under_International_Criminal_Law_Over_Legal_Persons_Lessons_from_the_Rome_Conference_on_an_International_Criminal_Court?auto=download> accessed 4 July 2016

Clopton ZD, 'Replacing The Presumption against Extraterritoriality' (2013)

Coleman J, Hershovitz S and Mendlow G, 'Theories of The Common Law of Torts' (2003)

CORE, 'The Bottom Line: UK Corporate Abuse Overseas' (2015) <http://corporate-responsibility.org/wpcontent/uploads/2015/10/The-Bottom-Linereportfinal-digital-version.pdf> accessed 26 December 2016

Cunningham S, 'Taking Causing Serious Injury by Dangerous Driving Seriously' (2012)

D'Ascoli S and Scherr KM, 'The Rule of Prior Exhaustion of Local Remedies in The International Law Doctrine and Its Application in The Specific Context of Human Rights Protection' (2007))

De La Vega Connie, Amol Mehra & Alexandra Wong, Holding Businesses Accountable for Human Rights Violations: Recent Developments and Next Steps (2011) <https://perma.cc/8WAA-SGCC > accessed 13 June 2016

De Schutter O, 'The Accountability of Multinationals for Human Rights Violations in European Law' (2005) <default/files/files/resources/banking_while_borneo_burns_0.pdf> accessed 26 December 2016

Deutschland Gebiet unter Alliierter Besatzung Kontrollrat, 'Enactments and Approved Papers of The Control Council and Coordinating Committee' (1947)

Deva S, 'Fictitious Separation, Real Injustice: Why and How to Tame the Twin Principles of Corporate Law (2017)

Dodge WS, 'Alien Tort Litigation: The Road Not Taken' (2014)

Dorich A, 'Parent Company Responsibility of Corporations for The Acts of Their Overseas Group Subsidiaries: The European Union/United Kingdom Perspective' (2015)

Duff A, '5 Legal Liability' (2003) http://platform.rgs.org/NR/rdonlyres/A1732337-720E4FCC-950D-0BC094B57FDA/0/06ch5.pdf accessed 30 October 2016

Duff RA, 'Intention, Agency and Criminal Liability: Philosophy of Action and The Criminal Law' (1990)

Earth Charter http://www.earthcharterinaction.org/content/pages/Read-the-Charter.html accessed 9 August 2017

Earth Negotiations Bull., Dec. 13, 1999, at 1, 13 <http://www.iisd.ca/download/pdf/enb2006e.pdf > accessed 12 January 2017

Edward DW and Tomic S, 'In The Supreme Court of Canada' (1990)

Engle E, 'Alien Torts in Europe? Human Rights and Tort in European law' (2005)

Enneking LFH, 'Foreign Direct Liability and Beyond-Exploring The Role of Tort Law in Promoting International Corporate Social Responsibility and Accountability' (2012)

European Commission of Human Rights, Application No. 788/60, Austria v. Italy, decision of 11 January 1961 on the admissibility, (1961) 4 Yearbook of the European Convention on Human Rights

Florey KJ, 'State Law, US Power, Foreign Disputes: Understanding The Extraterritorial Effect of State Law in The Wake of Morrison v. National Australia Bank' (2012)

Foakes J, 'Immunity for International Crimes, Developments in The Law on Prosecuting Heads of State in Foreign Courts' (2011)

French PA, 'Collective and Corporate Responsibility' (1987)

Friends of the Earth, 'Briefing: Corporate Accountability' (2005) from http://www.foe.co.uk/resource/briefings/corporate_accountability1.pdf accessed 5 July 2017

Glasbee H, 'Looking for Responsibility in The Corporate World or The Corporation's Multiple Personality Disorder' in Directors' Personal Liability for Corporate Fault a Comparative Analysis. Austin/Boston/Chicago/New York/The Netherlands: Wolters Kluwer (2008)

Gov't Comm'r of the Gen. Trib. of the Military Gov't for the French Zone of Occupation in Germany v Roechling, Indictment, 14 Trials of War Criminals Before the Nuernberg Military Tribunals Under Control Council Law No. 10 1061 Appendix B (1950)

Grasso C, 'Peaks and Troughs of The UK Deferred Prosecution Agreement: The Lesson Learned from The First-Ever DPA between The SFO and ICBC SB PLC' (2016) <https://uel.academia.edu/CostantinoGrasso> accessed 5 July 2017

Griffiths R, 'Theodor Meron, Henry's Wars and Shakespeare's Laws' (1996) 198-200

Hasselback D, 'Investigating a Target Company's CSR Claims is Now a Standard Part of Transaction Due Diligence, Lawyers Say' (2015)

Hayajneh AZ, 'Civil Liability for Environmental Damage: A Comparative Study between Jordanian and English Legal Systems' (2004)

Hoffman P and Stephens B, 'International Human Rights Cases Under State Law and in State Courts' (2012)

House of Representatives Report No. 102-367, at 4. II and Senate Report No. 102-249, at 3(1991)

International Commission of Jurists, Report of The Expert Legal Panel on Corporate Complicity in International Crimes: Volume 3 (Civil Remedies) 4 (2008) <https://perma.cc/Q94M-FPZY> [hereinafter ICJ Report] accessed 15 September 2017

International Conferences (The Hague), Hague Convention (IV) Respecting the Laws and Customs of War on Land and Its Annex: Regulations Concerning The Laws and Customs of War on Land, 18 October 1907 <htpp//www.refworld.org/docid/4374cae64.html> accessed 5 November 2016

International Criminal Court, Policy Paper on Case Selection and Prioritisation (2003) <https://perma.cc/SDL9- A7B2 > accessed 8 March 2017

International Criminal Tribunal for Rwanda Press and Public Affairs Unit, Fact Sheet No.1; The Tribunals at A Glance (1999) http://www.ictr.org/ENGLISH/factsshee,htm accessed 13 November 2016

International Humanitarian Law' (2010) United Nations Audiovisual Library of International Law New York, United Nations <https://perma.cc/7U38- HQ8F> accessed 2 September 2017

International Law Commission, 'The Charter and Judgment of the Nürnberg Tribunal – History and Analysis' (United Nations 1949). Memorandum Submitted by The Secretary General A/CN.4/5, 75

Jaafari S, 'Lack of Political Will Stands in The Way of Bringing Assad to Court' (2017) https://www.pri.org/stories/2017-04-06/lack-political-will-stands-way-bringingassad-court accessed 8 July 2017

Karen CfJ, 'Alter, The New Terrain of International Law: Courts, Politics, Rights' (2014) 5

Kathryn Gordon, 'The OECD Guidelines and Other Corporate Responsibility Instruments: A Comparison' (OECD Working Papers on International Investment 2001/05) <https://www.oecd.org/corporate/mne/WP-2001_5.pdf> accessed 18 March 2016

Keitner, CI, 'Conceptualizing Complicity in Alien Tort Cases' (2008)

Kirshner JA, 'Why is The US Abdicating The Policing of Multinational Corporations to Europe? Extra Territorialism, Sovereignty, and The Alien Tort Statute' (2011)

Knepper WE and Bailey DA., Liability of Corporate Officers and Directors. § 2-07 at 2-18-2-21 (2004)

Koranteng K A, 'Ghana: Injustice At Tema Steel Company' (2014) <https://www.newsghana.com.gh/ghana-injustice-tema-steel-company/> accessed 22 January 2017

Kuijer M, 'Effective Remedies as A Fundamental Right Seminar on Human Rights and Access to Justice in The EU, Barcelona' (2014)

Lambooy T, 'Legal Aspects of Corporate Social Responsibility' (2014) Browser Download This Paper

LC, Summary Records of the Eighteenth Session, Yearbook of the International Law Commission (1966) I/2, p. 188 <http://untreaty.un.org/ilc/publications/yearbooks/Ybkvolumes(e)/ILC _1966_v1_p2_e.pdf > accessed 21 September 2017

Leary JC, 'Talisman's Sudanese Oil Investment: The Historical Context Surrounding Its Entry, Departure, and Controversial Tenure Diss' (2007)

Letter from Yadh Ben Achour to Pamela Hamoto, Permanent Representative of The United States to The United Nations (Oct. 6, 2015) <https://perma.cc/Z9HG-9C43 > accessed 4 September 2017

Levin D, 'Daimler Lends VW a Hand to Manage Scandal Clean up, Fortune' (Oct. 20, 2015) http://fortune.com/2015/10/20/vw-daimler-board-scandal/ [https:// perma.cc/U4NXEYAF accessed 15 July 2017

Loblaw Companies Limited, Company Statement "Lonlaw Companies Limited Update Statement on Bangladesh" (2014) <www.loblaw.ac/English/MediaCentre/announcement/default.aspx> accessed 22

Maduna, PM, 'Declaration by Justice Minister Pennell Maduna on Apartheid Litigation in The United States' 11 July 2003 <www.info.gov.zajotherdocs/2003/apartheid.pdf >15 November 2016

Markoff G, 'Arthur Andersen and The Myth of The Corporate Death Penalty: Corporate Criminal Convictions in The Twenty-First Century' (2012)

Marsden C, 'Corporate Responsibilities in Times of Civil Unrest: The Case of Egypt and Vodafone' (2011) <file:///C:/Users/Emmanuel/Downloads/Corporate%20Responsibilities%20in%20Times%20of%20Civil%20Unrest%20the%20case%20of%20Egypt%20and%20Vodafone.pdf> accessed 26 December 2016

McManus FS, The MacBride Principles, The University of Minnesota Human Rights Library (2016) <https://perma.cc/JA8X-5HCM> accessed 8 January 2016

McNulty PJ, Deputy Attorney General, US Dep't. of Just., Memorandum to The Heads of Department Components and US Attorneys on Principles of Federal Prosecution of Business Organizations, 2 (Dec. 12, 2006) <https://www.justice.gov/sites/default/files/dag/legacy/2007/07/05/mcnulty_memo.pdf[https://perma.cc/9VNVW583]> accessed 15 July 2017

Meier B, 'In Guilty Plea, OxyContin Maker to Pay $600 Milliion' (2007) New York Times <http://www.nytimes.com/2007/05/10/business/11drug-web.html> accessed 14 September 2017

Murray O, Kinley D, and Pitts C, 'Exaggerated Rumours of The Death of An Alien Tort: Corporations, Human Rights and The Peculiar Case of Kiobel' (2011)

Newsletter: Criminal Complaint against Senior Manager of Danzer: Accountability for Human Rights Violations in the Democratic Republic of Congo, European Centre for Constitutional and Human Rights (Apr. 25, 2013) https://perma.cc/26CW-57UV accessed 16 September 2017

Open-Ended Intergovernmental Working on Transnational Corporations and Other Business Enterprises with Respect to Human Rights, UN Human Rights Council (2014) <https://perma.cc/GY7A-JB3R > accessed 18 September 2015

Organisation for Economic Cooperation and Development, 'Organisation for Economic Cooperation and Development: Convention on Combating Bribery of Foreign Public Officials in International Business Transactions, Paris, November 20, 1997: 1–8' (1998) 3 Trends in Organized Crime 77, 82

Osofsky HM, 'Climate Change and Environmental Justice: Reflections on Litigation over Oil Extraction and Rights Violations in Nigeria' (2010)

Paust JJ 'Non-State Actor Participation in International Law and The Pretense of Exclusion' (2010)

Perutz MF, Redress: 'Torture Survivors Perceptions of Reparation: A Preliminary Survey' (2001) <http://www.redress.org/downloads/publications/TSPR.pdf> accessed 4 July 2017

Peters K, The Corporate Responsibility Doctrine: Handling Matters When Corporate Executives Are Involved in Criminal or Civil Matters, in Protecting Corporation against Management Liability Claims: Leading Lawyers on Analysing Development in Employment Regulation, Investigating and responding to Allegation, and Creating Effective Compliance Strategies (2013). 7 <https://www.gordonrees.com/Templates/media/files/pdf/The%20Corporate%20Responsibility%20Doctrine.pdf> accessed 15 September 2017

Politheor GM. UN Guiding Principles & Proposed Binding Treaty Will Reinforce Human Rights Protection from Corporate Abuses (2016) https://businesshumanrights.org/en/commentary-un-guiding-principles-proposed-binding-treaty-willreinforce-human-rights-protection-from-corporate-abuses accessed 10 January 2017

Pop AI, 'Criminal Liability of Corporations Comparative Jurisprudence' (2006) <http://www.law.msu.edu/king/2006/2006_Pop.pdf> accessed 24 April 2016

Power S, 'Raising The Cost of Genocide' (2003) Dissent Magazine <http://www.dissentmagazine.org/article/raising-the-cost-of-genocide> accessed 8 July 2017

Re South African Apartheid Litigation' (MDL 1499) <http://www.kosa.orgjdocuments/09~09~OJ_MinJusticeRSAto_JudgeBcheidlin.pdf > 15 November 2016

Report of the International Commission of Equity on East Timor to The Secretary-General, 30 January 2000, UN Doc. A/54/726-S/2000/59

Report of the Secretary-General on The Establishment of a Special Court of Sierra Leone, UN Doc. S/2000/915, 9

Roberts CL, 'The Case for Restitution and Unjust Enrichment Remedies in Patent Law' (2010)

Rocard M, "What Is The International Community?" (2013)

Scherer AG and Palazzo G, 'Globalization and Corporate Social Responsibility' (2008)

Scott CM, 'Translating Torture into Transnational Tort: Conceptual Divides in The Debate on Corporate Accountability for Human Rights Harms' (2001)

Shotter J, 'Social Accountability and Selfhood' (1984) http://philpapers.org/rec/SHOSAA accessed 20 November 2016

Silvia Fernández de Gurmendi President of the International Criminal Court, Remarks to The 25th Diplomatic Briefing Check against Delivery The Hague (2015) <https://www.icccpi.int/iccdocs/db/25DB-Pres-Eng.pdf> accessed 5 November 2016

Skinner G, 'Nuremberg's Legacy Continues: the Nuremberg Trials' Influence on Human Rights Litigation in US Courts under The Alien Tort Statute' (2008)

Skinner G, 'Rethinking Limited Liability of Parent Corporations for Their Subsidiaries' Extraterritorial Violations of Human Rights Law' (2016) http://clsbluesky.law.columbia.edu/2016/02/10/rethinking-limited-liability-ofparent-corporations-for-their-subsidiaries-extraterritorial-violations-of-human-rightslaw/ Accessed 20 April 2017

Social Accountability International, 'SA8000 Standard Documents' (2014) http://www.sa-intl.org/index.cfm?fuseaction=Page.ViewPage &PageID=937 accessed 26 December 2016

Special Representative on Business and Human Rights, United Nations Guiding Principles on Business and Human Rights: Implementing The United Nations "Protect, Respects, and Remedy" Framework, adopted by The Human Rights Council, 17th Sess., Mar. 21. 2011, U. N. Doc. A/HRC/17/.L.17/31 (2011)

Steinitz M, 'The Case for An International Court of Civil Justice' (2014)

Stenning A and Walton S, 'Introduction' (2017) iii-x <http://www.tandfonline.com/doi/full/10.1080/14688417.2017.1310440> accessed 15 June 2017

Stephens B, 'Translating Filartiga: A Comparative and International Law Analysis of Domestic Remedies for International Human Rights Violations' (2002)

Stevenson DD and Wagoner NJ, 'FCPA Sanctions: Too Big to Debar?' (2011)

Summers M, 'The International Court of Justice's Decision in Congo v Belgium: How Has It Affected the Development of a Principle of Universal Jurisdiction That Would Obligate All States to Prosecute War Criminals' (2003)

Taylor M, 'Leigh Day Claims £105m Costs for Trafigura litigation' (2010)

The Global Sullivan Principles, The University of Minnesota Human Rights Library (2016) <https://perma.cc/JU6X-WGCT > accessed 24 May 2016

The ICRC Advisory Services on International Humanitarian Law, 'General Principles of International Criminal Law' (2015) https://www.icrc.org/eng/assets/files/2014/general-principles-of-criminal-icrceng.pdf accessed 8 July 2017

The President of The United Nations Security Council Addressed to The Secretary-General, UN Doc. S/2000/1234, 22 December 200

Secretary-General Addressed to The President of The United Nations Security Council, UN Doc. S/2001/40, 13 January 2001

The Trafigura Case (2015) Environmental Justice Organisations, Liabilities and Trade <http://www.ejolt.org/wordpress/wp-content/uploads/2015/08/FS-45.pdf > accessed 26 December 2016

Thompson RC and Ramasastry A and Taylor MB, 'Translating Unocal: The Expanding Web of Liability for Business Entities Implicated in International Crimes' (2009)

Transparency International (Berlin), 'Africa: Judicial Corruption Fuels Impunity, Corrodes Rule of Law, Says New Report' (2007) <http://allafrica.com/stories/200705241122.html> accessed 18 January 2017

Triponel AF, 'Comparative Corporate Responsibility in The United States and France for Human Rights Violations Abroad' (2010)

UK National Contact Point for The OECD Guidelines for Multinational Enterprises, 'Complaint Regarding The Conduct of G4S and Subsidiaries in The Occupied Palestinian Territory and Israel, Raised by Lawyers for Palestinian Human Rights' (2013) <http://lphr.org.uk/wpcontent/uploads/2015/06/LPHR-OECDComplaintMaster-no-contact-details.pdf> accessed 26 December 2016.

UN News Centre, 'Open-pit Coal Mine Project in Bangladesh Threatens Human Rights UN Experts' (2012) <http://www.un.org/apps/news/story.asp?NewsID=41398#.V7Wnw1srKmy> accessed 26 December 2016

UN Security Council, 'Begins Negotiations on New Syria Resolution' (2016) <http://www.cbsnews.com/news/united-nations-security-council-begins-negotiationson-new-syria-resolution/> accessed 21 November 2016

US Department of Justice. (2009). Criminal RICO: 18 USC. 1961-1968: A Manual for Federal Prosecutors. Washington, D.C.: US Dept. of Justice, Criminal Division, Organized Crime and Racketeering Section 2(23) 12

US Gov't Printing Off., 5 Trial of War Criminals before The Nuremberg Military Tribunals under Control Council Law No. 10 1052 (1950)

Wagner G, 'Punitive Damages in European Private Law' (2011)

Walsh G, 'Tort of Negligence definitions' (2011.)

War Criminals, 'Law Report' (1949) <http://www.loc.gov/rr/frd/Military_Law/pdf/Law-Reports_Vol-12.pdf> accessed 11 September 2017

Warin JF, Diamant MS and Root V, 'Somebody's Watching Me: FCPA Monitorships and How They Can Work Better' (2011)

Watson GR, 'Or a Treaty of the United States: Treaties and the Alien Tort Statute After Kiobel' (2013)

Weber RH and Baisch R, 'Liability of Parent Companies for Human Rights Violations of Subsidiaries (2015) <https://ssrn.com/abstract=2625536 or http://dx.doi.org/10.2139/ssrn.2625536> accessed 25 September 2017

Weston, 'Human Rights' ('International Human Rights in Domestic Courts') in Encyclopaedia Britannica Online (last updated 19 March 2014) <http://britannica.com/EBchecked/topic/275840/humanrights> accessed 22 August 2017

Wolf ML, 'The Case for An International Anti-Corruption Court' (2014) 5 Brookings Institution 8 <http://www.brookings.edu/~/media/research/files/papers/2014/07/international%20anti%20corruption%20court%20wolf/anticorruptioncourt wolffinal.pdf> accessed 20 September 2017

World Development Movement, 'Banking While Borneo Burns' (2013) <http://www.globaljustice.org.uk/sites/> accessed 2 December 2017

World Development Movement, 'UK Urges GCM Resources to Assess Human Rights Impactof Bangladesh Coal Mine' (2014) <http://www.globaljustice.org.uk/news/2014/dec/8/uk-urges-gcm-resourcesassesshuman-rights-impact-bangladesh-coal-mine> accessed 26 December 2016

World Trade Report, 'Speeding Up Trade: Benefits and Challenges of Implementing The WTO Trade Facilitation' (2015) <https://www.wto.org/english/res_e/booksp_e/world_trade_report15_e.pdf> accessed 12 August 2016

Wright GR, "Negotiating The Terms of Corporate Human Rights Liability under Federal Law' (2016)

Yadh Ben Achour to Pamela Hamoto, Permanent Representative of the United States to the United Nations (Oct. 6, 2015) <https://perma.cc/Z9HG-9C43> accessed 3 September 2017.

Younge G, 'Go Tell It On The Mountain' (1997) The Guardian, accessed 4 January 2016

Web pages

<http://blogs.wsj.com/law/2012/11/15/bp-statement-on-deepwater-horizon-settle ment-withu-s/

<[https://perma.cc/AVF9-3J9S]> accessed 15 July 2017

<http://www.icty.org/> accessed 13 November 2016

<http://www.oecd/document/0,3343,en_2469_201185_1889402_1_1_1_1, 00.html> accessed 15 January 2017

<http://www.fcpablog.com/blog/2010/7/7/snamprogetti-eni-in-365-mil lionsettlement.html

[https://pema.cc/CC8B-UD4T]> accessed 16 September 2012

ABOUT THE AUTHOR

Dr Emmanuel Nartey, Ex Solider, Executive Adviser for BAME-British Army, Olympian, Athletes Commissioner, Member of International Scientific Committee of Social and Business Studies, Member of International Association of Psychological Scientist, Member of Charted Management Institution, Researcher, BA, LLB lecturer in law, MBA and LLM lecturer in public international law, international trade law, human rights law, corporate accountability, international law, corporate social responsibility and corporate governance, former Head of Business and Law at Private Schools. I have BA in Business and Management, Member of the Inner Temple Court (Bar), Master in Laws, MSc International Politics and Comparative Policy and PhD within the legal sector of international law and human rights law.

Visiting Scholar at Centre for Financial and Corporate Integrity Coventry University, Law Lecturer Cardiff Metropolitan University and Reviewer of the Journal; Journal of Accounting, Auditing and Taxation. Dr Nartey is also a Ghanaian judoka. He competed in the men's 73 kg event at the 2012 Summer Olympics and was eliminated by Dex Elmont in the second round. He was the first judoka to represent Ghana at the Olympic Games. Nartey studied at the University of East London on Sport Scholarship, University of the West of England, and the University of Law.

He serves in the British Army. He is the author of a book titled *My Olympic Dream*.

In 2005 Emmanuel became the first Ghanaian Judoka to contest the World Championships, held in Cairo. The 2013 World Championships in Rio were his sixth World Champs. He has produced some impressive performances in the last few years, including a bronze medal at 2013 African Championships in Mozambique and another bronze at the Asian Open World Cup event in Chinese Taipei.

Career highlights: 10 x world championship representative 3x world cup gold medalist 1 x world cup silver 3 x bronze 1 x European cup bronze Selected to represent Ghana at Commonwealth Games in Glasgow, 2014 Bronze – Under 73kg, Pan-American Open, Buenos Aries, Argentina, 2013 Selected to represent Ghana at Olympic Games in London, 2012